CONTEMPORARY MUSICIANS

ISSN-1044-2197

CONTEMPORARY MUSICIANS

PROFILES OF THE PEOPLE IN MUSIC

LAURA HIGHTOWER

LEIGH ANN DeREMER, Project Editor

VOLUME 29
Includes Cumulative Indexes

GALE GROUP

Detroit
New York
San Francisco
London
Boston
Woodbridge, CT

STAFF

Leigh Ann DeRemer, *Project Editor*
Luann Brennan, *Contributing Editor*

Laura Avery, Aaron J. Oppliger, *Associate Editors*

Laura Hightower, *Senior Sketchwriter*
Barry Alfonso, Carol Brennan, Gerald E. Brennan, Gloria Cooksey,
Daniel Durchholz, Lloyd Hemingway, Francis D. McKinley,
Nathan Sweet, *Sketchwriters*

Bridget Travers, *Managing Editor*

Maria L. Franklin, *Permissions Manager*
Julie Juengling, *Permissions Assistant*

Mary Beth Trimper, *Manager, Composition and Electronic Prepress*
Gary Leach, *Composition Specialist*
Dorothy Maki, *Manufacturing Manager*
Stacy Melson, *Buyer*

Robert Duncan, *Imaging Specialist*
Randy Bassett, *Image Database Supervisor*
Dean Dauphinais, *Senior Editor, Imaging and Multimedia Content*
Pamela A. Reed, *Imaging Coordinator*
Michael Logusz, *Graphic Artist*
Cover illustration by John Kleber

ISBN 0-7876-3254-6
ISSN 1044-2197

10 9 8 7 6 5 4 3 2 1

Contents

Introduction ix

Cumulative Subject Index 265

Cumulative Musicians Index 291

Introduction

Fills in the Information Gap on Today's Musicians

Contemporary Musicians profiles the colorful personalities in the music industry who create or influence the music we hear today. Prior to *Contemporary Musicians,* no quality reference series provided comprehensive information on such a wide range of artists despite keen and ongoing public interest. To find biographical and critical coverage, an information seeker had little choice but to wade through the offerings of the popular press, scan television "infotainment" programs, and search for the occasional published biography or expose. *Contemporary Musicians* is designed to serve that information seeker, providing in one ongoing source in-depth coverage of the important names on the modern music scene in a format that is both informative and entertaining. Students, researchers, and casual browsers alike can use *Contemporary Musicians* to meet their needs for personal information about music figures; find a selected discography of a musician's recordings; and uncover an insightful essay offering biographical and critical information.

Provides Broad Coverage

Single-volume biographical sources on musicians are limited in scope, often focusing on a handful of performers from a specific musical genre or era. In contrast, *Contemporary Musicians* offers researchers and music devotees a comprehensive, informative, and entertaining alternative. *Contemporary Musicians* is published four times per year, with each volume providing information on about 80 musical artists and record-industry luminaries from all the genres that form the broad spectrum of contemporary music—pop, rock, jazz, blues, country, New Age, folk, rhythm and blues, gospel, bluegrass, rap, and reggae, to name a few—as well as selected classical artists who have achieved "crossover" success with the general public. *Contemporary Musicians* will also occasionally include profiles of influential nonperforming members of the music community, including producers, promoters, and record company executives. Additionally, beginning with *Contemporary Musicians 11,* each volume features new profiles of a selection of previous *Contemporary Musicians* listees who remain of interest to today's readers and who have been active enough to require completely revised entries.

Includes Popular Features

In *Contemporary Musicians* you'll find popular features that users value:

- **Easy-to-locate data sections:** Vital personal statistics, chronological career summaries, listings of major awards, and mailing addresses, when available, are prominently displayed in a clearly marked box on the second page of each entry.

- **Biographical/critical essays:** Colorful and informative essays trace each subject's personal and professional life, offer representative examples of critical response to the artist's work, and provide entertaining personal sidelights.

- **Selected discographies:** Each entry provides a comprehensive listing of the artist's major recorded works.

- **Photographs:** Most entries include portraits of the subject profiled.

- **Sources for additional information:** This invaluable feature directs the user to selected books, magazines, newspapers, and online sources where more information can be obtained.

Helpful Indexes Make It Easy to Find the Information You Need

Each volume of *Contemporary Musicians* features a cumulative Musicians Index, listing names of individual performers and musical groups, and a cumulative Subject Index, which provides the user with a breakdown by primary musical instruments played and by musical genre.

Available in Electronic Formats

Diskette/Magnetic Tape. *Contemporary Musicians* is available for licensing on magnetic tape or diskette in a fielded format. The database is available for internal data processing and nonpublishing purposes only. For more information, call (800) 877-GALE.

Online. *Contemporary Musicians* is available online as part of the Gale Biographies (GALBIO) database accessible through LEXIS-NEXIS, P.O. Box 933, Dayton, OH 45401-0933; phone: (937) 865-6800, toll-free: (800) 543-6862.

We Welcome Your Suggestions

The editors welcome your comments and suggestions for enhancing and improving *Contemporary Musicians*. If you would like to suggest subjects for inclusion, please submit these names to the editor. Mail comments or suggestions to:

The Editor
Contemporary Musicians
Gale Group, Inc.
27500 Drake Rd.
Farmington Hills, MI 48334-3535

Or call toll free: (800) 347-GALE

Nat Adderley

Cornetist, composer

A major player in hard bop jazz during the 1950s, Nat Adderley pioneered the genre of soul jazz. He commanded an extraordinary range of tones on the cornet, and possessed a distinctive ability to play "way down low" on the horn, without losing the agility to discharge powerful notes in the upper registers in rapid succession. He toured the world as a bandleader and wrote compositions that were performed and recorded by many of the greatest names in the jazz world. Among Adderley's most popular songs were "Jive Samba," "Hummin'," and "The Work Song," and during his 50-year career he played on nearly 100 albums. Adderley's accomplishments in many areas paralleled those of his older brother, alto saxophone player Julian "Cannonball" Adderley, and the two siblings collaborated for many years, both in the Cannonball Adderley Quintet and on selected projects.

Adderley was born Nathaniel Adderley in Tampa, Florida on November 25, 1931, the second of two sons. He was still an infant when the family moved to Tallahassee in order for his parents, Sugar and Julian Adderley Sr., to teach at Florida A&M University. Nat Adderley's first musical endeavor as a youngster was as a singer, and he was in fact a boy soprano until his voice deepened in adolescence.

While the Adderley brothers were growing up, Julian Adderley Jr. played trumpet. As Nat Adderley entered his teens however, his brother abandoned the trumpet and switched to playing the saxophone. With an idle trumpet in the Adderley house it was not long before Nat Adderley appropriated the instrument for himself. Beginning in 1946 he studied the trumpet, receiving assistance from both his father—a professional musician—and his older brother.

Adderley played his trumpet locally with various bands in Florida until joining the army in 1950, at which time he switched instruments and began to play the cornet. He played with an army band during his military tour of duty in Korea, and after his discharge in 1953 he enrolled at Florida A&M, intending to study law at his mother's urging—Adderley's parents were well educated and held high expectations for their children's academic success. Adderley nonetheless abandoned his plans indefinitely in order to accept an unanticipated invitation to tour Europe with the Lionel Hampton band.

He left for Europe in 1954, and when he returned in the following year he joined his brother on an impromptu excursion to New York City where one of the legendary moments of jazz awaited them upon their arrival. Before the end of their first evening in New York, the two brothers were performing at Café Bohemia in Greenwich Village with featured stars Kenny Clark, Horace Silver, and Oscar Pettiford. Nat Adderley, who left Florida with his brother on a whim and with only tentative plans to explore the big city jazz scene, was heard on three separate recordings within weeks of his arrival in New York. He contributed to *Bohemia after Dark* and to *Cannonball Adderley: Spontaneous Combustion.* Additionally, Nat Adderley released his own album, *Nat Adderley: That's Nat.* The latter recording featured Nat Adderley's classic compositions, "Work Song," "Sermonette," and "Jive Samba." The following year he released, *To the Ivy League from Nat,* on EmArcy, a four-star album according to *All Music Guide.* The younger Adderley maintained a low profile behind his older brother's fame but went on nonetheless to record dozens of albums, including a number of recordings as a bandleader and many with his brother's ensemble, the Cannonball Adderley Quintet. During the 1960s, Nat Adderley recorded most frequently with Riverside Records; additionally he was heard on Capitol, Milestone, Atlantic, and Original Jazz Classics. Some of his albums were later re-issued by Original Jazz Classics.

Formed A Legendary Quintet

Nat and Julian Adderley initially formed an ensemble in 1956 but disbanded the group by the following year. After the split-up, Nat Adderley played with Woody Herman and trombonist J. J. Johnson until late in 1959 at which time Cannonball Adderley assembled a new band, the Cannonball Adderley Quintet. With the endorsement of trumpeter Miles Davis, who was impressed with the Adderleys, the brothers secured the assistance of agent John Levy and their prospects improved accordingly. Scott Yanow of *All Music Guide* said of Nat Adderley that he "was at the peak of his powers ..." during those formative years of the quintet.

Nat Adderley, a charter member of the Adderley quintet, remained with the group until its demise after the death of Cannonball Adderley in 1975. During the nearly 20-year history of the quintet, the ensemble left its mark on the *Billboard* charts, with 12 albums on the charts between 1962 and 1975. The group's classic album, *Mercy, Mercy, Mercy,* was released by Capitol in 1967 and reached number 13 on the music charts. The featured title song on that album not only reached number 11 on the pop singles listing but also hit second place on the rhythm & blues singles chart. In February of 1968, the *Mercy* album won an award from the National Academy of Recording Arts and Sciences (NARAS Grammy Award) for the best instrumental jazz performance by a small group.

Many Accomplishments

Adderley's exploits veered beyond the Adderley quintet, as he worked additionally as a sideman with Wynton Kelly, drummer Kenny Clarke, and saxophonist Jimmy Heath between 1960 and 1975. During the 1970s, Adderley and his brother collaborated on a cohesive "concept" album called "Big Man—The Legend of John Henry." That work, which was released as a musical on the Fantasy label, was performed at Carnegie Hall in 1976 as a tribute to the untimely death of Cannonball Adderley; Joe Williams starred in the concert. In later 1980s productions of *John Henry,* Adderley expanded the work into a full-blown musical. The expanded version was performed in 1986 at both the Kennedy Center for the Performing Arts in Washington D.C. and at the La Jolla Playhouse in Southern California. Nat Adderley himself appeared off-Broadway in a play on the life of Mahalia Jackson not long after his brother's death.

Also after his brother's death, he formed his own band. The new ensemble, including Vincent Herring on saxophone and Walter Booker on bass, performed together for approximately 20 years. Additionally, Sonny Fortune joined Adderley as a sideman during the 1980s, and Adderley toured both as a soloist and as a bandleader in Europe and Japan. Through all of his concert tours, Adderley experienced an enthusiastic reception worldwide and especially in Europe. He was inspired by the ambience and encouraged that jazz stood in the threshold of an international awakening during the 1990s.

In 1975, Adderley went to Florida Southern College for a sojourn as artist-in-residence. In that capacity he performed as a headliner at A&M's Child of the Sun Jazz Festival. His regular appearances at the festival spanned more than ten years—into the mid-1980s. Approximately ten years later, in 1996, he joined the school faculty. He taught music at Harvard, performed an annual stint at Sweet Basil in New York City, and toured with Luther Vandross on occasion.

Adderley traveled everywhere—Australia, New Zealand, Japan—with his most frequent venue in Zurich, Switzerland during his later years. The early 1990s saw a Broadway production of his 1986 adaptation of the John Henry musical, *Shout Up a Morning*; and in 1994 Adderley contributed cameos on Antonio Hart's tribute album, *For Cannonball and Woody*. In 1995, a *Mercy, Mercy, Mercy* reprise appeared on Evidence Records, with Antonio Hart on saxophone, pianist Rob Bargad, bassist Walter Booker, and Jimmy Cobb on drums.

A Jazz Purist

In the mid-1980s Adderley dispensed with exclusive engagement agreements and ceased signing recording contracts, preferring instead to work on a less confining, per album basis. Ultimately he recorded on more than a dozen labels including Enja, Landmark, and Atlantic during the four-decade span of his recording career between 1955 and 1995. In an interview with Amy J. Moore of *Down Beat,* he discussed the implications of freedom and total involvement for jazz musicians. He affirmed that collaboration and spontaneity combine to comprise a special synergy that is the essence of jazz, a circumstance that endows the genre with its unique interpretive characteristics and that distinguishes jazz from all other music. Adderley said also that memorable jazz performances elicit guts and bravery from the performers, because not all improvisations succeed. Truly devoted musicians learn to accept derision equally with adulation during those unpredictable times when a spontaneous collaboration fails to please the listener—when people say stuff like, "What was that ricky-tick crap?" as Adderley related the emotion.

In 1997, the jazz world honored Nat Adderley with an induction into the Jazz Hall of Fame. Two years later, in 1999, his colleagues in music paid a grand tribute to him at the Playboy Jazz Festival in 1999 with a moving presentation by Longineu Parsons on trumpet, bassist Walter Booker, and percussionists Airto Moreira and Roy McCurdy. George Duke and Michael Wolff shared the piano duties, and Adderley received a standing ovation as Parsons and the group performed a selection of Adderley's most recorded compositions, including "Jive Samba" and "Work Song."

Years of Declining Health

In 1997, Adderley had his right leg amputated as a result of diabetes, and three years later he died from complications of the disease. On the day before he died, he crossed the bridge into the twenty-first century, ultimately expiring on January 2, 2000. Adderley was survived by his son, Nat Adderley, Jr. who is a pianist and musical director. Also surviving Adderley were his wife, Ann; his daughter, Alison Pittman; and five grandchildren. Philip Elwood noted in the *San Francisco Examiner* that Adderley was one of the "friendliest and most cordial guys any of us jazz camp followers ever encountered." According to the unassuming Adderley, he was just an "old bebopper."

Selected discography

Singles

"Mercy, Mercy, Mercy" (with Cannonball Adderley Quintet), Capitol, 1967.

Albums

Bohemia After Dark (with others), 1955.
That's Nat Adderley, Savoy, 1955.
Branching Out, Original Jazz Classics, 1958.
Much Brass, Original Jazz Classics, 1959.
That's Right, Original Jazz Classics, 1960.
Worksong, Riverside, 1960.
In the Bag, Original Jazz Classics, 1962.
Mercy, Mercy, Mercy (with Cannonball Adderley Quintet), Capitol, 1967.
The Old Country, Enja, 1990.
Good Company, Challenge Records, 1995.
Mercy, Mercy, Mercy, Evidence (reissue), 1995.

Sources

Periodicals

Billboard, July 22, 1995, p. 56; January 15, 2000, p. 6.
Down Beat, February 1994, p. 50; March 1994, p. 40 (2); March 1996, p. 39; January 1997, p. 58; July 1997, p. 62.
Jet, August 4, 1997, p. 40.
Los Angeles Times, June 15, 1999, p. 2 (Home Ed.); January 4, 2000, p. 17.
San Francisco Examiner, January 8, 2000, p. B-3 (First Ed.).
Washington Post, January 5, 2000, p. B–8 (Final Ed.).

Online

"Jazz Profiles – Nat Adderley," http://npr.org/programs/jazz profiles/adderley.html (June 8, 2000).
"Nat Adderley," *All Music Guide,* http://allmusic.com (April 27, 2000).

—Gloria Cooksey

Marc Almond

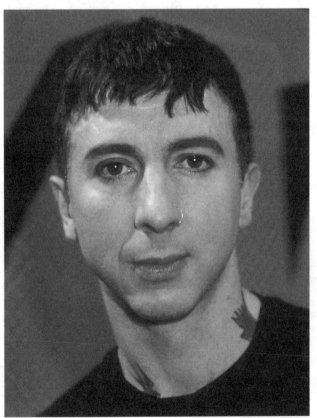

Singer, songwriter

Before vocalist and songwriter Marc Almond commenced his acclaimed and prolific solo career, he earned fame as a member of Soft Cell, the pioneering electronic duo that created the smash hit "Tainted Love." But Almond's talents go beyond his ability to produce number-one songs. Instead, the internationally revered artist has made his most important contribution to music as a successful singer, songwriter, and performer adored by critics throughout Europe and the United States. "Listeners who acknowledge Marc Almond only as the voice behind Soft Cell's 'Tainted Love' do the English singer a great disservice," wrote Kurt B. Reighley in a profile for the *Trouser Press Guide to '90s Rock.* "Since that electro-pop landmark in 1981, Almond has steadfastly devoted his career to exploring the art of the song."

Throughout his career, Almond has always been happy to interpret other songwriters music, regardless of the style. For example, he successfully covered the music of Jacques Brecht, tunes from the 1960s intended to be performed by female vocalists, and even pop superstar Madonna with his rendition of "Like a Prayer." Almond has collaborated with a wide range of artists as well, some of which included Gene Pitney, Nico, Nick Cave, The The, P.J. Proby, Coil, Bronski Beat, Jim "Foetus" Thirlwell, Psychic TV, Sally Timms of the Mekons, and Andi Sex Gang. And while he bounced from label to label as a solo recording artist, Almond, known as one of the most uncommercial yet commercial musicians in the pop world, maintained a devoted following and occasionally made a hit on the European and British charts.

Peter Marc Almond was born on July 9, 1956, in Southport, Lancashire, England. In 1979, in Leeds, England, Almond, acknowledged as the city's leading futurist and looking for a musician to accompany his cabaret act, teamed with keyboardist Dave Ball to found Soft Cell, Great Britain's first successful electro-pop duo. Their success resulted from Soft Cell's mix of personality—a bow-tied Ball aside Almond's whipping boy persona—and warm and shining but sometimes painful music. Although the press loathed Almond's overly stylized mannerisms, fans reveled in his on-stage antics. In just four years together, Soft Cell enjoyed a string of international hits, arriving in 1981 with their most successful, the multi-million selling version of Gloria Jones' northern soul song "Tainted Love." As popular two decades later as it was in the early-1980s, the single was followed by other popular hits like "Bedsitter," "Numbers," "Torch," and "Say Hello, Wave Goodbye." Soft Cells' first single, 1981's "Memorabilia," was the very first techno record, setting the stage for a whole new movement in pop music.

When Almond and Ball disbanded in 1984, Soft Cell had sold in excess of ten million records worldwide, and their style would influence the next generation of bands that followed, from the Pet Shop Boys and the

For The Record . . .

Born Peter Marc Almond on July 9, 1956, in Southport, Lancashire, England.

Member of Soft Cell, 1979-84; founded Marc and the Mambas, 1982; released first solo album, *Vermine in Ermine,* 1984; released the controversial *Mother Fist... and Her Five Daughters,* 1987; released greatest commercial success, *The Stars We Are,* 1988; released *Twelve Years of Tears,* documenting 1992 farewell performance at London's Royal Albert Hall, 1993; released *Open All Night,* a book of poems entitled *A Beautiful Twisted Night,* and the autobiography *Tainted Life,* 1999. Performed and recorded with a wide range of artists including Gene Pitney, Nico, Nick Cave, The The, P.J. Proby, Coil, Bronski Beat, Jim "Foetus" Thirlwell, Psychic TV, Sally Timms of the Mekons, and Andi Sex Gang.

Addresses: *Record company*—Instinct/Shadow, 26 W. 17th St., Ste. 502, New York City, NY 10011, phone: (212) 727-1360, fax: (212) 366-5878, e-mail: instinct@compuserve.com. *Management company*—M.A.W. Management, New York City, NY, and London, England. *Website*—Theatre of Marc Almond—The Official Marc Almond Website, http://www.marcalmond.co.uk.

Divine Comedy to Pulp, Blur, and others. Critics point to the duo's 1981 album for Sire Records, *Non-Stop Erotic Cabaret,* as Soft Cell's best offering. "Sandwiched between the steamroller of 'Tainted Love' and the used hanky of 'Say Hello, Wave Goodbye' is every shag Marc ever had, every tear ever cried and every rose dropped in the gutter," concluded Brian Connolly in *Rock: The Rough Guide.* "Almond takes every song by force, while Ball's arrangements have a simplicity that belies their age."

Meanwhile, beginning in 1982, Almond had put together an offshoot project called Marc and the Mambas as a less commercial outlet for his ideas. With fellow musicians Billy McGee and the classically trained Annie Hogan (both of whom remained with Almond during his solo pursuits throughout the 1980s), Almond recorded two double albums released in 1983: *Untitled* and *Torment and Toreros.* Featuring a mainly acoustic lineup and a small orchestra—an element influenced by musicians and bands from My Life Story and Rialto

to Tricky—both in the studio and in concert, the Mambas firmly established Almond's credibility as an artist. Moreover, the project enabled Almond to explore a variety of styles other than electro-pop. With *Untitled,* for example, Almond covered songs by Jacques Brel, Scott Walker, and Lou Reed.

After retiring the Mambas, Almond announced that he was leaving the music business. However, his retirement was short-lived, as 1984 saw the release of a single entitled "The Boy Who Came Back," as well as his first solo album, *Vermine in Ermine.* The transition from band leader to solo artist proved fruitful, with Almond forging ahead to produce a string of diverse and critically noted albums that always took his audience in a new direction. He followed his debut, after leaving the Phonogram label and signing with Virgin Records, with *Stories of Johnny,* an album that displayed Almond's undoubted power as a torch singer rather than a traditional rock/pop performer, but managed to reward him with a hit single for the LPs title track.

Although Almond's mainstream popularity started to diminish, his reputation within the music business and among critics and colleagues only strengthened. They took notice of his improving vocals, his interpretive powers and willingness to perform others' songs, and his sense of humor and irony combined with a hint of bitterness. In 1986, Almond released the mini-LP *A Woman's Story,* an obscure collection of cover songs that, given the singer's open bisexuality and fascination with cross-dressing, proved he could tackle songs intended for women without changing the gender. The twisted, controversial but musically stunning *Mother Fist...and Her Five Daughters,* arrived in 1987 to supportive reviews.

In reference to the above efforts, *Melody Maker*'s Ben Myers insisted that "Almond created a number of masterpieces which easily rivaled anything by the likes of Edith Piaf, Otis Redding and Rogers & Hammerstein. Add to this the destructive wit of Oscar Wilde and you'll be fleetingly touched by moments of genius." The performer's greatest asset, Myers continued, "is his willingness to absorb the past to create albums which are not merely a collection of songs, but a series of instances as immediate as the greatest of cinema and as lasting as a classic novel." Nonetheless, chart action still eluded the performer, and Virgin decided not to renew his contract.

Ironically, Almond's first release for the Parlophone label, 1988's *The Stars We Are,* became his greatest commercial success; the duet "Something's Gotten Hold of My Heart," sung with George Pitney, gave both artists their first number-one hit as soloists. In 1990, Almond returned with an album of Jacques Brel songs, *Jacques,* followed by *Enchanted.* But despite including some of Almond's finest work, neither received much popular attention. However, Almond returned to the charts in 1992 when a remake of David McWilliams' "The Days of Pearly Spencer," from Almond's *Tenement Symphony,* entered the British top five.

In the fall of 1992, Almond made a second attempt to bid farewell to a high-profile career by performing two retrospective concerts at London's Royal Albert Hall, documented on the 1993 album *Twelve Years of Tears.* A low-key album entitled *Absinthe: The French Album,* a collection of old French songs and arrangements of poems by Baudelaire and Rimbaud, arrived that year as well. Then two years later in 1995, Almond released *Treasure Box,* featuring the glam-rock single "The Idol" and returned to the stage with a new band. The following year, the performer released *Fantastic Star,* recorded in New York City with a larger band and offering a lush, more traditional pop sound. A less conventional effort with Jim Thirlwell that mixed camp and industrial music, the disturbing *Flesh Volcano/Slut* appeared in 1998.

In March of 1999, Almond released *Open All Night,* "a mature, meditative journey, each track outstanding and definitely Marc Almond today, more relevant than ever," according to the musician's website. Tackling an array of styles, including the jazz-inspired "When Bad People Kiss" and the poignant "Tragedy," the album drew from a well of musical sources, including rhythm and blues, trip hop, Latin, and gospel. The album also featured two duets: "Threat of Love," with Siouxsie Sioux and the Creatures, and "Almost Diamonds," with Sneaker Pimps' vocalist Kelly Dayton.

To add to his long list of musical credits, Almond also wrote an anthology of poems and lyrics entitled *A Beautiful Twisted Night,* made available in April of 1999 by the publishers Ellipsis, and an autobiography entitled *Tainted Life,* published by Macmillan.

Selected discography

Solo

Vermine in Ermine, Phonogram, 1984, reissued, 1998.
Stories of Johnny, Virgin, 1985.
A Woman's Story, Virgin, 1986.
Violent Silence (EP) Virgin, 1986.
Melancholy Rose (EP), Virgin, 1987.

Mother Fist... and Her Five Daughters, Virgin, 1987.
Singles 1984-1987, Virgin, 1987.
The Stars We Are, Parlophone, 1987.
Jacques, Rough Trade, 1989.
Enchanted, Parlophone, 1990.
Tenement Symphony, WEA, 1991.
A Virgin's Tale Vol. I, Virgin, 1992.
A Virgin's Tale Vol. II, Virgin, 1992.
Twelve Years of Tears, Warner, 1993.
Absinthe: The French Album, Thirsty Ear, 1994.
Treasure Box, EMI, 1995.
Fantastic Star, Mercury, 1996.
Live in Concert, Thirsty Ear, 1998.
(With Jim Thirlwell) *Flesh Volcano/Slut,* 1998.
Open All Night, Blue Star/Instinct, 1999.

Marc and the Mambas

Untitled, Phonogram, 1983, reissued, 1998.
Torment and Toreros, Phonogram, 1983, reissued, 1998.

Soft Cell/Marc Almond

Memorabilia: The Singles, Polydor, 1991.

Sources

Books

Buckley, Jonathan and others, editor, *Rock: The Rough Guide, Rough Guides,* Ltd., 1999.
Robbins, Ira A., editor, *Trouser Press Guide to '90s Rock,* Fireside/Simon & Schuster, 1997.

Periodicals

Advocate, November 9, 1999.
Billboard, September 25, 1999.
Los Angeles Times, November 24, 1999.
Melody Maker, December 16, 1995; December 13, 1997; August 8, 1998; May 1, 1999; July 31, 1999; November 3-9, 1999.
New York Times, November 30, 1999.

Online

Sonicnet.com, http://www.sonicnet.com (May 22, 2000).
Theatre of Marc Almond—The Official Marc Almond Website, http://www.marcalmond.co.uk (May 22, 2000).

—Laura Hightower

Asleep at the Wheel

Country band

Since the early-1970s, Asleep at the Wheel has been the standard bearer for western swing music. Country music's counterpart to big band music, western swing, like swing in general, experienced a revival in the late 1990s. While the Wheel benefited from this sudden upsurge in interest, it didn't impress their front man and founder Ray Benson. He told Michelle Nikolai of *Country.com*, "I don't believe in fads, fads come and go and this is our 30th year. We try not to worry too much about trends." By not following the latest fads, the band had to survive lean times of low sales and no recording contracts. Their persistence paid off, though, in the form of Grammy awards and the widespread respect of music critics and fellow musicians. The Wheel's authenticity became so highly regarded that in the 1990s, when the Wheel decided to record two albums consisting entirely of the music of western swing legend and pioneer Bob Wills, they were able to recruit some of the biggest names in country music to collaborate with them.

Throughout their long history, Asleep at the Wheel's driving force has been Benson, the only member to remain through all the years. Leading the band through changes that have seen more than 80 members,

AP/Wide World Photos. Reproduced by permission.

For The Record . . .

Members include **Ray Benson** (born Ray Benson Seifert on March 16, 1951, in Philadelphia, PA; original member), guitar, vocals; **Chris Booher**, piano; **Cindy Cashdollar**, dobro; **Floyd Domino** (born Jim Haber; joined group 1972; left group 1978), piano; **Michael Francis**, saxophone; **Danny Levin** (born 1949, in Philadelphia, PA; joined group 1974; left group early 1980s), fiddle, mandolin; **Bill Mabry** (joined group 1975; left group late 1970s), fiddle; **David Miller**, bass; **Lucky Oceans** (born Reuben Gosfield on April 22, 1951, in Philadelphia, PA; original member, left group c. 1980), steel guitar, drums; **Chris O'Connell** (original member, left group in late 1980s), guitar, vocals; **Leroy Preston** (original member, left group c. 1978), guitar, drums, vocals; **Jason Roberts**, fiddle, mandolin; **Pat "Taco" Ryan** (born July 14, 1953, in Texas; joined group 1976; left group in early 1980s), saxophone, clarinet; **David Sanger**, drums.

Group formed in West Virginia, 1969-70; moved to San Francisco Bay area, 1971; signed with United Artists and released first album, *Comin' Right at Ya'*, 1971; group moved to Austin, TX, 1974; had first single on the country charts, "The Letter Johnny Walker Read," 1975; started doing television commercial and movie soundtracks to pay off debts, 1980; released first studio album in five years, *Asleep at the Wheel*, 1985; released *A Tribute to Bob Wills and the Texas Playboys*, Liberty, 1993; nominated for album of the year by the Country Music Association, 1993; celebrated twenty-fifth anniversary with special performance for the PBS television series *Austin City Limits*, 1995; released second Bob Wills tribute album, *Ride With Bob*, 1999.

Awards: Grammy Awards for "One O'Clock Jump," 1978; "String of Pars," 1987; "Sugarfoot Rag," 1988; "Red Wing," 1993; "Blues for Dixie," 1994; "Hightower," 1995; "Bob's Breakdowns," 1999; Academy of Country Music Award for Best Touring Band, 1977.

Addresses: *Record company*—DreamWorks Records, 9268 W. 3rd St., Beverly Hills, CA 90210. *Website*—www.asleepatthewheel.com. *E-mail*—aatw@gte.net.

Benson has kept true to the sound of the band that he started far from the land of western swing. Benson grew up in suburban Philadelphia, where he was friends with Lucky Oceans, who played steel guitar. The band formed when Benson met drummer LeRoy Preston and moved with him and Oceans to a farm in West Virginia to live rent-free and play music. Benson brought in another high school friend, singer and guitarist Chris O'Connell, giving birth to the first incarnation of Asleep at the Wheel. While they performed traditional country songs and early rock and roll, they had not yet developed the blend of American pop music genres that would mark their mature work.

This quartet played the area bar scene and then moved onto the Washington, D.C. circuit, where rising country rock talents such as Emmylou Harris were getting their start. But the Wheel soon moved to the San Francisco Bay area, persuaded by the manager of fellow country rocker Commander Cody during a tour through the D.C. area. Of course, the Wheel wasn't the only band trying to make it in San Francisco in 1971, and the crowded music scene forced them to play just for their food sometimes. Their sound was still taking shape, and with the addition of Floyd Domino on keyboards, they brought in a jazz element that they had previously lacked. Persistence paid off, and the band landed a regular gig at the Longbranch Saloon in Berkeley. But their biggest break, though, came when Van Morrison saw them and then praised them in an interview in *Rolling Stone.* This brought the attention of record companies, and late in 1972 the band signed with United Artists.

First Album Went Nowhere

The Wheel's first album, *Comin' Right at Ya,* came out in March of 1973 and received almost no attention from the public. For Benson, though, the most significant event of that year may have been his first and only encounter with his idol, Bob Wills. Wills, in ill health, had finished a recording session for what would be his last album. Benson introduced himself in the hallway at the studio, but Wills was so exhausted that he could only grunt in acknowledgment. According to Benson, that night Wills fell into a coma from which he never recovered. The next year, on the evening Wills died, the Wheel had a gig at the legendary Cain's ballroom in Tulsa, which Wills had founded. In tribute they played nothing but his songs that night. Describing the event, Benson told Jeffrey B. Remz of *Country Standard Time,* "Somehow this mantle has been lovingly handed to us, and it's a real honor."

In the meantime, the band had relocated again, moving to Austin, Texas, having found appreciative audiences, a supportive environment, and plenty of places to perform. This period also saw the group adding members, giving them more flexibility in their arrangements.

Stand-up bassist Tony Garnier, drummer Scott Hennige, and fiddler and mandolin player Danny Levin, who had played briefly with the band back in West Virginia, all joined. With this expanded lineup, they released *Asleep at the Wheel,* now on the Epic label. The lack of sales led them to try yet another label, Capitol, for their third album, *Texas Gold.* In these lean times, Benson showed his skill at keeping the band going. Domino told Cartwright how Benson kept finding contracts for the band: "A record label would drop us and Ray would pull out his little book and flip to the phone numbers of two or three other labels."

This time the Wheel reached a larger audience, with the album making the top ten on the country charts. They also released three singles from the album, including "The Letter That Johnny Walker Read." The commercial success did not translate into complacency, though, as Benson continued to expand the band and its sound. They brought in fiddler Bill Mabry, which gave them two fiddles, just like the Texas Playboys, and Link Davis, playing both saxophone and fiddle, bringing a Cajun influence and adding horns for a sound that could cover both strains of swing, western and jazz.

Became Keepers of the Flame

As the band became better known, their reputation as the preservers of western swing tradition also grew. Their success earned them an appearance on the PBS television series *Austin City Limits* in 1976, for which they invited members of Wills' band, the Texas Playboys, to perform with them. This collaboration with their musical idols did more for the Playboys than merely honor them. Several of them received new recording contracts on the basis of this performance. The Wheel themselves received a unique recording opportunity the next year because of their faithfulness to their musical roots, recording for the Smithsonian Institution's Americana series, which is dedicated to preserving the musical heritage of the American people.

The band continued to expand its range, though, by increasing their membership. Pat "Taco" Ryan joined on clarinet and saxophone, giving the band the leeway to perform big band arrangements. Even with eleven members, the Wheel continued their collaboration with the Texas Playboys on their 1976 album, *Wheelin' and Dealin'.* The album's cover of the classic "Route 66" showcased their ability to blend big band and western swing and garnered a Grammy nomination. Their stage performances also began to earn honors from the music industry, and the Wheel was named the Best Touring Band by the Academy of Country Music in 1977.

Even while receiving all this recognition for their work, relations were not always smooth within the band. In 1978 Benson and Domino had a falling out, and Domino became the first early member to leave, a complicated matter because his wife managed the band at that time and also had disputes with Benson. Instead of replacing Domino, Benson trimmed the size of the band, with two new members—John Nicholas on guitar, piano, harmonica, mandolin, and vocals; and Fran Christina on drums—joining Benson, O'Connell, Oceans, Ryan, and Levin. These changes did not slow the Wheel's rising reputation, and their version of "One O'Clock Jump," from the album *Collision Course,* earned the band their first Grammy award.

Awards and success did not translate into financial success, though, and the next few years would be difficult ones for the Wheel. Although 1980 saw the release of their seventh studio album, *Framed,* a five-year drought would follow. Membership changes continued, as Oceans left. A more serious problem surfaced when the band discovered that they had more then $200,000 worth of debt. Without a recording contract, the group turned to providing the music for beer commercials and movie soundtracks, even appearing occasionally on film. Benson also turned his hand to producing, working with Willie Nelson, Aaron Neville, and Bruce Hornsby.

The band eventually returned to the studio, releasing *Asleep at the Wheel* in 1985. In many ways, they picked up right where they left off, releasing a top 20 country single in "House of Blue Light" and receiving an award as Band of the Year from the National Association of Campus Activities. With their next album, *10,* the Wheel entered a period when they consistently earned recognition for their unique work with nominations and awards. In 1988 and 1989, they took home Grammy awards for Best Country Instrumental Performance. By this time Benson was the only remaining original member, although O'Connell had rejoined them after a maternity leave. The rest of the band consisted of fiddler Larry Franklin, fiddler Johnny Gimble, bass player Jon Mitchell, pianist/accordionist Tim Alexander, steel guitarist John Ely, saxophonist Mike Francis, and drummer David Sanger.

The band continued their pace, touring extensively and releasing new material every year or two. They also continued the pattern of changing record companies after an album or two, and Benson continued to change the lineup for the band. He told Cartwright that he modeled his band leadership after the likes of Duke Ellington: "They used books so that they could change personnel without losing that consistency. My book's up here—in my head." Benson used that book not only to find musicians for the band, but also to enlist guest performers from the elite of country music. Following 1990's *Keepin' Me Up Nights* and 1992's *Route 66,* Benson brought together a wide variety of talent for 1993's *A Tribute to Bob Wills and the Texas Playboys.*

Recorded with Guests and Old Friends

This album, consisting entirely of covers of Wills' songs, not only honored Benson and the Wheel's main musical inspiration; it also acknowledged the high regard that the country music world held for the band. The musicians on the album included Dolly Parton, Willie Nelson, Chet Atkins, Garth Brooks, and Lyle Lovett. The Wheel's collaboration with Lovett on "Blues for Dixie" earned a Grammy for Best Country Performance by a Duo. But perhaps the most important guests on the album were former band members Oceans, Domino, and O'Connell, reuniting with Benson for this special project. Otherwise, the lineup was much different than it had been even six years earlier. Only Benson and Francis remained. The newer members included Tim Alexander on piano, accordion, and vocals; Cindy Cashdollar on Hawaiian steel guitar; Ricky Turpin on fiddle, electric mandolin, vocals; David Earl Miller on bass; and Tommy Beavers on drums.

In spite of all the personnel changes, Asleep at the Wheel as an entity celebrated its twenty-fifth anniversary in 1995. To mark the occasion, former members and a gallery of country stars joined the band on stage for a special episode of *Austin City Limits.* The band continued their extensive touring, releasing the live album *Back to the Future Now.* They didn't return to the studio until they put together another Bob Wills tribute, this time entitled *Ride With Bob,* released in 1999. Again a wide range of guests appeared with the band, ranging across the spectrum of musical styles, including a collaboration between country legend Merle Haggard and swing revivalists Squirrel Nut Zippers. The motivation for doing another Wills tribute came from not having room for as many songs as Benson wanted the first time around. The first time they never got around to Wills' greatest hits, but this time they did.

The Wheel's lineup for this outing saw a few changes, with Jason Roberts and Chris Booher taking over as fiddlers and David Sanger taking the drums. A bigger change for the band was that they recorded the album in the studio they built in Austin. They especially designed their equipment to evoke the sounds of recordings from Wills' heyday while maintaining the sharpness of the digital age. Benson described the process to Michelle Nikolai of Country.com: "We build a lot of our own gear. And it's old tube gear, so basically we recreate the old tube sound. Although it's recorded on a digital format, it fattens everything up and makes it sound warm and beautiful." As before, the project received wide praise and recognition, earning five Grammy nominations, including one for a video documenting the recording sessions, which Benson directed.

The two albums of Bob Wills material show Benson just as firmly rooted as when Asleep at the Wheel started almost 30 years earlier. Benson explained why western swing still has such a strong hold on him, telling Jeffrey B. Remz of *Country Standard Time,* "The reason we were drawn to western swing is you can do a huge variety of music. You can play from big bands to ballads." Through all the years and changes, Benson and his band have thoroughly explored that variety. Their creativity in showing their respect for this traditional country music style has earned them respect throughout the music world.

Selected discography

Comin' Right at Ya, EMI America, 1973.
Asleep at the Wheel, Epic, 1974.
Texas Gold, Capitol, 1975.
Wheelin' & Dealin', Capitol, 1976.
The Wheel, Capitol, 1977.
Collision Course, Capitol, 1978.
Served Live, Capitol, 1979.
Framed, MCA, 1980.
Asleep at the Wheel, Dot/MCA, 1985.
10, Epic, 1987.
Western Standard Time, Epic, 1988.
Keepin' Me Up Nights, Arista, 1990.
A Tribute to Bob Wills and the Texas Playboys, Liberty, 1993.
The Wheel Keeps on Rollin', Capitol Nashville, 1995.
Back to the Future Now—Live at Arizona Charlie's, Sony, 1997.
Ride with Bob, DreamWorks, 1999.

Sources

Books

Comprehensive Country Music Encyclopedia, Time Books, 1994.
Romanowski, Patricia and Holly George-Warren, editors, *The New Rolling Stone Encyclopedia of Rock and Roll,* Fireside, 1995.
Stambler, Irwin, *Country Music: the Encyclopedia,* St. Martin's, 1997.

Periodicals

Billboard, February 5, 2000, p. 56.
Texas Monthly, November 1995, p. 78.

Online

"Asleep at the Wheel," *All-Music Guide,* http://allmusic.com (April 10, 2000).
"Asleep at the Wheel," *Country.com,* http://www.country.com (April 10, 2000).
"Second Time's a Charm: Asleep at the Wheel Takes Care of Unfinished Business," *Country.com,* September 14, 1999, http://www.country.com (April 10, 2000).
"With Bob Wills Along, Asleep at the Wheel Keeps Rolling," *Country Standard Time,* July 1999, http://www.country standardtime.com (April 10, 2000).

—Lloyd Hemingway

John Barry

Composer

For more than three decades, the music of composer John Barry contributed intrinsically to the definition of the American film experience. He created award-winning soundtracks that wafted in the background of dozens of cinema's more memorable film attractions and into the mainstream of American culture. Through his musical scores he effectively defined the emotional backdrop for the most watched movies of the 1960s, 1970s, and 1980s, including *Born Free, Midnight Cowboy, Out of Africa,* and *Dances with Wolves.* The list of John Barry movie soundtracks is as impressive as it is lengthy, including *Lion in Winter,* the remake of *King Kong, The Deep, The Cotton Club, Chaplin,* and *Mercury Rising.* Altogether Barry earned a total of four Oscars for his motion picture scores, and for generations of moviegoers his name was closely associated as the composer of the soundtracks to more than a dozen James Bond spy thrillers. The James Bond music scores, at times enervating and always seductive, captivated moviegoers who became spellbound at the adventures of the unstoppable spy hero in *Goldfinger, Octopussy,* and other films based on the novels of author Ian Fleming about an unusually capable British agent, code-named 007 and otherwise known as "Bond, James Bond."

Barry was born Jonathan Barry Prendergast in York in northern England. He was the youngest of four siblings, including two other boys and a girl. His father owned a string of eight movie theatres in the town where the family lived, and Barry quit school in his mid-teens to go to work in the projection booth of one of his father's cinemas. Barry, having studied classical piano and harmony, was fascinated with the dramatic appeal of theatrical music. He sometimes composed his own personal soundtracks to the movies he saw, and he became determined even as a young man to work as a composer and to write film scores. When the cinema hosted live musical concerts, Barry enjoyed the jazz music above all and embraced every opportunity to make the casual acquaintances of some of the great jazz artists of the times.

When Barry joined the army around 1950, he continued to write and to study music even from the remote locations in Cypress and Egypt where he was stationed. He used borrowed money to purchase a correspondence course on jazz arrangement through a mail-order advertisement in a magazine. The course, guided by jazz artist Stan Kenton's arranger, William Russo, kept Barry engrossed for two years.

In 1955, after leaving the army, Barry collected his own musical ensemble and eventually billed the band as the John Barry Seven. Barry played a trumpet in the septet; nonetheless his musical scores focused squarely on guitar as the lead instrument. According to Barry, he allowed the guitar to take center stage because the instrument symbolized contemporary music and was indisputably the most popular of all the instruments. During the late 1950s Barry and his band recorded for Columbia (EMI) and one of their songs, "Hit and Miss," reached the top ten echelon of the hit chart in Britain. Also during that time he accepted a position as musical director for EMI Records, a situation that led to a further opportunity to write his first professional movie score for Adam Faith's *Beat Girl* in 1959. For that movie, Barry developed contemporary jazzy themes, in keeping with the times. In 1960, he wrote the soundtrack of the Peter Sellers movie, *Never Let Go,* and in 1962 Barry wrote the music for *The Amorous Mr. Prawn.*

In 1962, Barry accepted an offer to rework the score of a new movie called *Dr. No,* which at that time was the first in a series of immensely popular films to be based on Ian Fleming's novels about an exotic and debonair British spy, James Bond. In retrospect the score was widely attributed to Barry who rewrote the score to better suit the movie's producers. Years later Barry's involvement in creating the score was publicly acknowledged, although he never received formal credit for the *Dr. No* project. The James Bond film series, which for many years starred the smooth lead actor, Sean Connery, developed into a cultural phenomenon. Over the course of the next two decades Barry scored 11 out of the 19 subsequent movies in the series, catapulting his name into the forefront of the film music industry in the process.

Barry's dynamic Bond themes augmented the rare blend of culture, danger, and adventure that was

For The Record . . .

Born Jonathan Barry Prendergast on November 3, 1933, in York, England; married Jane Birkin, 1966; divorced; married Laurie; children: four daughters, one son. *Education:* Instruction via correspondence with jazz arranger William Russo.

Selected movie soundtracks: *Born Free,* 1966; *Goldfinger,* 1963; *Thunderball,* 1963; *Lion in winter,* 1968; *Mary, Queen of Scots,* 1971; *The Deep, 1976; Somewhere in Time,* 1980; *Out of Africa,* 1985; *Dances with Wolves,* 1990; *Mercury Rising,* 1998; signed with Universal Classics and Jazz, 1998.

Awards: Best Film Scores (*Born Free, Lion in Winter, Out of Africa, Dances with Wolves*), Best Songs ("Born Free"), Academy of Motion Picture Arts and Sciences; Songwriters Hall of Fame, 1998; Frederick Loewe Award, Palm Springs International Film Festival, January 1999; Officer of the Order of the British Empire, July 1999; Honoree, British Music Industry Trusts, July 1999.

Addresses: *Management*–The Kraft-Benjamin-Emgel Agency, 9200 W. Sunset Blvd., Suite 321, Los Angeles, CA 90069-3505.

inherent to the Fleming novels. Barry's music constituted an essential factor in the evolution of the James Bond persona. A generation later, composer David Arnold succeeded Barry as the composer for the James Bond scores. As quoted by Paul Sexton in *Billboard,* Arnold noted that, "For me the success of the Bond series was 50 percent Sean Connery and 50 percent John Barry." Among Barry's greatest hits from the Bond movies was the title song from the 1963 feature, *Goldfinger.* Also among the more popular Bond melodies were Barry's collaborations with lyricist Don Black that resulted in the hit title songs, "Thunderball" and "Diamonds are Forever." Barry also created the soundtrack to *Casino Royale,* and *Never Say Die,* two later films about the secret agent James Bond, by other producers.

Barry collaborated with lyricist Don Black again in 1966 for the soundtrack to the movie *Born Free,* a James Hill docudrama on human interaction with the lions of Africa. Barry's score won the Academy of Motion Pictures Arts and Sciences "Oscar" award that year.

The title song of the movie became enormously popular and was heard everywhere; it too won an Oscar. Also nominated for an Oscar was his 1971 score for *Mary, Queen of Scots.*

During the 1980s, Barry suffered a series of emotional trials, including the death of his parents in close proximity to one another in 1980, followed by the accidental death of his older brother five years later. It was suggested that during that time a morose and melancholy atmosphere shrouded his film scores, including *Out of Africa* and *Somewhere in Time.* Barry's 1985 score for *Out of Africa* won the Oscar award for the best soundtrack that year. The drama, which starred Meryl Streep, was set around the exotic backdrop of a coffee plantation in Africa; Barry dedicated the sentimental soundtrack to the memory of his late brother.

Barry himself suffered a serious accident in the late 1980s, brought on by a toxic reaction to a drink he was consuming. Ironically, it was a so-called health potion that caused the affliction, which resulted in a critical injury when his esophagus ruptured. He underwent life-saving surgery and a lengthy recovery period, including a series of follow-up operations. His recuperation lasted two years, from 1988-1990. He returned to cinematic composing with the subsequent release in 1990 of an Oscar-winning soundtrack for the Kevin Costner production, *Dances with Wolves.* Again in 1992 he received an Oscar nomination for the music from *Chaplin.*

Barry, in addition to his stature in the film industry, found enjoyment throughout the years in composing works of his own inspiration and volition—music not associated with any story or screenplay, but rather the spontaneous music of his heart. Among his early productions, an album named *Moviola* was released in 1966. A compilation of his own works and arrangements, the recording presents Barry conducting the Royal Philharmonic Orchestra. Also among his sporadic non-cinematic releases was his 1998 album, *The Beyondness of Things,* released by Universal Classics (Decca). *Beyondness* was his first major non-film project after a number of years. It offered a romantic respite of symphonic music, specifically intended *not* to portray a visual image and likewise to distinguish itself from his film scores, according to the composer.

Throughout his lifetime Barry earned a reputation for his tireless dedication to his work. In the late 1990s he performed to a sellout crowd at London's Royal Albert Hall, his first concert in more than two decades. Also during the 1990s his many compositions experienced a resurgence of popularity for a variety of reasons. In particular, several young pop stars discovered his music and incorporated his songs into their own performances, and the compositions that he created for the James Bond movies experienced a revival because they evoked a special nostalgia for many performers of the 1990s. Also in 1999, Barry began a project to record Celtic songs and dances featuring vocals from guest artists.

Barry was inducted into the Songwriters Hall of Fame in 1998, and in complement to his sizable collection of Oscars, he received the Frederick Loewe Award at the Palm Springs International Film Festival in January of 1999. He was honored as an Officer of the Order of the British Empire in July of 1999, and that same month he was honored by the British Music Industry Trusts. That same year saw the publication of two full-length biographies documenting the life of Barry—Sansom & Co.'s *John Barry: A Life in Music* by Geoff Leonard and others, and *John Barry: A Sixties Theme* by Eddi Fiegel. Barry, according to *Entertainment Weekly,* stands among the "living legends" of film composers.

Barry married actress Jane Birkin in the 1960s; they were later divorced, and Barry remarried. He has three daughters and one son. He lives on Long Island with his wife, Laurie.

Selected discography

Albums

Across the Sea of Time, Epic, 1996.
The Beyondness of Things, Universal Classics and Jazz (Decca), 1998.

Movie soundtracks

Thunderball, 1963.
Goldfinger, 1963.
Somewhere in Time (platinum), 1980.
Out of Africa (platinum), 1985.
Dances with Wolves (platinum), 1990.
Music of John Barry, Vol. Two, Silva America, 1996.
Playing by Heart, 1999.

Sources

Periodicals

Billboard, July 3, 1999; October 2, 1999, p. 81.
Entertainment Weekly, March 13, 1998, p. 30.
Los Angeles Times, January 8, 1999, p. 16.

Online

"John Barry," http://www.filmmusic.dk/barry2/html (June 6, 2000).

—Gloria Cooksey

Basement Jaxx

Techno rock group

With the release of 1999's *Remedy,* the British house music duo Basement Jaxx—DJs Felix Buxton and Simon Ratcliffe—set the dance world on fire with a sound they call punk garage, turning the pair into club land messiahs. Given the pair's diverse musical influences—Timbaland, Larry Heard, George Duke, Lonnie Liston-Smith, and Thomas Bangalter, one of the driving forces behind both Daft Punk and Stardust—Basement Jaxx's music reflected a myriad of musical styles. And as illustrated by *Remedy,* Buxton and Ratcliffe display an apparent penchant for creating original, exciting music without limitations. "There's the ragga and the Latin, and a bit of disco, funk and noise," Buxton explained, as quoted *Rolling Stone.* "We were tired of music that didn't have any joy about being alive at all—just dreary going-on music," added. "We definitely wanted to celebrate life a bit. We're happy to be alive, and we want to make music that can give you hope and dreams: something raw, something emotional, something real."

Not only did the full-length debut sell millions of copies worldwide, but *Remedy* also turned out to be one of the most critically acclaimed albums of the year, garnering the kind of positive reviews usually reserved for traditional rock groups. *Rolling Stone* gave it a four-star "excellent" rating, *Spin* named it as one of the top albums of the 1990s, and numerous others listed *Remedy* as one of the best albums of the year. Upon the LP's release in America, the first single from the album, "Red Alert," hit number one on the *Billboard* Dance Music/Club Play chart. According to the music

press, Basement Jaxx's success arose because, unlike other techno outfits who focus primarily on drum loops and samples, Buxton and Ratcliffe decided to reintroduce melody, structured songs, and real vocalists onto the world's dance floors.

And while Basement Jaxx's music does resemble other house music imports such as the Chemical Brothers or Fatboy Slim, there nonetheless exists a noticeable difference. "We really respect what Fat Boy Slim does. But what he's doing is very different from what we're doing. His music is more like 'Zap, here it is.' It's not music of depth and longevity. It's music of this moment. Our music is less throwaway," said Buxton in an interview with *Boston Globe* correspondent Christopher Muther. In other words, the difference between Basement Jaxx's sound and other techno-styled music is, "Its soul, its depth," Buxton added. "There are very few acts where I can feel the emotion in their music. For me, music needs to move you, that's what it's all about. That's what we're trying to do."

A Passion for House Music

Although unrecognized among mainstream audiences until the phenomenal arrival of *Remedy,* the hardworking team, who spend most of their time off in the studio, had already made a name for themselves behind the scenes. The pair first met in 1993 through mutual friends at a bar in the multi-ethnic Brixton neighborhood of London, England (some sources state they met at a Thames riverboat party organized by Buxton). At the time, Buxton, the son of a vicar in the Anglican church—a "rather strict father," he revealed to *Rolling Stone*'s Matt Hendrickson—was employed by a publicity firm boasting such clients as Tupperware, but he really wanted to make house and garage music. Ratcliffe, who grew up in Holland and Wales, was a student at the University of London and working like Buxton outside of the music business in an electronics store, though he had recently begun creating his own jungle and house records in his basement studio.

Not long after their initial meeting, the duo started recording together at Ratcliffe's flat, combining their musical inspirations into a single ideal: to return to the roots of house music. Whereas Ratcliffe gravitated to the deep Latin funk of groups like War and George Duke, Buxton found his inspiration in Chicago house music, thus resulting in Basement Jaxx, a mixture of several different styles. In 1994, the pair formed their own label, Atlantic Jaxx Records, and recorded their first two EPs. Although they went unnoticed in England, the recordings did manage to attract recognition from some of their heroes, including DJ legend Tony Humphries, who played the song "Da Underground" from Basement Jaxx's first EP on his New York City mix show during 1994 and 1995, as well as American house DJ Louie Vega. "We were two skinny white

Members include **Felix Buxton** (born in 1971 in London, England; son of an Anglican church vicar) and **Simon Ratcliffe** (born in 1970; raised in Holland and Wales; attended the University of London).

Formed Basement Jaxx in Brixton, South London, England, 1993; founded Atlantic Jaxx Records, 1994; signed with XL Recordings, released *Remedy,* 1999.

Awards: Two awards at the Winter Music Conference 2000 (WMC2000) in Miami, FL, for Best Newcomers and Best Dance Act.

Addresses: *Record company*—Astralwerks/Caroline, 104 W. 29th St., New York City, NY 10001, (212) 886-7500. *Management*—Andrew Mansi and Mark Pickin, West Management, London, England. *Booking for North America*—Sam Kirby, Renaissance Entertainment, New York City, NY. *Booking for other markets*—Peter Elliott, Primary Talent, London, England.

English guys," remembered Ratcliffe, as quoted by Hendrickson. "And we had Americans calling and telling us that what we were doing was dope. That gave us the push to continue."

Jaxx Night Set in Motion

In addition to receiving complimentary words from other DJs, the pair also earned a reputation for their live performances. A crucial factor to their eventual success, the two held regular "Basement Jaxx" nights at various locales around Brixton, making their very first of such events at Taco Joe's, a seedy, hole-in-the-wall Mexican restaurant frequented by drug dealers and situated beneath a railway. As word spread about the duo, Jaxx night at Taco Joe's and other small venues became popular attractions, with more than 100 people from all walks of life crammed into dimly lit rooms built to hold just 50 patrons.

A typical show would include Basement Jaxx spinning all types of music, from Whitney Houston and Public Enemy to the twosome's own originals. "Posh people, people off the street, drug dealers, everyone came together. The system was booming, and it was really raw. It was wicked," Buxton told Hendrickson. How-

ever, the two decided to quit holding Jaxx nights in the late-1990s, at the peak of the events' popularity. From the beginning, Basement Jaxx had held strong to the ethos: "Check your attitude at the door, and throw your coat on the floor." So, when Jaxx night later became known as the "cool place to go," Buxton and Ratcliffe thought it best to pull the plug. "Before, we could just play the music we wanted. That disappeared," explained Ratcliffe. "Everyone started coming with this attitude of 'You're cool, let's see what you can do.'" Buxton further noted, "It was a bit fashion-overload. 'This magazine is coming this week, this one the next.' We could see it changing. So you have to move on."

Meanwhile, Basement Jaxx had concentrated on recording, too, and in 1995, their club classic "Samba Magic" caught the attention of Virgin Records. After the label picked up the song for distribution, the duo started drawing praise from both the American and British house community as one of the top production units around. As a result, Basement Jaxx spent much of 1996 remixing songs for several well-known acts: the Pet Shop Boys, Roger Sanchez, and Lil' Mo Yin Yang, just to name a few. That same year, they also released a third EP containing the club favorite "Flylife," which reached the British Top 20 and was one of the most popular dance anthems of the year after the Multiply label re-released the single in 1997. Soon thereafter, the pair released a compilation of their best Atlantic Jaxx efforts that led to offers from several major record companies.

A Four-star Album

Weighing their long list of options, Buxton and Ratcliffe decided to sign to the independent XL Recordings, with Astralwerks distributing Basement Jaxx's records in the United States. In May of 1999, after the arrival of "Red Alert," Basement Jaxx released *Remedy* in the United Kingdom. Subsequently, in August of that year, the duo's full-length debut arrived in America to rave reviews. *USA Today,* for example, listed *Remedy* on its list of the ten best albums of the year, while *Rolling Stone* reviewer Rob Sheffield described Basement Jaxx as "a pair of daft punks whose wholly original 'punk garage' style melds old-school Chicago house with Latin salsa, ragga, jazz discord and anything else that isn't nailed down." Compared to other techno acts, "They blow the DJ boffins right out of the booth with the dirty-mind party bounce of 'Red Alert' and 'Same Old Show,'" Sheffield further remarked. "For these guys, dance music belongs to the true believers, and on *Remedy* they take you to church."

The success of the unique Basement Jaxx sound brought Buxton and Ratcliffe's live act—featuring a live band, dancers, and singers—to fans across the globe, from Japan and Australia to California, New York, and Canada. The duo's popularity continued to escalate, and they scored their second number-one *Billboard* Dance Chart hit with "Rendez-Vu." In 2000, Basement Jaxx earned three Brit Award nominations: Best British Album for *Remedy,* Best Dance Act, and Best British Single for "Red Alert." They picked up two awards at the Winter Music Conference 2000 (WMC2000) in Miami, Florida, taking home honors for Best Newcomers and Best Dance Act.

Selected discography

"Red Alert," (maxi single), XL/Astralwerks, 1999.
Remedy, XL/Astralwerks, 1999.
"Bingo Bango," (single), XL, 2000.

Sources

Periodicals

Atlanta Journal-Constitution, August 5, 1999; December 26, 1999.

Billboard, May 29, 1999; July 3, 1999; August 14, 1999; October 9, 1999; October 30, 1999; November 6, 1999; January 1, 2000; February 12, 2000; March 4, 2000; March 18, 2000.
Boston Globe, September 10, 1999; September 16, 1999.
Los Angeles Times, June 27, 1999; October 4, 1999; December 12, 1999; January 2, 2000.
Melody Maker, July 10, 1999; July 24, 1999; October 23, 1999.
Rolling Stone, August 19, 1999; September 22, 1999; December 16-23, 1999.
USA Today, August 31, 1999; December 28, 1999.
Village Voice, March 2, 1999; August 3, 1999.
Washington Post, August 22, 1999; October 24, 1999.

Online

Basement Jaxx at Astralwerks, http://www.astralwerks.com/basementjaxx/ (May 17, 2000).
Sonicnet.com, http://www.sonicnet.com (May 17, 2000).

—*Laura Hightower*

The Bluetones

Pop band

After the release of their debut, the number-one hit album *Expecting to Fly,* the Bluetones were unwillingly pushed onto the Britpop bandwagon. "I was never sure what Britpop was in the first place, to be honest," lead singer Mark Morriss said to Paul Sexton of *Billboard.* "We were lumped in with so many bands we had nothing in common with, apart from the fact that we all hold guitars." Moreover, the Bluetones, despite critical raves, have never felt like they fully belonged. "It's because we've always been reluctant to follow the path," guitarist Adam Devlin agreed in an interview with *Independent*'s Nick Hasted. "We're not celebrity people. We don't do the things other pop stars do. We get a bit of a hard time for it, too; we'd get ridiculed as awkward and dull. We can live with that. It's just that we don't hang around with Christ Evans, we don't put our songs on commercials, we don't go on compilation albums. It's a cut-off point we've got. We're not willing to whore ourselves. It comes with a bit of a price."

Consequently, unlike so many Britpop bands, who appear to do nothing musically and still sustain the public's interest, the Bluetones, despite making good records, had a problem maintaining their profile, largely because they never really developed a specific image.

For The Record . . .

Members include **Eds D. Chesters** (born on October 24, 1971; former member of Puppy Dogs From Hell, Brando, and SOHO; studied chemistry at Newcastle University before dropping out to concentrate on music), drums, percussion; **Adam P. Devlin** (born on September 17, 1969; former member of the Bottlegarden), six- and twelve-string guitars; **Mark James Morriss** (born on October 18, 1971; former member of the Bottlegarden), vocals, harmonica; **Scott Edward Reginald Ilanthriy Morriss** (born on October 10, 1973; former member of the Bottlegarden), bass guitar, vocals; **Richard Payne** (joined band in 2000; former member of Dodgy and the Unbelievable Truth), keyboards, guitar.

Formed as a quartet just outside London, England, in Hounslow, in 1994; released number-one album *Expecting to Fly,* 1996; released *Return to the Last Chance Saloon,* which entered the British charts at number 11, 1998; released *Science and Nature,* 2000.

Addresses: *Record company*—Superior Quality Recordings, website: http://www.superiorqualityrecordings.co.uk. *Publicity company*—Hall Or Nothing, 11 Poplar Mews, Uxbridge Rd., London, England W12 7JS, website: http://www.hallornothing.com. *General contact for mailing list*—The Bluetones, P.O. Box 3836, London, England NW3 4XF. *Websites*—The Bluetones Official Website: http://www.blue tones.co.uk, The Bluetones Unofficial Homepage: http://www.bsm.ndo.co.uk/The Bluetones.

But Morriss calculated that remaining not the least bit contrived will work to the band's advantage. "The longer people take to get a handle on us, the longer it will take for people to get bored with us truly," he pointed out to *Melody Maker* in March of 1998. "I love reading Oasis and Black Grape interviews," he added. "And all the naughtiness they get up to, I enjoy it, but we're not that type of character. It doesn't suit the way we look, we're quite unassuming blokes, but no one has hit the nail on the head as far as we go." Likewise, noted Devlin, "We're quite keen to steer it away from our personal lives. We're rock 'n' roll; we just don't advertise it."

The Bluetones formed just outside London, England, in Hounslow, in 1994, as a foursome. Originally, the group consisted of guitarist Adam Devlin, drummer/percussionist Eds Chesters, and brothers Mark Morriss, the band's lead vocalist and harmonica player, and Scott Morriss, the Bluetones' bass guitarist and vocalist; all, except Chesters, played together before as the Bottlegarden, and Richard Payne, a keyboardist and guitarist, joined in 2000. "We all made a collective gamble," Devlin, who, along with the other members, gave up their various jobs and educational pursuits to concentrate on the band, told *Melody Maker* in March of 1998. "We all quit what we were doing and went on the dole. We spent a good few years on the dole before we got signed. If nothing had happened, we'd have been stuck at 27 years old with no experience of anything."

Drawing from a well of classic and modern pop/rock influences—such as Buffalo Springfield, Jeff Buckley, Led Zeppelin, the Band, Randy Newman, Arthur Lee, Love, Scott Walker, the Smiths, and the Stone Roses—the band started playing local clubs and writing songs for their debut album. *Expecting to Fly,* named after an old Buffalo Springfield song, was released in the United Kingdom on February 12, 1996, on Superior Quality and, upon the strength of the band's previously released singles, entered the British charts at number one on February 18, 1996. Suddenly, the Bluetones were thrust into the limelight, heavily touted by the music press, as well as by the influential John Peel.

The album—which included the tracks "Bluetonic," "Slight Return," and "Cut Some Rug," all British-released singles—was later released by A&M Records in the United States in August of that year. However, Mark Morriss, for one, realized that the chances of breaking through to American audiences wouldn't happen overnight. "We don't expect to walk into America, for them to roll out the red carpet, and for us to say 'What's wrong with you guys? We've had a big song,'" he conceded to Sexton. "That's the wrong attitude that too many people have." But while the group's debut didn't top the sales charts in America, it nonetheless received favorable critical responses. *Expecting to Fly,* commented Mike Flaherty in *Entertainment Weekly,* "arrives with all of Britpop's requisite emphasis on strong song craft—then goes it one better. Conjuring a hybrid of once-influential forebears—the textured thoughtfulness of Aztec Camera with the hip-swaying buoyancy of the Stone Roses—accusation and introspection entwine in their sprightly, energized odes."

After touring extensively to promote their first album, the Bluetones took a year off in 1997 to concentrate on a follow-up record, arriving the following year with *Return to the Last Chance Saloon.* Released in the United Kingdom on March 9, 1998, the second effort entered the British album charts at number 11 on

March 15, 1998. "It's loads different," Chesters, who began drumming at age 11, explained in an interview with *Rhythm* magazine. "We felt a lot more comfortable second time round, and we were definitely wiser, stronger and more relaxed about everything." The drummer further added, "We really needed a break after the first album, and it's paid off. As far as the four of us were concerned though, there wasn't any pressure—in spite of what people were saying about difficult second albums. We knew the songs would come, we just needed some time, and once we'd written a couple of good ones, we knew the album was going to be great."

Four of the album's songs—"Solomon Bites the Worm," "If...," "Sleazy Bed Track," "4-Day Weekend,"—were released as singles in the United Kingdom, and despite speculation that the Bluetones could not match the quality of their debut, *Return to the Last Chance Saloon* was a hit with fans as well as critics. Although James Delingpole in a review for *Q* magazine complained about Mark Morriss's "unbearably whiny" vocals on the slow, sensitive numbers, the writer overall described the record as "pretty impressive—especially the guitar work, which nods variously toward the Smiths, Led Zeppelin and Radiohead."

And while sales were not quite so impressive as the Bluetones' debut, the slight difference never shook the band's confidence. "I think, after the success of the first album, we were not prepared for the public gaze being fixed on us quite as much as it was," Mark Morriss admitted to Carol Clerk and Ben Knowles of *Melody Maker* in December of 1999. "Now we've learned to live without it and drift into the background a bit. It's just fashion. Things move on. It was really no surprise to us that things leveled off, and I'm glad they did. We'd rather play to people who really want to hear us than sell ourselves to people who aren't interested."

Unfortunately, the States continued to elude the Bluetones, but they found audiences in Japan more receptive. The group's third album, *Science & Nature,* hit store shelves first in Japan on April 12, 2000, and the Japanese version included a bonus track entitled "It's a Boy." Then the next month, on May 15, 2000, *Science & Nature* was released in the United Kingdom and included videos of the songs "Keep the Home Fires Burning" (a.k.a. "KTHFB") and "Autophilia." Both songs were previously released as singles. According to Mark Morriss, as he told *Melody Maker* earlier in February,

Science & Nature "isn't a major change in direction, but it's got the most variety and it'll give people a different perspective on the band. There's country and western and there's folk, there's kind of dark reggae, but it always sounds like us."

In addition to expanding their music beyond the confines of pop, the Bluetones also intended to spice up their live shows with visuals and film when they hit the road to support the release. "We're putting together something that's more of an audio-visual thing than just an audio thing," Mark Morriss continued. "In the past, we've tried to eliminate the stage sets as best we can, but we haven't taken it further than that. This time there'll be more for you to look at than just our ugly mugs."

Selected discography

Expecting to Fly, Superior Quality/A&M, 1996.
Return to the Last Chance Saloon, Superior Quality/A&M, 1998.
Science and Nature, Superior Quality/Mercury, 2000.

Sources

Periodicals

Billboard, March 16, 1996; February 22, 1997.
Bradford Telegraph & Argus, January 15, 1999.
Dallas Morning News, July 7, 1996, p. 7C.
Entertainment Weekly, August 23, 1996, p. 124.
Independent, February 4, 1996, p. 3; February 16, 1996, p. 13; February 23, 1996, p. 13; May 13, 1996, p. S20; May 24, 1996, pp. 2-3; March 13, 1998, p. 14; April 10, 1998, p. 11.
Los Angeles Times, September 14, 1996.
New Musical Express, February 10, 1996; November 1998; January 29, 2000; February 19, 2000.
Q, March 1998.
Rhythm, July 1998.
Rolling Stone, September 5, 1996.

Online

The Bluetones Unofficial Homepage, http://www.bsm.ndo.co.uk/TheBluetones (May 16, 2000).

—Laura Hightower

Boss Hog

Rock band

Established by the husband-and-wife team of singer/guitarist Christina Martinez and Jon Spencer, a well-known guitarist and founder of the acclaimed Blues Explosion, Boss Hog became the toast of Lower East Side night clubs in New York during the early 1990s, and by the middle of the decade had attracted alternative music fans from across the United States. Although Spencer anchored the band, it was Martinez's vocals—ranging throughout the emotional spectrum from sensitive, sexual, and romantic, to fierce and powerful—that defined the Boss Hog sound. And whereas the John Spencer Blues Explosion featured beats and art-school concepts, Boss Hog placed their musical emphasis on full-force rock and abrasive pop-punk.

Boss Hog rose from the ashes of Pussy Galore, a celebrated low-fidelity, neo-blues cult band formed in Washington D.C. in 1985 by Spencer and fellow guitarist Julie Cafritz. The two musicians had met while Spencer was studying semiotics and history of art in Provincetown, Rhode Island, eventually deciding to drop out of college, head for the city, and form a band. "I hated the people, the course, everything," Spencer recalled, as quoted by *Rock: The Rough Guide* contributor Susan Compo. "I just wanted to play rock 'n' roll." Taking the band's moniker from the villain in the James Bond movie, Spencer and Cafritz teamed with drummer John Hammill to release the group's 1985 four-song debut EP entitled *Feel Good About Your Body* on their own Shove label.

Feeling ignored in the nation's capital, Pussy Galore soon relocated to New York, where Spencer and Cafritz hired a third guitarist, Neil Haggerty, as well as a new drummer to replace Hammill named Bob Birt, formerly of Sonic Youth. By 1986, Martinez, a former photographer for the band, joined as a fourth guitarist, remaining with Pussy Galore until September of that year, just long enough to appear on the group's *Exile on Main Street* album. The band's notorious internal tensions caused her to leave. After Martinez departed, Pussy Galore continued on for the remainder of the 1980s until their dissolution in 1990. Their albums during this time for Caroline Records included 1987's *Right Now;* 1988's *Sugarshift Sharp,* produced with Steve Albini; 1988's *Dial M For Motherf***er,* considered the band's consummate moment and recorded without Cafritz, who had meanwhile also quit the band; and 1990's *La Historia De La Musica Rock.* A compilation album entitled *Corpse Love* was released in 1992.

Founded Boss Hog

After disbanding Pussy Galore, the members went their separate ways. At the time Martinez and Spencer formed Boss Hog in 1989 before the split, both were working with various other groups. Originally, the group

emerged hastily in order to fill a vacant slot at the legendary CGBG's night club in New York, culling the name Boss Hog from a biker magazine—not after the corrupt politician from the *Dukes of Hazzard* television show as many often assumed. Trading in Pussy Galore's trash aesthetic for retro punk-rock and a mixture of sexploitation and sleaze—rumor has it that Martinez performed entirely nude for their first gig at CGBG's— Boss Hog were an instant hit. Within no time, the group, along with like-minded bands such as Unsane and Railroad Jerk, ruled New York's Lower East Side music scene.

Signing with the Amphetamine Reptile label soon thereafter, Boss Hog—completed by an "All-Star" lineup of Kurt Wolf, Charlie Ondras, Jerry Teel, and Pete Shore in addition to Martinez and Spencer— hooked up with Albini again in Chicago to release in 1989 a mini-LP entitled *Drinkin', Lechin' and Lyin'*, a collection of distorted bass and guitar riffs. Most eyes, however, were drawn to the record's provocative cover: a pose of Martinez clad only in boots, gloves, and lipstick. Shore departed before Boss Hog recorded

their second album, the full-length *Cold Hands,* released in 1990. Martinez again graced the album cover naked, sharing the spotlight this time with her clothed bandmates. By now, Martinez and Spencer had married, and the latter was also enjoying rising stardom through his primary project, the John Spencer Blues Explosion.

Boss Hog experienced several changes in 1992. Following numerous "All-Star" departures and additions, as well as the unfortunate death of Ondras from a heroin overdose, Spencer and Martinez dropped those remaining from the roster and brought in bassist Jens Jurgensen, a German design student and former member of the Swans, and a then-inexperienced drummer named Hollis Queens. "[Queens] took us out of a sad part of our lives," Martinez recalled to *Magnet* magazine's John Elsasser. "She made us all excited about playing again. She's still the cheerleader of the band." With a new lineup solidified, Boss Hog recorded their final effort for Amphetamine Reptile, 1993's mini-LP entitled *Girl +.* An obvious turning point in the band's development with a more mature, structured sound, the record's success attracted major-label interest. Thus, both Martinez and Spencer left their day jobs working on magazines at Condé Nast to concentrate on music full time.

Signed with Geffen

After cementing a record deal with Geffen (DGC), Boss Hog in 1995 released their self-titled, major-label debut, which earned the band wider recognition and critical acclaim. *Rolling Stone* contributor Rob O'Connor, for one, noted, "It's the kind of sound you would expect to hear if there were such a thing as a futuristic juke joint. When the harmonica flashes through 'Walk In,' clashing perfectly with the descending guitar line, you hear [blues guitar great] John Lee Hooker and [punk legend] Johnny Rotten mesh in the jukebox—a match you would never expect but one with which it's hard to argue." Likewise, Jonathan Bell in *Rock: The Rough Guide* called *Boss Hog* "as fine a '90s rock album as you're likely to hear, utterly bereft of bombast and pretension."

Despite such an impact, Boss Hog fell out of sight for the next two years, largely as a result of delays associated with Geffen's merger and record-industry downsizing, as well as scheduling conflicts that arose with Spencer's work with the Blues Explosion. Furthermore, Martinez had given birth to the couple's first child, Charles Henry Spencer, who took precedence over her role as a rock star. "My primary goal is to be a good mother—it's completely my focus and my priority," she told John Elsasser. "I would not have had a child otherwise. I knew what a great responsibility it would be. I didn't enter into that lightly."

Nonetheless, Martinez still missed working, but toward the end of 1998, heard discouraging rumors about Geffen's future and a supposed merger of record-industry conglomerates. And while executives at Geffen tried to assure Martinez that her band had nothing to worry about, she eventually learned that only eight of the label's 60-plus artists would survive such a merger. "So I looked at the roster," said the frontwoman to Elsasser. "And I'm like, 'Hmm, Beck, Hole.' I went through the list, and it became obvious to me that if they had to keep eight, we weren't going to be on that list. They were going to keep the moneymakers, and everyone else was going to go."

Persevered on Their Own

The following year, six major record companies became five; Seagram merged its Polygram Music Group with its Universal Group, while Geffen, A&M, Interscope, MCA, Island, Mercury, Universal, Motown, and Def Jam were reconstructed, leaving many bands without a contract in the process. Subsequently, Geffen released Boss Hog officially in February of 1999, just as Martinez had predicted.

However, after signing with the indie label In The Red and adding ex-Goats keyboardist Mark Boyce to the lineup, Boss Hog returned in 2000 with a new album, *White Out,* oddly enough the group's most commercially appealing record thus far. And with Spencer spending so much time with Blues Explosion, Martinez had the opportunity to implement more of her own ideas. She also mixed and sequenced the entire album, which was produced by a well-known team of musicians: Tore Johansson, Andy Gill, and Roli Mosimann. "On this record, it came together so beautifully," she told Elsasser, "with the exception of losing my record label."

White Out, still hard-hitting and abrasive, nonetheless showed that Boss Hog were more than a punk band. "While the band experiments in sometimes garage-rock style a la Sonic Youth," wrote Amy Steele for the *Boston Globe,* "Martinez's passion and intensity filter through every song, as she manages to be both fierce and feminine." In support of the album, Boss Hog in December of 1999 played their first live show in more than a year, with more dates planned on the East Coast and in Japan. Even in the absence of a major-label contract, Boss Hog seemed well-equipped to survive on their own.

Selected discography

Boss Hog

Drinkin', Lechin' and Lyin', (mini-LP), Amphetamine Reptile, 1989.
Cold Hands, Amphetamine Reptile, 1990.
Girl +, (mini-LP), Amphetamine Reptile, 1993.
Boss Hog, DGC, 1995.
White Out, In The Red, 2000.

Pussy Galore

Feel Good About Your Body, (EP), Shove, 1985.
Exile on Main Street, Shove, 1986.
1 Year: Live (tape), Shove, 1986.
Pussy Gold 5000 (EP), Shove/Buy Our, 1987.
Right Now, Caroline, 1987.
Sugarshift Sharp, (EP), Caroline, 1988.
*Dial M for Motherf***er,* Caroline, 1989.
Historia de la Musica Rock, Caroline, 1990.
Corpse Love, Hut/Caroline, 1992.

Sources

Books

Buckley, Jonathan and others, editor, *Rock: The Rough Guide,* Rough Guides Ltd., 1999.
Robbins, Ira A., editor, *Trouser Press Guide to '90s Rock,* Fireside/Simon & Schuster, 1997.

Periodicals

Atlanta Journal-Constitution, December 15, 1995.
Billboard, September 14, 1996; December 21, 1996.
Boston Globe, March 2, 2000.
Harper's Bazaar, October 1996; March 2000.
Magnet, April/May 2000.
Rolling Stone, November 16, 1995; March 2, 2000.
Washington Post, March 24, 2000.

Online

Insound.com, http://www.insound.com (May 4, 2000).

—Laura Hightower

Lester Bowie

Trumpeter, fluegelhornist

Lester Bowie was a rarity in jazz. As a charter member of the Art Ensemble of Chicago, he was a card-carrying member of the avant-garde and made a significant contribution to extending the vocabulary of his instrument—the trumpet—and of jazz itself. At the same time, the music he created was enjoyed by a broader listening public. One reason for this was his openness to materials that other jazz artists would have sneered at—songs by the Spice Girls or Marilyn Manson, for instance. A large part of his accessibility stemmed from Bowie's sense of humor. "His recordings often seemed like prankish arguments," wrote Ben Ratliff in the *New York Times*, "that the only way to understand jazz is to see it both in carnivalesque and intellectual contexts, to play circus music and modernist post-bop, pure hit-parade pop and nearly academic composition."

Bowie was born on October 11, 1941, in Frederick, Maryland, and first picked up a horn when he was five years old. His father, a trained classical trumpeter and a high school teacher in St. Louis, Missouri, worked with Lester daily. An apocryphal story has it that Bowie practiced by an open window in the hope that his hero, Louis Armstrong, would discover him. While still a

Born on October 11, 1941, in Frederick, MD; died on November 8, 1999, in Brooklyn, NY; married twice: Fontella Bass (divorced), Deborah Bowie, six children. *Education*: Attended Lincoln University and North Texas State College.

Toured with R&B stars Albert King, Little Milton, Ike Turner, Gene Chandler, Jerry Butler, Gladys Knight, and Jackie Wilson, early-1960s; married soul singer Fontella Bass, mid-1960s; moved to Chicago, worked as studio musician for Chess Records and other labels, joined Muhal Richard Abrams Experimental Band, 1965; joined Roscoe Mitchel's Art Ensemble, 1966; moved to France with Art Ensemble, Bowie composition "Gettin' To Know Y'All" performed by the Baden-Baden Free Jazz Orchestra, 1969; returned to United States, 1971; moved to Lagos, Nigeria, lived and performed with Fela Kuti, 1977; formed New York Hot Trumpet Quintet, The Root To The Branch, and the Sho Nuff Orchestra, early-1980s; formed Brass Fantasy, 1986; performed regularly with The Leaders, late-1980s; performed last project *Out Of The Gray Haze*, a tribute to Louis Armstrong, 1999.

teenager, Bowie formed his own group the Continentals, which played doo-wop and popular music which remained a important influence on him throughout his performing life, even after he had established his reputation as the premier avant-garde trumpeter of his time. The '50s hit "The Great Pretender," for example, remained part of his repertoire until the end of his life.

In 1959, after graduating from high school, Bowie entered the Air Force. It was in the military in Texas that he decided he was serious about music. "I locked myself away for six months to work on creating my own sound," he told Mike Joyce of the *Washington Post*. "I worked on these things for six months, things I knew I invented myself. Then one day a friend talked me into listening to a Blue Mitchell record. It just knocked me out. Blue Mitchell was playing all these things I thought I made up. That's when I knew you have to be able to absorb all influences to come up with anything original."

After his discharge, Bowie returned to St. Louis where he hooked up with drummer Philip Wilson and pianist John Chapman. The trio played hard bop, but jazz gigs

were few and far between in St. Louis. To support himself, Bowie took to touring with R&B artists such as Albert King, Little Milton, Ike Turner, Gene Chandler, Jerry Butler, Gladys Knight, and Jackie Wilson. In 1961 he met Oliver Sain and soul singer Fontella Bass, and the three went out on the road together. Bowie married Bass a little later, took over as her musical director, and helped produce her big hit, "Rescue Me." In 1965, Bowie and Bass moved to Chicago. "He used to say 'All musicians from St. Louis wanted to go to Chicago.' That's where new music was happening," his second wife Deborah told Howard Reich of the *Montreal Gazette*. In the Windy City, Bowie supported himself with studio work, most notably at Chess, the most important blues label of its day.

But as much as he loved blues and R&B, he yearned for greater musical challenges. In the mid-'60s, on the advice of a friend, he attended a workshop offered by pianist Muhal Richard Abrams. Abrams' home was a focal point for Chicago jazz players in the 1960s. Every week, Abrams held jam sessions there with the Experimental Band, a loose conglomerate of local musicians that included future stars like Jack DeJohnette, Anthony Braxton, and Henry Threadgill, as well as three local students: Roscoe Mitchell, Joseph Jarman, and Malachi Favors. After a while, the Experimental Band metamorphosed into the Association for the Advancement of Creative Musicians (A.A.C.M.). Later, Mitchell formed the Art Ensemble with Bowie, Favors, and Jarman.

The Art Ensemble quickly established itself as a force to be reckoned with. Favors and Jarman took to performing with painted faces and African costume, while Bowie began wearing the white lab coat that became one of his trademarks. The players explored the expressive limits of their instruments and introduced whistles, sirens, bull horns, noisemakers, and other "little instruments." Because it was neither free jazz, bop or other traditional forms, the music was met with incomprehension. Bowie once calculated that when the Art Ensemble was getting started, it rehearsed about 300 times a year but had only a few actual performances. In response to the limited opportunities in their native country, the group packed its bags and moved to France in 1969. The curiosity about American jazz, especially new jazz, was intense in France and within days they had gigs. In their two years in Europe, the group—under its new name the Art Ensemble of Chicago (A.E.C.)—made 12 albums, gave hundreds of concerts and played on radio and TV. When they returned to the United States in 1971, their reputation had preceded them and they were signed almost immediately by a major label, Atlantic Records.

Even while with the AEC, Bowie continued to work on projects of his own and with other musicians, like Sunny Murray, Archie Shepp, Jimmy Lyons and Cecil Taylor. His extended piece, "Gettin' To Know Y'All," was performed in 1969 by the Baden-Baden Free Jazz Orchestra. He maintained his membership in the AACM—he served as the group's second president, succeeding Abrams—and continued to take part in AACM concerts and other events, even after moving to Brooklyn on 1975. "He never really lost that connection to Chicago," Bowie's wife Deborah told the *St. Louis Post Dispatch*. "It was really part of who he was." Bowie himself had a clear idea of the difference between the two cities. "Chicago is a place where music is created," he told Phil Johnson of the *Independent*, "New York is a place where it is sold."

Despite his growing reputation as a trumpeter and demand as a sideman in other jazz projects, his musical wanderlust often led him to travel to new places, confident that as long as he had his horn he would survive. He lived in Jamaica for a year, where the natives would inquire about his health if a period passed when they didn't hear him practicing. In 1977, he moved to Lagos, Nigeria where things didn't go as well as Bowie had hoped. He was on the verge of leaving for home when someone recommended he call on the great Nigerian star, Fela Kuti. "I took a cab to Fela's place," Bowie told John Fordham of London's *The Guardian*, "and a little African guy comes out and says: 'You play jazz? You from Chicago? Well, you've come to the right place, 'cause we're the baddest band in Africa.' Then Fela tells me to play [the] blues, my speciality. I played a couple of bars and he says: 'Go get his bags, he's moving in.' I stayed with him about a year, and it was fantastic.' Bowie ended up playing on three of Fela's records.

The 1980s were a fertile period for Bowie. Besides his ongoing involvement in the Art Ensemble, he put together a number of solo projects—and usually ran both the artistic and musical sides himself, without the help of a manager. Early in the decade he formed the New York Hot Trumpet Quintet, a group which included Wynton Marsalis for a short time. The Root To The Branch was Bowie's gospel-tinged group. He mounted a legendary performance at New York's Symphony Space by the 59-piece Sho Nuff Orchestra—a virtually unheard of size for a jazz group. He performed regularly with his old friend, drummer Philip Wilson. Later in the 1980s, he played in an all-star band called The Leaders.

His primary musical vehicle outside the AEC was Brass Fantasy. He got the idea for the group in the early 1980s, but was not able to actually bring it off until 1986. "I'd been working on that concept for years," he told Amy Duncan of the *Christian Science Monitor*, "but it wasn't until then that I was able to do it on the level that I wanted to do it, because I wanted to have the best brass players in the city, and that costs a lot of money." Brass Fantasy took the brass bands of New Orleans as its model; its line-up included trumpets, trombones, tubas, a French Horn and percussion, and was occasionally augmented with steel drums and the like. Bowie created Brass Fantasy to create opportu-

nities to play and improvise using standards and the pop hits of the '50s and '60s. The group drew on an incredibly broad range of material from sources most jazz purists looked down on. Among the music covered by Brass Fantasy was "The Great Pretender," "2 Becomes 1" by the Spice Girls, "Thriller" by Michael Jackson, James Brown's "Papa's Got A Brand New Bag," "Beautiful People" by Marilyn Manson and "Don't Cry for Me Argentina" from *Evita* by Andrew Lloyd Webber. The group displayed its range on the latter, wrote John L. Walters in the *Independent*. [The song] is "a brilliant arrangement that proceeds from abstract gongs and cymbals, through a delicate Gil Evans-ish brass filigree, to tango to rip-roaring stomping funk."

While recognized as one of the finest trumpeters of his generation, Bowie frequently drew critical flak for the humor he injected into his work. Besides the squeaks, squawks, grunts and moans he was able to coax from his horn, he sported a flat-top haircut and Fu-Manchu goatee that tailed off into two points, and gave his compositions irreverent titles like "Miles Davis Meets Donald Duck." He completely rejected the idea that jazz had to be solemn and unsmiling. "Sometime in the '60s," Bowie explained to Paul A. Harris of the *St. Louis Post-Dispatch*, "the humor got away from jazz. It got intellectual, and nobody could smile. And it wasn't just the humor that got away—the life was taken out. The whole life was taken out of the music. I think, because of that, we've lost a lot in the music. The music doesn't reach a lot of people for that reason. They think jazz is this very intellectual stuff, and you've got to know all about it to appreciate it." Bowie possessed a deep respect for jazz and its tradition which was revealed in projects like his last, *Out Of The Gray Haze*, an orchestral homage to his boyhood hero, Louis Armstrong. At the same time he never lost his adventurousness. At the time of his death, he was involved in Hip-Hop Feel-Harmonic, a group made up of rappers and musicians from his neighborhood in Brooklyn.

In the summer of 1999, Lester Bowie was diagnosed with cancer of the liver. He continued touring, despite bad health. While touring Europe with Brass Fantasy in October 1999, he suddenly fell ill. His wife Deborah flew to London and returned with him to the United States. Back in New York, they went directly from the airport to the hospital. "Lester knew this would be his last tour," Deborah Bowie told Howard Reich of the *Montreal Gazette*. "He knew there was a chance he might not complete it, but he had the spirit to try." Two weeks later, on November 8, 1999, Lester Bowie died.

Selected discography

Numbers 1 & 2, Nessa, 1967.
Rope-A-Dope, Muse, 1975.
Esoteric, Hat Hut, 1980.
The Great Pretender, ECM, 1981.

I Only Have Eyes For You, ECM, 1985.
Avant Pop, ECM, 1986.
Serious Fun, DIW, 1989.
The Organizer, DIW, 1991.
The Fire This Time, In & Out, 1992.
Odyssey of Funk & Popular Music, Vol. 1, Atlantic, 1999.

With Art Ensemble of Chicago

Stance a Sophie, Nessa, 1970.
With Fontella Bass, America, 1970.
Bap-Tizum, Atlantic, 1972 (reissued by Koch 1999).
Live at Mandel Hall, Delmark, 1972.
Nice Guys, ECM, 1978.
Full Force, ECM, 1980.
Urban Bushmen, ECM, 1984.

With Roscoe Mitchell

Sound, Delmark, 1966.
Congliptious, Nessa, 1968.

With Fela Kuti

No Agreement, Celluloid, 1977.

With The Leaders

Mudfoot, Black Hawk, 1986.
Out Here Like This, Black Hawk, 1986.
Unforseen Blessings, Black Hawk, 1988.

With Defunkt

Avoid The Funk, Hannibal, 1988.
Cum Funky, Enemy, 1994.

Sources

Chicago Sun-Times, November 10, 1999; January 22, 2000.
Christian Science Monitor, January 19, 1990.
Gazette (Montreal), November 11, 1999.
Guardian (London), November 11, 1999.
Independent (London), November 10, 1995; May 15, 1998.
New York Times, November 11, 1999.
St. Louis Post-Dispatch, June 30, 1989; March 14, 1993; November 10, 1999.
Times (London), November 11, 1999.

—*Gerald E. Brennan*

Glenn Branca

Composer

Glenn Branca is a completely self-taught musician who made himself into one of the most controversial composers of the late 20th century. He established his name writing serious avant-garde music for groups that came to be known as "guitar orchestras": four or more electric guitars, some of his own invention, along with percussion and keyboards, that looked like a rock band, but which played high volume sheets of raw sound which apparently contained no melodies, themes, or development. "The Glenn Branca experience is an explosive one," wrote Geoff Smith and Nicola Walker Smith, adding that if Branca had written his music in the 1600s, he would surely have been hanged for witchcraft.

Branca was born on October 6, 1948 in Harrisburg, Pennsylvania. His first musical love was Broadway musicals which he was able to see during regular visits with his parents to New York City. Branca decided to study theater and in 1971 received a degree in stage direction from Emerson College in Boston. He formed his own theater group, the Bastard Theatre, while he was in Boston. Although he had no musical training except for a few rudimentary lessons on the classical guitar, Branca began writing experimental music for his theater group, and before long he was splitting his time between theater and music. At one point, he considered putting together a rock band. He realized, however, that he had no chance of finding gigs in Boston clubs for the sort of austere band he imagined, and he gave up the idea.

In 1976, Branca gave up the idea of music entirely, got rid of his guitar, and moved to New York City to concentrate his energies on doing theater. In New York, he met Jeffrey Lohn, who shared his interest in cutting edge theater and avant-garde rock. They formed the Theoretical Girls, a combination theater/music project, whose work Branca described to William Duckworth in *Talking Music*, as "loosely rehearsed, high energy music." It was a time when punk, new wave, and then no wave was sweeping New York, and the Theoretical Girls played all the famous spots, especially Max's Kansas City and CBGB's. Unsurprisingly perhaps, they realized in short order that audiences were responding to them as a rock band far more than theater, and they forged boldly ahead in that direction. Branca later admitted it was his experience in the Theoretical Girls that changed him from a theater person to a music person. Branca and Lohn eventually began moving in different directions and Branca left the group, forming The Static, a band based on a musical group he had conceived of while studying in Boston.

But in 1979, when Lohn's Theoretical Girls were offered a gig at Max's, Branca asked if he could open the show. Instead of The Static, however, he brought a group of guitarists who played a composed work Branca had written, called *Instrumental for Six Guitars*. The piece had startled Branca as much as it did the first audiences to hear it. He had his guitarists tune their instruments in a non-standard tuning that Branca had devised. It led to some completely unexpected musical dynamics. "I didn't really know what six guitars playing in this tuning was going to sound like before I heard it in rehearsal," Branca told Duckworth. "The piece went through four varied sections. All of them sounded good, but the last section sounded stunning. The last section was so amazing that I actually stopped in the middle of the first rehearsal. I couldn't continue." The specially tuned guitars combined with the music's high volume brought out overtones that are not normally heard. "You could hear voices and choruses and horns and strings," Branca recalled for Duckworth, "all of this happening separately from anything I had written, conceived or even knew was there."

He set out to discover what was responsible for the strange musical phenomena he was hearing for the first time. When he learned that close harmonies tended produce the extra voices, he wrote even closer ones. Sonic intensity—loudness—was also a factor, so he added instruments and cranked them up. In 1980, about six months after *Instrumental* was first performed, Branca organized a permanent group to perform his compositions, the Glenn Branca Ensemble. He began writing longer and longer pieces for the Ensemble.

The process culminated in 1981 with the composition of *Symphony No. 1*, for guitars, keyboard, drummer and percussion. Until then, Branca still thought of his

For The Record . . .

Born on October 6, 1948, in Harrisburg, PA. *Education*: Attended Emerson College, in Boston, MA.

Moved to New York City, 1976; formed Theoretical Girls with Jeffrey Lohn, 1976; composed first piece, *Instrumental for Six Guitars*, 1979; composed first large scale work, *Symphony No. 1*, 1981; composed *Symphony No. 2*, for own invention, mallet guitar, 1982; studied acoustics, mathematics and music theory, 1980s; first work for traditional orchestra (commissioned), an opera based on play *Woyzeck* by Georg Büchner, 1985; completed first large-scale work for symphony orchestra, *Symphony No. 7*, 1989; composed ballet, *The World Upside Down*, 1990; composed *Symphony No. 8 (The Mystery)*, 1992; composed *Symphony No. 9 (L'Eve Future)*, 1993; composed *Symphony No. 10 (The Mystery Pt. 2)*, 1994; composed *Symphony No. 11 (The Netherlands)*, 1998; composed *Symphony No. 12 (Tonal Sexus)*, 1998.

Addresses: *Record company*—Atavistic Records, P.O. Box 578266, Chicago, IL 60657, email: info@atavistic.com.

work as a "rock music." And that was reinforced by some of the music press which referred to his group as a "guitar orchestra." But when he started calling his work "symphonies," the serious music establishment, which until then had dismissed Branca as a pop musician, began to take notice, as if that moniker alone sufficed to give the music respectability. Branca explained to the *New York Times'* Steven Holden why he chose the name: "A symphony to me is a full-length, large-scale piece with a variety of instrumentation and orchestral range. I've never dealt with any kind of sonata form. But in the density of texture, the sense of slow movement and the development of thematic ideas, I think of my music as symphonic." Branca was clearly moving into the territory of minimalism and the modern avant-garde. At the same time his music retained all the trappings of rock: electric guitars played at bone-quivering volume.

Other symphonies followed. *Symphony No. 2* used an instrument of Branca's own invention, the mallet guitar, a modified hammer dulcimer, with electric pick-ups and more strings than a guitar so a single guitarist could play many more notes. At the same time, his interest in music theory was growing. For *Symphony No. 3*, he modified harpsichords with guitar amplifiers and added them to his ensemble. He became absorbed in the harmonic series, which he discovered seemed to imply—mathematically almost—certain music. He developed new tunings for guitar to take advantage of his discoveries, and used them in his next symphonies. His study of the harmonic series led him to the science of acoustics, which in turn led to mathematics and its applications to his music. He plunged in with an abandon, and only emerged when he realized that his actual composition had nearly ground to a halt.

After *Symphony No. 5* was written, the *Christian Science Monitor* wrote about Branca's "cascades of sound you've never heard before." And for Branca himself, that was exactly the point of his music. He told Geoff Smith and Nicola Walker Smith that he was "trying to make some kind of music that I've never heard before. Admitting that such a goal was inherently difficult, he added, "it seems I never get it right which means I just have to try again... I'd say there are four or five kinds of pieces that I want to hear, none of which I've successfully written yet."

He pushed on though, into the study of musical theory, and was eventually able, in the mid-1980s, to write for conventional orchestra. He and choreographer Greta Holby were commissioned by the Opera Tomorrow Festival to write an opera based on *Woyzeck* by Georg Büchner. The collaboration with Holby did not work out, but Branca completed one scene of the opera, entitled *In Passion's Tongue* which was performed at the festival in 1986. Branca recycled other material composed for the opera in his first large-scale work for full orchestra, *Symphony No. 7*. After that work, Branca threw himself into composing for symphony orchestra, producing pieces for dance, theater and film. He was attracted to the broader sonic palette that the orchestra offered. For years, he avoided writing for guitar ensemble. He accepted the commission for *Symphony No. 8*, a guitar work, in the late 1980s, but only with great reluctance.

By the early 1990s, he was looking forward to some indefinite future when he would be able to write for a huge musical group he called a "Strange Orchestra:" a kind of super orchestra comprised of instruments from every musical tradition on earth. "I want to write for more interesting timbres than are available to me in the orchestra," he told Cole Gagne. "I want to put together an orchestral sound—you see, I love the orchestral sound—but I want to introduce all kinds of other instruments that I love too... But I'm not talking about just a hurdy-gurdy or bagpipes. I'm talking about hurdy-gurdy, bagpipes, sarangi, sitar, tamboura, musette, steel drums—a whole spectrum, a massive orchestra that would include all the orchestral instruments as well and would be treated as a western orchestra." In other words, Branca sees his place solidly within the Western avant-garde tradition; he is not interested in writing world music.

By the mid-1990s, however, Branca had returned to the guitar compositions and aural assault that had made his name. By the end of the century he had inhabited a musical no-man's-land where no conventional label seemed to apply to his music, which was how he liked it. Critics, when not outright hostile, were frequently mystified by the music. David Toop of the *Times of London,* for example, wrote: "The beauty, or horror, of Branca's art is that all of it is much the same… This is music frozen in a null-point between agony and ecstasy, but good fun, nonetheless." Even composers differ. John Cage denounced Branca as fascistic after hearing *Indeterminate Activity of Resultant Masses*; composer Ben Johnston, who heard the same performance, later said with fascination: "It was like looking through a microscope at a world I've never seen." For Branca, however, all that matters is the sometimes quixotic search for music he has never heard before.

Selected discography

The Ascension, Robi Droli, 1980.
Symphony No. 1 (Tonal Plexus), ROIR, 1981.
Music For The Dance 'Bad Smells', GPS Records, 1982.
Symphony No. 2 (The Peak Of The Sacred), Atavistic, 1982.

Symphony No. 3 (Gloria), Atavistic, 1983.
Symphony No. 5 (Describing Planes Of An Expanding Hypersphere), Atavistic, 1984.
The Belly Of An Architect, Crepuscule, 1987.
Symphony No. 6 (Devil Choirs At The Gates Of Heaven), Atavistic, 1988.
The World Upside Down, Atavistic, 1991.
The Mysteries (Symphonies No. 8 + No. 10), Atavistic, 1994.
Symphony No. 9 (L'eve Future), Point Musi, 1994.

Sources

Books

Anderson And Five Generations Of American Experimental Composers, Schirmer Books, 1995.
Gagne, Cole, *Soundpieces 2: Interviews With American Composers,* Scarecrow Press, 1993.
Smith, Geoff, and Nicola Walker Smith, *New Voices: American Composers Talk About Their Music,* Amadeus Press, 1995.

Periodicals

Christian Science Monitor, August 1, 1983; November 23, 1984.
New York Times, December 23, 1983.
Times of London, February 28, 1994.

—*Gerald E. Brennan*

Michael Brecker

Tenor saxophonist

© Jack Vartoogian. Reproduced by permission.

For nearly 20 years, fusion jazz superstar and "reedman" Michael Brecker left his mark on thousands of studio recordings and collaborations in jazz, pop, and rock & roll. The tenor saxophonist staked out a solo career beginning in the late 1980s to a welcoming round of applause. Yet even as he recorded on his own, he upheld family ties in 1992, to stand beside his elder sibling, trumpeter Randy Brecker, for a reunion album, *Return of the Brecker Brothers,* and for a series of live appearances. Michael Brecker, who was influenced largely by John Coltrane and mentored by Horace Silver among others, successfully achieved "crossover" status between fusion, post-bop, and contemporary jazz. For his first solo album he worked with Pat Metheny, Elvin Jones, and Charlie Haden, and as a solo artist and bandleader he toured with McCoy Tyner. Brecker worked with Adam Rogers, Clarence Penn, and Larry Goldings, and played with popular stars from Joni Mitchell and Paul Simon to Steely Dan. In 30 years, Brecker earned an impressive seven Grammy awards from the National Association of Recording Arts and Scinces.

A native of Philadelphia, Pennsylvania, Michael Brecker was born on March 29, 1949. For Brecker's father, attorney Robert Brecker, jazz was a way of life. The family owned an Hammond organ, and Brecker enjoyed playing with his father who doubled as a jazz pianist between courtroom gigs. Michael Brecker studied the clarinet and played some alto saxophone before settling on tenor saxophone in high school. His teenage years were a succession of jazz dreams come true for the boy. After school he spent free afternoons with his father listening to Coltrane records and playing drums and horns at home, or else making the rounds of Philadelphia clubs where Brecker jammed with professional musicians like Eric Gravatt. It was Gravatt who first taught Brecker the meaning of endurance.

Brecker followed behind his older brother in attending college at the University of Indiana in 1966. There Brecker majored in fine arts before moving to New York City in 1969, where he picked up session work and played in rehearsals. He recalled for *Down Beat* the atmosphere in New York City when he first arrived there in the 1960s, "It was a special time to be in New York. That's when the so-called boundaries between what was then pop music and jazz were becoming very blurry."

In New York, trombonist Barry Rogers befriended Brecker and mentored him through the newness of living in the big city. From Rogers, Brecker learned about Cajun music, African rhythms, and Latin sounds. Together Michael Brecker, Randy Brecker, and Rogers founded a band called Dreams in 1969. Along with the main trio, Dreams included a strong rhythm section comprised of John Abercrombie, Billy Cobham, Don Grolnick, and Will Lee. Also during those early years Brecker joined with approximately two dozen others in

For The Record . . .

Born on March 29, 1949, in Philadelphia, PA; son of Robert Brecker. *Education*: University of Indiana.

Co-founder of Dreams, recorded with Columbia, 1969; with Horace Silver, 1973-74; with Randy Brecker (Brecker Brothers), 1975-79; co-founder of Steps (later known as Steps Ahead), mid-1970s; session musician, 1969-1986; solo debut, Impulse! Records, 1987; signed with GRP, 1990; toured and recorded with Paul Simon, 1991; reunited with Brecker Brothers, 1992; collaborations with Herbie Hancock, McCoy Tyner, and Horace Silver, 1995-96.

Awards: Grammy awards, National Academy of Recording Arts and Sciences, 1987, 1993 (two awards), 1994 (two awards), 1995 (two awards); Album of the Year, *Down Beat*, 1986; Album of the Year, *Jazziz*, 1986

Addresses: *Management*—International Music Network (IMN), Kate McLaughlin, Northeast Agent, e-mail: kate@imnworld.com

an organization called Free Life Communication. The organization, comprised of performing artists, perpetuated their art by giving free concerts throughout the city.

In 1973 and 1974, Brecker and his brother joined Horace Silver's band, an experience that Brecker likened to attending college because there was so much to learn from Silver. After breaking with Silver's band, the brothers set out to forge their own identity, billing themselves generically as the Brecker Brothers. Thus Michael Brecker, in tandem with his brother, pioneered what was a new jazz form at the time, called fusion or electro-fusion jazz. The brothers performed together habitually between 1974 and 1979. They recorded six albums together for Arista, and reportedly the duo contributed instrumental accompaniment on more than 1,800 records. The brothers opened a club, called Seventh Avenue South, where the initial jamming took place for the Breckers' next band, called Steps (later known as Steps Ahead). That group featured Mike Manieri, Eddie Gomez, Don Grolnich, and Steve Gadd. Additionally there was a brief tenure with Bob Mintzer's band and some work with guitarist Mike Stern.

Throughout the 1980s, Brecker worked intensively as a session musician in New York. It was largely such studio work that kept him gainfully employed until the release of his solo debut album in 1986. By that time, Brecker was anxious to work independently, as he felt a need for greater artistic freedom, which might be achieved most readily in solo work. He staked out his proverbial territory as a solo artist and a bandleader, and he joined in collaborations with Joey Calderazzo around that same time. Brecker's efforts reached fruition with the release of *Michael Brecker* in 1986, his first solo album after a 20-year career as a sessions saxophone player and sideman. The recording, released on MCA/Impulse!, was nominated for a Grammy award as best solo jazz instrumental. In 1990, he released *Don't Try This at Home* on Impulse!, and he toured and recorded with singer and composer Paul Simon in 1991.

Brecker and his elder sibling, having achieved considerable success as an early fusion duo in the 1970s, kept the family tradition alive with a follow-up album in 1992. *Return of the Brecker Brothers* was a long-overdue sequel to their original *Brecker Brothers* album and their earlier collaborations. The brothers appeared together in live performance on a number of occasions following the release of their comeback album, including a performance to help christen the renovated Five Spot in Manhattan early in 1993. *Newsday's* Martin Johnson welcomed the return of, "[t]heir hard-driving, expansive sound," and the funk and fusion reunion between the siblings gave fans and critics cause to cheer.

Brecker's "African Skies" took the Grammy as best instrumental composition of 1993. He was also a member of the 1994 Grammy-award-winning GRP All-Star Band under the direction of Tom Scott. Brecker's Grammy fever raged again in 1995, when *Tales from the Hudson,* a pairing with Pat Metheny, won two awards, including the award for the best instrumental solo performance for "Cabin Fever."

As Brecker's solo career solidified, a pairing between him and pianist McCoy Tyner made the bill at Yoshi's in Oakland, California. The booking, arranged by Jason Olaine, led to a Grammy-winning collaboration between Brecker and Tyner on their 1994 Impulse! release, called *Infinity*. Brecker assembled other impressive lineups as well, including Adam Rogers on guitar, Clarence Penn on drums, and Larry Goldings on organ. In 1997, Samuel Fromartz for *Reuters* called Brecker's solo work, "passionate but not pretty," and described a Brecker concert as a "feeding frenzy."

As a bandleader and solo artist in the late 1990s, Brecker led a quartet with Calderazzo on piano, James Genus on bass, and drummer Jeff "Tain" Watts. The dynamic foursome recorded a sizzling contempo-style album, *Two Blocks from the Edge,* only after a yearlong tour of performing and perfecting the material. The compilation, written largely by Brecker and with assistance from Calderazzo, went to market as Brecker's fifth on the Impulse! label in 1998 and included the popular Brecker composition, "Delta City Blues," that evolved into his personal theme song. University of Kentucky jazz professor Miles Osland said of the song in *Down Beat*, "...[A] textbook example of exemplary musical artistry combined with superlative technical prowess." John Janowiak labeled the song more succinctly, as "down-and-dirty soul."

Creatively speaking, Brecker's muse went into overdrive in 1998. He debuted as a bandleader at the Catalina Bar & Grill in Los Angeles, California and played a spectacular solo concert in Italy's Dolomite Mountains. The Dolomite venue was accessible only by means of a one-hour hike from a depository chairlift landing preceded by a rugged hour-long drive. The performance lasted merely 60 minutes, but the spectacular view on the mountaintop justified the extreme conditions required to reach the site. The concertgoers, not surprisingly, harbored no anxieties for the music to stop, and Becker's performance ended in overtime.

Following his appearance in Rhode Island at the JVC Jazz Festival in August of 1998, Josef Woodard labeled Brecker as a "reluctant giant in music ... [a] preeminent and influential saxophonist of his generation, blessed with fearsome technical finesse as well as melodic charms ... [who] continues to pursue the path of greatest personal reward, not necessarily the greatest commercial good." The commentary appeared in *Los Angeles Times*.

As the 1990s wound to a close, Brecker released *Time Is of the Essence* on Verve. The album, hailed as a long-awaited breakthrough, features Larry Goldings on organ, in complement to the piano styles of Pat Metheny. Also heard on the album are Jones, Tain, and Bill Stewart. Ted Panken said in *Down Beat* of Brecker's performances on that release, "Brecker plays with ... clarity, a hungry master searching for—and often reaching—the next level."

Brecker's work in 2000 brought additional reunions with Metheny, Jones, and Haden, with Brecker booked to perform at the Monterey Jazz Festival.

Brecker lives on the Hudson River and maintains an office in Manhattan. His master class laurels include a session at the University of Kentucky in October of 1998.

Selected discography

Solo

Swish, EWCD, 1980.
Smoking' in the Pit (with Steps Ahead), NYC Records, 1980.
Cityscape, Warner Brothers, 1983.
Michael Brecker, MCA/Impulse!, 1986.
Don't Try This at Home, MCA/Impulse!, 1987.
Now You See It... Now You Don't, Impulse!, 1990.
All Blues (with GRP All-Star Band, Tom Scott leading), GRP, 1994
Live In Tokyo (with Steps Ahead), NYC Records, 1994.
Infinity (with McCoy Tyner Trio), Impulse!, 1994.
Tales from the Hudson (with Pat Metheny), Impulse!, 1995.
Two Blocks from the Edge (with Calderazzo, Genus, and Watts), Impulse!, 1998.
Time Is of the Essence, Verve, 1999.

Brecker Brothers

Brecker Brothers, One Way, 1975.
Back to Back, One Way, 1975.
Blue Montreux, Bluebird, 1978.
Heavy Metal Be-Bop, One Way, 1978.
Don't Stop the Music, One Way, 1980.
Straphangin', One Way, 1980.
Detente, One Way, 1980.
Return of the Brecker Brothers, GRP, 1992.
Out of the Loop, GRP, 1994.
Electric Jazz Fusion, Jamey Aebersol, 1999.

Appeared on

Hardbop Grandpop (Horace Silver), 1996.
The Promise (Johnny McLaughlin), 1998.

Sources

Down Beat, September 1994, p. 47; December 1994, p. 57; October 1998, p. 53; April 1999, p. 72, February 2000, pp. 27-33.
Entertainment Weekly, November 6, 1992, p. 68.
Los Angeles Times, May 28, 1998, p. 45; June 18, 1998, p. 31; November 21, 1999, p. 73.
Minneapolis Star Tribune, April 14, 2000, p. 7; April 17, 2000, p. 5B.
Newsday, February 18, 1993, p. 88.
Reuters, March 10, 1997.
San Francisco Chronicle, May 15, 1999, p. E3; March 31, 2000, p. D6.

—Gloria Cooksey

Dennis Brown

Reggae singer

Early in his career as a child star during the late 1960's, reggae singing legend Dennis Emmanuel Brown, received the nickname of "boy wonder of Jamaican music." In 1981, reggae fans unanimously ordained Brown with a new title, "Emmanuel, the Crown Prince of Reggae" and the undisputed heir apparent, following the death of reggae "king" Bob Marley. Brown, with his extremely powerful tenor and distinctive singing voice, established himself easily as one of the most impressive reggae artists of the twentieth century. A happy and friendly man, Brown amassed a loving and loyal following throughout his career, and upon his death at the early age of 42, he was widely eulogized for his outgoing personality. He recorded more than 100 records, including over 50 albums, from the time he was in this teens. The world of reggae music lost a "towering talent," noted *Billboard* magazine, when Brown passed away on July 1, 1999.

Dennis Brown was born Dennis Emmanuel Brown on February 1, 1957 in Kingston, Jamaica; he grew up in Chocomo Lawn in West Kingston. Show business in a sense was his birth right, as he was the son of Arthur Brown, a prominent Jamaican actor. Dennis Brown was well-known as a child star, and some hailed the young boy as a prodigy during the 1960s. By the age of nine years old he sang regularly with Byron Lee and the Dragonaires, standing on beer crates in order for the admiring audiences to get a glimpse of his small frame.

During the course of his lifetime, Brown worked with virtually every one of the noted producers of contemporary reggae and ska. Initially, during his childhood career, he maintained an association with Derrick Harriot and Byron Lee before earning a reputation as a recording artist while a teenager in the 1970s. He signed his first recording contract in the late 1960s with the legendary Clement S. "Sir Coxsone" Dodd of the Studio One label.

Brown's first hit with Dodd, "No Man Is an Island," sold well also as an album, and during his extensive career with the innovative Dodd, Brown earned a reputation as a versatile talent, capable of performing a variety of different styles. Brown, known as one of the most melodious voices in reggae, proved himself to be not only a crooner and a wailer, but a raucous dance music afficionado as well. "Brown is blessed with a lithe, crooning tenor that gives him more-than-passing resemblance to Marvin Gaye," wrote J.D. Considine in *Rolling Stone,* "something that set many hearts aflutter in the reggae community." Throughout the 1970s, his recordings were produced on the Impact! and Aquarius labels, including numerous collections of his single hits which accounted for much of his popularity during that era. He went on to record on many of the prominent reggae labels of his time.

As Brown approached adulthood during the 1970s, he recorded with the Observer label with producer Winston "Niney" Holness, a collaboration that resulted in such albums as *Just Dennis* in 1975, and *Wolves and Leopards* in 1978. Through his association with Holness, Brown achieved a level of international stardom and set the stage for superstardom in the field. From 1977-82, Brown worked extensively with the prominent reggae producer Joe Gibbs. The two collaborated on a variety of songs, including "Visions," "Words of Wisdom," and "Joseph's Coat of Many Colours." Brown was heard repeatedly with Gibbs's partner Errol "ET" Thompson as well, their most popular hit together by far being the 1979 release, "Money in My Pocket."

Additionally, Brown went on contract with the mainstream label, A&M Records, in 1980 and near the end of that decade the crooner worked for King Jammys, and for "Gussie" Clark's Music Works. "Big All Around," Brown's 1989 duet with Gregory Isaacs, was recorded by Clark's Music Works and surfaced as a global hit. At the time of his death, Brown had recorded most recently for Don One Sound, and his final release, *Believe in Yourself,* appeared on that label.

Throughout the 1980s and 1990s, Brown's presence at the Montego Bay Sunsplash Festivals was a regular occurrence. His 1983 appearance at Sunsplash was long after regarded as one of his finest moments. After signing with A&M Records, he released two albums for the label in 1983 and also embarked on a venture into producing independently around that same time, under his DEB Music and Yvonne's Special labels. He moved to London, England for a time where he was associ-

Born Dennis Emmanuel Brown on February 6, 1957, in Kingston, Jamaica; son of Arthur Brown; married to Yvonne; 13 children; died on July 1, 1999, in Kingston, Jamaica.

Signed with Studio One, 1970; with producer Joe Gibbs, 1977-82; albums released on RAS Records, Shanachie, A&M Records. Early in his career as a child star during the late 1960s, Brown received the nickname of "boy wonder of Jamaican music." In 1981, reggae fans unanimously ordained Brown with a new title, "Emmanuel, the Crown Prince of Reggae" and the undisputed heir apparent, following the death of reggae "king" Bob Marley. Brown, with his extremely powerful tenor and distinctive singing voice, established himself easily as one of the most impressive reggae artists of the twentieth century. He recorded more than 100 records, including over 50 albums, from the time he was in his teens.

ated with producers Robbie Shakespeare and Sly Dunbar during the early 1980s and recorded with that duo on their Taxi label. The bass and drum duo of Sly & Robbie was heard later on Brown's 1990s hit, "Cosmic Force."

In 1995, Brown's rendition of "Light My Fire" received a Grammy nomination from the National Academy of Recording Arts and Sciences. Additionally, in 1978, Brown appeared in the movie *Heartland Reggae.*

Brown assumed the billing of "Emmanuel, the crown prince of reggae" in deference to "king" Bob Marley, who prior to his own death had acknowledged Brown as a personal favorite. Brown's untimely death occurred after he and several members of his tour group became ill during a visit to Brazil with Gregory Isaacs, Max Romeo, Lloyd Parker, and We the People in May of 1999. Romeo, Isaccs, and Parkes were said to have fully recovered. However, Brown was not so fortunate as his colleagues. Upon his return to Jamaica, he was rushed to the hospital on the evening of June 30, 1999, in serious distress and suffered cardiac arrest. He died on July 1, 1999 in Kingston, Jamaica, of a collapsed lung at the University Hospital.

Brown, who was survived by his wife, Yvonne, was father to at least one dozen children. Elena Oumano of *Billboard* remembered him upon his death as "a tow-ering talent and beloved son." The country of Jamaica afforded Brown one of its highest honors, with burial in the National Heroes Park in Kingston. Posthumously, on March 7, 2000 Hip-O Records released *Dennis Brown: The Ultimate Collection* as an addition to its compilation series.

Selected discography

Singles

"No Man Is an Island," Dodd, 1968.
"Money in My Pocket," Joe Gibbs, 1979. "Big All Around" (with Gregory Isaacs), Music Works, 1989.
"Liberation," Alvin Ranglin, 1994.

Albums

No Man Is an Island, Dodd, 1968.
Just Dennis, Trojan, 1975.
Visions, Shanachie, 1977.
Westbound Train, Third World, 1978.
Wolf & Leopards, EMI, 1978.
Live in Montreux, Laser, 1979.
Joseph's Coat of Many Colours, Laser, 1979.
Words of Wisdom, Shanachie, 1979.
Spellbound, Laser, 1980.
Foul Play, A&M, 1981.
Love Has Found Its Way, A&M, 1982.
The Prophet Rides Again, A&M, 1983.
Satisfactory Feeling, Tad's, 1983.
Money in My Pocket, Trojan, 1983.
Walls & Letters, Joe Gibbs, 1984.
Love's Got a Hold on Me, Joe Gibbs, 1984.
Reggae Superstars Meet, Striker, 1985.
Halfway Up, Halfway Down, A&M, 1986.
Hold Tight, Live & Learn, 1986.
Brown Sugar, RAS, 1986.
Slow Down, Shanachie, 1987.
Inseparable, VP, 1988.
My Time, Rohit, 1989.
Good Vibrations, Rohit, 1989.
No Contest, VP, 1989.
Unchallenged, VP, 1990.
Go Now, Rohit, 1991.
Sarge, VP, 1991.
Overproof, VP, 1991.
Victory Is Mine, RAS, 1991.
Cosmic Force, Heartbeat, 1992.
Blazing, Shanachie, 1992.
Friends For Life, Shanachie, 1992.
Some Like It Hot, Heartbeat, 1992.
Another Day In Paradise, Trojan, 1992.
Live in Montego Bay, Sonic Sounds, 1992.
General, VP, 1993.
Hotter Flames, VP, 1993.
Unforgettable, VP, 1993.
Early Days, Sonic Sounds, 1994.
Light My Fire, Rounder, 1994.
3 Against War, VP, 1994.
Vision of a Reggae King, VP, 1994.
Blood Brothers, RAS, 1994.

Joy in the Morning, Lagoon, 1995.
Dennis Brown & Friends, JA, 1995.
Love Light, Blue Moon, 1995.
Live at Montreux, Magnum America, 1995.
I Don't Know, RAS, 1995.
Musical Heatwave, Trojan, 1995.
Nothing Like This, RAS, 1995.
Open the Gate, Heartbeats, 1995.
Temperature Rising, VP, 1995.
Super Reggae, Rooney, 1996.
Songs of Emanuel, Sonic Sounds, 1996.
Dennis, Burning Sounds, 1996.
Could It Be, VP, 1996.
Lover's Paradise, House of Reggae, 1996.
Beautiful Morning, World, 1996.
Milk and Honey, RAS, 1996.
He's One of a Kind, Imaj, 1998.
Tracks of Life, Recall, 1998.
Watch This Sound, Jamaican Vibes, 1998.
Tribulation, Heartbeat, 1999.
Love Is So True, Prestige World, 1999.
Generosity, Gator, 1999.
Bless Me Jah, Ras, 1999.
Stone Cold World, VP, 1999.
Believe in Yourself, Don One Sound, 1999.
Live in Montreux, Magnum Collect, 1999.
Here I Come Again, Culture Press, 2000.
Academy, Orange Street, 2000.
Dennis Brown: The Ultimate Collection (posthumous), Hip-O, 2000.

Sources

Periodicals

Billboard, July 10, 1999.
Los Angeles Times, July 2, 1999, p. 32.
Rolling Stone, April 16, 1992, p. 81; February 24, 1994, p. 41.

Online

"Dennis Brown," http://www.artistsonly.com/dennis.htm (May 4, 2000).
Jamaica Gleaner (online), July 1, 1999, http://dev.go-jamaica.com/gleaner/19990701/f6.html (May 4, 2000).
"In Memory of Dennis Brown, the Crown Prince of Reggae," http://www.onedroprecords.com/welcome.html (May 4, 2000).

—Gloria Cooksey

Norman Brown

Jazz guitarist, composer

Modern jazz guitarist Norman Brown revealed in his art the soul of a dedicated musician. In concert and on records, Brown's music generated adult appeal as he presented a delicate style that he successfully optimized through production and performance of his own compositions. Brown's career evolved from a boyhood affinity for guitar music—ignited by the sounds of Jimi Hendrix, and rekindled through the music of George Benson. Brown's family recognized his ability early and encouraged and assisted him in carving a niche among his contemporaries. He honed his talent at the Musician's Institute of Hollywood and remained with that organization in a teaching capacity for a decade, composing works and nurturing other musicians along the way. Through his recorded performances, released throughout the 1990s, Brown came to the attention of a diverse audience, including rhythm & blues, pop, and jazz fans. His understated personal style and cultivated jazz rhythms brought him worldwide recognition as a polished adult artist.

Norman Brown was born and raised in Kansas City, Missouri. As a child, he enjoyed the music of Jimi Hendrix and took inspiration from that artist. Brown's interest in playing the guitar flourished when he heard his older brother playing some tunes on a borrowed guitar, and he began to play in secret whenever the guitar was idle, in his brother's absence. Brown's brother, five years older, overheard Norman Brown's secret practice sessions one day, and was so impressed with the younger boy's delicate touch on the strings that he essentially stopped playing, opting instead to help his younger sibling learn to play better. Neither did Norman Brown's natural talent go unrecognized by his father, Roy Brown Sr., who also helped to nurture the talent, encouraging the budding musician to listen to Wes Montgomery and George Benson.

It was Benson's music in particular that that inspired young Brown, and he was sometimes compared to the popular guitarist as his own style matured. Brown's father purchased a new guitar and amplifier for the boy, who then stepped up from the acoustic guitar into a new realm. In high school Brown played rhythm & blues and other popular music styles. While his early repertoire was comprised largely of Earth, Wind, and Fire songs, performed mostly with local bands, Brown progressed rapidly into contemporary jazz, and played with quartets. The Brown brothers nurtured a close sibling relationship, and Brown's older brother used money from his first job to purchase a professional-quality electric guitar and an amplifier for the younger boy, not long before his own death in 1980.

On To Southern California

In 1984, Brown joined the Musician's Institute of Hollywood as a staff instructor, having completed the school's one-year vocational curriculum. For ten years thereafter he taught guitar technology, for two days every week, as many as ten sessions per week. Brown became a devoted educator, teaching guitar lessons privately, organizing and hosting guitar seminars, and performing outreach in general.

In 1990, Brown signed a contract with Motown Records on a jazz label that was newly launched at that time, called MoJazz. He wrote and co-produced his debut album, *Just Between Us,* which appeared in 1992. The recording, with nine tracks of his own upbeat compositions, saw its way to number 51 on the rhythm & blues charts. The album's successful showing led to critical approval as well as a promotional tour in Europe. The success of that initial release helped to define Brown's image as a serious jazz artist, with adult appeal.

Again he included nine new compositions of his own in 1994 on a follow-up album, *After the Storm.* The springtime release explored a variety of moods, including a sense of solitary moodiness that was absent from his debut release. Without getting lost in the somber atmosphere, however, Brown included a variety of rhythms, including Latin dance tunes for color. Within three weeks of its release, the album found its way to number two on the Top Contemporary Jazz albums chart, while simultaneously showing respectably at the number 22 position on the rhythm & blues charts. Among the *Billboard* listings, Brown's album nested securely within the Top 200, at number 141. *All Music Guide* listed *After the Storm* as a four-and-a-half-star album.

Among the album's featured songs, the popular single, "That's the Way Love Goes," was eventually released on video and was seen on VH-1. The song introduced listeners of a new audience niche to Brown's pleasurable guitar as the album earned a following among adult alternative music fans. Overall, *After the Storm* was the vehicle that brought Brown to prominence as a serious artist. The record brought continued success for Brown throughout 1994. He opened that year at the House of Blues in New Orleans, Louisiana, and his touring engagements brought him to Tuscaloosa, Alabama where he kicked off what would ultimately be an international promotion for *After the Storm.*

That summer he rounded out his tour on the festival circuit and made appearances at the Capital Jazz Festival as well as Philadelphia's Melon Jazz Festival. Brown's refreshing and sophisticated contemporary music came to the attention of the National Association of Recording Merchandisers, who invited him to perform at their conference in San Francisco. Likewise he took a detour through Los Angeles on his tour, in order to perform for the Black Radio Executives at their conference in Los Angeles that spring.

Brown was gratified, but uninspired by the administrative aspects of record producing. As an escape from the tedium and to enhance his sound, he added his own scatlike vocals to his music. He released a final MoJazz album, appropriately named, *Better Days Ahead,* in 1996, then switched labels and signed a contract with Warner Brothers.

Brown's first release on the new label, an album called *Celebration,* was released on August 10, 1999. Critics approved; *All Music Guide* rated it a four star effort.

Brown discredits perennial comparison between himself and Benson and remains eager to distinguish his style from his predecessor. Although both musicians play on Ibanez guitars (Brown's model is GB 10), Brown's own music by his own definition is more traditional from a rhythmic standpoint, oftentimes slower and with less verve, when compared to Benson's flowing jazz movements. Brown, whose repertoire encompasses both contemporary and traditional jazz styles, was described as "R&B fusion with a jazz base," according to J. R. Reynolds, who quoted MoJazz director, Bruce Walker, in *Billboard.*

Selected discography

Singles

"That's the Way Love Goes," MoJazz, 1994.

Albums

Just Between Us, MoJazz, 1992.
After the Storm, MoJazz, 1994.
Better Days Ahead, MoJazz, 1996.
Celebration, Warner Bros., 1999.

Sources

Periodicals

Billboard, June 11, 1994, p. 1; August 7, 1999, p. 36.
Ebony Man, August 1994, p. 6.

Online

"Norman Brown," *All Music Guide,* http://allmusic.com (May 4, 2000).
"The Robertson Treatment: Norman Brown," *Brooklyn Boy Books & Entertainment,* http://www.brooklynboy.com /news/rob3.htm (May 4, 2000).

—Gloria Cooksey

Catatonia

Pop band

Although Catatonia boasts a wide range of influences, from classic rock bands to jazz and soul singers, the Welsh-based Britpop band earned recognition not as imitators of the past, but for their own spirited music. At the source of the group's appeal stands vocalist/guitarist Cerys Matthews, a brassy singer with an extraordinary voice, as well as a back-to-basics approach to entertaining audiences and having a good time. "Cerys has the sort of voice that sends over-emotional hacks dizzying off into reams of praise," wrote Paul Whitelaw in a review for *Melody Maker.* "She's soul without bluster, skipping desultorily from tender-as-a-bruise cooing to a scabrous taunt, from awestruck glee to impossible sadness, sometimes in the space of a single syllable. At times it's truly astonishing—painfully beautiful, naked, helpless and entirely uncontrived. Like Bjork, there are times when she sounds like a 10,000-year-old child, weary and wise, yet wide-eyed and crackling with the sheer wonder of being alive."

However, Matthews can't take all the credit for bringing Catatonia so much notoriety and a string chart-topping albums and singles in Great Britain and throughout Europe. The other members of the quintet, likewise, contribute greatly in making Catatonia such a huge success. They include guitarist Mark Roberts; bassist Paul Jones, a former member, along with Roberts, of the Welsh-language punk band Y Cyrff; guitarist Owen Powell; and drummer Aled Richards, who replaced original drummer Dafydd Iuean, now a member of another popular Welsh band known as the Super Furry Animals.

Catatonia formed in 1992 after Roberts encountered Matthews performing acoustic versions of Jefferson Airplane and the Jam songs on a street corner in Cardiff, the capitol city of Wales. The two subsequently found that they shared similar musical influences—a diverse list of performers that included Billy Holiday, Eric Cantona, John Lennon, Rolf Harris, Abba, Soft Machine, Bob Marley, and Dolly Parton—and decided to form a band. Next, Matthews and Roberts hooked up with Jones, Powell, and Iuean, and within a few short months as an official group, Catatonia had signed with the independent Welsh label Crai. In 1993, the band released their first two singles, "For Tinkerbell" and "Hooked," the first of which was named *NME* (*New Musical Express*) "Single of the Week."

An instant favorite of the British music press, who adored Matthews' bluesy voice and enthusiastic persona, Catatonia followed their debut outings with "Whale," another *NME* "Single of the Week" in 1994, and "Bleed," the band's first top ten hit on the British indie chart released in early-1995 on the independent Nursery label. In April of 1995, after Iuean departed and Richards joined on drums, Catatonia signed with the Blanco Y Negro label, an A&R source run by Rough Trade founder Geoff Travis and owned by WEA United

Kingdom, which handles marketing, sales, and promotion. Travis had previously cut the song "Whale" for his Rough Trade Singles Club.

Outshined Other Newcomers

Soon after signing, Catatonia started touring relentlessly with bands like Marion, Salad, and Puressences, acts which at first received greater press attention than the Welsh newcomers. However, Catatonia pressed on, and eventually left the others in their wake. In the meantime, Catatonia set about writing songs and recording a debut album with producers Stephen Street—who worked with the Smiths and Blur, among others—and Paul Sampson at Maison Rouge Studios in London. With 1996's *Way Beyond Blue,* Catatonia enjoyed their first taste of success. The album, propelled by singles such as "Bleed," "You've Got A Lot To Answer For," and the band's theme tune titled "Sweet Catatonia," brought the band major exposure, including extensive airplay, an appearance for the Radio 1 road show, and a place in the United Kingdom top 40. The group became favorites, too, as subjects for

Britain's gossip columnists, largely for Matthews' celebrating the group's success about town.

In addition to performing in the United Kingdom, Catatonia made an attempt to break through in America, crossing the Atlantic to play shows in New York City, Los Angles, and Austin, Texas. But because of record company chaos and bad timing, their debut never saw release in the United States. Nonetheless, back home Catatonia's popularity continued to escalate, and by May of 1996, they had completed two national sell-out tours.

Scored Hits with *International Velvet*

The later months of 1997 brought the band even greater success with two major hit singles. The witty "I Am the Mob" came first, followed quickly by "Mulder and Scully," a song inspired by the *X-Files* television show that entered the United Kingdom singles chart at number three. Then, in early 1998, Catatonia released a second LP, the critically applauded *International Velvet.* "The new songs are some of the saddest, most righteous, tough/forlorn classics you'll hear all year," wrote Whitelaw in his review of the collection. Making its chart debut at number 11 in Britain, *International Velvet* cemented Catatonia's pop-star status, with *Q* magazine eventually listing the record as one of their "90 Best Albums of the 1990s" and *Melody Maker* naming the outing "Album of the Year." The song "Road Rage" was named best single at the *Q* Awards. The band also scored three Brit Award nominations that year for best group, best album, and best single for "Road Rage," as well as a Mercury Music Prize nomination for the celebrated release.

"Right after we finished recording, I think we knew that *International Velvet* was a special album," said Matthews, as quoted by Atlantic Records. "We had stumbled an awful lot until that point and we had been working so hard. There was a desperation about it. We'd been on the road pretty much solid two years. When it came time to record, we were just spilling our guts, really."

Catatonia continued to tour non-stop in support of the album, including a sold-out headlining tour and several music festival appearances. After *International Velvet*'s European release, Catatonia landed several high-profile gigs, playing at the Lisbon Expo, the World Cup in Paris, and fashion week in Milan. "We did a press conference in Denmark," marveled Powell, as quoted by Mark Jenkins in the *Washington Post,* "and there were people there from Latvia, Lithuania and Poland, all of them saying, 'Two of your records are in the top 10 in our country.' I didn't even know that we'd released records in Poland and Latvia. The fact that you can communicate with people in those countries without ever having been there is quite a thing to get your head around."

In the summer of 1998, barely a month after the album's American release, Catatonia came to the United States to participate at the H.O.R.D.E. festival, joining well-known acts like Blues Traveler, the Barenaked Ladies, and Paula Cole. Most of the audience had never heard of them, despite them being one of the biggest-selling acts in their native Great Britain. But the band themselves admitted they knew little of the other bands. "People say, 'Oh yeah, you're playing with Blues Traveler. That must be great,'" Powell told Jenkins. "To be honest with you, none of us know anything about Blues Traveler. What do they sound like?"

Topped the British Album Chart

The group concluded 1998 with a British arena tour with another well-known Welsh band, the Manic Street Preachers, then traveled to Australia and New Zealand for the first time to perform. Here, the band tested some of their new material, songs—including the top ten hit "Dead From the Waist Down"—that would later appear on their next album, *Equally Cursed and Blessed*. Produced by Catatonia and Tommy D (who previously worked with the Sugarcubes, A Tribe Called Quest, and the Shamen) and released in Britain in 1999, the album debuted on the United Kingdom chart at number one and showed the group's growing confidence in their songwriting abilities. "It's a much more reflective album than *International Velvet*," explained Matthews for Atlantic Records. "It's a lot more thoughtful. That sort of made sense at the time because everything was happening so quickly and *International Velvet* had gone so madly. So yeah, they're more thoughtful songs altogether … darker maybe even."

After switching to Atlantic Records to distribute *International Velvet*, Catatonia finally began to win over fans in the United States. The album was released in March of 2000, and Matthews appeared on the cover of the April issue of *Details* magazine, as well as in feature stories in both *Interview* and Nylon. "I've got absolutely no expectations," Matthews said, however, in an interview with Los Angeles Times writer Marc Weingarten about the group reaching the same level of success in the United States "I did two or three years ago. I wanted to come here and mesmerize everybody, but it's a big country and you've got a lot of good acts now. I just want to enjoy it."

Selected discography

Way Beyond Blue, (United Kingdom) Blanco Y Negro/WEA, 1995.
Catatonia 1993/1994, (United Kingdom) Crai, 1998.
International Velvet, (United Kingdom) Blanco Y Negro/WEA, 1998; Vapor, 1998.
Equally Cursed and Blessed, (United Kingdom) Blanco Y Negro/WEA, 1999; Atlantic, 2000.

Sources

Periodicals

Billboard, July 4, 1998; November 6, 1999; March 11, 2000.
Los Angeles Times, August 21, 1998; January 27, 2000; January 29, 2000.
Melody Maker, November 8, 1997; January 31, 1998; March 28, 1998; December 15-21, 1999.
Rolling Stone, May 25, 2000.
US Weekly, April 10, 2000
Washington Post, August 9, 1998.

Online

Atlantic Records, http://www.atlantic-records.com (May 24, 2000).
Sonicnet.com, http://www.sonicnet.com (May 24, 2000).

—Laura Hightower

Lyor Cohen

Record producer, promoter

Behind-the-scenes music executive Lyor Cohen is a mover and shaker of modern music. During the 1980s he popularized "street rap" music, also called "gangsta' rap," by taking the genre from an underground art form to a legitimate mainstream music style. Prior to the arrival of Cohen, with his personable attitude and easy business style, rap artists had difficulty establishing their legitimacy within the lucrative mainstream media environment because of the violent lyrics and gang imagery portrayed in their songs. As a promoter for Def Jam Records, Cohen successfully brought its performers to the forefront of the American music scene by superimposing his own innate sense of organization and stability onto the chaotic aura that shrouded rap musicians and their art. His innovative "street marketing" advertising strategy brought a new visibility to Def Jam, where as a co-partner at the record label, he assisted in steering Def Jam to profitability and in handling some of the most prominent recording artists of the 1990s in the process.

Additionally, Cohen was the driving force behind "99 Hard Knock Life," the most successful rap tour in history. Later, when Seagram Universal purchased Cohen's interest in Def Jam for a considerable sum, the global music conglomerate placed him at the helm of its newly formed Island/Def Jam label where his responsibilities overflowed beyond the world of rap and into other music styles, including heavy metal, pop, and movie soundtracks.

Cohen, who was born in New York City in 1960, spent his early childhood in Israel with his parents. He was still a young boy when the family returned to the United States and relocated to Los Angeles, California, where he graduated from Marshall High School in 1977. He attended the University of Miami in Florida majoring in global marketing and finance, then spent the year after graduation with some Ecuadorian schoolmates in their homeland where they attempted to start a shrimp-farming enterprise. The inexperienced, albeit well-connected, entrepreneurs failed in their ambitious venture. Subsequently Cohen returned to the United States, where he worked as a nightclub promoter in Los Angeles. Soon after his return he seized an opportunity to invest $1,000 into an independent rap venture that realized a profit of $36,000 and set him on the road to profitability.

In the early 1980s, after booking the rap act Run DMC and maximizing the profits for a 36-fold return, Cohen established a business relationship with rap record producer Russell Simmons. Simmons, who had co-founded the Def Jam Record label in 1983, brought Cohen into the business, and by 1985 the two worked closely together, with Simmons as chairman and Cohen intimately involved in all aspects of the Def Jam production. Cohen brought a new innovation to the record advertising business by shunning the mainstream advertising venues, and opting instead to promote Def Jam's rap records directly to the consumers on the streets. In time the pair of Simmons and Cohen managed several of the most popular acts in rap music.

By outward appearance, the Israeli-descended Cohen seemed to be an anomaly in the largely African American rap music scene, where with his imposing stature of six-feet-five inches tall, he came to be known affectionately, if sardonically, as "Little Israel" by his rapper clients. His high-energy work style earned him the additional nickname of "Mr. Handle-It-Make-It-Happen." For 17 years he operated Def Jam with Simmons, persistent in promoting the record label via innovative "street marketing" tactics including passing out sample tapes to local disc jockeys while simultaneously plastering posters and fliers throughout the city to advertise his clients. Cohen's strategy brought the Def Jam message to the listener on the street and appealed to rap fans in particular because of the non-traditional and rebellious character of the music and its followers.

Cohen managed a coup for rap music when he arranged for Run DMC to appear on the cover of *Rolling Stone,* a prestigious honor in the music world. Not long afterward, DMC climbed into the top ten range on the pop charts. In 1986, Cohen negotiated an endorsement deal between Run DMC and Adidas; the pact was a breakthrough for the legitimacy of rap music. In 1988, following the departure of Def Jam's co-founder Rick Rubin, Cohen assumed a 50 percent ownership of the company as a co-partner with Simmons. Soon Def Jam's reputation swelled along with company earnings.

By mid-1997, Def Jam's profitability reversed course and soared upward. The following year, in 1998, the label's popular rapper, Jay-Z, won a Grammy Award from the National Academy of Recording Arts and Sciences. Also contributing to Def Jam's newfound popularity was Def Jam rapper DMX who earned a $40 million profit for the record label, from $180 million in record sales. Def Jam reported not only a tripling of sales in 1998, but also the company moved out of debt and into profitability. Cohen, who by then was well known for his non-traditional strategies, successfully broke with standard record promotion policies when he released two DMX albums in rapid succession. Against all precedent Cohen followed the DMX debut album that sold 3.4 million albums that year by reverberating within eight months to release a follow-up album that quickly recorded sales of 2.5 million. Def Jam, which had grown impressively since mid-1997, by 1998 had established its reputation as a dominant force in the recording industry and controlled four percent of all album sales by 1999.

Cohen's company, which had distributed records through Sony Music's Columbia Records during the early 1990s, cancelled its distribution agreement with Sony in June of 1994, opting to turn over distribution rights to PolyGram. Soon afterward the new distributor paid $33 million to acquire a 50 percent interest in Def Jam and eventually purchased an additional 10 percent of the company for another $11 million. Def Jam continued with Cohen as president and chief operating officer and Simmons as chief executive, and late in 1998 Seagram Co. made a move to purchase PolyGram—including the distributor's 60 percent share of Def Jam. When Def Jam drew the attention of executives at Seagram Co. who were eager to bargain with the small private rap label, the two companies successfully negotiated a merger.

Def Jam merged with Seagram not once, but twice, initially as part of the massive restructuring by Seagram whereby it purchased 60 percent of Def Jam in the form of PolyGram distribution company and again after Seagram reorganized. With the initial acquisition finalized, Seagram immediately reorganized its music interests into Seagram's Universal Music, the largest recording company worldwide. By February of 1999, a second agreement was reported in the offering between the Cohen-Simmons team and Seagram's Universal by which the Def Jam owners negotiated for Seagram to purchase the remainder of the all-rap record label for more than $100 million.

As Seagram's Universal took possession of the whole of the Def Jam enterprise, the conglomerate wasted no time in merging Def Jam and Island Records into an all-new label, called Island/Def Jam. The new label, a $350 million enterprise, brought Def Jam out of the limited niche of rap music. In the process Seagram's moved Cohen into a highly influential position in the new company, placing him at the forefront of new environments, including heavy metal, pop, rock, and other popular styles. Even in the face of an extensive downsizing effort that resulted from Seagram's aggressive mergers, Cohen's promotional skills were recognized immediately.

Seagram assigned him to commandeer a collection of the company's biggest name stars, including pop stars such as Elton John, Sisqo, and Hanson, plus rocker Jon Bon Jovi, along with the perennial rap and hip-hop stars with whom Cohen was firmly established: DMX, Jay-Z, Foxy Brown, Montell Jordan, and others. Cohen later backed former world heavyweight champion Mike Tyson in an enterprise to launch his own record label in the spring of 1999 and was largely responsible for bringing new-millenium songwriter and vocalist Jeff "Ja Rule" Atkins to the public spotlight. Additionally, Cohen received credit as executive producer of the *Notting Hill* soundtrack, and in 2000 he introduced Sum-41, a new rocker, to the music scene.

As co-president of the newly formed Island/Def Jam label, Cohen assembled the "99 Hard Knock Life" rap road show, a production that earned $11 million from 37 performances and ranked as the most successful rap road show ever produced. He first announced the Southern California Hard Knock tour in January of 1999, with the event scheduled to start the following month. The inviting song bill included some of the top stars of rap, including Method Man, Redman, and DJ Clue. Historically rap music tours had a tradition of poor organization, and other problems. Cohen, with his high sense of organization, oversaw every detail to of the Hard Knock tour. The result was a successful program that attracted audiences not only from the inner city echelons, but also from among the estimated 70 percent of rap music consumers other than back street denizens, including many who hailed from the upper middle class suburbs.

Cohen is married and has one son. He lives with his family in New York City's Upper East Side and has an office in midtown Manhattan. He is active in programs to help disadvantaged youth. He sits on the boards of trustees of Camp Hill in Roscoe, New York. Camp Hill, in the Catskills Mountains, provides two-week (overnight) programs for at-risk youth to foster self-esteem and cultural awareness. Similarly he is active in the Refugee Project.

Selected discography

Albums produced

Nutty Professor (soundtrack), PGD/PolyGram, June 1996.
Notting Hill (soundtrack), 1999.

Sources

Advertising Age, March 20, 2000, p. 12.
Billboard, November 26, 1994, p. 6.
Los Angeles Times, January 26, 1999, p. 1; February 19, 1999, p. 1.
Newsweek, January 31, 2000, p. 40(4).

—*Gloria Cooksey*

Dark Star

Psychedelic rock band

For more than a decade, Christian "Bic" Hayes, Dave Francolini, and Laurence O'Keefe searched for the ultimate psychedelic rock sound, first as Levitation, then in the formation of Dark Star. When Levitation dissolved in 1994, most assumed, including the band members themselves, that their days of making music together had ended. Drug dependencies, among other problems, caused Levitation to fall apart, leaving the group a common subject of ridicule throughout Great Britain. Feeling defeated after Levitation's drug-induced implosion, the trio entered a two-year black period. "Dole, acid, alcohol, mourning," admitted Francolini, as quoted by *Melody Maker*'s Neil Kulkarni. "Sat around listening to PiL and Swans at deafening volume, just talking. It means something now. We'd been through real highs with Levitation: at that stage we three were at a low, just the saddest, darkest time of my life." In fact, one member was forced to check himself into rehab in order to overcome his addictions. Then, after years of destitution and personal struggles, the three men started rehearsing together again, recorded and released singles and a debut album, and finally earned their vindication when, in January of 2000, they played live as Dark Star on the hit show *Top of the Pops,* joining an elite group of British pop/rock groups—such as PiL and New Order—to have done so.

The surreal, wildly expansive acid-rock group Levitation existed on the brink of chaos, both on stage and off, though their albums consistently won positive criticism. The group's story began in 1990 when vocalist/guitarist Terry Bickers quit his former band, the House of Love, after a much-publicized falling out with that band's lead singer, Guy Chadwick. Angered and unhappy with the constraints the House of Love placed on his guitar playing, as well as Chadwick's mainstream approach to making music, Bickers left to follow his own instincts, teaming in London with fellow space cadets Robert White on keyboards/guitar, Hayes on guitar, Francolini on drums, and O'Keefe on bass to form Levitation, a band intent on shaking up the music scene with incendiary live shows, not to mention Chadwick's discussions with the British music press on odd subjects like prog-rock revivals, flying saucers, reincarnation, and Egyptology.

Levitation also took the idea of the "rock 'n' roll lifestyle" to the extreme limits. The group's out-of-control behavior, marked by narcotic excess, would leave not one member unscathed. Bickers, for example, would reportedly carry a bag of Es in his pocket on stage, chewing his way to the bottom of the bag throughout the course of a show, while O'Keefe appeared permanently spaced-out. Francolini, notorious for his complex drumming patterns as well as for his semi-nude appearance in the first Levitation video—writhing in the middle of the woods eating soil—was the self-admitted member who used more drugs than anyone else.

Earned Acclaim

Somehow, Levitation managed to keep the group together for a few short years, even recording some brilliant songs along the way. The band's first recording, a stunning EP entitled *Coppelia,* arrived in April of 1991 on the Rough Trade label. Opening with the shimmering "Nadine," turning more reflective with "Rosemary Jones," and illustrating vigorous, exhilarating guitar-playing with "Paid In Kind," *Coppelia* won significant critical praise, and the anthemic track "Smile" became a live favorite among fans. An even more expansive EP, *After Ever,* followed later that summer, and in 1992 the two records were combined, along with some live tracks and a new song, "It's Time," and released as the mini-LP *Coterie.* However, critics agreed that the compilation, in spite of rave reviews, seemed merely an introduction to the group's abilities in comparison to the explosive *Need For Not,* Levitation's debut full-length album. Released just a few months after *Coterie* and produced by the Cardiacs' Tim Smith, the album further propelled Levitation's rising popularity.

The following year, the band released another heralded EP, *World Around,* but troubles within the band had also begun to intensify. Finally, in mid-1993 soon after the release of the stale single "Even When Your Eyes Are Open," the group's major-label debut on Chrysalis, Bickers announced that he was leaving the band, refusing to enlighten the press with a specific

For The Record . . .

Members include **Dave Francolini**, drums; **Christian "Bic" Hayes**, vocals, guitar; **Laurence O'Keefe**, bass.

Trio played as members of the London-based band Levitation, 1990-94; after a period of overcoming drug addictions and personal tragedies, the former bandmates re-grouped as Dark Star, 1996; signed to Harvest imprint of EMI Records, released singles and debut album *twenty twenty something,* 1999; appeared on *Top of the Pops,* 2000.

Addresses: *Record company*—EMI-Capitol Records, 1750 N. Vine St., Hollywood, CA 90028, phone: (213) 462-6252, fax: (213) 467-6550.

reason. And in 1994, halfway through a gig at London's Tufnell Park Dome, he quit and walked offstage.

Hoping to move forward without Bickers, the remaining members recorded in Wales with new lead vocalist Steven Ludwin another album entitled *Meanwhile Gardens.* The largely instrumental LP, released only in Australia, included re-makes of old songs, added instrumentation such as horns and strings, and some patchy new offerings. After receiving lukewarm reviews for the album and an ill-fated tour of Germany, the band decided to call it quits. By the mid-1990s, the members of Levitation were all unemployed, with the tough times about to begin in earnest.

Battled Failure and Addiction

"When the band broke up, I had a desperate time," Hayes revealed to James Oldham for a *New Musical Express* feature story. "My mother died and I had a lot of personal problems with illness. I just couldn't get anything together at all." Similarly, Francolini struggled to cope with his drug dependency. "I was heavily into narcotics and alcohol at the time," he recalled. "During that period, Bic moved up on Goldhawk Road in the thinnest house in London. In the confines of that corridor we sat drinking inordinate quantities of alcohol and taking lots of acid and just being really upset."

For the next two years, the members of Levitation more or less lived without any sense of direction, although Hayes worked with Heather Nova and O'Keefe with Dead Can Dance's Brendan Perry and Heidi Berry. Francolini, meanwhile, opted to put his drumsticks aside, focusing instead on management and production. Still, they all carried over their heads the failure of Levitation, along with a bothersome reputation: the spaced-out casualties of drug addiction. "It was redundancy. All the people around us suddenly didn't want to talk to us or even see us. We felt like failures," Hayes painfully recalled.

Drug-free Music

Toward the end of 1996, however, after attending a Sonic Youth concert, Hayes, Francolini, and O'Keefe felt inspired—realizing they had nothing to lose—to try and get back together again. From there, they scraped together enough money to book space in a North London basement to rehearse. For the first time, the three musicians were creating psychedelic rock tunes with a clear head, writing on their first day back "Graceadelica," the 1999 single that would later enter the British charts at number 25. "Those rehearsals just gave us this massive vent for all our frustrations: every time we got back into that room, all our past f***ups and dreams just got belched out," O'Keefe explained to Kulkarni. "All the aggressiveness and anger we felt about what had happened to us came out; when we got back together and tapped into it, it was an amazing feeling. Not like therapy. More like a dirty protest."

After searching for a new singer to no avail, Dark Star decided in October of 1997 that no one else but Hayes should front the band, and after hammering out songs for what would become their debut album, *twenty twenty something,* they saw their luck begin to change. Not only did they find a new manager, but also received a record deal with EMI to release the record in April of 1999 on the company's recently reactivated Harvest imprint. "I think the Dark Star album sounds raggedy, rough, and punky," Francolini, who claimed the group could play every note on the album live, told Oldham. "You can really feel it. When you put that album on, it sounds like we're in the room with you."

Earning rave reviews for the effort, the members of Dark Star were poised to redeem themselves. The songs compiling *twenty twenty something,* wrote Kulkarni, are "mired in that murky sound world where every moment depends on real alchemy, where every switch to a positive emotion carries with it enormous dramatic gravitas, a sound where anything can happen." And despite the trio's newfound freedom from drugs, their live performances remained just as earth-shattering. "A lot of people haven't seen a band like ours before," Hayes noted to Oldham. "The age of the kids who come to see us means most of them have grown up during Britpop… and when they're confronted by us playing at this insane volume, they're blown away."

Since re-affirming themselves, Dark Star felt confident about the future. "It came out of real pain, but it's infinite: we can go anywhere we want to with Dark Star," Hayes professed, as quoted by Kulkarni. The singer/guitarist further explained to Oldham how Dark Star have discovered a new sense of seriousness about their music the second time around: "I don't want people to think we aren't committed. This is serious. It's art, for want of a better word."

Selected discography

Dark Star

"Graceadelica," Harvest/EMI, 1999.
twenty twenty something, Harvest/EMI, 1999.

Levitation

Coppelia, (EP), Ultimate, 1991.
After Ever, (EP), Ultimate, 1991.

Coterie, (mini-LP), Rough Trade, 1992.
Need For Not, Rough Trade, 1992.
"Even When Your Eyes Are Open," (single), Chrysalis, 1993.
Meanwhile Gardens, Festival, 1994.

Sources

Books

Buckley, Jonathan and others, editor, *Rock: The Rough Guide,* Rough Guides Ltd., 1999.
Robbins, Ira A., editor, *Trouser Press Guide to '90s Rock,* Fireside/Simon & Schuster, 1997.

Periodicals

Melody Maker, November 21, 1998; February 20, 1999; March 27, 1999; June 5, 1999; November 17-23, 1999.
New Musical Express, January 29, 2000, p. 22.

—*Laura Hightower*

Dead Kennedys

Punk rock band

Actions speak louder than words. The band name alone indicated the intention of punk rock group Dead Kennedys' music. Infamous for their shocking methods of expressing liberal political views, the Dead Kennedys plastered a place for themselves in the hall of fame for 1980s punk. However, the Dead Kennedys may have impacted society of the 1980s more by their behavior than their music. Steve Knopper from *Music-Hound Rock* summarized the Dead Kennedys' impression upon culture by stating, "The Dead Kennedys, purposely provocative with their name, album covers, and titles … were more influential for what they did than how they sounded." Starting by sadistically naming themselves after a family considered royalty by many Americans, the Dead Kennedys jammed their nine-year career as a band with outrageous stage antics, controversial songwriting, poignant album releases, and surprising community service. Dead Kennedys was the forum for political expressions against conservative politics, the religious right, and many social injustices. The group broke through barriers which helped form their legendary status in the underground punk scene of the 1980s. Their legacy inspired many other groups such as The Adolescents, Bad Brains, Henry Rollins, and Megadeth.

Photograph by Roger Ressmeyer. Corbis. Reproduced by permission.©

Jello Biafra (born Eric Boucher), moved from Boulder, Colorado to attend college at the University of California at Santa Cruz. Shows by the Sex Pistols and the Ramones set fire to the furnace within Biafra which fueled groundbreaking accomplishments in the punk music community. The energy and politics of the San Francisco punk scene impressed Biafra. According to an account from the group's record label web page, "After seeing early performances of The Saints and Wire, among others in London that summer, Biafra discovered that the early San Francisco punk scene (Avengers, Dils, Zeros, etc.) was far more raw and primal than anything he had seen so far."

The Dead Kennedys formed in San Francisco in July 1978 after Biafra answered an ad in a music paper placed by East Bay Ray. Klaus Fluoride joined Biafra and Ray to play bass, a second guitarist, named 6025 joined. Bruce Slesinger (a.k.a. Ted) pounded out the beat on drums. Boucher chose a name which signified glaring social injustices which his own country was involved in during the late 1960s and early 1970s. Jello reflected the disgusting western consumerism his culture was thriving on while Biafra referred to the desperate republic in Africa whose struggle for independence was crushed through a food blockade by British and United States governments.

Antics Began

It began in San Francisco's North Beach area in July 1978. Mabuhay Gardens, a Filipino restaurant which was a spot for punk music for close to a decade, was the location of the Dead Kennedys' first gig. Dead Kennedys performances were chaotic and full of theatrics, with Biafra's political lessons thrown at the crowd throughout the set. Police often showed up at shows because of the group's antics. Not surprisingly, the band's conduct chased away mainstream record labels. They played in the Bay Area for the first couple of years, gaining a faithful underground following. A tour in Britain in late 1980 established the Dead Kennedys as a prominent band in the underground scene, as well as attracted Sex Pistols and Clash fans.

The Dead Kennedys' initial offering was similar to British punk rock in that it featured, according to Andy Lewis from the *Rough Guide to Rock,* "all beefy guitar, rumbling bass, and enthusiastically whacked bass." Lyrical content of the songs separated Dead Kennedys' art from other punk rock groups. Scathing sarcasm about issues such as corporate deception, racism, and policies of the Reagan administration made up the majority of the odes. "California Uber Alles," written about then-California governor Jerry Brown, was the first single released by the Dead Kennedys and rose to the top of punk playlists in 1979, becoming popular enough for release in Britain on Fast Records. The Dead Kennedy song titles were often brash if taken literally, which caused commotion in their overseas listeners where the sarcasm sometimes failed to carry over in translation. Several conservative and religious groups were outraged by the music and actions of the liberal band. Notorius titles such as "Let's Lynch The Landlord," "Kill The Poor," "Nazi Punks F*** Off!" and "Too Drunk To F***," caught many people's attention.

The Dead Kennedys' notorious behavior was epitomized at the Bammies, which were the Grammies of San Francisco. The band was invited to play in front of a crowd which included music industry executives and mainstream groups. Instead of playing their hit "California Uber Alles," Dead Kennedys surprised the audience with a freshly written song attacking the music industry called "Pull My Strings." Biafra served his local community by entering the mayoral race of San Francisco in 1979. He ran under the humorous motto, "There's always room for Jello." Surprising many, he finished fourth out of ten with 6,000 votes.

Fed the Masses

Fresh Fruit for Rotting Vegetables, released in 1980 by IRS and Cherry Red in England was the Dead Kennedys' debut album. Revealing the taboo nature of their music, their record label web page stated, "That's why Faulty Products was started...as a branch of IRS, because originally *Fresh Fruit...* was supposed to go out through A&M, but A&M wouldn't touch it, so they created an American arm of the very appropriately named Faulty Products." *Fresh Fruit* contained humor and sarcasm in A-sides of their first singles, in a cover of Elvis' "Viva Las Vegas," and in new material such as "Forward to Death" and "I Kill Children." It was the only album the group did not own the rights to, thus allowing many pirate copies to appear. Other albums were recorded on the group's own label, Alternative Tentacles, and are still in print. Ted left the band after *Fresh Fruit...* was released and was replaced by drummer Darren H. Peligro.

Music listeners caught on when "Too Drunk to F***," a single released in 1981, saw surprising popularity at home and abroad. In the United States it became a favorite among the fraternities on various campuses and in the United Kingdom it made the top 40 list despite being banned from airplay.

The band's disgust with popular religion was expressed in a 1982 EP, *In God We Trust, Inc.*, with songs that described organized religion as corrupt and fascist. The music was thrash punk—very fast and short songs. Meanwhile, the group's label, Alternative Tentacles, continued to grow and penetrated the music scene with classic releases by D.O.A., T.S.O.L., and in the United Kingdom, 7 Seconds, Bad Brains and Husker Du.

Plastic Surgery Disasters, released in late 1982, showcased an expansion of the Dead Kennedys' musical repertoire, which even included a piece by Fluoride on the clarinet. The album included a song on anti-pollution which was probably closest to a ballad that a Dead Kennedys song reached. After *Plastic Surgery Disasters* was released, the group took a hiatus, which allowed Alternative Tentacles to fluorish and establish itself as a cornerstone in the underground music scene in the United States.

Down the Tubes

Frankenchrist, released in 1985, was perhaps the band's most notorious release of their career, which ultimately pointed the group toward a breakup. It included a poster of European artist H.R. Giger's "Landscape #XX: Where We Are Coming From." It portrayed a landscape of genitalia in explicit positions. Biafra stated that the poster was merely an expression of the ugliness of a consumer-oriented society, but many did not find it humorous. The label even included a sticker that read : "WARNING: The inside foldout to this record cover is a work of art by H.R. Giger that some people may find shocking, repulsive or offensive. Life can sometimes be that way."

Biafra was prosecuted for distributing pornography to minors during 1986-1987 and the legal saga lead to the demise of the band. Biafra established the No More Censorship Defense Fund, which along with helping with the legal fees in the Frankenchrist case, made available copies of articles dealing with censorship and plans to help others who were being harassed. The case against Biafra was eventually dismissed after a 7-5 jury vote of acquittal. However, the group had disbanded before the release of their final album, *Bedtime for Democracy,* which came out in 1986. *Give Me Convenience or Give Me Death* was released as a compliation in 1987.

Continuing the Tradition

All of the members remained active musically after the Dead Kennedys broke up. Among many spoken word projects, Biafra put out music in collaboration with Al Jourgensen and Paul Barker of Ministry under the title of Lard. Ray joined Algerian Cheika Rimitti on an album and formed a band called Candyass. Klaus Fluoride released several solo albums, while D.H. Peligro formed a band named after himself. Fluoride and Ray also played in an instrumental surf band called Jumbo Shrimp.

Biafra embarked on spoken word tours speaking about censorship and opposing the PMRC, against the Persian Gulf War, conservative political and social agendas among other topics. He felt the repercussions of his outspoken nature in 1994 when his leg was broken in an attack by a group of skinheads at the East Bay 924 Gilman club in San Francisco. The cause of the attack was allegedly because he was considered a sellout. Biafra continued his activism when he ran for United States President in 2000 under the Green Party.

A vicious legal battle was launched by Ray, Peligro, and Fluoride in October of 1998. Dissatisfied with the results of handshake agreements from the past, the three members charged Biafra with underpaying them royalties. They sued to part with Alternative Tentacles and take their master recordings with them. The issue was due for trial in May 2000. Those antics were enough to shock even diehard fans.

A jury in San Francisco ruled on May 19, 2000, that Biafra underpaid the rest of the band and failed to promote the group's back catalog. The other three Dead Kennedys were awarded $200,000 in actual damages and $20,000 in punitive damages. In a countersuit Biafra filed against Ray, the jury found Ray guilty of mismanaging their partnership. Ray had to pay Biafra $5,000.

Selected discography

Fresh Fruit for Rotting Vegetables, IRS Records, 1980.
In God We Trust, Inc., EP, Alternative Tentacles, 1982.
Plastic Surgery Disasters, Alternative Tentacles, 1982.
Frankenchrist, Alternative Tentacles, 1985.
Bedtime for Democracy, Alternative Tentacles, 1986.
Give Me Convenience or Give Me Death, Alternative Tentacles, 1987.

Sources

Books

MusicHound Rock, Visible Ink Press, 1999.
Robbins, Ira A. editor, *Trouser Press Guide to '90s Rock,* Fireside/Simon & Schuster, 1997.

Periodicals

Spin, February, 2000, pp. 73-78.

Online

All Music Guide, http://www.allmusic.com (April 17, 2000).
The Rough Guide to Rock, http://www.roughguides.com (April 17, 2000).

—Nathan Sweet

Joey DeFrancesco

Organist

Although keyboardist Jimmy Smith, regarded as the master of the Hammond B-3 organ sound in jazz, never gave up on his instrument during the 1980s when the popularity of synthesizers overshadowed the organ, most critics cite a younger player by the name of Joey DeFrancesco as the musician most responsible for bringing the organ back to the forefront of the jazz scene. A brilliant, energetic player who helped the Hammond organ regain respectability since his arrival in the late 1980s, DeFrancesco was born on April 10, 1971, in Springfield, Pennsylvania, spending most of his childhood in the city of Philadelphia. DeFrancesco, an established organist by the time he was 20 years old, came from a line of distinguished musicians: his grandfather, a multi-instrumentalist; his father, an accomplished organist and trumpeter; and his brother, a blues guitarist, all enjoyed respected careers.

DeFrancesco's musical roots can be traced back to the organist's Sicilian-born grandfather, Joe DeFrancesco, Sr., who, unlike his grandson, didn't even enter the music world until the age of 29. Nonetheless, the elder musician displayed a seemingly innate ability to learn just about any instrument he picked up, leading him eventually to spend eight years playing with the swing band the Dorsey Brothers. Describing his grandfather's talent, DeFrancesco recalled, "He'd get a call, maybe it was Wednesday, for Wednesday night, to do a piano gig," as quoted by interviewer Pete Fallico for the organist's official website biography. "Well, he'd go rent a piano and learn how to play it during the day and go do the gig that night!"

Following in the footsteps of DeFrancesco, Sr., eldest son "Papa" John DeFrancesco (DeFrancesco's father) became an accomplished musician as well. He started his career playing trumpet in Niagara Falls, New York, but after seeing a performance one night by organist Jimmy Smith, Papa John laid down his horn in favor of the other instrument. His supportive wife, Laurene DeFrancesco, agreed to the new instrument—and large piece of furniture—as an addition to the family home, and Papa John, teaching himself how to play and practicing nights after work, soon became a proficient player. Listening to albums and watching other noted organists play live at clubs to improve his technique, he commenced his professional career as an organist by performing at local venues in Niagara Falls, then moved the family to Buffalo, New York, a town known for its "organ fever." From there, the family finally settled in Philadelphia, considered by many the jazz organ capital of the world. It was here that DeFrancesco's father, leading his trio, established himself on the jazz scene.

An Organ Prodigy

Watching his father on stage and hearing music at home, DeFrancesco likewise took to the organ and was so young when he started that his legs dangled from the bench, his feet unable to reach the pedals. A natural musician and born entertainer like his grandfather and father before him, DeFrancesco started playing piano at the age of five, but quickly gravitated to the organ. Soon thereafter, the prodigious youngster made his first public appearance. He recalled to Fallico about the first time his father took him—at the age of six—to one of his gigs to sit in at a club called the Grid Iron in Philadelphia: "I knew 'Groove's Groove,' Jimmy Smith's 'The Sermon' and a couple of things … I remember walking into that place and hearing that organ, you know… they were playing some blues: 'Red Top' … and I was a nervous wreck (laughing) … I was so nervous that when they brought me up there to play, I only played the bottom manual; I didn't even play the top keyboard. My dad had to adjust the volume for me 'cause there was no way I could reach the bass pedals or the volume pedal … and that was like the greatest experience I'll ever have."

Realizing his son's unmistakable gift and desire to play, Papa John began taking his young son to clubs in and around Philadelphia, where the heroes of the jazz organ would appear on a regular basis. Such early exposure, in particular his first encounter with one of the legends of groove-organ music, a self-taught player named Jack McDuff, proved an important catalyst for DeFrancesco's subsequent development. That evening, at a club called the Flight Deck in Wilmington, Delaware, DeFrancesco had the opportunity to play for a few minutes at the end of the show with the renowned player. "I came up there and played 'Rock

Candy' and Jack was..he was laughing... He got behind me, like he was shooting me and stuff. We traded off and it was great. He picked me up when I was done and kept saying; 'Ten!... Ten years old!'... you know, things like that, I'll never forget." Following this impressionable night, DeFrancesco would go on to meet and learn from some of the greatest organists of the time, including McDuff, Richard "Groove" Holmes, Trudy Pitts, Shirley Scott, Don Patterson, Jimmy Mc-Griff, and others.

DeFrancesco studied music during high school in Philadelphia, but decided against continuing formal training when an invaluable learning experience was offered to him: to play with Miles Davis, inarguably one of the most important jazz musicians to have ever lived. The young organist had met the legendary trumpeter/bandleader when he was asked to play his instrument, along with other high school students, on a local television show which boasted Davis as a guest. So impressed was Davis with DeFrancesco, then only 16 years of age, that he later asked the young musician to join his band in New York. DeFrancesco made other strides while still in high school as well; he won numerous awards as a teen, including the Philadelphia Jazz Society's McCoy Tyner Scholarship, and at the first ever Thelonius Monk International Jazz Piano Competition held in 1987, the then-16-year-old De-Francesco placed third.

Emulated the Jazz Masters

By the time DeFrancesco left high school, the promising organist's future seemed certain. Already, he had secured a contract with Columbia Records for five albums and was playing by 1988 with Davis, accompanying the renowned bandleader for a European tour and playing keyboards for "Cobra" from Davis's *Amandla.* Working with Davis changed DeFrancesco's playing in many ways. For instance, the organist started to concentrate with more determination on the techniques used by the jazz masters. Applying what he was learning from Davis directly to the organ, DeFrancesco would solo with his right hand to emulate the sound of Davis's horn, and he even picked up the trumpet as a second instrument. Moreover, his association with Davis served as a boost for his popularity, and jazz enthusiasts from around the world recognized DeFrancesco's name.

In 1989, DeFrancesco debuted with *All of Me,* though the album received lukewarm reviews for its poor choice of material and overblown arrangements. However, he redeemed himself the following year with *Where Were You.* Recorded at the renowned Van Gelder studios with guest appearances by bassist Milt Hinton, Kirk Whalum, guitarist John Scofield, and Illinois Jacket, *Where Were You* presented DeFrancesco as a young artist among his new peers. After this, DeFrancesco recorded three more albums for Columbia: 1991's *Part III,* recorded with the organist's touring band, 1992's *Reboppin',* which included an appearance by DeFrancesco's father and brother for the track "Family Jam," and 1993's *Live at the Five Spot.*

Jazz and Beyond

After leaving Columbia, DeFrancesco continued to record for other labels, applying his talent to a variety of formats. For 1994's *All About My Girl,* the organist and his backing band—guitarist Paul Bollenback and drummer Byron Landham—delved into the blues, soul, and rockabilly in addition to the jazz style, easing into slower numbers with guest tenor saxophonist and producer Houston Person. DeFrancesco stretched his musicianship further with 1995's *The Street of Dreams,* an album dedicated to his mentor, McDuff. With this effort, DeFrancesco illustrated his versatility by also playing piano and trumpet and even singing. Next, the organist teamed with McDuff for the 1996 recording *It's All About Time,* which included a version of the elder player's funk gem "Rock Candy," the same tune De-Francesco played for McDuff as a 10-year-old boy.

In the spring of 1998, DeFrancesco, along with his father, released the acclaimed *All in the Family.* Of the album, Herb Boyd in a May 1998 review for *Down Beat* insisted: "If your pulse does not quicken at the first quiver and sumptuous quake of the combined organs of Joey and Papa DeFrancesco, then there must be something wrong with your ticker." DeFrancesco followed this project with three more well-received albums: a collection of standards entitled *All or Nothing at All,* released in 1998; a tribute to one of his influences entitled *The Champ: Dedicated to Jimmy Smith,* released in 1999; and a concept album recorded with guitarist Frank Vignola and drummer Joe Ascione in celebration of his Italian roots entitled *Goodfellas,* released in 2000. "I always wanted to do this album," the then 28-year-old organist told Jason Koransky in an interview for *Down Beat.* "The album goes with the Italian-American heritage, the music we listen to. They're tunes that you hear from the movies, like 'Speak Softly Love.' You know we're talking about *The Godfather* once you hear that. These are the songs you love if you're Italian. They're tradition. If you're Italian, Frank Sinatra is president and 'Fly Me To The Moon' is a staple."

Leaving his childhood home of Philadelphia in 1998, DeFrancesco relocated to Phoenix, Arizona, where he lives with his wife and young daughter. In the fall of 1999, DeFrancesco had the opportunity to play at the San Francisco Jazz Festival with his idol, Smith, a realized dream for the younger musician. A live recording of the show—which marked the first time Smith ever recorded with another organist—was set for future release on Concord Jazz, DeFrancesco's current label.

Selected discography

All of Me, Columbia, 1989.
Where Were You, Columbia, 1990.
Part III, Columbia, 1991.
Reboppin', Columbia, 1992.
Live at the Five Spot, Columbia, 1993.
All About My Girl, Muse, 1994.
The Street of Dreams, Big Mo, 1995.
(With Jack McDuff) *It's All About Time,* Concord Jazz, 1996
All in the Family, High Note, 1998.
All or Nothing at All, Big Mo, 1998.
The Champ: Dedicated to Jimmy Smith, High Note, 1999.
Goodfellas, Concord, 2000.

Sources

Books

Swenson, John, editor, *Rolling Stone Jazz & Blues Album Guide,* Random House, 1999.

Periodicals

Down Beat, July 1994, p. 77; September 1994, p. 36; December 1994, pp. 56-57; November 1995, p. 46; February 1997, pp. 49-50; May 1998, pp. 62-64; December 1999, p. 80; February 2000, pp. 45-47; March 2000, p. 64.

Online

"Joey DeFrancesco Biography," *All Music Guide,* http://www.allmusic.com (April 10, 2000).
Joey DeFrancesco Home Page, http://www.joeydefrancesco.com (April 10, 2000).

—*Laura Hightower*

Dave Douglas

Trumpeter, composer

AP/Wide World Photos. Reproduced by permission.

Dave Douglas may be the signature musician of the 1990s. By mid-decade, his work with groups as dissimilar as Horace Silver's band and John Zorn's Masada had revealed him to be a jazz trumpeter of great promise. At the same time, he was leading a large number of his own groups which played music of considerable breadth. "He pushes the music into other areas, building to suit his instincts, into the classical chamber mode, into Eastern European folk idioms, or quirky rock riffage, abutting uncharted improv sections", wrote Josef Woodward in *Jazz Times*. In 1998, *Down Beat*'s Critics Poll named Douglas Talent Deserving Wider Recognition both for his trumpet playing and for his overall jazz artistry; in 1999, *Jazz Times* voted him jazz artist of the year. Douglas reached these peaks while working at a frenetic pace: by 2000 he had some 100 recording credits under his belt.

Douglas's eclectic musical tastes have their roots in his early life in Montclair, New Jersey, where he heard the rock and pop albums of his older brothers and sisters, and the swing records in his father's collection. "Stevie Wonder was fed to me with as much validity as the Beatles or Coleman Hawkins or Beethoven," Douglas told James Hale in *CODA* magazine. "I developed an inner world of hearing music at a very early age." Indicative of his relationship to jazz is the fact that he came to the great Miles Davis groups of the 1950s and 1960s only after hearing Davis's funk and rock-infused later work. Rather than a museum piece based on forms of the 1940s and 1950s, Douglas would make an extremely plastic form that could accept all the diverse musical styles that interested him.

He took up piano not long after starting grade school. At the age of seven he began studying trombone and at nine switched to trumpet. He first studied the classical repertoire. When he was eleven, however, he made two important discoveries while rooting through his father's collection of LPs: *The Smithsonian Collection of Classic Jazz* set gave him an introduction to the history of jazz forms, while *Music Minus One* albums gave him an opportunity to improvise with a band in his own home. By the time Douglas had reached his teens, music had assumed a central place in his life. He took a tape player and music on family vacations, and while still in high school made up his mind to become a professional musician.

His relationship to his instrument was a complicated one, not withstanding the virtuosity he eventually displayed. "I'm just trying to get the sound that's in my head," he told the *Toronto Star*'s Geoff Chapman, "and often the sound in my head doesn't have a lot to do with the trumpet itself. For a long time, I was just trying to ignore the fact that I was playing this obnoxious instrument." He told Hale that for a long time, until late in the 1990s, in fact, it was a tenor sax he was hearing. "Until recently, I never thought I was playing the trumpet. I was hearing tenor saxophone in my head, and that's why to this day I so often use the low register. I want to be down there where a Coleman Hawkins, Ben Webster and Dexter Gordon were." After a high school year abroad in Spain, where he was able to play with real gigging musicians, Douglas first attended the Berklee College of Music where he studied jazz harmony and arranging, and then the New England Conservatory of Music where he learned the Carmine Caruso trumpet method. In 1984 he moved to New York City where he enrolled in New York University and began studying with Caruso himself. While in school in New York, he honed his performance chops in one of the toughest venues imaginable, as a Times Square street musician. In 1986, while working with a theater group in Switzerland, he discovered Romanian folk music, part of a tradition that would be an important part of his work through most of the 1990s. "It was like

a new language for me," he told Hale, "it added to everything else I was hearing."

The jazz world got its first look at Douglas in 1987 when he joined the Horace Silver quintet. The job provided Douglas with valuable experience in hard bop, but the trumpeter never fully gelled with Silver's group. "I don't think Horace was thrilled with the way I was playing," Douglas told Lloyd Sachs of the *Chicago Sun-Times*. "I was 23 and still thought I was single-handedly changing modern American music. I was trying to play modern when he wanted something more literal. It wasn't the smoothest ride, but ultimately, learning that language was very important to me."

His recording career took off in earnest in 1993 when he joined a group put together by Don Byron to play the music of Mickey Katz. The same year Douglas cut the first album of his own, a work called *Parallel Worlds*. The line-up, highly unusual for a jazz record, included Mark Feldman on violin, Erik Friedlander on cello, Mark Dressler on bass and Michael Sarin on drums. Douglas's string group ended up that way by accident. "I remember Dave had a gig at the (original) Knitting Factory and he called me at the last minute to come to a rehearsal because his trombone player couldn't make it back from the West Coast in time," Friedlander told Hale. "I ended up performing with Dave for the first time and the string band was born." The group recorded two other CDs, *Five* and *Convergence*, both on the Soul Note label.

Rough tapes of the *Parallel Worlds* sessions reached saxophonist John Zorn, who called Douglas not long afterward and invited him to join the group Masada, which Zorn was putting together. Masada was a brilliant hybrid in which the sound and spirit of the early Ornette Coleman quartet met klezmer music. With Zorn on sax, Douglas on trumpet, Greg Cohen on bass, and Joey Baron on drums, Masada turned out to be one of the super-groups of the nineties. A large part of Masada's success and popularity was due to the fiery chemistry and near-telepathic awareness that existed between Douglas and Zorn. Masada became Zorn's most popular group and helped launch Douglas into wider prominence.

By the mid-nineties, Douglas was one of the busiest, unheralded musicians working. In 1994 his Tiny Bell Trio, comprised of guitarist Brad Schoeppach and drummer Jim Black, released its first CD, entitled simply *The Tiny Bell Trio*, followed by 1995's *Constellations*. Douglas also put together a sextet in 1995 which released *In Our Lifetime*. 1996 saw the release of *Five*, and a collaboration with Dutch percussionist Han Bennink. Douglas brought out three albums in 1997, including *Sanctuary*, a free jazz composition utilizing electronics. He released another three in 1998, including the premier CD by his group Charms of the Night Sky, made up of Feldman on violin, Cohen on bass, and Guy Kucevsek on accordion. This burst of work all took place while Douglas was touring with Masada and his own bands and working as a sideman with musicians such as Myra Melford, Anthony Braxton, Fred Hersh, Ned Rothenberg, Uri Caine, and David Shea.

Douglas's career entered a new phase in late 1997 when his sextet played a six night stand at New York's Iridium Club. The gig, compared by some to Ornette Coleman's 1959 date at the Five Spot, was a sign that Douglas had left the downtown music ghetto and entered the jazz mainstream. In the wake of the Iridium shows, he was named *Down Beat*'s Jazz Artist of the Year in 1998, and the *Jazz Times* Artist of the Year in 1999. The payoff came later in 1999, when RCA Records offered Douglas a two-year contract that allowed him to release four records, each by a different group, together with full control over production. Steve Gates, RCA's vice-president of A&R told Hale why the company was willing to grant Douglas such a degree of freedom: "I think of Dave as pushing the limits of titles because he is as much a creator of world music as he is of jazz. The improvised nature of his music pushes it toward jazz, but I think he brings world and classical repertoire into his work, as well. I think Dave will be one of a few artists who will reshape jazz in the coming few years."

All the accolades have not slowed Douglas's energetic pace. Despite continued reports of its demise, Masada continues to be active. In early 2000 his sextet released *Soul on Soul: Celebrating Mary Lou Williams*, the first of his releases for RCA. Douglas also formed two new groups, Magic Triangle, a quartet, and a nonet called Witness. Douglas was also commissioned to write music for the Tricia Brown Dance Company, compositions which were to be performed by Charms Of The Night Sky on Douglas' second RCA release. And there are always new projects. "There are just a lot of ideas floating around, many thankfully unfulfilled, for each of my projects," Douglas told the *Boston Globe*'s Bob Blumenthal. "And while I wish there was some kind of secret for getting it all out, the way that I do it is just to work every day. Composition is like long-distance running, or any other activity that requires developed muscles."

Selected discography

As bandleader

Parallel Worlds, Soul Note, 1993.
In Our Lifetime, New World/Countercurrents, 1995.
Five, Soul Note, 1996.
Sanctuary, Avant, 1997.
Stargazer, Arabesque Jazz, 1997.
Moving Portrait, DIW, 1998.
Charms of the Night Sky, Winter & Winter, 1998.
Magic Triangle, Arabesque Jazz, 1998.
Convergence, Soul Note, 1999.
Leap of Faith, Arabesque Jazz, 2000.
Soul on Soul, RCA, 2000.

With the Tiny Bell Trio

The Tiny Bell Trio, Songlines, 1994.
Tiny Bell Trio—Constellations, hatHUT, 1995.
Live in Europe, Arabesque Jazz, 1997.
Songs for Wandering Souls, Winter & Winter, 1999.

With Masada

Alef, DIW, 1994.
Beit, DIW, 1994.
Gimel, DIW, 1994.

With Hans Bennink

Constellations, Songlines, 1996.

Sources

Boston Globe, January 23, 2000.
Chicago Sun-Times, September 15, 1996.
CODA, 1999.
Down Beat, August 1998.
Jazz Times, February 2000.
Los Angeles Times, February 20, 2000.
New York Times, December 7, 1997.
Toronto Star, August 26, 1999.

—Gerald E. Brennan

Harry "Sweets" Edison

Jazz trumpeter

Harry "Sweets" Edison, a smooth and suave trumpeter, was a cohort of orchestra leader Count Basie, a favorite of bandleader Nelson Riddle, and a noted backup artist for the most prominent vocalists of his time. Edison, with his energetic yet reticent blowing style, bridged a genre gap between the early classic jazz sound of Louis Armstrong and modern bebop modes. Edison, who played equally well in both styles, had a special talent for sustaining his trumpet notes and injecting each single tone with expression and soul never heard before or after. The special quality of his trumpet playing earned him the nickname "Sweets" because of the sweetness of the tones. Likewise his ability to control the tone of his trumpet brought him to the forefront as a session musician, playing accompaniments for the most respected vocalists of his time.

Edison was a true pioneer of jazz. An old-time homespun boy, born in Columbus, Ohio, he never knew with certainty even the year of his birth. According to his best knowledge, he was born in 1919, although some sources list the date as early as 1915. Edison knew even less about his own father, a Native American of the Hopi (Apache) tribe and a drifter who stayed only a few weeks with Edison's mother before taking to the road and was rarely heard from afterward. Edison spent his early years with an uncle, who was a coal miner and a farmer, in Louisville, Kentucky. It was Edison's uncle who taught the boy to play the pump organ and to play scales on an old cornet. Edison, who also listened to his uncle's records, was especially inspired by the music of Louis Armstrong and Bessie Smith.

At the age of 12, Edison returned to Ohio to live with his mother, following a bout with typhoid fever that nearly killed him. His mother, pleased with his musical ability, bought him a trumpet and outfitted him with a tuxedo. He joined with a local bandleader, named Earl Hood, who encouraged Edison to play but refused to compensate him initially for the trouble. Eventually Edison managed to wangle 35 cents per night from Hood before moving to St. Louis, Missouri, in 1933 to play with a new group called the Jeter-Pillars Orchestra. From there he moved to New York City in 1937 to play with Lucky Millinder's band on the recommendation of a friend who was impressed with Edison's natural ability. Edison lost his job with the high-strung and opportunistic Millinder when a new horn player, named Dizzy Gillespie, joined the band; but Millinder rescinded and rehired Edison when Gillespie quit and left Millinder stranded.

Edison and the Count

In 1938, within months of his arrival in New York, Edison assumed a spot in William "Count" Basie's band as a replacement for Bobby Moore who fell ill. The band performed largely out of Kansas City and

Born on October 10, 1919 in Columbus, OH; married; one daughter, Helena; died on July 27, 1999 in Columbus, OH.

Earl Hood Band, semi-professional; Jeter Pillars Orchestra, 1933-1937; Lucky Millinder Band, 1937; with William "Count" Basie's Orchestra, 1938-1950; quintet leader and solo artist; screenplay composition, with Benny Carter; as a studio musician accompanied Frank Sinatra, Billie Holiday, Ella Fitzgerald; played with bands/orchestras of Buddy Rich, Quincy Jones, Louis Bellson, Henry Mancini, Nelson Riddle; Yale University, Ellington Fellowship (seminar program).

Awards: National Endowment for the Arts Award, "Master Musician," 1991; Jazz Hall of Fame, 1997.

traveled extensively. Edison spent 12 years with Basie's unique ensemble in which all of the musicians were treated as soloists and each in turn received an opportunity to bask in the spotlight. During those years with Count Basie, Edison developed the sultry sound of his trademark horn style, spontaneously, while performing with the great masters of jazz: Frank Foster, Thad Jones, and Lester "Prez" Young. Jazz was young, and the dearth of written music for the bands never worried Edison because he never learned to read music in the first place. Neither was Basie worried as he instructed Edison, "[Y]ou sound good … if you find a note that sounds good … play the same damn note every night!"

On the road, Edison and Young lived as roommates, and in 1944 the two appeared together, in a film called *Jammin' the Blues.* It was Young who first took to calling Harry Edison by the nickname of "Sweetie Pie," a commentary on Edison's musical style. According to Edison, the nickname was a tribute to his trumpeting, which Young said was a sound "so sweet it could rot a baby's teeth." The nickname stuck with the trumpeter and in time his colleagues shortened the name to "Sweets."

In all, Edison spent 12 unforgettable years with the Basie orchestra, performing virtually every night, often in dancehalls. They traveled extensively throughout the United States, from the Fox Theatre in Detroit, Michigan, to make-shift dance arenas in tobacco warehouses in the Carolinas, frequently with blues diva Billie Holiday as their vocalist. The mood of the times inspired spirited musical battles for dance-floor supremacy between the big bands of the era, and Edison proudly recalled the elan of those days for critic Stanley Crouch. Crouch quoted Edison for *Knight-Ridder /Tribune,* "If you messed with us, you found your hindquarters on the floor at the end of the night. We didn't play around. We swung, and we kept swinging … you were in a big natural mess if you came up against us."

Studio Sessions and Solos

Basie's band dissolved inadvertently in 1950, according to Edison, while the group was in New Jersey and ran out of work for a time. Basie left his musicians in a hotel and set out to find a gig for the orchestra but got sidetracked in Chicago where he ended up working with a different group. Edison, upon learning of Basie's extended side gig, packed his own bags and moved to Los Angeles, California, where he made contact with an old acquaintance, a quick-witted friend who was well acquainted with Nelson Riddle. With a generous recommendation she introduced Edison to the prominent bandleader, and Riddle repeated the recommendation to a popular singer named Frank Sinatra who insisted upon auditioning the trumpeter. Sinatra was gratified—so impressed in fact that he funded music lessons for Edison to learn to read music. Edison accompanied Sinatra regularly for years afterward.

Throughout the 1950s and the 1960s Edison worked as a studio musician and as a soloist, eventually establishing permanent residency in Los Angeles because of the volume of studio work that brought him there repeatedly. He had a beautiful, softly muted horn style, of which Geoff Chapman said in the *Toronto Star,* "Harry Edison can probably say more with one note than any jazz player alive…. [A]n approach that stresses simplicity, glorious tone, natural potency and an unmatched affinity with the … mute." Edison's ability to accompany singers without drowning out their voices behind the trumpet was a rare feat; his soft tone distinguished him from the others and kept him in demand as a background musician, especially for female singers such as Ella Fitzgerald and Billie Holiday.

Additionally he recorded dozens of albums and performed on television specials. He collaborated on movie soundtracks with Benny Carter, and during the 1950s he toured with Norman Granz's Jazz at the Philharmonic. Edison spent time working behind the scenes as a musical director for the acclaimed Josephine Baker, and he played with an assortment of great bandleaders and orchestras, including Buddy Rich, Quincy Jones, Louis Bellson, and Henry Mancini. In later years, the kindly and understated Edison had little but good things to recall about Basie, Holiday, and his jazz colleagues; and although the Basie orchestra dismantled itself in 1950, Edison and the other members joined the Count in performances on many occasions.

As an octogenarian and in failing health Edison never faltered but continued to perform. He recorded a live album, 's Wonderful, at Club House 33 in Japan, and he toured Europe repeatedly on an annual basis. In 1998, he appeared in Toronto, Ontario at the Montreal Bistro during the JVC Jazz Festival. Additionally, he performed regularly in New York City, even while maintaining his residence in California, and through the Duke Ellington Fellowship Program Edison taught seminars at Yale University.

The Nicest Guy

In 1991, Edison received the National Endowment for the Arts Award of Master Musician, and he was inducted into the Jazz Hall of Fame in 1997. *New York Amsterdam News* called him "a celebrated elder statesman" of the jazz world, and his *Live in Copenhagen* album earned a gold record.

According to some, Edison earned the nickname Sweets in part because of his affinity for women. A proverbial ladies' man, he appreciated women and his fans above all else, never taking either for granted. Modest, but content with his special soft trumpet tones, Edison was very at ease with himself and with others. He never sought accolades and was not competitive by nature. He was a musician above all else, making music for the sake of the music. He was absorbed with playing and performing according to his own personal style, a style that brought him the respect and admiration of fellow colleagues and fans alike. Former Basie trombonist Benny Powell, who came to appreciate Edison as a mentor, maintained that he learned one lesson above all else from the classic trumpeter: "economy of notes."

Edison was dapper and debonair yet sensible and thrifty; he loved life and lived well. Early in 1998, he left California and returned to Columbus to reside with his daughter, Helena, to whom he was known as a devoted father. He died in his sleep on July 27, 1999 in Columbus, Ohio, culminating a 14-year battle against cancer. He was the last surviving member of the Count Basie band from the 1930s.

Afterthoughts

During an interview with Chapman in the summer of 1998, Edison confided his concern over modern electronic music forms that smothered the spirit of jazz. He bemoaned the synthetic music machines that prevailed in the background of recording sessions and acquiesced his concern for the future of jazz as an art form. He cautioned against lack of innovation among turn-of-the-century jazzmeisters and extolled the virtue of singularity of sound, a jazz player's greatest asset. Edison, according to reports, practiced his horn regularly throughout his lifetime, until the eve of his death.

Selected discography

Albums

Harry Edison Quartet, Pacific Jazz, 1953.
The Inventive Harry Edison, Pacific Jazz, 1953.
Sweets at the Haig, Pacific Jazz, 1953.
Sweets, Clef, 1956.
Gee Baby, Ain't I Good to You?, Verve, 1957.
The Swinger, Verve, 1958.
Harry Edison Swings Buck Clayton, Verve, 1958.
Harry Edison Swings Buck Clayton and Vice Versa, Verve, 1958.
Mr. Swing, Verve, 1958.
Sweetenings, Roulette, 1958.
And Vice-Versa, 1960.
Patented by Edison, Roulette, 1960.
Ben Webster and Sweets Edison, Columbia, 1962.
Jawbreakers, Original Jazz, 1962.
Home with Sweets, Vee-Jay, 1964.
Sweets for the Sweet, Sue, 1965.
When Lights Are Low, Liberty, 1965.
Just Friends, Black & Blue, 1975.
Edison's Lights, Pablo, 1976.
Opus Funk, Storyville, 1976.
Harry "Sweets" Edison - Eddie "Lockjaw" Davis & Richard Boone, Storyville, 1976.
Harry Sweets Edison and Eddie Lockjaw Davis, Vol. 1, Storyville, 1976.
Harry Sweets Edison and Eddie Lockjaw Davis, Vol. 2, Storyville, 1976.
Blues for Basie, Pablo, 1977.
Simply Sweets, Pablo, 1977.
's Wonderful (recorded live at Club House 33 in Japan), Pablo, 1982.
Jazz at the Philharmonic, Pablo, 1983.
For My Pals, Pablo, 1988.
Can't Get out of This Mood, Orange Blue, 1988.
The Best of Harry Sweets Edison, Pablo, 1990.
Swing Summit, Candid, 1990.
Arte Amada, Bons Ritmos, 1991.
Swinging for the Count, Candid, 1995.
There Is No Greater Love, Jazz Hour, 1995.
Live at the Iridium, Telarc, 1997.
Live in Copenhagen, Mobile Fidelit, 1997.
Harry "Sweets" Edison, Giants of Jazz, 1998.
Sweets and Jaws, Black & Blue, 1998.
Whispering, E.J., 1999.
Harry "Sweets" Edison and Jonah Jones, LRC, 1999.

Sources

Periodicals

Billboard, August 7, 1999.
Independent (London, England), July 29, 1999.

Knight-Ridder/Tribune, July 30, 1999.
Los Angeles Times, October 8, 1999, p. 24.
New York Amsterdam News, August 5, 1999, p. 19; September 23, 1999, p. 23.
Toronto Star, August 20, 1998.
Village Voice, April 30, 1996, p. 5.

Online

AMG All Music Guide, http://allmusic.com (June 22, 2000).
Vanguard Records, http://www.vanguardrecords.com/s2s /Harry.html (May 5, 2000).

—*Gloria Cooksey*

eels

Pop band

The singer, songwriter, guitarist, multi-instrumentalist, and producer known simply as E—the man responsible for eels who says his moniker is an old nickname gone too far and the reference to "eels" is just an ever-changing vehicle for his songs—returned in 2000 with his group's third offering, *Daisies of the Galaxy,* marking the musician's first big step toward embracing life after personal tragedy: the deaths of his sister, mother, and father. Regarded as an upbeat coda to 1998's *Electro-Shock Blues,* the album that dazzled critics but repelled record buyers with its grueling tour of suicide, cancer wards, and funerals, this third offering from eels took a more optimistic view of the world. As E himself concluded, according to DreamWorks Records: "If *Electro-Shock Blues* was the phone call in the middle of the night that the world doesn't want to answer, then *Daisies of the Galaxy* is the hotel wake-up call that says your lovely breakfast is ready."

Throughout *Daisies of the Galaxy,* like previous eels records, runs a list of poignant characters. When asked if he has always felt so empathetic toward others, E said that yes, he does appreciate the good in others and tries to understand their hardships and problems. "I can be very cynical, but deep down I don't believe there's such a thing as bad people," he told Mark Healy in an interview for *Rolling Stone.* "People do bad things and get led astray, but if you take any person and follow the line backward from the bad thing they did, you can usually start to understand them." And just how did he arrive at such a hopeful view? "Well, if you've been through some of the experiences I've been through these last few years, you cling to any shred of optimism you can muster," he continued. "Once I felt like the dust was settling and I hadn't been to any funerals for awhile, I realized you have a choice: You can stay down in the muck, or you can tighten your belt and move on. It's like, 'OK, time for some carefree years. Time to have some fun.'"

A native of Virginia who later settled in Los Angeles, California, E was born Mark Oliver Everett on April 9, 1963. Several years before forming eels, he released two underrated solo albums for Polydor Records. In 1995 in Los Angeles, after Polydor agreed to release the veteran songwriter and producer from his contract, E teamed with his touring drummer, Butch Norton, and bassist/multi-instrumentalist Tommy Walter to record as eels, hoping that an expanded lineup would enable him to produce a fuller sound more akin to his greatest influence—singer, songwriter, and pianist Randy Newman—and to add trip-hop technology to the idiocratic pop sensibility of his prior work. Taking his new project to DreamWorks Records, the label established by film director/producer Steven Spielberg, E, along with his group, became one of the first acts to sign a contract with the newly formed record company.

A Diverse Debut

E's new band debuted in mid-1996 with the eclectic *Beautiful Freak,* an album noted for its intelligent pop sound and intriguing lyrics. Each song of E's revealed a heartfelt, personal edge and underpinning humor, a mix that appealed to a young, literate audience dissatisfied with the slacker culture. Because of these elements, eels' first album often drew comparisons to another fresh-sounding songwriter, Beck. However, E, who friends describe as cantankerous, resisted such charges: "The only similarity is that we're white guys using samples. We're coming from a completely different angle," he argued, as quoted by *Rock: The Rough Guide* contributor Alex Ogg. Regardless of the similarities, *Beautiful Freak* earned rave reviews for its fresh mix of classic pop, country, rock, and hip-hop beats, with *Q* magazine calling the work a "complete musical vision, a genre-spanning soundscape that reels you in with its myriad of hooks." And after the album's 1997 release in Great Britain, *Melody Maker* ranked *Beautiful Freak* number 43 on that year's list of best albums, while a *New Musical Express* critics' poll listed it at number 33.

Record buyers, both in America and Europe, embraced eels' debut as well. The ironic single "Novocaine for the Soul" became a modern rock hit at home as well as abroad, and the band in 1996 started touring the United States and Europe, opening for the likes of the Screaming Trees and playing music festivals such as the Inrock Festival in France and the Rockpalast in Germany. By 1997, eels were touring as a headlining

For The Record . . .

Members include **E** (born Mark Oliver Everett on April 9, 1963, in Virginia), songwriter, producer, multi-instrumentalist, guitar, vocals; **Butch Norton** (born Jonathan Norton), drums; **Tommy Walter** (left band in 1997), multi-instrumentalist, bass.

Formed in Los Angeles, CA, 1995; signed with Dream-Works Records, released *Beautiful Freak,* 1996; released dark album *Electro-Shock Blues,* 1998; released the more upbeat *Daisies of the Galaxy,* 2000.

Addresses: *Record company*—DreamWorks Records, 9268 W. 3rd St., Beverly Hills, CA 90210, phone: (310) 234-7700, fax: (310) 234-7750, website:http://www .dreamworksrec.com.

act, quickly gaining a reputation for their impressive live shows, especially in Europe, where the band's popularity soared. That same year, eels also toured in the United States with Lollapalooza, then returned to Europe for another round of sell-out concerts. Despite eels' breakthrough, Walter left the band soon after touring in order to form his own band, Metromax, later known as Tely.

Revealed Personal Hardships

The eels' next album, *Electro-Shock Blues,* arrived in 1998. Primarily a solo effort by E with a noticeably darker feel than the group's debut, the album was inspired largely by the suicide of E's sister Elizabeth, who died just before the release of *Beautiful Freak,* and the long illness and imminent death of his mother, who suffered from cancer. While not received well in terms of record sales because of its anguished subject matter, *Electro-Shock Blues* nonetheless garnered stellar reviews. *CMJ* (*College Music Journal*) called the work "one of 1998's most oddly powerful pop albums, demonstrating that weighty, tearful emotions, pretty melodies and groovy tempos can harmoniously complement one another." To support the album, E enlisted My Head frontman Adam Siegal (a former member of the Suicidal Tendencies) to play live with him on bass, but the American leg of the tour was cut short when his mother succumbed to cancer in November of 1998. But in spite of E's personal difficulties, eels did return to Europe later as Pulp's supporting act, then returned home to conclude the *Electro-Shock Blues* tour.

E spent most of 1999 writing and producing *Daisies of the Galaxies* in his Los Angeles basement with eels drummer Norton, Grant Lee Buffalo's Grant Lee Phillips on bass, and R.E.M.s Peter Buck on piano, guitar, and bass. The sessions were interrupted, however, when E had to return to Virginia to clean out his parents' house and settle their estate, documented in the song from the album "Estate Sale," written with Buck. While at his parents' house, E also came across a 1950s-era Greek children's book, which he used for the album's artwork.

Returned to Happier Music

After all his recent tragedies, E, now the only living member of his immediate family, felt the need to focus on the positive. "I needed to make something in love with life for my own sanity," he related, as quoted by DreamWorks. "It became important that I make simple, pure, sweet music." And although *Daisies of the Galaxy* opened with the sound of funeral music, E, who says he is happiest while making a record, opted to use a New Orleans-styled groove. "I wanted to make a fun, pretty record that was full of life," E added. "During the *Daisies* sessions I realized we were making two different records. One was loud, dark and scary and full of feedback; the other was more acoustic and positive. I only wanted to put out the latter now—even if it doesn't have any big guitar on it, or a guy going 'heeYYY-YEAAAAAHHHH!' "

Released in March of 2000, *Daisies of the Galaxy* brought E further acclaim. "Like its predecessor," concluded Jim Wirth in *New Musical Express, Daisies of the Galaxy* "mixes humor and humility, hope and fear, and stands as quiet testimony to one of modern music's most gifted writers…. Here is an album that, in its wit, humility and calmness in the face of a firing squad of terrors, justifies the existence of pop albums. In almost every respect a masterpiece." Soon thereafter, eels started touring again, this time just E, Norton, and a couple of string and horn players. They traveled first to Europe, then opened for singer/songwriter/ pianist Fiona Apple in the United States. Already, E had made plans for a fourth record, and soon after completing Daisies, started working on new, louder songs again with Siegal. Judging by the past, the next eels release was sure to draw similar admiration from both fans and critics. As *Los Angeles Times* reporter Richard Cromelin said of the songwriter: "E refuses to codify emotional reality into a convenient package. His determination to capture life's complex, ambiguous, paradoxical contours is what makes his songs so true and touching."

Selected discography

Beautiful Freak, DreamWorks, 1996.
Scream 2, (soundtrack), contributed song "Your Lucky Day in Hell," Capitol, 1997.
Electro-Shock Blues, DreamWorks, 1998.
Daisies of the Galaxy, DreamWorks, 2000.

Sources

Books

Buckley, Jonathan, and others, editor, *Rock: The Rough Guide,* Rough Guides Ltd., 1999.

Periodicals

Atlanta Journal-Constitution, December 18, 1997.
CMJ, January 11, 1999, p. 5.
Los Angeles Times, February 5, 2000; March 16, 2000; April 30, 2000.
Melody Maker, February 16-22, 2000, p. 46.
New Musical Express, February 19, 2000.
Q, December 1996, p. 147.
Rolling Stone, April 27, 2000; May 25, 2000.

Online

a band called eels, http://planetorg.com/eels (May 20, 2000).
eels at DreamWorks Records, http://www.dreamworksrec .com (May 20, 2000).
Sonicnet.com, http://www.sonicnet.com (May 20, 2000).

—Laura Hightower

Elastica

Punk rock/pop band

When Elastica released their self-titled debut album in 1995, the British rock group enjoyed great success in their homeland as well as in the United States. Known for their quirky, catchy songs driven by interlocking guitar rhythms, Elastica reworked the sound and image of new wave punk rockers like Adam and the Ants, Wire, the Buzzcocks, and Blondie, arriving at a more pop-oriented, hook-driven musical formula than most of their influences and a more detached, earthier presence than their predecessors. Elastica differed from their modern-day counterparts as well, allowing them to receive a warmer welcome from American audiences than most other British bands. "Unlike the punkish posturing of bands like Oasis and Echobelly, Elastica are the most Americanized of the British group, devoid of arrogant attitude, pompous self-devotion or disdain for their musical peers," *Rolling Stone* contributor Kara Manning said of the group. "There's a kind, open-hearted quality about all four musicians, even though [Justine] Frischmann exudes an elegant cool any woman would envy."

Although touted by the music press as the "Next Big Thing" both at home and abroad, watching a string of singles climb the British and American charts, Elastica and their future soon became the subject of much media speculation. Problems arose among the band members; unable to finish writing songs for a follow-up album, Elastica reportedly folded in 1998, though a spokesperson for the group later said that the group never officially disbanded. However, after numerous lineup changes and overcoming writers block, Elastica returned in 2000 with a new album entitled *The Menace.* And while the rock world, known for its short attention span, usually forgets about groups after prolonged absences, fans and critics alike enthusiastically welcomed Elastica back into the fold.

Lead vocalist and guitarist Justine Frischmann, couldn't be happier that the group decided to tough it out, rather than give up altogether. "Everything went ridiculously right with the first record; absolutely everything seemed to fall into place," she explained to Paul Sexton in *Billboard* magazine. "Then, as life has a habit of doing, it went just as wrong. For me, it was a process of growing up and working out what it was that attracted me to making music in the first place. It became kind of an obsession." But in 1999, Frischmann regrouped Elastica, joined by a new lineup comprised of original members Annie Holland and Justin Welch on bass guitar and drums respectively, plus new members Paul Jones on guitar, Dave Bush on keyboards, and Sharon Mew (also known as "Mews") on keyboards and backing vocals. They made their "comeback" performance debut that summer at the Reading Festival, a pivotal moment that reinvigorated Elastica, leading them to scrap the recordings they had made up to that point and start anew. Soon thereafter, the band released an EP, followed by their long-overdue sophomore effort.

For The Record . . .

Members include **Dave Bush** (former member of the Fall; joined band in 1977), keyboards; **Sheila Chipperfield** (born on June 17, 1976; joined band in 1997; left band in 1998), bass guitar, backing vocals; **Justine Elinor Frischmann** (born on September 16, 1969; daughter of a singer and an architect; studied architecture at University College London; former member of Suede), lead vocals, guitar; **Annie Holland** (born on August 26, 1965; left band in 1995; rejoined band in 1998); bass guitar; **Paul Jones** (former member of Linoleum; joined band in 1998), guitar; **Donna Lorraine Matthews** (born on December 2, 1971, in Wales; left band in 1998), guitar, backing vocals; **Sharon Mew** (also known as "Mews"; former member of Heave; joined band in 1998), keyboards, backing vocals; **Abby Travis** (born on November 10, 1969; played with Beck and Mommy; member of the Abby Travis Foundation and Botanica; joined band in 1995; left band in 1996), bass guitar; **Justin Welch** (born on December 12, 1972; son of a drummer; former member of Suede and Spitfire; member of side project called Me Me Me), drums.

Frischmann and Welch formed band in 1992 in London, England; released debut self-titled album, joined Lollapalooza tour, 1995; released sophomore album *The Menace*, 2000.

Addresses: *Record company*—Deceptive Records, London, England.

Perseverance and self-preservation are nothing new to Frischmann, who, as one of the original members of Suede, experienced the glare of the limelight firsthand. Although that group hadn't quite hit it big by the time Frischmann left, she would later gain much publicity, often negative, for living with Suede singer and co-founder Brett Anderson, then dumping him in favor of Blur's Damon Albarn. The daughter of a singer and a well-known architect, the engineer of London's NatWest skyscraper, Frischmann meanwhile decided to drop her musical aspirations after her relationship with Anderson and Suede ended, and went on to study architecture at University College London.

However, one day while listening to P.J. Harvey and designing a car park, Frischmann realized how much she missed music and, in 1992 in London, formed Elastica with Welch, whom she befriended during his very brief tenure in Suede. Annie Holland, a guitarist, borrowed a bass guitar for her audition, while Welsh-born guitarist Donna Matthews answered a *Melody Maker* advertisement calling for a player influenced by the Fall, the Stranglers, and Wire. She impressed Frischmann first by not mentioning Suede as an influence, but most importantly with her gutsy, lead-guitar finesse. Matthews, who "plays all the complicated parts," confessed Frischmann to Manning, immediately got the job.

Elastica Become Pop Stars

When Elastica hit the club circuit, they quickly established themselves with a brittle, high-tempo sound and a collection of short, yet well-crafted songs. At the end of 1993, after signing with the independent Deceptive label, Elastica released their first single, "Stutter," a limited-edition record that sold out in just one day thanks to radio play and rave reviews. The band's second single, "Line Up," released in 1994, went straight to the British top 20, and the subsequent follow-ups, 1994's "Connection" and 1995's "Waking Up," reiterated Elastica's punk origins.

These songs, although instant hits, nevertheless suffered criticism for sounding too much like songs of previous bands. Some critics claimed that with the single "Line Up," Elastica appropriated the melody from Wire's "I Am the Fly." Likewise, "Connection," the band's biggest hit, was accused by some reviewers for taking the keyboard riff from Wire's "Three Girl Rhumba." Consequently, in March of 1995, on the eve of the release of their full-length debut, Elastica was taken to court by Wire's publishers, as well as the publishers of the Stranglers, who claimed that "Waking Up" used the guitar riff from that group's "No More Heroes." Elastica hurriedly settled both cases out of court before the release of the album.

In spite of these legal troubles, *Elastica* earned rave reviews and entered the British album chart at number one. Moreover, the record became the fastest-selling debut in British chart history, beating the record set by Oasis' *Definitely Maybe* just seven months earlier. Issued on Geffen Records in the United States, the album also fared well in America, where "Connection" became a modern rock radio hit. Elastica spent much of 1995 cracking the United States, including a stint on the Lollapalooza tour as Sinead O'Connor's replacement.

However, Elastica would also begin a series of lineup changes that year. Holland, who readily admits to disliking gigs, was unable to cope with constant touring and the overall lifestyle that accompanies playing in a popular band. Her replacement, an American named Abby Travis, known for her work with Beck, Mommy, the Abby Travis Foundation, and a new band called Botanica, filled in during Lollapalooza. After about a year with Elastica, she too departed, finding that traveling between the United States and England just didn't work out. In 1997, the band enlisted Sheila Chipperfield as Elastica's new bass player, then recruited Dave Bush, formerly of the Fall, as a permanent keyboard player.

A Breakup?

Still trying to hold the band together, Elastica were nonetheless by now under considerable speculation by the media, who questioned whether or not the group would endure. Although they had played some songs for the *Radio One* "Evening Session," Elastica had not released any new material since 1995. By 1998, Elastica's future still appeared questionable; Holland rejoined the band on bass, Chipperfield, no longer needed, departed; Matthews left the group because of a breakdown in personal and creative relationships, Paul Jones, formerly of Linoleum, replaced Matthews on guitar, and Mew, a former member of Heave, joined as an additional keyboard player and vocalist.

Amid continued rumors of a breakup, Elastica struck back in April of 1999 with a six-song EP of unreleased and new material, featuring songs written in 1996 and 1997 while Matthews and Chipperfield were still members of the band. All of the songs, according to the band, reflected different phases of Elastica's development; "Nothing Stays the Same" is a home tape by Matthews, "Miami Nice," is a home recording by Frischmann and Lawrence Hardy of the now-defunct band Kingmaker, and "Operate" is a live recording with Matthews. The remaining tracks, "Generator," "How He Wrote Elastica Man," and "KB" were recorded with the new Elastica lineup.

With Elastica apparently intact and feeling a renewed sense of enthusiasm for their music, the band in April of 2000 released *The Menace.* Expected hits from the album, which are more evolved, noted critics, than the band's debut, included "Mad Dog" and "Love Like Ours." Frischmann, who has since mended her relationship with Matthews, felt confident about the new lineup. "It's really great," she said to Carol Clerk of *melody Maker.* "It just feels like a lot of wounds have healed, and I think we just all feel a bit older, and it just doesn't seem as serious. It's more fun."

Selected discography

Elastica, Deceptive/Geffen, 1995.
The Menace, Deceptive, 2000.

Sources

Books

Buckley, Jonathan and others, editors, *Rock: The Rough Guide,* Rough Guides Ltd., 1999.

Periodicals

Billboard, April 1, 2000
Los Angeles Times, March 16, 1995; December 30, 1995; February 16, 1997.
Melody Maker, November 8, 1997; July 31, 1999; August 7, 1999; September 4, 1999; February 2-8, 2000.
New Musical Express, February 12, 2000.
People, May 8, 1995.
Rolling Stone, May 4, 1995; January 25, 1996.
Stereo Review, September 1995.

Online

Sonicnet.com, http://www.sonicnet.com (June 19, 2000).
Spas2000—An Elastica Fan Homepage, http://www.geocities.com/SouthBeach/Lights/2253 (June 19, 2000).

—Laura Hightower

The Fastbacks

Punk rock band

Since their inception more than 20 years ago, the Seattle-based punk group the Fastbacks have watched many bands rise and fall in their hometown. Perhaps one explanation for the Fastbacks' longevity in the wake of so many failures is the group's apparent disregard for trends or fashion, always refining their own brand of punk rock—amazingly with the same intensity and excitement of their youth—while never falling prey to music industry hype or self-parody. Arguably one of the best punk bands in America, the Fastbacks have enjoyed a long, yet not always commercially fruitful career, one that stemmed not from the want of monetary gain, but from a deep-seeded friendship and a strong desire to make music. As chief songwriter Kurt Bloch explained, as quoted by Sub Pop Records, the quartet's former label, "there's nothing better than having an idea for a song take over your life."

Throughout the 1980s, 1990s, and beyond, the Fastbacks, in the tradition of other long-haul Seattle bands like the Walkabouts, Young Fresh Fellows, and Green Pajamas, endured like an old married couple secure in their relationship. In a true test of the band's commitment, they emerged unscathed by the grunge scene that swept across the Northwest in the early 1990s. Although bystanders to the firestorm, the Fastbacks claim that the music-industry and mainstream frenzy over grunge actually benefited the group in a sense. "The whole movement helped the Fastbacks," explained bandmember Lulu Gargiulo to Jud Cost in *Magnet.* "We got a lot more local exposure because of grunge. There was an explosion of people coming out to see any Seattle band. Before that, we had absolutely nobody come to see us."

Despite the growing audiences, the Ramones-inspired Fastbacks nevertheless missed out on the celebrity offered to Seattle's grunge-era acts. However, the lack of popular recognition never bothered Bloch. "At the end of the day, all of the bands who were big back then—except for Pearl Jam—aren't even around any more," he noted. "You'd watch most of those groups after they'd made it big," added Gargiulo, "and they didn't even look like they were having a good time." Thus, to many Seattle natives, bands like the Fastbacks represent the city's real music scene. Even Eddie Vedder, Pearl Jam's lead singer and songwriter who invited the Fastbacks to open some stadium-sized shows for his group, counts the Fastbacks among his personal favorites.

The Fastbacks formed in 1979 when Kurt Bloch, a guitarist who was already in a group called the Cheaters, enlisted his friends from Seattle's Nathan Hale High School, vocalist and bass guitarist Kim Warnick and second guitarist and vocalist Lulu Gargiulo, to play in a side project. In the beginning, Bloch served as the Fastbacks' drummer in addition to writing songs. However, he soon switched to guitar after talking a 15-year-old neighbor boy into sitting in on drums. That neighbor, Duff McKagan, would later move to Los Angeles and join a group called Guns N' Roses. Since McKagan's departure, the Fastbacks went through approximately 15 drummers before finding Mike Musburger, the group's current drummer who joined in 1992.

Consistent with their long-time friendship and disregard for industry trends, the Fastbacks' music—largely the result of Bloch's songwriting prowess—likewise maintained an unfaltering energy over the years. "We're still doing this because Kurt writes such good songs," said Warnick to Cost. "Kurt lives and breathes music," Gargiulo further noted. "His only fault may be that he's a musical junkie." Bloch began feeding his addiction with the Fastbacks with the group's debut EP, *The Fastbacks Play Five of Their Favorites,* released in 1982, and the *Every Day Is Saturday* EP, released in 1984. Both of these EPs were compiled on the Fastback's debut, 1987's *...and His Orchestra,* an album loaded with melodies and casually unpretentious songs.

In 1989, Bloch took on another job serving as a guitarist for the Young Fresh Fellows after that band's Chuck Caroll departed, but continued to focus on his primary concern, the Fastbacks. In 1990, the band released a second album, *Very Very Powerful,* which was rated at number 93 on the *Alternative Press* list of "Top 99 of '85-'95." That same year, both Warnick and Gargiulo took time off from the Fastbacks as well to play guitar and drums, respectively, for Motorhoney.

For The Record . . .

Members include **Kurt Bloch**, guitar, songwriting; **Lulu Gargiulo**, guitar, vocals; **Mike Musburger** (joined band in 1992), drums; **Kim Warnick**, vocals, bass guitar.

Formed band in 1979 in Seattle, WA; released debut EP *The Fastbacks Play Five of Their Favorites,* 1982; released *Very Very Powerful,* 1990; signed with Sub Pop Records, 1992; released *Zücker,* 1993; released *Answer the Phone, Dummy,* 1994; released *New Mansions in Sound,* 1996; signed with SpinART Records, released *The Day that Didn't Exist,* 1999.

Addresses: *Record company*—SpinART Records, P.O. Box 1798, New York City, NY 10156, (212) 343-9644.

Resuming work with the Fastbacks in 1991, Bloch continued to split his time between his own band and the Young Fresh Fellows, two bands that Warnick said can easily co-exist. "The Fellows don't play that often," she explained to Cost, "and even though we've been around a long time, neither do we. You might think by now we've been to every club in America, but we really haven't toured all that much."

In 1992, concurrent to signing with the Seattle-based label Sub Pop Records, the group released another album entitled *The Question is No.,* an anthology of 14 songs drawn from singles, compilations, and unreleased material recorded between 1980 and 1992. The following year, the foursome released *Zücker,* an album that hinted at a mainstream breakthrough with standouts such as "Gone to the Moon" and "Never Heard of Him." "Incorruptible and irresistible," concluded a review in *Entertainment Weekly,* "this blend of melodious girl-group vocals and furious 3-chord punk rock makes Seattle's illustrious Fastbacks a possible candidate for the next big thing." But the above-mentioned magazine wrongly assumed that the Fastbacks' guitar lines were simplistic by design. In fact, Bloch's songs have so many chord changes that he often puts Warnick and Gargiulo's fingers on their strings for them. "I'm so glad he writes hard songs," Gargiulo, who doesn't mind the allegation, said to *LA Weekly*'s Gina Arnold. "They take forever to learn—but we've got forever to learn them."

In 1994, the Fastbacks released *Answer the Phone, Dummy,* which included "In the Observatory" and "On the Wall." The sounds on this critically successful album were mined from the same punk-pop territory as its predecessor. In 1996, the Fastbacks returned with *New Mansions in Sound,* an album that earned even greater acclaim. Three years later, the Fastbacks arrived on a new label, SpinART Records, for *The Day that Didn't Exist,* released in 1999. Here, "Kurt Bloch continues to pen some of the most infectious, non-wuss choruses known to man," according to *CMJ,* "executing them with a supercharged strum that alleviates any potentially off-putting cuteness."

Although the Fastbacks have yet to become a huge commercial success, they prefer their low profile to the pressures that accompany major-label support. Gargiulo, for example, still feels a rush when she mingles with the group's small network of devoted followers. "We have this handful of dedicated fans all over the country," she explained to Cost. "They encourage us when we come through town. At the show in L.A. last night, there were these two guys who were so excited to see us that, even though it was a pretty terrible place to play, it made the whole trip worthwhile."

Selected discography

The Fastbacks Play Five of Their Favorites (EP), No Threes, 1982.
Every Day Is Saturday (EP), No Threes, 1984.
...and His Orchestra, PopLlama, 1987, reissued, 1991.
Very Very Powerful, PopLlama, 1990, reissued, 1992.
The Question is No., Sub Pop, 1992.
Zücker, Sub Pop, 1993.
Answer the Phone, Dummy, Sub Pop, 1994.
New Mansions in Sound, Sub Pop, 1996.
The Day that Didn't Exist, SpinART, 1999.

Sources

Books

Robbins, Ira A., editor, *Trouser Press Guide to '90s Rock,* Fireside/Simon and Schuster, 1997.

Periodicals

CMJ, November 1, 1999, pp. 20-21.
Entertainment Weekly, February 26, 1993, p. 56.
LA Weekly, January 30-February 5, 1998.
Magnet, January/February 2000, pp. 53-54.
Rolling Stone, April 29, 1993.

Online

Fastbacks Frenzy, http://www.accessone.com/~maxima/ index.htm (June 14, 2000).

Fastbacks at SpinART Records, http://www.spinartrecords.com/fastbacks.html (June 14, 2000).

Sonicnet.com, http://www.sonicnet.com (June 14, 2000).

Sub Pop Bands—Fastbacks, http://www.subpop.com/ bands/ fastbacks/website/index.html (June 14, 2000).

—Laura Hightower

Flying Saucer Attack

Post-rock band

Arriving on the independent music scene in the early to mid-1990s, Flying Saucer Attack—with its folk songs and feedback sculptures—was the new band of choice among underground hipsters and space-rock enthusiasts throughout the United Kingdom and the United States. After performing at the inaugural Terrastock music festival, as well as releasing a long-awaited studio album in 1997, the acclaimed *New Lands,* Flying Saucer Attack seemed poised to take on the world with their trance-like, cerebral sound. However, two and a half years passed before Flying Saucer Attack's return. As David ("Dave") Pearce, now the project's sole commander, told Fred Mills in an interview for *Magnet,* "I cracked up for a little while, basically."

While exaggerating the circumstances of his self-imposed exile from music, the time off nonetheless proved beneficial, evidenced by Pearce's impressive step forward with 2000's *Mirror.* "I think this one has *something,*" the musician agreed. "And it's a blessed relief, because all these years down the line you worry that you may have completely blown it." By nature, Pearce, in spite of critical accolades, has always second-guessed his talent, a common trait of many artists that can, paradoxically, either further creative development or stop the flow of ideas completely. Indeed, self-doubt was part of the reason why Pearce, who had spent months meticulously recording and editing *New Lands,* began to fall apart. "But it wasn't only a feeling of, 'Oh, my music's all wrong.' It was also more... stuff. About that time, things just weren't working upstairs in the attic, either."

Besides the harsh self-criticism, Pearce was also, he soon discovered, in the midst of a bout with clinical depression, a case that grew so deep that he quit altogether playing guitar and turning on his tape machine for a full 12 months. And when Pearce finally did pick up his instrument again, his return to music was usually marked by short bursts of playing followed by hours of just listening to the recordings. "It's like I didn't have an approach anymore," he revealed to Mills. "My sort of sense of purpose and even my musical purpose just, I don't know... The last two years have disappeared completely. Prozac probably explains why I'm still here. [Depression] is something that runs in my family." Unlike so many who live with such an affliction for years, Pearce eventually recovered his purpose, uncovering some of the best compositions of his career.

At the onset of his artistic journey, however, Pearce had no problem in keeping his creative juices flowing. The history of Flying Saucer Attack, also known as FSA, is intertwined with various other bands—Crescent, Movietone, AMP, Third Eye Foundation, and others—that formed in and around Bristol, England, in the late 1980s and early 1990s. Pearce, who from 1983 through 1986 was involved with a school band called HaHaHa and later Mexican Embassy, on occasion played with but was not a formal member of these groups. Nonetheless, they all shared a common bond. As a student in the late 1980s attending Farnham Art College, Pearce met a number of musically inclined fellow students and friends. Together, they formed a band called the Secret Garden, but never released any material. Secret Garden only recorded rehearsal tapes and played just two gigs before Pearce, along with Secret Garden member "Richard" (who later formed AMP), decided to focus on their own project called Distance. Pieces of their collaborations, demo tapes recorded in 1991, would crop up from time to time on AMP and Flying Saucer Attack material.

Between 1991 and 1992, Pearce joined another band that recorded only rehearsal tapes called Lynda's Strange Vacation. The bass player for that group, Rachel Brook, was Pearce's girlfriend, and in the summer of 1992, they decided to leave Lynda's Strange Vacation in order to follow their own musical instincts. Initially, the duo, taking the moniker Flying Saucer Attack from the title of a Los Rezillos song, was a studio-based project for Pearce and Brook to explore their art-psychedelic influences, most notably Can, Syd Barrett, Wire, John Coltrane, Nick Drake, Roy Harper, A.R. Kane, and especially Krautrockers Popul Vuh.

"In many ways, it was a nice time," Pearce reminisced, as quoted by Mills, about FSA's beginnings. "It was different with those early records. It was a 'we.' Rachel was 19 or 20, and I was in my mid-20s. And I was still working in a record shop, a shop not many people came into but most of the people who did knew each

For The Record . . .

Members include **Rachel Brook** (left band in 1995), bass guitar; **David Pearce**, guitar, vocals, other instruments.

Formed Flying Saucer Attack in Bristol, England, 1992; released self-titled debut album, 1993; released *Chorus,* marking the end of the project's "phase one"; Pearce returned alone as FSA to release the acclaimed *New Lands,* gave high-profile performance at Terrastock, 1997; released *Mirror,* 2000.

Addresses: *Record company*—Drag City, P.O. Box 476867, Chicago, IL 60647, (312) 455-1015, e-mail: dragcity@mcs.com. *Website*—Flying Saucer Attack: Phase Two: http://www.dsl.org/fsa.

other. Movietone (Brook's other band) was getting together at the same time. Crescent was, too. Third Eye Foundation was starting and was involved in everyone's bands. And, OK, we might have been playing gigs to 30 people in a back room in Bristol, but there was always something going on. There would be the odd trek up to London to play a gig, and there were all these little records coming out. The point is, everyone was seeming to do something. So all those early FSA records were fueled by that."

In March of 1993, Flying Saucer Attack released the single "Soaring High/Standing Stone," followed in June of that year by a second single entitled "Wish/Oceans." Both singles were recorded for their own FSA label (distributed by VHF in America in 1994). In November of 1993, FSA made their full-length debut with the home-recorded *Flying Saucer Attack.* Centered around the pair's sonic explorations—dense and feedback-loaded one moment and pastoral the next—and notorious for a fuzzy guitar cover of Suede's "The Drowners," the vinyl-only album sold out within no time to fans starved for Spaceman 3 and My Bloody Valentine.

Winning a small underground following in the United Kingdom and the United States for their unique blend of British folk/pop driven through odd effects, Flying Saucer Attack followed with the single "Land Beyond the Sun," released in October of 1994, and a second album of their first few singles and other material entitled *Distance,* released in November of that year on VHF. "Fuzzy, experimental and gloomily atmospheric," described Richard Fontenoy in *Rock: The Rough Guide,* "each track is a still-life approximation of a waking dream-state—drumless and post-rock." Stand-

out tracks included the acoustic "Instrumental Wish" and the tempered-rock "Standing Stone."

Signing with Chicago's Drag City label to distribute in the United States, FSA returned with *Further* in 1995, an album that retained the duo's lo-fidelity recording methods. Like their previous work, *Further* was recorded at home on a four-track without digital assistance. The music press showered the album with favorable reviews. *Alternative Press,* for example, declared that the record revealed "some of the sparsest, most emotional music you ever want to astral project to." *Chorus,* a compilation of radio sessions and singles from before and after *Further,* arrived in 1995. With this album, Flying Saucer Attack ambiguously declared the end of "phase one" of their existence, hinting at a mysterious "phase two" to come.

By now, the romantic relationship between Pearce and Brooks had begun to deteriorate, and after the release of *Chorus,* Brooks departed FSA in order to fully concentrate on her other project, Movietone. Subsequently, Pearce returned solo under the Flying Saucer Attack name to release the *Sally Free and Easy* EP in 1996, followed by the highly anticipated *New Lands* in 1997. The second phase of FSA, more of a gradual change in direction than a radical departure, won the same critical support of the project's prior efforts. "Pearce taps into a mood that is at once mystical and effusive," commented *Magnet* in its review, "murmuring sweet nothings over elongated, shimmering riffs that send molten jets of harmonics and undertones in all directions."

Following Pearce's unfortunate absence from music, Flying Saucer Attack made a comeback of sorts in 2000 with *Mirror,* revealing some of the artist's most folk-inspired pieces to date. *Mirror* "finds him tinkering with his trademark lo-fi, drumless drone formula—some numbers clank and crunch with an ominous rock/techno flair—and replacing his usual intangible vocal mumbling with gently forthcoming, folk-styled singing on the album's most haunting tunes." Apparently back to making music without interruptions, Pearce, at the time of *Mirror's* release, had already started work on his next LP, rumored to be a mostly acoustic set.

Selected discography

Flying Saucer Attack, (United Kingdom) FSA, 1993; VHF, 1994.
Distance, VHF, 1994.
Further, Drag City, 1995.
Chorus, Drag City, 1995.
Sally Free and Easy, (EP), Drag City, 1996.
New Lands, Drag City, 1997.
Mirror, Drag City, 2000.

Sources

Books

Buckley, Jonathan and others, editors, *Rock: The Rough Guide,* Rough Guides Ltd., 1999.

Periodicals

Alternative Press, August 1995, p. 85.
Magnet, March/April 1998, p. 65; April/May 2000, pp. 51-54.
Melody Maker, October 14, 1995.
Rolling Stone, August 24, 1995; April 4, 1996.
Village Voice, February 20, 1996; May 6, 1997.

Online

Flying Saucer Attack: Phase Two, http://www.dsl.org/fsa (June 12, 2000).
Rolling Stone.com, http://www.rollingstone.com (June 12, 2000).
Sonicnet.com, http://www.sonicnet.com (June 12, 2000).

—*Laura Hightower*

Laurent Garnier

DJ, producer

French DJ and producer Laurent Garnier is a member of an unofficial, though highly selective, professional fraternity: he is among modern dance music's most celebrated European turntable artists. *New Musical Express* writer Andy Crysell called him "a passionate character in danceworld … [who] invariably, strikes hyper-life into dancefloors." Garnier's heady, hypnotic style has won him a devoted following across Europe, but his studio efforts, released under his own label, have collected unanimously positive reviews. As the principal of F Communications, his Paris-based company, Garnier has also been involved in the surprise success of a television commercial for Levi's Sta-Press jeans: in a clip directed and soundtracked by one of the label's artists, an endearing yellow puppet rides as a passenger in a car, nodding his furry head to "Flat Beat," a song that sold more than two millions copies for F Communications and the song's creator, Mr. Oizo.

Garnier was born in Boulogne-sur-Seine, France, in 1966. His father ran a bumper-car and amusement-ride business. One of Garnier's babysitters worked for a major record company, and he began to amass a collection of countless record albums as a result. Even at an early age, he was intensely devoted to music; so much so that his parents took him to discotheques when he was 12—a scene that fascinated him. "The music was thumping, the lights, everything was marvelous. It was really beautiful to watch someone with the power to make people dance," he told *Mixmag* writer Tony Marcus. Garnier's grandmother owned a restaurant, and his first real DJing gig came when she allowed the teen to spin for its New Year's Eve party.

Catering College

At the age of 14, Garnier founded his own "pirate" or unlicensed radio station, which he called Radio Teenager. He built the transmitter himself, and broadcasted only on Friday nights. He and his friends, however, didn't feel they had enough of the right kind of records to play, so they taped music off of other stations' broadcasts. Acquiescing to his parents' wishes to find a more stable profession, Garnier attended a catering college in France, but to escape the compulsory national service for young men in France, he moved to England in the mid-1980s. He worked for a time at the French embassy in London, but eventually migrated to the northern city of Manchester in 1987.

There, he found work managing a restaurant, but also found himself in the throes of a crucial moment in music history with the birth of a new genre. Garnier was both a DJ and frequent patron at the epicenter of the burgeoning house-music scene, Manchester's Hacienda club. "I was playing disco, hi-NRG, Village People, Taylor Dayne, go-go, cha-cha. It was very open," he recalled in the *Mixmag* interview.

For The Record . . .

Born on February 1, 1966, in Boulogne-sur-Seine, France.

Worked as a DJ in Manchester, England, 1987, and in Paris, France, after 1988; founded F Communications (record label), 1994; made first record, "Acid Eiffel," for the FNAC in 1993 with fellow DJs Shazz and Ludovic Navarre; released first full-length solo LP, *Shot in the Dark,* on F Communications, 1995.

Addresses: *E-mail*—fcom@wanadoo.fr.

But it was a series of records played by another DJ one night that greatly impacted the direction of Garnier's career. The tracks that evening included cuts from the New York City duo Mantronix, who were gathering a huge British following with their unique blend of turntable wizardry and rap beats, and Farley Jackmaster Funk, a Chicago DJ who released a cover version of a classic soul track from Isaac Hayes, "Love Can't Turn Around," that made it all the way into the British charts in 1986. "It blew my mind," he recalled of the moment in the *Mixmag* interview. "I was dancing in the Hacienda … [a]nd you know when you can get punched by someone and it hits you heavy? Well I was on the dance floor and I felt this massive punch. I went straight over to the DJ box, I just knocked on the door saying … 'What kind of stuff is this.' I never heard anything like it before."

Soon, Manchester emerged as ground-zero for the explosion of what was being termed "acid house" by 1988. "It was the future of disco music and disco wasn't there anymore," Garnier recalled in *Mixmag* about that time. "House was talking to everybody, to gays, straight, blacks and whites. So it was a good thing." Garnier became one of the first DJs to spin records from Detroit techno pioneers Derrick May, Kevin Saunderson, and others—records that would make the American artists legends in the genre across Europe a decade later.

In the end, Garnier was not able to avoid his mandatory stint in the French army, and signed on as a chef. Fortunately, the posting allowed him to continue his DJing: he spun at Paris's gay clubs until early in the morning, and then rushed to catch the train back to his barracks. "Every night for one year I slept only two or three hours each afternoon," Garnier remembered in an interview for *New Musical Express* with Piers Martin. Returning to the Hacienda in 1990, he found the Manchester music scene had created a tremendous

cultural force with young people, but one that also seemed to revolve around illicit substance abuse, too. "They don't even listen to the music anymore, they just get the rush off their drugs and they lose themselves in their own little world," he said in the *Mixmag* interview. "It bores me."

Founded Record Label

In the early 1990s, Garnier became one of the most sought-after DJs across Europe, and spun at large-scale outdoor events and in the most popular dance clubs in cities like Berlin and Brussels. In Paris, he began his own underground event, which he called Wake Up in Paris. In 1993, he scored his first hit with a record he made with two other French artists, Shazz and Ludovic Navarre. "Acid Eiffel" was released on the FNAC label, and did well, but within a year the label had dissolved; in 1994, Garnier and Eric Morand, who had run FNAC, formed F Communications in Paris.

Garnier's first record on his imprint was issued in 1995. *Shot in the Dark* was a full-length album, and each track a homage to either a subgenre in the dance scene or to a well-known turntable artist. "Every single track on it corresponds to a different time of the night or to a different time of my life," Garnier told *Mixmag*. "It's a very personal thing. I just made music I believed in and music I'd liked for years," he told Marcus in the same interview. "I just wanted to see if I could do it myself. All the other records I'd made before had been with somebody in the studio helping me or collaborating. Now I can say that nobody helped me, nobody mixed anything for me."

Garnier's next record, *30*, was so titled because he spent an entire year—his thirtieth—in the studio working on it. It had a minor hit with the track "Crispy Bacon" in 1997, a track that *New Musical Express* reviewer John Perry described as "a thumping slice of road-drill techno." A 15-minute short film was produced by Mr. Oizo, a recording artist whose real name is Quentin Dupieux. The two had met when Garnier bought a car from Dupieux's father; a studio artist as well, the younger Dupieux's first tracks were released on F Communications. In 1999, the label had a massive success with one of Mr. Oizo's tracks, "Flat Beat," that was used for a television commercial for Levi's Sta-Press jeans.

The spot, directed by Dupieux, featured a memorable yellow puppet—Flat Eric, as he became known—riding in a car and nodding his head to the music. Sales for "Flat Beat" skyrocketed, and the single went on to sell two and a half million copies. "Without that puppet it would never have sold five percent of what it did," Garnier told Martin in the *New Musical Express* interview. "So we can say a good 90 percent of people who bought it believes the puppet made the music! And that proves how stupid people are today. You know, they will buy a tune because of a puppet."

"I Can't Please Everyone"

In 2000, Garnier released another full-length work on his label. Titled *Unreasonable Behaviour,* the work was somewhat of a departure for his style with its dark, apocalyptic mood. Its first single was "The Sound of the Big Babou;" that song, "Cycles D'Opposition" and "Last Tribute from the 20th Century" won praise from reviewers. "Last Tribute" featured Garnier's own electronically enhanced voice intoning the names of cities where techno first emerged—New York, Chicago, Detroit. A track called "The Man with the Red Face" took its name from Garnier's rather infamously brutal production techniques—in the studio one day, he instructed his saxophone player to play so hard that after a while the veins in the musician's forehead were frighteningly visible. *New Musical Express* writer David Stubbs called *Unreasonable Behaviour* "an album of gloomy, almost gothic techno splendour. Beneath its typically sleek, deep urbane house grooves, it beats nervously with foreboding, fear and loathing for humanity as a whole."

Garnier was pleased with the end result of *Unreasonable Behaviour,* and felt that by this point in his career, he had achieved a certain peace with his creative energies. He declared that he cares little about critical reaction, or whether or not one of his records is a commercial success. "If people don't like it, well, I can't please everyone and I'm not trying to," Garnier told Martin in *New Musical Express.* "But I feel happier, much stronger about it. Maybe that's why everyone likes the new album."

Selected discography

(With Shazz and Ludovic Navarre) "Acid Eiffel," FNAC, 1993.
Shot in the Dark, F Communications, 1995.
Compil Techno, Wotre Music, 1996.
30, F Communications, 1997.
Unreasonable Behaviour, F Communications, 2000.

Sources

Mixmag, November 1994.
New Musical Express, December 7, 1996; March 29, 1997; February 12, 2000, p. 42; March 4, 2000, p. 27.

—Carol Brennan

God Is My Co-Pilot

Rock band

Under the leadership of the openly bisexual husband-and-wife duo of vocalist, clarinetist, and keyboardist Sharon Topper and guitarist Craig Flanagin, God Is My Co-Pilot emerged as one of the most crucial voices in the underground music community of the 1990s. Along with a loose, revolving cast of downtown New York City players, Flanagin and Topper explored lyrical themes ranging from sexuality to radical politics to religious enlightenment, while their hard-to-define musical sound meshed no-wave noise, hardcore thrash, post-funk, avant-garde jazz, and even occasional touches of Middle Eastern chants, Finnish folk music, and Jewish music.

Although God is My Co-Pilot can at times seem dogmatic, their taintless passion, ever-growing musical scope, desire to approach the creative process without boundaries, and astonishingly prolific output have certainly challenged traditional assumptions about how musicians produce and, in turn, audiences consume the musical form. In short, as God Is My Co-Pilot stated in their anthem, the scat-hop song "We Signify" from 1993's *Straight Not,* "We're co-opting rock, the language of sexism, to address gender identity on its own terms of complexity. We're here to instruct, not to distract. We won't take your attention without giving some back."

In just a decade's time, God Is My Co-Pilot released more than 15 full-length albums, as well as numerous singles and EPs, and toured extensively the world over. Growing in strength and number over the years, the band's membership swelled to unheard of propor-

tions in an attempt to explore the collective nature of music. New York luminaries and artists of the avant-garde such as John Zorn, Anthony Coleman, Elliott Sharp, and many others offered their talents as guest members. These musical visionaries, alongside independent rockers such as Jad Fair, Catpower's Chan Marshall, and the Boredoms' Yoshimi P-We, allowed for God Is My Co-Pilot to sound fresh and exciting each time out—the direct result of changing personnel. Topper, who writes most of the lyrics and sings lead vocals, and Flanagin, the project's musical director who plays guitar among other instruments, represent the only two musicians who have appeared consistently on every God Is My Co-Pilot record.

The idea to form God Is My Co-Pilot came about in 1990 when Flanagin, who grew up on a farm in New York, and Topper, a native of Long Island, found themselves feeling increasingly alienated from modern music. A true "Do It Yourself" (D.I.Y) spirit, Flanagin, who knew very little about music, subsequently bought his first guitar and taught himself to play. Soon, he developed his own improvisational technique that defied standard chord progressions and other accepted musical patterns, then started jamming with a bassist named James Garrison. They invited Topper, at that time Flanagin's girlfriend, to join in for the impromptu sessions. Excited by the trio's results, Flanagin went in search of a drummer, eventually finding Siobahn Duffy, who would sporadically leave the group. Thus, they enlisted percussionist Michael Evans to fill in, and when Duffy would return, God Is My Co-Pilot used two drummers; others such as Fish and Roses' Rick Brown and Carbon's David Linton also filled in from time to time, and bassists Fly and Daria Klotz and drummer Fredrik Haas have also played with the group.

According to critics, die-hard fans, and God Is My Co-Pilot themselves, re-creating an entire list of every musician who has participated in one form or another with the group would prove time-consuming and nearly impossible, though Flanagin did at one time make a "family tree" for a fanzine article that went unpublished. "Michael Evans, drummer, etc., says it's like a basketball team," Flanagin offered to Janne Maki-Turja in an interview with Finland's *Mutiny!* magazine, "where there are a certain number of people in training, and then the coach (that would be me in this metaphor) picks who are the starters, who's the traveling squad, who to put in to make special plays, and so on."

The band's personal lives, rather than professional needs, usually influence who will participate. "Our creative collaborations mainly come out of our social lives," Topper explained to Andrew Utterson of the British publication *Perpee.* "Our friends are musicians—some 'famous,' some not. As we spent more time on music, our rehearsals and recording sessions began to be our only time to socialize and have fun, so we invite our friends to come and do this

For The Record . . .

Members include **Craig Flanagin** (born in New York), guitar, other instruments, musical director; **Sharon Topper** (born on Long Island, NY), lyrics, vocals, clarinet, keyboards. Flanagin and Topper are married.

Formed group in 1990 in New York City, NY; God Is My Co-Pilot, with a revolving cast of guest musicians, released more than 15 full-length albums, as well as numerous singles and EPs, and toured extensively the world over, 1990—; released debut album *I Am Not This Body,* 1992; released *Mir Shlufn Nisht,* 1994; released *Sex Is for Making Babies,* 1995; released *Get Busy,* 1998.

Addresses: *Home*—God Is My Co-Pilot, P.O Box 490, Cooper Station, NY, 10276. *Email*—godco@earthlink.net.

with us when we feel they have something musically to contribute and it also helps turn recording and rehearsal into a party. Also, the continuous exchange of musical ideas with new people keeps the music interesting for us—the audience with the shortest attention span. As far as the music goes, Craig is the musical director, and one of his favorite things is the challenge of matching different musical personalities to best effect."

With their revolving door of percussionists and other musicians, Flanagin and Topper, the latter known for her ability to shift from sweet to savage vocals at any given moment, started playing live throughout New York City, where they became a favorite act at the Knitting Factory, as well as other famous avant-garde clubs. The performance aspect of God Is My Co-Pilot remained of primary importance over the years. They held regular shows in and around their home base of New York and toured across Europe and Japan as well.

"We play more often in New York than any other band, I think … certainly if you remember that we have averaged more than one show per week in the city since 1990," said Flanagin to Maki-Turja. "We can play so much partly because there's not just one kind of place for us to play; we love doing gigs that aren't just like a 'rock show' in a 'rock club.' Naturally, we play at CBGBs and Knitting Factory and places like this… At least once every summer we play at the Sideshows by

the Seashore at Coney Island, which we always enjoy; the carnival atmosphere is already in place! We've played at three Radical Jewish Culture festivals now … we like that, because in addition to letting us play for people who like us but would never have come to see us at ABC, the different context lets us hear our own music in a very different way, and makes us pay a lot of attention to things like how we relate to an audience."

In 1991, God Is My Co-Pilot started releasing an endless series of records on their own The Making of Americans as well as other independent labels. The group's debut album, the wildly eclectic, 34-song *I Am Not This Body,* arrived in 1992. In 1993, the band released more than ten records, including the EP *When This You See Remember Me,* the live set *Tight Like Fist: Live Recording,* the *Straight Not* album, and the cassette-only *What Doctors Don't Tell You.*

God Is My Co-Pilot, longtime participants in John Zorn's Radical Jewish Culture series, in 1994 released *Mir Shlufn Nisht,* a collection of traditional Hebrew and Yiddish songs. The group even adhered to the Orthodox directive that the word "God" not be written down, altering the group's name to read G-d Is My Co-Pilot. That same year also brought forth the 23-song album *How to Be.* In 1995, the group released *Sex Is for Making Babies,* considered one of God Is My Co-Pilot's most bracing albums for its outright attack on conventional sexual mores. That same year, along with a flurry of new EPs and singles, they released the "party record" *Puss 02.* 1996 saw the release of two volumes of early singles and EPs for the compilation *The History of Music.* That same year, *The Best of God Is My Co-Pilot* surfaced as a notable introduction to the group's work. The band rounded out the decade with other standouts including 1997's *Excuse Me, Don't Squeeze Me,* a collaboration with Melt-Banana, and 1998's *Get Busy.*

Although such a proliferation of music may seem daunting to many bands, God Is My Co-Pilot insists that developing songs isn't all that overwhelming. "It's the urge to work through ideas and not to create 'the perfect song' so much as to apply different ideas to old songs and to create new songs within the framework and rules of the new idea," Topper, explaining the group's work ethic, said to Utterson. Likewise, Flanagin picked up the guitar for one simple reason: "I never wanted to be a rock star," he said in earnest to Jason Pettigrew of *Alternative Press.* "I heard these noises, and I wanted to be able to make these noises."

Selected discography

God Is My Co-Pilot (EP), The Making of Americans, 1991.
On A Wing & A Prayer (EP), Funky Mushroom, 1992.
I Am Not This Body, The Making of Americans, 1992.
Gender Is as Gender Does (EP), Funky Mushroom, 1992.

How I Got Over (EP), Ajax, 1992.
Pissing and Hooting (EP), The Making of Americans/Seze, 1993.
Speed Yr Trip, The Making of Americans, 1993, reissued, DSA, 1995.
When This You See Remember Me, Dark Beloved Cloud, 1993.
My Sinister Hidden Agenda (EP), Blackout, 1993, reissued, The Making of Americans, 1995.
What Doctors Don't Tell You (cassette tape), Shrimper, 1993.
Straight Out, Outpunk, 1993.
Tight Like Fist: Live Recording, Knitting Factory Works, 1993.
How to Be, The Making of Americans, 1994.
Kittybait (EP), Ajax, 1994.
Mir Shlufn Nisht, Avant, 1994.
Sex Is for Making Babies, DSA, 1995.
No Fi, The Making of Americans, 1995.
Puss 02, Dark Beloved Cloud/ The Making of Americans, 1995.
The History of Music, Vol. 1, 1996.
The History of Music, Vol. 2, 1996.
The Best of God Is My Co-Pilot, Atlantic, 1996.
Excuse Me, Don't Squeeze Me, 1997.
Get Busy, Atavistic, 1998.

Books

Robbins, Ira A., *Trouser Press Guide to '90s Rock,* Fireside/Simon & Schuster, 1997.

Periodicals

Alternative Press, October 1992.
Fever Pitch, Spring/Summer 1996.
Rolling Stone, May 18, 1995.
Village Voice, August 18, 1992.

Online

God Is My Co-Pilot Information, http://www.io.com/~hise/godco/info.html (June 16, 2000).
Mutiny!, http://www.io.com/~hise/godco/articles/mutiny .html (June 16, 2000).
Perpee, vol. 2, http://www.io.com/~hise/godco/articles/ per-pee.html (June 16, 2000).

—*Laura Hightower*

Trilok Gurtu

Percussionist

Watching Trilok Gurtu perform live is a mesmerizing experience, an event that captures all the senses. "Seated amid a panalopy of drums, shaker, cymbals, rattles and other indefinable sound producing objects, he moves from one to the other," wrote Don Heckman for the *Los Angeles Times* in 1999. "Tapping the tabla drums with his fingers, stroking cymbals and bells, occasionally bashing a snare or a bass drum, he is unrestricted by style, a true world music artist." And while many link the musician to jazz based on his work touring with John McLaughlin in the 1980s and 1990s and for joining the band Oregon as Colin Walcott's replacement, Gurtu himself, musically speaking, sees the whole world as his stage.

"We're just trying to say that music is one," the Indian-born percussionist extraordinaire commented to *Down Beat*'s Larry Birnbaum in 1993, upon the release of his third solo outing entitled *Crazy Saints*. "It's not West and East anymore; it's gone universal. It's possible to play with anybody, if you are open and you adapt." And when asked whether critics should classify his music as jazz fusion or world music, Gurtu replied: "It's very hard to categorize not only my music but the music of anybody who is trying to do something different. I think it's the experience that you have gathered from everywhere. In my experience, I gathered a lot from Africa, South India, jazz, Jimi Hendrix, Cream. I heard everything in Bombay—Motown, Otis Redding, Sly Stone."

For his latest album, an homage to Africa released in 2000 entitled *African Fantasy,* Gurtu continued to indulge in his appreciation for all forms of music and culture. "*African Fantasy* is about Africa and India, two great nations for music, and what each has contributed to music," Gurtu, who recorded the album with his band The Glimpse, explained to Meg Dedolph of *Down Beat.* "When I was in America, I said, 'Please don't forget African music. That's why America's on the map. Because of the funk, because of the jazz, it's African. Keep that. You owe something to these people.'"

A three-time winner of *Down Beat* magazine's best percussionist award, Trilok Gurtu, born on October 30, 1951, in Bombay, India, came from a long line of musicians. His father's father was a sitar player, his mother's mother a singer and dancer. His own mother, Shobha Gurtu, a frequent guest on Gurtu's later solo albums, was a prominent singer of ghazal and thunzri music, a semi-classical North Indian style. "It's also based on dancing," Gurtu offered further, as quoted by Birnbaum. "In India, a big part of playing the drums is how to accompany the dancer. That's why I loved James Brown, doing all those steps."

Trained in Indian Music

Although always receptive to an array of musical forms, Gurtu's earliest influences were rooted in the

For The Record . . .

Born on October 30, 1951, in Bombay, India; son of Shobha Gurtu, a famous Indian vocalist. *Education*: Studied Indian classical music with Ustad Abdul Karim Khan Saheb and Ahmed Jan Thirakwa.

Started formal training in tabla at age six; discovered rock, soul, and jazz as a teen and started playing drums and other percussion instruments; toured Italy with an Indian crossover group, 1973-76; traveled to New York City with Indian pop singer Asha Bhoshle and began an association with saxophonist Charlie Mariano, 1977; played with various musicians in Europe, 1978-c. 1979; moved to Woodstock, New York, to teach at Karl Berger's Creative Music Studio, 1980; joined jazz group Oregon, 1984; joined John McLaughlin's trio, released debut album *Usfret*, 1988; released *Crazy Saints*, 1993; released *African Fantasy*, 2000. Worked with Archie Shepp, Jan Garbarek, Philip Catherine, Indian violinist Lakshminarayana Shankar, Gil Evans, Airto Moreira, and Paul Bley, and recorded with Catherine, Shankar, Moreira, Bley, Barre Phillips, John McLaughlin, and Oregon, among others.

Awards: Named *Down Beat* Magazine percussionist of the year, 1994, 1995, and 1996.

Addresses: *Record company*—Blue Thumb/MCA Records, 1755 Broadway, 8th Fl., New York City, NY 10019, (212) 841-8000, website: http://www.mca records.com.

rhythmic rules and structures of Indian classical music. At the age of six, he began formal training in tabla, an eloquent percussion instrument that provides the pulse of the Indian musical tradition, with his initial tutor, Ustad Abdul Karim Khan Saheb. A strict disciplinarian who would give his young student a good hiding when he made mistakes, as well as reward him with gifts when he played properly, Khan Saheb nevertheless knew that Gurtu possessed magic in his fingers when in the right mood. As a youngster, Gurtu also studied with Ahmed Jan Thirakwa, and in 1965, formed a percussion group with his brother. "Trilok became a kansen (one who learns music by ear) rather than Tansen," his mother said to Nandita Chowdhury of *India Today Music*. "Whatever the gharana, whatever the music, he played on."

As for other significant influences, Gurtu likewise feels indebted to composers light years away from India, namely Bach and Mozart, who he considers the masters of accessible music. "Everyone's still playing their music," including jazz and pop artists, he noted to Dedolph. "If you take Bach, you have the best bass lines." However accessible Bach and Mozart were to Gurtu, it was American jazz and rock and roll that really made his heart race. And when Gurtu, along with the rest of the world's teenage population, fell under the seductive spell of the rock and soul sounds of Jimi Hendrix, James Brown, Sly and the Family Stone, and the Supremes, his traditional instruments were gradually augmented by all manner of kit drums and percussion, and he gained a reputation experimenting in the burgeoning Indian pop and jazz scenes.

"When I was young, I earned money backing singers, and when I was about 16 I started working in movies. I also worked in five-star hotels; that's when I heard John Coltrane and Hendrix and everything. I came across the record *Coltrane Plays The Blues,* and Elvin Jones knocked me out," he recalled to Birnbaum. "At 20 or 21, I went to Paris with a progressive group, Waterfront. I used to play Hendrix tunes on tabla, but nobody gave a damn." Returning to Bombay from France, Gurtu played the Jazz Yatra Festival with alto saxophonist Charlie Mariano. "Charlie was the first Western musician I played with."

Played with Jazz Greats

In 1973, Gurtu toured Italy with an Indian crossover group, remaining there through 1976. In 1977, he traveled to New York City with Indian pop singer Asha Bhoshle. While in New York, he also forged a long-term association with Mariano. "I loved the music and the positive competition—that hunger and enthusiasm for music—but I couldn't stand the one-upmanship, so I left and went to Germany," he said to Birnbaum of his stay in New York, which lasted until 1978. In Germany, Gurtu played drums and tabla for a rock group, but made little money. Thus, he relocated to Sweden to work with Don Cherry, who introduced the percussionist to the music of Ornette Coleman, the genius who invented an entire school of jazz known as the avant-garde; Cherry had played trumpet with the alto saxophonist's powerhouse quartet in the 1950s. During his time in Europe, Gurtu went on to work with Archie Shepp, Jan Garbarek, Philip Catherine, Indian violinist Lakshminarayana Shankar, Gil Evans, Airto Moreira, and Paul Bley, and recorded with Catherine, Shankar, Moreira, Bley, and Barre Phillips.

After living in Europe for a year or two, Gurto returned to the United States, settling in Woodstock, New York, to teach percussion at Karl Berger's Creative Music Studio. Here, he met drummer/percussionist Jack De-Johnette, fusion guitarist Pat Metheny, percussionist

Nana Vasconcelos, and a multi-instrumentalist named Collin Walcott, who studied both tabla and sitar and played with the group Oregon, a jazz-influenced world music quartet that used, among a range of instruments, Indian percussion, as well as Eastern modalities and compositions derived from classical forms. Walcott, after meeting the young percussionist, casually mentioned to his bandmates one day that should he ever leave the band, Gurtu would make a fine replacement, and when Walcott died in 1984 car accident, his suggestion by coincidence eerily came true. "People are still moved by that," Gurtu revealed to Birnbaum.

However, walking in Walcott's shadow amid questions by friends and fans surrounding the strange chain of events grew tiring as time passed. Thus, when English guitarist John McLaughlin, having seen Gurtu perform at a jazz festival once in Germany, asked the percussionist to join his trio in 1988, Gurtu immediately accepted the invitation, leaving Oregon soon thereafter. Joining McLaughlin also coincided with the release of Gurtu's first solo album, 1988's *Usfret,* an open-ended session—with parts written for percussion only—recorded with his mother, Cherry, Shankar, guitarist/multi-instrumentalist Ralph Towner, Jonas Hellborg, and pianist Daniel Goyone, who Gurtu regards as his "musical brother." A second, more structured album, *Living Magic,* arrived in 1991, featuring Vasconcelos on percussion, Goyone on keyboards, and stellar saxophone by Jan Garbarek.

Career Blossomed in the '90s

In 1993, Gurtu released his acclaimed *Crazy Saints,* for which the percussionist recruited Metheny and Austrian keyboardist Joe Zawinul, as well as his mother. The following year, his rising status in jazz was confirmed in 1994, the year he won his first of three consecutive *Down Beat* poll awards for number-one percussionist. The next year, Gurtu returned with *Believe,* followed by *Bad Habits Die Hard* in 1996 and *The Glimpse,* a tribute to Cherry and his role in exploring world music, in 1997. In 1999, Cherry's daughter, Neneh, guested on Gurtu's *Kathak,* a collection of mostly original compositions that drifts easily, yet convincingly, across various cultural boundaries.

With the release in 2000 of *African Fantasy,* Gurtu paid tribute to the music of Africa and its danceable quality, an important element he sees as lacking in jazz today. "The dance feeling in jazz is gone, the swing. It's getting very intellectual," he insisted, as quoted by Dedolph. "Everybody plays like somebody, but nobody plays like himself. I'm an outsider watching this, not a jazz historian or an American who grew up around jazz. It's too tricky and everyone wants to show their chops, wants to show their technique. Jazz is about listening, not about watching technique. I feel that jazz is very

African and should remain like that. Like blues, it's danceable, and … wow … it's African!"

In the late 1990s and into the next decade, samples of Gurtu's music began to show up in dance mixes in clubs throughout the world, but the percussionist doesn't mind sharing his work, even with those who most likely don't consider themselves jazz or world music fans. "For me it's a privilege," he said to Dedolph, though he asks DJs and producers to respect what they choose to sample. "If you're going to use Indian music, use it properly," he added. "Keep the integrity, don't make it *el cheapo.*"

As the third decade of his accomplished career approached, Gurtu, who says that Americans—a culture always open to new ideas in music—seem to understand his sensibilities the most, held strong to his creative goals. "You know," he told Heckman, "my first name—Trilok—means 'King of the Three Worlds,' basically, that is, your body, your consciousness and the beyond. And I try to find that kind of integration in my music. Because, even with the most difficult things, if you can make them simple, they will reach a big audience. Everybody should like what you do. That's my view. I don't try to play high flown, I don't try to be complicated just to be complicated. I just try to touch my listeners with my music."

Selected discography

Usfret, CMP Records, 1988.
Living Magic, CMP Records, 1991.
Crazy Saints, CMP Records, 1993.
Believe, CMP Records, 1995.
Bad Habits Die Hard, CMP Records, 1996.
The Glimpse, Silva America, 1997.
Kathak, Mintaka, 1999.
African Fantasy, Blue Thumb Records, 2000.

Sources

Periodicals

Down Beat, March 1993; January 1994; December 1997; April 2000, pp. 43-47.
India Today Music, December 15, 1997.
Los Angeles Times, September 6, 1996; September 2, 1999.

Online

Europe Jazz Network—Trilock Gurtu, http://www.ejn.it/mus/gurtu.htm (May 15, 2000).
Sonicnet.com, http://www.sonicnet.com (May 15, 2000).

—Laura Hightower

Guster

Rock band

In the late-1990s, Guster, a Boston-bred, New York-based trio, became one of the most successful indie/college rock bands to gain a strong following and sell thousands of albums without commercial support. Instead, they built their reputation up and down the East Coast through relentless touring and humorous exchanges with audiences, which in turn provided Guster a solid and ever-growing grass-roots fan base. As their popularity spread by word of mouth across the United States, Guster—who sold collectively around 90,000 copies of their first two independent albums, *Parachute* and *Goldfly,* with the help of fans alone—eventually landed a major-label record deal with Sire Records, but promised to stay true to their original vision. Selling a lot of records, the indie-rock trio insisted, doesn't necessarily mean selling out.

One of the most unique aspects of Guster, aside from their penchant for writing short, infectious songs about love, self-doubt, suicide, and the absurdities of the rock-star lifestyle, is their unique sound—a mix of roots rock, folk, and experimental pop—and refusal to abide by industry pigeonholing. Whereas most rock bands typically center around a lead guitar, bass guitar, and drums, Guster defied the usual conventions with two acoustic guitars and a bongo set. "This thing was born out of friendship," explained Brian Rosenworcel, Guster's percussionist, to *Boston Globe* correspondent Joan Anderman. "We all happened to play instruments that didn't quite add up to a band. But we made it our mission to make it add up to a band." Even with their first album for Sire, 1999's *Lost and Gone Forever,* for

which they had access to a top-notch producer and an unrestrained budget, Guster refused unlike so many newly signed groups to fall prey to giddy overproduction. "Actually, instead of focusing on what we needed to complement the Guster sound," Rosenworcel added, "we focused on making the Guster sound as good as we could."

Rosenworcel, a native of Hartford, Connecticut, who lived with his two bandmates for four years until he finally moved into his own apartment in the fall of 1999, met Ryan Miller and Adam Gardner, who both play guitar and sing for Guster, in 1992 at Tufts University near Boston. "The band started very informally in our dorm rooms when we were college freshman," said Miller, a Texas native who graduated with a degree in religion, to John Roos of the *Los Angeles Times.* "All we had were our guitars and some bongos, and so that's what we played. We never really set any rules or had this subversive plot to be gimmicky. But when people kept telling us, 'You can't make it without a real rhythm section or electric guitar,' it only strengthened our resolve to prove them wrong."

Guster, whose members graduated from Tufts in 1995, honed their skills playing clubs around the Boston area during their college years, drawing in more and more fans with each subsequent performance. They originally went by the name Gus, but later adopted the moniker Guster after learning that several other national touring acts played under the same name. After recruiting producer Mike Denneen, Guster debuted in 1994 with a self-released album entitled *Parachute* on Aware Records. Because the three friends lacked a record label, their enthusiastic fans, known as the Guster Rep, essentially promoted and distributed Guster's first record. "We'd get them 10 CDs, they'd sell them, and send us a hundred bucks," Rosenworcel recalled to Anderman.

Over time, the trio amassed more than a thousand Rep members nationwide, who they compensated for their efforts with T-shirts and free concert tickets. In total, *Parachute,* thanks to Guster fans spreading the word, sold a remarkable 35,000 units. Later that year the *Boston Globe* named *Parachute* Best Local Debut Album of 1995. By now, Guster had become one of the most popular acts in the area. As a result of the trio's celebrated live shows, Guster—hailed as one of the biggest indie-rock successes of the 1990s—went on to win the honor for Best Live Act at the Boston Music Awards in 1997.

In March of 1997, Guster released *Goldfly* on Hybrid Recordings, an album distributed by Aware and sold mostly at shows and through the fans. They maintained a relentless touring schedule, deciding to take their show to cities across the country. More often than not, Guster sold out clubs in every town they visited, thanks in large part to the Rep program. The dedi-

For The Record . . .

Members include **Adam Gardner**, guitar, vocals; **Ryan Miller** (born in Texas; graduated from college with a degree in religion), guitar, vocals; **Brian Rosenworcel** (born in Hartford, CT), bongos, vocals. All graduated from Tufts University in 1995.

Formed at Tufts University in Medford, MA, 1992; debuted with *Parachute,* 1995; signed with Sire Records, 1998; released *Lost and Gone Forever,* toured with the Dave Matthews Band and performed at Woodstock '99, 1999.

Addresses: *Record company*—Sire Records, 936 Broadway, 5th Floor, New York City, NY 10010, phone: (212) 253-3900, fax: (212) 253-2950. *Website*— Official Guster website: http://www.guster.com.

cated, entirely voluntary Guster Reps continued a roots-level marketing campaign, distributing flyers and spreading the word about the quirky trio from the Northeast.

Soon, Guster earned a reputation nationwide for marrying sometimes dark subject matter, such as relationship woes, alienation, and the worship of false idols with upbeat, melody-rich music. "My challenge is figuring out what I have to say that hasn't already been said—and said better than I ever could—by someone else," Miller, Guster's primary songwriter, revealed to Roos. "I'm a 25-year-old college graduate from a white middle-class family … so I'm not about to get preachy about the more complex issues of the day. I'm just trying to express the range of my personal feelings— love, jealousy, anger, guilt—for whatever they're worth."

Like Guster's grass-roots following, major labels took interest in the trio as well, and in 1998, the band signed an agreement between Sire Records Group and Hybrid Recordings. Sire, under the major-label contract, reissued *Goldfly* soon thereafter, and the album went on to sell a total of 55,000 copies according to Sound-Scan, with the single "Airport Song" peaking at number 35 on *Billboard*'s Modern Rock Tracks chart.

In 1999, Guster made their major-label debut with *Lost and Gone Forever.* Co-produced with Steve Lillywhite, the influential producer of albums by top acts such as U2, the Dave Matthews Band, and Peter Gabriel (who first noticed Guster in 1998 during two sell-out shows

at Irving Plaza in New York), the record earned rave reviews. That same year, Guster sold out venues across the United States, such as the Hammerstein Ballroom in New York, brought their show to Canada, and played at Woodstock '99. In 2000, the band toured with the Dave Matthews Band, gaining even broader mainstream recognition.

Despite their high-profile backing and increasing exposure, Guster retained their own unique sound, unconventional lineup, and unorthodox approach to songwriting. "I didn't want our records to be disposable pop," Miller said to Roos. Their differences from other pop/rock groups are arguably what makes Guster so appealing, "I don't think we really sound like anybody else, and sometimes, it takes more than one listen to get a handle on what we're doing," he added. "It's probably easier to determine what we're not, like a conventional rock band. We don't improvise, so we're not a jam or hippie band either."

However, Guster doesn't consider their style groundbreaking by any means. "We do put a lot of thought into what we do, but it's not this real sophisticated stuff you'll hear from the Flaming Lips, Mercury Rev or Beck," Miller further noted. "More than anything else, with our harmonizing and sense of melody, we just aspire to be a good pop band like Crowded House or Squeeze—one that packs each record with a little smarts and a lot of ear candy."

Selected discography

Parachute, Aware, 1995.
Goldfly, Hybrid, 1997, reissued, Hybrid/Sire, 1998.
Lost and Gone Forever, Hybrid/Sire, 1999.

Sources

Periodicals

Billboard, January 24, 1998; August 14, 1999.
Boston Globe, February 8, 1996; May 23, 1997; September 24, 1999; November 1, 1999.
Los Angeles Times, January 19, 2000.
New York Times, November 30, 1999.

Online

All Music Guide, http://www.allmusic.com (June 6, 2000).
Guster Official Website, http://www.guster.com (June 6, 2000).
Sonicnet.com, http://www.sonicnet.com (June 6, 2000).

—Laura Hightower

Beth Hart

Singer, songwriter

Photograph by Tim Mosenfelder. Corbis. Reproduced by permission. ©

Los Angeles native Beth Hart, a blues-styled rock singer and former street performer, made her debut in 1995 with *Immortal,* attracting attention for her raw, outspoken nature, gifted musicianship, emotion-filled live shows, and a voice compared to the likes of Janis Joplin. "Hart is the epitome of the natural woman," wrote Chuck Taylor for the October 2, 1999, issue of *Billboard* magazine, "bawdy and funny, chatty and free-wheeling with her choice of spiced language. But that's white bread compared to her onstage presence, where the tall, gaunt singer/songwriter struts and squalls out songs with the vim of Mick Jagger... At other times, she takes her place at the piano or center stage, where she sits without a shred of pretense, legs straddled over the sides of a chair, conjuring a voice so delicate and pained, you wonder if she's going to cry—or if you will."

Drawing reactions such as this from the moment she took the stage for amateur contests as a teen, Hart nonetheless experienced misgivings about the music business when her career finally took off. Eventually, touring the world over proved detrimental to her band, and Hart dropped out of sight for nearly four years, time spent soul-searching and dealing with problems through writing music. Then, ready to give her professional career a second chance, she resurfaced in 1999 with the acclaimed *Screamin' for My Supper,* an album that saw Hart's songwriting skills mature with vulnerable, honest tunes about facing life's issues.

Born around 1972, Hart took up the piano at the age of four, studying classical composers such as Beethoven and Bach. As the years passed, however, her tastes grew to include noted rock acts of the day, namely Led Zeppelin and Rush, as well as legendary soul and blues artists, from Aretha Franklin and James Brown to Otis Redding, Billie Holiday, and Etta James. All of these musicians, and particularly James' soulful voice, would greatly influence Hart's own personal style. She explained, "It's funny because my favorite male influences are classical guys like Beethoven or Bach," as quoted by Ami Sheth in an interview for *HITS* magazine. "Those guys made some pretty sexy music, but the females are like the soul! Etta James, Aretha Franklin, Billie... Where does that come from? Etta James is definitely my favorite. I love her so much. She's such a bad ass—she's gotta be in her late 60's and still tours all the time. She's such a hard worker."

Determined to work hard herself, Hart saw her creative vision begin to take shape by the time she reached her teens and enrolled at the Los Angeles High School for the Performing Arts for her tenth grade year as a vocal and cello major. Encouraged by a classmate, the young singer started honing her skills on stage, regularly performing during open mic nights at the Belly Room of the Comedy Store nightclub. And soon thereafter, feeling right at home in front of an audience, the seemingly natural entertainer was singing at local venues up to five nights per week. In addition, Hart entered various talent contests at local clubs as a solo act throughout the South Central Los Angeles area; more often than not, she brought home the grand prize for her captivating presence.

Seduced by the Stage

"When I'm up there and the crowd is right there with me, it's like being breast-fed by my mother; like feeling so much love from the sexiest, most honest, kindest man; like the best drugs in the world; like God putting his hand on your back and loving you," she told Taylor, describing her attraction to performing live. "It is the best."

But while Hart was gaining valuable experience and making a name for herself on the club circuit, her performance as a student suffered. Staying out until all hours on school nights marred her attendance record, and officials, consequently, eventually asked the promising musician to leave. After this, Hart attended real estate school for a brief time, then decided to give up academics all together in order to devote her energies entirely to music.

By the summer of 1993, the aspiring songwriter had formed a loose-knit backing band and expanded her performance territory to include well-established, greater Los Angeles-area clubs like the Roxy, the Troubadour, and Club Lingerie. While working this circuit, Hart met her future collaborator, Tel Aviv-born bassist Tal Herzberg, a former member of Israel's 17-piece Air Force Orchestra. Following his military

service, Herzberg within two years had become the most-recorded bassist in Israel, contributing to more than 60 albums. And when he relocated to the United States in 1992, the experienced bassist immediately developed a reputation as one of the country's top session players.

Intrigued by Hart's raw, soulful style, Herzberg teamed with the young songwriter and also recruited guitarist Jimmy Khoury to join the group. Khoury, a native of Fall River, Massachusetts, had previously played with several bands in the Boston area, touring extensively up and down the East Coast before moving to Los Angeles. Despite the trio's experience and individual talents, they opted to take a more subdued approach in working together, and rather than continuing to play within the local club scene—where Hart was already a recognized performer—they instead took their music to the streets.

Moving from smoke-filled Los Angeles night spots to the carnival-like atmosphere of Santa Monica's Third Street Promenade, Hart and her new band rolled out a carpet, set up candles, and played to passersby and lucky crowds of people six night a week. Soon, word of these intimate street performances spread throughout the community, bringing Hart to the attention of 143 Records, who promptly signed the young songstress. "Beth isn't just any artist. She is an unbelievably gifted singer/songwriter. She is the reason why many of us get in the business," asserted 143 president Larry Frazin, as quoted by Carrie Bell in the July 3, 1999, issue of *Billboard.* "She is a throwback to the days of Joni Mitchell and Bob Dylan. And live she is completely electrifying."

From the Street to the Studio

Upon securing a contract, Hart, along with her band that by now included drummer Sergio Gonzalez, who joined in early 1994, recorded her debut record for 143/Lava/Atlantic with distinguished producers Hugh Padgham (noted for his work with pop singer Phil Collins), Mike Clink (who previously worked with rockers Guns N' Roses), and 143 founder David Foster. Released in 1995, *Immortal* made an instant impression, and the band embarked on a nine-month tour, performing in cities across the United States, on stage at Lollapalooza, as the opening act for the Scorpions in Germany, and as a headlining act at clubs in Denmark and South Africa.

However, Hart soon realized that evolving into the music business was not an easy task, for herself as well as for the other band members. "You assume when you get signed that the rest of your life will be a fantasy. Instead, I was a miserable bitch because we weren't ready," the singer admitted to Bell. "We had a buzz to live up to. I kept getting compared to people who I couldn't live up to. Then, we shipped out on Lollapalooza, which was fun but stressful.... In the beginning it was great. But we hit the road and started fighting. It was such a heavy ride that the band needed time apart. I spent a good year and a half in a state of heavy depression. I got such a severe sense of failure."

Witnessing her band fall apart after returning to Los Angeles, Hart dropped out of sight for a while to deal with the circumstances of her career. Traveling to Birmingham, Alabama, where she had met friends during the 1995 tour, Hart believed that here she could recuperate and focus on songwriting. "I didn't want to face home, so I didn't. I was partying a lot," she recalled to Bell. "But eventually I realized lots of other people in the world have it worse than me and I could either kill myself or try again. In doing that, I was ready to try again, and a lot of songwriting came about."

Hart's period of contemplation and uncertainty lasted five months, after which time she returned to Los Angeles to resume her career and complete songs for a follow-up album. "Instead of thinking what I wanted to do, I did it. I wanted to have more balls," she said to Bell. For what would become *Screamin' For My Supper,* Hart first joined forces with producer Oliver Lieber (who also worked with the Corrs) to record a handful of new tunes, including "Delicious Surprise" and the autobiographical "L.A. Song (Out of This Town)." However, the songwriter wanted to produce some of the record as well—to add something of herself rather than rely solely on a producer to interpret her songs—and to this end teamed again with Herzberg, whose past studio experience proved invaluable.

A Producer and a Performer

Together, Hart and Herzberg booked time at a studio called the Sound Chamber in North Hollywood, re-enlisted Khoury on guitar, and brought in new drummer Rocco Bidlovski. "We went in with the idea that we were going to listen to each other," stated Hart, who produced 11 tracks with Herzberg for her sophomore effort, according to her official website. "This wasn't about us being brilliant producers, because we ain't. It was about going in and just letting it fly." Unlike sessions for the first album, during which time Hart felt nervous, the studio experience the second time around was more relaxed. "I spruced up the studio with candles, rugs, and flowers," she recalled to Bell. "We drank some wine and had a big party in there for three months.... I had a ... good time, and I think it shows."

Indeed, *Screamin' for My Supper,* released in August of 1999, won rave reviews for Hart's self-inspired songs about hope and enlightenment. "I wasn't making an album for people to hear," the songwriter admitted to Taylor. "I was more making an album to heal and talk about family, friends, God, the demons, my addictions,

things that make me the happiest and things that make me the saddest. This was the first time in my life where I was willing to say just what I think and not worry so much about how people will judge me. At that point, I had nothing to lose, so why not tell the truth?" Learning to assert herself, not to mention collaborating with important tunesmiths such as Lanny Cordola, the Los Angeles-based songwriting team of Gregg Sutton and Bob Thiele, and New Jersey native Glen Burtnick (best remembered for writing Patti Smyth and Don Henley's number one hit "Sometimes Love Just Ain't Enough"), helped Hart evolve into a respected artist with *Screamin' for My Supper* and to re-ignite her promising career.

After recording her second album, Hart broadened her creative interests and started preliminary work with filmmaker Richard Donner for a biopic about the late Janis Joplin; the young singer eventually declined to act in the film, deciding that movies were not the appropriate medium for her spontaneous artistic nature. However, when invited to audition for a stage musical entitled *Love, Janis,* Hart, who had been interested in stage acting since her childhood, jumped at the opportunity and subsequently landed her first theater role. "I auditioned for Janis' sister, Laura, and the director, Randall Myler," Hart recalled for her website. "The show is great because every single word of the show is by Janis. Nothing is written by anyone else. It's all her interviews and all her letters to her family. I do some acting and sing all the songs, and another girl does the letters. It's been great. We've been getting standing ovations every performance."

Following the success of *Love, Janis,* Hart toured the United States and selected European cities with labelmate Edwin McCain. Then, beginning in October of 1999, Hart headlined the newly launched Hard Rock Café tour. The tour visited American cities where the restaurant/bar chain has franchises, including Los Angeles, New York City, Miami, Boston, and Chicago, with all proceeds benefiting VH1's Save the Music program. The initiative works to improve the quality of education in public schools by restoring and supporting music programs. Supporters of Save the Music, including Hart herself, stress the importance of music participation for America's youth. "If it weren't for music programs when I was in school, I would definitely be in jail," commented Hart, as quoted in an Atlantic Records press release.

With Hart's popularity rising since the release of her second album, her role in *Love, Janis,* and headlining at Hard Rock Cafés across the country, many wondered if the singer would receive an invitation and/or accept the opportunity to perform with the all-female Lilith Fair concert series. "I don't know," she told Sheth. "I love a lot of the artists on it. I think Sheryl [Crow]'s got a really cool voice and she writes great radio songs. Sarah [McLachlan] is such a ... talented female, it's sick. All of them are, but it's just a little light for me, to be honest with you. My favorite music is Godsmack and Tool. I'll be going to Ozzfest… You won't see me at Lilith."

Selected discography

Immortal, 143/Lava/Atlantic, 1995.
Screamin' for My Supper, 143/Lava/Atlantic, 1999.

Sources

Periodicals

Billboard, July 3, 1999, p. 15; July 19, 1999; October 2, 1999, p. 108.
Entertainment Weekly, September 10, 1999, p. 152.
HITS, August 1999.
Request, September 1999.
Songwriters Monthly, August 1999.
Spin, September 1999.

Online

Beth Hart—Official Website, http://www.bethhart.com (April 10, 2000).
"Beth Hart," *Ultimate Band List,* http://www.ubl.com/ ubl_artist.asp?artistid=5533 (April 10, 2000).

—Laura Hightower

Screamin' Jay Hawkins

Singer

© Jack Vartoogian. Reproduced by permission.

Fifties wild man Screamin' Jay Hawkins was a precursor to some of the more exotic rock and roll acts of the later part of the century. Hawkins, with his special combination of what critics unanimously called "shock and schlock" simultaneously entertained, bewildered, and bemused rock and roll fans with voodoo-evoking images of death, shrunken heads, and bone-rattling sound effects. Bigger than life, Hawkins attained legendary stature, learning to play piano and read music as a toddler, and ultimately studying opera in emulation of his idols Paul Robeson and Enrico Caruso. Ultimately Hawkins found his career niche in 1950s rock and roll where with his classically trained bass-baritone singing voice, he conjured up ghoulish images on stage and on record.

Born Jalacy J. Hawkins on July 18, 1929 in Cleveland, Ohio, Hawkins was adopted from an orphanage at 18 months of age and raised by a Native American family of the Blackfoot Tribe. Hawkins, a prodigy by many standards, developed his musical literacy very young. He easily taught himself to play the piano as a toddler, and read music adeptly by age six. At age 14 he learned to play the saxophone. Although as a teenager he took up the sport of professional boxing, winning a Golden Gloves championship in 1943, he also attended the Ohio Conservatory of Music, indulging a yearning desire to study opera. He dropped out of high school in 1944 and joined the war effort, enlisting in the United States Army. During his tour of duty he was assigned to entertain the troops as a member of the special services. He was reportedly taken as a prisoner of war following a paratroop landing off the island of Saipan.

Rock and Roll Forever

Hawkins continued to box and won a middleweight championship in Alaska in 1949, although by 1950 he had abandoned his interest in the sport and elected to pursue a musical career exclusively as a rhythm and blues pianist. Around that same time he changed his name to Screamin' Jay, a nickname inspired when an enthusiastic fan in West Virginia cried out, "Scream, baby, scream!" in reaction to the Hawkins aura. In 1952, discharged from the military, Hawkins found employment as a chauffeur for jazzman Tiny Grimes and eventually joined Grimes' band, the Rockin' Highlanders, as a vocalist and piano player. Grimes, who recorded for Atlantic Records at the time, provided Hawkins with the opportunity to record an original composition, "Why Did You Waste My Time," and miscellaneous other songs on some of the Highlanders recordings.

The highly spirited and energetic Hawkins was constantly at odds with recording executives over his rowdy compositions such as "Screamin' Blues," which conflicted with the producer's perceived audience preference for soothing, mellow sounds. Later, Hawkins played piano with Fats Domino's band in 1954 until problems arose between Domino and Hawkins. The unlikely combination of Screamin' Jay Hawkins' uninhibited style and Domino's easy beat clearly did not work, and the combination failed to congeal. Domino ultimately let Hawkins go when he showed up to perform in a loud leopard skin suit.

Hawkins debuted as a solo performer at Small's Paradise in New York City's Harlem district, and eventually moved into performing at the clubs on Atlantic City's boardwalk. He signed with Okeh Records in 1955 and recorded his first hit, "I Put A Spell On You." The song, a lamentation of unrequited love, was written in the tone of a ballad. Hawkins, however, recorded the composition in the midst of a drunken binge that resulted in his addition of bellowing, hollering, and other bizarre sound effects. He claimed, in fact, that the extent of his inebriation was such that upon hearing the taped version of the record, he had no recollection of the recording session. Amazingly, the original recording, for all its insanity, was extremely inhibited in contrast to a subsequent version of the song recorded by Columbia Records the following year. Whereas the Okeh recording failed to sell, the much rowdier Columbia version became a hit single for Hawkins in 1956. Both versions were edited for radio play, with the bone-rattling sound effects stripped out of the record-

ing, as many found the noises offensive and reminiscent of cannibalistic culture.

Elaborate Gimmicks a Trademark

It was the popular New York City disc jockey, Alan Freed, inspired by the audio antics of "I Put A Spell On You," who came up with the elaborate gimmicks that came to be associated with Hawkins' trademark performance style. Freed paid Hawkins generously to make his stage entrance in a coffin and to escalate the horror images throughout the performance. Hawkins' act evolved into a zany freak show. He was carried on stage in a blazing coffin decorated with zebra skin, often dressed as a vampire. Other assorted props and paraphernalia included his cigarette smoking skull-on-a-stick, affectionately dubbed Henry, with flames rising from his head. Electrically ignited explosions punctuated the act, and Hawkins suffered severe burns on more than one occasion during the spectacular performances.

Hawkins carried his image to extremes, scrawling lipstick advertisements in the ladies rooms along Atlantic City's Boardwalk. At times he appeared with a bone through his nose, dressed in loincloth and carrying a spear and a shield, or wearing a turban. Such antics served to increase his popularity, but led to criticism from conservative factions. The National Association for the Advancement of Colored People (NAACP) voiced displeasure, concerned that the trashy cannibalistic illusions might become associated with the African American population. On occasion Hawkins' concerts were picketed not only by mothers, complaining of the poor taste, but even by the National Coffin Association, insisting that Hawkins poked fun at the dead. Concert-goers and record-buying audiences loved the special effects regardless, and even in the absence of bone-rattling sound effects, which were stripped entirely from the United States release of "I Put A Spell On You," the recording sold over one million copies.

In the wake of such controversy, Hawkins admitted that the performances, specifically the entrance by coffin, gave him chills. Despite his compensation of $2,000 for a performance, he found himself unable to proceed with his act without the assistance of alcohol and drugs. Hawkins as result developed a substance dependency over time.

The novelty of the voodoo-inspired performances peaked in the 1950s, and by the early 1960s, the popularity of Hawkins' act waned. He continued to perform, touring largely in Europe where he maintained a following among avant-garde crowds, especially in England. He performed frequently in Asia and Hawaii and toured military bases entertaining the United States troops. Around that time Hawkins moved to

Hawaii. Among his hit records during the 1960s were "I Hear Voices" and "Feast of the Mau Mau," released in 1967. Hawkins and his scary, screaming style earned a reputation as "fun horror."

His tours in Europe, Hawaii, and New York City continued into the 1970s, and in 1974 Hawkins successfully conquered his alcohol and drug dependency. His "spell" song meanwhile experienced a revival, and was recorded by several jazz and rock stars, resulting in a substantial royalties income for Hawkins. Hawkins collaborated informally with the Rolling Stones and in 1980 performed as the opening act for the Rolling Stones at a major concert in Madison Square Garden. Also during the 1980s Hawkins worked at the Palomino Club in the San Fernando Valley where he earned a ghoulish reputation among his friends because he kept his coffin prop in his kitchen, next to the refrigerator, as a makeshift storage cabinet.

Film Career

In 1978 Hawkins appeared as himself in the feature film *American Hot Wax,* a docu-drama about the disc jockey Freed. Later, in 1984, Hawkins' "spell" recording was incorporated into the soundtrack of the cult film *Stranger Than Paradise* by Jim Jarmusch, and once again "spell" experienced a resurgence of popularity. In 1990 Hawkins appeared as an eerie and eccentric hotel manager in Jarmusch's *Mystery Train,* and the 1991 film *Rage in Harlem* included a scene in which Hawkins sang "Spell." Hawkins also played the character of Reggie in the Andres Vicente Gomez production, *Perdita Durango,* in 1997. *Perdita,* a Spanish film characterized by tongue-in-cheek humor, horrific brutality, and voodoo overtones was at once bizarre and highly typical of the persona that was Screamin' Jay Hawkins.

In 1990 Hawkins organized and starred in a band called the Fuzztones, which toured the United States and Europe. Also during the 1990s he signed with Demon Records and released some miscellaneous recordings, including "Heart Attack and Vine." He did commercials in Japan where his popularity was immense, and in the late 1990s he moved to Paris, France.

Hawkins died at the Ambroise Pave clinic in the Parisian suburb of Neuilly-sur-Seine following aneurysm surgery and subsequent massive organ failure on February 12, 2000. It was his wish that his body be cremated because he had been in "too many damn coffins already." Additionally he left instructions for his ashes to be scattered over the ocean. Hawkins, who was married an estimated six times, fathered untold numbers of children, as many as 57 by his own estimation. A search for his dozens of children was held after his death in an effort to provide closure.

Among the many who eulogized Hawkins with awe, Chris Morris of *Billboard* recalled the singer's "career of distinctive musical dementia." Critics and observers, in retrospectives of rock and roll, credited Hawkins for his unique style that predated later artists with gothic overtones including Kiss, Marilyn Manson, Alice Cooper, and England's Black Sabbath.

Selected discography

At Home with Screamin' Jay Hawkins, Epic, 1958.
Feast of the Mau Mau, 1967.
Screamin' Jay Hawkins, Philips, 1970.
Frenzy, Edsel, 1982.
Real Life, EPM, 1989.
Voodoo Jive: The Best of Screamin' Jay Hawkins, Rhino, 1990.
Black Music for White People, Bizarre, 1991.
Cow Fingers & Mosquito Pie, Epic/Legacy, 1991.
The Night & Day of Screamin' Jay, 52 Rue Est. 1992.
Portrait of a Man, Demon, 1995.
Somethin' Funny Goin' On, Bizarre, 1995.
At Last, Last Call, 1998.

Sources

Books

Contemporary Musicians, volume 8, Gale Research, Inc., 1993.

Periodicals

Associated Press, February 12, 2000.
Billboard, February 26, 2000, p. 8.
Entertainment Weekly, February 25, 2000, p. 79.
Jet, April 3, 2000, p. 18.
New Musical Express, February 26, 2000.
Reuters, March 3, 2000.
Rolling Stone, November 27, 1997, p. 30.
Variety, October 6, 1997; February 21, 2000.
Washington Post, February 15, 2000.

Online

"Screamin' Jay Hawkins," *All Music Guide*, http://hallmall.com/cgi-bin/redirect/go2.cgi?search=Screamin' JayHawkins&site=BIOGRAPHY (June 26, 2000).

—Gloria Cooksey

Ofra Haza

Singer

The first Israeli recording artist to achieve international renown, Ofra Haza was also a phenomenon in the Middle East with the wide crossover appeal of her music. Haza sang in Hebrew, Arabic, and English, and her songs bridged a cultural gap in this strife-ridden part of the world between its Jewish, Muslim, and Christian music-lovers. In 1988, she scored a massive hit with "Im Nin'alu," a Yemeni prayer set to a catchy disco beat; it sold more than a million copies and remained a dance-floor staple for months across Europe and North America. Her music, a *People* reviewer once wrote, merges "the coiling quarter-tone melodies of traditional Yemenite folk music to the crisp electronics of modern dance-pop in a remarkably satisfying fusion." Over her 20-year career, Haza became one of the most successful recording artists Israel had ever produced, and when she entered a Tel Aviv hospital in February of 2000 for an undisclosed illness, fans gathered outside to hold vigil.

Born in the late 1950s in Tel Aviv, Israel, Haza was one of nine children born to parents who had emigrated from Yemen some years before. An impoverished and for many years unstable nation at the tip of the Arabian Peninsula, at one point Yemen once banished its Jewish population to the desert; Haza's parents were then rescued by military airlift and granted entry visas into Israel. But Jews from Yemen are generally among Israel's poorest citizens; Haza and her family lived the slum area of Tel Aviv, a neighborhood known as Hatikva. Back in Yemen, however, her mother had been a professional singer, and Haza remembered her singing to her children from an early age. Haza herself began to exhibit the same musical inclination, and at the age of 12, joined a local protest theater group recently founded by a neighbor of hers, Bezalel Azoni.

Protest Lyrics

Azoni would become an integral part of Haza's singing career as a songwriting partner and manager over the years, recognizing in the teenaged Haza a unique talent. She soon emerged as one of the most gifted performers in the company—also called Hatikva—and recorded four albums with other members. She even won a national singing contest in Israel. Many of these early songs of hers were characterized by lyrics that protested the discrimination Yemeni Jews and other immigrants from Arab countries faced when in Israel.

Like all young people in Israel, male and female alike, Haza entered the Israeli army at the age of 18 for two years of compulsory service, which she spent as a secretary. Afterward, she was signed to a record label as a solo artist. Her first album featured tracks like "The Tart's Song," a musical rant in which a young woman rejects the conservative values of her society. Initially, Haza's albums achieved only nominal success, and received little or no airplay on the radio, but her defiant

For The Record . . .

B orn c. 1959; died of internal organ failure related to AIDS, February 23, 2000, in Tel Aviv, Israel; married Doron Ashkenazi, 1997.

Began career in the theater in Tel Aviv, c. 1971; appeared on four LPs with members of theater troupe Hatikva, early 1970s; released first solo LP in Israel, c. 1978.

Awards: Named best female singer in Israel in 1980, 1981, 1986.

lyrics caught on with young people, and her records began selling well. She was named Israel's best female singer in 1980, 1981, and 1986. In 1983, she was chosen to represent her country in the well-publicized Eurovision song contest. Producers there liked her voice, and invited her to record an album for European distribution.

This period of Haza's career coincided with her desire to return to the music of her particular heritage. As she later told a *New York Times* journalist, Peter Watrous, "Yemenite music has a good, special dance rhythm. Nobody can hear it and stand, without dancing." She began adapting traditional songs, adding modern percussion and electronic instrumentation, and *50 Gates of Wisdom: Yemenite Songs* was the result. Its lyrics were borrowed from a famous liturgical poem dating back to the sixteenth century. She and Azoni had simply wanted to make a record that their older, tradition-minded parents would like, and were taken by surprise when the record became an underground hit in European dance clubs. The English group Coldcut heard one of the songs, and sampled it into a remix they did for rappers Erik B. and Rakim. "That gave my song a big push," Haza told the *Wall Street Journal*'s Amy Dockser Marcus. "People that didn't know me heard my voice on a rap song." Watrous wrote of the catchy, intriguing sample in this particular song, "Paid in Full," in his *New York Times* article. "Out of left field comes a woman's wailing voice, obviously Middle Eastern in its gentle, hilly melismas," he observed. "But her voice fits in perfectly, suggesting different cultures colliding and yet having fun." Some of Haza's vocals were also remixed into another notable track from this era, "Pump Up the Volume," from M/A/R/R/S. That particular track from *50 Gates of Wisdom*, "Im Nin'alu, (If the Gates of Heaven Closed)" was remixed and released as a single in the United States in 1987. It went on to sell a million copies worldwide.

Success Abroad

Haza's emergence onto a more global stage coincided with the rise of a new genre, which quickly came to be tagged "world beat." Signed to Sire Records, Haza recorded *Shaday*, released in 1988. Many of its tracks were based on another famous liturgical poem, the Song of Solomon. It would become her most successful album to date, selling a million copies globally with its mix of songs in Hebrew and English. A review by Michael Small in *People*, however, faulted the work for the overly sentimental balladry in its English tracks. "It's too bad Haza doesn't rise above musical clichés more often because her sparkly clear voice, sometimes resembling Barbra Streisand's, seems able to handle something more challenging," opined Small.

Haza toured the United States in 1988, and for a time, lived in Los Angeles. In 1990, she released *Desert Wind*, her first full English-language album. Yet as she told the *Wall Street Journal*'s Marcus, "it may be in English, but it's still my message." One track, "Fatamorgana," was a homage to her parents' tragic experiences in Yemen years before. The song contains a chant in Arabic, courtesy of her mother, who sang it into the telephone for Haza from Israel while the album was being made. The song won particular praise from Marcus. "Haza's lilting contralto evokes the rhythm of her people's march into desert exile, the heat, the mirages, the sadness," observed the *Wall Street Journal* writer.

Grammy Nomination

Around this time, Haza also made a video that aired on the music-video network MTV, making her the first Israeli artist on the channel. Her 1992 album, *Kirya*, again featured songs in Hebrew, Arabic, and English, and was produced by acclaimed studio genius Don Was; rock stalwarts Lou Reed and Iggy Pop made guest appearances for Haza. The album took its title from the ancient nickname for the holy city of Jerusalem, and Haza had hoped to make a record that could serve as a reminder that peace in the Middle East was long overdue. "So many of our sons have to die every day because of you," she sang in the title track. The album was nominated for a Grammy award in the World Music category.

By the mid-1990s, Haza was a bona-fide celebrity in the Middle East. Both Israeli and Palestinian teens bought her records, and she was hailed as a positive role model. After a 1993 peace accord between Palestine and Israel—who had fought bitterly for decades over territory that both considered their ancient homelands—the signers of the pact were awarded the Nobel Prize for peace. One of the three recipients, Israeli Prime Minister Yitzhak Rabin, invited Haza to perform at the ceremony in Oslo, Norway. A year later, in 1995, Haza also sang at the memorial service for Rabin after he was assassinated.

In 1998, Haza recorded the theme song, "Deliver Us," to the 1998 Disney animated film, the *Prince of Egypt*, as the voice of Moses's mother. The following year, she appeared on a multilingual compilation of holy songs, *The Prayer Cycle: Music for the Century by Jonathan Elias*, that also featured Alanis Morissette and Perry Farrell. She sang a duet on it with Pakistani singer Nusrat Fateh Ali Khan.

Tragic Death

Haza was a beloved public figure in Israel, so when she checked in to Tel Aviv's Tel Hashomer hospital on February 10, 2000, there was much speculation about the cause. Fans stood outside the hospital in a round-the-clock vigil, and it was suspected that the 41-year-old singer was suffering from cancer. She died on February 23 of internal organ failure. As testament to her importance, even the current Israeli Prime Minister, Ehud Barak, made an official announcement. "I had the honor of knowing Ofra and was impressed by her shining personality and her great talent," Barak said, according to *Billboard* magazine, on the night that Haza died. "Her contribution to Israeli culture was great, and the honor she brought this country will never be forgotten."

A few days later, however, a Tel Aviv newspaper revealed that Haza had been suffering from Acquired Immune Deficiency Syndrome (AIDS). *Ha'aretz*, the paper, wrote about the anger of some hospital workers because Haza had tried to keep the nature of her illness a secret; they worried that they had been exposed to HIV-positive blood. Haza had been adamant about preserving the confidentiality of her medical records, even after her death. The *Ha'aretz* story ignited a minor controversy over patients' rights in Israel, and many felt that the privacy of the singer—who likely wished to spare her conservative Yemenite family the reason behind her fatal illness—had been needlessly violated. As the British medical journal *Lancet* explained, complaints that hospital employees may have been at risk of infection were dubious, since Tel Hashomer "follows orders from the [Israeli] Health Ministry to treat all patients as if they are carriers of an infectious disease unless proven otherwise." The newspaper, however, defended itself against charges of sensationalism. "Ofra Haza was a public figure and to a certain extent public property in her life," *Ha'aretz*'s managing editor, Yoel Esteron, told *New York Times* writer Deborah Sontag. "In her death it is impossible to leave this chapter in darkness. We are talking about a human disease like any other, and there is no reason to demonize it."

Selected discography

50 Gates of Wisdom: Yemenite Songs, Shanachie, 1988.
Shaday, Sire, 1988.
Desert Wind, Sire, 1989.
Kirya, Shanachie, 1992.
Yemenite Songs, Cleopatra, 1998.
(With others) *The Prince of Egypt* (soundtrack), DreamWorks, 1998.
(With others) *The Prayer Cycle: Music for the Century by Jonathan Elias*, Sony Classical, 1999.

Sources

Billboard, March 11, 2000, p. 4.
Ha'aretz (Tel Aviv), February 28, 2000.
Lancet, March 18, 2000, p. 998.
New York Times, March 18, 1988, pp. C1, C25; February 24, 2000, p. A22; February 29, 2000.
People, February 6, 1989, p. 25; October 19, 1992, p. 21.
Rolling Stone, March 22, 1990; April 1, 1999.
Wall Street Journal, February 15, 1990, p. A12.

—*Carol Brennan*

Charles Ives

Composer

Charles Ives was arguably the first and greatest American composer. Although aware of the work of European composers such as Schubert, Brahms, and Schumann, Ives broke with their traditional style. He instead used distinctively American materials in his works. He utilized New England hymns, folk tunes, military marches and popular songs of the day to evoke places in the United States, such as Central Park and Concord, Massachusetts, and typical American holidays, such as Thanksgiving, Decoration Day and the Fourth of July. Far from writing comfortable, homespun music, however, Ives' work ranks among the most advanced and experimental of the twentieth century, anticipating by years innovations eventually introduced by giants like Stravinsky, Schoenberg, Debussy, and Darius Milhaud.

Charles Ives began his musical education at an early age. His father, George E. Ives, was also a musician. He was the youngest bandmaster to serve in the Union Army during the Civil War, and General Grant reportedly told President Abraham Lincoln that Ives' band was also the best in the Army. When Charles was five years old, George started a comprehensive musical instruction that ranged from piano, organ, and cornet, to theory, ear training, composition, orchestration, and sight reading. George Ives, like his son later, was also interested in experimenting with music, for example using more than one key or more than one rhythm simultaneously. He encouraged these interests in Charles. He had his son play a melody in one key while he accompanied it in a completely different one; similarly he had Charles play two melodies in different keys on the piano simultaneously. According to *Composers Since 1900,* the elder Ives told his son, "you've got to learn to stretch your ears."

When Charles was 13 years old he took a job as the organist at St. Thomas Church in Danbury, Connecticut. Not long after, he composed his first piece, *Holiday Quick Step*, which was performed by his father's band. He was a seemingly talented football and baseball player while in high school, but he gave up athletics when he entered Yale University because his father realized his grades would suffer otherwise. Ives nonetheless graduated from college in 1898 with barely passing grades, presumably because he had devoted himself so single-mindedly to music. While at Yale, he composed some 80 pieces, including work for organ, songs, and a string quartet. He continued to study composition and organ at the same time. Ives' compositions were not warmly received by his teachers at Yale, though. They criticized his already widespread use of unresolved dissonance.

After graduating from college, Ives was faced with the question how he should support himself. His father had believed Charles had such great talent he could become a famous pianist. His near pathological shyness prevented him from taking up a life of public perfor-

Born on October 20, 1874, in Danbury, CT; died on May 19, 1954, in New York City, NY; married Harmony Twichell. Education: Yale University, bachelor of arts degree.

Accepted job as organist at St. Thomas Church, Danbury, CT, 1887; composed first piece, *Holiday Quick Step,* 1888; composed first song, "Slow March," 1888; composed first choral composition, *Psalm 67,* 1898; composed Second Symphony, 1897-1901; composed *From the Steeples and Mountains,* 1901; composed Third Symphony, 1901-03; composed *New England Holidays,* 1904-13; co-founded his own insurance company, Ives and Company, 1906; composed *Central Park in the Dark,* 1907; composed *The Unanswered Question,* 1908; Ives and Company became Ives and Myrick, 1909; composed Piano Sonata No.2, *Concord,* 1909-15; composed Fourth Symphony, 1910-16; performed Third Symphony for the first time, 1946; published Piano Sonata No.2 himself, 1919; published *114 Songs,* 1922; gave first performance of Second Symphony, 1951; gave debut performance of both *From the Steeples and Mountains* and Fourth Symphony, 1965.

Awards: Pulitzer Prize in music for Third Symphony, 1947.

mance, however. Instead, he moved to New York City with friends and took a job clerking at an insurance company while continuing to play organ at the Central Presbyterian Church in Manhattan.

In 1901 he composed *From the Steeples and Mountains,* his most radical piece yet. It used two groups of bells, four trumpets and four trombones. The bells, tuned in different keys, were meant to suggest bells tolling from different church towers. The effect was discordant, polytonal, and eerie. The work would not be premiered until the New York Philharmonic played it in July of 1965, more than eleven years after Ives' death. Also in 1901 Ives finally completed his Second Symphony which he had been working on for more than four years. *Composers Since 1900* called Ives' Second Symphony the composer's "first significant attempt to make use of authentic American materials." It quotes a number of tunes popular at the time,

including "Columbia, the Gem of the Ocean," "America the Beautiful," and the Stephen Foster songs "Old Black Joe," and " Camptown Races." The symphony was not performed until 1951.

Ives left the Mutual Insurance Company in 1906 to form his own insurance firm, Ives and Company, which three years later became Ives and Myrick. The company did very well, eventually growing into one of the largest agencies of its kind in the country. Ives was senior partner of the firm and was quite proud of his business success, feeling that experience contributed something important to the music he was composing. "My business experience revealed life to me in many aspects that I otherwise might have missed," he is quoted in *Composers Since 1900.* "I have experienced a great fullness of life in business. The fabric of existence weaves itself whole."

In June of 1908, he married Harmony Twichell, and they eventually adopted a daughter. The family settled in New York, and Ives spent weekdays working in his insurance company, and evenings, weekends and holidays composing. Mrs. Ives, quoted in *Composers Since 1900,* said "He could hardly wait for dinner to be over, and he was at the piano. Often he went to bed at 2 or 3 a.m." Music was everything in his life. He never owned a radio or a phonograph. He did not read newspapers. He did not attend concerts, not even the few dedicated to his own music. He avoided most social functions. Fortunately, his wife supported him completely. "Mrs. Ives," he is quoted in *American Composers,* "never once said or suggested or looked or thought that there must be something wrong with me. She never said, 'Now why don't you write something nice, the way they like it?' Never. She urged me on my way to be myself and gave me her confidence."

Ives wrote his greatest works between 1904 and 1920. *Three Places in New England,* Ives' first orchestral piece to be performed, made its debut in 1931 in a version for chamber orchestra, though its original scoring for full orchestra was not heard until 1974. *New England Holidays,* completed between 1904 and 1913, is a kind of musical memoir by Ives, intended to conjure up, through snatches of familiar melodies, his boyhood in New England on holidays like the Washington's Birthday, Decoration Day, the Fourth of July, Thanksgiving Day, and Forefather's Day. 1907's *Central Park in the Dark* is "a picture of sounds of nature and happenings that men would hear ... when sitting on a bench in Central Park on a hot summer night," Ives is quoted in *American Composers*. Again, the instrumentation and collage of melodies suggested the sounds surrounding a visitor in the park.

Ives wrote his Piano Sonata No. 2, *Concord,* between 1909 and 1915. Like many other Ives pieces, the sonata is both deeply philosophical in nature and intended to conjure his native New England. The four movements are entitled "Hawthorne," "Emerson," "The Alcotts," and "Thoreau," all writers from Concord, Massachusetts. The piece includes some of Ives' boldest technical experiments, such as a portion of "Hawthorne" that calls for the pianist to play a cluster of notes using a wooden ruler. Lawrence Gilman, writing in the *New York Herald Tribune* at the time of the piece's debut in 1939, called the sonata "the greatest music composed by an American, and the most deeply and essentially American in pulse and implication."

Ives' final symphony, the Fourth Symphony, was completed in 1916 but did not premiere until Leopold Stokowski conducted a performance by the American Symphony Orchestra in 1965. Part of the reason was the piece's complicated rhythms—27 different rhythms are heard at the same time in one section. Another is the size of the ensemble called for by Ives. Besides a greatly expanded orchestra, the symphony is written for a huge percussion section, a chorus, and a brass band. Between the sheer size of the group of musicians and the technical demands placed on them, three conductors are called for. Afterward Stokowski called the Fourth Symphony the most difficult piece of music he had ever played.

Few of Ives compositions were performed during his own lifetime, in part because he made no effort to have them published. Once a work was complete, he seemed satisfied to file it away and move on to the next one. He published the Piano Sonata No. 2 *Concord*, himself in 1919, distributing it among friends, and in 1922 paid for the publication of an anthology of his songs, entitled *114 Songs*. As a consequence, he remained largely unknown, except among a group of younger composers interested in the innovations he pioneered. In a tantalizing "what if," Gustav Mahler was said to have discovered a score of Ives' Fourth Symphony which he copied out and was taking back to Vienna where he planned to perform it. Unfortunately, Mahler's death put an end to the plan.

In 1918 Ives suffered a heart attack. By 1928 diabetes and nervous trembling in his hands which made transcription impossible, ended his composing. He attempted some pieces in the mid-1920s, but by 1926 his confidence was unalterably shaken. His wife, quoted in the *New Grove Dictionary of Music and Musicians*, related "he came downstairs one day with tears in his eyes and said he couldn't seem to compose any more—nothing went well—nothing sounded right." He never composed again. After that, his music slowly attracted more and more attention, championed by composers such as Henry Cowell and Aaron Copland. Copland and Hubert Linscott gave a performance of Ives songs in 1932 that attracted a good deal of attention and helped make Ives' name known among young composers. In 1947 Ives was awarded a Pulitzer Prize for his Third Symphony. In 1951 Leonard Bernstein gave the premier performance of the Second Symphony.

But the shy Ives did not emerge from his home to hear his music or to accept the honors he was given. He even declined Bernstein's offer of a private performance by the New York Philharmonic. On May 19, 1954, while recovering from a minor operation, Ives suffered a stroke and died.

Selected works

First Symphony, 1895-98.
Second Symphony, 1900-02.
From the Steeples and the Mountains, 1901.
New England Holidays, 1903-14.
Three Places in New England, 1903-1914.
Third Symphony, *The Camp Meeting*, 1904.
Fourth Symphony, 1909-16.
Piano Sonata No. 2, *Concord*, 1909-15.
Central Park in the Dark, 1907.
The Unanswered Question, 1908.
114 Songs, 1922.

Sources

Books

Ewen, David, *American Composers*, 1982.
Ewen, David, *Composers Since 1900,* 1969.
Stadie, Stanley, *New Grove Dictionary of Music and Musicians*, 1980.
Staines, Joe and Jonathan Buckley, editors, *Classical Music: The Rough Guide.*

Online

"Charles Ives," *All Classical Guide*, http://allclassical.com/cg/x.dll?UID=10:28:32¦&p=acg&sql= 1:7494~D[|7]257#WORKS (June 27, 2000).

—*Gerald E. Brennan*

Lord Kitchener

Singer, composer

Lord Kitchener was the calypso name of Trinidad native Aldwyn Roberts. Kitchener was also known as the Grandmaster of Calypso and the Road March King. Freewheeling and lighthearted, the singer and composer emoted his vitality through a vast repertoire of songs, largely in celebration of life in the Caribbean islands. After moving to Britain for some years following World War II, Kitchener perpetuated the everyday sentiments of life through his music and memorialized his experiences as a Caribbean native transplanted to England. Throughout his sojourn abroad, he continued to send his songs home to Trinidad, where his many fans received them eagerly as mementos from their idol. Upon his return to Trinidad in 1963, he received a hero's welcome and continued to inspire his fellow countrymen with the brusque tone and sometimes gruff wit that characterized his songs, more than 1,000 in all, most of them about the sights and sounds of his everyday life. Throughout his lifetime and even after his death in 2000 at age 77, Kitchener was highly esteemed by his fellow countrymen and by the calypso community worldwide.

Kitchener was born Aldwyn Roberts, in Arima, Trinidad on April 18, 1922. He was one of six siblings, the offspring of a blacksmith. After attending school, Kitchener entered his father's trade, but rapidly lost interest in smithing. Instead Kitchener, who had been writing songs since the age of five, began singing nickel sessions in the bamboo tents of his hometown at age 16. The carnival celebrations and calypso tradition were rooted deeply into the the culture of the Caribbean, and the tent venues comprised an integral part of the Trinidad carnival scene. Whenever the teenager performed, audiences were highly receptive to his smooth and easy voice.

His effortless singing style was in fact uncanny, given that he suffered from a severe speech impediment as a child and never was able to overcome the debility altogether. Remarkably, the deficiency never surfaced in his singing, and he performed with a pleasant voice and with near-perfect diction. His popular performances at carnival time led eventually to an invitation to sing at the Victory calypso tent in Port of Spain, the capital city of Trinidad. There Kitchener, still known as Aldwyn Roberts, performed in the company of formidable calypso stars including Atilla the Hun, Roaring Lion, and Growing Tiger, as the calypso singers called themselves. Over time his love of singing developed into a serious vocation. Following one particularly successful concert at the Victory tent in 1944, the 21-year-old Roberts adopted a calypso pseudonym, in the style of his contemporaries. He selected the name Lord Kitchener in tribute to Horatio Kitchener (1850-1916), a British hero from the Boer War, whose memory was revered by the population of Trinidad.

By 1946, Kitchener's popularity was firmly established in Trinidad where through the lyrics of his songs he

For The Record . . .

Born Aldwyn Roberts on April 18, 1922, in Arima, Trinidad; one of six siblings; adopted the name of Lord Kitchener, 1944; married, 1953; died on February 11, 2000, in Trinidad.

Performed at carnivals' tents, Arima and Port of Spain, Trinidad, 1938-1947; immigrated to England, 1948; EMI Records (Melodisc), 1950s; returned to Trinidad, 1962.

Awards: Trinidad Carnival Road March King, 1946, 1947, 1954, 1963-68, 1970-73, 1975-76.

kept alive the memories of island life during the years of the Second World War. In 1945, following V-E Day in May and V-J Day in August, Kitchener took particular inspiration from the din of the celebratory street music created by young boys pounding on inverted steel containers. Although steelband music, as the phenomenon was called, was officially banned in Trinidad because of its disruptive nature, Kitchener glorified the young steelband musicians through his songs like "Yes, I Heard the Beat of a Steelband." Likewise he mimicked the sound of the steel drums with lyrics such as, "Jumbem bajubalam jumbem," and he immortalized a particular street musician named Zigilee, calling him the "leader of the ping-pong."

On one occasion, following a lavish celebration among the Chinese population in Port of Spain in October of 1945 to celebrate the bombing of Hiroshima and the subsequent defeat of the Japanese forces, Kitchener wrote his "Lai Fook Lee" tune for the carnival of 1946. That song earned the distinction as the Road March of the carnival that year—the Road March being an honor designating the most popular song among the steelband musicians during the carnival season. Kitchener's songs earned such popularity among the steelband musicians that the winners of 19 out of 37 consecutive Panorama steelband competitions performed tunes by Kitchener. Thus he contributed to popularize the raucous steelband musical style and bring its performers to artistic legitimacy.

Indeed the underground character of calypso music preceded the innovation of steeldrums, when calypso as a musical form originated as a belligerent practice during the era of slavery in the West Indies. The musical genre, although native to Trinidad, is founded in the African kaiso tradition and gained prominence among African slaves who were prohibited from speaking to each other while they toiled in the fields. In retaliation, the slaves devised a set of musical rhythms with spoken accompaniment whereby they expressed their sentiments to each other in song, thus communicating without violating the rules of their masters and escaping retribution. As a result the lyrics to Calypso music are characteristically nonsensical, intensely repetitive, and oftentimes political in nature.

During the war years, many calypso singers fled the political climate of Trinidad, with some seeking refuge in England in search of artistic freedom and economic fortune. Kitchener in the late 1940s—having performed already in Aruba, Curaçao, and Jamaica—immigrated to England. He secured passage on a ship called the Empire Windrush with others of his peers, including Atilla, Tiger, and Lion. The boat sailed into Tilbury, arriving in June of 1948, where upon its arrival Kitchener was filmed on a newsreel, dressed in the natty double-breasted suit and hat that became his trademark over the years. On that occasion he sang and strummed the guitar, performing one of his own tunes, called "England is the Place for Me." While in England he composed many songs depicting his life as an immigrant from the Caribbean living in England.

Among the contemporaries of Lord Kitchener during his years in England was Egbert Moore (Lord Beginner). Together they recorded the first professional calypso tapes in history at the EMI Abbey Lane studio in London in 1950. The recording sessions between Kitchener and Moore continued for many years afterward, and the finished products were released on Melodisc. Additionally, Kitchener collaborated freely with others of his exiled colleagues, including Fitzroy Coleman, Rupert Nurse, Shake Keane, and Clarrie Weir. Kitchener's songs by far were intended for accompaniment by steelband music, and while abroad he continued to export his records home to Trinidad where his friends and followers comprised an eager and receptive audience, and the hum of his voice became a familiar sound on Trinidad radio. After some years, the demise of the Melodisc record label resulted in the unfortunate loss to history of the Kitchener master tapes, including the Kitchener classic "Underground Train" that was taped during the original recording session in 1950.

Kitchener, unmistakable for his impeccable diction, experienced great popularity while in England. Through an association with an impresario, named Emile Chalet, Kitchener's performance venues evolved from small pubs around London where he regularly attracted substantial audiences, eventually to a club of his own in Manchester. The British audiences received him warmly, and in 1953 he married an Englishwoman, yet he never came to accept England as his home. Regardless, his following extended even to the British royal family, and he performed at the coronation of Her Royal Highness Queen Elizabeth II.

The queen's sister, Princess Margaret, reportedly purchased 100 copies of his recording of "Ah, Bernice!"

During his sojourn in England, Kitchener cherished fond thoughts of his homeland. Continually he sent his songs back to the people of Trinidad as a show of solidarity, and they never forgot him. Despite his soaring popularity in England, a phenomenon called rock and roll overtook Britain during the 1960s, and Kitchener opted to return to the West Indies to mingle once more with his fellow countrymen, the people he loved. Huge crowds and immense festivity accompanied his return to the Caribbean in 1962. His popularity had never waned during his absence, and he remained a hero over the course of the ensuing years. His carnival tunes repeatedly earned the distinction of Road March songs—including in 1954 while he lived in England. Eventually he earned the nickname of the Road March King. His "The Road Make to Walk on Carnival Day" won in 1963, and "Mama This Is Mas" won in 1964. "My Pussin'" won in 1965. Kitchener won again in 1967, 1968, and 1970 and then wrote both of the top two songs in 1971, winning the Road March title that year with "Mas In Madison Square Garden." Kitchener's 1975 Road March, "Tribute to (Winston) Spree Simon," told the tale of the nine-year-old youth who in 1939 devised a technique to make distinguishable notes on the pans used by steelbands. "Winston Spree" was Kitchener's final Road March.

In 1976, he stepped aside voluntarily, simultaneously encouraging a new generation of younger musicians and composers to assume the position of honor that he held for so many years. He encouraged the musicians who touted a new dance rhythm, called soca, and brought newcomers into the Trinidad musical traditions and to the attention of the Trinidad audience and encouraged women to represent their viewpoints by creating original calypso works along with the men. Even as Kitchener shed the spotlight, he continued to compose. His songs remained extremely popular and he continued to win the annual Panorama prize, winning again in 1976 and three times during the 1980s: in 1982, 1984, and 1985.

During the 1970s, Kitchener built an expansive home for himself in Diego Martin outside Port of Spain. He lived his later years on the estate, which he called Rain-O-Rama after one of his popular tunes. There Kitchener enjoyed a healthy lifestyle and simple pleasures along with his family. His greatest indulgence was in his enjoyment of racing, and he owned a stable of horses. He was known to his friends as Bing, and it was his personal philosophy to always look forward to the future, never looking back. He was in fact known to forget the words and melodies to his compositions virtually immediately after performing each tune for the first time.

In 1994, he was honored with a postage stamp bearing his image. That same year marked the erection of a seven-foot statue of Kitchener by Pat Chu Foon. The work, called "Grandmaster of Calypso," stands at the entrance to St. James, outside Port of Spain. In 1997, Kitchener, still active, wrote "Guitar Pan," and in 2000 he wrote his final song, "Pan Birthday."

Kitchener, who suffered from bone marrow cancer, died on February 11, 2000 in Trinidad, following kidney failure. On two occasions he was under consideration for a Trinity Cross of Trinidad & Tobago, and the issue had yet to be put to rest upon the occasion of his death.

Selected discography

Singles

"Green Fig Man," 1944.
"The Underground Train," EMI, 1950.
"Mama Look a Band Passing," Road March, 1954.
"The Road Made to Walk on Carnival Day", Road March, 1963.
"Mama This Is Mas," Road March, 1964.
"My Pussin'," Road March, 1965.
"Mas in Madison Square Garden," Road March, 1971.
"Tribute to (Winston) Spree Simon," Road March, 1975.

Albums

'67 Kitch, RCA, 1967.
Kitchener Goes Soca, Charlie's, 1981.
Roots of Soca, Charlie's, 1984.
Master At Work, Kalico, 1985.
Honey in the Kitchen, Wads Music, 1992.
Still Escalating, JW Prod, 1994.

Sources

Periodicals

Daily Telegraph (London), February 15, 2000.
New Musical Express, February 26, 2000.

Online

"Kitchener: Life is a Calypso," Media and Editorial Projects Ltd., revised August 12, 1999, http://caribbeanbeat.com /archive /kitchener.html (May 19, 2000).
"Lord Kitchener," *Express*, February 23, 2000, http://www .nalis.gov.tt/history/History_LORDKITCHENER_PeopleOfThe Century.htm (May 19, 2000).

—Gloria Cooksey

Femi Kuti

Singer, saxophonist, bandleader

© Jack Vartoogian. Reproduced by permission.

Growing up the son of a famous father can be a mixed blessing, and Femi Kuti, the son of Nigerian Afrobeat pioneer Fela Kuti, who died of an AIDS-related illness in 1997, spent much of his life in his father's considerable shadow. By the mid- to late-1990s, however, the younger Kuti finally emerged in his own right as one of Africa's most dynamic performers, soon gaining a solid following in Western Europe to match his domestic audience in Nigeria. His most recent album recorded with his 18-piece band Positive Force entitled *Shoki Shoki*—released in Europe by the French record label Barclay in 1997 and on MCA Records in the United States in 2000—swirled together African funk and dance rhythms to create a bold, brass-driven, and slick sound all his own.

"I'm not Fela," he told *Boston Globe* correspondent Paul Robicheau. "Nobody can ever get Fela's flavor again. But if you're sincere with yourself, you can get your own flavor, and you can be known, or people will love you for your own flavor." And with *Shoki Shoki,* Kuti flavored his sound with touches of hip-hop—with a remix by the Roots of his anthemic "Blackman Know Yourself"—techno, and even jazz. "You can't avoid listening to Coltrane, Charlie Parker, and everybody like that… The moment you listen to anything, you are automatically influenced, subconsciously or consciously. I listen to everything. I'm going to start going crazy for classical music, to show you how crazy my mind works sometimes. I heard some classical tune on the plane, and it sounded so cool."

Kuti's emergence as a recording and performance artist who mixed music of the past with that of the present unexpectedly resulted in a renewed interest in his father's music, and he worked steadily not only to fuel his own career, but also to work with Barclay on a massive reissue program of the vast Fela Kuti catalog. On February 1, 2000, MCA issued *The Best of Fela Anikulapo-Kuti,* a two-CD compilation of classic Fela material. Then, later that month and into March and April, the label released a total of ten double-album packages comprising 20 albums recorded by the Afrobeat legend between 1970 and 1981, collections previously released in 1999 by Barclay in France and Talkin' Loud in the United Kingdom. "Those reissues have made a whole new generation of sample madness," the Roots' beat expert, Ahmir Thompson, told Vivien Goldman in *Spin.* "The race to use the tracks has started already: Q-Tip, Lauryn [Hill], D'Angelo, Black Star, Mos Def, and myself. Afrobeat is the next crop of funk to get appetized."

Kuti's work, like the music of his father, draws from his African roots, but steps beyond with the addition of more contemporary grooves, resulting in Afrobeat crossing over to the dance floors of London, Paris, and other major cities across Europe and America. "When Fela died, something told me I had to fill his space," Kuti, who joined his father's band while still in his teens, told *Billboard* in 1999. "I am destined to play Afrobeat because it is part of who I am and where I come from. But I love rock, rap, house and jungle. I want to introduce those sounds into my music. I don't believe in barriers, I want to take Afrobeat into the future."

Forged an Individual Identity

Born in 1963, Kuti was destined to follow in his Fela's footsteps, though he wanted to forge an individual identity rather than imitate his father. He picked up the saxophone at the age of 16, and joined his father's band at the age of 18, perhaps as the only way to bond with the elder Kuti, held in awe by many Africans for simultaneously wedding 27 women—many of whom danced for his band—and fathering dozens of children. One of his wives was a British-born pianist of African American, Native American, English, and Nigerian descent named Remi, mother of Kuti and his sisters Yeni and the late Sola. However, Kuti, unlike Fela, remained a one-wife man. "I have my wife Funke in the band with me," he revealed to Goldman, an arrangement "which controls my sexual powers and makes sure I'm not a maniac on the streets." Kuti also swore off smoking cigarettes and using marijuana as part of a spiritual cleansing in 1984, both habits his father enjoyed throughout his lifetime.

In addition to remaining monogamous and smoke-free, Kuti differed from his father in other ways as well. Fela Kuti, born in 1938 in Abeokuta, Nigeria, and educated at Trinity College of Music in London, helped revolutionize the politics as well as the music of his homeland. In 1969, the saxophonist/keyboardist/vocalist brought a band to Los Angeles, where he evolved a new style, later dubbed Afrobeat, that fused radical black politics, African rhythms, and American jazz, soul, and funk. When he returned to Nigeria in 1973, Fela opened the famed Shrine club in the town of Lagos, recording prolifically there with his 20-plus member group Africa 70 (later named Egypt 80). Like reggae legend Bob Marley in Jamaica, Fela became a voice for his country's poor and disenfranchised, and an outspoken critic of Nigeria's repressive political regime. His songs regularly provoked legal harassment, imprisonments, and police beatings, which only fueled further inflammatory recordings and punitive actions by the authorities in power. In 1977, his opposition to the government culminated when soldiers sacked his Lagos compound, a sort of state-within-a state he had formed known as Kalakuta Republic.

Kuti, by comparison, chose a less contentious, agenda-free direction. For example, his single "Beng Beng Beng" was banned in Nigeria not for its political message, but instead for its sexual explicitness. And while *Shoki Shoki* features politically informed songs such as "Truth Don Die," "Blackman Know Yourself," and "What Will Tomorrow Bring," the album adapts a significantly tempered version of Fela's intense anti-establishment stance. Willing to work within the system to accomplish his objectives, in 1998 Kuti formed an organization called M.A.S.S.—Movement Against Second Slavery—a student-focused activist group promoting Pan-Africanism and the preservation of African culture.

"I'm trying to find a way for people to really understand what is going on in Africa, for our corrupt leaders to look back and see that they are not helping Africa by what they're doing," he said in an interview with Richard Harrington of the *Washington Post*. "There's no way the masses are going to get them out of power except by violence and yet there is no way to be successful because they have the arms. We know that a revolution will not help Africa, that another war will not help Africa, so how do we get out of this mess we're in? We have to find another way of making [the leaders] understand that everything is wrong. So I'm just brainstorming with M.A.S.S."

And while his father's free-form tracks could thunder on for an hour or more, Kuti prefers catchy rhythms that span a more moderate length of time. "I used to get bored playing long songs," he said to Goldman. "The problem was cutting them down and not having a problem at home!" he mused, imitating his father: "'So! You're not playing Afrobeat anymore!' I still wanted to be a part of my father, y'understand, but doing *Femi Anikulapo-Kuti*."

Rooted in His Father's Tradition

Undeniably, father and son had much in common. Although Kuti, the son of an almost regal figure, sometimes revolted against his father with an aristocratic haughtiness of sorts, their relationship mellowed over the years, and both men loved and felt intensely proud of one another. However, Fela could seem overbearing at times and detested disobedience. Moreover, while the elder bandleader supported his son's solo career, he nonetheless made Kuti earn his position in the band, with little encouragement besides his often brutal criticism.

Regardless of Fela's methods, Kuti was poised to take over where his father left off and had been laying the groundwork for his own global success for nearly two decades. In 1984, after his father and Fela's then-manager, Pascal Imbert, served jail time for trumped-up currency charges, Kuti, then just 21, ran the Shrine, took over Egypt 80, and became an enthusiastic and forceful frontman. During a later stretch in prison, Kuti ran the club so well that Fela wanted his son to stay on after his release, but the younger musician refused. Although the men did not speak for a good five years after he declined the offer, Kuti, who had by now developed far too musically and wanted to concentrate on his own career, insisted that it was one of the best decisions he ever made. He went on to record several records for European labels, including a self-titled album released by Motown Records—during the label's brief foray into world music—in the United States in 1995.

Finally, in the mid-1990s, the two reconciled after a chance meeting at the Lagos club, but some family members kept the feud alive even after Fela's death. Some band members, for instance, refused to play with Kuti because he was not full-blooded African. "I nearly cried," Kuti admitted to Goldman, recalling the band's reaction, who continued to play Fela's old repertoire in Lagos clubs with Kuti's half-brother Seun as the frontman. Nonetheless, Kuti kept in mind his own mission. "I'm fighting for my people, I'm fighting for the world," he continued. "I believe the sin in life is not to try."

Kuti as a Father

When not touring with his band throughout the world, Kuti—who draws wild cheers from women as he takes off his shirt on stage—lives in Lagos with his wife, son, sister, mother, grandmother, and various children in a large family home in the working-class neighborhood of Ikeja. The Afrobeat star admits that when he discovered that his son Omrinmade, born in 1995, had musical gifts as well, he was not entirely thrilled. On the one hand, he could imagine the thrill of one day taking the youngster on the road with him, keeping in the family tradition. "But I don't want to make the mistake some people make," Kuti, who felt the pressure growing up with his father's band, said in an interview with *Los Angeles Times* writer Steve Hochman. "He should go to school, be with friends. He has to experience life, make mistakes, have his successes. Maybe he wants to do football in school, play tennis. He needs that and needs to just be happy."

Selected discography

Femi Kuti, Motown, 1995.
Shoki Shoki, MCA, 2000.

Sources

Periodicals

Billboard, August 14, 1999; January 8, 2000.
Boston Globe, July 7, 1995; March 25, 2000.
Los Angeles Times, April 2, 2000.
Maclean's, May 1, 2000, p. 68.
New York Times, September 20, 1999.
Rolling Stone, March 2, 2000.
Spin, February 2000, pp. 80-84.
Village Voice, March 28, 2000.
Washington Post, March 17, 2000; March 25, 2000.

Online

Femi Kuti, http://www.mcarecords.com/artists/artist.asp?artistid=174 (May 13, 2000).

—Laura Hightower

Lambchop

Country, soul-rock band

Since their formation in 1993, Nashville outcasts Lambchop have been considered the strangest country-inspired outfit, with the arguable exception of Palace, to play a brand of country or country-rock music that aims for the hearts of alternative-rock listeners. But while most mid-1990s alternative country-rockers—namely Son Volt, Wilco, Freakwater, and Richard Buckner—draw directly from the roots of country music, Lambchop took a different route. Far from the back-to-basics blueprint of the increasingly popular alternative-country sub-genre, Lambchop by comparison made the smooth and sleepy Nashville style central to their songs. Nonetheless, one won't find Lambchop sharing the stage with Music Row big shots—they instead toured regularly with alternative band Yo La Tengo and acoustic-folk singer/songwriter Vic Chesnutt—and it seems doubtful that Garth Brooks fans would take to Lambchop's sly tales of suicide, death, aging, alcoholism, deception, or faceless souls trying to survive another mundane day. Consider these lines from "The Old Gold Shoe," a track off 1999's *Nixon:* "Like painful Southern bliss the kids out in the street/poured upon like caramel take their toys and break them/and garnished with some crushed pecans look at them, then walk away."

At Lambchop's forefront stands singer/guitarist Kurt Wagner, the one mainstay member who writes nearly all of the band's material and delivers his songs in warm, gentle tones that make no effort to conceal the emotional heart of the matter at hand, whether it be one of bitterness, lust, or spite. Although he prefers to classify his group as a country outfit, with pedal steel guitar and acoustic guitar being an important element of the group's overall sound, Lambchop at times appears more akin to an improvisational jazz collective than a traditional country combo, complete with a horn section that provides Wagner's songs with lush, often string-laden arrangements. The ever-changing and expanding lineup, which has numbered anywhere from 10 to 15 members and has boasted some of Nashville's top session musicians, draws on Nashville's "countrypolitan" period, when singers like Patsy Cline and Jim Reeves were provided with big-city accompaniment. Wagner and his crew likewise draw on the sounds of nearby Memphis, late-1960s rock-country-rhythm and blues fusion and the early-1970s soul of Al Green, and also make use of the dramatic "Philly soul" sound, a prominent style of the same era.

"It's not the most practical idea, that's for sure, but we're trying to do it in a realistic way," the singer/ songwriter admitted to *Independent* writer Andy Gill, referring to Lambchop's unwieldy lineup. "We're all friends, a collective of people who enjoy each others' company and just like doing things together. Members join and leave, but the line-up just seems to grow—I think when we hit 20 members, we can have our own union. It just takes a little give and take on everybody's part. It helps that we're more adults than little kids, and

5that everybody has a good foundation in their lives. I don't want this to be a burden on anybody; I just want it to be something people can enjoy."

Modern Country Sound

Such diversions—spoken-word monologues and homemade instruments included—represent Wagner's attempt to fix what he feels is wrong with modern-day country music. "There are so many things wrong with country music," asserted Wagner with a don't-get-me-started sigh, as quoted by Gill, "the main one being that it doesn't reflect the time we're living in. It reflects the world of commerce and the idea of formula…. If the guys who wrote these songs actually wrote about what was happening in their lives, they'd be writing about doing too much coke, screwing around on their wife, about their four divorces and all the alimony, and how

they've screwed up their lives. And," he concluded with a smile, "country music would be much richer for it!"

Although born and raised in Nashville, Tennessee, Wagner growing up never gravitated toward the city's rich musical heritage. "In Nashville, if you're not just this incredibly gifted technician—be it a singer or guitar player or whatever—they really have trouble getting past that," he explained to *Washington Times* writer Jim Patterson. "It really just bugs them. I think that's one of the reasons I got into art instead of music."

After high school, Wagner left Nashville to study sculpture, earning undergraduate and graduate degrees in fine art from the Memphis Academy of Arts and Montana State University, respectively. With his artwork, Wagner focused mainly in environments, installations where all the walls and objects in a room would have writings or drawings added to them. Later on, when he started recording songs, the same approach carried over into his music, which often probes the different levels of perception. The concept of space and time, a technique Wagner learned while studying sculpture, was likewise applicable to music, he discovered. "It's very much the same deal," he told Gill. "I just tried to apply those same learnings, those teachings, into the things I do now. One way or another, I'm still talking about experience and life, and how you perceive that—and how it comes out of my twisted mind."

Chet Atkins Meets the Velvet Underground

While in art school, Wagner like many of his peers played music, but never thought of it as much more than a side interest. Upon graduation, he returned to Nashville, following a brief stay in Chicago, and started inviting friends for informal get togethers to play music. Over time, the group progressed from making home tapes to recording singles and then CD's, eventually landing them a recording contract with the independent, Chapel Hill, North Carolina label Merge Records. Lambchop's debut album, *I Hope You're Sitting Down* (also titled *Jack's Tulips*), arrived in 1994, illustrating the band's dedication—in the same vein as Chet Atkins—to the steel guitar and the string-laden sound of Nashville country. However, the band also drew from the well of post-punk irony, occasionally breaking from country arrangements with thrashing drums, Velvet Underground-like guitar lines, and shaking organ.

Two years later saw the release of *How I Quit Smoking*, an album owing more to mainstream country, drawing upon the glossy 1970s Nashville productions of Billy Sherrill, famous for his work with Charlie Rich, Tanya Tucker, and Tammy Wynette. The album also featured string arrangements by John Mock, known for his work with straight country singer Kathy Mattea. Nonetheless, Wagner's obscure lyrics remained prominent, rendering song titles like "The Scary Caroler" and "Your Life as a Sequel"—not the stuff of Top 40 country radio.

A more accessible outing, an EP entitled *Hank* recorded at various festivals during 1995, also arrived in 1996.

The group's next full-length album, however, took obscurity a step further. More rock-inspired than its predecessors, 1997's *Thriller* took subtle steps into the avant-garde. The record's opening songs, "My Face, Your Ass" (the answer to the classic question "Got a Match?") and "Your F***ing Sunny Day" (re-titled for the single release "Your Sucking Funny Day"), especially showed the more aggressive side of Lambchop. And Wagner, who maintains his day job in the construction industry among "hard-core" workers, sanding and finishing hardwood floors, made no apologies about his use of foul language. "It's my personality; it's not so much about shock value, I just speak the way I speak," he said to Gill. "I feel bad about it, because I suppose I should have the command and presence of mind to find other words to use," Wagner continued. "But what [straight] country music doesn't reflect is the fact that these singers cuss like madmen, and for them to not put that in, yet at the same time claim they are the voice of the working man or whatever, is ridiculous—it's more like the voice of the working man who's having dinner at his mother-in-law's house."

Brought Soul to Nashville

Late 1998 saw the release of *What Another Man Spilled,* an album that continued with the country style. However, Lambchop added their own touches again, blending elements of jazz, tropicalia, and even soul—with intriguing, vivid renditions of Curtis Mayfield's "Give Me Your Love" and Frederick Knight's "I've Been Lonely for So Long"—with their traditional Nashville sound. *What Another Man Spilled* also featured guest vocals by singer/guitarist/songwriter Vic Chesnutt, whom Wagner had met some ten years prior at one of his shows. Lambchop, in turn, collaborated with Chesnutt for his 1998 album *The Salesman and Bernadette,* and toured with the musician that year for 25 European shows. "I'm a big fan of Lambchop," Chesnutt said to *Boston Globe* staff writer Jim Sullivan. "They're a big band that can play quiet. Their older records were meandering dirges and they progressed into a soul band and I like both sides. This album was a complete collaboration, and sounds like a Lambchop record in a way. They're friends, and I love 'em as people."

In early 2000, the Nashville supergroup released *Nixon,* the title referring to an affinity for 1970s-era orchestral country and soul music rather than to the former United States president. Winning rave reviews as did their prior efforts, *Nixon,* wrote Dennis Lim of the *Village Voice,* is "intricate, and remarkable in its detail." And Greg Kot of *Rolling Stone* called Wagner's offbeat phrasing and doleful humor "profoundly Southern and affectionately universal." Featuring songs such as the Philly soul "Grumpus" and the celebratory centerpiece song "Up With People," alongside gloomier pieces like

"Butcher Boy" and "The Petrified Forest," Lambchop again covered several bases, from soul and country to indie-rock and Wagner's own heartbreaking beatnik poetry.

While major labels often inquired about signing Lambchop, Wagner always insisted that his band is not up for sale. With all the members of Lambchop's members having wives, children, and other jobs that must take precedence, regular touring—a music business priority—remains impossible. "They shouldn't have to sacrifice the quality of their lives in order to just be a musician or to make music. I just think that concept is sort of ludicrous…. You may not be 'successful,' but you can certainly have a normal life—a house, a home, a family, dogs, a job—and make music," Wagner explained to Patterson. "I'd rather not have to go out and grind floors everyday," he added, "but is that a good enough reason to sacrifice the quality of what you think you're doing musically? I don't think so."

Selected discography

I Hope You're Sitting Down, Merge, 1994.
"The Man Who Loved Beer" (seven-inch single), City Slang, 1996.
How I Quit Smoking, Merge, 1996.
Hank (EP), Merge, 1996.
Thriller, Merge, 1997.
What Another Man Spills, Merge, 1998.
Nixon, Merge, 2000.

Sources

Periodicals

Atlanta Journal-Constitution, May 7, 1995; December 18, 1998.
Boston Globe, April 23, 1999.
Independent, July 5, 1996, p. 11; September 13, 1997, p. 5; October 3, 1997, p. 17; September 5, 1998, p. 43; September 11, 1998, p. 16.
Los Angeles Times, January 30, 1999.
Melody Maker, September 12, 1998.
New York Times, January 12, 1999.
Rolling Stone, March 2, 2000; April 27, 2000.
Tampa Tribune, March 24, 2000, p. 19.
Village Voice, January 19, 1999; February 29, 2000.
Washington Post, February 25, 2000.
Washington Times, March 15, 2000, p. C4.

Online

Merge Artist—Lambchop,http://www.mrg2000.com/merge /bio.html?id=lambchop (May 1, 2000).
Official Lambchop Site, http://www.landlocked.net/lambchop/ (May 1, 2000).

—Laura Hightower

Jim Lauderdale

Singer, songwriter

AP/Wide World Photos. Reproduced by permission.

Though he spent much of his career based in Los Angeles, California, Jim Lauderdale has nevertheless made a name for himself as one of Nashville's leading songwriters. He landed eight cuts with the platinum-selling country artist George Strait, including "Where the Sidewalk Ends" and "King of Broken Hearts." Other hit-makers who covered Lauderdale's songs include Vince Gill, Mandy Barnett, Kathy Mattea, and Kelly Willis, among others. Country singer Mark Chesnutt scored a number-one hit with Lauderdale's "Gonna Get a Life," co-written with frequent partner and Nashville veteran Frank Dycus, while Patty Loveless notched two chart-topping songs with "Halfway Down" and the Grammy-nominated "You Don't Seem to Miss Me."

Unfortunately, the same popular success Lauderdale enjoyed behind the scenes never carried over into his pursuits as a recording artist, despite pages upon pages of press raves about his albums, his soulful voice, and confessional songs about life. As an explanation, many point to the fact that, although Lauderdale has released his own albums since the late-1980s in addition to writing scores of songs for other country artists, the artist's most admirable virtue as a solo performer may also be his curse—his ability to mine from a wide range of musical influences. Known for his eclectic tastes, from country and bluegrass to jazz, blues, folk, and rock and roll, the singer seemed too restlessly creative for mass marketing. "His literate style of country," commented Mark Schone for a profile in the *Encyclopedia of Country Music,* "applies the progressive mind-set of Gram Parsons to the musical legacies of Memphis [Tennessee] and Bakersfield [California]."

Thus, the very diversity of Lauderdale's style resulted in country radio usually ignoring his own recorded efforts. "Someone would say, 'How do you describe this album?'" he said to Chris Morris of *Billboard,* referring to his 1994 release *Pretty Close to the Truth.* "They'd say, 'Are you country? Is this alternative? Are you alternative country?' I think the music is pretty eclectic, to the point where it's several different things." Lauderdale, without any hint of snobbery, noted the differences between the music that inspired his own writing and the styles that nurtured his contemporaries as the reason why his records sound so unlike mainstream country. "One of my takes about country music these days is that there are songs that are really kind of soft-rock—what would be like early '70s California country, or Eagles-type stuff. That's really kind of one of the main styles in country. Some of these country guys right now grew up listening to some of the softer rock, or the Eagles or Styx or Kiss or whoever," he added. "But my influences were rawer. Of course there was the Beatles and the Stones and everything, but also Muddy Waters and Howlin' Wolf. Maybe there will be a time in country music when maybe it's OK to have those influences and show them."

Influenced by Southern Musical Heritage

Born on April 11, 1957, in Troutman, North Carolina, James Russell Lauderdale, the precocious son of a minister, was influenced by the musical heritage of the South from an early age. Raised on the songs pouring from his father's scratchy radio and the music performed at regional bluegrass festivals, Lauderdale as a teen studied the vocal turns of George Jones, admired and understood the oaky baritone of Johnny Cash, embraced the emotional appeal of Buck Owens, and took in the subtle confessionals of Merle Haggard. After college, Lauderdale became a journeyman song-man, singing, writing, and accruing life experience as he moved from New York to Texas to Tennessee—where he stopped in Nashville long enough to record an unreleased album with bluegrass great Roland White—before settling down in Los Angeles.

All the while, Lauderdale carried with him the true country music that defined his childhood, yet also appreciated the music that infiltrated the various regions in which he lived. Because of this open-mindedness, the songwriter was able to expand the definition of country music without compromising his roots. "Great music—whether it's George Jones, Hank Williams, Muddy Waters, or Bob Dylan—is great music because it's so real," Lauderdale noted on his website, though he adds, "And part of being real is being true to who you are. Maybe you pick up some new influences, but you can never become something else."

After recording a second unreleased album for Columbia Records in 1987, Lauderdale finally made his way into record stores in 1991 with a cut on the second *Town South of Bakersfield* compilation, an anthology of the Southern California alternative country music scene. Since then, all of Lauderdale's solo efforts, while they did not earn mass acceptance, nonetheless garnered favorable critical response. His debut outing entitled *Planet of Love,* a stunning "hard country album," he said, exhibiting Lauderdale's vocal and compositional gifts and co-produced by Rodney Crowell and John Leventhal, arrived on the Warner Brothers label in 1991.

Western Beat Star

By now, Lauderdale was a favorite within the Los Angeles area country music scene, though he was often linked to artists from a seemingly dissimilar genre—like Lucinda Williams (with whom he later toured in 1999), Dave Alvin, Rosie Flores, and Chris Gaffney—under the label "Western beat." As Lauderdale explained to Morris, "That concept came up when a bunch of us guys were playin' at the Montreux Jazz Festival a few years ago. They had a country night. I thought that was a cool tag."

Next, Lauderdale moved to Atlantic Records to release a pair of equally impressive, though more roots-oriented efforts: 1994's *Pretty Close to the Truth* and 1995's *Every Second Counts.* The first Atlantic album was hailed by several reviewers as one of the best country-rock efforts of the decade. On the latter, wrote Alanna Nash for *Entertainment Weekly,* "Between the chiming guitars and from-the-gut vocals you can hear traces of everyone from Cream to Van Morrison to Al Green. It took Lauderdale to make eclecticism this seamless." Likewise, Tony Scherman in *People* concluded, "Few singer-songwriters have Lauderdale's talent, curiosity and spine. He remains one of pop's best-kept secrets."

In 1996, Lauderdale returned with *Persimmons,* considered his rawest-sounding album to date. Like his previous releases, the album built upon styles from across the musical spectrum: from straight country, "Some Things Are Too Good to Last" sung with Emmy-lou Harris, mid-1960s garage-band rock, "Tears So Strong," to blues, "Optimistic Messenger," to near metal-rock, "Jupiter's Rising." Released by the small Upstart label, Lauderdale had recorded *Persimmons* just before signing with RCA Records.

Mainstream Country

With RCA, Lauderdale released a more mainstream country album in 1998 entitled *Whispers* with the help of some of country music's finest songwriters: Nashville heavyweights Dycus, Harlan Howard, Melba Montgomery, and John Scott, as well as California friend Buddy Miller. In 1999, the singer/songwriter released two more records, another straight-country album for RCA entitled *Onward Through It All* and a bluegrass duet album, *I Feel Like Singing Today,* with Ralph Stanley on the Rebel label. Lauderdale had also recently guested on Stanley's *Clinch Mountain Country,* and Stanley sang as a guest on Lauderdale's *Whisper.* "I've been wanting to do a bluegrass thing for years and years," Lauderdale told Jim Bessman of *Billboard,* "and to finally have one with Ralph Stanley is mind-blowing."

Again, Lauderdale raked in stellar reviews, but still lacked popular sales support. However, the musician felt satisfied and fortunate for what he had accomplished. "As day jobs go, [songwriting] isn't so bad. Realistically, all an artist can hope for is to get a chance to release a record and have support behind him. The rest is really gravy," he told David Sprague of *Billboard.* "There seems to be a growing crossover [appeal]," Lauderdale continued. "There are people who've heard my name in relation to Mark Chesnutt and people who know me from seeing me open for Hootie & the Blowfish. But I don't worry about making a niche for myself. It may be someone's job to do that, but it's not mine."

Selected discography

Planet of Love, Warner Bros., 1991.
Pretty Close to the Truth, Atlantic, 1994.
Every Second Counts, Atlantic, 1995.
Persimmons, Upstart, 1996.
Whisper, RCA, 1998.
Onward Through It All, RCA, 1999.
(With Ralph Stanley) *I Feel Like Singing Today,* Rebel, 1999.

Sources

Books

Kingsbury, Paul, editor, *Encyclopedia of Country Music,* Oxford University Press, 1998.

Periodicals

Billboard, June 25, 1994, pp. 13-14; June 29, 1995, pp. 11-12; July 17, 1999.
Entertainment Weekly, September 15, 1995, p. 108; August 20, 1999, p. 128.
People, October 23, 1995, p. 23; September 23, 1996, p. 25; February 23, 1998, p. 28

Online

Jim Lauderdale Official Website, http://www.jimlauderdale .com (May 11, 2000).

—*Laura Hightower*

Leftfield

When the progressive dance act Leftfield released their debut album *Leftism* in 1995, the duo of Paul Daley and Neil Barnes completely reinvented British house music. An album that stretched beyond the boundaries of dance music, *Leftism,* four years later in 1999, was declared the "Greatest Dance Album of All Time" in a poll by the world's foremost DJs. Even as the years passed, the ground-breaking record, with its timeless mix of shaking dub, imposing techno, and dynamic, motion-inducing splendor, has retained a modern dance sound. Paving the way for future dance/techno music acts like the Chemical Brothers and Prodigy, *Leftism* is regarded as the album that redrew the genre's borders by pioneering the hybrid of dub and house music long before the invention of big beat. The album also introduced the use of guest vocalists from a broad spectrum of musical backgrounds—like gothic torch singer and former Curve vocalist Toni Halliday and reggae artist Earl Sixteen—who performed over rhythms borrowed not only from dub, but from reggae and African music as well.

Because *Leftism* was considered a defining moment in dance music, similar to the influence of Pink Floyd's

For The Record . . .

Members include **Neil Barnes** (raised in London, England; former member of London School of Samba, DJ at the Wag Club, and teacher at Paddington College) and **Paul Daley** (raised in Margate, England; former member of A Band Called Adam and contributor to the Brand New Heavies).

Formed Leftfield, 1989; released debut single "Not Forgotten," 1990; formed Hard Hands label, c. 1992; released untimely hit single "Open Up," 1993; produced soundtrack for *Shallow Grave,* 1994; released groundbreaking debut album *Leftism,* 1995; contributed to *Trainspotting* soundtrack, 1996; released acclaimed *Rhythm and Stealth,* 1999.

Addresses: *Record company*—Columbia Records, 550 Madison Ave., New York City, NY 10022, (212) 833-5212, website: http://www.sony.com. *Publishing company*—Hard Hands/Chrysalis Music (ASCAP). *Management*—Hard Hands, c/o Lisa Horan, London, England. *Website*—Leftfield Online, http://www.leftfield-online.com.

Dark Side of the Moon on rock, many speculated whether Leftfield could follow with an album of the same magnitude. However, the duo returned in late 1999 with *Rhythm and Stealth*, an album just as vital and challenging as their debut. But whereas *Leftism* succeeded upon its larger-than-life sound, *Rhythm and Stealth* showcased the duo's more tailored, minimal approach to dance music as they refined their nu-house foundation while experimenting with Jamaican dub, Detroit techno, skewed electronica, and rays of ambient textures. Judging by Leftfield's more atmospheric tracks on *Rhythm and Stealth,* wrote *Village Voice* contributor Frank Kogan, "Leftfield could make a leaking faucet sound dramatic." He went on to describe the album in its entirety as "rhythm, clang, beauty."

Daley and Barnes, both of whom dabbled in punk, dub, industrial, and funk before appearing on the emergent house scene, joined forces as Leftfield in 1989. Hinting at a subversive punk attitude, the duo's goal was to earn themselves a place—alongside acts like Orbital and Sabres of Paradise—in the progressive house camp, a crew of artists who concentrated more intently on reinterpreting musical influences than merely cranking out dance beats. Prior to the formation of Leftfield, Daley, who grew up in Margate, a borough in the

southeast of England, worked at a hair salon in London's Kensington Market and was a former member of A Band Called Adam on the Rhythm King label and contributor to the Brand New Heavies. Meanwhile, Barnes, who spent his childhood in London's Islington, was a member of Elephant Stampede, played bongos for the London School of Samba, and worked as a DJ at the Wag Club. He also earned a degree in modern history and taught for five years at Paddington College.

Formed Leftfield

The two first met at an acid jazz club called Violets in the late-1980s. "We were both percussionists in different areas," Barnes, explaining why they decided to start making music together, stated for the duo's website. "But we both realised that we couldn't express ourselves properly. You can only take it so far, using live instruments, but samplers and sequences opened up new worlds creatively." Leftfield debuted in 1990 on Rhythm King with the deeply resonant single "Not Forgotten," a song inspired by the *Mississippi Burning* soundtrack. A remix of the track appeared as a B-side of the duo's second single, "More Than I Know," released in 1991. However, when both songs broke big in Great Britain, a dispute with the duo's label ensued, forcing Leftfield to put their recording career on hold.

In the meantime, Daley and Barnes, unable to release new songs because of contractual restraints enforced by Rhythm King, embarked on a career as remixers. Working for acts such as React 2 Rhythm, Ultra Naté, and Inner City, Leftfield were able to maintain a prominent reputation, even in the absence of their own recorded material. Eventually, after legal wranglings with Rhythm King came to an end, Leftfield set up their own imprint, Hard Hands, named after a 1960s hit by percussionist Ray Barretto. In 1992, now free to release their own music, Leftfield returned with two more singles, the reggae-tinted "Release the Pressure" and the trance-based, minor chart hit "Song of Life," both of which became underground dance classics.

Leftfield especially caught public and critical attention with the 1993 single "Open Up." Recorded with John Lydon—formerly of the Sex Pistols and PiL—on guest vocals and remixed by Andy Weatherall and the Dust Brothers, "Open Up" was a major crossover success. The song probably would have risen to the top of the British charts had it not been for bad timing. Containing the line "Burn Hollywood! Burn!," the single was released, by coincidence, during the same week forest fires raged throughout Southern California, affecting many in the Los Angeles area. Radio stations, seeing the line as too provocative, placed a virtual blanket ban on the song. Nevertheless, "Open Up" made enough of an initial impact to reach the British top 20, and the song was widely regarded by the music press as one of the finest records of the year.

Broke Ground with Debut Album

After producing the soundtrack for the 1994 British film *Shallow Grave,* Daley and Barnes released their long-awaited debut album, the acclaimed *Leftism.* Featuring exploratory moments as well as upbeat numbers, the album proved just as suitable for the front room as the dance floor and featured a range of guest vocalists, from Lydon, Curve vocalist Toni Halliday, and Manchester poet Lemn Sissay to African rap artist Djum Djum and reggae vocalist Earl Sixteen. The song performed by Halliday, "Original," was released as a single, charted in the United Kingdom at number 18, and occasioned Leftfield's debut performance on *Top of the Pops.* Considerable recognition followed, and *Leftism* climbed into the British top 10.

Within months after the album's release, Leftfield started remixing for musicians and groups like David Bowie, Renegade Soundwave, and Yothu Yindi, then received Britain's much-coveted Mercury Prize for their debut album. One year later, in 1996, the duo scooped up a Brit Award for Best Dance Act. And four years past its debut, Mark Sutherland in *Melody Maker* recalled *Leftism* as one of 1995's best releases. "It was funny," recalled Daley, as quoted by *Billboard* writer Michael Paoletta. "After we won the awards, our label asked us, 'So, are you ready to be pop stars?' And we were like, 'Uh, no.' You don't have to always be in the public eye and be a pop star."

In spite of wanting to remain underground, Leftfield gained further publicity in April of 1996 after contributing the otherwise unavailable "A Final Hit" to the soundtrack for cult film *Trainspotting,* based on the best-selling drug culture novel by Scottish writer Irvine Welsh and directed by Danny Boyie. The duo was also featured on the compilation album *Wipeout XL* for the Astralwerks label. Released in December of 1996, it included some of the world's most prominent techno/trance acts—Leftfield along with the Future Sound of London, Fluke, the Chemical Brothers, Underworld, Photek, and Orbital—offering some of their best efforts.

An Album of the Future

Daley and Barnes spent the next three years recording and re-recording their follow-up album, 1999's *Rhythm and Stealth,* which was preceded by the CD-5 single "Afrika Shox," which featured guest vocals by electro pioneer Afrika Bambaatta. "Bambaataa was a very strong influence on my early interest in electronic music," Barnes told Carol Clerk of *Melody Maker.* "It was great fun working with him, because he is very open-minded and he keeps in touch with what is happening. He had part of his posse with him, the Zulu Nation, who came down to the studio as well, and the whole thing had a really happy atmosphere." The

shocking video for "Afrika Shox," directed by Chris Cunningham, known for his work with Madonna, Björk, Portishead, and Aphex Twin, also drew attention. Referring to the single's video as a "black comedy," Barnes further explained, "I mean it's ridiculous, the guy walks around and bits of his body drop off—it's not to be taken seriously. You could say it was a reflection on society, that nobody is willing to help him until the end, when Afrika Bambaataa says, 'Do you need a hand?' and he hasn't got any. A lot of people don't think it's funny, but we do."

With *Rhythm and Stealth,* which debuted at number one on the British album chart and included the track "Afrika Shox," Leftfield created an extraordinarily diverse, yet at the same time totally homogeneous panorama of techno/ambient sounds, maintaining the duo's solid reputation and penchant for experimentation. Other standout songs, performed with an array of guest vocalists, included "Dusted" with Roots Manuva, "Chant of a Poor Man" featuring Cheshire Cat, "Swords" with Nicole Willis, and "Rino's Prayer" sung by Rino Della Volpe. "I hope people like it—time will tell," added Barnes. "It's a much tougher album than the first one, it's much rawer and has a more stripped-down sound. It's not like *Leftism* at all, it's a very different album and I'm very proud of it as a record … It's definitely an album of the future, rather than of the past."

"Quite frankly," Barnes told Paoletta, "we wanted to go against the musical grain with the new album. When we started working on it, we both knew that we wanted to take it in another direction and develop our sound. In fact, this album was heavily influenced by all that early-'80s electro stuff like Ultravox, Human League, and Visage." In agreement with his partner's recollections, Daley added, "We didn't want to turn into a stadium techno band. It was important for us to keep our feet firmly planted in London's underground club scene, because there's a lot going on there." And despite the duo's growing popularity, Barnes insisted, "In England, it's possible to sell lots of records and maintain your credibility. To do that, you just have to make music that keeps you credible. You can't turn your back on what got you to where you are. These days, hype and imagery have a tendency to overtake the music. With [*Rhythm and Stealth*], we didn't want that."

In addition to making records, Daley and Barnes also develop music for software for computer games, such as for *Music 2000.* Leftfield's "Phat Planet," from their follow-up album also became the theme song for a new Saturday-morning animated show on the Fox network called *Beast Machines.* The duo also composed the opening musical sequence for the 2000 film *The Beach,* starring Leonardo DiCaprio.

Selected discography

(Contributor) *Shallow Grave* (soundtrack), EMI, 1994.
Leftism, Hard Hands/Sony, 1995.
(Contributor) *Trainspotting* (soundtrack), includes Leftfield's "A Final Hit," EMI/Capitol, 1996.
(Contributor) *Wipeout XL* (compilation), Astralwerks, 1996.
Rhythm and Stealth, Hard Hands/Higher Ground/Columbia, 1999.

Sources

Periodicals

Billboard, April 27, 1996; December 7, 1996; May 24, 1997; August 14, 1999; December 11, 1999; December 25, 1999-January 1, 2000.

Melody Maker, December 5, 1992; March 18, 1995; August 28, 1999; September 4, 1999; October 2, 1999; December 1-7, 1999; December 22, 1999-January 4, 2000.
Village Voice, December 14, 1999.

Online

Leftfield Online, http://www.leftfield-online.com (May 31, 2000).
Sonicnet.com, http://www.sonicnet.com (May 31, 2000).

—*Laura Hightower*

John Lewis

Pianist, composer, arranger

As the musical director and primary composer of the Modern Jazz Quartet throughout the group's entire history, pianist/arranger John Lewis proved that a weakness for the classics can lead to greatness in contemporary music. Searching for an outlet for his interests in bop, the blues, and jazz, as well as the compositions of classical composers such as Bach, Lewis, in 1952, formed the enduring and highly influential quartet, consisting of a usual lineup featuring a piano, bass, drums, and vibraharp. In the December 30, 1953 issue of *Down Beat* magazine and quoted by Eugene Holley of *Down Beat*, Nat Hentoff interviewed the young pianist about his new combo. In describing the outlook he wanted to take with the Modern Jazz Quartet, Lewis articulated, "I think that the audience for jazz can be widened if we strengthen our work with structure. If there is more of a reason for what's going on, there'll be more overall sense and, therefore, more interest for the listener."

In the five decades that followed this statement, Lewis, possessing a "cool" piano playing style like that of the legendary bandleader Count Basie, a technique that made every single note count, watched his single idea become a reality. Along with his partners in the Modern

Born John Aaron Lewis on May 3, 1920 in La Grange, IL; married to Mirjana. *Education:* Earned Bachelor's degree in music and anthropology from the University of New Mexico; earned Master's degree in music.

Started playing local gigs as a teenager in Albuquerque, NM; served in the United States Army during World War II; moved to New York City, 1945; member of Dizzy Gillespie's big band, 1946-48; played with Miles Davis and others, 1948-49; incorporated the Modern Jazz Quartet, January 14, 1952; disbanded quartet, 1974; reunited quartet, 1981; co-founded and conducted Orchestra U.S.A., 1962-65; conducted the American Jazz Orchestra, 1985; headed the faculty at Lenox School of Jazz, 1957-60; taught jazz improvisation at Harvard University and City College, 1975-82; disbanded the Modern Jazz Quartet and focused on solo work, released *Evolution,* 1999.

Addresses: *Record company*—Atlantic Records, 1290 Avenue of the Americas, New York City, NY 10104, (212) 707-2144.

Jazz Quartet, vibraharpist and featured soloist Milt Jackson, bassist Percy Heath (who replaced original member Ray Brown soon after the quartet's formation), and drummer Connie Kay (who replaced original drummer Kenny Clarke in 1955), Lewis helped jazz gain a new respectability within the classical community, but always kept each performance new and exciting. Throughout the 20th century, the quartet reigned as one of the jazz world's most appealing and innovative small combos, attracting a world-wide audience. The Modern Jazz Quartet would have stretched their longevity even further had it not been for Jackson's passing from liver cancer on November 9, 1999. His death marked the end of the group.

While most groups lose their enthusiasm over time, the Modern Jazz Quartet, through their legendary interplay and Lewis's synthesis of American and European musical forms, was able to maintain an energy that lasted, excluding a hiatus between 1974 and 1981, nearly half a century. "We enjoyed making music. When we played on stage, we played for our pleasure first," Lewis offered as an explanation for the quartet's perseverance, as quoted by Eugene Holley in *Down*

Beat. "If somebody else enjoyed it, fine, but it wasn't created for that purpose. We had a responsibility for playing for the public, to let them participate by understanding and gaining pleasure from what we did. But that's not the primary thing. The primary thing for us was the interplay, which took a long time to achieve. The whole point of a composition is to make a piece that incorporates improvisation into it as seamlessly as possible, so you won't know what's improvised and what's not. It took a long time for that to happen, but that was the goal we worked toward achieving."

John Aaron Lewis was born on May 3, 1920 in La Grange, Illinois, but after his father died, he moved with his mother to Albuquerque, New Mexico. At the time, Albuquerque differed from most other American cities, given the community's unique mix of people from a variety of cultures and no real rules of segregation. In addition to blacks and whites, Albuquerque also had a large population of Mexican and Spanish Americans, as well as Indians. According to Lewis, the group that suffered the greatest hardships in New Mexico were the Hispanics, rather than the African Americans. Lewis's new multicultural environment in the Southwest also mirrored his own heritage. "In my family you found everything you could imagine," he informed Holley. "Cherokee, Comanche, Irish and the French part came from Martinique. My great grandmother's husband was one of the Buffalo Soldiers from the 7th Cavalry. My grandmother and great-grandmother spoke Spanish and French."

Lewis, whose mother died when he was four years old, took his first piano lesson from his aunt at the age of seven and was soon playing all the time with his cousins. "We had pianos in our houses, no TVs. You had to find other was to entertain yourself. We belonged to the Methodist Church, but on some Sundays, these people from the Holy Rollers church would ask my grandmother, who raised me, if I could come and play, and they paid me 50 cents," Lewis recalled to Holley. During his teenage years, Lewis and his cousins played gigs with several older, influential musicians, including a local pianist and arranger named Eddie Carson. In addition to local musicians, the Count Basie big band, Lester Young, and Duke Ellington played in Albuquerque from time to time. One performance by Ellington, in particular, left Lewis speechless. "The most incredible visual experience I've ever had was with Duke Ellington's orchestra in 1939, 1940.... He's still my role model."

After high school, Lewis enrolled at the University of New Mexico, graduating in 1942 with a Bachelor's degree in music and anthropology. Then, he served in the United States Army during World War II. While stationed in Europe, he played in a special services band with an innovative drummer from Pittsburgh named Kenny "Klook" Clarke, an original member of the Modern Jazz Quartet. Following his military discharge in 1945, Lewis relocated to New York City in order to pursue a career in music. He was especially intrigued by the emergence of several small groups, the most well-known led by Dizzy Gillespie and Charlie Parker, that were adding classically-inspired melodies to their music instead of simply taking lines from the day's popular songs, a trend that had dominated jazz up to that time.

Thus, from 1946 until 1948, Lewis played with the Dizzy Gillespie big band as a member of the rhythm section, which also included Clarke, Jackson, and Brown. His earliest memories of blending jazz and classical music occurred during a September 1947 appearance with the orchestra at Carnegie Hall, for which Lewis had contributed two arrangements, "Emanon" and "Two Bass Hit," and debuted his "Toca-cata for Trumpet." That same year he toured with Gillespie in Paris, then returned to the United States to work as a sideman with Illinois Jacket, Lester Young, Miles Davis, Ella Fitzgerald, and Charlie Parker, for whom he recorded an important solo on "Parker's Mood." After leaving Gillespie's orchestra, Lewis from 1948 to 1949 played with a group of other young, forward-thinking musicians, including Davis, baritone saxophonist Gerry Mulligan, drummer Max Roach, and composers John Carsi, George Russell, and Gil Evans. Their musical efforts resulted in Davis's influential *Birth of the Cool* recordings.

Continuing to broaden the possibilities of jazz, Lewis, Jackson, Clarke, and Heath, who replaced Brown, who left in order to work with his wife Ella Fitzgerald, began recording together in the early-1950s and officially incorporated the Modern Jazz Quartet on January 14, 1952. After Lewis earned his Master's degree in music in 1953, the quartet worked steadily in New York, performing in clubs and recording for the Prestige label. In spite of some early criticism that they weren't playing "true jazz," the group pressed on. However, Clarke left in 1955 and moved to Paris, where he lived until his death in 1985. His replacement was a versatile drummer named Connie Kay, already known for his sessions work for Atlantic Records.

Just one year later in 1956, the Modern Jazz Quartet received a significant boost when they embarked on the historic Birdland tour to Paris with Davis, Lester Young, and Bud Powell. By the time they returned to America, the members of the quartet had become major stars, as audiences marveled at the group's telepathic interplay and regal stage clothes. From the mid-1950s until the mid-1970s, the quartet enabled Lewis to explore a wide range of musical concepts. He wrote and arranged over 100 compositions—most of which were released by Atlantic Records—during this 20-year period, including blues numbers, ballads, tone poems, soundtracks, concertos, and orchestral works.

Some of the quartet's most acclaimed recordings included the soulful *Pyramid* released in 1959, the Latin-tinged *Collaboration* released in 1964, the swinging *The European Concert* released in 1960, and *Blues on Bach* released in 1973. However, years of constant touring had taken a toll on the Modern Jazz Quartet as the 1970s got underway. Thus, the group called it quits in 1974. Jackson cited financial frustrations as his reason for wanting to break up the quartet, but Lewis called attention to more personal reasons: "I didn't have an opportunity to know my children," he explained to Holley.

Following the split, Lewis continued to work on outside projects, interests he had started pursuing long before the group's so-called retirement. He released his first orchestral album, *European Windows,* in 1958, followed by *Improvised Meditations & Excursions* and *Wonderful World of Jazz,* two of his early piano-based albums. Around this time, Lewis also served as director for the Monterey Jazz Festival, and went on to co-found and conduct Orchestra U.S.A., from 1962 through 1965, and the American Jazz Orchestra in 1985. Also a strong believer in the value of music education, Lewis headed the faculty at the Lenox School of Jazz in Massachusetts from 1957 to 1960 and taught jazz improvisation at Harvard University and City College from 1975 to 1982.

Although officially disbanded, the Modern Jazz Quartet continued to play occasional gigs. Then in 1981, after an offer came to tour Japan, the group decided to get back together. Some highlights from their "comeback" years included 1988's *For Ellington,* 1991's *MJQ At 40,* a four-CD retrospective, and *MJQ and Friends,* recorded with the late Harry "Sweets" Edison. After the death of longtime drummer Kay on November 30, 1994, the quartet operated on a semi-active basis until Jackson's death in late-1999.

Throughout most of his career, Lewis's exceptional work with the Modern Jazz Quartet tended to take precedence over his solo aspirations. However, the late-1990s saw a renewed interest in Lewis as a pianist. He started performing solo recitals and conducting orchestras, and several of his early recordings have been reissued. In 1999, he released an acclaimed piano solo CD entitled *Evolution* that included a haunting version of his classic ballad "Django," an elegy for the Gypsy guitarist Django Reinhardt. Lewis resides with his Croation-born wife, Mirjana, in New York on Manhattan's East Side. A humble, soft-spoken man, Lewis say he doesn't dwell to much over his accomplishments as a composer and pianist. "I don't even think about that," he said to Holley. "I'm to busy trying to make music and be with my family. Now, I have one grandchild, Samuel. And I have time to spend with him."

Selected discography

John Lewis

Modern Jazz Society, Verve, 1955.
Grand Encounter, Pacific Jazz, 1956.
The John Lewis Piano, Atlantic, 1956.
Afternoon in Paris, Atlantic, 1956.
European Windows, RCA, 1958.
Improvised Meditations & Excursions, Atlantic, 1959.
Odds Against Tomorrow, United Artists, 1959.
Wonderful World of Jazz, Atlantic, 1960.
John Lewis Presents Jazz Abstractions, Atlantic, 1960.
Original Sin, Atlantic, 1961.
A Milanese Story, Atlantic, 1962
Essence, Atlantic, 1962.
European Encounter, Atlantic, 1962.
Animal Dance, Atlantic, 1962.
P.O.V., Columbia, 1975.
Bach Preludes and Fugues, Verve, 1984.
The Bridge Game, Philips, 1984.
The Chess Game, Vol. 1, Verve, 1987.
Delaunay's Delemma, EmArcy, 1987.
The Chess Game, Vol. 2, Verve, 1988.
Midnight in Paris, EmArcy, 1988.
The American Jazz Orchestra, East-West, 1989.
Evolution, Atlantic, 1999.

Modern Jazz Quartet

Modern Jazz Quartet, Original Jazz Classics, 1951.
The Modern Jazz Quartet Plays Jazz Classics, Prestige, 1952.
The Modern Jazz Quartet Plays for Lovers, Prestige, 1952.
The Modern Jazz Quartet, Fantasy, 1952.
The Artistry of the Modern Jazz Quartet, Prestige, 1952.
Django, Original Jazz Classics, 1953.
Modern Jazz Quartet, Vol. 2, Prestige, 1954.
Concorde, Original Jazz Classics, 1955.
Fontessa, Atlantic, 1956.
Modern Jazz Quartet at the Music Inn, Vol. 1, Atlantic, 1956.
One Never Knows, Atlantic, 1957.
No Sun in Venice, Atlantic, 1957.
Third Stream Music, Atlantic, 1957.
Modern Jazz Quartet at the Music Inn, Vol. 2, Atlantic, 1958.
Pyramid, Atlantic, 1959.
Odds Against Tomorrow, Blue Note, 1959.
European Concert, Vol. 1, Atlantic, 1960.

European Concert, Vol. 2, Atlantic, 1960.
Dedicated to Connie, Atlantic, 1960.
The Comedy, Atlantic, 1960.
Patterns, United Artists, 1960.
Lonely Woman, Atlantic, 1962.
A Quartet Is a Quartet Is a Quartet, Atlantic, 1963.
The Sheriff, Atlantic, 1963.
Jazz Dialogue, Atlantic, 1965.
Blues at Carnegie Hall, Atlantic, 1966.
Under the Jasmine Tree, Apple, 1967.
Space, Apple, 1969.
Plastic Dreams, Atlantic, 1971.
Blues on Bach, Atlantic, 1973.
The Last Concert, Atlantic, 1974.
More from the Last Concert, Atlantic, 1974.
The Complete Last Concert, Atlantic, 1974.
Together Again at Montreux Jazz, Pablo, 1982.
Echoes, Pablo, 1984.
Topsy: This One's for Basie, Pablo, 1985.
Three Windows, Atlantic, 1987.
For Ellington, East West, 1988.
Rose of the Rio Grande, Capitol, 1989.
Celebration, Atlantic, 1992.
Night at the Opera, Jazz Anthology, 1994.
In Concert, Prelude, 1996.

Sources

Books

Swenson, John, editor, *Rolling Stone Jazz & Blues Album Guide,* Random House, 1999.

Periodicals

American Visions, February/March 2000.
Commentary, January 2000.
Down Beat, October 1997; April 2000.
New York Times, September 7, 1997.

Online

All Music Guide, http://www.allmusic.com (June 22, 2000).

—Laura Hightower

Los Hombres Calientes

Jazz group

The "Hot Men" of jazz, Los Hombres Calientes persist in delighting audiences with innovative multicultural entertainment, even tossing instruments to their audiences to encourage participation with the fun-loving and spirited band. This sensational New Orleans-based group hit the top 20 echelon of popular recording charts with their first album release, even prior to its distribution outside the state of Louisiana. The group performed initially as a one-night stand in 1998 and elicited such positive response, that it booked subsequent engagements. Barely two years later it had performed in France, England, and Mexico, with a United States tour scheduled for the spring of 2000. With its high-energy, New Orleans style dance-party format, Los Hombres Calientes consistently attracts a non-jazz crowd along with jazz purists.

The serendipitous six-member ensemble is a combination of some of the finest talent in the world of modern jazz, with trumpeter and founder Irvin Mayfield reverberating his horn against the rhythms of drummer Jason Marsalis and percussionist Bill Summers. Yvette Bostic-Summers enhances the percussion and adds vocals, with Victor "Red" Atkins on piano and Edwin Livingston on bass.

Mayfield, the driving force behind the band, was born in New Orleans in the late 1970s. He received a classical music education initially on the piano, and then on the trumpet, which he embraced at age seven. He attended high school at the distinguished New Orleans Center for the Creative Arts (NOCCA) and took part in the University of New Orleans Jazz Program along the way. He was a veteran performer before he was out of his teens, having jammed with Algiers Brass Band and Kermit Ruffins; Mayfield honed his horn sounds by performing at Donna's and at Snug Harbor in New Orleans, Louisiana. In addition to his affiliation with Los Hombres, Mayfield performs with his own quintet and has appeared with the multi-talented Marsalis, including the Jason Marsalis Quintet, with Wessell Anderson, Nicholas Payton, Ruffins, and others. In 1999 Mayfield received *New Orleans* magazine's honor as a Jazz All-star for contemporary and traditional jazz, and in 1999 he was filmed behind the scenes and during performances with Los Hombres for the *Jazz Dreams* documentary. Mayfield has recorded for Basin Street Records, Half Note, and for STR. He is a perennial performer in New Orleans—at Snug Harbor and the Funky Butt, in the French Quarter at Tipitina's, in the Storytown district, and elsewhere around the area. Mayfield acknowledges Wynton Marsalis and Terence Blanchard as his mentors.

Drummer Jason Marsalis, born on March 4, 1977, is the youngest member of Los Hombres Calientes. He along with Mayfield and Summers, receives credit as one of the three core members of the band. Marsalis, who makes a lasting impression for his rhythmic rapport with percussionist Bill Summers, was highly influenced by Jeff "Tain" Watts. Additionally, Marsalis is the youngest of the talented Marsalis siblings, the sons of jazz master Ellis Marsalis. Barely into his twenties, Jason Marsalis during his early career performed with the Casa Samba percussion group and contributed to the Celtic styles of the Poor Clares. Marsalis, who released his first two solo albums on Basin Street Records, also performs regularly as a member of pianist Marcus Roberts's band. Additionally Marsalis contributed to recordings with father and brother Branford, and with Harolde Battiste among others. In 1997 Jason Marsalis was listed among *New Orleans* magazine All-Stars.

Percussionist Bill Summers contributes bongo, conga, and timbale to the unique sound of Los Hombres Calientes. Summers, another core member of the ensemble, was born in the late 1940s in Detroit, Michigan, and studied piano at the Detroit Observatory for ten years. As a young man he moved to San Francisco and signed with Prestige Records in 1977, and with MCA in 1981. His 1981 MCA hit song, "Call It What You Want," reached number 16 on the top 20 jazz chart. He is best known for his Afro funk fusion style. In addition to his own funk band, Summers' Heat, he is well remembered for his membership in Herbie Hancock's Headhunters band and was heard on *Chameleon,* the Headhunters' classic electro-fusion album released in the mid-1970s. Additionally, Summers worked with Johnny Hammond, Patrice Rushen, and Carl Anderson. Summers contributed to the soundtrack of the television miniseries *Roots* under the direction of Quincy Jones.

Members include **Victor "Red" Atkins**, piano; **Yvette Bostic-Summers**, vocals, percussion; **Edwin Livingston** (born in 1970 in Texarkana, TX; *Education*: Studied with Roger Fratena and Mark Foley; graduated Wichita State University; attended Southwest Texas State University), bass; **Jason Marsalis** (born on March 4, 1977; son of Ellis Marsalis; one of four siblings), drums; **Irvin Mayfield** (born in New Orleans, LA; *Education*: New Orleans Center for the Creative Arts; University of New Orleans), trumpet; **Bill Summers** (born in the late 1940s in Detroit, MI; *Education*: Detroit Observatory), bongos, conga, timbale.

Debuted at Snug Harbor in New Orleans, Louisiana, on February 7, 1998; signed with Basin Street Records, 1998; notable appearances at New Orleans Jazz & Heritage Festival, 1998, 1999; Nantes, France, 1999; London, England, 1999; Jazz Aspen, 1999; Dominican Republic Jazz Festival, 1999.

Awards: Best of the Beat, Best New Latin Band, *OffBeat*, 1998; Best of the Beat, Best New Contemporary Jazz Band, *OffBeat*, 1998; Best of the Beat, Best Contemporary Jazz Album, *OffBeat*, 1998; Album of the Year, Jazzusa.com, 1998; *Billboard* Latin Music Award for Contemporary Latin Jazz Album of the Year, 1999; Best New Latin Band, *OffBeat*, 1999; Best New Contemporary Jazz Band, *OffBeat*, 1999; Talent Deserving Wider Recognition, Acoustic Jazz Group, *Down Beat;* Talent Deserving Wider Recognition, Beyond Group, *Down Beat.*

Addresses: *Record company*—Basin Street Records, 4151 Canal Street, Suite C, New Orleans, LA 70119, website: www.basinstreetrecords.com.

Sidemen and Ladies

Vocalist Yvette Bostic-Summers is a regular member of the lineup, despite the group's "Hombres" name that implies all men. In complement to her vocals, she also displays her skill as a percussionist. Additionally, Bostic-Summers, along with her husband (Bill Summers) produced *Los Hombres Calientes Volume 2.*

Edwin Livingston ultimately settled into the bass player's seat behind original member David Pulphus. Livingston, like Marsalis and Mayfield, is a child of the 1970s. He was born in Texarkana, Texas, and was raised in Garland, a suburb of Dallas. He played saxophone in the sixth grade, but soon discovered a discarded bass guitar around the house and started to take lessons. At Lakeview Centennial High School he switched to double bass at the urging of his music instructor. Livingston studied under Roger Fratena of the Dallas Symphony, a disciplined experience that excited Livingston's interest in a career as a professional musician. After high school he attended Wichita State University where he studied under Mark Foley. After completing college, Livingston remained in Kansas where he served as artist-in-residence at Garden City Community College under the World Residency Act. He moved briefly to Colorado and then to Austin, Texas, where he performed in clubs while continuing his music education at Southwest Texas State University. In addition to Los Hombres, Livingston appears with alto saxophonist Wessell Anderson at assorted venues in Louisiana.

Also in Los Hombres' lineup, pianist Atkins was the only non-core member to perform at the group's exciting Snug Harbor debut in 1998; he was cited by *New Orleans* for his work on Los Hombres' debut album, "a first class recording with classy keyboard work by Atkins."

Sizzling Hot

The group is a sum of parts that include of some of the finest entertainers in jazz, which makes for a special event whenever the entire sextet can see clear of their respectively busy individual schedules to perform together. Since the group's February 7, 1998, debut at Snug Harbor, it has received warm welcomes at jazz clubs and rock clubs alike. Los Hombres Calientes effectively interprets samba, tango, bossa nova, blues, funk, reggae, and a new rhythm called songo, among other styles. Michael Point said in *Down Beat* that Los Hombres "tie together cultures with seamless sonic stitching."

Yet even while the band members maintain the purity of Latin rhythms, they meld the dance songs with undertones of jazz, always to a gratifying effect. By March of 1998, Los Hombres Calientes was a headline act at the House of Blues and signed a contract with Basin Street Records. The band released a debut album not long afterward, which scaled the charts to settle in the top 25 on the *Billboard* jazz listing. In May of 1998 the group made a splash at the New Orleans Jazz & Heritage Festival, and their album became the number one seller at the festival, not only that year, but for two years in succession, 1998-99. Additionally the group is well known at New Orleans' Funky Butt on Congo Square.

November of 1999 brought the release of their second album, *Los Hombres Calientes Volume 2,* on which they introduced Livingston as bassist for the group. Also contributing to the mood on the 18-track follow-up album were the Louisiana Philharmonic String Quartet, Derwin Perkins on guitar, Cornell Williams on bass, Ronald Markham on keyboards, and Philip Manuel and Alain Fernandez on vocals.

Awards and Adulation

Within two years of the Los Hombres Snug Harbor debut, the group won an impressive collection of awards and nominations. In *Down Beat,* Los Hombres was cited in the critic's poll as the Talent Deserving Wider Recognition in both the acoustic jazz and "beyond group" categories. The *Times-Picayune* of New Orleans cited the *Los Hombres Calientes* debut album as the Local CD of 1998, and the album was named Album of the Year by Jazzusa.com. Particularly impressive were the group's five wins in the *OffBeat* Best of the Beat competition, as winner for Best New Latin band, Best New Contemporary Jazz Band, and Best Contemporary Jazz Album, along with runner-up citations for Best Contemporary Jazz Band and Best Latin Album. Additionally Los Hombres was nominated twice in 1999 for the *Gambit* Big Easy Entertainment Award. *Los Hombres Calientes* also received the award for Contemporary Latin Jazz Album of the Year at *Billboard*'s Latin Music Awards for 1999. The Summerses and Mayfield accepted the award on April 27, 2000.

Selected discography

Los Hombres Calientes, Basin Street Records, 1998.
Los Hombres Calientes Volume 2, Basin Street Records, 1999.

Sources

Periodicals

Billboard, November 27, 1999, p. 52; April 15, 2000, p. 42.
Down Beat, December 1998, p. 99; March 2000, p. 44-47, p. 67.
New Orleans, July 1998, p. 44; April 1999, p. 58.

Online

All Music Guide, http://allmusic.com (May 19, 2000).
"*Billboard*'s Latin Jazz Album of the Year!" http://www.basinstreetrecords.com/loshombres.html (May 19, 2000).
"Congruent Angles," *Austin Chronicle,* http://www.auschron.com/issues /vol18/issue07/music.Livingston.html (May 20, 2000).

—*Gloria Cooksey*

Shelby Lynne

Singer, songwriter

Shelby Lynne, like musicians such as Lyle Lovett and k.d. lang who preceded her, was destined to become famous as an exceptionally gifted singer and songwriter whose talent proved too broad for the confines of country music. "Unlike many more popular artists," noted Miriam Longino in the *Atlanta Journal-Constitution,* "whose pleasant voices tend to sound interchangeable on radio, Lynne can wrap her pipes around a song to squeeze every choke, growl and he-done-me-wrong out of it. She has the guts and delivery of Patsy Cline laid over the choo-choo boogie of Asleep at the Wheel." Though she walked away with the Academy of Country Music Award for best new female artist in 1991 and was hawked as a mainstream country singer early in her career, Lynne's roots are nonetheless firmly planted in history, beckoning back to Dusty Springfield's Memphis-era recordings, as well as the nearly-forgotten western swing, big-band sound of Bob Wills. At the same time, however, Lynne mines the past sparingly, most notably on her acclaimed 2000 release *I Am Shelby Lynne,* enabling her own identity to filter through.

A teen phenomenon in the 1980s who was signed the day she arrived in Nashville, Lynne, a small girl with a grand, soulful voice, seemed poised for stardom. However, after three record deals—none of which yielded significant radio hits—Nashville's Music Row had given up hopes of making Lynne the next Patty Loveless or Tanya Tucker. Not only could she belt out torch songs and country standards on a par with the best, Lynne could also sing in other tones: "a drooping twang, a bluesy moan, conversational asides or the confiding delicacy of a jazz singer," wrote John Parles in a *New York Times* review. A notorious Nashville rebel to boot, Lynne failed to fit into the country music industry's cookie-cutter ideal. "I was a miserable son of a bitch," she admitted to *Spin* magazine's Mark Schone, recalling the days when she felt as though her singing career had ended. "I was quitting the business; I didn't feel anybody believed in me as somebody who had something *real* to offer." Nonetheless, Lynne never held any doubts about her unquestionable talent or career choice. "I was born a star," she added. "That's not the issue."

Born on October 22, 1968, in Quantico, Virginia, Shelby Lynne Moorer was raised in the South Alabama swamp town of Jackson in the even smaller settlement of Frankville, population 150. Lynne discovered her love for music and performing at the tender age of four, when her father, a high school English teacher, lifted the youngster onto a table at Shakey's Pizza in Mobile and she sang "You Are My Sunshine" for all the other patrons. "I've always been serious about my music, since I picked up the guitar when I was 8 and taught myself to play," Lynne told Longino. "Anything I do musically is natural, and I sing it the way I feel at the time. Each song usually takes me somewhere, and I go."

Born Shelby Lynne Moorer on October 22, 1968, in Quantico, VA; daughter of a high school English teacher and a legal secretary; married and divorced.

Started singing at age four and playing guitar at age eight; recorded at the age of 15, with her mother and sister Allison Moorer, a cover of the Four Knights song "Couldn't Stay Away From You"; Lynne's father, in front of his two teenage daughters, shot his wife to death and then killed himself, 1986; moved to Nashville at the age of 18; appeared on TNN's *Nashville Now*, 1987; released three albums for Epic Records, 1989-91; released Western swing album *Temptation*, 1993; released her most celebrated album, *I Am Shelby Lynne*, on Island Records, 2000.

Addresses: *Record company*—Island Records, 825 8th Ave., 24th Fl., New York City, NY 10019, (212) 333-8000.

Found Comfort in Her Music

A self-described tomboy and outcast at school who, by the age of ten preferred listening to old Elvis Presley records, singing, and playing guitar over making friends and studying, Lynne found comfort from an unhappy childhood in her music. She grew up on her father's Willie Nelson and Waylon Jennings albums, as well as rock and roll music from the 1950s and 1960s, compliments of her mother, a legal secretary. At home, the young singer also discovered her grandmother's 78s, memorizing songs by Bob Wills, Jimmie Rodgers, and the Mills Brothers.

With her records spinning, Lynne would practice singing, using a hairbrush for a microphone and dreaming of one day becoming a star herself. Her mother, along with sister Allison, would on occasion join in, and when Lynne was 15, the harmonizing trio cut a single, a cover of the Four Knights song "Couldn't Stay Away From You." Although the recording made little impact, it did help spark two careers: that of Lynne, and eventually that of her younger sister Allison Moorer, who in 1999 won an Academy Award nomination as co-writer of the song "A Soft Place to Fall" from the film *The Horse Whisperer,* and by 2000 had recorded two country albums for MCA Records. Lynne's father also contributed to the project, the flip side of the single being one of his own originals. "His songs were kind of that whole Dylanesque, I'm-a-travelin'-man type of

thing," she recalled to Schone. "When I look at them, I can see this dude was sharp."

However, Lynne's father, a heavy drinker who abused his wife, didn't live to see whether the record would spark his career. "I loved and admired him," Lynne said softly of her father in an interview with *Los Angeles Times* writer Robert Hilburn. "But we just fought all the time. We were too much alike. Daddy had a drinking problem, and I was the only human being on Earth who ever stood up to him. I think he was a brilliant man with no outlet, very frustrated." In 1985, her mother fled with the two girls to nearby Mobile, but her father soon discovered their whereabouts. And in 1986, in front of a 17-year-old Lynne and her sister, he shot his wife to death before taking his own life.

Lynne refused to discuss the details of her parents' deaths with the media, but did explain the impact of the tragic event on her life and career. Critics repeatedly made the narrow assumption that her pain caused her talent and artistry to surface, a connection that Lynne always detested. "Everyone says, 'She's so good [a singer] because this happened' or 'She's so difficult because…,'" Lynne, known for her own drinking and rebellious nature, forcefully said to Hilburn. "Maybe so, but only partially. I was just as damn difficult when I was 7 years old as I was when I was 18. My father always told me to be an individual, and I've remembered that every day of my life."

Nashville Bound

After the incident, the girls moved in with their grandmother who broadened Lynne's musical interests to include rhythm and blues and jazz singers. However, Lynne wanted to be on her own, and at 18, she married and moved to Nashville. The marriage lasted less than two years, but Lynne had already made important strides with her career. In the wake of a buzz generated by demo tapes as well as a chance appearance in October of 1987 singing on the TNN network's *Nashville Now,* she found herself recording a duet entitled "If I Could Bottle This Up" with George Jones and working with Billy Sherrill, one of the most influential producers in country music. The hit-making artists he worked with included, among others, Jones, Tammy Wynette, Charlie Rich, Tanya Tucker, David Houston, Barbara Mandrell, Janie Fricke, and Johnny Paycheck.

"Isn't she something?" Sherrill said to Hilburn, recollecting his days of working with Lynne. "I thought she was the best thing I ever heard in my life, country-wise, but I couldn't get across to the people who ran the company how good she was. She's definitely her own person, but people are wrong when they say she'd never listen to reason. What she wouldn't listen to is idiots." Country superstar Willie Nelson, who shared a label, manager, and eventually a stage with the young singer expressed a similar sentiment to Schone. "To me, she's as good as Billie Holiday, but I knew she was going to have trouble being commercially successful in Nashville. They don't know what to do with someone that talented."

Thus, Lynne's five Nashville albums for various labels revealed only occasional moments of interest. Signing with Epic Records—for whom she recorded three country-pop albums—Lynne released the Sherrill-produced *Sunrise* in 1989. "It's a record by a little-bitty, green, eager singer who's desperate to please," she told *Uncut*'s Nigel Williamson, as quoted by Eric Weisbard in the *Village Voice*. Lynne dismissed her second Epic release, 1990's *Tough All Over,* as "crap commercial country," though it contained traces of rhythm and blues as well. Lynne called her final album for Epic, the tepid *Soft Talk* released in 1991, "my rebellion."

By 1992, Lynne began to chafe at the style of music Epic pushed her to record. "I was very headstrong and a little crazy," the singer recalled to Marc Weingarten of the *Washington Post*. "I wanted to have things right for me, but I didn't know what right was. There are good songs in Nashville, but you have to have the patience to find the right tunes. I wish I had known that then." Frustrated with her label's demands, Lynne left Epic: "That was when I started taking control of how I wanted to make records. I had at that point decided I'm not gonna be able to do this until I do it for me."

Disillusioned with Music Row

Striking out on her own, Lynne remained without a label for two years. During this time, the singer focused on writing songs for the first time. Those originals ended up on her acclaimed 1993 album for the short-lived Morgan Creek label entitled *Temptation,* an album that sought to recreate the big-band Western swing era and demonstrated Lynne's versatility. After Morgan Creek folded, Lynne moved to Nashville's most impacting independent label, Magnatone Records, to record 1995's *Restless.* Here, Lynne mixed country, bluegrass, big band, and blues into an electrifying concoction, but she would later disavow the stab at another mainstream country album.

Tired of Nashville, Lynne put her singing career on hold in 1997 and moved into a rented "camp" house in Mobile Bay. Soon thereafter, she found hope in Bill Bottrell, whose roots-tinged production on Sheryl Crow's 1995 debut *Tuesday Night Music Club* she greatly admired. Through a former manager, Lynne had sent a demo tape to Betty Bottrell, the producer's wife and manager. From the onset, Bottrell encouraged Lynne to drop the pretense of her upbeat songs and face the tragedies in her life through her writing, including what her father had done. "I don't know if she'd want me saying this," Bottrell ventured to Schone, "but I kind of forced her to do that, and we spent months on it. The song [about the death of Lynne's parents] is called 'The Sky Is Purple,' and it's not on the album. But that's sort of how she learned to do confessional songwriting."

A creative breakthrough, the painful song helped the developing songwriter to further explore her own feelings about ruined relationships and self-doubt. Other songs that explored the darker side included "Why Can't You Be?", a tune she scribbled while upset and drinking on a plane, as well as "Life Is Bad," a song full of images of blood, tombs, and sinking ships that she wrote in ten minutes one morning. Lynne also returned to some of her musical roots, aside from country, as well, spending hours re-examining the songs of Springfield, Nina Simone, Aretha Franklin, and the Band, all of which influenced the music for her personal lyrics.

Won Acclaim and Validation

When Lynne and Bottrell took the album to label executives, *I Am Shelby Lynne* was met with enthusiasm. "We were knocked out," recalled Island Records executive Jim Caparro to Hilburn. "We all felt she made a brilliant record." However, not wanting the album to fall through the cracks, Island took time to put together a special marketing plan, which included releasing *I Am Shelby Lynne* first in England, hoping to attract attention across Europe before bringing it to the United States. The plan worked, and reviews and sales in England—and later back home—were sensational. "When the reviews started coming in from Europe, she finally felt validated," noted Bottrell.

While patiently awaiting the album's release in America, Lynne, in the spring of 1999, moved to Palm Springs, California, well outside the orbit of the major music cities. "The sun is out all the time, and nobody's here," she explained to Weingarten, adding, "the only way to make a change is to do it radically." Here, Lynne lives in a sleek, retro-modern house modeled on the landmark residences built by legendary Palm Springs architect Albert Frey. Reveling in a solitary lifestyle, Lynne spends most of her time writing songs, reading, cruising the desert highways in a black 1960s Cadillac listening to hip-hop, or hanging out at a Rat Pack-era bar/restaurant called Melvyn's.

Selected discography

Sunrise, Epic, 1989.
Tough All Over, Epic, 1990.
Soft Talk, Epic, 1991.
Temptation, Morgan Creek, 1993.
Restless, Magnatone, 1995.
I Am Shelby Lynne, Island, 2000.

Sources

Atlanta Journal-Constitution, June 9, 1995; April 20, 2000.
Billboard, March 23, 1996.
Fortune, February 21, 2000.
Los Angeles Times, February 13, 2000.
New York Times, April 15, 2000.
People, November 22, 1993; February 26, 1996.
Rolling Stone, September 30, 1993; February 17, 2000.
Spin, March 2000, pp. 109-10.
Village Voice, April 11, 2000.
Washington Post, March 12, 2000; April 14, 2000.

—Laura Hightower

Rita MacNeil

Singer, songwriter

Photograph by Gunter Marx. Corbis. Reproduced by permission. ©

Against the odds and following years of determination, singer and songwriter Rita MacNeil has become one of the biggest, brightest, and most beloved stars in her native Canada, where many considered her a musical legend. But while her popularity soared over the years—not only in Canada, but in other countries across the globe as well—one would find it all but impossible to locate a Rita MacNeil album in the United States, except through her website. Most agree that her absence in the American market comes down to externals. A large woman with a faint yet noticeable cleft palate who has battled a weight problem along with teasing throughout her life, MacNeil has yet to find her place in an image-conscious industry, despite her wide-ranging talents. Nonetheless, MacNeil understands the pressures of working in a business set on appearances, even though such factors have nothing to do with her music. As David Napier in *Saturday Night* noted, "it's the music—heart-wrenching lyrics backed by a haunting voice—that has brought the middle-aged mother of two to the brink of international stardom."

MacNeil took the often malicious attacks and jokes about her weight in stride, working throughout her 20-year career to overcome preconceptions. "We all look different in this world and should have the right to do what we love to do, no matter what," said the award-winning singer to *World & I* contributor Linda Joyce Forristal. While MacNeil has encountered difficulties throughout her lifetime, including intense shyness and dealing with sexual abuse as a child at the hands of an uncle, her struggles have served as the impetus for her songwriting, and for this she remains grateful. Within the lyrics and melodies of her numerous hits—rich, emotional recollections that never fail to rouse her endearing fans such as "Working Man," "Flying on Your Own," "I'll Accept the Rose," and "She's Called Nova Scotia"—live MacNeil's own personal experiences and the tragedies of those around her.

Because of her unique ability to relate to others' hardships, MacNeil has acted as a source of inspiration for millions of listeners worldwide, including fans from Sweden, Japan, Australia, the United Kingdom, and her own homeland. Her frequent concert tours, both at home and abroad, always sell out. In Canada, the singer's 15 albums have consistently exceeded the platinum sales mark, and she saw several top ten hits in both Britain and Australia. An artist known for her wide range of styles—from Celtic, country, and folk to rhythm and blues, pop, and rock—MacNeil appeals to a variety of fans. Like so many modern-day songwriters, she has gained much of her musical nourishment from the radio. "I'd listen to everything from Celtic to rock to Hawaiian music," she recollected, according to her website. "As a teenager, I could hardly wait to be able to come home from school and put the radio on. I liked everybody, that was the whole premise of my life."

Born on May 28, 1944, in the town of Big Pond in Cape Breton, Nova Scotia, Canada; daughter of Renee and Neil MacNeil; siblings: three brothers, four sisters; married and divorced; children: Laura and Wade.

Began recording career in Toronto and Ottawa playing in small clubs and at feminist rallies; released self-produced and distributed debut album *Born a Woman,* 1975; returned to hometown of Pig Pond, late-1970s; performed 72 shows at the Expo '86 in Vancouver and became an "overnight" success; signed with Virgin Records (Canada) after high sales of independent album *Flying on Your Own,* 1987; performed at the Royal Albert Hall in London, 1991; signed with EMI Music, 1995; published autobiography *On a Personal Note* and released album *A Night at the Orpheum,* 1999.

Awards: Three Juno Awards for Most Promising Artist, 1987; Female Vocalist, 1990; and Female Country Vocalist, 1991; four Canadian Country Music Awards for Country Fan Choice of the Year, 1991 and 1992, as well as for Top Selling Album, 1990 and 1991; five honorary doctorates from the University of New Brunswick, St. Mary's University, Mount St. Vincent, St. Francis Xavier, and University College of Cape Breton; inducted into the Order of Canada, 1992; Gemini Award for television show *Rita & Friends,* 1996.

Addresses: *Record company*—EMI-Capitol Music Group, 1290 Avenue of the Americas, New York City, NY 10104, (212) 253-3000. *Website*—Rita MacNeil: http://www.ritamacneil.com.

Bestowed with several honors and awards for her contributions to the world of music, MacNeil won three Juno Awards for Most Promising Artist in 1987, Female Vocalist in 1990, and Female Country Vocalist in 1991; four Canadian Country Music Awards for Country Fan Choice of the Year in 1991 and again in 1992, as well as for Top Selling Album in 1990 and 1991; and received five honorary doctorates from the University of New Brunswick, St. Mary's University, Mount St. Vincent, St. Francis Xavier, and University College of Cape Breton. One of MacNeil's proudest moments occurred when she was inducted into the Order of Canada in 1992. In a career filled with accomplish-

ments, two other highlights stand out for MacNeil: a 1991 performance at the Royal Albert Hall in London, England, and a prior 1986 appearance at Expo '86 in Vancouver, British Columbia, Canada. "Vancouver is one of my favorite places," MacNeil stated on her website. "It's where I got my big break and it will always have a special place in my heart. The press were very kind and I think they were responsible for getting people out to the shows. It was the springboard that enabled me to continue and opened up a lot of doors for me."

Determined to Sing

Most of the credit for a performer's rise to fame, however, is due to the singer's own perseverance. MacNeil, the fifth of eight children born to Renee and Neil MacNeil on May 28, 1944, in the town of Big Pond in Cape Breton, Nova Scotia, Canada, started singing with her extended family, who immigrated to North America from the Isle of Barra in Scotland four generations before. On a regular basis, family members and friends would get together for informal "kitchen parties," during which someone would play an instrument and everyone would sing. By the age of six, MacNeil realized that she wanted to spend the rest of her life in music. "I sang first because I was compelled to," wrote MacNeil in her 1999 autobiography entitled *On a Personal Note,* "as if I were freeing my spirit." Both MacNeil's father, a hard-working carpenter and shop owner who inspired the singer to later write the song "Old Man" (available on 1981's *Part of the Mystery* and 1992's *Thinking of You*), and especially her mother, who stayed busy raising MacNeil and her three brothers and four sisters, supported their daughter's aspirations from the beginning.

In 1952, MacNeil moved with her parents and siblings from Big Pond to Sydney, Nova Scotia, in order for her father to find more work. But despite an industry boom in that town, carpentry work remained scarce, and her father continued to struggle to make ends meet. It was during these years that MacNeil developed a case of severe shyness, a condition intensified by her harelip and teasing by classmates. Even though singing around those she knew well came easily as a child, when she tried to take formal music lessons, the bashful MacNeil was unable to utter a single note for her teacher. Later on, she entered a local Kiwanis Music Festival, but froze midway through her performance and wept all the way home.

As a result, MacNeil never learned to read, write, or play a musical note. Instead, she learned to create songs in her head, a technique she continued to use as an adulthood. According to MacNeil, she sings and hums words, and the melodies just comes to her. After composing songs by memory, she then sings them to her band, who help MacNeil mold each tune into a polished product.

Faced Stage Fright

Although MacNeil, at the time still desperately afraid to perform in public, spent most of her early life practicing songs by singing to her mother and using a broom handle as a microphone, she made up her mind during her teens to overcome her stage fright in order to fulfill her longtime dream. At the age of 17, in the early-1960s, she left home and moved to Toronto, Ontario, believing that the big city would provide her more opportunities to sing. In Toronto, MacNeil started singing in small clubs and bars and eventually married and had two children, Laura and Wade. During these years, MacNeil was also involved in the women's movement and became a sort of musical spokesperson, performing regularly at feminist rallies around Toronto. However, worried that she might be pigeonholed, MacNeil later removed herself from the activist scene. "I can use the word feminist, it's other people who don't understand it that make me nervous," she explained to Napier.

MacNeil's marriage ended in divorce after six years, and she moved with her children to Ottawa, Ontario, where she spent her darkest days a single mother. Forced to support her children on her own, MacNeil took various jobs as a janitor, sales clerk, and waitress, in addition to occasional performances, to earn enough money for her family. "A lot of songs come out of those hard times and you learn a lot about yourself," she recalled on her website. "You learn about what it's like being on both sides of the fence as far as trying to meet your bills and make a living. Then when things start to go well, and things are easier you can look back on those hard times to give you strength to get through everything. It's great inspiration for writing."

Returned to Her Roots

Feeling homesick, MacNeil in the late-1970s returned to her first childhood home, Big Pond. Soon thereafter, her luck began to change, and after giving a total of 72 performances during the Expo '86 in Vancouver, she became an "overnight" sensation. Prior to this breakthrough, though, MacNeil had already begun her recording career, releasing her early albums independently. Her debut, 1975's *Born a Woman,* was produced and distributed with help from MacNeil's friends, who collected money to finance the project. In 1981, the singer arrived with *Part of the Mystery,* then released her third album, *I'm Not What I Seem,* in 1985. All of her self-produced records—with the latter album partially produced by the CBC (Canadian Broadcasting Company) and distributed by the College of Cape Breton—did relatively well, selling around 10,000 copies each. Although now out of print, her early recordings are available for download via her website.

MacNeil forged ahead with a fourth album, 1987's *Flying on Your Own,* a record she hoped would attract major-label interest. Although record companies rejected the effort, she released *Flying on Your Own,* the title-track being her signature song about a woman's inner strength after a failed relationship, by herself. Eventually, the release sold so many copies that Virgin Records (Canada) offered to distribute. Now signed to EMI Music, MacNeil continues to publish her songs through her own Lupins Productions, headquartered in Sydney and managed by her son.

Continuing to record—including a performance with the Vancouver Symphony Orchestra entitled *A Night at the Orpheum,* released in 1999—and touring almost non-stop throughout the 1990s, MacNeil also worked in television during these years on her own hit variety show on CBC called *Rita & Friends* (winner of a 1996 Gemini Award) from 1994 until 1997. Over the three seasons it aired, *Rita & Friends* entertained more than one million viewers each week and featured an eclectic mix of guests such as songwriter Joni Mitchell, rock singer Jeff Healy, and alternative acts like the Crash Test Dummies and Sloan. Other side projects included toying with the idea of her own line of plus-size clothing and opening her famous Tea Room, a popular tourist stop in a renovated school house in her hometown. Completed in the early-1990s and run by MacNeil's daughter, the well-known destination serves baked goods, teas, and Rita MacNeil memorabilia.

Selected discography

Born a Woman, Boot Records Ltd., 1975.
Part of the Mystery, Lupins, 1981.
I'm Not What I Seem, UCCB Press, 1983.
Flying on Your Own, Lupins, 1987.
Reason to Believe, Lupins/Virgin Music Canada, 1988.
Now the Bells Ring, Lupins/Virgin Music Canada, 1988.
Rita, Lupins/Virgin Music Canada, 1989.
Home I'll Be, Lupins/Virgin Music Canada, 1990.
Thinking of You, Lupins/Virgin Music Canada, 1992.
Once Upon a Christmas, Lupins/Virgin Music Canada, 1993.
Songs from the Collection, Lupins/Virgin Music Canada, 1994.
Porch Songs, EMI Music Canada, 1995.
Joyful Sounds, EMI, 1996.
A Night at the Orpheum, EMI Music Canada, 1999.

Sources

Books

MacNeil, Rita, *On a Personal Note,* Key Porter, 1998.

Periodicals

Billboard, February 12, 1994, p. 27.
Maclean's (Toronto), November 2, 1992; March 3, 1997, p. 15; November 24, 1997, p. 118; January 18, 1999.
Saturday Night (Toronto), October 1995.
World & I (Washington), October 1998.

Online

All Music Guide, http://www.allmusic.com (April 29, 2000).
Rita MacNeil Official Website, http://www.ritamacneil.com (April 29, 2000).

—Laura Hightower

Mint Condition

R&B band

Mint Condition, known for ballads such as the gold singles "Swingin'" and "Breakin' My Heart (Pretty Brown Eyes)," arrived on the music scene in 1991 with *Meant to Be Mint,* progressively carving a niche for themselves in the world of rhythm and blues over the years that followed. The Minneapolis sextet built a fanbase the old-fashioned way: through live performances. Taking cues from groups before them like the Gap Band and Earth, Wind, and Fire, Mint Condition remained one of the genre's few acts that play as a self-contained live band—a rare occurrence in today's market-driven music industry.

Whereas many contemporary R&B and soul-inspired groups arrive on the musical landscape solely as an "album act," Mint Condition, a union of dedicated musicians who believe that playing their own instruments helps to vocalize their art, have always preferred to "keep it real," usually opting to record in a live studio. For this reason, Mint Condition stand apart from their peers, courageously resisting the temptation to implement formula over function. Their 1999 album, *Life's Aquarium,* a collection of songs that centers on life experiences, continued to showcase Mint Condition's unique dedication to an ideology that was conceived a full decade prior.

The members of Mint Condition include Larry Waddell on keyboards, Homer O'Dell on guitar, Stokley Williams on lead vocals and drums, Jeff Allen on saxophone and keyboards, Kerri Lewis on keyboards, and Ricky Kinchen on bass. All of the members, excluding Kinchen, who came to the group from Chicago, gradu-

ated from Central High School in St. Paul, Minnesota. Before joining forces as Mint Condition, all the band members played in various bands and backed singers around the Minneapolis-St. Paul area. The products of a similar musical environment, the members of Mint Condition also shared a musical sensibility that transcended cultural and generational boundaries. Not only do they remain respectful and indebted to the rich African American musical tradition, but they also recognize the countless varieties of expression from around the world.

Mint Condition, who dabble in funk, jazz, and rock in addition to R&B, admire and pay tribute to a myriad of artists from the past as well as the present. "We came up listening to all those bands from the '70s—Cameo, Funkadelic, Led Zeppelin, a bit of everything," Williams recalled in an interview with *USA Today*'s Steve Jones upon the release of the group's 1996 album *Definition of a Band.* "On a lot of the songs we just set up and played in a circle and recorded mistakes and all because that's what musicianship and real music is about—the element of surprise." This sense of musicianship, note many critics, lacks in much of the hip-hop and producer-driven vocal acts that dominated the R&B scene throughout the 1990s.

Formed in Minneapolis, Minnesota, in 1989, Mint Condition started out performing in local clubs before attracting the attention of producers Jimmy Jam and Terry Lewis of Perspective Records, a subsidiary of A&M Records. "There was definitely a kinship there," Williams told Jones, adding that Mint Condition received a lot of useful advice from the production duo. "After they came out to see us at a live show, they told us we had a deal." After signing a record deal, Mint Condition set about their dream of revitalizing the live band sound.

Mint Condition viewed this as an important mission, Williams said, given the fact that so many public schools have cut music programs out of the curriculum altogether, leaving many musically inclined youngsters to become either rappers or DJs as outsets for musical self-expression. However, Williams does admit that there are some positive signs emerging from the rap scene. "We see a lot of changes even within the hip-hop community. They are actually starting to have bands and they are actually helping a lot of the old bands to come back out just by using their samples and reviving the whole sound."

In 1991, the sextet debuted with *Meant to Be Mint,* an album containing the hit songs "Breakin' My Heart (Pretty Brown Eyes)," which rose to number one on the *Billboard* R&B chart, and "Forever in Your Eyes." Mint Condition returned in 1993 with *From the Mint Factory,* which yielded another hit single that reached number two on *Billboard's* Hot R&B chart entitled "U Send Me Swingin'." However, both albums, with regards to sales, failed to achieve a mainstream breakthrough for the group.

Hoping to attracted more buyers, record company executives and Mint Condition made a concerted effort—without sacrificing quality—to propel the group's third album, 1996's *Definition of a Band,* higher up the charts. The first single off the album, "What Kind of Man Would I Be," about remaining faithful in a relationship, smashed the *Billboard* Hot R&B top five. The video received regular television rotation and featured the musicians playing their instruments. "We would show up for shows, and they wouldn't have any instruments for us," O'Dell explained to Jones. "They would have six mikes set up and we'd say, 'Where're the drums? Where're the keyboards? So for this album we wanted to make sure that we got that point across."

Another single, "Let Me Be the One," featured lyrical/vocal flavor by Q-Tip from A Tribe Called Quest. Overall, the album won critical praise for its mixture of R&B, rock, soul, jazz, funk, and Caribbean and African sounds. Most importantly, the members of Mint Condition were thankful to have survived the ups and downs of the music industry. "This is our third album, and a lot of people we came out with in '89 are not here now. To me, that's more successful than selling a million albums," observed Williams, as quoted in *Jet* magazine. "We haven't won a Grammy," remarked Kinchen in agreement, "but we kind of have when you get Stevie Wonder calling you saying he likes your stuff. It keeps

you going when you have the support of your peers and musicians who have paved the way for you."

After a three-year absence and a switch to a new label, Elektra Entertainment, Mint Condition resurfaced in September of 1999 with *Life's Aquarium,* on which the band continued to serve up a blend of funk, jazz, rock, R&B, and even Latin rhythms. In addition to the uptempo romance track and first single "If You Love Me," the album also included a song entitled "Pretty Lady," recorded with one of Mint Condition's idols, Gap Band lead singer Charlie Wilson. The collaboration came about after Mint Condition attended one of the Gap Bands shows in Minneapolis. "It was an honor recording with someone we've always listened to," Williams told *Billboard*'s Gil Griffin. "I learned humility, staying down to earth, and practicing my craft from him."

Selected discography

Singles

"Breakin' My Heart," Perspective, 1991.
"Forever in Your Eyes," Perspective, 1992.
"Are You Free," Perspective, 1992.
"U Send Me Swingin'," A&M, 1993.
"Nobody Does It Betta," A&M, 1993.
"Someone to Love," A&M, 1994.
"So Fine," Perspective, 1994.
"What Kind of Man Would I Be," A&M, 1996.
"You Don't Have to Hurt No More," Perspective, 1997.
"Let Me Be the One," Perspective, 1997.
"If You Love Me," Elektra, 1999.
"If You Love Me" (maxi single), Elektra, 1999.

Albums

Meant To Be Mint, Perspective, 1991.
From the Mint Factory, Perspective, 1993.
Definition of a Band, Perspective, 1996.
The Collection (1991-1998), Perspective, 1998.
Life's Aquarium, Elektra, 1999.

Sources

Periodicals

Billboard, August 10, 1996; September 7, 1996; January 11, 1997; June 28, 1997; August 14, 1999; August 21, 1999.
Jet, February 24, 1997.
USA Today, October 28, 1996.

Online

Mint Condition: Life's Aquarium, http://www.mintfactory.com (June 14, 2000).
Sonicnet.com, http://www.sonicnet.com (June 14, 2000).

—*Laura Hightower*

Phil
Minton

Singer, trumpeter

© Jack Vartoogian. Reproduced by permission.

Phil Minton may possess one of the most remarkable voices ever recorded, either in a musical or nonmusical setting. While he has had notable outings singing traditional lyrics, particularly settings of the poetry of William Blake, fans of improvisational music know him best for his plethora of vocal sounds not normally associated with singers—an assortment of mumbles, gargles, swizzles, burps, hiccups, and screams that many would be hard-pressed to interpret as artistic. "It's remarkable how horrible it is," Kenneth Goldman of the *New York Press* said about Minton's solo CD, *A Doughnut In One Hand*, an album that does not contain a single musical instrument, not a single melody, indeed not a single musical note, at least not in any traditional sense, "but it's equally remarkable how you can't tear yourself away from it; it has the effect of a Warhol *Electric Chair* or a car crash: You know you shouldn't look but you can't stop staring… Minton, for the first time, forces us to ponder the musical qualities of noises that we'd rather not deal with and that fact alone makes this an important recording."

Phil Minton was the product of a family of singers in the United Kingdom. His father and uncle were both members of a Welsh male choir in the town of Torquay, England, and his mother is reputed to have possessed an impressive soprano voice. "Singing and choirs were always a talking point in our house," Minton told Brian Marley of *Rubberneck*. Minton displayed vocal talent from an early age, and not just as a singer. He was able to impersonate the voices of various celebrities and family members, and to produce a wide range of miscellaneous sounds, which quickly cut short his time at the local boys choir. "I was probably a bit too disruptive to be a choirboy for very long," he admitted to Marley.

Minton wasn't interested in much musically except singing and whistling until he turned 15. Around that time, he heard Louis Armstrong for the first time, which sparked a desire to learn trumpet. The decision was made easier, Minton told Marley, because a trumpet "had three valves and looked easier than saxophone." He started listening to Dizzy Gillespie, Miles Davis and other contemporary jazz artists. But it was hearing John Coltrane on Davis's album *Cooking* that opened Minton's ears to the possibilities of jazz. "Coltrane's sound was just about the most exciting thing I'd ever heard," he told Marley. "I was completely and utterly hooked on music by then."

Unable to find a teacher in Torquay who could explain the dynamics of the new jazz, Minton was forced to fall back on his own resources. He taught himself trumpet and singing while performing in local jazz and blues bands. His interests turned to improvised music, inspired in large part not by music but by the so-called "action paintings" of abstract expressionist Jackson Pollack, which Minton decided were exactly what music should sound like. Anxious to improvise, Minton

Born on November 1, 1940, in Torquay, England.

Learned trumpet as a teenager; member of the Brian Waldron Quintet, 1959-61; performed as trumpeter and vocalist with Mike Westbrook Band, 1963-64; singer and trumpeter with the English group Jonston Macphilbry on Canary Islands, 1964-65; rejoined Mike Westbrook Band, 1971; worked with theater groups Welfare State, IOU, and others, 1970s; formed group Voice with Maggie Nicols and Julie Tippetts, 1975; worked with artists such as Fred Frith, Roger Turner, Peter Brotxmann and Junter Christmann's Vario, 1979-84; performed in Konran Boermer's opera Apocalipsis cum figuris, Lindsay Cooper's Oh Moscow, and Sally Potter's film Gold, late 1980's; first worked with Vervan Weston, 1987; Weston and Minton's *Songs From a Prison Diary* commissioned by the Le Mans Festival, 1989; *SongsFrom a Prison Diary* premieres, 1990; made guest appearances wih Geörg Graewe's Grüben Klang Orchester, Trio Raphiphi with Radu Malfatti and Phil Wachsmann, John Butcher and Erhard Hirt, and Oxley's Celebration Orchestra, 1990s. Feral Choir project initiated in Stockholm and Berlin, 1994; toured the United States with Bob Ostertag's piece, Say No More, 1994.

Awards: Voted Best Male Singer in Europe by International Jazz Forum, 1988; Cornelius Cardew Composition Prize for *Songs From a Prison Diary*, 1991.

Addresses: *Record company*—FMP, Postfach 100 227, D-10562, Berlin, Germany. *E-mail*—Phil Minton, pminton@dircon.co.uk.

formed a group with two friends and began playing "action music" that saw him engaging in both vocal and physical gymnastics; he sang his repertoire of different mouth sounds while jumping and twisting across the stage. The group held a single public concert—which drew no audience. "Although it was very exciting to us, we didn't quite know what we were doing," Minton confessed to Paul Dutton in *Coda*. "I never thought I'd end up making a living doing such wonderful things."

In the early 1960s, Minton played trumpet in English dance bands to earn his living. Then, in 1963, he was asked to join the Mike Westbrook Band, one of the seminal bands of the British free jazz movement. Working with Westbrook enabled Minton to focus on performing the kind of music he truly loved. "I then started seriously but tentatively to explore, and I tried to do it with my voice," he told Marley. "I wasn't too successful at first because I didn't have the technique for it. So I stuck to the trumpet." Minton was becoming dissatisfied with the limitations of the instrument, however. Listening to his shortwave radio, he had become aware of the range of techniques used by other singers: Italian opera, blues, Tuvan throat singing of Mongolia, Yojk music of Sweden, along with the song traditions of India, the Middle East and Africa. "I was hearing all this and I really couldn't get the sounds I wanted on the trumpet," he told Marley, "and I had basically to own up to myself what was happening. I'd learned trumpet to gain credibility, to give me … the confidence to do what I'd always been doing naturally since I was a kid, playing with my voice, making different sounds, different timbres and colourings, and techniques for producing my sort of music."

Mintón left the Westbrook band in 1964 and moved first to the Canary Islands where he played trumpet and vocalized with the group Johnston Macphilby, then to Sweden where he stayed for five years. He returned to England in 1971 and rejoined Mike Westbrook's band. From the 1970s, Minton worked on a large number of projects, his own and others. He performed with most of the luminaries of the world improv scene, including Fred Frith, John Zorn, Lindsay Cooper, Lol Coxhill, Tom Cora, and the Tony Oxley Celebration Orchestra. A noteworthy collaborator was pianist Veryan Weston. Besides two albums of standards interpreted by Minton, they also composed *Songs from a Prison Diary*, a work, based on poems written by Ho Chi Minh while in French captivity. The work for 22 voices premiered in 1990 and a year later won the Cornelius Cardew Composition Prize.

Songs was an unusual work for Minton. It is "composed," meaning that it exists on paper rather being a purely improvised work. The method of composition, however, was for Minton to improvise, which Weston then transcribed. Minton does not typically base his work on literary sources, although one of his most successful works, *Mouthful of Destiny,* recorded by his quartet in 1996, used sections of James Joyce's *Finnegan's Wake*. But anyone who has heard Minton perform knows that he rarely sings "words." Instead he produces a stream of—among other sounds—barks, squeals, coughs, hiccups, rasps, belches, snorts and screams, that Goldsmith, in a review that actually managed to praise Minton's solo CD *A Doughnut in One Hand* in the *New York Press*, described as "the grossest noises [Minton] can possibly think of." But, as Goldsmith notes, that is only because Minton is working territory no other musician is working.

In his review, Goldsmith perceptively compared Minton to a Samuel Beckett character slowly disintegrating before our eyes. Minton's musical partners often become part of his devolutionary scenarios. Peter Brötzmann, for example, at a duo performance with Minton in Berlin abruptly found his clarinet in two pieces. Minton, however, never let up and Brötzmann finished the last three or four minutes of the piece squawking and braying through his bare mouthpiece, while Minton mimicked every sound he made.

Minton sees improvisation as "a natural state" for all musicians. "But music education knocks the improvisation out of most people," he told Marley, "and people nowadays can go on jazz courses to learn to be 1950s jazz musicians, which is sad and rather tragic." In response to this state of affairs, Minton began offering a vocal workshop called Phil Minton's Feral Choir. Minton's publicity material defines "feral," as "in a wild state after escape from captivity." He describes the workshop as "not only for singers but for anyone who takes a delight in the freedom to experiment ... the courage to take a vocal leap and enjoy expanding the borders of your own voice will equip you more than any formal training." The workshop has been held in Stockholm, Sweden, Berlin, Germany, Cardiff (United Kingdom), Rotterdam, Netherlands, Munich, Germany and Tokyo, Japan where 80 voices took part.

Minton stayed active during the 1990s by working with his quartet, comprised of Veryan Weston, Robert Turner and John Butcher. In 1993 he contributed to Bob Ostertag's electronic piece, *Say No More,* as well as taking part in Ostertag's tour called Say No More In Person. In 1996 he released his first solo album, *A Doughnut In One Hand.* Now in his sixth decade of performing, Minton continues to push musical boundaries.

Selected discography

Solo

A Doughnut In One Hand, FMP CD 91, 1996.

With others

Up, Umea Blue Tower BTCD 07, 1969.
(With Mike Westbrook Band) *Solid Gold Cadillac*, RCA SF 8311, 1972.
Goose Sauce, Original Records ORA 001, 1977.
Bright as Fire, Original Records ORA 003, 1980.
The Cortege, Original Records ORA 309/Enja 7087-22, 1982.
Off Abbey Road, Tip Toe 888805, 1989.
(With Fred Frith) *A Doughnut In Both Hands*, Rift3/, 1975, 1980.

(With Lol Coxhill) *Couscous*, Nato 157, 1983.
Vario, Moers Music 02048, 1983.
(With Roger Turner) *Ammo*, Leo LR 116, 1984.
Dada da, Leo CD LR 192, 1993.
On Duke's Birthday, Hat Art 2012/6021, 1984.
The Berlin Station, FMP SAJ 57, 1984.
Vario, Moers Music 02048, 1985.
(With The Ferrals) *Ruff*, Leo LR 138, 1986.
Plan Eden, Creative Works CW 1008, 1986.
(With AMM) *IRMA*, Matchless MR16, 1988.
(With GrubenKlang Orchester) *Songs and Variations*, Hat Art CD 6028, 1988.
Flavours, Fragments, ITM Classics 950014, 1992.
(With Lindsay Cooper) *Oh Moscow*, Victo cd015, 1989.
Sahara Dust, Intakt CD 029, 1992.
Trio Raphiphi, ITM 1465, 1990.
Concert Works, Random Acoustics RA 003, 1991.
Songs From a Prison Diary, Leo CD LR 196, 1991.
State of Volgograd, FMP CD 57, 1991.
AngelicA 91, CAICAI 001, 1991.
Cactuscrackling, FOR 4 EARS CD 411, 1991.
GoTo, Sans Soleil, 1991/1995.
(With the Dedication Orchestra) *Spirits Rejoice*, Ogun OGCD101, 1992.
(With Veryan Weston) *Ways*, ITM 1420, 1992.
Ways Past, ITM 1468, 1992.
(With Christian Munthe) *Muntmunt*, Blue Tower CD04, 1993.
(Bob Ostertag) *Say No More*, RecDec 59, 1993.
Say No More In Person, Transit 444444, 1994.
Verbatim, Rastascan BRD 029, 1996.
AngelicA 1994, CAICAI 006, 1994.
(With Tony Oxley Celebration Orchestra) *The Enchanted Messenger*, Soul Note 121284, 1994.
AngelicA 1995, A1 007, 1995.
(With John Butcher and Erhard Hirt) *Two Concerts*, FMP OWN 90006, 1995.
(With Jon Rose) *Techno mit Stoerungen*, Plag Dich nicht 002, 1995.
(With Phil Minton Quartet) *Mouthful of Destiny*, Victo cd041, 1996.
(With Roof) *The Untraceable Cigar*, Red Note 04, 1996
Trace, Red Note 7, 1997.
(With Bob Ostertag) *Improvisation*, Resonance 51, 1996.
(With David Moss) *Time Stories*, Intakt CD 054, 1997.
Verbatim, Flesh and Blood, SeeLand 512/Rastascan BRD 035, 1998.
(With André Goudbeek Quartet) *As It Happened*, WIMprovijf CD 310399, 1998.

Sources

Boston Globe, January 29, 1999.
Coda, September/October 1996.
New York Press, November 17, 1998.
Rubberneck, undated.

Additional information provided by Phil Minton.

—*Gerald E. Brennan*

The
Mr. T
Experience

Punk-pop band

The unsung heroes of northern California punk music, the Mr. T Experience emerged from the same Berkeley/East Bay Gilman Street punk rock music scene that eventually spawned Operation Ivy and Green Day. However, they are often overlooked, failing to figure prominently into the punk rock genealogy. In truth, the Mr. T Experience—known as MTX to fans—has been playing their brand of pop-punk, inspired largely by the Ramones, the Buzzcocks, and the Descendents, since the mid-1980s, nearly a decade before their Gilman Street peers Green Day and Rancid became mega-superstar acts. Although the Mr. T Experience never achieved the commercial success of their contemporaries, their extensive catalog of upbeat punk love songs influenced countless other similar bands nationwide. Not simply purveyors of the same punk style played by multiple bands before them, the Mr. T Experience fueled a new punk-pop sound with goofy pop culture references and catchy melodies.

The origins of the Mr. T Experience date back to the early days of the now-legendary Gilman Street music scene of Berkeley, California. The East Bay was, and still is, a mostly working-class, area located on the "wrong side" of the San Francisco Bay. Often referred to as "East Berlin" by the more upscale residents across the water in San Francisco, the East Bay was nonetheless poised to become the next breeding ground for punk rock. Beginning around 1985 and 1986, a small group of young people started performing in garages, basements, pizza parlors, and anywhere else they could find to play. These shows were

an alternative to the violent, testosterone-driven tendencies of traditional punk and hardcore, and emphasized instead a lighter-hearted, upbeat variety of punk rock.

Eventually, such efforts would evolve into the Gilman Street Project, a Berkeley warehouse that would catalyze the careers of bands like Operation Ivy, Crimpshrine, Soup, Corrupted Mortals, and Isocracy. But before these acts—their founders barely in their teens—the Mr. T Experience had already recorded the style of classic pop-punk the East Bay is now famous for. After a career that spanned well over a decade of pop-culture jokes, wistful stories about romantic complications, political satire, and grand schemes that fizzle into just stupid ideas, MTX mainstay member singer/songwriter/guitarist Dr. Frank (born Frank Portman) continued to maintain his uncompromised enthusiasm for punk music, surviving near-breakups in order to record well into the late-1990s and beyond. In fact, Dr. Frank was the only original member of the group left by the time they released *Revenge Is Sweet, and So Are You* in 1997, leading him to jokingly refer to the group as MTX "Starship."

Dr. Frank, along with guitarist Jon Von, formed the Mr. T Experience in 1985 and self-released their first album in 1986. Recorded and mixed in a single day in July, *Everybody's Entitled to Their Own Opinion,* went for tunefulness rather than overall quality. After changing drummers and enlisting Kent Steedman of the Celibate Rifles as producer, MTX returned in 1987 with a faster, harder, and more love-minded collection of 17 songs entitled *Night Shift at the Thrill Factory.* Two years later, in 1989, the Mr. T Experience released the seven-song *Big Black Bugs Bleed Blue Blood,* which included the ode to "Gilman Street." All of the band's early recordings went out of print, but were later reissued by their long-time label, Lookout! Records.

After signing to their new home, the Mr. T Experience rose to national prominence with *Making Things with Light,* released in 1990. By pushing the vocals to the forefront and placing the rhythm guitars in a more supportive role, Dr. Frank was finally able to fully realize his melodic designs, exemplified in the leading track "What Went Wrong." In addition to stronger musical design, the songwriter also moved somewhat away from characteristic punk, revealing some of himself in songs such as "I'm Breaking Out" and commenting on relationships in "She's No Rocket Scientist" and "Parasite." Another giant step forward in musical complexity, *Milk Milk Lemonade,* followed in 1992. Departing further from standard pop punk, the album entertwined vocals and guitars with even greater skill, showing more diversity than MTX had previously displayed. Alongside the rootsy "Two-Minute Itch" and the hard-rocking "Christine Bactine," Dr. Frank also invested in simple melodies with the catchy "Last Time I Listened to You" and "I Love You But You're Standing on My Foot."

For The Record . . .

Members include **Aaron** (left band in 1992 to join Samiam), bass guitar; **Alex** (left band in 1992 to join Samiam), drums; **Jym** (joined band in 1993), drums; **Dr. Frank Portman,** vocals, guitar; **Joel Reader** (joined band in 1994), bass guitar, backing vocals; **Jon Von** (left band in 1992 to join the Rip Offs).

Dr. Frank and Jon Von formed band in Berkeley, CA, in 1985; self-released debut album *Everybody's Entitled to Their Own Opinion,* 1986; signed with Lookout! Records, released *Making Things with Light,* 1990; released *Milk Milk Lemonade,* 1992; released folk-influenced *Our Bodies, Our Selves,* 1994; released *Love Is Dead,* 1996; released *Revenge Is Sweet, and So Are You,* 1997; released *Alcatraz,* 1999.

Addresses: *Record company*—Lookout! Records, P.O. Box 11374, Berkeley, CA 94712. *Website*—The Mr. T Experience at Lookout! Records: http://www.lookout records.com.

Despite these accomplishments in intricacy and ambition, the Mr. T Experience failed to beak through into the pop mainstream, due in large part to a series of lineup problems. After the release of *Milk Milk Lemonade,* the band seemingly broke up; MTX co-founder Jon Von departed in 1992 to join the Rip Offs, and bassist "Aaron" and drummer "Alex" both left soon thereafter for Samiam. However, Dr. Frank, determined to forge ahead, regrouped as a trio to record *Our Bodies, Our Selves.* Released in 1994, the calmer, more folk-influenced album, compensating for a slimmed-down lineup, focused instead on Dr. Franks's consistently improving songwriting. Critics noted "The Dustbin of History," "More Than Toast," and "Game Over" as evidence of his creative momentum.

Still, the Mr. T Experience remained in danger of disbanding for good after further personnel shifts. At a crucial moment in 1994, a then 17-year-old bassist named Joel Reader ran into Dr. Frank on Gilman Street. When Reader learned that MTX was in danger of breaking up for want of a bassist, he casually mentioned that he had been playing along with Mr. T Experience records since the age of 11, and it seemed as if the young guitarist was perfect for the job. Thus, MTX, in a sense, underwent a rebirth, with Reader playing bass guitar and singing backing vocals and "Jym," who had replaced the band's original drummer a year earlier, alongside sole original member Dr. Frank.

The trio, in 1995, released *The Mr. T Experience !... And the Women Who Love Them,* relaunching themselves as a pure pop-punk outfit. Highlights included "My Stupid Life," "All My Promises," and "Tapin' Up My Heart." That same year, MTX released a four-song EP entitled *Alternative Is Here to Stay,* a reaction to the rising mainstream success of East Bay punk rock acts. They then threw themselves into touring—including trips to Europe and Japan—like never before. 1996 saw the release of *Love Is Dead,* an album filled with loud, catchy singalongs such as "Dumb Little Band" and "I'm Like Yeah, but She's All No" that won praise from critics. Dr. Frank's "grimsmirk spirit infects the whole wonderful album," wrote Ira A. Robbins in the *Trouser Press Guide to '90s Rock,* "which mates spunk, hooks and insightful intelligence as if inventing a new musical form."

The Mr. T Experience followed this with *Revenge Is Sweet, and So Are You,* another bubblegum-punk album, in 1997. *Alcatraz* arrived in 1999 and included bits of roller-rink organ, the sincere yet paradoxical "Two Of Us," and the ringing "We're No One," a song that "cops 1999's trophy for most arcane songwriting influence," wrote Jud Cost in *Magnet.* Also that year, Dr. Frank released a bossa nova-sounding solo album entitled *Show Business Is My Life.*

Selected discography

The Mr. T Experience

Everybody's Entitled to Their Own Opinion, Disorder, 1986, reissued, Lookout! 1995.
Night Shift at the Thrill Factory, 6th Int'l/Rough Trade, 1987, reissued, Lookout! 1996.
Big Black Bugs Bleed Blue Blood, Rough Trade, 1989.
Making Things with Light, Lookout! 1990.
Milk, Milk, Lemonade, Lookout! 1992.
Gun Crazy, (EP7), Lookout! 1993.
Our Bodies, Our Selves, Lookout! 1994.
The Mr. T Experience!... And the Women who Love Them, Lookout! 1995.
Alternative Is Here to Stay, (EP), Lookout !, 1995.
Love is Dead, Lookout! 1996.
(With others) *The Duran Duran Tribute Album,* (contributed song "Is There Something I Should Know"), Capitol, 1997.
Revenge Is Sweet, and So Are You, Lookout! 1997.
Alcatraz, Lookout! 1999.
(With others) *Lookout! Freakout!,* (contributed song "Tomorrow Is a Harsh Mistress"), Lookout! 2000.

Dr. Frank

Show Business Is My Life, Lookout! 1999.

Sources

Books

Robbins, Ira A., editor, *Trouser Press Guide to '90s Rock,* Fireside/Simon and Schuster, 1997.

Periodicals

Atlanta Journal-Constitution, October 23, 1997.
Audio, July 1996.
Boston Phoenix, September 25-October 2, 1997.

Los Angeles Times, March 12, 1996.
Magnet, October/November 1999, pp. 85-86.
Melody Maker, May 1, 1999.

Online

The Mr. T Experience at Lookout! Records, http://www.look outrecords.com (June 9, 2000).
Rolling Stone.com, http://www.rollingstone.com (June 9, 2000).

—Laura Hightower

Pharoahe Monch

Rap/hip-hop artist

Defining what "underground" means always results in debate. For some, the term refers to the "chitterling circuit of hip-hop," as noted by Marci Kenon in *Billboard,* or the beginning stages of an individual's career. "Once you get to a certain point, you cannot be considered underground anymore, even if you are doing what some define as underground music," said Domino, a hip-hop producer and CEO of Hieroglyphics Imperium Records, an underground label based in Oakland, California. "At one point, hip-hop in general was underground. It wasn't in the magazines. It wasn't on television. It wasn't in the movies. It was rarely on the radio. It hadn't come to the surface; it wasn't available to everyone." Thus, according to this view, once a person builds a foundation and fan base, he moves from the underground into the mainstream. In other words, when a relatively unknown innovator progresses and breaks into the mainstream, making way for the next wave of new talent to begin their own careers, the rap/hip-hop artist is no longer an associate of the underground scene.

However, some observers consider commercial successes like Jay-Z and Redman underground, or "true to the streets," though they agree that highly commercialized stars like Puff Daddy and Will Smith represent the antithesis of what the underground scene stands for. Pharoahe Monch as well believes that a rap artist can remain true to his roots. And despite the mass popularity of hip-hop music, a genre once reserved for a smaller, urban audience, he still considers his creations of and for the "underground" scene. "Some people feel that if you sell, you are not underground anymore," he told Kenon. "I disagree with that. I think that underground is an approach that you take to making a song." Take for example "Simon Says," his hit single that sold in excess of 125,000 units according to SoundScan from the artist's 1999 album *Internal Affairs.* "The beat is very underground," Pharoahe continued. "I didn't expect it to get as much radio play as it did. It's not in the format of a typical rap song. I wanted to be direct with people, lyrically, and not give them anything to think about."

Regardless of whether critics and fellow hip-hop artists now consider his music commercial because of the rapper's widespread popularity, Pharoahe unquestionably spent years enduring the trials and tribulations of the underground/streetwise scene before making it big. Born Troy Jamerson in 1972 in Jamaica, Queens, New York, the future rapper received the latter part of his nickname early in life. The girls at school used to call him "Monch" after a doll popular at the time, and the youngster, known for his easy-going nature, happily accepted the moniker. He added "Pharoahe" some years later while studying Egyptian history in college.

Meanwhile, the young Pharoahe had also developed an interest in rap music. An enthusiastic fan of rap and hip-hop, he regularly attended the "rap jams" taking place around Queens. "I'd have a beer and listen to the cutting and scratching, and feel *reaal* good," he smiled, as quoted by Andy Crysell of *New Musical Express.* "But then you'd go home and normal life would resume." Soon, however, a normal life wasn't enough, and Pharoahe decided to set his sights on a career in rap music, beginning by recording his own muffled and amateurish tapes at home.

After improving his technique, Pharoahe commenced his recording career, spending the next eight and a half years as one half of one of rap music's most revered and enduring underground duos, Organized Konfusion. He met his partner, Prince Poetry, while attending Manhattan's Art and Design High School, where he studied illustration and photography. Both drew inspiration musically from Queens rappers Run DMC and A Tribe Called Quest, but also wanted to apply the techniques they learned at art school to create their own brand of hip-hop. "We learned that everything is art," he explained to Crysell. "Dance, spoken word, garbage cans, people talking on the block, the architecture around you. Everything feeds the rhymes."

Outside the mainstream, Pharoahe and Prince Poetry worked without guidelines, never abiding by anyone else's standards but their own. Therefore, only devoted to themselves and their core audience, Organized Konfusion usually made music against the grain. The duo's much-lauded, self-titled debut arrived in 1991, and their critical second effort, *Stress: The Extinction Agenda,* followed in 1994. Taking a rebellious ap-

---

For The Record . . .

Born Troy Jamerson in 1972 in Jamaica, Queens, NY.

Recorded with Prince Poetry as Organized Konfusion, 1991-97; disbanded Organized Konfusion and signed with Rawkus Records, 1998; released debut solo album, *Internal Affairs*, 1999.

Addresses: *Record company*—Rawkus Entertainment, 676 Broadway, 4th Floor, New York City, NY 10012, phone: (212) 358-7890, fax: (212) 358-7962, website: http://www.rawkus.com.

---

proach to this album, Pharoahe and Prince Poetry ignored music industry rules, releasing a dark, striking first single from the record called "Stress." An explicit song, "Stress" never received much radio play, but Organized Konfusion persisted in spite of lackluster record sales.

Undeterred, the duo, hailed by fans for their expressive wordplay and state-of-the-art production skills, switched labels from Hollywood to Priority for their third album, 1997's *The Equinox*. However, after another record failed to sell as well as expected, Pharoahe grew frustrated and started to question his involvement in the music business. Subsequently, he took some time off to rethink his next move, eventually deciding to try again as a solo artist. Pharoahe and Prince Poetry parted amicably in 1998, soon after Priority terminated their contract. "When I signed with Rawkus [Records], I was like, 'I'll give you two songs that you can work, I guarantee you,'" he told *XXL* contributor Bonsu Thompson in an interview with fellow hip-hop artist Mos Def. "You see, Mos and I need to sell records to set a standard for the music industry. For a little 14 year old coming up to have the opportunity to be like, 'I want to be like Pharoahe, Mos, Talib, or G Rap' because they're hearing it. That's what sales mean to me."

Upon signing with Rawkus, Pharoahe contributed songs to two benchmark compilations—*Soundbombing II* and *Lyricists Lounge Vol. I*—then started work on his debut solo album, *Internal Affairs*. Released in late 1999, the album included the party tune "Simon Says," which became a hit, ranking alongside such prior songs as House of Pain's "Jump Around," in cities across the United States and later in Great Britain. Suddenly, after nearly a decade in rap, Pharoahe's quiet life came to an end, as he found himself dashing down the streets of Queens to avoid mobs of fans. "I

am an introverted guy who enjoys solitude," Pharoahe admitted to Crysell, though he realized that a successful career in hip-hop would make it difficult to retain a sense of anonymity. "Through the TV and radio, I'm now in people's faces 24 hours a day. I hope they don't mind that."

For *Internal Affairs*, Pharoahe enlisted the help of several top names in the business, such as Redman, Method Man, Canibus, and Busta Rhymes, who also returned to produce the video for "Simon Says." All say that it wasn't the lure of money that drew them into the project, but rather a common respect for Pharoahe's work—his extreme individualism—with Organized Konfusion. Like his outings with Prince Poetry, *Internal Affairs*, also Pharoahe's most accessible album, won high praises for its "adrenaline-fueled tracks that pack more punch than Mike Tyson in his prime," wrote Thompson. Just as impressive is Pharoahe's remarkable ability to match the lyrical and vocal wits of a diverse range of fellow rappers, especially considering his life-long health condition: chronic asthma.

"In light of the fact that he's a chronic asthmatic, he's probably the greatest MC living, because he's working against a huge deficit physically," Mos Def told Thompson. "People who have full capacity of their lungs can't repeat his rhymes." According to Pharoahe, the asthma usually never affected his performance, but when he suffered complications during a Rock Steady concert in 1998, he vowed to live a healthier life through exercise and good eating habits. Pharoahe also says that breathing is also important in enabling him to rap. "Sometimes you hear music and you have an interpretation of what part you play as an instrument in that piece," he explained. "You gotta know how to breathe and you gotta know when to breathe. There are saxophone players who play continuously and get their inhalation in simultaneously to continue their flows."

Content with his rise from the underground to wider recognition, Pharoahe, who successfully enlightened rap listeners without alienating them and succeeded commercially without sacrificing his individual integrity and street sensibility, nonetheless hoped to one day try his hand in other areas of entertainment, namely writing books and screenplays. "I had a great imagination as a kid. I used to think about autobahns and 007 and now I'm in those places," he told Crysell. "And when I'm old and grey, I'll be talking to my own kids about these days in Europe."

Selected discography

Solo

Internal Affairs, Rawkus, 1999.
"Simon Says," (single), Rawkus, 1999.

Organized Konfusion

Organized Konfusion, Hollywood, 1991.
Stress: The Extinction Agenda, Hollywood, 1994.
The Equinox, Priority, 1997.

Sources

Periodicals

Billboard, April 1, 2000.
New Musical Express, February 26, 2000, p. 25.
Rolling Stone, December 9, 1999.
Vibe, December 1999/January 2000, p. 135.

Village Voice, March 9, 1999; November 16, 1999
Washington Post, December 4, 1999; January 12, 2000.
XXL, January 2000, pp. 73-76.

Online

Rawkus Entertainment, http://www.rawkus.com (May 29, 2000).
Sonicnet.com, http://www.sonicnet.com (May 29, 2000).

—Laura Hightower

Morphine

Rock band

How low can you go? That's the musical question posed by Morphine, purveyors of "low rock," a bottom-heavy, cacophonous rumble you can feel in your bones. It's produced by a decidedly unusual grouping of instruments: a baritone sax, drums, and a unique two-string bass that's played like a slide guitar. Unlike most rock bands, Morphine doesn't use a guitar or piano to carry the melody or fill sonic space. Instead, those notes are implied, like in certain jazz tunes, but the overall impact of Morphine's music can't be denied. Like the band's name implies, low rock's effect is disorienting, feels somewhat illicit, and it totally addictive.

The concept of the low-rock sound was created by Mark Sandman, who died of a heart attack while performing in Italy on July 3, 1999. In some ways, he was the ultimate scenester among the Boston/Cambridge music community, maintaining numerous side projects before and during his tenure in Morphine. Creatively restless, he began experimenting with low sounds when he played in the Boston blues-rock quartet Treat Her Right. There, Sandman played a conventional six-string guitar, but did so through an octave-shifting effects pedal that made the instrument sound more like a bass.

He then switched to a conventional bass, but one with just a single string, reasoning (somewhat Zen-like) that all the notes he'd need to play were on that one string. By the time Morphine took off, he'd added a second string. Later, he would add a third, albeit one from a guitar, and call the invention the Tritar. Obviously, experimentation and innovation came naturally to Sandman, who was just 46 when he died.

Songwriting came naturally, too, and to hear a tune by Morphine is to hear something that's quite removed from mainstream pop and rock. Besides "low rock," Morphine's sound is sometimes called "beat noir," in reference to its jazzy feel—in a perfect world, the sound you'd hear emanating from a smoky bar at unreasonable hours of the morning—but also its lyrical content, which is often dark, hard-boiled, and full of intrigue.

Sandman played with his Treat Her Right bandmates David Champagne, a guitarist and the leader of that group, harmonica player Jim Fitting, and drummer Billy Conway who would later join Morphine on the albums *Treat Her Right,* released in 1986, *Tied to the Tracks,* released in 1988, and *What's Good For You* released in 1991. The first was released independently, but the second was recorded for RCA, who didn't know how to market the band's quirky sound and sensibility. For the third, they were back to indie status, working with Boston-based Rounder Records.

As Treat Her Right was in its final throes, Sandman was gigging all over the place, most frequently at

For The Record . . .

Members include **Dana Colley**, baritone saxophone; **Billy Conway** (joined 1993), drums; **Jerome Deupree** (left band 1993), drums; **Mark Sandman** (died July 3, 1999), bass, vocals.

Group formed in Boston/Cambridge, Massachusetts area in 1992; released debut album *Good* on independent Accurate/Distortion label. It was later picked up by larger indie Rykodisc. Ryko also released albums *Cure for Pain*, 1993, and *Yes*, 1995, plus an album of rarities *B-sides and Otherwise*, 1997. The group was represented on numerous movie soundtracks, and built up a solid cult following through insurgent touring campaigns. Signed with DreamWorks label in 1996, resulting in *Like Swimming*, 1997, and their swan song, *The Night*, 2000.

Addresses: *Record company*—DreamWorks Records, 100 Universal Plaza, Bungalow 477, Universal City, CA 91608.

Cambridge nightspots the Plough & Stars and the Middle East. His various bands included Supergroup, a collaboration with Seattle-based Chris Ballew, who would eventually rise to fame with the Presidents of the United States of America. There was also Treat Her Orange (later the Pale Brothers), which found Sandman playing with mandolinist Jimmy Ryan of the Blood Oranges, and the Hyposonics, whose membership included future Morphine saxman Dana Colley and Either/Orchestra leader Russ Gershon.

Morphine, too, started out as just one among many of his projects, but Sandman was quick to recognize its potential. He formed the trio with Colley and drummer Jerome Deupree. As Boston Phoenix columnist Matt Ashare wrote of Morphine, "[It] best captured the essence of Sandman's singular style: his deadpan delivery, his wry pulp-noir vignettes, his 'less is best' aesthetic, and his love of loose R&B grooves rooted equally in the deep meaty blues of Howlin' Wolf and Muddy Waters and the savvy pop funk of an artist like Prince, who was one of his all-time favorites."

The band's debut album was released through Russ Gershon's Accurate/Distortion label in 1992. The next year, it was picked up by the independent but nationally distributed Rykodisc label, based in Salem, Massachusetts. There was nothing special about the songs themselves—"We write pretty standard three-minute rock songs with verses, choruses, and hooks," Sandman told the *Boston Phoenix*—but the vibe of those songs was as indelible an individual stamp as a rock band can hope to muster these days.

Just as their music stood outside the mainstream, so did Morphine's approach to the business of music. They didn't open shows for larger acts very often; instead, they did their own modest headlining tours, setting up short residencies in various towns and allowing their audience to develop organically. Sandman knew how to exploit what he had to work with, and let the press run with the band's oddities—he invented the term "low rock" for that very purpose—but kept the particulars of his private life out of the papers.

While they were recording their second album, *Cure for Pain,* Deupree was replaced with Treat Her Right skinsman Billy Conway. The album, released in 1993, was less than a commercial sensation, but gained much wider exposure when some of the songs were used prominently in the film *Spanking the Monkey.* That, and almost universal critical praise, raised the group to a level of popularity that it was able to maintain until its untimely end.

"Listening to early Morphine creates a sensation similar to slowly burning yourself with a cigarette," wrote *Addicted to Noise* contributor Seth Mnookin around the time of the release Morphine's third album, *Yes* in 1995. "It's a little scary, very intense, and impossible to stop because you're so determined to feel what's going to happen next." That sort of response was typical of a Morphine fan, and the group sated its public's desire for material with numerous singles sprinkled with bonus tracks and songs on various soundtracks. A collection of such odds and ends, *B-Sides and Otherwise,* surfaced in 1997.

Just before that, Morphine became the second act signed to DreamWorks records, the music arm of the entertainment conglomerate owned by Steven Spielberg, David Geffen, and Jeffrey Katzenberg. The album *Like Swimming* found the band varying the low-rock sound to a degree, incorporating instruments such as guitar, tritar, mellotron, and female background vocals into the mix. Ultimately, though, low rock was Morphine's hook, not an end in itself, and there were no hard and fast rules about what could and couldn't be done within the context of the band.

That became even more the case on *The Night,* the album Morphine had finished just before Sandman collapsed on a stage outside Rome and was pronounced dead-on-arrival at a local hospital. *The Night* seems a fitting epitaph, however, because its music finds Morphine's sound taken to its logical conclusion as a unique brand of chamber-rock—adding more, and somehow ending up with less. Only Morphine could do that. Keyboards, violin, cello, and double bass, acoustic and electric guitars, oud, and various hand drums are played on the album. Drummer Deupree is back, too, playing in tandem with Conway on nearly every track. In some ways, the album is the lowest of the low, which is meant as both a compliment and a tribute to Sandman, who brought something unique to music—something not very many musicians can claim.

The Night may have been Sandman's final work, but it was not the last word on his legacy. In late 1999, Morphine's surviving members—Conway, Colley, and Deupree as well—formed Orchestra Morphine, a big band that toured the country, playing Sandman's music in a new, and wholly fleshed out fashion. Sidemembers included Either/Orchestra leader and Accurate Records executive Russ Gershon, trumpeter Tom Halter, keyboardist Evan Harriman, bassist Mike Rivard, and singers Laurie Sargent and Christian McNeill.

Whether Orchestra Morphine can go on to create new music without Sandman seems unlikely, though not entirely impossible. "He was a visionary," DreamWorks chief Lenny Waronker said of the fallen musician. "He invented a sound that was unique. He was one of a kind; he was uncompromising. It might be a cliché to call someone the real thing, because too many say that these days, but in his case it's the truth. He was truly the real deal."

Selected discography

Albums

Good, Accurate/Distortion, 1992; Rykodisc, 1993.
Cure for Pain, Rykodisc, 1993.
Yes, Rykodisc, 1995.
Like Swimming, Rykodisc, 1997.
B-Sides and Otherwise, Rykodisc, 1997.
The Night, DreamWorks, 2000.

Soundtrack appearances

"You Look Like Rain," *The Best of Mountain Stage, Vol 7,* Blue Plate, 1994.

"Yes," *National Lampoon's Senior Trip Original Soundtrack,* Capricorn, 1995.
"I Had My Chance," "Bo's Veranda," *Get Shorty,* Antilles, 1995.
"Radar," *Safe and Sound,* Mercury, 1996.
"Gone for Good," *2 Days in the Valley Original Soundtrack,* 1996.
"Kerouac," *Kerouac: Kicks Joy Darkness,* Rykodisc, 1997.
"This Is Not a Dream (with Apollo 440)," *Spawn: The Album,* Epic, 1997.
"11 O'Clock," *Phoenix Original Soundtrack,* Will Records, 1998.
"Honey White," *MTV 120 Minutes Live,* Atlantic, 1998.
"Hanging on a Curtain," *La Femme Nikita Original TV Soundtrack,* TVT, 1998.
"I Had My Chance," "Murder for the Money," *Wild Things Original Soundtrack,* Varese Sarabande, 1998.
"You're an Artist," *The Mod Squad Original Soundtrack,* Elektra, 1999.
"Sheila," *IFC—In Your Ear Volume 1: Original Soundtracks,* Hybrid, 1999.
"Radar," *Condo Painting: Life From a Different Angle Original Soundtrack,* Gallery Six, 2000.

Sources

Periodicals

Billboard, July 17, 1999.
Boston Phoenix, July 9-15, 1999.
Seattle Post Intelligencer, May 12, 2000.

Online

Addicted to Noise, http://www.addict.com/issues/1.05/Features/Morphine/ (June 23, 2000)
Boston Rock Storybook, http://www.rockinboston.com/morphine.htm (June 26, 2000)

—*Daniel Durchholz*

Mickie Most

Producer

Although he started out as a rock-and-roll performer, finding success with a string of hits in South Africa, Mickie Most made his mark in music as one of the most successful British producers of the 1960s and 1970s. He discovered and was the first producer for the Animals and Herman's Hermits, and he also produced for Donovan and the Yardbirds, helping to create hits on both sides of the Atlantic. He focused more on singles than albums, especially at RAK records, which he founded in 1969. After retiring from active record production when the punk movement swept England in the late 1970s, he has stayed active with song publishing and talent scouting. The value of his legacy has been debated, lauded by some for the landmark music he produced and reviled by others for the commercial nature of his work.

Born Michael Hayes, Most knew early on that he wanted to make a career in show business after he lasted less than a day at a factory job. He changed his last name when he joined up with Alex Wharton to form the Most Brothers, a late 1950s act that got a recording contract but didn't generate any commercial success. Most's life took a turn when he fell in love with a South African girl whose family returned to their home country. Her parents made clear that if Most was serious about her, he would have to follow them. He did so, and spent four years in South Africa performing with Mickie Most and the Playboys, recording several songs that were hits there.

Opportunity Knocked

Once married, he and his wife returned to England, where he again took up performing. But he had spent his studio time in South Africa learning the ropes of record production, and he watched for the chance to get into that end of the music business. His opportunity came in 1963 when he spotted the Animals playing at the Club-A-Gogo in Newcastle. He made them a unique offer: he would pay them royalties if they let him produce their records. For that arrangement to pay off for either of them, he needed to make a deal with a record company, which he was able to do, thanks to his connections in the industry.

The big breakthrough for the Animals and Most came out of 15 minutes in the studio and plenty of perseverance on Most's part. "House of the Rising Sun" had long been a part of the band's stage repertoire before they committed it to tape in 1964. But clocking in at over four minutes, the song defied conventional wisdom about hit singles, which had a standard length of three minutes at the time. Most persisted, though, and the label relented. The song went to number one on both sides of the Atlantic and became the band's signature tune.

Despite the song's success, later singles showed that the Animals' rhythm and blues sound didn't necessarily translate into pop success. Most turned to a solution that would become one of the keys to his hit making: tirelessly searching the song writing factories for potential hits. He told Richarrd Buskin in the book *Inside Tracks,* "I used to spend every other week in New York or Los Angeles, scouring around places such as the Brill Building for material." For the Animals, he brought back such songs as "We Gotta Get Out of This Place" and "It's My Life." For the first time, but not the last, Most found himself in the position of having produced hits in both England and the United States with songs that the performers disliked. Even as these songs made their way up the charts, Eric Burdon of the Animals decried them in public as being too pop, and the Animals split with Most when their contract expired in 1965.

Discovered Herman's Hermits

By this time Most had found other acts who were more willing to perform the songs that he had been snatching up from songwriters in the States. He had signed a new group, the Nashville Teens, who had a huge hit in 1964 in the United States and the United Kingdom with "Tobacco Road," but they never rose to such heights again. Most's other new discovery at the time, Herman's Hermits, had more staying power. Unlike his discovery of the Animals, this time Most had the songs first and then looked for the act that would make the right vehicle for them.

Born Michael Hayes on June 20, 1938, in Aldershot, Hampshire, England.

Changed his name while playing in the Most Brothers, late 1950s; moved to South Africa, 1959; had eleven number one hits in South Africa with Mickie Most and His Playboys, 1959-63; returned to England and signed production deal with the Animals, 1964; produced the Animals' "House of the Rising Sun" and the Nashville Teens' "Tobacco Road," both of which went to number one on the charts in the U. S. and U. K., 1964; produced first Herman's Hermits work, 1964; began producing Donovan, 1966; formed RAK records, 1969; started producing Hot Chocolate, 1975; sold RAK label but kept ownership of music publishing, 1983.

Most purchased the rights to a Carole King and Gerry Goffin song, "I'm Into Something Good," and started looking for a youthful band to perform the song. He saw a picture of Herman's Hermits lead man Peter Noone, and went to watch them. He liked what he saw in Noone, but before agreeing to produce the band, he requested that two members of the group be changed. Noone complied, and Most produced "I'm Into Something Good" for them, starting a string of hits in both the United States and the United Kingdom. When the demands of a song proved too much for the Hermits' musicianship, Most would bring in session players such as guitarist Jimmy Page and bassist John Paul Jones, who would later play together in Led Zeppelin.

With his reputation as a hit-maker established, Most began to expand his stable of talent, taking over production duties for some acts who had already established themselves. One such group, the Yardbirds, became known for starting a trio of innovative and influential guitarists—Eric Clapton, Jeff Beck, and Page—on the road to stardom. Most produced the band through the period that saw Page briefly in the line-up with Beck before the latter moved on to his solo career. While Most recorded songs that showed off the inventiveness and skills of the Yardbirds' guitarists, he usually consigned those songs to the B-sides of the singles, putting more generally accessible tunes on the A-sides.

He did the same for Beck after he became a solo act, and although Beck scored some hits in Britain under Most's production, some of the B-sides contained material that became part of rock and roll legend, such as "Beck's Bolero," which featured Beck, Page, and Jones playing with the 1960s most prominent session pianist, Nicky Hopkins, and Who drummer Keith Moon. But when Beck formed the Jeff Beck Group, with Rod Stewart and future Rolling Stone Ron Wood, no American label showed interest in releasing their debut album, *Truth,* until a member of Most's staff sent a review of one of the band's shows to Epic.

Although Most tried to pick the most accessible songs for his artists to release as singles, his approach wasn't formulaic. His work with Donovan revealed Most's flexibility. When the two joined forces, Donovan's reputation had taken a beating. Having started out in the folk-rock mode as a more gentle version of Bob Dylan, he had reached a lull in his career. In the studio with Most, he proceeded to turn out a string of folksy yet psychedelic hits, most notably "Sunshine Superman" and "Mellow Yellow" in 1966. Their collaboration would continue to be lucrative throughout the rest of the 1960s. At the same time, Most kept active in the pop mainstream, also producing for Lulu, who had several hits in the United Kingdom in the late 1960s.

Started His Own Record Label

By now Most had earned widespread recognition for his talents. In 1969, critic Nik Cohn wrote in his book *Rock from the Beginning,* "In the whole of pop, he's the only man I can think of who has unnatural powers, who really knows what will hit and what won't. He rarely misses." Most decided to make the most of his powers by starting his own record label, RAK records, in 1969. He also knew what market he wanted to corner. He told Buskin, "I decided that, as all of the major companies were now leaning towards dumping singles and signing artists with the album concept in mind, I would take care of the singles market myself." While few of the acts that he signed to RAK made it big in the United States, he claimed that the first 27 records released by the label made it at least into the top 50 in Britain.

RAK developed a reputation for producing bubblegum pop, most notably written and produced by Nicky Chinn and Mike Chapman, who had been Most's rivals for the catchy pop market in Britain. However, Most himself produced the band that had the largest commercial success for RAK: Hot Chocolate. Their singles "Emma" in 1974 and "You Sexy Thing" in 1975 became international hits, and the latter experienced a resurgence in 1997 when it appeared on the soundtrack of the movie *The Full Monty.* Throughout the 1970s, Most remained an active figure in the British music industry, appearing as a regular panelist on the British talent-scouting television show *New Faces.*

In the late 1970s, though, the music environment in Britain underwent a significant change with the rise of punk. The entire punk culture stood in rebellion against the kind of music that Most had produced. Johnny Rotten of the Sex Pistols, the first big punk band, took on Most in an interview for *Melody Maker,* as recounted in Nicholas Schaffner's *The British Invasion*: "I don't believe in love, and I never will. It's a myth brought on by Micky [sic] Most & Co. to sell records." Most evidently had a similar distaste for the music that Rotten and company made, and in 1983 he sold RAK's catalog to EMI and became much less active in the recording industry.

Though less active, he never left the recording business entirely. He continued to buy songs for RAK music publishing, remaining on the lookout for the tune that could break out and become the next big hit. He even went back behind the board a couple of times in the 1990s, but the public and press paid little notice to the acts that he produced. Still, 35 years after he first entered record production, Most remained certain of what makes pop music work. In 1999 he told Nigel Hunter of *Billboard,* "Music is very important to young people because it's their language and a good way of communicating." He had an uncanny understanding of how to make records that successfully pulled off that communication on a large scale throughout the 1960s, making him an integral part of rock and roll history.

Selected discography

As performer

The Best of Mickie Most & His Playboys, Rock-n-Beat, 2000.

As producer

The Animals

Animal Tracks (U. K. version), Columbia, 1965, reissued, EMI, 1999.
Complete Animals (contains all of Most's work with the group), EMI, 1990.

Jeff Beck

Truth, Epic, 1968.
Beck-Ola, Epic, 1969.

Donovan

Sunshine Superman, Epic, 1966, remastered and reissued, 1996.

Mellow Yellow, Epic, 1967.
Gift from a Flower to a Garden, Epic, 1967.
Hurdy Gurdy Man, Epic, 1968.
Barabajagal, Epic, 1969.

Herman's Hermits

Introducing Herman's Hermits, MGM, 1965.
Both Sides of Herman's Hermits, MGM, 1966.
Blaze, MGM, 1967.
Their Greatest Hits, ABKCO, 1973.

Hot Chocolate

Hot Chocolate, Big Tree, 1975.
Man to Man, Big Tree, 1976.
Every 1's a Winner, Infinity, 1978, reissued, EMI, 1993.

Nashville Teens

Tobacco Road, London, 1964; reissued, Repertoire, 2000.

Yardbirds

Little Games, Epic, 1967; reissued in expanded version, EMI, 1996.

Sources

Books

Buskin, Richard, *Inside Tracks,* Avon, 1999.
Clarke, Donald, editor, *The Penguin Encyclopedia of Popular Music,* Viking, 1989.
Cohn, Nik, *Rock from the Beginning,* Stein and Day, 1969.
Larkin, Colin, editor, *The Encyclopedia of Popular Music,* Muze, 1998.
Schaffner, Nicholas, *The British Invasion: From the First Wave to the New Wave,* McGraw-Hill, 1983.

Periodicals

Billboard, July 10, 1999, p. 31.

Online

"Mickie Most," *All Music Guide,* http://www.allmusic.com (April 10, 2000).
"Mickie Most, Man of Many Millions," *Capetown Sunday Times,* http://www.suntimes.co.za (April 10, 2000).

—Lloyd Hemingway

My Bloody Valentine

Thrash-pop band

My Bloody Valentine started out as a fairly mundane indie band, often drawing criticism for imitating other pop-rock acts before them. However, the group would eventually reinvent themselves to develop a truly original style—in fact, a whole new sub-genre of rock music. With their groundbreaking hybrid of ethereal melodies and studio-oriented, discordant sounds, My Bloody Valentine perfected the art of creating heady, non-specific hypnotic trance-rock melded with thrash-rock and usually indiscernible lyrics, influencing the independent music scene in the late-1980s and beyond. "My Bloody Valentine produce a sound that is at once familiar yet unrecognizable. Their guitars sputter and wobble like a melted data disk flung from an exploding starship," wrote Alan DiPerna for *Guitar World*. "But somewhere in the din, traces of human life are detectable—pop melodies! It's like hearing pop music for the first time—the way a visitor from another planet might hear it."

Thus, in the end My Bloody Valentine proved themselves as an individual force in avant-pop music, rather than as mere clones of their predecessors. Instead, other rock bands sought to pattern themselves after My Bloody Valentine, known as MBV to fans. After releas-

Photograph by Steve Jennings. Corbis. Reproduced by permission. ©

For The Record . . .

Members include **Bilinda Butcher** (joined band in 1987), vocals, guitar; **Dave Conway** (left band in 1987), vocals; **Debbie Googe** (joined band in 1986), bass guitar; **Colm O'Ciosoig** (born in Dublin, Ireland), drums; **Kevin Shields** (born on May 21, 1963 on Long Island, New York; relocated with his family to Dublin, Ireland, at the age of ten; siblings: sister, Ann Marie Shields, who later served as MBV's touring manager, and younger brother Jimi Shields, a former member of Rollerskate Skinny before joining Lotus Crown), vocals, guitar, songwriting; **Tina** (left band in 1985), keyboards.

Shields and O'Ciosoig formed My Bloody Valentine in Dublin, 1984; released *Ecstasy and Wine,* 1989; released pivotal album *Isn't Anything,* 1988; released *Loveless,* 1991.

Addresses: *Record company*—Sire Records Group, 936 Broadway, 5th Floor, New York City, NY 10010, (212) 253-3900, website: http://www.sirerecords.com. *E-mail*—BloodyVal@aol.com.

ing the pivotal *Isn't Anything* in 1988, MBV saw their major breakthrough with the acclaimed *Loveless.* Released in 1991, the meticulously produced album filled with gravity-defying textures stands alone, without argument, as one of the decade's most important audio statements. Since then, however, MBV, well-known for their perfectionist tendencies, have yet to release a follow-up to their grand statement. As of 2000, fans and critics alike continued to wait patiently for MBV's forthcoming record.

The primary source for MBV's sonic inventions and adventures is from the mind of a quiet, American-born Irishman named Kevin Shields, the group's principal songwriter as well as vocalist and guitarist. Born on Long Island, New York, on May 21, 1963, Shields relocated with his family to Dublin, Ireland, at the age of ten. His sister, Ann Marie Shields, later served as MBV's touring manager, while younger brother Jimi Shields was a former member of Rollerskate Skinny before joining Lotus Crown. Shields, forced to leave his comfortable American childhood and acclimate himself to a new culture, at first found it difficult to adjust, but he eventually managed to shake his identification in the neighborhood as the American kid on the block, emerging from his shell by age 13 with a vengeance to

join one of Dublin's many street gangs. "Nothing serious," the musician explained to *Melody Maker.* "We used to invade other people's estates.... It wasn't exactly Ice-T and his homeboys, but it was exciting."

After moving to Ireland, Shields also learned of the glam rock phenomenon via the English television show *Top of the Pops.* "When I was a kid in America the only rock bands kids were into were, like, Three Dog Night, bands like that," he recalled in an interview with *Options Magazine*'s Mark Kemp. "In England, even little kids were totally into glam rock, like T-Rex and even Roxy Music. Because it was glam rock. It was pop music." Around the same time, Shields befriended Colm O'Ciosoig (pronounced "o-COO-sak"), a shy boy who shared Shields' interest in punk and glam rock, and at the age of 14, together with O'Ciosoig, Shields decided to form a band. Back then, O'Ciosoig, who went on to play drums for MBV, played bass guitar and encouraged Shields to learn to play lead guitar. Shields, who really wanted to play bass, reluctantly agreed. The two friends led various punk and pop bands during their teenage years, and upon leaving school, O'Ciosoig took a job as a bus conductor and Shields as a driver's mate, all the while delving further into their own musical experimentations and noise-rock sounds.

Followed Whims

However, Shields went through a period of questioning his skills on guitar. Now considered a wildly original player who implements texture more than technique, he advises other guitarists not to put so much pressure on themselves to become innovators. "About ten years ago, I virtually gave up playing guitar because I thought I could never do anything as truly different as most of the guitarists I liked. You meet a lot of people who are obsessed with originality; they feel it's unworthy to play anything that's vaguely familiar. They think it's cheap somehow," Shields said to DiPerna. "I guess I fell into that. I gave up the guitar in favor of synthesizers for a couple of years and then got literally bored out of my mind with the idea of being original. It seemed like a tedious, self-righteous thing to do. So I decided to just follow my whims, play for a laugh, go out and jam on garage rock. That's how this band started."

Thus, in 1983, with Shields on guitar and O'Ciosoig on drums, the duo gathered a revolving door of other musicians and started playing Cramps and Birthday Party-inspired music around Dublin. In 1984, they officially formed My Bloody Valentine—a moniker inspired by a Canadian B-grade horror flick—with a more stable lineup that included Dave Conway on lead vocals and Conway's then-girlfriend, Tina (last name unknown), on keyboards. Soon thereafter, the newly established quartet moved to Berlin, Germany, where they recorded and released their debut mini-album,

This Is Your Bloody Valentine. Making little impression in Berlin, MBV, without their keyboardist, returned to Great Britain and settled in London, recruiting Debbie Googe as a new member on bass guitar. In mid-1986, MBV released a second predominantly pop-oriented record, a 12-inch EP entitled *Geek* that, like the debut, lacked originality.

Later that year, MBV signed with Joe Foster's fledging Kaleidoscope Sound label and released *The New Record by My Bloody Valentine* EP, a record that saw the group using a broader musical palette and revealed a new influence, the Jesus and Mary Chain. After this, the group switched to the Primitives' label, Lazy, and released in 1987 the *Sunny Sundae Smile* EP, Conway's final record with the group. Here, My Bloody Valentine married bubblegum pop with buzzing guitar noise, a formula maintained for both the *Strawberry Wine* EP and the mini-album *Ecstasy,* released later that year. Both of these records were later compiled and released as the LP *Ecstasy and Wine* in 1989.

Meanwhile, after Conway's departure and before recording *Strawberry Wine* and *Ecstasy,* MBV had enlisted guitarist/vocalist Bilinda Butcher, who had recently dropped out of dancing school and given birth to son Toby, the product of a former relationship, at the time she joined the group. By now, the MBV lineup had stabilized to include Shields, O'Ciosoig, Googe, and Butcher. Shields, who became romantically involved with Butcher, recalled the day she joined MBV: "Bilinda couldn't play the guitar when she joined the band," he noted to DiPerna. "She initially joined as a singer, and she just kind of learned guitar. First she played really simple textured things—only a few notes. Now she essentially plays what you might call 'rhythm guitar.' On the records, I tend to play most of the instruments, mainly because of the way we write. I tend to write the music as I go along, and it's just easier for me to play it. We don't really think in terms of whose part is whose when we're recording. Later on, we'll arrange it for live playing and work out who will do what."

Unearthed a New Sound in Rock

Conway's leaving and Butcher's arrival, as well as a move to Creation Records (Sire Records distributed for the United States market), also signaled a major shift in musical direction and recording techniques; a typical MBV performance would consist of slowly gyrating feedback and distortions, from which emerged the sighing harmonies, or fragile melancholia, of Shields and Butcher. The drastic change was first apparent on the formidable *You Made Me Realise* EP and the pivotal album *Isn't Anything,* which included the guitar barrage "Feed Me With Your Kiss," both released in 1988. Finally, after years of struggling for recognition, MBV had unearthed a completely new sound, and their status skyrocketed. "*Isn't Anything* is the most impor-

tant rock album of the '80s," wrote *Alternative Press,* who ranked the effort number 46 on its list of top 99 albums of 1985 through 1995. "Guitarists Kevin Shields and Bilinda Butcher introduced a new aesthetic, creating unbearably sensual, alien environments through furious tremolo-bar wrenching and outrageous distortion." In agreement, *Entertainment Weekly* awarded *Isn't Anything* with an "A+" rating.

It took three years for MBV to perfect songs for a follow-up album. In the interim, they released two EPs: the richly-textured *Glider* in 1989 and *Tremelo,* an extreme piece of music which reached the British Top 30 in 1990. By this time the leaders of the avant-pop soundscape, MBV had a profound impact on other up-and-coming "shoegazing" bands, such as the Boo Radleys, Slowdive, Chapterhouse, and more, who tried to imitate their on-stage persona of looking downward while performing and drone-swarm sound using methods—flangers, chorus pedals, etc.—that Shields despised as facile. "I always feel I'm disclaiming what we do. Our music is very simplistic, although people rarely perceive it that way," the songwriter pointed out in an interview with *Guitar Player.* "People also assume that I use tons of effects, but the only effect I use that you really perceive as an effect is backwards reverb."

When *Loveless* finally arrived in 1991, the music world was blown away, reinforcing MBV's influence on the independent scene in both Great Britain and America. "A challenging storm of bent pitch, undulating volume and fractured tempos, *Loveless* has a calm eye at its center, an intimate oasis from which guitarists Bilinda Butcher and Kevin Shields gently breathe pretty tunes into the thick, sweet waves of droning distortion," wrote Ira Robbins in *Rolling Stone.* "Despite the record's intense ability to disorient—this is real do-not-adjust-your-set stuff—the effect is strangely uplifting. *Loveless* oozes a sonic balm that first embraces and then softly pulverizes the frantic stress of life."

Moreover, legendary pop/rock artists such as Bono of U2 and David Byrne declared MBV as the most intriguing band on the music scene, and Brian Eno told *Rolling Stone* that MBV, one of his favorite bands, "set a new standard for pop" with "Soon," the closing track of *Loveless.* Honored with a multitude of press recognition as well, *Loveless* was included in *Rolling Stone's* "Essential Recordings of the '90s," *Spin* ranked it at number 16 for the publication's "90 Greatest Albums of the 1990s," and *Melody Maker* listed the album at number seven on its list of the "Top 30 Albums of 1991."

A Decade-long, and Counting, Hiatus

However, during the recording process of *Loveless,* MBV had run up massive studio bills with Creation, and thus made another label switch to Island Records.

Although both Island and Sire fully supported the group's next venture, MBV embarked upon a long gestation period. "In retrospect," Shields told Simon Reynolds of *Alternative Press* in 1995, "we had a totally overambitious plan to find a premise, build our own studio, and get the record out by July 1993. We'd just completed the ten-month *Loveless* tour, and we'd all this nervous energy. Not sleeping a lot puts me in a manic state." Thus, because of equipment trouble in their own, newly constructed studio in south London, along with Shields wanting to distance MBV from the band's imitators and a preoccupation with jungle music—the fusion of hip-hop, dub, ragga, and techno that emerged from London's underground scene in the mid-1990—MBV have not released a new album since *Loveless.* However, some articles reported that the band actually did finish an album, but Shields decided it was not good enough and shelved the tapes.

While waiting to record, the members of MBV took on other side projects. Shields produced, remixed, and guested with other bands, such as Yo La Tengo and J. Mascis of Dinosaur Jr., and worked with Sonic Boom for his side project Experimental Audio Research, releasing *Beyond the Pale* in 1996; Googe started working with Snowpony as a bass player, O'Ciosoig did some engineering and began drumming for the group Clearspot, and Butcher made guest appearances singing with various bands.

Selected discography

This Is Your Bloody Valentine, (mini-album), Tycoon, 1985; reissued, Dossier, 1988.
Geek, (12-inch EP), Fever, 1986.
The New Record by My Bloody Valentine, (EP), Kaleidoscope Sound, 1986.

Sunny Sundae Smile, (EP), Lazy, 1987.
Strawberry Wine, (EP), 1987.
Ecstasy (mini-album), Lazy, 1987.
Feed Me With Your Kiss, Creation, 1988.
You Made Me Realise (EP), Creation, 1988.
Isn't Anything, Creation/Relativity/Warner Brothers, 1988; reissued, Creation/Sire/Warner Brothers, 1994.
Ecstasy and Wine, Lazy, 1989.
Glider (EP), Creation, 1989; Sire, 1990.
Tremelo (EP), Creation, 1990; Sire/Warner Brothers, 1991.
Loveless, Creation/Sire/Warner Brothers, 1991.

Sources

Books

Robbins, Ira A., editor, *Trouser Press Guide to '90s Rock,* Fireside/Simon and Schuster, 1997.

Periodicals

Alternative Press, October 1995.
Guitar Player, May 1992.
Guitar World, March 1992.
Melody Maker, January 4, 1992.
New Musical Express, December 10, 1988.
Options Magazine, 1992.
Rolling Stone, February 6, 1992; March 5, 1992; April 2, 1992; March 23, 1995; May 13, 1999.
Select, February 1992.
Stereo Review, June 1992.

Online

Sonicnet.com, http://www.sonicnet.com (June 11, 2000).
Unofficial My Bloody Valentine WWW Site, http://www.expect delay.com/mbv/index.html (June 11, 2000).

—*Laura Hightower*

Mystikal

Rap artist

In truth, Mystical does not technically rap. "He howls, he bellows, he barbarically yawps himself raw, all at a volume and velocity as unrelenting as any hardcore punk or metal outfit," wrote Mark Binelli in *Rolling Stone.* Yet Mystikal's talents lie far beyond his original style of rapping. By the late-1990s, the United States Army veteran who saw action as a combat engineer in the Gulf War (also known as Operation Desert Storm) cemented his reputation as one of the most promising MCs in rap music, supporting his blasting delivery with witty lyrics and a crafty flow. "Mystikal's appeal rests in his unyielding vocal intensity, his ability to maintain his scream-like delivery at any speed, his vivid imagery and his utilization of self-created sound effects to accentuate his point," noted Soren Baker of the *Los Angeles Times.* "To the uninitiated, he may come off as a Busta Rhymes imposter, but Mystikal is one of rap's most gifted and distinctive artists."

Although he catapulted to stardom with Master P's No Limit Records, Mystikal had already established himself as a rising star long before millions of hip-hop fans purchased his first 1997 album for the label entitled *Unpredictable.* His independent, self-titled debut, as well as the reissued version *The Mind of Mystikal,* both released in 1995, sold more than 500,000 units collectively. And after copies of *Unpredictable* flew off record store shelves, Mystikal's star continued to shine on 1999's *Ghetto Fabulous,* the rapper's third outing. Winning stellar reviews for its broad thematic scope—most No Limits artists dedicate their work primarily to gangster topics—*Ghetto Fabulous,* like his

prior records, stood apart from other hardcore rap albums. Here, Mystical delivered a touching tribute to his mother, as well as stories from his childhood and high school days. "Mystikal is one of the few artists who sound fresh and exciting with each listen," concluded Baker, "regardless of topic."

Mystical was born Michael Tyler in New Orleans, Louisiana, a city rich in musical tradition. Growing up in New Orleans "gives you a different rhythm, since it's a different style of music," he told Binelli, but the southern town also held other advantages as well. "New Orleans is different from everywhere," he explained to Charlie Braxton in an interview for *XXL.* "We didn't have gangs like in California, so you didn't have to worry about all that. It was kinda like the *Cosby Show* without all the money. I was around the poverty and everything, but my mom kept all that away from me. She didn't let me know how poor we were. I never did feel that."

Nonetheless, Mystikal did spend his childhood in one of the most impoverished and violent communities in New Orleans, the city's uptown area known as the 12th Ward. Many young African Americans in the neighborhood fell into selling drugs to make money, but Mystical was fortunate. His mother Marie Tyler, a single parent, along with a large extended family, showered Mystikal and his two siblings—older sister Michelle and younger brother Maurice—with love and affection, encouraging the children to excel in school, attend church regularly, and stay away from crime.

Developed Own Rapping Style

Although he had been rapping as a casual hobby for a long time, Mystikal learned about the competence one needs to rap in high school, when a more competitive rapper challenged him in the hallway one day. When the other student showed him up, Mystikal realized that an important element to the art of rapping, in addition to knowing how to tell a story, included knowing how to boast for attention. Soon thereafter, Mystikal began overwhelming the other MCs in his neighborhood with his rhymes. "I wanted to get a certain reaction…. If you laugh, that's like a 'whoooo' to me because I done said something hard. That's why I evolved into such a live performer," Mystikal stated for Jive Records. "To every word there was an action for it. After watching so many plain rappers, then watching good rappers, then putting my whole interpretation into the whole situation, that's what my style came out to."

Despite his lyrical talent, Mystikal first earned a name for himself around New Orleans not for rapping, but for breaking with a group called the Converse Crew. Through dancing, however, Mystical eventually hooked up with Beats By the Pound producer KLC, who would later serve as an important figure in his rap career.

When the popularity of dancing started to fade, Mystikal, like other southern hip-hop artists, turned to other areas of the culture such as rapping and producing in order to express themselves. In New Orleans, KLC stood at the forefront of rap as producer and DJ of a local group called the 3-9 Posse. Recognizing Mystikal's unique style, KLC brought the young rapper into the studio and recorded and produced some of his early demo tapes.

However, after graduating from Cohen High School and trying to supplement his artistic pursuits with a series of odd jobs, Mystikal decided to put his rap career on hold and enlisted in the United States Army. During his time with the military, he served in the Gulf War and kept up with the New Orleans rap scene by visiting his home whenever possible. When he completed his service with the Army, Mystikal returned to New Orleans, where local groups and labels were starting to receive national attention. To Mystikal, it looked as if his former hobby could turn into a full-time career, and he immediately called upon KLC for help.

The producer, though busy working with several other hip-hop acts, nevertheless welcomed Mystikal back into the fold. KLC promised to produce an album for the hopeful rapper after the release of records for 3-9 Posse and Lil' Slim—now known as Soulja Slim. But an impatient Mystikal, while waiting his turn, signed with another local label called Big Boy Records. In early-1995, he arrived with his self-titled debut, but local acceptance alluded the young rapper. At the time, a new homegrown style of hip-hop music called Bounce had taken over the New Orleans scene. "I had to

compete with the Bounce artist [popularity] that was going on in New Orleans," he told Braxton. "I love Bounce. I definitely love it. But it was just frustrating trying to get people to listen to me. I knew if I could please New Orleans' fans, it was on."

Success and Tragedy

Soon, local audiences did take notice of Mystikal, and their support helped land the rapper a distribution deal with New York's Jive Records, who reissued his debut, plus a few extra tracks, as *The Mind of Mystikal* in February of 1995. The album sold more than 500,000 copies and earned radio play nationwide, but Mystikal found himself in financial trouble. Adding to his frustrations, Mystikal was in the midst of dealing with the loss of his sister Michelle to domestic violence. Michelle, who had seen her brother through his struggling years, was killed in 1994 by her boyfriend Damion Neville, the grandson of Neville Brothers mainstay Charles. "Losing my sister in '94, that changed my whole perspective," Mystikal recalled to Braxton. "We grew up spiritual with a strong Baptist background. My family was tight. Then all of a sudden, that happened. September 22, 1994—losing my sister—that was my birthday present. Happy birthday to me."

Although left with a deep emotional and psychological scar after Michelle's death, Mystikal nonetheless pushed on with his rap career. Fortunately, his debut caught the attention of fellow rap artist Master P (born Percy Miller), the CEO of No Limit Records. Besides rap music, Mystikal had another connection with the No Limits chief. Master P, too, had lost a sibling, younger brother Kevin, who died in a drug-related murder. Thus, with Mystikal's first album for No Limits entitled *Unpredictable,* Master P encouraged him to explore his feeling surrounding the tragedy. The album, released in 1997, contained a tribute to his sister, "Shine," as well as a song addressed to Damion Neville called "Murderer 2."

In 1999, Mystikal returned with *Ghetto Fabulous,* produced by No Limit's production team known as Beats by the Pound, and featuring guest appearances by No Limit artists as well as Busta Rhymes and Naughty By Nature, two of the rapper's personal influences. In early-2000, Mystikal, reunited with KLC at the producer's spacious home studio to start work on his next album, *Let's Get Ready to Rumble,* expected for release later in the year. Now a successful rap star with financial security, Mystikal lives in a large home in New Orleans in an exclusive gated community. The humble, religious rap artist credits God, rather than himself, for all his accomplishments him. "My talent is spiritual," he cried as he looked toward the sky, as quoted by Braxton. "It's not just me putting words together. This is a gift."

Selected discography

Mystikal, Big Boy, 1995.
The Mind of Mystikal, (reissue of *Mystikal* plus extra tracks),
   Big Boy/Jive, 1995.
Unpredictable, No Limit/Jive, 1997.
Ghetto Fabulous, No Limit/Jive, 1999.
Let's Get Ready to Rumble, Jive, 2000.

Sources

Periodicals

Billboard, July 13, 1996; November 29, 1997.
Los Angeles Times, December 13, 1998.

Rolling Stone, November 27, 1997; March 18, 1999.
XXL, January 2000.

Online

Mystikal at Jive Records, http://www.peeps.com/jiverecords
   /index.html (June 5, 2000).
Sonicnet.com, http://www.sonicnet.com (June 5, 2000).

—*Laura Hightower*

Bif
Naked

Singer, songwriter

Vancouver, Canada's Bif Naked, a skateboarding theater student turned punk rocker, does not shy away from most subjects, no matter how painful, disturbing, or provocative. "I've written about being raped, my parents' divorce, necking with girls, doing it with boys, terminating a pregnancy, my own divorce. I've written a song about my bicycle, too. It's all the same to me," she told *Interview* magazine's Dudley Saunders. "I just don't believe in hiding anything. Life's too short."

A full-strength rock singer often compared to Ronnie Spector, Joan Jett, Pat Benatar, and Chrissie Hynde, Naked nevertheless carries a quirky wit, distinctive vocal style, and allure that makes her truly unique. Moreover, Naked's honesty and fearlessness about sharing her personal triumphs and tragedies have made her a critical and popular success. One song in particular entitled "Chotee," off Naked's Lava/Atlantic debut *I Bificus,* rose from an emotionally painful abortion while married to her former husband. "I got talked into terminating the pregnancy by my husband, which I resented even though now I realize it was the right thing to do. In fact, the only time I've ever been nervous about a song was when I had to sing 'Chotee' in front of him. Then it turned out he didn't even get it: He thought the baby in the song was him. After that, I was never too nervous about singing it again."

Beth (maiden name Torbert) Hopkins was born in 1971 in New Delhi, India, the illegitimate child of teen-age private school students. Prior to her birth, two young American missionaries had heard that a young child would soon be born and given up for adoption. Her Canadian-born birth mother was banished to a mental hospital in order to hide her pregnancy, then flown to a hospital in New Delhi to have her baby. Full of anticipation when they arrived to pick up their new child, her adoptive parents later discovered that the newborn was handed over to them without the necessary documentation to prove ownership. Hence, the family spent two years waiting in India for a proper birth certificate, then departed for the United States.

Naked's first new home was in Gettysburg, South Dakota, where her adoption was finally made official. From there, the family moved to Lexington, Kentucky, then to Minneapolis, Minnesota, before her father, a professor of dentistry, took a new job in Winnipeg, Manitoba, Canada. Naked, then 13 years old, started to rebel after the move. Her teen years, she admits, were nothing short of "hellacious" and saw Naked trading in her ballet classes in favor of loitering at a local arcade and skateboarding. However, Naked, a huge fan of Madonna, also dreamed of stardom. Therefore, after high school she enrolled at the University of Winnipeg as a theater major, a decision that caused her parents to breathe a sigh of relief.

Not long after her college career began, Naked joined her first band, Jungle Milk, a local troupe that performed oddball cover songs. She eventually married Jungle Milk's drummer, who was also a member of another band called Gorilla Gorilla, and when that group's lead singer quit on the eve of an important gig supporting Canadian punk heroes D.O.A., Naked stepped in to take over vocal duties. As front woman for Gorilla Gorilla, she decided to invent a name for herself. Thus "Bif," an old high school nickname, was augmented by the last name of "Naked," a moniker she deemed sexy and very punk rock. Naked, it seemed, was a natural from the start, and the group started accumulating more and more fans through constant touring.

Life on the road and partying, however, began to take a toll on Naked. During Gorilla Gorilla's first tour, for example, she was treated several times for alcohol poisoning, and her marriage, a union that she said was really over before it began, ended in divorce after just six months. In spite of these difficulties, Naked, determined to learn professionalism by working through difficult situations, remained with the group after they relocated to Vancouver. Now a straight-edged fitness fanatic who doesn't smoke, drink, use drugs, or eat red meat, Naked said that prior to her personal turnaround in 1995, alcohol led her to make a lot of unhealthy decisions. Back in Manitoba, Naked had once dated a bodybuilder who turned the singer on to fitness. "But I still drank and did drugs on those early tours, and I was losing my voice all the time," she recalled to Saunders. "I even got alcohol poisoning. I was trying to keep up with the guys, and I did have a great time. But I also made bad decisions when I drank—whether it was to do drugs or to have sex with someone. Impaired judgement was no friend of mine."

After stints with two more bands, the high-energy punk combo Chrome Dogs and Dying to Be Violent, Naked struck out on her own in order to escape the boundaries that had been placed on her lyric-writing. In 1994, she released an independent EP entitled *Four Songs and a Poem,* followed by her debut self-titled album. With *Bif Naked,* the young songwriter grasped the opportunity to explore all the issues and experiences that shaped her own life. The honesty of her songs, as well as her strong, punk-rock persona, made her an instant icon to thousands of young women worldwide. The same kind of independent attitude had also provided another artist, Tori Amos, a similar kind of fanbase. "I do get really heartfelt letters from some of my fans who can relate to it," Naked informed Saunders. "It reminds me of what Madonna meant to me when I was 14 years old: She was not afraid of anything, man."

Following her debut, Naked toured Canada, the United States, and Europe. In 1995, Naked, whose label had gone under soon after *Bif Naked*'s release, reissued the album on her own label, dubbed Her Royal Majesty's Records. That same year, the singer/songwriter also tossed aside her punk-rock lifestyle, eschewing all her destructive activities. "Because of my addictive personality, I couldn't just go on the wagon," she stated, as quoted by Atlantic Records. "It had to be something that was almost a religion…. I also felt that I suddenly had a social responsibility, because the kids that were coming to my gigs were really young."

In addition to serving as an example to younger fans, Naked also became the national spokesperson for Stop the Violence-Face the Music. In the summer of 1997, she hosted "Bif Naked's Rap Punk Pop Invitational" with SNFU, Raggadeath, and Face the Pain, a tour that traveled to 18 Canadian cities. She also performed as the only female act on the main stage at Edgefest, an annual gathering in Canada of alternative bands, alongside the likes of Green Day, the Foo Fighters, and Creed.

In 1999, Naked returned with a second album, her major-label debut entitled *I Bificus,* featuring autobiographical songs about loss, betrayal, and elation. *Billboard* hailed the release a "truly great rock debut," describing Naked as a "bold, big-voice, but beautifully nuanced performer." Following this success, Naked performed that summer with Lilith Fair, then toured with the Cult and Kid Rock.

In addition to pursuing a musical career, Naked landed several acting jobs as well on television series and made-for-television movies. In May of 2000, she started filming *Lunch With Charles,* a feature film by writer/director Michael Parker. Co-starring with Hong

Kong film star Sean Lau, Naked plays the role of Natasha, a woman who struggles to explore her voice as a Celtic singer without losing her own identity.

Selected discography

Bif Naked, Aquarius, 1994; reissued, 1995.
I Bificus, Lava/Atlantic, 1999.

Sources

Periodicals

Billboard, July 3, 1999; August 14, 1999.
Interview, December 1999.
Rolling Stone, October 14, 1999.

Online

Official Bif Naked Fan Page, http://www.angelaudio.com/bif /index.html (June 23, 2000).
Sonicnet.com, http://www.sonicnet.com (June 23, 2000).

—Laura Hightower

Nine Inch Nails

Industrial rock band

Nine Inch Nails (NIN), the elaborate brainchild of auteur Trent Reznor, shattered the concept of popular music by crafting songs from sounds which could easily have been heard in a metal fabrication plant. Along with the industrial nature of the music, dark, tortured lyrics completed the product seemingly forged on an anvil by a furious blacksmith. Even though the music fabricated by NIN was mechanical and often created on a hard drive of a computer instead of a traditional instrument, deeply emotive lyrics gave evidence that the creator was indeed human. The *Trouser Press Guide to '90s Rock* described NIN by stating that Reznor, "virtually perfected the tantrum-rock genus, spewing lyrical vitriol at an astounding array of targets (not the least of which being himself) and obsessively sequestering himself, Macintosh at the ready, to craft the caustic isolationist anthems that made him the anti-hero to a bleaker-than-bleak generation of young devotees."

Perhaps NIN was the perfect expression of how even the great advent of the information age at its best can only be used to improve the human condition by revealing it. Even so, Reznor impacted 1990's rock music in a huge way. Chris Norris of *Spin* stated, "his

Photograph by Steve Jennings. Corbis. Reproduced by permission.©

For The Record . . .

Members include **Charlie Clouser**, keyboards; **Jerome Dillon**, drums; **Robin Finck**, guitar; **Danny Lohner**, guitar, keyboards, bass; **Trent Reznor**, vocals, guitar, bass, drums, electronics, computers; and **Chris Vrenna**, drums.

Formed in 1988 in Cleveland, OH; Reznor wrote, arranged, performed, and produced most all of the material on Nine Inch Nails albums, enlisting band members for touring; debut album, *Pretty Hate Machine,* released 1989, went triple-platinum; formed Nothing Records, 1991; played in first Lollapalooza tour, 1991; released both *Broken* and *Fixed* EPs, 1992; *The Downward Spiral,* with controversial lyrics and video released, 1994, went quadruple platinum; produced soundtrack for *Natural Born Killers*; headlined Woodstock '94; *Further Down the Spiral,* remixes from previous album, released 1995; opened for David Bowie on United States tour; released *The Fragile,* 1999.

Awards: Grammy for Best Metal Performance for "Wish," 1993; Grammy for Best Metal Performance for "Happiness in Slavery," 1996; *Spin* magazine Album of the Year for *The Fragile,* 1999.

Addresses: *Record company*—Nothing/Interscope Records, 10900 Wilshire Blvd., Ste. 1230, Los Angeles, CA 90024.

brand of post-grunge introspection and self-disgust were central to that era's alternative-rock ethos." Reznor was considered the most artistically consistent innovator of industrial music along with Ministry, Skinny Puppy, and KMFDM. A description by *Rolling Stone* stated, "Reznor is widely regarded as one of the most influential voices in alternative music, earning himself a slot in a canon of musical auteurs previously carved out by the likes of Bowie, Reed, and Eno."

Trent Reznor grew up in Mercer, an isolated rural town in Pennsylvania. Born on May 17, 1965, he studied classical piano as a child, taught himself tuba and saxophone and dove into the keyboard as a teen. His career began as many other rock stars have—in garage bands in his home town. Reznor briefly studied computer engineering at Allegheny College before moving to Cleveland in 1987, where his career truly caught fire. He released singles with several bands while in Cleveland and Erie, Pennsylvania. Those groups were techno driven such as the synth-pop sound of the Exotic Birds, pomp-pop enunciations of Innocence, and dance beats of Slam Bam Boo. While with Problems, small success was earned when one of their songs, "True Love Ways," was performed by Joan Jett in the film, *Light of Day.*

Nine Inch Nails formed in Cleveland, Ohio in 1988 while Reznor worked at a recording studio as a general assistant. The studio job provided him with crucial experience to create and record music. He began NIN when he was 23 years old, as a modern, technological one-man band. TVT, an independent label, signed Reznor based on the demo he wrote, arranged, performed, and produced. Assistance from other musicians was mainly for touring. Members of the touring Nine Inch Nails included at one time or another Robin Finck on guitar; Danny Lohner on keyboards, guitar, and bass; Charles Clouser on keyboards; Chris Vrenna on drums; and Jerome Dillon on drums.

Started the Machine

Nine Inch Nails burst onto the scene in 1989 with the debut release, *Pretty Hate Machine.* It was coproduced by Flood (Depeche Mode, U2), John Fryer (Cocteau Twins), Adrian Sherwood, and Keith LeBlanc. Three college radio hits came from the album, which charted in 1990, stayed on for a couple of years and eventually went triple- platinum. The release fed the glowing ember of a Gothic scene and brought it to a rage as hoards of teenage fans wore black eyeliner and black trenchcoats. *Pretty Hate Machine* turned out to be a turning point in the industrial-pop genre. "Head Like A Hole," with its ferocious digital sound, screamed incessantly from radio and MTV. "Sin," a song with darker content, was refused for play on MTV due to its graphic sexual content; however, it further expanded the concept of pop music. NIN's ascension to stardom was helped by their live shows on the first Lollapalooza tour in 1991. Machine gunning across the country, Reznor introduced a stage persona that was full of energy, power, and anger, revealing frustrations that lay deep within.

Some of those frustrations were with his label at the time, TVT. Reznor spent three years at odds with TVT, stating it was an antagonistic relationship, which did not support him artistically or financially. Finally, Interscope came up with a deal to core-lease the group, and he eventually broke away from TVT and set up his own studio along with his manager, John Malm: Nothing Records. Soon, Pop Will Eat Itself and Marilyn Manson were signed, and were symbolic of Reznor's energy. Most notable was the production of Marilyn Manson's *Antichrist Superstar,* during which he and Manson became close friends.

Broken, released in 1992, was the first release from Nothing. Debuting in the *Billboard* Top Ten, the project was harder and more abrasive than *Pretty Hate Machine.* Again bringing in Flood, who produced three tracks, the EP included raging songs like "Last" and "Wish," which earned a Grammy for Best Metal Performance in 1993; and "Happiness in Slavery," which earned a Grammy for Best Metal Performance in 1996. "Happiness in Slavery" also drew attention because of the accompanying video which portrayed a man being sexually tortured and then destroyed by a machine. "Down In It" was more extreme, as the origin for a video clip which was so lifelike that the FBI investigated it under the premise of it being a snuff film.

Fixed, an EP also released in 1992, was the second project from Nothing. J.G. Thirwell, Butch Vig, and others assisted Reznor on this collection of remixes from *Broken.* Reznor expanded his synthesizing by working with other industrial bands during 1992 such as Pigface, and Revolting Cocks, which was lead by Al Jourgensen and Paul Barker of Ministry. A live tour in 1993 saw a full band thrash through sets with the wrath of a chainsaw. So impressive was NIN's show, that they opened for Guns-n-Roses on a tour in Europe. Creativity continued however, as they recorded a song by Joy Division, "Dead Souls," for the soundtrack to *The Crow.* Industrial Supremacy

The Downward Spiral, from 1994, took five years to create but debuted at number two on the charts and went quadruple platinum. It included segments which were recorded in his home studio, the same house where members of the Charles Manson family murdered Sharon Tate nearly 25 years earlier. Reznor claimed he realized the house's significance only after recording had begun despite accusations of distaste by the media. With Flood again coproducing, it featured ex-King Crimson guitarist Adrian Belew. This album included more variety than previous work. "A Warm Place" reflected a softer side of Reznor, whereas "Closer" revealed the primitive desires of physical attraction. Perhaps alluding to Charles Manson, "pig" was mentioned throughout the album. Harsh and scarred as the album was, it even had its limits. Reznor recalled in 1995 that he almost included "Just Do It," a song about suicide on *The Downward Spiral,* but Flood persuaded him from it. Reznor later stated that, "I had a story to tell [with The Downward Spiral], and I was—and still am—very pleased with how it turned out. I didn't realize at the time, however, that it was about to become a self-fulfilling prophecy."

Success was roaring and NIN was impacting many. In 1994, Reznor produced the soundtrack for Oliver Stone's *Natural Born Killers.* It included three NIN songs: "Burn," "A Warm Place," and a remix of "Something I Can Never Have." Reznor even recorded a song with Tori Amos, "Past the Mission," for her *Under the Pink* album. The band epitomized and directed the

alternative rock scene by headlining at Woodstock '94. Rage let loose on stage and from the studio inspired artists like Chuck Palahniuk, author of the story *Fight Club.* He admitted, "I listened to *The Downward Spiral* and *Pretty Hate Machine* constantly while I was writing *Fight Club;* there were cuts on it that I would put on "repeat" to the point that my housemates were just insane. "Hurt" was one of the big ones."

Further Down The Spiral, an EP released in 1995, offered remixes of several tracks from *The Downward Spiral.* Rick Rubin, Thirwell, and Coil joined in on the companion album. The band gained additional attention when they toured with David Bowie in the United States. Feeling the vibe, Bowie joined Reznor on the rendition of his own "Scary Monsters" and on NIN's "Hurt" and "Reptile." Another success was "The Perfect Drug," released in 1997, which was on the *Lost Highway* movie soundtrack and received a Grammy nomination for Best Hard Rock Performance.

Wrench in the Works

Reznor hit a low period during the late 1990s. His grandmother, who raised him since he was five, died in 1997, leaving him with even less personal stability than that which produced the sordid songs of *The Downward Spiral.* A falling out with close friend Marilyn Manson left him staggering. Writer's block set in and even a retreat to Big Sur, California did not turn out the work he wanted for his next album. Alan Moulder, the engineer/co-producer for *The Fragile,* guided Reznor to the producer of *The Wall,* Bob Ezrin. Ezrin helped Reznor sort through a huge mass of sonic expression recorded at Nothing Records, which was in a former funeral home in New Orleans, to pull together a double album. It was a full 100-minute autobiographical masterpiece.

The Fragile, which took two years to complete due in part to writer's block, debuted at number one on the charts and went platinum within ten months. Reznor brought in David Bowie, pianist Mike Garson, guitarist Adrian Belew and Ministry drummer William Rieflin as contributors. Chris Norris of *Spin* described *The Fragile* when he stated, "Rather than the lurid thrills of *The Downward Spiral*—whose catchy tunes about sex and death fueled many study-hall fantasies—*The Fragile* chronicles, in slow, torturous movements, an unglamorous descent into depression and self-negation. It deals with aging, numbness, disillusionment, and uneasy self-acceptance." Whereas the work contained some familiar anger such as in the discourse about his split from Manson in "Starf***ers, Inc." many of the lyrics were the most optimistic of his career. *Spin* magazine selected *The Fragile* as the 1999 album of the year.

Completing *The Fragile* must have been somewhat therapeutic for Reznor as he set out on several more projects. He and Manson showed some sign of making up when Manson appeared on the "Starf***rs, Inc." video. A slight step back in complexity, but still challenging, he was slated for a collaboration with hip-hop auteur Dr. Dre. In addition, he began to form a band with a female vocalist so that he could still create music, but enlist someone else to perform vocals.

Selected discography

Pretty Hate Machine, TVT, 1989.
Broken, EP, Nothing/TVT/Interscope, 1992.
Fixed, EP, Nothing/TVT/Interscope, 1992.
The Downward Spiral, Nothing/Interscope, 1994.
Further Down the Spiral, Nothing/Interscope, 1995.
The Fragile, Nothing/Interscope, 1999.

Sources

Books

Ira A. Robbins, editor, *The Trouser Press Guide to '90s Rock,* Fireside/Simon & Schuster, 1997.
MusicHound Rock, Visible Ink Press, 1999.

Periodicals

Rolling Stone, May 31, 1990, p. 34; July 9-23, 1992, pp. 32-33.

Online

All Music Guide, http://www.allmusic.com, (April 17, 2000).
MTV Online, http://www.mtv.com, (May 10, 2000).
NIN Web Page, http://www.nin.com, (May 22, 2000).
Rock On the Net, http://rockonthenet.com/artists-n/nineinch nails_main.htm, (May 2000).
Rolling Stone.com, http://www.RollingStone.com, (May 7, 2000).
The Rough Guide to Rock, http://www.roughguides.com, (April 17, 2000).
Smashedupsanity.com, http://www.smashedupsanity.com/chronology/, (May 25, 2000).
Spin Magazine Online, http://www.spin.com, (May 6, 2000).

—*Nathan Sweet*

Papas Fritas

Pop band

With a name like Papas Fritas, a moniker meaning "fried potatoes" in Spanish, one may expect to hear Latin music. But the band, bound together by a common affection for pop songs and known for their geeky charm, embrace simple, powerful melodies and carefree lyrics. Tony Goddess, who does most of the songwriting for the group, said that he sometimes wishes he could pen harsh thrashers like Korn and other hard-edged rock acts. "Coming up with something with snappy energy is harder than atonality," he told Jim Sullivan for a *Boston Globe* interview, while at the same time admitting to his teenaged metal-rock phase. "But I'm not the kind of person that dwells on negative emotions. Music can help you transcend rather than dwell… I never felt we were one of the 'cooler' bands, but when people talk about us, they'll say we aren't trying to put anything over on them—we're just trying to make music."

In 1992, the members of Boston's Papas Fritas formed a band together with one goal in mind: to create catchy, simple, and honest pop music that makes people feel good. Tony Goddess, the group's guitarist and vocalist and the bandmember who came up with the group's name one day in his Spanish class, and Shivika Asthana, a drummer and vocalist raised by parents who emigrated from India, both originated from Delaware, where they played in a high school marching band together, while bassist and vocalist Keith Gendel moved to the East Coast from the southwestern city of Houston, Texas. The trio met while attending college at Tufts University in Somerville, Massachusetts—Goddess majored in English and music, and Asthana and Gendel majored in bio-psychology.

In the beginning, the three students viewed their band as a mere hobby, spending their first couple of years together playing at basement parties and recording tapes for friends on Goddess's Tascam four-track machine. But their focus started to shift when Matt Hanks of Sunday Driver Records released three of the band's songs in 1994 on a seven-inch single entitled "Friday Night." The band's last four-track production, "Friday Night" fully illustrated the band's live sound and included a song that caught the attention of Minty Fresh Records called "Smash This World" when it received airplay on a Chicago radio station.

As word of the record spread, Papas Fritas decided it was time to start acting like a "real" band with regular touring, promoting themselves, and improving their singing. In the summer of 1994, the trio signed with Minty Fresh and progressed to an eight-track studio—affectionately named Hi-Tech City—that they built in the basement of their house on Electric Avenue in Somerville. After recording two new songs for a seven-inch single, 1995's "Passion Play/Lame to Be" (*Passion Play* was also issued as an EP with three additional songs from old tapes), the band concentrated on their debut album.

Determined to give the record a sonic identity all its own, Papas Fritas spent nearly six months perfecting the 13 songs that would compile their self-titled debut, and in October of 1995, *Papas Fritas* finally hit store shelves. With childlike innocence and enthusiasm, the group's first outing focused on sunny melodies, re-creating in a referential way the classic pop sounds of the Beatles, the Beach Boys, the Mamas and the Papas, and the Kinks. The album's release also coincided with the trio's college graduation, leaving Papas Fritas ample time for promotion and tours. Thus, they performed for audiences across the United States, then traveled to Europe, where the group toured with the Flaming Lips, and finally Japan. Returning home after months on the road in September of 1996, Papas Fritas settled down to focus on the next record. This time, they relocated their studio to a wooded area in Gloucester, Massachusetts, setting up in an old, rustic school house they dubbed The Columnated Ruins. The new location proved complimentary to the band's desire to make a more organic and natural-sounding record, and in April of 1997, Papas Fritas released their second full-length LP, *Helioself.*

A direct result of the trio taking the band to a more serious level, the album generated favorable reviews from the mainstream press, including *Melody Maker* and *Rolling Stone.* "*Helioself* offers more than just clowning around…," wrote *Village Voice* critic Rob Brunner, for example. "Papas Fritas have created a sort of grown-up version of little-kid music, capturing

For The Record . . .

Members include **Shivika Asthana** (born in Delaware; daughter of Indian immigrants; graduated with a degree in bio-psychology from Tufts University), drums, vocals; **Chris Colthart** (touring member; joined band in 1999), guitar; **Donna Coppola** (touring member; joined band in 1999), keyboards, percussion; **Keith Gendel** (born in Houston, TX; graduated with a degree in bio-psychology from Tufts University), bass, vocals; **Tony Goddess** (born in Delaware; graduated with degrees in English and music from Tufts University), guitar, vocals.

Formed band in 1992 while attending Tufts University in Somerville, Massachusetts; released single "Friday Night" on Sunday Driver, 1994; signed with Minty Fresh Records, released "Passion Play/Lame to Be" and debut, self-titled album, toured Europe with the Flaming Lips, 1995; released *Helioself,* 1997; released *Building and Grounds,* 2000.

Addresses: *Record company*—Minty Fresh Records, P.O. Box 577400, Chicago, IL 60657. *Publicist*—Matt Hanks: press@autotonic.com, Anthony Musiala: musiala @mintyfresh.com. *Website*—Papas Fritas Home Page: http://www.papasfritas.com. *E-mail*—Keith Gendel: kgendel@biofoot.com, Shivika Asthana: shivika @ibm .net

the knowing naivete of a precocious child... These painstakingly constructed songs fondly evoke childhood silliness without simply aping it; the fun is in hearing familiarly goofy sounds recast as sophisticated pop music." Soon after the album's release, Papas Fritas hit the road again, spending the better part of the year on tour in support of *Helioself.* They returned home exhausted, and for the first time felt unsure of their next move. "After touring on *Helioself,* that's when we all went through that postcollegiate 'What am I going to do with my life?' thing," Goddess told the *Boston Phoenix.* "We had a manager at the time who didn't think that anything could be accomplished on an indie label, and he messed with our thinking a little bit."

"It wound up getting pretty tiresome," Asthana further explained to *Magnet* magazine's Jud Cost, "so we got away from each other for about a year, got jobs and settled down. And that's definitely helped. We're like a family that sometimes doesn't get along, but we still care about each other a lot." Since then, and after negotiations with major labels DreamWorks and Geffen fell through in the midst of record company megamergers, the group decided to concentrate on their music, rather than worrying about making it big in the record industry. "We used to have this mindset of, 'Let's get big—let's get really huge,'" the drummer continued. "But we've gotten away from all that. It just didn't fit our personalities."

After the band's self-imposed sabbatical, during which time they reappraised their purpose and identity, the trio returned to the studio in June of 1999 to mix a third album. Two months later, in mid-August, Papas Fritas introduced two new members that would join them for live shows: guitarist Chris Colthart and keyboardist/percussionist Donna Coppola. With the new additions, Papas Fritas then traveled to New York in September to perform at the *CMJ* (*College Music Journal*) festival for "Minty Fresh Night."

Completed in October of 1999 and released in March of 2000, the more immediate and slower-paced *Buildings and Grounds* revealed a new side of Papas Fritas. "We made a concerted effort to write more songs in minor keys," revealed Goddess to Cost. "And we tried to make this record more sophisticated, so I've been able to play four- and five-note chords instead of just three-note chords." Likewise, Gendel described the outing as a conscious effort by the band to leave behind the childlike overtones of their prior albums. Made of "sterner stuff," noted Marc Weingarten of the *Village Voice* and described by Cost as "a spooky, minor-chord gem that glows with the intensity of a peat fire in a cemetery," *Buildings and Grounds* won praise as Papas Fritas' most consistent and stimulating album.

Although Goddess is content with remaining independent and the group's new album, the songwriter, who at one time worked at a local record store in Gloucester called Mystery Train, realizes the importance of knowing what music buyers are listening to. "It's cool being aware of what young kids are listening to," he told Cost, "because I know how much music meant to me at that age. It's one thing I've always loved about pop music: I love a record, and seven million other people like it, too. It makes me feel like we have something in common. I don't like music to set me apart from people. I like it to make me feel I'm not alone. I love that Christina Aguilera song 'Genie In A Bottle,' for example. I wish I'd written it."

Selected discography

"Friday Night," (seven-inch single), Sunday Driver, 1994.
"Passion Play/Lame to Be," (seven-inch single), Minty Fresh, 1995.

Passion Play, (EP), 1995.
Papas Fritas, Minty Fresh, 1995.
Helioself, Minty Fresh, 1997.
Buildings and Grounds, Minty Fresh, 2000.

Sources

Periodicals

Boston Globe, March 10, 1997; July 24, 1997; March 18, 2000.
Boston Phoenix, March 2, 2000.

Guitar Player, August 1997.
Magnet, April/May 2000, pp. 39-41.
Melody Maker, December 9, 1995; October 4, 1997.
Rolling Stone, May 29, 1997.
Village Voice, May 13, 1997; April 11, 2000.
Washington Post, March 10, 2000.

Online

Papas Fritas Home Page, http://www.papasfritas.com (May 12, 2000).

—Laura Hightower

Harry Partch

Composer

Harry Partch was perhaps the most radical of all American composers. He developed a theory of music vastly different from that upon which Western music of the last 500 years is based. He designed his own musical scale, which consisted of 43 tones instead of the 12 used by traditional Western music. He invented over 20 unique musical instruments capable of playing the music he composed, and produced and distributed recordings of his music on his own record label. Partch rejected most trends in twentieth century classical music, such as serialism and chance as utilized by John Cage, and he had a difficult, uneasy relationship with academia. In fact, despite the avant-garde character of his work, Partch did consider his music as something new in a revolutionary sense. As he saw it, his work stretched back to ancient sources, in particular the music of the Greeks. He was not moving forward, but instead backward to sources of music more authentic than anything being created by modern composers.

Harry Partch was the son of ex-missionaries and grew up in the American Southwest. His first rudimentary musical training came from his mother, a church organist. By his own account, he studied piano and harmony with various private teachers in the Arizona, New Mexico, Los Angeles, and Kansas City, and entered the University of Southern California—for a few months at least—where he studied under concert pianist Olga Steeb. He began composing as a teenager, and in his early twenties worked in traditional classical forms: a piano concerto, a symphonic poem, and a string quartet, among other pieces.

The turning point in his musical life came in the spring of 1923 when he discovered *On the Sensations of Tone*, a book by Hermann Helmholtz which explained the foundations of music through the science of acoustics. Helmholtz related musical intervals—in their most basic form, the difference in sound produced by two adjacent keys on a piano—to the mathematics of a vibrating string. For Partch, this explanation led to the revolutionary conclusion that implied that the 12 tones used for hundreds of years in Western music—the black and white keys on a piano—were not the only way to compose. A scale could be divided into as many distinct tones, known as microtones, as one wanted. Additionally, Partch believed that the roots of music in the ancient world actually laid in such microtonal systems that were very different from the Western scale, a scale which was artificially based on the mechanics of the piano. With this in mind, he developed his own scale, comprised of 43 distinct tones, rather than 12.

Because most conventional Western instruments were incapable of playing such a scale, Partch began inventing his own. The first was built in 1930 from a viola body and a cello fretboard. Called the Adapted Viola, Partch played it upright between his knees with a bow. Partch's biographer, Bob Gilmore, called the instrument "the true point of no return in Partch's early musical development." It gave him the means to work in his new system and it was around this time that he burned all his earlier work. Partch's first compositions in his new system were settings of poems by Li Po for intoned voice and Adapted Viola. Other instruments followed over the years, including an Adapted Guitar, a keyboard instrument called the Chromelodeon that could play Partch's scale, the Kithara based on an ancient Greek stringed instrument, and various marimbas, such as the Bass Marimba, the Diamond Marimba and the Boo, a bamboo marimba.

In 1934 and 1935, with money from a grant from the Carnegie Foundation, Partch traveled to Europe. In the British Museum, he researched ancient and non-Western music for a book that laid out his theory of music, published some 15 years later as *Genesis of a Music*. While in Europe Partch also met poet William Butler Yeats, whose translation of Sophocles' *Oedipus Rex* he hoped to adapt for his instruments and intoned voice. Yeats responded with enthusiasm to the private concert Partch performed for him and gave his permission to use the translation. Although it was not completed or performed for many more years, *King Oedipus* marked the beginning of Partch's work for theater. For the rest of his career, most of his work would have a strong narrative element, whether it was the relatively simple settings of hobo graffiti for voice and Adapted Guitar in *Barstow*, or a full-scale theatrical event with

Born on June 24, 1901, in Oakland, CA; died on September 3,1974, in San Diego, CA. *Education*: Attended the University of Southern California.

Invented first instrument, the Adapted Viola, and wrote settings of Li Po poems for Adapted Viola and voice, 1930; traveled to Europe, 1934; lived as a hobo, 1935-43; built Chromelodeon, 1942; first public concert, April 1944; moved to Madison, WI, to complete his book *Genesis of a Music*, 1944; *Genesis of a Music* published, 1949; *King Oedipus* premiers at Mills College, Oakland, CA, 1952; *Plectra & Percussion Dances* composed, 1952; Gate 5 Ensemble founded and first recording, *Plectra & Percussion Dances* released, 1953; received commission from University of Illinois to compose *The Bewitched*, 1956; began work with filmmaker Madelain Tourtelot, 1957; composed music for *Windsong*, 1958; *Music Studio*, a film about Partch, released, 1958; *Revelation in the Courthouse Park* premiered at the University of Illinois, 1961; film version of *United States Highball* completed, 1963; *And On the Seventh Day the Petals Fell in Petaluma* composed, 1964; Composers Recordings Inc. released first commercial recording of Partch's work, 1964; Columbia Records released *The World of Harry Partch*, 1969; Harry Partch Foundation established, 1970; *The Dreamer That Remains—A Study in Loving*, a film about Harry Partch with music by Harry Partch completed, 1972.

musical ensemble, actors and dancers of *Revelation in the Courthouse Park*.

The spring of 1935, at the height of the Great Depression, was the beginning of several years Partch spent hoboing, riding the rails, living in hobo jungles, and occasionally earning money picking fruit or doing other odd jobs. Partch's homelessness effectively ended his composing for the time. But the journals he kept were later used as texts for works like *The Letter, Barstow*, and *United States Highball*. Despite the fact that his life as a hobo ended in 1943, Partch was never financially secure. He lived from one small grant, commission or personal loan to the next and he moved to a different house practically every year of his life.

The first public performance of Partch's work took place in April of 1944 under the auspices of the League of Composers in New York City. Partch presented *Barstow, United States Highball, San Francisco*, and *Y.D. Fantasy*, first at Carnegie Chamber Music Hall and a few days later at Columbia University. The concerts were widely reviewed and Partch was even profiled in the *New Yorker*. To the composer's disappointment and frustration, however, the performances were forgotten almost as soon as the ink had dried on the reviews, and they did not lead to any further offers.

Partch spent the late 1940s finishing his book, *Genesis of a Music*, in Madison, Wisconsin. The university's press published the book in 1949. The stay in Madison, typical of Partch's relationship with academic music, was marked by suspicion on both sides. Partch belittled the musical establishment in both his writings and musical satires, while music departments had little use for a self-educated "crackpot" whose ideas about music went against the grain of everything they stood for and were teaching to their students. Consequently it was only through the graces of friends and admirers, such as Gunnar Johansen and Ben Johnston, that Partch was able to win short-term affiliations with a few universities.

From Wisconsin, Partch returned to California, first Gualala on the state's remote northern coast, and then to the area around the San Francisco Bay. In 1952, *King Oedipus*, the Yeats translation Partch had been working on since the 1930s, was finally produced at Mills College in Oakland. Scored for voices, Marimba Eroica, Chromelodeon, and cello, the performance drew mixed reviews in the press in San Francisco and New York. But the "intoned voice" Partch wrote for—a sort of heightened speech rather than singing—put great demands on the audience over the course of the 75-minute long work. Although personally satisfying to see his work finally performed, *King Oedipus* led to further disappointments for Partch. First, the college failed to offer the appointment he was hoping for. Then the Yeats estate refused to allow him to issue a recording of the work, despite assurances he had received in writing from Yeats himself 20 years earlier. Partch's involvement in theater would continue through the 1950s and 1960s with large scale works such as *The Bewitched, Revelation in the Courthouse Park, Water! Water!*, and *Delusion of the Fury*.

In 1952 Partch entered another fertile period of composition. With *Plectra & Percussion Dances*, the focus of his work moved away from human speech to the instrumental, rhythmic music that would increasingly characterize his last two decades of work. In 1954, friends found him a studio in Sausalito, and at the same time they solicited subscriptions that were used to establish a trust fund to finance recordings of Partch's music. The records, in turn, were meant to provide Partch with an income that if small, was at least regular. The plan worked. To make the recordings, Partch assembled a group of musicians from nearby San Francisco, tagged the Gate 5 Ensemble after the name of Partch's studio. He taught the group how to play his exotic collection of instruments which had grown steadily over the years until they filled whatever space Partch happened to be living in. He released more than ten recordings on his Gate 5 label in the 1950s and 1960s. "His role as producer and distributor of recordings of his own work impressed fellow artists such as Anais Nin," Bob Gilmore wrote, "and served as a model for several younger composers in the 1960s and 1970s."

In the fall of 1957, Partch began an association with Chicago filmmaker Madelaine Tourtelot that would last through the 1960s. They agreed to collaborate on a film version of *United States Highball*. In the middle of work, however, he saw some footage she shot at sand dunes on Lake Michigan and conceived a score based on the myth of Apollo and Daphne. It was used in Tourtelot's film 1958 *Windsong* and later revised as the 1969 ballet *Daphne of the Dunes*. *United States Highball* was finally completed in 1963. Partch moved from Illinois back to Petaluma, California, in September of 1962. The falling of blossoms from the trees inspired him to begin one of his rare instrumental works, *And On the Seventh Day the Petals Fell in Petaluma*. Eventually completed in 1966, *Petals* is a series of duos, trios, quartets, quintets and a septet, a showpiece for Partch's different instruments.

Partch's instruments were a blessing and a curse for him. Without them, his music would have been unperformable. But as it was his music could only be performed on them, and there was but a single set. Before he could accept invitations to perform, arrangements had to be made to transport the fragile, often unwieldy pieces. Once they were moved, musicians had to be found and trained to play them. Notating music for his 43-note scale was also a problem that plagued Partch. These issues continue to pose questions for Partch's legacy. Can a music survive that depends on delicate instruments most musicians have never seen, much less used, that depends on an arcane notation most musicians are just as unfamiliar with?

In December of 1964, Composers Recordings Inc. (CRI) released the first commercial recording of Partch's music, a sign he thought that the need for private issues had ended. CRI continued, at irregular intervals, to bring out Partch's work. In the late 1990s the label launched a plan to release a series of retrospective CDs. In the mid-1960s, Partch began another theater piece that would become *Delusion of the Fury*. Based on a Japanese Noh play and an Ethiopian folk tale, whose theme was the futility of anger, the work premiered at the UCLA Playhouse in January 1969.

The last years of Partch's life were made easier by his friend Betty Freeman, who arranged for him to receive a small regular annual income. Health problems were complicated by musical problems. He organized a new ensemble to play his work, but rehearsals at his new studio in Venice were frustrated by what he perceived as a lack of seriousness in many of the musicians he recruited. At the same time he was plagued by concerns for his instruments. They required constant maintenance which he was too old to provide. What is more, he might not have a home, but the instruments *had* to have one. He tried to find a university willing to take over their storage and care, but in vain. In the end, he willed everything to his long-time disciple and collaborator, Danlee Mitchell, who later became the head of the Harry Partch Foundation, one of the main keepers of the Partch flame.

Partch's last big project was music for *The Dreamer That Remains*, a film about him and his work made by Stephen Pouliot. He died on September 3, 1974, in San Diego, California.

Selected discography

(With Gate 5 Ensemble of Sausalito), *Plectra & Percussion Dances*, Harry Partch Trust Fund First Edition, 1953.

Oedipus, A Harry Partch Trust Fund First Edition, Oedipus, 1954.

(With Gate 5 Ensemble of Sausalito), *Plectra & Percussion Dances*, second edition, Gate 5 Records, 1957.

(With Gate 5 Ensemble of Evanston, Illinois), *U. S. Highball*, Gate 5 Records, Issue 6, 1958.

Thirty Years of Lyric and Dramatic Music, Gate 5 Records, Issue A, 1962.

(With Gate 5 Ensemble of Evanston, Illinois), *The Wayward*, Gate 5 Records, Issue B, 1962.

(With Gate 5 Ensemble of Sausalito), *Plectra & Percussion Dances*, Gate 5 Records, Issue C, 1962.

(With Gate 5 Ensemble of Sausalito), *Oedipus*, Gate 5 Records, Issue D.

(With Gate 5 Ensemble from University of Illinois), *The Bewitched* (excerpts), Gate 5 Records, Issue E, 1962.

Revelation In The Courthouse Park, Gate 5 Records, Issue F.

Water! Water!, An Intermission, Gate 5 Records, Issue G, 1962.

The World of Harry Partch-Quadraphonic, Columbia Records, 1972.

Enclosure II, innova 401, 4 CD set, 1995.

The Harry Partch Collection: Volume 1, CRI, CD 751, 1997.

The Harry Partch Collection: Volume 2, CRI, CD 752, 1997.

The Harry Partch Collection: Volume 3, CRI, CD 753, 1997.

The Harry Partch Collection: Volume 4, CRI, CD 754, 1997.

Enclosure V, innova 404, 3 CD set, 1998.

Videos

Enclosure I, includes films *Rotate the Body in All Its Planes*, *Music Studio—Harry Partch*, *United States Highball*, and *Windsong*.

Enclosure IV, includes *Delusion of the Fury* and *The Music of Harry Partch*.

The Dreamer That Remains: A Study in Loving, New Dimension Media, Inc.

Books

Partch, Harry, *Bitter Music: Collected Journals, Essays, Introductions, and Librettos*, edited by Thomas McGeary, University of Illinois Press, 1991.

Partch, Harry, *Enclosure III*, edited by Philip Blackburn, American composers Forum, 1997.

Partch, Harry, *Genesis of a Music: An Account of a Creative Work, Its Roots and Its Fulfillments*, University of Wisconsin Press, 1948.

Sources

Books

Gilmore, Bob, *Harry Partch: A Biography,* Yale University, 1998.
Hitchcock, H. Wiley and Stanley Sadie, editors, *New Grove Dictionary of American Music*, Macmillan, 1986.

Online

"The Meadows Guide to Partch Recordings, Videos and Books," http://www.corporeal.com/freshpix.html#recordings (June 26, 2000).

—*Gerald E. Brennan*

Prince Paul

Hip-hop artist, producer

It is hard to imagine, but one of hip-hop's true revolutionaries is a person whose name you may not know and whose face you would likely not recognize. Until recently, he has seemed to exist only in album credits—a deejay on one album, a producer on some others, and a remixer of singles here and there. But Prince Paul's work has made an impact on the hip-hop universe, and though he stepped out front in the last couple of years, he is still one of rap's most enigmatic and elusive figures.

So what has he done that is so special ? For one thing, Paul brought hip-hop out of the era where the only thing that could be sampled was the same old "funky drummer" snippet from a James Brown record. The joints he produced featured samples from all kinds of crazy sources—Johnny Cash songs, jazz albums, TV shows, foreign language instruction records, whatever. He turned hip-hop records from a forum for old-school boasting into a new medium for psychedelic collage. Beyond that, he also invented the hip-hop skit. Granted, it didn't take long for this particular feature of rap records to seem totally played out, but back when Paul inserted the game-show sections into De La Soul's *3 Feet High and Rising*, it was something totally new. Along with De La Soul, Paul also opened the way for a new spirit of positivity to enter the rap game.

Prince Paul was born Paul Huston on April 2, 1967 on New York's Long Island. His love of music came from his father, a truck driver (now deceased) who played jazz records for his infant son. As a tribute, Paul included a sample of "Moody's Mood for Love," a favorite of his father's, into his album *A Prince Among Thieves*. Paul's mother was a home health aide. His upbringing was suburban and mostly without incident. He took clarinet lessons for a time, but quickly gave up. His musical heroes were funk musicians, such as George Clinton and his band Parliament-Funkadelic, and hip-hop forefathers like Biz Markie and Rakim. In junior high school, Paul began deejaying, and quickly showed his gift for innovation, dropping samples of television show theme songs into his mixes, and spinning records backwards for odd effect. Paul attended Amityville High School, ironically the same school attended by the members of De La Soul, though they didn't know each other at the time. He earned a degree from Five Towns College and worked a day job at an insurance company called General Accident after graduating.

By night, however, Paul's hip-hop dreams continued unabated. He played a house party in Brooklyn where members of the band Stetsasonic approached him about working with them. He produced the title track for their 1988 album *In Full Gear.* "Delight [of Stetsasonic] was like, 'You gotta quit college 'cause Stetsasonic is going to blow up and you need more time with the group and you need to quit your job,' " Paul told *Urb* magazine. He refused, convinced that hip-hop, like so many musical trends, was just a passing phase.

Paul changed his mind in 1989 after producing De La Soul's landmark album *3 Feet High and Rising*. Its songs were far different from the self-promotional boasts and proto-gangsta threats that dominated the genre up to that point, and in-between them, Paul inserted unusual samples—Steely Dan and Hall and Oates—and hilarious quiz show questions like "How many feathers on a Perdue chicken?" The album was a critical and popular success, ultimately selling more than a million copies. The follow-up, *De La Soul is Dead,* was less successful, but still managed to earn gold status. Another collaboration, *Buhloone Mindstate,* was widely praised by critics, but rap's ever-fickle public had moved on by then.

In his spare time, Paul had been producing and remixing tracks for the likes of Boogie Down Productions, Big Daddy Kane, and the most legitimate white rappers of their time, 3rd Bass. Following the split with De La Soul, Paul joined Wu-Tang Clan producer RZA, rappers Too Poetic and Fruitkwan, and formed Gravediggaz in 1994. The group released the album *Six Feet Deep* in 1994, and album that represented quite a turn for Paul, who up to that point had seldom dealt in gangsta clichés. Gravediggaz actually went past the violence and mayhem of most gangsta rap, though, creating a mix of over-the-top gore and heavy metal some dubbed "horrorcore." Nevertheless, it produced the hit single "Diary of a Madman." Paul, whose pseudonym in Gravediggaz is Undertaker, went on to make two more albums, *The Pick, the Sickle, and the Shovel* in 1997, and *Scenes from the Graveyard* in 1998.

Before those records came out, however, Paul took a step toward finally making a solo record. He combined samples of a psychoanalytic self-help album with the recorded dreams and fantasies—many of them incredibly explicit—of friends and various rappers, and turned it all into an album called *Psychoanalysis (What Is It ?)*. The disc shocked many who were not ready for an album from Paul that dealt with things like date rape and murder. "It was a joke that went too far," Paul told the *New York Times*. "The next thing, I'm getting write-ups about people getting shocked. I thought that record was the end of my career. Next thing, all the work comes in." Paul produced tracks for his old hero Biz Markie as well as Living Colour guitarist Vernon Reid and comedian Chris Rock (the Grammy-winning *Roll With the New*). "One reason Chris and I are friends is that we're both nerds," Paul told the *New York Times*.

After the *Psychoanalysis* album, Paul set out on a much more ambitious project. His 1999 album *Prince Among Thieves* was nothing short of a hip-hop opera. It has a story line running all the way through, laid out in between song skits and musical numbers that show off Paul's mastery of many different hip-hop styles. The story involves a nascent rapper, Tariq, who needs $1,000 to finish a demo tape he is sending to Wu-Tang producer RZA. His best friend True hooks him up with some drug dealing associates, and soon the previously upright youth is seduced into selling vast quantities of dope for drug kingpin Mr. Large. True helps him buy a gun, a pimp named Count Mackula sets him up with a prostitute, and eventually, he is busted by the police. His mother sends a minister to bail him out, but when he hits the streets once again, he discovers that True has stolen his music and his appointment with RZA. As it turns out, it was True that had played him all along, setting him up in the drug game and then calling in his corrupt police buddies. Tariq finds True and the two shoot each other, but True survives because he was wearing a bullet-proof vest. Tariq, wounded but with nothing to live for, takes his own life. Though a grim tale, *A Prince Among Thieves* earned major critical praise and may someday become a movie; Chris Rock has negotiated to buy the film rights.

At the same time he was working on *Prince,* Paul was moving in another direction altogether. He teamed with deejay Dan "The Automator" Nakamura (of Dr. Octagon fame) in the group Handsome Boy Modeling

School. The name is taken from an episode of Chris Elliot's short-lived Fox television sitcom *Get a Life*. There is a loose concept to the album, but basically, it is a framework for Paul's wildly entertaining tracks, featuring cameo appearances by Grand Puba, Sadat X, Encore, DJ Shadow, Cibo Matto's Miho Hatori, Sean Lennon, Del tha Funky Homosapien and Beastie Boy Mike D. Like *A Prince Among Thieves, How's Your Girl* was named on many critics' lists of the best recordings of 1999.

Despite all his success, Paul seems able to keep it all in perspective. As he told *Urb,* "People are like 'Yo Paul, you're like a legend.' It doesn't sink in. I'm happy that I have the opportunity, but I still live by how-long-is-this-going-to-last? I've seen the roller coaster up and I've seen it down, so I never want to get too comfortable with success."

Selected discography

Solo

Psychoanalysis (What Is It?), Tommy Boy, 1997.
A Prince Among Thieves, Tommy Boy, 1999.

With Gravediggaz

Six Feet Deep, Gee Street, 1994.
The Pick, the Sickle, & the Shovel, Gee Street, 1997.

With Stetsasonic

On Fire, Tommy Boy, 1986.
In Full Gear, Tommy Boy, 1988.
Blood, Sweat, and No Tears, Tommy Boy, 1991.

With Handsome Boy Modeling School

So How's Your Girl ?, Tommy Boy, 1999.

As producer

De La Soul, *3 Feet High and Rising*, Tommy Boy, 1989.
Big Daddy Kane, "Ain't No Stoppin' Us" / It's a Big Daddy Thing," from *Big Daddy Thing*, Cold Chillin'/WB, 1989.

3rd Bass, "The Gas Face" / "Brooklyn Queens," from *The Cactus Album*, Def Jam, 1989.
MC Lyte, "MC Lyte Likes Swingin'" from *Lyte as a Rock*, First Priority/Atlantic, 1990.
De La Soul, *De La Soul Is Dead*, Tommy Boy, 1991.
3rd Bass, "Derelicts of Dialect" / "Herbeiz in Your Mouth" / Come In" / "No Static at All" / "Green Eggs & Slime," from *Derelicts of Dialect*, Def Jam, 1991.
Boogie Down Productions, "Drug Dealer" / "Sex and Violence" / "How Not to Get Jerked, from *Sex & Violence*, Jive, 1992.
De La Soul, *Buhloone Mindstate*, Tommy Boy, 1993.
Justin Warfield, "Dip Dip Divin'"/ "K Sera Sera"/ "Thoughts in the Buttermilk," from *My Fieldtrip to Planet 9*, Quest/WB, 1993.
Biz Markie/Chubb Rock, "No Rubber, No Backstage Pass," from *America Is Dying Slowly*, EastWest, 1996.
Vernon Reid, *Mistaken Identity,* 550 Music, 1996.
Chris Rock, *Roll With the New,* DreamWorks, 1997.
Chris Rock, *Bigger & Blacker*, DreamWorks, 1999.

As remixer

Cypress Hill, "Latin Lingo," Ruffhouse /Columbia, 1991.
Beastie Boys, "Root Down," Grand Royal/Capitol, 1995.
Alliance Ethnik, "Simple et Funky," DeLabel, 1996.
Dr. Octagon, "Blue Flowers," DreamWorks, 1996.
"If Nine Was Six" from *Altered Beats: Assassin Knowledge of the Remanipulated*, Axiom, 1996. Imani Coppola, "Legend of a Cowgirl," Columbia, 1997.
Keziah Jones, "African Space Craft," DeLabel, 1998.

Sources

New York Times, April 12, 1999.
Urb, May/June, 1999.

Additional information used from Tommy Boy promotional materials.

—*Daniel Durchholz*

Ustad Alla Rakha Qureshi

Tabla drummer

© Jack Vartoogian. Reproduced by permission.

Drummer Ustad Alla Rakha Qureshi, also known as Ustad Allarakha Khan, popularized the musical genre of solo tabla as a concert form. Beginning in the 1960s, Qureshi and sitar master Pandit Ravi Shankar were recognized for their accomplishments in bringing classical Hindustani music to Western audiences. For approximately 20 years, between the late 1950s and through the 1970s, Qureshi (a Muslim) and Shankar (a Hindu) toured the world, thus popularizing the special music of a socially diverse and politically fragile region of northern India. Often the two played in a musical style, called *sawaal-jawaab,* or "question and answer." In *sawaal-jawaab* the musicians enter into a dialogue, not unlike a Western-style musical "dueling duet." Qureshi's esteemed performance venues included the Monterey Jazz Festival, the Woodstock Festival of 1969, and Carnegie Hall, where he frequently performed as a duo with Shankar.

Ustad Alla Rakha Qureshi was born Alla Rakha Qureshi, by most accounts in 1919 in Gurdaspur, Punjab, and was raised in Phagwal, near Jammu. He was the eldest of seven brothers. Qureshi's father, Hashmali, was a farmer, and his father before him was a soldier. Although their first-born son loved Indian classical music and was drawn to the performing arts, Qureshi's parents steadfastly opposed his inclination. As a boy he experienced great pleasure in watching the performances of classical Hindu theatre groups. In his early adolescence—as young as 12 years old according to some sources—after teaching himself rudimentary drumming and spending time in study with Lal Mahamed, Qureshi ran away to Lahore to study at the Punjab school of classical music (gharana). There he became a student of Ustad Mian Khadarbaksh Pakhawaji (Mian Quader Bakshi), and with "Bakshi" as a mentor, Qureshi studied voice for ten years under the direction of Ustad Ashiq Ali Khan.

It was tabla studies, however, that consumed his interest. The tabla is a double-headed drum of Hindustani tradition. With its dual drumheads, the tabla commands a total range of approximately one octave, combined from the lowest tone of the baiya (larger drum) to the highest tone of the tabla (smaller drum). The musical art form of tabla drumming is steeped in oral tradition, and tabla drummers do not play or learn from written music. Through skill and concentration Qureshi developed the expertise to play nuances and bend the notes with varied pressure from the base of his hand.

A Lifetime of Music

Qureshi lived for a time in Pathanko as a member of a theater company, and in 1930 he worked at a radio station in Lahore. Six years later, in 1936, he moved to Delhi to accept a position with All India Radio. In 1940, he worked with Shankar and again on All India Radio.

For The Record . . .

Born Alla Rakha Qureshi on April 29, 1919 in Ratangarh, India; married Bavi Begum; father of Razia, 1959-2000; Zakir Hussain, born March 9, 1951; Fazal Qureshi, born 1961; Taufiq Qureshi, Kurshid Aulia; died on February 3, 2000 in Bombay, India. *Education*: Punjab Gharana.

All India Radio, 1936-42, "Rangmahal Studios, 1943; performed as a duo with Ravi Shankar, 1950s, 1960s, 1970s; recorded on Moment Records.

Awards: Chowdaiah Award for distinguished lifetime musicianship, government of Karnataka, 2000.

He went on to Bombay, and during that same decade he learned to play raga. In Bombay in 1943 he worked for the Rangmahal Studios as a musical director, where he contributed to more than two dozen productions based in popular music. He composed music under the name of A. R. Qureshi and made appearances in films, performing both as a vocalist and as an instrumentalist. He worked with accomplished Kathak dancers, including Sitara Devi and Birju Mahara. Devi, who worked extensively with Qureshi during his years in the filmmaking industry, recalled Qureshi's exceptional talent and ability to play complex rhythms. Devi told Celia W. Dugger of the *New York Times*, "I used to say, 'Sahib, please don't play difficult, or I won't be able to follow you!"

Upon taking his leave from Rangmahal, Qureshi resumed his art as a classical musician of tabla. In the early 1950s he teamed with Shankar. The two performed as partners in an immensely popular musical duo. By 1958, they made their first appearance in the Western Hemisphere, at the Royal Festival Hall in London. Their fame spread across the Atlantic, and they performed at the Monterey Pop Festival in 1967. The two traveled worldwide, representing their homeland at international music festivals everywhere; in 1969 they performed at the original Woodstock Festival in New York, and in 1971 they appeared at Madison Square Garden at a benefit concert for Bangladesh. Qureshi recorded an album with American jazz drummer Buddy Rich, and, as a result of the tabla player's extensive experimentation with fusion music, ultimately came to be categorized as a popular musician because of the nature of his early work in films and his lengthy association with popular musicians in the United States and Great Britain.

Regardless, his work was almost exclusively Hindu and classical in bent. He inspired and collaborated with many prominent rock and roll artists of the 1960s and the 1970s, including former Beatle, George Harrison, and Grateful Dead drummer, Mickey Hart. Hart, in *Drumming at the Edge of Magic,* recounted Qureshi's adept ability to juxtapose conflicting rhythms using a tabla technique called *lamchar gat. Lachmar gat* was a specialty of Qureshi's, learned at the Punjab gharana and mastered through years of concentration. Hart acknowledged Qureshi's influence with unique praise, "Alla Rakha was a rhythm master—my first. He was a Mozart of my instrument." According to Hart, Qureshi's complex rhythms mimicked the sounds of multiple simultaneous drummers in a remarkable fashion. Following a private session with Qureshi, Hart explained, "I returned from that hotel room feeling as if I'd been shown the Golden Tablets." Yet despite his crossover aura as a star of modern media, Qureshi upheld a belief in traditional performance. It was his preference that music might be enjoyed by small, intimate groups of people who bestowed total attention on the music, without distraction. In his role as a teacher, too, he was demanding and required his students to spend lengthy sessions in his tutelage in order to become absorbed with his presence and thus with the art.

Qureshi came to be highly respected by his colleagues and students and earned the respected title of Ustad, an honor denoting an honored teacher or guru. By means of his performances with Shankar, he brought new recognition to the art form of playing tabla, which prior to Qureshi, was relegated to a background instrument rather than a solo concert instrument of itself. With the support of Shankar, the two developed a concert repertoire wherein at times Qureshi's powerful tabla usurped the spotlight. Qureshi performed his tabla on an unprecedented equal footing with Shankar's stringed sitar, competing adeptly with the more extensive tonal range of Shankar's instrument. The solo capabilities of Qureshi's tabla were further emphasized when the two performed their *sawaal-jawaab* selections "in dialogue." In addition to Shankar, Qureshi also performed in concert with Vilayat Khan and Ali Akjar Khan. In 1976, Qureshi received a Grammy Award nomination from the National Academy of Recording Arts and Sciences for the best chamber music performance for *Improvisations, West Meets East, Album 3,* an Angel Records release featuring Ravi Shankar, Yehudi Menuhin, Jean Pierre Rampel, Martine Gelliot, and Qureshi. He recorded in later years for Moment Records under the direction of the Zakir Hussain Management firm.

Outside the Concert Hall

Qureshi was the teacher and father of Zakir Hussain, who was widely recognized as the greatest living tabla player of the late 20th and early 21st century. As a young man in the 1930s, Qureshi married Bavi Begum, and the couple had three sons, Zakir Hussain, Fazal Qureshi, and Taufiq Qureshi. Qureshi taught each of his sons to play tabla, but only after each displayed the appropriate seriousness of interest and regard for the instrument. Qureshi fathered two daughters, but taught neither to play tabla because of a strict gender-biased religious precept that precluded him from teaching females.

In 1986, he established the Alla Rakha Institute of Music in Bombay and used the school as a vehicle to impart his musical knowledge to hundreds of students daily. He was at his school in Bombay, India, February 3, 2000 when he was stricken by a heart attack upon hearing the news of the death of his daughter, Razia, who served him as a companion and caretaker during his later years of failing health. She died in an untimely fashion following routine cataract surgery, and the shock of the news caused her father to succumb. He immediately slipped into a coma from which he never recovered. Qureshi's surviving daughter, Kurshid Aulia, lives in London. Additionally he was survived by nine grandchildren.

Sad Farewells

Only one week before his death, Qureshi received the Chowdaiah Award for distinguished lifetime musicianship from the government of Karnataka. The award, named after T Chowdaiah, was instituted in 1994; Qureshi was only the fifth recipient of the honor. His colleagues remembered him for his calm and unassuming demeanor, for his devotion to perfection, and for his extreme powers of concentration. Critics concurred that a special joy emanated from Qureshi during his performances; he evoked a revelatory specter as he played and sang. Shankar said of Qureshi, "His specialty was a very loving personality." The *Telegraph* called him, " …a musician of formidable energy and invention and … one of the most celebrated figures in Indian classical music."

Selected discography

Albums

Rich a la Rakha (with Buddy Rich), World Pacific.
Improvisations, West Meets East, Album 3 (with Ravi Shankar, Yehudi Menuhin, Jean Pierre Rampel, Martine Gelliot), Angel, 1976.
Master Drummers (with Zakir Hussain), 1991.

Tabla Duet, Chhanda Dhara, 1994.
Ultimate in Taal-vidya, Magnasound/OMI, 1996.
Magical Moments of Rhythm (with Zakir Hussain), Eternal Music, 1997.

Appeared on

Concert for Bangladesh (George Harrison), 1971.
Rolling Thunder (Mickey Hart), 1972.
At the Monterey International (with Ravi Shankar), 1993.

Sources

Periodicals

New York Times, February 6, 2000 (Late Ed.); February 14, 2000 (Late Ed.), p. A4.
Telegraph, February 8, 2000.
Wall Street Journal, February 9, 2000 (Eastern Ed.), p. A24.

Online

"About Ustad Alla Rakha," http://easternharmony.com/talla.htm (May 1, 2000).
"Magical Moments of Rhythm," *Eternal Music – Eternal Music Productions,* http://www.eternalmusic.com/albmagic.html (May 1, 2000).
"Following another beat," *Music Magazine,* 2000, http://www.themusicmagazine.com/allarakha.html (May 1, 2000).
"Ustad Alla Rakha," *All Music Guide,* http://allmusic.com (May 1, 2000).
"Ustad Alla Rakha Dies at 81" (including excerpts from *Drumming at the Edge of Magic*) http://www.mhart.com/pages/Artists/allarakha.HTML (May 1, 2000).

—Gloria Cooksey

Rancid

Punk rock band

Rancid, who cut their brand of punk music—a formula heavily influenced by the Clash—with ska, reggae, and sometimes rockabilly and pop elements, helped put northern California's East Bay on the musical map. Although some critics dismiss the group as mere throwbacks to the early days of punk music, loyal supporters often call them the Rolling Stones to Green Day's Beatles. In truth, most punk enthusiasts place Rancid somewhere in between these two descriptions; while Rancid, known for sporting bondage trousers and colored mohawks, does often mine guitar riffs from their forebears, the street-smart group nonetheless produced short, clever songs that always sounded exhilrating.

As a result of their solid punk-pop songwriting platform, Rancid—formed in Albany, California, in 1990—was able to break into the mainstream in the mid-1990s, finding their way on to modern rock radio and MTV with the hit songs "Time Bomb" and "Ruby Soho" from their third album *...And Out Come the Wolves.* For Rancid, comprised of lead vocalist/guitarist Tim Armstrong, guitarist/vocalist Lars Frederiksen, bass guitarist Matt Freeman, and drummer Brett Reed, reviving punk music meant more than the dyed hair, tattoos, and

Members include **Tim Armstrong** (born in 1966 in Albany, CA, the youngest of three brothers; son of a maintenance worker and a cookie factory worker; member of Operation Ivy, 1987-89), lead vocals, guitar; **Lars Frederiksen** (born in 1972 and raised by his mother, a former nanny, in Campbell, CA; former member of Slip and the UK Subs; joined Rancid in 1993), guitar; **Matt Freeman** (born in 1966 in Albany, CA, and raised by his father; member of Operation Ivy, 1987-89), bass guitar; **Brett Reed** (born in 1972; son of divorced parents), drums.

Formed band in Albany, CA in 1990; signed with Epitaph Records and released debut self-titled album, 1993; released platinum-selling *Let's Go*, 1994; released the acclaimed album *...And Out Come the Wolves*, 1995; released *Life Won't Wait*, 1998.

Addresses: *Record company*—Epitaph Records, 2798 Sunset Blvd., Los Angeles, CA 90026, phone: (323) 413-7353, fax: (323) 413-9678, website: http://www.epitaph.com. *Publisher*—I Want to Go Where the Action Is Music/BMI. *Website*—Rancid: http://www.rancidrancid.com.

body piercing. The band's gritty lyrics and hard-edged sound reminded everyone just what punk rock was all about. And despite all the attention, Rancid, without fail, remained true to their craft.

"We really haven't changed," said Armstrong, discussing the group's 1998 album *Life Won't Wait* in an interview with *Rolling Stone*'s Lorraine Ali. "We're still loyal to the scene that gave us so much. We started a record label, signed all our favorite bands and still go to shows. We're just trying to give back what we got out of it." Indeed, punk rock literally saved the members of Rancid, all of whom grew up in a world of blue-collar poverty. "It's such a cliché to say that music saves lives, but for me it's really true," Frederiksen revealed in an interview with *Rolling Stone,* as quoted by Fred McKissack in the *Progressive.* "Two years ago I was shooting dope and drinking myself to death. I wouldn't be here today if these guys hadn't become my family."

Rancid's roots lay in the East Bay scene centered on Gilman Street, a club in Berkeley, California. The nonprofit, all-volunteer operation provided groups like Green Day and Rancid, as well as Rancid's precursor Operation Ivy, with a supportive environment and an opportunity to play in the late-1980s and early-1990s, times when options for the new breed of punk bands were limited. Reed, who had previously been hanging out in the more hard-core clubs of San Francisco, saw Gilman Street as a revelation. In Berkeley, people were accepted into the fold, whether they were hardened street kids or not. "You could have fun at shows instead of having to deal with the whole violence thing," the drummer recalled to Alec Foege in *Rolling Stone.*

Since then, however, Gilman Street has more or less become a shrine to popular punk bands from the East Bay, as well as a hangout for greedy major-label A&R representatives. After Green Day and the Offspring, bands that hailed Operation Ivy as a major influence, became platinum-selling superstar acts, it wasn't long before record industry representatives in search of the next big thing started showing up at Rancid gigs. Sure enough, by December of 1994 Rancid, too, was considering a lucrative offer: a 1.5 million record deal with Epic Records, along with a $500,000 publishing contract. Finding themselves surrounded by a mob of managers and booking agents, Rancid in the end decided to stay with their original home, Epitaph Records, the Los-Angeles based independent label that also fostered the careers of the Offspring, NOFX, and Pennywise. "Staying on Epitaph put so much fire in us, man," Armstrong told Foege. "During all the bullshit, we developed a Rancid motto: The only people that are happy with us are us."

Operation Ivy

Friends since high school, Armstrong—who then went by the moniker "Lint"—and Freeman from 1987-89 played together in Operation Ivy, one of the early bands that launched the scene at Gilman Street. Formed in Oakland, California, with drummer Dave Mello and vocalist Jesse Michaels, Operation Ivy drew inspiration from the Ruts and the Clash, as well as Great Britain's Two-Tone movement. The band released the *Hectic* EP in 1988 and the full-length *Energy* in 1989, both on Lookout ! Records, before succumbing to the pressures of local success and unbroken touring and calling it quits. During their two short years of existence, Operation Ivy amassed a passionate following around the East Bay. Armstrong remembered the night before one sold-out show in particular, when he was approached by a 15-year-old fan. "I can't get in," the youngster told him, as quoted by Foege, "but I love you guys, and we have the same last name." Without pausing to think, Armstrong led him in through the kitchen entrance. That young fan, Green Day's Billie Joe Armstrong (of no relation), still considers that night one of the most important and inspiring events of his life.

After Operation Ivy disbanded, Armstrong and Freeman formed a few more short-lived bands. Then Freeman joined a band called MDC (Millions of Dead Cops), a decision the bassist admitted had a lot to do with his strained relationship with his father, a Berkeley police officer, while Armstrong worked as a roadie for the same group until his serious drinking problem prevented him from adhering to the schedule. His worsening addictions finally resulted in five trips to a detoxification facility in nearby Richmond, followed by a stint with the Salvation Army collecting unwanted clothes and furniture. Then, with just two weeks of sobriety under his belt, Armstrong contacted Freeman, informing his pal that he wanted to regroup. Freeman, by this time employed at a truck-rental company, immediately agreed.

Returned to Punk as Rancid

"Armstrong's street clothes—blue-green bondage pants, cherry-red combat boots, a white muscle T-shirt and a shredded jean jacket held together by safety pins—scream London 1977," wrote Foege. "But unlike the average zonked-out anarchist, Armstrong exudes a distinctly Brandoesque magnetism. Dark, gentle, brooding, Rancid's leader and main lyricist cuts a rangy, handsome profile. He talks as if he's got marbles in his mouth and walks with a slacker slump; but when he speaks, his eyes glow, and he chooses words with the utmost care."

Born the youngest of three brothers in 1966 in Albany, a lower middle-class town just north of Berkeley, Armstrong grew up in a decent neighborhood in an old house his mother inherited from her father. However, the family remained poor. Armstrong's father, a maintenance worker, also had a drinking problem, and his mother, a worker at a cookie factory, eventually had to support the entire household on her meager income alone. "Mom's a real hard worker," Armstrong said. "Even though we had no money, she was too proud to go on welfare. And she'd try to take us nice places like the Oakland Zoo."

Armstrong formed his first band with older brother Greg, who later became a career sergeant in the United States Army. Listening to his brother's extensive record collection, which included the Ramones, the Clash, the Dead Kennedys, and the Circle Jerks, Armstrong became a huge fan of punk music. His all-time favorite band, however, was the Specials, a British ska outfit. Like Armstrong, the other members of Rancid shared a similar background, both musically and socially. Freeman, raised by his father, a single parent, was also born in 1966 and grew up in Albany, and Reed, born in 1972, spent his childhood shuffling back and forth between his divorced parents' homes.

Frederiksen, born in 1972, came from a broken home as well. His mother, a native of Denmark, came to the United States as a nanny and worked for many wealthy New Yorkers and celebrities, including, at one time, Gene Kelly. The son of an absent father, Frederiksen, a high school dropout, spent most of his childhood in Campbell, California, a small town near San Jose with a predominantly Mexican American population. Well-known for his red mohawk haircut, Frederiksen grew up listening to bands like Crass, Discharge, and the Subhumans, who, he admits, scared him a little at first. Today, Frederiksen outshines all his bandmates as the one with the most tattoos.

At the time Armstrong and Freeman recruited Reed to join Rancid, the aspiring drummer, who had just bought a used drum kit from a junkie in San Francisco, hardly knew how to play at all. But within a month, Rancid played its first show as a three-piece. In 1992, Lookout ! released the trio's first seven-inch single, "I'm Not the Only One." Initially, Rancid flirted with the idea of using Billy Joe Armstrong as a second guitarist. But in the meantime, Rancid received an offer from Brett Gurevitz of Epitaph Records to record their debut album, and during the sessions, they met Frederiksen and invited him to join the group. Rancid released their self-titled debut album in April of 1993, then embarked on their first national tour, followed by an extended tour of Europe.

Sold Millions of Records

Frederiksen, who had played previously with Slip and the UK Subs, made his recording debut with Rancid in early-1994 on the single "Radio Radio Radio," a song co-written with Billy Joe Armstrong and released on the Fat Wreck Chords label. In February of that year, Rancid entered the studio to begin sessions for their second album. The twenty-three song *Let's Go*, released later that year on Epitaph, drew comparisons to the early Clash sound played at a frenetic pace. The album took flight immediately, earning gold, then platinum status. Not surprisingly, major labels started calling, but Rancid turned down offers from Maverick Records, home to Madonna, and Epic in favor of remaining with their friends at Epitaph. The entire staff at the company flew up from Los Angeles to celebrate upon hearing the news.

A return to the studio in March of 1995 resulted in that year's *...And Out Come the Wolves*. More fully formed and ska-influenced than its predecessors, though not exactly groundbreaking, Rancid's follow-up went platinum as well, won rave reviews, and showed up on several "best of" lists; *Spin* ranked *...And Out Come the Wolves* at number ten on its list of "20 Best Albums of '95," the *Village Voice* listen the album at number 16 for its annual critics' poll, and *Entertainment Weekly* ranked the album at number six on its "Top 10 Albums of 1995."

After Armstrong formed his own imprint label, Hellcat, Rancid returned in 1998 with *Life Won't Wait,* which included a collaboration with Mighty Mighty Bosstones vocalist Dicky Barrettt for the song "Cash, Culture & Violence." *Life Won't Wait* became a best-seller, too, and garnered the group further praise from the music press. Rancid announced that a fifth album featuring more straight-ahead punk would hit store shelves in August of 2000.

By the end of 1998, Rancid had played more than a thousand shows, canceling just one date since the group's formation because of an illness. "We've always gone everywhere," Frederiksen informed Mark Healy of *Rolling Stone.* "Even if it was Copperas Cove, Texas—where we played between pinball machines, 'cause the stage broke. It could be some kid just putting up this gig, renting out whatever he could get his hands on, just because he's excited about bands being able to come to his town. That's the beautiful thing about punk-rock touring: There's always a kid somewhere who will put on a show."

Selected discography

Rancid, Epitaph, 1993.
Let's Go, Epitaph, 1994.
...And Out Come the Wolves, Epitaph, 1995.
Life Won't Wait, Epitaph, 1998.

Sources

Periodicals

Billboard, June 6, 1998.
Boston Globe, June 4, 1998.
Guitar Player, September 1998.
Progressive, January 1996.
Rolling Stone, September 7, 1995; April 30, 1998; October 29, 1998.

Online

Sonicnet.com, http://www.sonicnet.com (June 17, 2000).

—Laura Hightower

Red Hot Chili Peppers

Rock group

From the time they formed in the early 1980s, the Red Hot Chili Pepper have played an innovative blend of punk, funk, rap, and metal. While they gained most of their notoriety for their energetic and mostly nude stage shows as well as their battles with addictions, their sound exerted a strong influence on alternative rock throughout the 1990s. With various members undertaking solo projects or touring with other bands, and their lack of permanency in the lead guitar spot, the Peppers always seemed on the verge of breaking up. In 1999, though, they reunited the lineup that appeared on their 1991 breakthrough *Blood Sugar Sex Magik* and released the album *Californication* to critical and popular acclaim.

The two men who have been Peppers from the beginning, vocalist Anthony Kiedis and bass player Flea, became close friends in high school in Los Angeles. They joined with fellow classmates Hillel Slovak on guitar and Jack Irons on drums to form the band Anthem. Anthem didn't last long, though. Flea left to play with the punk band Fear, while Irons and Slovak joined a group called What is This? Although all four of them remained busy with their own projects, they often crossed paths. One night they briefly reunited for a one-song jam performed on the spur of the moment at

For The Record . . .

Members have included **Flea** (born Michael Balzary, October 16, 1962, in Melbourne, Australia), bass; **John Frusciante** (born March 5, 1970, in New York; band member 1989-92; rejoined group 1999), guitar; **Jack Irons** (born July 18, 1962, in California; left band in 1988), drums; **Anthony Kiedis** (born November 1, 1962, in Grand Rapids, MI), vocals; **Arik Marshall** (born February 13, 1967, in Los Angeles; band member 1992), guitar; **Dave Navarro** (born June 7, 1967, in Santa Monica, CA; band member 1994-97), guitar; **Chad Smith** (born October 25, 1962, in St. Paul, MN; joined band in 1988), drums; **Hillel Slovak** (born March 31, 1962, in Israel; died June 25, 1988), guitar; **Jesse Tobias** (band member 1993), guitar.

Group formed in Los Angeles as Anthem, early 1980s; played first show as Red Hot Chili Peppers, 1983; released first album, *Red Hot Chili Peppers*, 1984; first reached the charts with the album *Mother's Milk*, 1989; released multi-million selling *Blood Sugar Sex Magik*, 1991; released *One Hot Minute*, 1995; released *Californication*, 1999.

Awards: *Rolling Stone* Music Award for "Scar Tissue," 1999.

Addresses: *Record company*—Warner Bros. Records, 3300 Warner Blvd., Burbank, CA 91505. *Website*— Official Red Hot Chili Peppers Web Site: http://www. redhotchilipeppers.com.

---

a Los Angeles club. This spontaneous gig went over so well that they soon became a regular presence on the Hollywood club circuit under their new name, Red Hot Chili Peppers.

They soon had a recording contract and a celebrity producer, Gang of Four guitarist Andy Gill. What they didn't have was the freedom to all perform together on their first album, 1984's *The Red Hot Chili Peppers*. Under contract with What Is This?, Slovak and Irons were replaced in the studio by Jack Sherman and Cliff Martinez, better known for his work with Captain Beefheart. The album flopped commercially and failed to capture the energy of their live performances, which

had become characterized by semi-nude bumping and grinding, with a lot of gymnastic leaping around the stage.

The band delved into their funk roots in picking the producer of their second album, putting the legendary George Clinton behind the board. The result, 1985's *Freaky Styley,* featured a horn section consisting of musicians who had played extensively with James Brown. While commercially not much of an improvement over their previous effort, musically the band showed signs of mastering their diverse and sometimes incompatible influences. Their next release, *The Uplift Mofo Party Plan* in 1987, found them with a more rocking sound than their previous effort. The album's lyrical content also cemented their raunchy reputation, which was either sexy or sexist, depending on one's point of view.

A Death in the Band

That reputation continued to grow with the cover of the 1988 EP *Abbey Road,* which had the band posed crossing the street in imitation of the famous cover of the Beatles' album of the same name. The Peppers, however, each wore nothing except a single, strategically placed sock While their audacious displays of public nudity gave them notoriety beyond their music, other excesses off-stage led to tragedy. That same year Slovak died of a heroin overdose. Distraught, Irons left the band. Kiedis and Flea, though, determined to carry on and recruited John Frusciante, a teenage fan of the band, to play guitar and Chad Smith on drums. They then dedicated their first album with this lineup, *Mother's Milk,* to Slovak's memory.

The Peppers' big breakthrough came in 1991 with the release of *Blood Sugar Sex Magik.* For this album they teamed up with producer Rick Rubin, who had made his reputation producing heavy metal bands such as Slayer and Danzig. While the album had its share of metal, rap, and punk, the ballads, especially "Under the Bridge," stood out as a new form that the band had mastered. In naming *Blood Sugar Sex Magik* one of the best albums of the 1990s, *Rolling Stone* said, "The alternating slap of extremes perfectly nails not only the giddy highs and drawn-out lows of life in a city built on illusions but also the Chili Peppers' fight to beat their own worst excesses." The album propelled the band to superstar status, selling two million copies.

But success didn't bring peace. Frusciante reacted against the sudden fame and fortune. Known for his near-obsession with guitar playing, the trappings of celebrity didn't sit well with his vision of what a musician should be. He would later tell David Fricke of *Rolling Stone,* "It got into my head that stardom was something evil. If you were a rock star, you were trying to put people on." Frusciante's tensions built to the point that he tried to quit the band right before a scheduled performance in Japan. Although Flea convinced him to stay for the show, Frusciante left soon afterward, opening what would turn out to be a revolving door for the lead guitar position in the band.

Guitarists Came and Went

Frusciante's first two replacements never appeared on a Chili Peppers album. First came Arik Marshall, who lasted for a year, and then came Jesse Tobias, who made it through a couple of months. Then in 1994 the band brought former Jane's Addiction guitarist Dave Navarro on board. Having not released an album in the four years since the incredible success of *Blood Sugar Sex Magik,* the band finally came out with *One Hot Minute* in 1995. Not everyone found the album worth the long wait. Although it went platinum, its sales fell well short of those for *Blood Sugar Sex Magik.* Critically, the verdict was mixed. Essi Berelian, in *Rock: the Rough Guide,* saw the songwriting as "a testament to a band at the peak of their creativity," while Rob Sheffield of *Rolling Stone* wrote that "they sounded like dinosaurs on 1995's miserable *One Hot Minute.*"

Once again, the band took a long break from the recording studio. In fact, the next couple of years were so trouble-filled that it became doubtful that there would be any more Chili Peppers. Following a tour that became notorious for the number of scheduled shows that never took place, the band members went their separate ways for a while. Then, in 1997 Flea served as the bass player when Navarro, Perry Farrell and others got together for a Jane's Addiction reunion tour. Besides these side projects, both Navarro and Kiedis relapsed into drug addictions. Then, to make matters worse, Smith and Kiedis both suffered injuries in separate motorcycle accidents.

The band's survival seemed even more unlikely when they once again lost their guitarist. Musical differences, and perhaps personal ones, between Kiedis and Navarro led to the latter's leaving. Working together in the studio had been difficult because the Peppers took a spontaneous approach to song writing and arranging, while Navarro liked to record several guitar tracks to work from for a song's final version. A threesome without a guitar player, the remaining band members began to doubt that they would continue as a unit. Flea told *Melody Maker* magazine, "I wasn't sure about the band's future and wasn't really interested. There was a point where it was feeling like a job and like no fun."

Instead of dissolving, though, the band improbably returned to the lineup that had brought them their largest success. Despite Flea's professed lack of interest in the band's future, he invited Frusciante to rejoin them. Frusciante himself had just gone through a long period of substance addiction that had landed him in the hospital in early 1998. Shortly thereafter, Flea negotiated Frusciante's return to the band, where he was literally welcomed with open arms by Kiedis. In describing their first rehearsal together, Kiedis told Gavin Edwards of *Rolling Stone,* "[W]hen he hit that first chord, it was so perfect—this blend of sounds from these people who I hadn't heard play together in so long."

The resulting album from this reunion, 1999's *Californication,* turned out to be one of the Chili Peppers' greatest successes. Working once again with Rubin as producer, the quartet put together a work that sold well and received some of the best reviews of the band's work. Sheffield called it "easily their best album ever." While familiar sexy funk and tender ballads filled the album, the songwriting displayed mature and thematic unity. Fricke described the album as "a bittersweet thing about bright possibility and broken promises." Kiedis himself told Fricke that the album's theme, from its title down to its individual songs, explores California as a place where reality doesn't live up to its romantic reputation: "[T]his weird, magical place that is really kind of the end of the world, the Western Hemisphere's last stop."

While they retained their flair, their frenzied gymnastics on stage, and their sense of humor, the Chili Peppers' lyrics showed the lessons of their years. The first single and hit off *Californication* was "Scar Tissue," a meditation on the past by Kiedis. While some doubted that the band would remain intact long enough to achieve anything more, the success of *Californication* demonstrated their resilience. Eight years after the Red Hot Chili Peppers first made their mark with music reviewers and buyers, they regrouped to do so again, establishing themselves as one of the major rock acts of the 1990s.

Selected discography

Red Hot Chili Peppers, EMI America, 1984.
Freaky Styley, EMI America, 1985.
The Uplift Mofo Party Plan, EMI America, 1987.
Mother's Milk, EMI America, 1989.
Blood Sugar Sex Magik, Warner Brothers, 1991.
One Hot Minute, Warner Brothers, 1995.
Californication, Warner Brothers, 1999.

Sources

Books

Buckley, Jonathan and Mark Ellingham, editors, *Rock: the Rough Guide,* Penguin, 1996.
Larkin, Colin, editor, *The Encyclopedia of Popular Music,* Muze, 1998.

Romanowski, Patricia and Holly George-Warren, editors, *The Rolling Stone Encyclopedia of Rock and Roll,* Fireside, 1995.

Periodicals

Guitar Player, November 1997, p. 53.
Melody Maker, February 9, 2000, p. 21.
Los Angeles Times, June 13, 1999, p. 3.
Rolling Stone, April 29, 1999, p. 38; May 13, 1999, p. 50; December 16, 1999, p. 217; April 27, 2000, p. 58.
Spin, August 1999, p. 111.
USA Today, December 18, 1997, p. 2D.

Online

"The Red Hot Chili Peppers," *All Music Guide,* http://www.allmusic.com (April 10, 2000).

—Lloyd Hemingway

Hans Reichel

Guitarist, daxophonist, inventor

Hans Reichel is one of the most unusual musicians at work in the world today. His work can be restrained, meditative, quirky, disturbing—or all of those at the same time. One of the authentic guitar innovators of the turn of the century, Reichel makes his music with a number of one-of-a-kind guitars of his own design, using performance techniques of his own invention, which enable him to coax a broad palette of sounds that previously lay hidden deep within the instrument. *Guitar Player* wrote of his impact: "Reichel is more than just a brilliant player, he has reconceptualized the instrument itself, opening up entirely new sonic possibilities." He broadened his sonic range even further with the astounding resources of the daxophone, an instrument of his own invention, one of such vocal versatility—albeit perhaps inhuman—that Reichel composed two "operettas" for it.

Hans Reichel was born in Hagen, West Germany, but makes his home in Wuppertal, a town the *Frankfurter Allgemeine Zeitung* called "the cradle of West German Free Jazz." He is one of a trio of musical giants from the Wuppertal—the others being saxophonist Peter Brötzmann and bassist Peter Kowald—who live within a couple blocks of each other. Wuppertal is also the birthplace of one of Germany's other important guitar pioneers, Caspar Brötzmann.

Reichel was a musical *Wunderkind*. When he was nine years old, he taught himself to play violin and played for a number of years in his school orchestra. As a teenager, he started listening to rock music, in particular Cream, the Beatles, the Rolling Stones, and Frank Zappa, along with various blues players, and soon took up guitar. "Jimi Hendrix is one of my major influences, although I don't try to copy him," Reichel told *Guitar Player*'s Mark Dery in 1988. "If anybody though, I feel related to Derek Bailey because, in a way, he's the old man who 'invented' improvised music, this kind of playing. I think he inspired me; I like his way of thinking about how improvised music can be done best, how it can function, and so on." When he was 15, he started playing bass in a local rock band. But he told *Guitar Player* that he gave up music altogether in 1970. He devoted himself instead to studying graphic arts and later worked as a typesetter. Since then, Reichel has also distinguished himself in graphic design and typography. He has designed a number of typefaces which are now used throughout the world, including FF Dax, FF Dax Condensed, FF Dax Wide, FF Schmalhans and FF Sari.

During his hiatus from music, Reichel did not own a guitar and did not plan to become a musician. He was eventually drawn back to music in 1972 when a visitor to his apartment left a cheap acoustic guitar behind. But, in typical contrarian form, Reichel did not start by playing the instrument—he took it apart first and started experimenting on its construction. Reichel's puttering about with the abandoned guitar had two results: first, he made a tape, barely three minutes long, of some of his guitar music, which he submitted to the German Jazz Festival in Frankfurt. What the judges heard was so remarkable, that Reichel was invited to perform in a special concert for newcomers, which in turn led to an offer to record for the German Free Music Productions (FMP) label and his first album, *Wichlinghauser Blues*, released in 1973. Second, he became a guitar builder. "I discovered that guitar-making is easy and fun," he told Dery, "and I've been doing it ever since."

Reichel built his first guitar around 1974 using the neck from the old acoustic guitar, a piece of wood from an unused table, a Fender pick-up and approximately 12 strings. "People thought I was crazy," he told Dery. "'He can go to a shop and buy a guitar, so why doesn't he do that?' But my guitars looked very different from store-bought ones." One of his early models was a double-neck electric guitar. But unlike other double-necks popular at the time, which looked like normal guitars, except they had two necks, one above the other on the left side of the instrument, Reichel's necks pointed in opposite directions, joining in the middle where the pick-up was, creating a mirror-like effect. Unsatisfied with only two necks, his next guitar had four necks, two on each side, with 23 strings—one neck, for reasons Reichel no longer recalls, had only five strings. Obviously these instruments couldn't be played like standard guitars, so Reichel invented new techniques that involved hammering the strings on the fingerboards, rather than plucking them. According to Reichel, it was much like playing a piano.

For The Record . . .

Born May 10, 1949, in Hagen, Germany. *Education:* Studied graphic design and typography.

Taught himself to play violin, 1958; taught himself guitar and bass, and played in local rock bands, mid-1960s; gave up music entirely and devoted himself to study of graphic arts and typography, 1970; tinkered with first guitar, 1972; submitted tape of his guitar playing to German Jazz Festival and was invited to perform there, 1972; released his first record album, *Wichlinghauser Blues*, for FMP label, 1973; began serious experiments with guitar modification, builds first behind-the-bridge guitars, mid-1970s; released solo guitar album, *Death of the Rare Bird Ymr*, 1979; invented daxophone, 1986; released *Shanghaied on Tor Road*, 1992; Kronos Quartet commissioned work which was performed at Talklaenge Festival in Wuppertal, 1997; work for orchestra and daxophone commissioned, 1997; received DM 25,000 Kunstpreis der Stadtsparkasse of Wuppertal, 1997.

Addresses: *Record company*—Free Music Productions, Postfach 100 227, D-10562 Berlin, Germany. *Website*—http://www.daxo.de.

"Finally," he told Dery, " I got tired of these multiplying necks and I returned to the simple thing—one neck, six strings." But though his newer instruments looked simple, they were revolutionary nonetheless. On standard electric and acoustic guitars, the strings extend from the nut, a small bar made of plastic or ivory at the top of the neck near the tuning machines, down the length of the guitar, and over another small bar of metal, plastic or ivory called the bridge near the end of the body. The strings are anchored in holes or slots usually an inch or less behind the bridge. Reichel had once seen a guitarist playing those short segments of strings behind the bridge which are not normally picked. Reichel wasn't particularly impressed with the music the guitarist made playing the short ends of the strings, but it gave him the idea of extending the strings on his guitar six inches or more past the bridge before anchoring them.

It created a brand new kind of musical instrument, with a sound all its own and which was very versatile. "When you play [one of my guitars] normally, it's a standard guitar," he wrote in a *Guitar Player* article on

his guitar designs. "But when the strings are plucked on the 'wrong' side of the bridge, it produces quite a different sound—subtle, ethereal, reverberated tones that float into each other. The timbres can sound very relaxed (it could be the ultimate new age guitar), although it allows you to forget about relaxation within a millisecond and blast out rock and roll, new age heavy funk, or whatever." Reichel built a series of "behind-the-bridge" guitars, both electric and acoustic, and later refined them further by putting a set of frets behind the bridge as well. The 1989 CD *Coco Bolo Nights* is a revealing collection of solos on Reichel's "homemade" guitars. Mike Joyce, writing about the record in the *Washington Post*, said, "Reichel has created an alternately soothing and restless suite, clearly fascinated and inspired by the peculiar tones, harmonics and percussive effects each instrument is capable of producing. The result is sometimes comforting, sometimes jarring and sometimes so exotic that it borders on world beat music."

In 1986, Reichel invented a entirely new instrument, which he christened the "Dachsophone" and later simplified to daxophone. The daxophone consists basically of four parts: one, a cello or violin bow; two, a small sound box equipped with a contact microphone; three, a board of indeterminate shape but on the average about a foot long, a little over an inch wide and about one-sixth of an inch thick; and, a "dax," a wedge-shaped block of wood with slightly curved sides. One end of the board was clamped to the sound box on a table. The other end extended out over the floor. That end was bowed with the right hand, while the left hand rocked the dax gently on the wood to alternate the pitch. The vibrations of the board resonated in the sound box and were amplified by the contact mic. Later, Reichel also designed a three-legged stand for the daxophone that could be dismantled and easily transported.

The sound of a daxophone is remarkably similar to a human voice or the cry of an animal. At the time he invented it, Reichel owned a Swedish record album entitled *Mammal Voices of Northern Europe, Vol. 1*, which included a badger—in German "Dachs." "I was impressed by the badger's astounding sonic range, from very low to very high notes," Reichel wrote in the liner notes to his 1992 CD *Shanghaied on Tor Road.* "Thus the dachsophone got its name—with echoes of Adolphe Sax." Sax was the inventor of the saxophone. Reichel later simplified the spelling of the instrument because, he claimed, he was tired of telling the badger story.

Like every person—and probably every badger—each daxophone possess its own individual voice, depending in particular on the kind of wood its board is made of and its shape. It can sound, for instance, like a boy soprano, a pipe organ, a man clearing his throat, or a mosquito buzzing around one's head. Since refining the instrument, Reichel has divided his time between it and guitar. Reichel performed on the daxophone on various albums, most notably *Lower Lurum* on the Rastascan label and *The Dawn of Dachsman* on FMP, a record Joe Gore writing in *Guitar Player* called "one of the avant guitar's high water marks." Not everyone took to the daxophone. Reichel described one response in his liner notes to *Shanghaied on Tor Road*: "A completely unnerved California critic once said it reminded him of tortured mules, monkeys, and poultry (i.e. animal testing) and the whole thing was really just annoying—like the neighbor's barking dog."

Reichel"s album *Shanghaied on Tor Road* is subtitled "The World's 1st Operetta Performed On Nothing But The Daxophone." And indeed all the wordless "singing" and accompaniment (except for one brief exception) is played—with over-dubbing—by Reichel on daxophone. His grunting, belching daxophones manage to recreate a number of familiar musical forms, including carny music, blues, early rock and roll, and the waltz. The idea for an all-daxophone recording came up after a 1990 concert at which Reichel, Canadian guitarist René Lussier, and Claude Simard played daxophone with the cello trio of Tom Cora, Anne Bourne, and Eric Longsworth.

Over the course of his career, Hans Reichel has performed with many of the heavyweights of improvising music. Besides Cora, he's played in duos with partners such as Fred Frith, German reed player and accordionist Rüdiger Carl, Keith Tippet, and Paul Lovens. "My favorite format is the trio," he joked with *Rubberneck's* Chris Blackford, "and quite often I play in a duo because I was lacking in an idea for who the third person could be." In the late-1990s, the Kronos Quartet encountered Reichel's music and commissioned a piece for daxophone and string quartet, which premiered in July 1997 at the fifth Talklaenge Festival in Wuppertal. The composer played the daxophone part in the work's first section, and Kronos joined in for a daxophone quintet in the second half. Ulrich Olshausen of the *Frankfurter Allgemeine Zeitung (FAZ)* wrote of the composition: "Its flowing imprecisions and flipped-out sonorities came from another world." Two days after the concert, according to *FAZ*, Reichel was given another commission, this time to write a piece for daxophone and symphony orchestra. Two years later, in 1999, he was awarded the Kunstpreis of the Stadtsparrkasse of his home town, Wuppertal.

As the twentieth century wound down, Hans Reichel's work, despite its inherent beauty and musicality, remained entrenched in the avant-garde ghetto, the result of its unconventional sound, the small record labels that have released it, and the fact that most other musicians seem willfully ignorant of his technical advances. "Reichel has opened up a lot of avenues in the last 20 years," Robert Iannapolo wrote in *Cadence*. "Unfortunately, few have been taken up by the mainstream. But given time, I think they will."

Selected discography

Wichlinghauser Blues, FMP, 1973.
Bonobo, FMP, 1975.
The Death of the Rare Bird Ymr, FMP 1979, (re-released on CD *Bonobo Beach/The Death Of The Rare Bird Ymr*, FMP, 1991).
Bonobo Beach, FMP, 1981 (re-released on CD *Bonobo Beach/The Death Of The Rare Bird Ymr*, FMP, 1991).
The Dawn of Dachsman, FMP, 1987 (re-released on CD 1994).
Coco Bolo Nights, FMP, 1989.
Shanghaied On Tor Road: The World's First Operetta Performed On Nothing But The Daxophone, FMP, 1992.
AngelicA 93, CAICAI, 1993.
Lower Lurum, Rastascan, 1994.

With others

Buben (with Rüdiger Carl), FMP, 1978 (re-released on CD, *Buben...plus*, FMP, 1994).
The Return of Onkel Boskop, Repertoire, 1983/1997.
Kino (with E.ROC), Teldec I.S., 1986.
Angel Carver (with Tom Cora), FMP, 1989.
Show-Down (with Wädi Gysi), Intakt, 1990.
Stop Complaining/Sundown (with Fred Frith and Kazuhisa Uchihashi), FMP, 1990/1991.
Kith 'n Kin (with Thomas Borgmann's Orkestra), Cadence Jazz Records, 1995.
King Pawns (with Kazuhisa Uchihashi), Zen, 1997.

Sources

Periodicals

Cadence, April 1993; March 1994; February 1996.
Frankfurter Allgemeine Zeitung, July 17, 1997; March 18, 1999.
Guitar Player, July 1988; January 1989; July 1994; January 1997.
Washington Post, July 17, 1989.

Online

European Improvisers Pages, http://www.shef.ac.uk/misc/rec/ps/efi/index.html (June 23, 2000).
Hans Reichel, http://www.daxo.de (June 23, 2000)

—Gerald E. Brennan

Sam Rivers

Composer, multi-instrumentalist

Composer, arranger, and multi-instrumentalist Sam Rivers, one of the most original and acclaimed voices in jazz, was often overlooked by the mainstream throughout his career. Rather than attempting to attract a wider audience for his music, Rivers instead concentrated on teaching younger generations of artists and developing new musical concepts. A versatile player known for his imaginative blending of jazz forms—from the blues and straight-ahead jazz to the avant-garde—Sam Rivers played with the greatest effect on soprano and tenor saxophone and flute, instruments on which he displayed his signature light, dancing style. However, he also became accomplished on piano, bass clarinet, and viola, all the while establishing himself as a composer and arranger of considerable talent. Rivers, a master improviser who frequently switches gears from liquid jazz to all-out funk, continued to record, perform, and influence fellow artists well into his seventies. Maintaining an obvious interest in all the styles jazz offers, Rivers explained to *Down Beat*'s Dan Ouellette, "I play the history of jazz because I've been through it all."

"Sam comes out of a school of saxophone playing that I can trace back to Coleman Hawkins and that I call 'the snake school,'" explained alto saxophonist Steve Coleman, who produced Rivers' albums during his time with RCA Records and played in the orchestra, to *Down Beat* writer Ted Panken. Represented by the likes of Lucky Thompson, Benny Golson, and Lockjaw Davis

as well, this "school" of players used an array of directional shifts in their lines and intervals. "Sam makes it even more pronounced because of his attack, the way he smears the notes," Coleman further commented. "You can instantly hear it's him. His sound and phrasing and rhythm are very slippery, sort of like he looks, kind of long and rangy. It goes beyond music; when he's directing the band and doing his little dance, for me that's like a snake dance. Before the band plays, he sings the music exactly like it should go. Nothing he could say would give you more information than watching him move."

Learned Traditional Music

Although in his later adulthood Rivers professed, "I'm one of the few musicians who plays free and plays changes. It takes a long time to be a traditional musician, but a few minutes to be a free one" as quoted by Panken. The master jazzman's roots stemmed from a more formal, as well as spiritual, source. Born on September 25, 1930, in El Reno, Oklahoma, to a family of musicians, Samuel Carthorne Rivers grew up surrounded by traditional influences. Rivers' grandfather, for one, published a book of hymns and African American folk songs in 1882, while his parents, both college graduates originally from Chicago, played and toured with the Silvertone Quartet, a gospel group in which his father sang and his mother accompanied on piano.

While still an infant, Rivers and his family returned to Chicago, where from the age of four the youngster sang in choirs directed by his mother and joined his father on excursions to famous South Side venues—namely the Regal Theater and Savoy Ballroom—to hear the top big bands of the day, from Duke Ellington and Count Basie to Earl "Fatha" Hines. Around the same time, in 1935, Rivers also learned piano and violin, an instrument he dropped two or three years later to concentrate solely on piano.

In 1937, Rivers' father died in an automobile accident (some sources state that the accident occurred around 1934 and left him incapacitated), and afterward his mother accepted a teaching position at Shorter College in Little Rock, Arkansas. Here, Rivers continued to develop his musical talent, playing trombone beginning at the age of eleven in the marching band of his school. Two years later, he picked up a saxophone. Finding the saxophone more to his liking than the trombone, Rivers, from that moment, considered that instrument his first love. In all, by the time the gifted young man graduated from high school in Little Rock at age 15, Rivers had learned, in succession, trombone, soprano saxophone, baritone horn, and eventually tenor saxophone, the instrument he discovered while a student at Jarvis Christian College in Texas.

For The Record . . .

Born Samuel Carthorne Rivers on September 25, 1930, in El Reno, OK; son of a singer and pianist, who toured with a gospel group called the Silvertone Quartet; married Bea. *Education:* Attended Jarvis Christian College in Texas; studied composition and theory at the Boston Conservatory of Music; also attended Boston University.

Formed first quartet, 1959; played with Herb Pomeroy's group, 1960-62; toured with Miles Davis, moved to New York City, released debut album, *Fuchsia Swing Song,* 1964; opened Studio Rivbea, 1971; moved to Orlando, FL, where he started his big band, an 11-piece wind ensemble, and a trio, 1991. Performed and appeared with artists from a variety of influences such as jazz musicians Dizzy Gillespie, Charles Mingus, McCoy Tyner, Max Roach, and Andrew Hill; blues masters T-Bone Walker, Jimmy Witherspoon, and B.B. King; as well as symphony orchestras including the San Francisco Orchestra with Serge Ozawa. Former faculty member and visiting artist at Wesleyan University, Dartmouth College, Cornish Institute, and the New School of Music in New York.

Addresses: *Record company*—Rivbea Music Productions, website: http://www.atlantic.net/~rivbea.html; RCA/BMG, 1540 Broadway, New York City, NY 10036, (212) 930-4000, website: http://www.bmg .com.

Discovered Improvisation

As a young man Rivers started improvising, later documenting these early origins for his poetic interpretation of "Body and Soul" from the 1991 album *Lazuli,* released on the Timeless label. "I had 'Body and Soul' down note for note," he said with a laugh to Panken. "I liked Coleman Hawkins' harmonic approach, but Lester Young was really the man because he was so melodic, floating all the time…. I analyzed Chu Berry's 'Stardust,' too. In those days there weren't many records, so you had to figure things out for yourself. That's why there were so many different sounding saxophone players then. Everybody had their own style because there wasn't anybody really to follow. Of course, after I heard Charlie Parker and Dizzy [Gillespie], that was the epitome." Rivers first heard

these jazz legends in the mid-1940s while working as a navy clerk stationed near San Francisco, California, where he spent off-hours moonlighting on gigs with singer Jimmy Witherspoon and participating in various jam sessions around the Bay Area. One record in particular, 1945's "Blue and Boogie" featuring the front line of Gillespie and Parker, intrigued Rivers. "It was the first bebop record I ever heard," he recalled, "and that sent me on…. I analyzed what they did with it in relation to the harmonic framework. Both were coming from the blues."

Inspired to take his musical training further, Rivers in 1947 enrolled in the Boston Conservatory of Music, where he studied composition and theory; he also attended Boston University. During his student years, he worked from time to time with other conceptually ambitious jazz musicians, among them Jaki Byard, Nat Pierce, Charlie Mariano, Gigi Gryce, Herb Pomeroy, and Alan Dawson. "Jaki was a very important in the early day," Rivers told jazz critic Leonard Feather, who wrote the musician's 1968 press information for Blue Note Records. "He was such an imaginative pianist that sometimes I found it hard to play with him. I was so busy listening to what he was doing. He is extraordinarily flexible, understanding every style of jazz just as I wanted to." These days also saw Rivers playing with an intermission trio at the RKO Theater, where musicians from touring big bands would often dine and hang, with Pomeroy's 13-piece band, and with a rehearsal bop-oriented band led by pianist/singer Jimmy Martin.

In 1952, Rivers dropped out of Boston University and fell ill for the next few years. Although he spent some time composing, he remained more or less inactive as a performer. Taking a hiatus from the Boston area after recovering, he then moved to Florida in 1955 and worked with his brother, bass player Martin Rivers, in Miami and toured the South with various rhythm and blues bands. Around 1957 or 1958, he returned to Boston, supporting himself by writing jingles before re-joining Pomeroy's group (1960-62) and forming a quartet in 1959 with pianist Hal Galper, bassist Henry Grimes, and a then 13-year-old drummer named Anthony (Tony) Williams, who Rivers predicted would enjoy a brilliant future.

Williams and Rivers would meet again in the summer 1964, when the saxophonist, upon Williams' recommendation, joined the Miles Davis Quintet to replace George Coleman in the tenor chair. During his two months with Davis, Rivers toured with the group in Japan and as part of the World Jazz Festival. Shortly after his brief stint with the group, that same year Rivers moved to New York City after finding that in Boston, where he set out to form his own band and had been composing seriously since 1957, most of his peers were so busy with teaching and performing that they lacked time for other responsibilities.

Debuted in New York

Arriving in New York, Rivers moved into two adjoining apartments on 124th Street and signed with Blue Note. In 1964, he made his debut as a bandleader with *Fuchsia Swing Song,* for which he performed music from the 1959-60 Boston quartet with Byard, Williams, and Ron Carter that demonstrated Rivers' movement from post-bop conception into the free-jazz zone. He followed this achievement with 1965's *Contours,* a quintet session with trumpeter Freddie Hubbard and pianist Herbie Hancock that adhered closer to mainstream jazz, then crossed back into free-jazz territory with 1966's *Involution.*

In the meantime, Rivers also grew increasingly interested in teaching, eventually workshopping his big band music at a Harlem junior high school. Among his group of eager, aspiring jazz players were baritone saxophonist Harriett Bluiett and tuba player Bob Stewart, both of whom joined Rivers on his later RCA recordings. Then in 1971, after touring with the Cecil Taylor Unit in 1969—he played with that group from 1968-73—as well as a six-month stint with McCoy Tyner, Rivers and his wife Bea opened Studio Rivbea, a performance and living space at 24 Bond Street in lower Manhattan for rehearsals and performances of his own original compositions as well as those of other deserving musicians. During the 1970s, the studio became a nurturing ground for numerous improvisers trying to make it in New York.

Between 1972 and 1982, after working again with Davis as well as Chick Corea's Circle, Rivers steadily performed and recorded in duos, trios, quartets, quintets, and big bands in a variety of settings, all the while continuing to foster his studio. "Rivbea was a very personal environment for the music to happen in," bassist Dave Holland, who collaborated with Rivers extensively during this time, including for an exchange that marked one of the greatest jazz albums of the 1970s entitled *Conference of the Birds,* recalled to Panken. "It put on these wonderful series of concerts that gave musicians a chance to focus on their ideas without any commercial constraints. So it was a breeding ground for a lot of interesting musical ideas which weren't being heard in New York. Of course, this kind of activity brought people together, and opportunities then came up for those groups to work in Europe and elsewhere."

As the next decade got underway, Rivers continued mostly as a bandleader, recording for Impulse! and for several lesser-known labels. His 1983 effort, *Colours,* showcased Rivers' unique ability to write music for large groups of saxophones, flutes, oboes, and piccolo with no other accompaniment. *Lazuli,* released in 1991, saw Rivers trying to gear his music for a wider audience, though it failed to make a satisfying impression on critics.

In 1991, soon after concluding four years of steady touring with Dizzy Gillespie's quintet and big band, Rivers left New York, settling with his wife in Orlando, Florida. The couple, while on vacation there, had discovered a talented network of musicians who worked in the area theme parks and studios. Throughout the 1990s, Rivers, in addition to forming his own record label called Rivbea, continued to complete one composition a month for each of three Orlando-based ensembles: a 16-piece big band, an 11-piece wind ensemble, and trio that is also the core rhythm section for the orchestra. "I'm writing more than ever," Rivers remarked to Panken. "I take in a composition, and we only need one rehearsal. When I first went to New York, we'd spend three hours on one tune. That doesn't happen here. Anything I write, they can play." In the summer of 2000, Rivers released a double-CD on Rivbea documenting his Orlando big band. This followed the release of two acclaimed albums for RCA, the 1999 Grammy Award-nominated *Inspiration* as well as *Culmination,* released in May of 2000.

Selected discography

Fuchsia Swing Song, Blue Note, 1964.
Contours, Blue Note, 1965.
Involution, Blue Note, 1966.
A New Conception, Blue Note, 1966.
Dimensions and Extensions, Blue Note, 1967.
Hues, Impulse!, 1971.
The Live Trio Sessions, I.A.I., 1972.
Configuration, Pelican Sound, 1973.
Streams: Live at Montreux, Impulse!, 1973, reissued, 1989.
Waves, Tomato, 1973.
Crystals, Impulse!, 1974.
Sizzle, Impulse!, 1975.
Capricorn Rising, Black Saint, 1975.
Dave Holland/Sam Rivers, I.A.I, 1976, reissued, 1992.
Dave Holland/Sam Rivers, Vol. 2, I.A.I., 1977.
The Quest, Pausa, 1976.
Paragon, Fluid, 1977.
Contrasts, ECM, 1979.
Colours, Black Saint, 1983.
Lazuli, Timeless, 1990.
Concept, Rivbea, 1997.
Portrait, FMP, 1997.
Live, GRP, 1998.
Inspiration, RCA, 1999.
Culmination, RCA, 2000.
The Complete Blue Note Sam Rivers Sessions, Mosaic, 2000.

Sources

Books

Swenson, John, editor, *Rolling Stone Jazz & Blues Album Guide,* Random House, 1999.

Periodicals

Boston Phoenix, August 5, 1999.
Down Beat, January 1997, p. 59; December 1997, pp. 78-79; January 1999, p. 67; April 2000, pp. 33-36.
Playboy, July 1984, p. 23.

Online

All Music Guide, http://www.allmusic.com (May 4, 2000).
Rivbea Music Productions,http://www.atlantic.net/~rivbea .html (May 4, 2000).
Sam Rivers Press Bio (1968), http://www.eclipse.net/~fitz gera/blakey/rivers1.htm (May 4, 2000).
Sonicnet.com, http://www.sonicnet.com (May 4, 2000).

—Laura Hightower

Royal Trux

Bobby Gillespie once called Royal Trux "the last great rock 'n' roll band," as quoted by Kitty Empire in *New Musical Express.* The primitive, yet futuristic band became infamous throughout the underground music world for deconstructing 1970s-era rock—the Rolling Stones, MC5, and others—and redelivering it warped and jumbled, capping each song with scraggly, menacing vocals. They have been dismantling rock and roll into blunt basics for well over a decade, overcoming drug addictions to enjoy a brief, yet important stint with Virgin Records, for whom they played relatively straightforward and accessible songs, before returning to the independent music scene and their original label, Drag City Records. Throughout their career, Royal Trux have drawn enthusiasm from fans and critics alike for their genre-defying music and impenetrable mystery.

Until the mid-1990s, Royal Trux consisted of a revolving cast of musicians orbiting around two imaginative songwriters: Neil Hagerty, a vocalist and guitarist, and junkie-priestess, one- time Calvin Klein model Jennifer Herrema, a vocalist as well who, early in the duo's career, also played a variety of thrift store instruments for the band. The seeds for what was to become Royal

For The Record . . .

Members include **Robbie Armstrong** (joined band in 1994, left band in 1995), drums; **Dan Brown** (joined band in 1994), bass; **Neil Hagerty** (former member of Pussy Galore with Jon Spencer), vocals, guitar; **Jennifer Herrema,** vocals; **Ken Nasta** (joined band in 1995 as Armstrong's replacement), drums; **Chris Pyle** (joined band in 1994; son of Artimus Pyle, a member of Lynyrd Skynyrd), drums.

Hagerty and Herrema officially formed Royal Trux in Chicago, released self-titled debut, 1988; released epic double-album *Twin Infinitives,* 1990; signed with Virgin Records, 1994; released major-label debut *Thank You,* 1995; returned to Drag City label, released pop classic album *Accelerator,* 1998; released rock, Latin, and jazz-influenced album *Veterans of Disorder,* 1999; released *Pound for Pound,* 2000.

Addresses: *Record company*—Drag City Records, P.O. Box 476867, Chicago, IL 60647, phone: (312) 455-1015, fax: (312) 455-1057, website: http://www.drag city.com. *Website*—http://www.royaltrux.com.

Trux were planted around 1984, when a 16-year-old Hagerty, a United States Army brat who grew up in cities around the world, met Herrema, then just 15 years old. At the time, Hagerty was still playing guitar with his former band, the now-defunct Pussy Galore, a garage, hardcore punk band led by the much-admired rock guitarist Jon Spencer.

In fact, Pussy Galore's 1987 album *Right Now* lists Royal Trux as a fifth band member, and rumor has it that it was Hagerty's idea for Pussy Galore to cover, in its entirety, the Rolling Stones' *Exile on Main Street.* The two band's coexisted until Hagerty and Herrema left in order to concentrate on their new project, and the supposed animosity between Royal Trux and Spencer became legendary. However, Hagerty finally set the record straight about his relationship with his old bandmate Jon Spencer. "There ain't ever been any animosity," Hagerty told Empire. "We never see each other. It means less than nothing to me. One year I'll just refuse to answer questions about it, and then the next year, I'll just deny that I was in Pussy Galore. Having feuds is always good. It's something for interviewers to write about."

Christening Royal Trux as an official group in 1988 in Chicago, Hagerty and Herrema started out performing as an odd, lo-fidelity "art" project. The pair's intent was to produce a union of free-form rock discord and garbled, science fiction-like imagery. "The duo's earliest work presented them as sort of a narcoleptic Sonny and Cher," wrote David Sprague in the *Trouser Press Guide to '90s Rock,* "disseminating the doctrine of 'better' living through chemistry on a scale that would earn a twenty-one-gun salute from [Beat writer] Bill [William S.] Burroughs." The results of Royal Trux's early intentions saw light on their 1988 debut, *Royal Trux,* a disjointed album that declared their goal of tracing the noise-rock scene back to its primal roots. Uncertain about whether the duo were trying to capture a musical form by tearing apart creativity and letting the pieces reassemble where they may, or just making an elaborate joke, the music press used words like "garage psychobilly punk" to define the Royal Trux sound.

An Epic Follow-up

After releasing a few 45-only records, Royal Trux relocated to San Francisco and recorded the epic, double LP *Twin Infinitives.* The sprawling album was released in 1990 on Chicago's newly founded Drag City Records and included such songs as the 15-minute "(Edge of the) Ape Oven" and "Yin Jim Versus the Vomit Creature." Lyrically based on the works of science fiction writer Philip K. Dick, *Twin Infinitives* musically included guitar riffs reminiscent of Led Zeppelin, the Rolling Stones, and AC/DC, bands that had inspired Hagerty and Herrema growing up. Immediately, the album, recorded in three months in a deserted warehouse, drew comparisons with other uncompromising avant-garde rock artists, namely Captain Beefheart and early Frank Zappa.

The tour that followed to promote the record saw the duo confronting members of the audience, physically as well as with words. In truth, as the duo later revealed, during this time both were heavily dependent on heroin. Their next album, also entitled *Royal Trux,* arrived in 1992. While a more disciplined attempt to create fully realized songs and to utilize more traditional music patterns, the pair's third album not surprisingly took a scary journey down a trail of narcotics-induced blues. According to Hagerty and Herrema, their great appetite for drugs was so large at one point that a fledging Matador Records advanced them $3,000 to produce an album and never heard a note of music. Instead, the duo, while residing in San Francisco, spent all the money on heroin. "Supporting our habit was a full-time job," Hagerty admitted to Empire. "They were really cool about it, and let us out of the whole thing."

Cleaned-up Their Act

In order to stop using, Royal Trux, by now living in New York City, decided to relocate to Washington, D.C., where heroin seemed less rampant. In 1993, the duo even decided not to play in New York because they felt the reality of being able to find heroin easily and at cheap prices would prove too tempting. After moving to a country home in Virginia, they recorded with session musicians that year's *Cats and Dogs,* an album that reined in the band's discordant guitar and primal yowling sound somewhat in favor of pure rock and roll. Their arsenal of blues-pop songs, injected with layers of noise, feedback, multi-layered guitar tracks, and Hagerty and Herrema's off-kilter vocals brought the duo major-label recognition. And in 1994, Royal Trux accepted an offer to sign with Virgin Records.

In a sense, Royal Trux underwent a rebirth of sorts that year, recruiting three new full-time members to serve as a rhythm section: bassist Dan Brown and drummers Chris Pyle, whose father Artimus Pyle was a member of Lynyrd Skynyrd, and Robbie Armstrong, who left the Royal Trux after appearing on just one album and was replaced by Ken Nasta. The new lineup, with the help of producer David Briggs, celebrated for his partnership with Neil Young, then began work on their 1995 Virgin debut entitled *Thank You.* Their most accessible album up to that time, *Thank You* included the single "Map of the City," as well as confident rhythm and blues and rock numbers such as "Shadow of the Wasp" and "Night to Remember." Another credible album, *Sweet Sixteen,* arrived in 1997, though the record's questionable subject matter led Virgin to release Royal Trux from their contract.

Indie Acclaim

Unscathed by their short-lived major-label career and financially sound after earning a more comfortable income, Royal Trux returned to indie life at Drag City. "Our whole interest was just to get a bunch of money," Hagerty explained to *Washington Post* writer Mark Jenkins, regarding the band's time spent with a big-name label. "We were able to get transportation, a place to live, musical instruments, that kind of thing. And we were able to pay the people who play with us; that's one thing that was really cool. We did put a little away in IRAs. And we were able to acquire the services of an accountant."

"We're just lucky that we didn't spend it on drugs," he added. "The timing of our big score was good, because we weren't using drugs anymore." The extra income also allowed Hagerty and Herrema to build a new studio at their Virginia home, where they recorded the pop classic *Accelerator* released in 1998 and *Veterans of Disorder* released in 1999, both of which were considered masterpieces by the music press and critics. The latter album opened with straight rockers and the Latin-influenced track "!Yo Se!," then veered into a looser, jazz-inspired direction. Royal Trux's latest record, *Pound for Pound,* was released in June of 2000.

Hagerty and Herrema continue to live in rural Virginia, and in addition to music, Hagerty published a book entitled *Victory Chimp.* "I think of it just as a comic book," he clarified to Empire. "I had a box full of stuff that I collected for ten years that I turned into a novel—stuff that I wrote, that other people wrote too. It just goes against all the rules of writing. It's just knitted together… It's about people's cognitive accumulation over time, when you go from being a teenager to being an adult. It kinda captures that period, like the Stones did with their records."

Selected discography

Royal Trux, (1st LP), Royal, 1988, reissued, Drag City, 1993.
Royal Trux, (EP7), Vertical, 1990.
Twin Infinitives, Drag City, 1990.
Royal Trux, (3rd LP), Drag City, 1992.
Cats and Dogs, Drag City, 1993.
Dogs of Love, (EP), Domino, 1993.
Thank You, Virgin, 1995.
Sweet Sixteen, Virgin, 1997.
Singles Live Unreleased, Drag City, 1997.
Three Song, (EP), Drag City, 1998.
Accelerator, Drag City, 1998.
Veterans of Disorder, Drag City, 1999.
Radio Video, (EP), Drag City, 2000.
Pound for Pound, Drag City, 2000.

Sources

Books

Robbins, Ira A., editor, *Trouser Press Guide to '90s Rock,* Fireside/Simon and Schuster, 1997.

Periodicals

Guitar Player, August 1998.
Los Angeles Times, April 15, 1995.
Melody Maker, May 23, 1998; September 12, 1998; September 4, 1999.
New Musical Express, February 12, 2000, p. 24.
Rolling Stone, September 2, 1993; June 15, 1995; June 29, 1995; December 28, 1995; April 3, 1997.
Washington Post, April 17, 1998; February 4, 2000.

Online

Sonicnet.com, http://www.sonicnet.com (June 2, 2000).
Royal Trux at Virgin Records, http://www.virginrecords.com (June 2, 2000).

—Laura Hightower

Rube Waddell

Street band

Rube Waddell is a throwback that emerged from the trash and drunks of San Francisco's Mission District; a jug band at the end of the Second Christian Millennium; a band of street musicians who, in an era of techno and sampling, insist on playing sea shanties, Hawaiian melodies, old blues, union songs, hillbilly ditties—and even the occasional Beethoven chorale. What's more, they play their music on whatever is at hand, be it junk or musical instrument, according to the Bay Guardian's John Paczowski, "harmonica, mandolin, trumpet, old buckets, Casio organs, and almost anything culled from abandoned streets and alleyways and capable of producing sound." Their only compromise to the electronic age was to set aside the jug in favor of battery-powered amplifiers strapped to their belts.

The original Rube Waddell—the first of the great flaky left-handed pitchers and a member of baseball's Hall of Fame—was born in rural Pennsylvania in the late 1800s. The band's origins, however, are shrouded in deep mystery. According to the group's official Web site, Rube Waddell spent time "tending bars at countless taverns along the eastern seaboard, wrestling alligators in the fetid swamplands and bayous of Louisiana, squatting at the feet of Guru Swami Sharma Prasad in the barren wastes of the great Ganges plain, appearing as 'The Doctor,' in Joop Kkonga's production of Buchner's 'Woyczeck' at the East Broadway Senior Citizens Center, and preaching to an audience of one at Cecil's Scrap and demolition Palace just off exit 20 on highway 43, 17 miles South of Little

Rock...After a brief stint at the Starkville City Jail, where he befriended a mysterious man in black, he began another extended period of hijinx and wanderlust, often appearing on select street corners throughout the county as the Rube Waddell Medicine Show and Musical Revue, featuring a wide variety of musical showmanship, recitations of pivotal works, divine augury and astounding feats of strength. And it is in this setting that Rube Waddell is most commonly seen today." Whatever the truth, the latter-day Rube Waddell, the heirs to the Hall of Famer, have become a fixture of the San Francisco music scene. Or as much of a fixture as street musicians, playing in the dead of night in one of the city's dingiest neighborhoods could hope to be.

Rube Waddell consists of three musicians: the Reverend Wupass, percussion, bass, and organ; Mahatma Boom Boom, guitar, trumpet, tablas, and accordion; and Captain Feedback one-string guitar, harmonica, and mouth harp. All the members sing. Though it later graduated to enthusiastic crowds in bars and restaurants, Rube Waddell got its start in the mid-1990s playing for change in front of tiny audiences on the streets of San Francisco. "The first couple of times we played on the street we were definitely a bit lonely," Reverend Wupass told the *SF Bay Guardian*. "We used to hook battery-powered amplifiers to our belts and wander around playing. Sometimes we'd go to this parking garage that had an enormous barred gate and we'd stand behind it playing 'Folsom Prison Blues.'" They also invaded Laundromats occasionally with their act; it got them out of the rain and they had a captive audience, at least until the clothes came out of the dryer. Unfortunately, they discovered that people there were not as free with their change as they were in the street.

They found their perfect gig playing at Leeds—not the hall where the Who cut *Live at Leeds*, but Leeds Shoes in San Francisco's Mission District, by day an area of poor Latino shops, by night a scene of drugs, alcohol, gangs and prostitution. Rube Waddell would set up in front of Leeds' entrance, under its eaves after the store had closed. "When we first played Leeds we set up out there on Mission Street and it was dirty and there were a bunch of people that had just been discharged from the S.F. General psych ward and a few drunkards standing out there watching us," Reverend Wupass related to the *SF Bay Guardian*. "There were other folks passing by—people going to bars, or home for the night—and we really had to create some sort of spectacle to keep people standing on that corner in that atmosphere and listening to us."

Eventually the word got out that something unusual was happening on Mission Street Saturday nights, "crazed musical revivals" the *San Francisco Weekly* called Rube's performances. Small crowds would gather at Leeds in expectation. If they were fortunate,

For The Record . . .

Members include **Captain Feedback**, one-string guitar, harmonica, mouth harp, vocals; **Mahatma Boom Boom**, guitar, trumpet, tablas, accordion, vocals; **Reverend Wupass**, percussion, bass, organ, vocals.

Began performing Saturday nights in front of Leeds Shoe Store in San Francisco Mission District, mid-1990s; released LP *Hobo Train*, Vaccination Records, 1997; released *Stink Bait*, Vaccination Records, 1998; nominated for Bay Area Music Award, 1999.

Addresses: *Record company*—Vaccination Records, P.O. Box 20931, Oakland, CA 94611.

Rube would eventually arrive, their noise-making gear in tow in shopping carts. They'd heap everything in front of the shoes displayed in the store windows, switch on their tiny amps, and cut loose. "It was worth traversing the horrors of Mission bars on a Saturday night," the *San Francisco Weekly's* House of Tudor reported, "just to catch their spiel on the stumble home. Drunken passers-by would dance or shout obscenities or just stare in disbelief. It was a good weekend when you could catch Rube Waddell."

The band did its best to enhance the performances. According to one report, its members even wrote a letter to Leeds' management, as concerned neighborhood residents asking that the store keep its display lights on to deter crime. By 1998, however, Leeds had closed its doors for good, and Rube had more fundamental concerns about its performance space. "Now that the store's closed," Captain Feedback told the *SF Bay Guardian*, "the area that we used as the stage has become absolutely disgusting. When we play Leeds now, we've got to go there early with a mop to clean up all the crap so we can actually set our instruments up."

Their instruments are a mix of old, new, found and homemade. Electric guitar is played through fuzzy battery-powered practice amps to the rhythm of Mahatma Boom Boom's tablas or a screwdriver banged on a hubcap. The band's trademark is Captain Feedback's main instrument, One-String Eddie. One-String Eddie was a homemade guitar: a single piece of wire stretched over a length of 2x6 board equipped with a pick-up, which was played by plucking the wire while sliding a bottleneck or knife blade along it. The name was taken from a real musician. "Eddie One String is a hero of mine," Captain Feedback explained to the *SF Bay Guardian*. "He was a homeless street musician who recorded in one brief session in L.A. in the '60s. He played a broomstick strung with a single piece of wire and attached to a tin bucket. I built the Eddie One String Guitar mostly in his honor but partially because I needed to design an instrument to address my limited needs as a musician."

As their popularity grew, Rube Waddell was able to move off the street and into San Francisco clubs and restaurants. They dragged their roots with them, continuing to play the same mix of old-time hillbilly songs, waltzes, blues, religious songs and such from early in the last century. They didn't much bother to upgrade their equipment either, which turned out to be a boon on occasion. "We did one show at the Stork Club in Oakland last year," Reverend Wupass told the *SF Bay Guardian*, "and there was a blackout right in the middle of our set. But we just kept on going because we were playing through battery-powered amps. We didn't even miss a beat. People appreciated that. They appreciated our survivalist qualities."

They have released two albums. The first, a one-sided LP called *Hobo Train*, came packaged in a ziploc bag, and besides a lyric booklet, included instructions for building a one-string guitar, facts about Rube Waddell the baseball legend, and recipes for okra gumbo. The band's second release, 1998's CD *Stink Bait*, packaged in a little metal bait tin, offers a taste of a Rube Waddell late-night hoe-down; the record sounds like it was recorded in 1929, just before the Big Crash. Among its songs are "Westward Rider" a combination blues-cowboy song arranged for One-String Eddie and tablas; "Roy Smeck" a tribute to the Hawaiian slack guitar great; "Mohandas" a bizarre ballad about a boy's mom's affair with her boss at the Hindustani restaurant; and an upbeat version of the old Wobbly rouser, "The Ballad of Joe Hill." The record closes with a harmonica-inflected version of the "Ode: An der Freude" from Beethoven's Ninth Symphony—sung entirely in German.

As the millennium ended, they had a number of new projects in the works. They hoped to do a theme record about the historical Rube Waddell and were working on something they termed "a sea exploration opera." They placed ads in San Francisco papers offering to set lyrics to music. They hoped to be able to put together an entire album from what they received. "We're looking for some really absurd mundanity," Mahatma Boom Boom told a reporter for the *San Francisco Weekly's* RiffRaff column. "The worse the better." But by mid-1999 they had only received four responses, and those four weren't particularly promising. Boom Boom described one contributor as "what seemed like a young teenage girl in Richmond" another as "a young, lonely, office-worker guy who really seemed pent up."

The group sees themselves as spiritual heirs of their namesake. "Rube was not a complex man. He was someone with a fundamental ability and a complete lack of professionalism," Captain Feedback told Paczowski. Mahatma Boom Boom added, "We don't really know how to do what we're doing. We play about 14 different instruments, but we play them all very simply… In that way we pretty much clearly reflect Rube's legacy."

And like the first Rube, the band once found itself on the field of a major league ballpark performing before thousands of spectators. They weren't playing ball, they were playing their music at a San Francisco Giants game. They proved that they could be just as flaky as any old Rube Waddell though. "We played a short set, and on our last song, right on the final note, the entire audience—like 35,000 people—started booing," Boom Boom explained to the *SF Bay Guardian*. "And we were standing there, and yelling back at them, giving them the finger in defiance. But when we turned around we realized that they were booing because the opposing team was taking the field. Still, for a moment it was invigorating to feel hated by that many people."

Selected discography

Hobo Train, Vaccination Records, 1997.
Stink Bait, Vaccination Records, 1998.

Sources

Periodicals

Ink, #11, November 1998.
San Francisco Weekly, September 2, 1998; June 23, 1999.
SF Bay Guardian, August 26, 1998.

Online

"Rube Waddell," http://www.girlyhead.com/RWaddell.html (July 5, 2000).
"Rube Waddell," http://www.imusic.com/showcase/indie/rube waddell.html (June 30, 2000).

—*Gerald E. Brennan*

Kate Rusby

Singer, songwriter

Emglish traditional folk singer Kate Rusby, despite her young age, performs with the same warmth, universal appeal, talent, and passion of her ancestors, winning acclaim throughout Europe and the United States with just two solo albums to her name. "The brightest light in English folk music, Rusby is blessed with a delightful voice, an engaging, down-to-earth personality, and refreshing musical integrity," wrote the *Daily Telegraph*, while *Billboard* magazine's Timothy White called her "hauntingly heartsore solo albums … among the finest expressions in the last quarter-century of the fast-reviving English folk tradition." Nonetheless, Rusby, a modest and humorous musician who shuns the limelight and all other formal pretensions, awards herself far less credit, even though she has good reason to celebrate her unquestionable musicianship. Although she won several honors, earned the praises of a range of artists from Bonnie Raitt to Andy Kershaw, and performed at Europe's most prestigious music festivals since the mid-1990s, the gifted singer/songwriter insisted on her website: "I'm just this wee Yorkshire lass who can't get up in t'morning."

Kate Rusby was born on December 1, 1973, in the ancient market town of Barnsley in Yorkshire, England. Her parents, dedicated musicians Steve and Ann Rusby—who met while frequenting the region's folk clubs and later formed their own "ceilidh" (party) dance band—heavily influenced the musical growth of their children. Rusby, who grew up listening to artists like Nic Jones when most of her schoolmates swooned over rock stars like Jon Bon Jovi, was the middle sibling of three. As soon as she was old enough, Rusby, along with her older sister Emma and later younger brother Joe, joined the family band to sing harmonies and play the fiddle, an instrument she picked up at the tender age of five. By the time she reached the age of 12, another folk icon from Barnsley named Dave Burland encouraged her to learn guitar.

Although Rusby loved music—drawn equally to the bluegrass sounds of the Del McCoury Band and to the pop/rock flavors of 10,000 Maniacs—she found herself uncertain about her future when her older sister left the music business in favor of the graphic design industry. "I was always in her shadow," said Rusby, as quoted by White. Still undecided, Rusby, at the age of 15, received an invitation to take her new guitar- and piano-based solo act to the Holmworth Folk Festival and gave a spectacular performance. From that moment onward, the young folk singer never looked back, although she did go on to study drama for a time as well.

Recorded First Album

A few years later, however, a music career began to crystallize when radio and record producer John Leonard introduced her to another Barnsley-based musician named Kathryn Roberts, who Rusby met years earlier at Irish dancing classes. With Roberts, Rusby formed a short-lived, yet fruitful partnership. In 1995, the pair released their first and only album, *Kate Rusby & Kathryn Roberts,* voted Folk Roots' Album of the Year that year. Immediately, major record companies tried to persuade Rusby to sign, but the young singer swiftly turned down every offer in order to concentrate on her own music. Instead, Rusby chose to remain with Pure Records, the small, cottage label she continues to operate with her parents.

On her own, Rusby held true to the English folk tradition, but developed her own distinctive writing style as well, taking acoustic music to new heights in popularity. And while Rusby proudly calls herself a folk singer, her striking persona nevertheless fits none of the usual stereotypes. "An unchanging tradition is a dying one," the talented storyteller told White, adding, "Young people today think of folk musicians as people with a finger in their ears, wearing heavy wool sweaters. But I find I can step into other people's shoes hundreds of years past when I play this music. Back then, people weren't afraid to show their emotions, and I have a passion for their passion."

Rusby showcased this passion for the first time on record as a soloist with *Hourglass.* Released in Great Britain on Pure Records in 1997 and issued by Nashville-based Compass Records in the United States in 1999, Rusby's debut received vast acclaim.

For The Record . . .

Born on December 1, 1973, in Barnsley, Yorkshire, England; daughter of musicians Steve and Ann Rusby, who met while frequenting the region's folk clubs and later formed their own "ceilidh" (party) dance band; siblings: older sister Emma and younger brother Joe.

Started playing fiddle at age five; picked up guitar at age 12; performed solo for the first time at the Holmworth Folk Festival at age 15; released debut solo album, *Hourglass,* 1997; released award-winning album *Sleepless,* 1999.

Awards: Technics Mercury Music Prize for *Sleepless,* 1999; BBC Radio 2 awards for Best Album for *Sleepless* and Best Folk Singer, 2000.

Addresses: *Record company*—Pure Records, P.O. Box 174, Penistone, W. Yorkshire, England, S30 6P, +44 (0)1226 790536. *Website*—Kate Rusby at Pure Records, http://www.purerecords.demon.co.uk.

producer John McCusker—the renowned Battlefield Band fiddler—on fiddles, were band members Michael McGoldrick on flute and whistles, Ian Carr on guitar, Andy Cutting on diatonic accordion, Tony McManus on guitars, Alison Kinnaird on cello, Donald Hay on percussion, Conrad Ivitsky on double bass, Alan Reid and Davy Steele on harmony vocals, and Eric Rigler on uillean pipes.

After performing to audiences throughout Europe and releasing a new single entitled "Cowsong" in November of 1998 with McCusker and musicians Carr, McGoldrick, Ivitsky, Cutting, and James Macintosh, Rusby returned in May of 1999 for the British release of her next album, *Sleepless.* Compass issued the album a few months later in American. Her band lineup this time included McCusker, Cutting, Carr, Ivitsky, McGoldrick, Donald Hay, Darrell Scott, Roger Wilson, Andy Seward, and Francis MacDonald; Dave Burland, Tim O'Brien, and Wilson made guest appearances on vocals. *Sleepless* proved just as emotionally penetrating as Rusby's debut. "The dark-hued tremble of Rusby's rich alto voice lends it a tone just one calm breath above the confidingly conversant, its effect abruptly warming or chilling those nearby, like a sudden hand at one's shoulder," wrote White. "Meanwhile, piano, harp, tin whistle, and squeezebox rustle around her words as if they were wafts of breeze from a door, or a heart, that's been left ajar."

Every track, whether a traditional folk tune or a Rusby original like the elegiac "A Rose In April," resonated with the singer's everyday revelations, bringing a calm universality to each lyric. "Barnsley's an old coal-mining town," Rusby, who seems to understand the depths of human emotion and life's hardships, explained to White. "All my family on my mum's side were miners. The mines closed 10 years ago, and there was a lot of unemployment at first. For us, storytelling is a form of escapism, songs of death or loss telling us our lives aren't so bad compared to another poor soul."

Traditional and Contemporary Sounds

Rusby didn't limit herself to songs steeped in the past. In addition to performing melancholy traditional folk ballads on *Hourglass,* Rusby offered other more contemporary stylings. Two examples included the meditative "Old Man," as well as the folk singer's eerie rendition of Sinead O'Connor's pioneering hip-hop/folk adaptation of the traditional "I Am Stretched on Your Grave."

Rusby, known for her warm, unselfish nature and self-depreciating sense of humor, also noted that she was really not alone in making her first solo album, expressing the importance of naming the other talented musicians involved. Joining Rusby, along with

Honored for *Sleepless*

Upon the strength of songs such as her own "Sleepless Sailor" and the traditional ballads "Our Town" and "Wild Goose," *Sleepless* earned significant acclaim. *Mojo* included the effort on its list of "Best Folk Albums" of 1999, while *Q* magazine named *Sleepless* one of its 50 Best Albums of 1999, as well as one of the Best Folk Albums of All Time. Her second offering went on to win in July of 1999 a Technics Mercury Music Prize, which named a short list of 12 Albums of the Year from a variety of genres; Talvin Singh won the overall honor for his Indian classical album *OK.* Subsequently, in February of 2000, Rusby took home the two top prizes at the national folk awards held by the BBC (British Broadcasting Company) Radio 2 network. Not only did she win the Best Album award for *Sleepless,* but was also named Folk Singer of the Year.

At the BBC awards, Rusby was praised for keeping the folk tradition fresh and new. And Rusby herself commented that in spite of the fact that Western culture has progressed to the digital/technological age, her songs, rooted in the traditional, resonate just as much meaning today as they did hundreds of years ago. "They're songs about people's emotions, falling in and out of love, being born and dying," she explained to the audience at the ceremony, as quoted by *Billboard*'s Nigel Williamson. "The songs might be 200 years old, but they have never seemed old-fashioned to me. They're as relevant today as the day they were written, and they always will be."

Selected discography

Kate Rusby & Kathryn Robert, (United Kingdom) Pure, 1995; Compass, 1999.
Hourglass, (United Kingdom) Pure, 1997; Compass, 1999.
Sleepless, Pure/Compass, 1999.

Sources

Periodicals

Billboard, October 3, 1998; July 3, 1999; July 10, 1999; August 7, 1999; October 23, 1999; February 19, 2000.

Melody Maker, August 7, 1999.
USA Today, March 16, 1999.
Wall Street Journal, December 2, 1998.
Washington Post, April 25, 1998.

Online

Kate Rusby, http://www.purerecords.demon.co.uk (May 29, 2000).
Sonicnet.com, http://www.sonicnet.com (May 29, 2000).

—*Laura Hightower*

Lalo Schifrin

Composer, conductor, arranger, pianist

Photograph by Derick A. Thomas; Dat's Jazz. Corbis. Reproduced by permission.©

One of the most versatile composers among contemporary musicians, Argentine-born pianist Lalo Schifrin not only earned acclaim for his robust playing, but for his adventurous yet tasteful composing and arranging talents as well. Moreover, he soared in a variety of different forms—from the world of jazz and orchestral music to his long list of film and television soundtracks. A musically imaginative writer who begins each day with a Bach prelude before composing because, as he told Catherine Applefeld Olson of *Billboard,* "It clears my mind," Schifrin seems to move effortlessly from one field of choice to the next and doesn't favor any particular genre over another. Rather, Schifrin thrives on the chance to try something new and invigorating, regardless of the style—the opportunity to invest his creations and playing with energy and enthusiasm. He feels equally at home conducting a symphony orchestra, performing at an international jazz festival, scoring a film or television production, or composing a work for the Los Angeles Chamber Orchestra or the London Philharmonic.

As a jazz musician, Schifrin made his initial mark working with Dizzy Gillespie's quintet from 1960 through 1962, penning for the legendary trumpeter/bandleader the renowned "Gillespiana," a piece for jazz quintet and jazz orchestra. Schifrin wrote the musical suite as both a tribute to Gillespie and as an exploration of the Latin rhythms that were an integral part of the trumpeter's repertoire. "It is based on two classical ideas," he explained to *Billboard*'s Steve Graybow. "The first idea is the concerto grosso, which is a group of soloists surrounded by a larger orchestra. The second is the suite of dances found in Baroque music. Together, it paints a musical portrait of Dizzy."

An accomplished classical composer as well—with numerous credits including "Cantos Aztecas," recorded by tenor Placido Domingo with orchestra and choir; "Piano Concerto No. 2," commissioned by the Steinway Foundation and performed by Mstilslav Rostopovich and Christina Oritz; and "Guitar Concerto," recorded by Angel Romero with the London Philharmonic—Schifrin combined his talents for the ongoing Jazz Meets the Symphony recordings and concert series. With this project, top-notch artists such as bassist Ray Brown, brassmen Faddis and James Morrison, alto saxophonists Paquito D'Rivera and Tom Scott, and more joined the pianist and various orchestras of note for performances worldwide.

In another aspect of his career that spanned over four decades—the area that brought him the greatest mainstream recognition—Schifrin composed soundtracks for some 120 films and television shows, winning numerous honors for his work including 20 Grammy Award nominations, four Grammy Awards, and six Academy Award nominations. His first score, for 1957's *El Jefe,* won the composer an Argentine Journalists Association Award for Best Score, and his

Born Lalo (Claudio) Schifrin on June 21, 1932, in Buenos Aires, Argentina; son of Luis (a violinist and conductor of the Teatro Colon in Buenos Aires); married, Donna; children: three. *Education*: Studied music in Argentina with Juan Carlos Paz and at the Paris Conservatory.

Formed own jazz group early in career; International Jazz Festival, Paris, Argentinean representative, 1955; Xavier Cugat's orchestra, arranger; Dizzy Gillespie's band, pianist and composer, 1960-62; moved to Los Angeles and focused on film work, mid-1960s though the 1980s; University of California, Los Angeles, teacher of music composition, 1970-71; developed Jazz Meets the Symphony series, early-1990s; focused on jazz and classical composing, 1990s. Guest conductor with philharmonic symphonies, including those in Los Angeles, Israel, Buenos Aires, and Mexico, the Indianapolis and Atlanta symphonies, and the Los Angeles Chamber Orchestra. Member: Young Musicians Foundation (president and musical director, 1983).

Awards: Received 20 Grammy Award nominations; winner of four Grammy Awards, including two for his theme from Mission: Impossible, 1967, 1969, 1986, and 1997; received six Academy Award nominations; Hollywood Walk of Fame Award; Hollywood Chamber of Commerce; Chevalier de l'Ordre des Arts et des Lettres, government of France.

Addresses: *Record company*—Aleph Records, website: http://www.alephrecords.com. *Agent for film and television scores*—Pero & Kaplan, c/o Philip J. Kaplan, Esq., 801 S. Flowers St., Los Angeles, CA 90017, phone: (213) 629-7124, fax: (213) 622-7575, e-mail: perokaplan@icnt.net. *Agent for personal appearances in the United States*—Ted Kurland Agency, Attn: Marilyn Rosen, 173 Brighton Ave., Boston, MA 02134, phone: (617) 254-0007, fax: (617) 782-3524. *Publicity information*—Maureen O'Connor, Rogers & Cowarn, phone: (310) 201-8816, fax: (310) 788-6633, e-mail: moconnor@shadwick.com. *Website*—Lalo Schifrin: http://www.schifrin.com.

breakthrough project arrived in 1965 with the music for the film *The Cincinnati Kid*. Since then, Schifrin went on to pen the unforgettable theme for the *Mission Impossible* television show, *Dirty Harry* (1971) and *Sudden Impact* (1983) starring Clint Eastwood, *Bullitt* (1968) with Steve McQueen, the Bruce Lee Saga *Enter the Dragon* (1973), *Rush Hour* (1998) featuring martial arts star Jackie Chan, and the Oscar-nominated film by Carlos Saura entitled *Tango* (1999). For his work in this medium, where he succeeded in bridging the worlds of traditional and film music like no other musician of his generation, Schifrin was regarded as the most important film composer of the post-Henry Mancini, post-*Psycho* era.

Discovered Jazz, Popular, and World Music

Born Claudio—he shortened his name to Lalo after emigrating to the United States—on June 21, 1932, in Buenos Aires, Argentina, Schifrin began studying classical music early in life with his father, Luis Schifrin, a violinist and the concert master of the Orchestra of the Teatro Colon in Buenos Aires, as well as Enrique Barenboim (father of concert pianist/conductor Daniel Barenboim). "It's a very unique city," he said of growing up in the South American capital, as quoted by Zan Stewart in *Down Beat*. "We absorb everything. Myself, I absorb like a sponge the music of other cultures, besides classical." Despite his father's rigid musical tastes, in addition to his own personal joy as a youthful piano student in the music of Igor Stravinsky, Béla Bartók, and Arnold Schönberg, Schifrin nonetheless was equally drawn to the sounds of jazz greats like Bud Powell and Thelonius Monk. "The first time I heard Monk was on a 78 at the record store," he recalled. "He was incredible, and I became mesmerized and started to learn jazz from records." Other interests blossomed too, including the Latin sounds of his native culture as well as music from around the world. An avid moviegoer as well during his childhood, Schifrin spent countless hours at the cinemas in Buenos Aires, where he found himself more captivated by the music than the stories themselves.

Winning a scholarship to attend the prestigious Paris Conservatoire (or Conservatory), where he studied with twentieth-century music great Olivier Messiaen and based his thesis of study on classical and African music, Schifrin traveled to France with the true intent of learning more about jazz. Thus, he led a double life of sorts throughout his stay in Paris; he studied classical music during the week at school, then spent the weekends playing with some of Europe's hottest jazz artists—people like piano legend Chet Baker and Belgian saxophonist Bobby Jaspar. In addition to jazz, Schifrin over the course of his stay in Paris developed eclectic tastes in modern, especially popular, music.

Performing with the pros overseas made a great impact on the younger pianist, and when Schifrin returned to Argentina in the mid-1950s, he continued to play jazz and started to write music for film. At the same time, Schifrin indulged in the more traditional music that had encompassed his formal training, writing chamber pieces, compositions for ballet, and even symphonies. In 1955, Schifrin represented Argentina in the Third Annual Jazz Festival held in Paris. Soon after that performance, in 1956, he formed his own big band, largely in the tradition of Count Basie and Dizzy Gillespie, through which Gillespie himself first heard Schifrin play. Schifrin recalled meeting Gillespie in Argentina, while the trumpeter/bandleader was in the midst of a United States State Department-sponsored tour: "Dizzy's was one of the first American jazz bands that came to Buenos Aires," he told Graybow. "My jazz band played for him at a reception, and he asked me if I had written the charts, which I had. Dizzy invited me to come to the United States to be his piano player. At first, I thought he was joking, because I was so surprised."

Followed Gillespie to New York

Realizing the sincerity of Gillespie's proposal, Schifrin followed the trumpeter to New York City in 1958. Focusing almost exclusively on jazz upon his arrival and through the early-1960s, Schifrin as a jazz performer worked with such big names as Sarah Vaughan, Ella Fitzgerald, Stan Getz, and Count Basie. By the mid-1960s, however, having moved to Los Angeles and landing a contract with Metro-Goldwyn-Mayer (MGM) to compose scores, Schifrin started to devote most of his energies to film work. And within no time, he had become one of the most prominent and productive of a new generation of film composers in Hollywood. While he maintained a love for jazz in his heart and mind during the height of his film career, Schifrin gave performances only on rare occasions.

However, Schifrin's career in Hollywood eventually grew stale over time. "They typecast me," said Schifrin to *Entertainment Weekly*'s Dave Karger. "They didn't trust me with a love story. I was too weird." Although Schifrin continued to score music for both television and film well into the 1990s—including, with Danny Elfman, for the 1996 film *Mission Impossible* based on the television series and for the 1998 film *Something to Believe In*—the composer turned to classical and jazz as his primary focus, beginning in the early-1990s with the development of Jazz Meets the Symphony, for which Schifrin served as the featured composer, pianist, and conductor.

According to Schifrin, the idea of combing the two genres—jazz and classical music—arose years before, during the composing of two early film scores. "In *The Cincinnati Kid*, Ray Charles sang backed by a symphony orchestra," he related to Stewart. "Then for the chase scene in *Bullitt*, I wrote a symphonic score combined with saxophone solos, all at very fast tempos. Years later, when I arranged music for Dizzy, Ray Brown, Grady Tate and myself to play for a tour with the Israel Philharmonic Orchestra, I began to fully realize that the two distinct musical forms could be combined." Since its formation, Jazz Meets the Symphony, represented by a total of four albums—plus a release combining the first four recordings entitled *Jazz Meets the Symphony Collection,* which garnered three Grammy nominations—has been Schifrin's primary focus. He planned to record a fifth installment in the autumn of 2000.

Each recording features shorter pieces, both covers and originals, alongside longer medleys that were written by or associated with Duke Ellington, Miles Davis, Charlie Parker, Fats Waller, Bix Beiderbecke, and, most notably, Gillespie. "I have to find pieces that adapt to the symphonic idiom without losing the jazz," Schifrin explained to Stewart. "The jazz comes first, and the music has to be interesting for the symphony players, so I don't do long notes for the strings and have the rhythm section moving with a guy improvising. Everybody has a challenging part. It's like walking a tightrope. If you walk too much on one side, it becomes completely classical and too academic. It it's too much jazz, the classical musicians can't play it."

Latin Music Meets Jazz

In addition to uniting jazz with classical influences, Schifrin also explored the blending of jazz with Latin elements for 1999's Grammy-nominated *Latin Jazz Suite,* recorded in Cologne, Germany and featuring the WDR Big Band, Jon Faddis, saxophonist David Sanchez, and drummer Ignacio Berroa. Using his upbringing in Buenos Aires as a point of reference, Schifrin for the project mixed jazz with Afro-Cuban, Caribbean, Pampas (a style of Argentine music), and Brazilian sounds. "All these influences and others were important to me, and in this suite I wanted to write things that, hopefully, are autobiographical, writing about my impressions or inventions based on my memories, based on what I know, or what I'm trying to know," he explained to Stewart.

Schifrin released *Latin Jazz Suite* on his own Aleph Records, a label he formed in 1998 that concentrated on his jazz, Latin, and classical recordings as well as his film and television scores; Schifrin's wife, Donna, with whom he shared a Beverly Hills, California, mansion once owned by Groucho Marx, headed the company. As Schifrin explained to Eileen Fitzpatrick of *Billboard*, he felt he needed an outlet for his work beyond that of his Hollywood years: "I have so many facets but have primarily been known for film scores," he noted. "I have great connections and friends in the

Latin and classical community, and forming the label enables me to take advantage of all these connections."

Although the tireless musician stayed occupied with Jazz Meets the Symphony as he approached the age of 70, he still maintained relationships within the classical realm. Among his works in this area include arrangements for the Three Tenors—José Carreras, Placido Domingo, and Luciano Pavarotti—like their debut performance as a trio in 1990 in Caracalla, Italy, as well as all three of the Grand Finale concerts celebrating the World Soccer Championships: Italy in 1990, Los Angeles in 1994, and Paris in 1998. Two of the tenors also commissioned Schifrin to arrange music for two successful Christmas programs, *Christmas in Vienna* in 1992 with Diana Ross, Carreras, and Domingo, as well as *A Celebration of Christmas* in 1995 with Carreras, Domingo, and Natalie Cole.

Along with his Grammy and Oscar nominations, Schifrin received numerous honors over the course of his career. Among them include the BMI Lifetime Achievement Award, a star on the Hollywood Walk of Fame, the Chevalier de l'Ordre des Arts et Lettres from the French minister of Culture, and more. Even as the years passed, Schifrin never slowed down. As he continued to record, compose music, and perform in the world's most renowned concert halls and at jazz festivals across the United States and Europe, Schifrin did so with the same enthusiasm of a much younger man. "For me this is not work," he said to Stewart. "It's the continuation of my teenage years when I discovered all the music I was totally blinded by. I'm still blinded by it and I'll die blinded by it."

Selected discography

Solo

Lalo Schifrin Y Su Orquestra, Columbia, 1956.
Spectrum, Epic, 1957.
Piano Espaol, Tico, 1960.
Piano, Strings & Bossa Nova, MGM, 1962.
Bossa Nova, New Brazilian Jazz, Audio Fidelity, 1962.
Lalo = Brilliance, Roulette, 1962.
Jazz Faust, 1962.
"7 Faces of Dr. Lao"/"The Wave" [45], MGM, 1963.
"Haunting"/"Theme from Dime with..." [45], MGM, 1963.
Between Broadway & Hollywood, MGM, 1963.
"Broken Date"/"The Good Life" [45], Verve, 1963.
(With Bob Brookmeyer) *Samba Para Dos,* Verve, 1963.
The Ritual of Sound, 1963.
The Living Cell, 1964.
Etude on Rhythm, 1964.
Lalo's Meditation, 1964.
New Fantasy, Verve, 1964.
(With Louie Bellson) *Explorations,* Roulette, 1964.
Once a Thief and Other Themes, Verve, 1965.
The Sphinx, 1965.

Three Pieces for Percussion And Strings, 1966.
Marquis De Sade (also known as Schifrin/Sade), Verve, 1966.
The Rise and Fall of the Third Reich, MGM, 1967.
Concerto for Trumpet, 1967.
There's a Whole Lalo Schifrin Goin On, Dot, 1968.
Dialogs for Jazz Quintet and Orchestra, 1969.
Improvisations for Jazz Soloists And Orchestra, 1969.
Variants on a Madrigal of Gesualdo, 1969.
Canons for String Quartet, 1969.
Grabado in Vivo!, RCA Victor, 1970.
Rock Requiem, Verve, 1971.
Pulsations for Electronic Keyboard, Jazz Band and Orchestra, 1971.
Madrigals for the Space Age, 1972.
"Latin Soul"/"Dirty Harry" [45], Verve, 1972.
"Bolero"/"Dona Donna" [45], Twentieth Century, 1975.
Towering Toccata, CTI, 1976.
Black Widow, CTI, 1976.
Continuum Journeys Voyage, Label X, 1977.
Gypsies, Tabu, 1978.
Canons, Entr'acte, 1978.
No One Home, Tabu, 1979.
Invocations, 1980.
Capriccio for Clarinet and Strings, 1981.
Ins and Outs, Palo Alto, 1982.
Resonances, 1987.
Double Bass Concerto, 1987.
Dance Concertantes for Clarient And Orchestra, 1988.
(With Placido Domingo) *Cantos Aztecas for Vocal Soloists, Orchestra and Chorus,* Pro Arte, 1988.
Les Solistes Francais Orchestre Philharmonique De Paris, Conducted by Lalo Schifrin, Cybelia, 1988.
Hitchcock: Master of Mayhem (also known as *Masters of Mayhem*), Pro Arte/Intersound, 1990.
Those Fabulous Hollywood Marches (also known as *Hollywood Marches*), Pro Arte/Intersound, 1990.
Kol Nidrei, 1990.
Grand Finale, 1990.
The Trial of Louis XVI, 1990.
Impresiones: Fantasy for Trumpet and Orchestra, 1991.
Carnaval of the Animals, Dove Audio, 1992.
Romancing the Film, Pro Arte, 1992.
Jazz Meets Symphony, Atlantic, 1992.
Cantares Argentinos, 1992.
Piano Concerto, 1992.
More Jazz Meets Symphony, Atlantic, 1993.
Bandido!, 1994.
Homage a Ravel, 1995.
Filmclassics (also known as *100 Ans De Cinema*), Aleph, 1995.
Lili'uokalani Symphony, Urtext, 1995.
Firebird, Four Winds, 1995.
Gillespiana, 1996.
Schifrin Meets Piazzolla—Jazz Meets Tango, 1996.
Concertos/trópicos, Auvidis, 1996.
Mission Impossible and More!: The Best of Lalo Schifrin, Motor, 1996.
A Rhapsody for Bix, 1996.
Psalms, 1996.
Dirty Harry Anthology, Aleph, 1998.
Jazz Mass, Aleph, 1998.
Metamorphosis: Jazz Meets the Symphony #4, Aleph, 1998.
The Reel Lalo Schifrin, Hip-O, 1998.
Represión, 1998.
Jazz Meets the Symphony Collection, Aleph, 1999.

Latin Jazz Suite, Aleph, 1999.
Talkin' Verve Lalo Schifrin, Verve, 1999.

With Dizzy Gillespie (as pianist, arranger, and conductor)

Gillespania, Verve, 1960.
An Electrifying Evening, Verve, 1961.
Carnegie Hall Concert, Verve, 1961.
A Night in Birdland Live, Vol. One, 1961.
A Musical Safari, 1961.
New Wave, 1962.
Dizzy on the French Riviera, 1962.
The New Continent, 1962.
Dizzy Gillespie/Double Six of Paris, Verve, 1963.
Free Ride, Pablo, 1977..

Film work (composer)

Rhino!, MGM, 1964.
Joy House (also known as *The Love Cage*), MGM, 1964.
The Cincinnati Kid, MGM, 1965.
Dark Intruder, Universal, 1965.
Once a Thief, MGM, 1965.
Blindfold, Universal, 1966.
Murder's Row, Columbia, 1966.
I Deal in Death, Twentieth Century-Fox, 1966.
Way Way Out, Twentieth Century-Fox, 1966.
The Liquidator, Metro-Goldwyn-Mayer, 1966.
Cool Hand Luke, Warner Bros./Seven Arts, 1967.
The President's Analyst, Paramount, 1967.
Who's Minding the Mint?, Columbia, 1967.
The Venetian Affair, Metro-Goldwyn-Mayer, 1967.
Sullivan's Empire, Universal, 1967.
The Fox, Warner Bros., 1968.
Where Angels Go, Trouble Fellows,Columbia, 1968.
The Rise and Fall of the Third Reich (documentary), 1968.
Mission Impossible versus the Mob (also known as *Mission: Impossible vs. the Mob*), Paramount, 1968.
Hell in the Pacific (also known as *The Enemy*), Cinerama, 1968.
The Brotherhood, Paramount, 1968.
Sol Madrid (also known as *The Heroin Gang*), Metro-Goldwyn-Mayer, 1968.
Coogan's Bluff, Universal, 1968.
Bullitt, Warner Bros., 1968.
Eye of the Cat (also known as *Wylie*), Universal, 1969.
Che!, Twentieth Century-Fox, 1969.
WUSA, Paramount, 1970.
Imago (also known as *How Now, Sweet Jesus?* and *To Be Free*), Magarac, 1970.
I Love My Wife, Universal, 1970.
THX 1138, Warner Bros., 1970.
Pussycat, Pussycat, I Love You, United Artists, 1970.
Kelly's Heroes, Metro-Goldwyn-Mayer, 1970.
Mrs. Pollifax-Spy, United Artists, 1971.
The Hellstrom Chronicle, Cinema V, 1971.
Pretty Maids All in a Row, Metro-Goldwyn-Mayer, 1971.
The Beguiled, Universal, 1971.
The Wrath of God, Metro-Goldwyn-Mayer, 1972.
Rage, Warner Bros., 1972.
Joe Kidd, Universal, 1972.
Prime Cut, National General, 1972.
Dirty Harry, Warner Bros., 1972.

The Neptune Factor (also known as *The Neptune Disaster* and *An Underwater Odyssey*), Twentieth Century-Fox, 1973.
Hit!, Paramount, 1973.
Harry in Your Pocket, United Artists, 1973.
Charley Varrick, Universal, 1973.
Enter the Dragon (also known as *The Deadly Three*), Warner Bros., 1973.
Magnum Force, Warner Bros., 1973.
Man on a Swing, Warner Bros., 1973.
Golden Needles (also known as *The Chase for the Golden Needles*), American International Pictures, 1974.
The Master Gunfighter, Taylor-Laughlin, 1975.
The Four Musketeers (also known as *The Revenge of Milady*), Twentieth Century-Fox, 1975.
Sky Riders, Twentieth Century-Fox, 1976.
Day of the Animals (also known as *Something Is Out There*), Film Ventures, 1976.
Special Delivery (also known as *Dangerous Break*), American International Pictures, 1976.
St. Ives, Warner Bros., 1976.
Voyage of the Damned, Avco-Embassy, 1976.
The Eagle Has Landed, Columbia, 1977.
Rollercoaster, Universal, 1977.
Telefon, United Artists, 1977.
The Manitou, Avco-Embassy, 1978.
Nunzio, Universal, 1978.
The Cat from Outer Space, Buena Vista, 1978.
Return from Witch Mountain, Buena Vista, 1978.
Boulevard Nights, Warner Bros., 1979.
Escape to Athena, Associated Film, 1979.
The Amityville Horror, American International Pictures, 1979.
Concorde: Airport '79 (also known as *The Concorde Affair, Airport '79, The Concorde-Airport '79* and *S.O.S. Concorde*), Universal, 1979.
Love and Bullets, Associated Film, 1979.
The Nude Bomb (also known as *Maxwell Smart and the Nude Bomb* and *The Return of Maxwell Smart*), Universal, 1980.
The Competition, Columbia, 1980.
The Big Brawl (also known as *Battle Creek* and *Battle Creek Brawl*), Warner Bros., 1980.
Brubaker, Twentieth Century-Fox, 1980.
Serial, Paramount, 1980.
When Time Ran Out (also known as *Earth's Final Fury*), Warner Bros., 1980.
Loophole (also known as *Break In*), Brent Walker, 1980.
Buddy Buddy, United Artists, 1981.
Caveman, United Artists, 1981.
The Fridays of Eternity [Argentina], 1981.
The Skin (also known as *La Pelle*), [Italy], 1981.
Airplane II: The Sequel, Paramount, 1982.
Amityville II: The Possession, Orion, 1982.
The Seduction, Avco-Embassy, 1982.
A Stranger Is Watching, MGM/United Artists, 1982.
The Class of 1984, United Film, 1982.
Fast-Walking, Lorimar, 1982.
Doctor Detroit, Universal, 1983.
The Sting II, Universal, 1983.
The Osterman Weekend, Twentieth Century-Fox, 1983.
Sudden Impact, Warner Bros., 1983.
Tank, Universal, 1983.
Bad Medicine, Twentieth Century-Fox, 1985.
The Mean Season, Orion, 1985.
The New Kids, Columbia, 1985.

Black Moon Rising, New World, 1986.
The Ladies Club, New Line Cinema, 1986.
The Fourth Protocol, Rank, 1987.
The Silence of Bethany, 1987.
Berlin Blues, Pathe Communications, 1988.
Little Sweetheart, Nelson Entertainment, 1988.
The Dead Pool, Warner Bros., 1988.
Return to the River Kwai, TriStar, 1989.
FX2—The Deadly Art of Illusion (also known as *FX2*), Orion, 1991.
The Beverly Hillbillies, Twentieth Century-Fox, 1993.
Manhattan Meringue, BMG Home Video, 1994.
The Scorpion Spring, New Line Home Video, 1995.
(With Danny Elfman) *Mission Impossible,* Paramount, 1996.
Money Talks, New Line Cinema, 1997.
Something to Believe In, Aleph, 1997.
Rush Hour, Aleph, 1998.
Tango, Hollywood Partners, 1998.

Television work (composer)

Series

The Big Valley, ABC, 1965.
T.H.E. Cat, NBC, 1966.
Mission: Impossible, CBS, 1966-73.
Mannix, CBS, 1967.
The Young Lawyers, ABC, 1970.
Petrocelli, NBC, 1974.
Starsky and Hutch, (pilot), ABC, 1974.
Bronk, CBS, 1975.
Starsky and Hutch, ABC, 1975-76.
Danger Theatre, Fox, 1993.

Movies

See How They Run, 1964.
The Doomsday Flight, 1966.
How I Spent My Summer Vacation (also known as *Deadly Roulette*), 1967.
The Young Lawyers, 1969.
The Mask of Sheba (also known as *Quest: Mask of Sheba*), 1970.
The Aquarians (also known as *Deep Lab*), 1970.
Welcome Home, Johnny Bristol, 1971.
Escape, 1971.
Earth II, 1971.
Hunter, CBS, 1973.
Night Games, 1974.
Back to the Planet of the Apes, 1974.
Guilty or Innocent: The Sam Sheppard Murder Case, 1975.
Delancey Street: The Crisis Within, 1975.
Foster and Laurie, 1975.
Brenda Starr, 1976.
Good Against Evil, 1977.
The President's Mistress, 1978.
The Nativity, 1978.
Institute for Revenge, 1979.
Chicago Story, 1981.
Victims, 1982.
Falcon's Gold (also known as *Robbers of Sacred Mountain*), 1982.
Rita Hayworth: The Love Goddess, 1983.
Starflight: The Plane that Couldn't Land (also known as *Starflight One*), 1983.

Spraggue (also known as *Spraggue: Murder for Two*), 1984.
Command 5, 1984.
Bridge Across Time (also known as *Arizona Ripperand Terror at London Bridge*), 1985.
Triplecross, ABC, 1985.
Beverly Hills Madam, 1986.
Kung Fu: The Movie, 1986.
Hollywood Wives, 1986.
Out on a Limb, 1987.
Shakedown on the Sunset Strip, CBS, 1988.
Original Sin, NBC, 1989.
Little White Lies (also known as *First Impressions*), NBC, 1989.
Face to Face, CBS, 1990.

Miniseries

A.D. (also known as *A.D.—Anno Domini*), NBC, 1985.
Earth Star Voyager, ABC, 1988.
The Neon Empire, Showtime, 1989.
A Woman Named Jackie, NBC, 1991.

Specials (composer, unless otherwise noted)

Jake's M.O., 1987.
Wolf Trap Salutes Dizzy Gillespie: An All-Star Tribute to the Jazz Master, PBS, 1988.
Music arranger, *Jose Carreras, Diana Ross, Placido Domingo: Christmas in Vienna,* Arts and Entertainment, 1992.
Music arranger, *Tibor Rudas Presents Carreras, Domingo, Pavarotti with Mehta: The Three Tenors in Concert 1994,* PBS, 1994.

Stage work (composer)

Jazz Faust (ballet), 1963.
The Trial of Louis XVI (opera), 1988.

Sources

Books

The Complete Marquis Who's Who, Marquis Who's Who, 1999.
Contemporary Theatre, Film and Television, Volume 5, Gale Research, 1988.
Contemporary Theatre, Film and Television, Volume 21, Gale Group, 1999.
International Dictionary of Films and Filmmakers, Volume 4: Writers and Artists, St. James Press, 1996.

Periodicals

Billboard, February 28, 1998, p. 80; July 18, 1998, p. 17; September 25, 1999, p. 65.
Down Beat, April 1995, p. 40; October 1996, p. 17; November 1998, p. 63; February 2000, pp. 49-51.
Entertainment Weekly, June 7, 1996, p. 38.
Time, June 3, 1996, p. 21.

Online

Lalo Schifrin Official Website, http://www.schifrin.com (April 27, 2000).

—*Laura Hightower*

Oliver Schroer

Violinist

Canadian-born new age acoustic violinist Oliver Schroer emerged as a significant creative force on the North American music scene during the 1990s, with four self-published albums and legions of professional collaborations to his credit. Yet Schroer, a "baby boomer," was a latecomer to the electronic technology that pervaded the music industry during the late twentieth century. Schroer grew up not only without daily television and radio, but also he was well into high school when he first discovered guitar amplification during in his mid-teens. Despite his traditional upbringing, musical classicism left him unmoved; as an eight-year-old he shunned his violin, and later as a teen-ager he left the instrument to collect dust while he practiced the guitar. He took a second look at his old violin only after painting it blue and learning to appreciate the diversity of authentic country music, at which point he capitalized on his early training and developed his natural talent to become a self-made man of music and melody, a musician's musician.

Schroer was born in the mid-1950s in Toronto, Ontario. He grew up approximately 100 miles northwest of the city, in the town of Flesherton. He learned to play the recorder at age six and the violin at age eight. As with young music students everywhere, he failed to appreciate the discipline, the monotony of the scales, and the perceived dullness of the classical repertoire. As a baby boomer in a modest family growing up in the 1950s and 1960s, Schroer remained unaccustomed not only to exotic electronics, but also to simple receivers and apparatuses as well. The family rarely watched television; likewise the wizardry of radio was a rarity in the Schroer household. He was in his mid-teens before he understood the specific role of a guitar amplifier in popular music.

Schroer was around ten years old when his older siblings embraced folk music, and his mother joined them. Not to be left out, Schroer listened too and was taken by the friendlier tunes. "Puff the Magic Dragon" was his self-admitted favorite. In early adolescence he noticed his siblings and friends turning increasingly to popular rock & roll music for entertainment. Some of them preferred country or blues, with Johnny Winter the unanimous favorite; thus Schroer's childhood interest in music developed into a captivating hobby when a friend with a folk guitar showed him how to play that instrument. Schroer virtually abandoned his classical training by age 13, and his violin repertoire dwindled to one single song, called "Orange Blossom Express," that he had gleaned from an old Mason Williams Band recording. Despite a personal preference for German classical music and the jazz of Louis Armstrong, Schroer's father conceded defeat, and presented his son with a new electric guitar on the boy's sixteenth birthday.

Schroer spent the following summer in the French-Canadian province of Quebec, through an exchange student program. A new world opened before him as he learned to speak French and discovered hard rock and other modern musical forms. His roommate at the school was a musical die-hard, with a record player stuck in perpetual motion. Through his new friend, Schroer discovered Frank Zappa and Jethro Tull; James Taylor made a debut into Schroer's life as well.

To a large extent Schroer's interest in music remained confined to playing the guitar for amusement. The notion of music as a profession existed beyond his idea of options. He viewed academic discipline as the solitary career base of life. According to that anticipation, he enrolled in college and studied history and philosophy, but his love for music and a new-found interest in jazz occupied his time. He became an avid follower of Chick Corea and Lenny Breau, and also developed an interest in the styles of guitarist Joe Pass and pianist Bill Evans.

As Schroer's musical taste matured, his violin—which he had by then painted blue—lay idle on the shelf; guitar remained his instrument of choice. He fiddled only sporadically, in jam sessions with friends, and on such rare occasions he plugged the violin into an amplifier (after he developed an understanding of the purpose of the electronic device).

First Gig

During his undergraduate years (and there were ten of them), Schroer joined the Traverston Band along with a

For The Record . . .

Born in the mid-1950s in Toronto, Ontario. *Education*: B.A. degree.

Performed with country music and other bands including Traverston Band, 1982; performed as a busker, 3-4 years, mid-1980s; established Eye Music (quartet), 1987; established Stewed Tomatoes; numerous collaborations including more than 75 albums; self-published CDs on Big Dog Music label.

Addresses: c/o The Post, Oliver Schroer, 589 Markham St., Toronto, Ontario, Canada M6G2L7; e-mail: oliver @oliverschroer.com.

friend named Jim Ryan; Schroer played his first professional performance at a New Year celebration in 1982. The thrill of playing appealed to him more than the $30 compensation that he received, and although he was hired to play the guitar, he enhanced the evening with samples of his fiddle playing. Traverston Band stayed busy, and the gigs were diverse. Schroer's repertoire grew quickly. He added more fiddling, square dance tunes, country songs—scores of compositions in all—enough to play all day and all night.

Schroer's next musical colleague was named Chris Sankey. Schroer along with Sankey, an acquaintance from a college philosophy class, favored open-air venues. They played in subways and on street corners, a practice known as "busking." Schroer enjoyed the lifestyle and continued as a solo busker for several years on his own. The art of a busker was demanding, and in time Schroer commanded a substantial repertoire—more than 600 tunes. He played most often in the subways during business commutes, and he enjoyed the unique audience intimacy afforded only by performing on the street. Interestingly, Schroer perceived that he charmed his audience more effectively with his violin than with his guitar.

New Take on His Old Fiddle

When Schroer and a friend enrolled in a square dancing class, Schroer carried his violin to the sessions and spent much of the time jamming with the musicians rather than strutting around the dance floor. The fiddlers shared techniques with Schroer who was eager to learn, and he developed his proficiency in Irish and French fiddle music.

Scandinavian, Balkan, and Asian jazz came next, as Schroer's curiosity for old fiddling styles was insatiable, or so it seemed. In 1987, he established a jazz quartet, called Eye Music. After the ensemble performed at the Montreaux Jazz festival in Switzerland in 1988, Schroer started a second band, called Stewed Tomatoes. He took Stewed Tomatoes around Canada, where they performed frequently at the various local folk festivals. The electrically charged Stewed Tomatoes featured Schroer's amplified violin playing plus horns and a rhythm section. Their galvanizing sound was a sellout at Bathurst Street Theatre in Toronto, and the group did the honors for a time as the house band at Stewart McLean's Vinyl Café as well. They appeared at the Northern Encounters Festival in Toronto, at the Canada Day celebration on Parliament Hill in Ottawa, at New York City's Lincoln Center, and with James Keelaghan on tour.

Individually, Schroer accompanied many popular folk singers and sat in with other ensembles as well: Thomas Handy, James Keelaghan, Marc Jordan, George Fox, Stephen Fearing, and Don Ross. Schroer played on recordings with Jimmy Webb, Barry Mann, the country "girl group" Quartette, and alternative rock's Great Big Sea. He was heard on James Keelaghan's *Road,* and on *Arc* with Thomas Handy. He contributed to Teresa Doyle's *Dance to Your Daddy,* which won the East Coast Music Award as best children's album of 1997, and he was heard on her album, *If Fish Could Sing.* Overall, Schroer contributed sounds or technical assistance to approximately 75 albums.

Big Dog Music

Schroer released albums of his own music in 1993, 1994, 1996, 1998, and 1999 through his Big Dog Music label. He contributed also to *Who's Forest,* an album from which profits were earmarked for the Partnership for Public Lands. He received a commission for 2000, to collaborate with three others in developing the music for the Canada Day celebration that year that was scheduled in Ontario at Toronto's Harbourfront. Additionally, 1996 saw the publication of Schroer's composition, "Horseshoes and Rainbows," in *Fiddler Magazine's Favorites.*

Schroer, through his assorted memberships in his own and other bands, including Muddy York and Rare, came to a clear recognition of his musical identity. Over time he unleashed the power of his violin in the process. He consistently proved himself unwilling to isolate music within the framework of one or two genres. He focused instead on optimizing the melody, regardless of musical style. His practice technique evolved effectively into a formula, albeit a creative concoction, whereby he recorded each melody repeatedly in order to preserve every subtle innuendo on tape, along with every flagrant improvisation of the respective play-through. In the seemingly endless repetition of recorded notes Schroer noted each minor discrepancy that distinguished one play-through from another.

Subsequently, he mentally spliced selected interludes, thus weaving a completed selection from the individual parts. In performance and on recordings, he reproduced the mentally spliced melodies for his unsuspecting audience. Schroer's focus on the intricacies of melody brought him from his early country fiddling days, through the folk styles of his numerous contemporaries, to what he called the *a cappella* violin style that he demonstrated repeatedly on his solo CDs on which he glided adeptly from Bach partitas, through bayou blues and traditional melodies, performing these and his own personal compositions with equal agility.

Schroer lives in Toronto and continues to shun television, videotape, and other complexities of the last century. He makes two concessions to technology in the form of his electrically adapted instruments, and his self-styled Internet site, a "funky web page," at http://www.oliverschroer.com.

Selected discography

Albums

Jigzup, Big Dog Music, 1993.
Whirled, Big Dog Music, 1994.
Stewed Tomatoes, Big Dog Music, 1996.
Celtica, Avalon, 1998.
O2, Big Dog Music, 1999.

Sources

Periodicals

Billboard, August 1, 1999, p. 80.

Online

"Oliver Schroer," http://www.oliverschroer.com/disco.html (May 17, 2000).

—Gloria Cooksey

Keely Smith

Singer

Archive Photos. Reproduced by permission.

Keely Smith could have easily been billed as "The Queen or First Lady of Las Vegas." For nearly half a century, Smith entertained thousands of people visiting the nation's home of gambling and entertainment. She first went to Las Vegas in the early 1950s and brought delight and pleasure to many who often stood in line to see her and spouse Louis Prima. As a headliner in only the most prestigious hotels in Nevada and elsewhere, Smith often began her act at midnight and five performances later wound her program to a close at 6 a.m. after bringing audiences to their feet. Many of her recordings over the years have been filled with upbeat tempos and high exuberance, but her presentation style of tenderness and perfect voice control has made her one of the best lyrical deliverers of ballads of all time.

Born Dorothy Jacqueline Keely on March 9, 1932, in Norfolk, Virginia, to Howard Keely and Fanny Stevens, she was the couple's only daughter and the youngest of three children. Her father was of native American Cherokee and Irish descent and her grandmother was a full-blooded Cherokee Indian. Her father was a carpenter and after her mother divorced him when Smith was nine years old, she later married Jesse Smith, who was also a carpenter. The Smiths later had a son. Keely recalled, "We lived in a very bad section of Norfolk called Atlantic City, and when I say bad, I mean every thief, every hooker, every anybody that did anything bad that landed up in jail came from this little section of town that I lived in."

She began singing as a child and started her career with Joe Brown's Children's Radio Gang show in Norfolk when she was eleven, and later Smith sang with Norfolk bands as a teenager. She had gone to Brown's studio to watch a friend, Rae Robinson, audition for his show and Brown asked her if she could sing. She tried out by singing "White Lies and Red Roses" and was selected, but her girlfriend was not. Each week she would go to the radio studio and pay $1 to learn a new song. Her family was very poor and her mother took in laundry to earn enough money to pay for the weekly song lessons. Brown used four to eighteen year old children to sing not only on his radio programs in Richmond and Norfolk, but at military bases on the weekends throughout Virginia. Using the skills she learned through song lessons, Smith participated in the programs. Although she received no pay, she learned the valuable lessons of microphone technique essential to the entertainment business. As Smith grew older, she became the group's secretary and participated in World War II United States savings bond rallies by singing off the back of a truck in Norfolk with other children from Brown's troupe. Smith never received vocal lessons during this time or throughout her career.

Smith's performances with Brown's group led to vocal performances at the Naval Air Station in Norfolk with

Born Dorothy Jacqueline Keely on March 9, 1932, in Norfolk, VA; daughter of Howard Keely, a carpenter, and Fanny Keely (nee Stevens); youngest of three children; married Louis Prima on July 13, 1953, and divorced October 3, 1961; married Jimmy Bowen, a record producer in 1965; divorced; married Bobby Milano, a vocalist and musical entertainer, April 1974; children, from her marriage to Prima: Toni, born 1955, and Louanne, born 1957.

Joined Louis Prima's orchestra and later changed her name to Keely Smith, using both her original surname and that of her step-father, late-1940s; entertained United States armed forces personnel in Europe and Japan, early-1960s; remained in the Nevada and California areas for most of her career until she retired from Las Vegas nightclubs in 1998; continued her recording career and renewed her appearances in nightclubs around the United States, including appearances at the House of Blues in Los Angeles, Chicago, and New Orleans, 2000. Smith has received over 30 awards and has often donated her time to charitable causes including the American Cancer Society and the Cedars of Lebanon Hospital in Los Angeles.

Awards: Grammy Award, Best Performance by a Vocal Group, 1958; City of Hope Award-Los Angeles; Golden Record for *I Wish You Love,* 1957; Hollywood Walk of Fame Star, 1999.

Addresses: *Business*—Keely Smith, c/o Keely Smith Enterprises, 3434 Oneida Way, Las Vegas, NV 89109.

Saxie Dowell and his Naval Air Station band three and four nights a week with no pay. Dowell was the composer of the 1939 hit song "Three Little Fishes." She left Dowell and joined a local band leader, Earl Bennett, and was paid $5 a night, enabling her to pay for all of her school clothes, books, and other personal necessities. She stayed with Bennett for several years performing in nightclubs in the Norfolk area including the popular Surf Club. Her devoted mother accompanied her everywhere because she was underage.

Met Louis Prima

When Smith was 15 years old, she and her family went to New York City on vacation during the summer of 1947, a trip she never dreamed would influence her life forever. Her family decided to abandon their New York vacation and go to Atlantic City instead where the seashore weather might provide a more favorable respite. One night she took her younger brother Busta to the famous Steel Pier because they were "jitterbug nuts" and she wanted to see which orchestra was playing. She recalled, "There was this man named Louis Prima, who we had never heard of before. We had never heard a record, never heard anything by him. And we heard this music coming in as we walked up to the ballroom and I looked at my brother and said, 'My goodness, who is this man? This band is wonderful.' But when we got in there, it was unbelievable what was going on. Half the people were dancing and the other half were standing around the bandstand. I edged my way up to the stage and placed my little brother on the stage, and I stood there absolutely mesmerized watching this man. I just stood there dumbfounded. I had never seen anything like it before. Besides being one of the best bands to dance to, they were funny. The comedy was unbelievable."

When she returned to Norfolk, she went to the Surf Club and talked to the manager, Mr. Cain, about the band she had seen that was so terrific, and she encouraged him to bring the group to his club. The Surf Club was known for always bringing in the very top bands, but Cain had never heard of Prima and his orchestra. The following summer the Surf Club was jammed when Prima made his debut. "The audience couldn't believe how good they were, and not only that, they were very funny," she recalled. During one of his performances, Prima announced he was looking for a female vocalist for his band. Six members of Joe Brown's troupe auditioned, but Smith did not. Prima had brought his wife on the tour and she learned from Smith's brother, Piggy Keely, that he had a sister who could sing. When Prima learned from his wife that Smith could sing, she was pulled off the beach on a Sunday afternoon and asked to audition on the spur of the moment. She was wearing a bathing suit and had to borrow a blouse and a skirt for the audition. Barefoot, Smith sang "Sleepy Time Gal" and "Embraceable You" and was hired on the spot. Before that week was out in August of 1948, she was on the road with Prima and his orchestra touring the country.

Prima suggested Smith change her name to Dottie Mae Smith since her nickname was Dot and Smith was her stepfather's name. But she said, "Why don't you call me Keely Smith, because in those days everyone in school called everyone by their last name. They never called you Dot or Dottie, it was always Miss Keely."

She began singing with Prima at the Paramount Theater in New York City, the Steel Pier in Atlantic City, Asbury Park, New Jersey, and returned for gigs in Virginia Beach, Virginia, and anywhere cities called for big band music. In 1949 when Prima and Smith returned to Virginia Beach, the Prima led band, as part of their act, left the stage and marched into the Atlantic Ocean playing and singing as they walked into the waves. By 1952 she was performing at the El Rancho in Las Vegas but big bands were coming to an end and the Prima and Smith act was having difficulty finding work. By November of 1954 Prima and Smith were married and had found work in the Sahara Hotel lounge in Las Vegas after driving across country where they remained together until 1961.

In 1954 Prima and Smith formed a team which became a tremendous night club attraction in New York, Chicago, Hollywood, and especially Las Vegas. They developed a new style that dealt with a wide range of songs, from jazz to pop ballads, that brought them and the Prima orchestra to the height of popularity in the country. Besides Keely, the Prima entourage also featured Sam Butera and the Witnesses, a group that made many records which ranked high on the teen-age lists in the 1950s and 1960s. Prima had formed a band in 1934 called Louis Prima and his New Orleans Gang, and the group made a long series of records for Brunswick and Vocalion. Prima to some came across as a musical clown, but those who worked with him almost invariably respected him for his first-rate musicianship and his contagious spirit.

Her movie career included appearances in three motion picture films including the classic 1958 film *Thunder Road*, for which she sang the soundtrack. Robert Mitchum got a hit record out of the title tune. Others included "Senior Prom" in 1958 and "Hey Boy! Hey Girl!"I in 1959 with Louis Prima in which Smith and Prima wrote part of the score. Her music has appeared in such films as *The Deerhunter, Raging Bull, Analyze This, That Old Feeling,* and *Mad Dog and Glory.*

Signed with Capitol Records

Smith was signed to Capitol Records with her own recording contract in the mid 1950s. During her first recording sessions, Mr. Gilmore, the producer for Capitol Records, began to play songs for the purpose of providing selection possibilities for her first album. When he got to one song, he remarked that he was going to play a pretty French song, but that it didn't mean anything. When Gilmore finished playing, Smith remembers remarking to Prima, "I'll sing any eleven songs y'all want me to but you gotta let me sing "I Wish You Love." Gilmore believed that the song was not among Smith's best options, but Prima insisted, "If she wants to sing "I Wish You Love," then she's going to sing "I Wish You Love." It has become one of the most

beautiful love songs of all time and one of her signature songs. Written by the noted French composer and singer Charles Trenet in 1955 and called "Que Reste-til de Nos Amoursa," it was featured by New York City cabaret singer Felicia Sanders. The song was also made popular by Gloria Lynne's 1964 Everest recording, but it is Smith's rendition that has delighted listeners for decades.

One of Smith and Prima's greatest hits was Johnny Mercer and Harold Arlen's "That Old Black Magic." Although written in 1942 and a number one hit for the Modernaires, Prima and Smith revived it in 1958, making it another million dollar seller and a longtime favorite of the public. Mercer said, "That one came from one of the early Cole Porter songs I heard when I first came to New York. It was a song called "You Do Something to Me," and it had a phrase in it—'do do that voo-doo that you do so well.' That thing about voodoo must have stuck with me, because I paraphrased it in "Old Black Magic." It won a Grammy Award in 1958 for Best Vocal by a Group.

Another of Prima and Smith's biggest hits was "Just a Gigolo." It had been a popular Viennese song written in 1930 by Leonello Casucci and originally titled "Schoner Gigolo." It was first introduced in the United States by Broadway singer Irene Bordoni and was a successful recording by Vincent Lopez and his orchestra. It later appeared in the 1946 musical film *Lover Come Back* that starred Lucille Ball before the Prima-Smith blockbuster revival.

In January of 1961, Prima and Smith appeared at the District of Columbia National Guard Armory for a gala to help raise money to pay off the Democratic campaign debt along with some of America's top talent, including Frank Sinatra. They later appeared at the inaugural ball for newly-elected President John F. Kennedy. Later that year Prima and Smith's marriage ended in divorce and she went solo beginning in 1962. In 1963 Smith had a top 20 hit in the United Kingdom, "You're Breaking My Heart," that remained on the top 20 British charts for five weeks, as well as a charted album of Beatles' compositions. That same year she switched to the Reprise label, where Nelson Riddle was her musical director. In 1964, after she had gone solo, she traveled to Germany and Japan entertaining United States military personnel. Later, she also assisted the National Guard in recruiting campaigns. In 1975 Prima was operated on for a brain tumor and fell into a coma. He died in New Orleans in 1978.

For most of her career she has appeared in Las Vegas, Lake Tahoe, Reno, Nevada and Palm Springs, California, nightclubs and hotels including the Desert Inn, The Thunderbird, The Sands, The Sahara in Las Vegas, as well as at the Paramount Theater, Apollo Theater, and Copacabana in New York City. She was a regular at the prestigious Mocambo Club in Los Angeles for years and in Atlantic City, New Jersey, as well as at many other nightclubs and venues around the United States.

Notable Collaborations

Smith has recorded over 25 LP vinyl albums on the Capitol, Dot, Jasmine, Applause, Fantasy, Reprise, and PAUSA labels. She has also performed songs by such notable composers and lyricists as Johnny Mercer, Harold Arlen, Sammy Cahn, Ira Gershwin, Jimmy VanHeusen, Jule Styne, Jimmy McHugh, George Gershwin, Joe Young, Harry Warren, Richard Rodgers, Oscar Hammerstein II, Johnny Burke, Rube Bloom, Brooks Bowman, Hoagy Carmichael, Einar A. Swan, Ruth Lowe, and Bernice Petkere. In 1958 Frank Sinatra recorded his last commercial issued 78 RPM record, which was a duet with Smith entitled "Nothing in Common" on the Capitol label. She has also worked with George Greeley, Don Menza, Dennis Michael Zuvich, Nell Carter, Bud Shank, Bill Perkins, Dinah Shore, Billy Vaughn, H. B. Barnum, Frank Sinatra, Billy May, Nelson Riddle, Ernie Freeman, Brad Benedict, Bill Miller, Kurt Reher, Alex Murray, Murray Kellner, Arthur Herfurt, Fred Falensby, Victor Bay, Eleanor Slatkin, Joseph Saxon, William Hinshaw, Alton Hendrickson, Alex Beller, Vincent DeRosa, Gerald Dolin and Juan Tizol.

Her television credits include the *Ed Sullivan Show*, the *Andy Williams Show*, and the *Dean Martin Show*, as well as many other guest appearances. In 1999 she appeared on an A&E cable television network biography special about the "Rat Pack." In addition, she played the part of Julie in a summer stock production of Jerome Kern's *Showboat*. After she appeared on the *Johnny Carson Show* in New York singing "Little Girl Blue," composer Richard Rodgers was so impressed that he offered her the lead role in the London production of his 1962 hit musical *No Strings*. It was his first production after the death of his partner Oscar Hammerstein II, but she turned it down.

In recent times she has appeared at the House of Blues in Hollywood and Los Angeles accompanied by a 14-piece orchestra. She is currently working on her autobiography, and a new tribute CD entitled *Keely Sings Sinatra* is scheduled for release in 2000. She has made Las Vegas, Nevada, her home for many years.

Selected discography

Albums

Be My Love, Dot DLP 3241
Because You're Mine, Dot DLP 3415
Dearly Beloved, Dot DLP 3387
The Hits of Louis & Keely, Capitol SM 1531

I Wish You Love, Applause APCL 3325
I'm In Love Again, Fantasy F9639
The Intimate Keely Smith, Reprise RS 6132
Keely Christmas, Dot DLP 3345
Keely Smith-I Wish You Love, PAUSA PR 9052
The Lennon-McCartney Songbook, Reprise 6142
Little Girl Blue, Little Girl New, Reprise R9-6086
Louis & Keely, Dot DLP 25210
Louis Prima Digs Keely Smith, Coronet CXS-121
On Stage, Louis Prima & Keely Smith, Dot DLP 25266
Politely!, Capitol ST 1073
Return of the Wildest, Dot, DLP 3392
Swing You Lovers, Dot DLP 3265
Swingin' Pretty, Capitol T-1145
That Old Black Magic, Reprise 6175
Together, Dot DLP 25263
Twist with Keely Smith, Dot DLP 3423
What Kind of Fool Am I, Dot DLP 3461
The Wildest! Applause, APCL 3324

CDs

Be My Love, Jasmine JASCD 321
Because You're Mine, Jasmine JASCD 333
CheroKeely Swings, Jasmine JASCD 323
Dearly Beloved, Jasmine JASCD 328
The Hits of Louis & Keely, Capitol 91208
Keely Christmas, Jasmine JASCD 329
Live Guard Sessions 1963, Jazz Band EBCD 2109-2
Sinatra 80th, All the Best, Capitol 35952-2
Spotlight on Keely Smith, Capitol 80327
Swing, Swing, Swing, Concord 48822
Swing You Lovers, Jasmine JASCD 322
Twist/Doin' the Twist, Jasmine JASCD 334
What Kind of Fool Am I, Jasmine JASCD 324

Sources

Books

Feather, Leonard, *The Encyclopedia of Jazz*, Horizon Press, 1960.
Gammond, Peter, *The Oxford Companion to Popular Music*, Oxford University Press, 1993.
Kelley, Kitty, *His Way*, Bantam Books Inc., 1985.
Lax, Roger and Frederick Smith , *The Great Song Thesaurus,* Oxford University Press, 1989.
Lissauer, Robert, *Lissauer's Encyclopedia of Popular Music in America 1888 to the Present*, Paragon House, 1991.
Maltin, Leonard, *Movie and Video Guide 1995,* Penguin Books Ltd., 1994.
McAleer, Dave, *The All Music Book of Hit Singles From 1954 to the Present Day*, Miller Freeman Books, 1994.
Osborne, Jerry, *Rockin Records,* Osborne Publications, 1999.
Simon, George T., *The Big Bands,* Macmillan Company, 1967.
Simon, William L. , *Readers Digest Treasury of Best Loved Songs*, Reader's Digest General Books, 1991.
Stambler, Irwin, *Encyclopedia of Popular Music*, St. Martin's Press, 1966.
Wilk, Max, *They're Playing Our Song*, McClelland & Stewart Ltd., 1973.

Online

"Dorothy 'Keely' Smith," *All Music Guide*, http://www.allmusic .com/cg/x.dll (February 2000).

Greg Purcott Productions, http://www.gpproductions.com /acts/grant.htm (January 2000).

"Jumpin Jive, A Tribute to Louis Prima," http://www.geo cities.com/BourbonStreet/Square/2077/page1.html (June 30, 2000).

"Keely Smith, " *All Movie Guide*, http://www.allmovie.com (February 2000).

Universal Stuidos, http://www.mca.com (February 2000).

Additional information was obtained through interviews with Keely Smith on October 13, 1999, and February 9, 2000.

—Francis D. McKinley

Hank Snow

Country singer

One of country music's biggest stars with over 70 million records sold, Hank Snow was a classic entertainer. A yodeling crooner from humble beginnings, he followed his own adolescent wanderlust and went to sea at the age of 12, during which time he developed the outlook and persona of a traditional rambling troubadour. Subsequently he learned to play the guitar and developed a following among his co-workers on the ships and docks of the North Atlantic. As a popular recording artist for RCA Victor in the 1930s, and later as a member of Nashville, Tennessee's Grand Ole Opry, Snow penned much of his own repertoire and endeared himself to listeners around the world. His upbeat songs depicted a romantic image of the lifestyle of a free and rambling spirit.

Some of Snow's classic compositions include his signature song, "I'm Moving On," and his 1962 hit song, "I've Been Everywhere." As Snow's talent matured he mastered the art of strumming ballads in addition to his natural affinity for writing and singing songs of the road. Likewise he was adept at performing rousting renditions of fast-paced rhumbas. During the 1950s, as a partner in a musical promotion partnership with Colonel Tom Parker, Snow was instrumental in bringing a then-unknown guitar picker named Elvis Presley from Mississippi to the stage of the Grand Ole Opry. Additionally, Snow was honored with numerous professional awards throughout his career, and in 1976 he established the Hank Snow Foundation for the Prevention of Child Abuse, a cause that he held dear throughout his life. *All Music Guide* said that Snow was a "country traditionalist who gave much more to the business than he took."

Snow was born Clarence Eugene Snow on May 9, 1914 in Queens County, Nova Scotia, Canada, in the small town of Brooklyn. As a child he went by the nickname of Jack, and he adopted the name of "Hank Snow" for theatrical purposes when he embarked on his career as a country music performer. His parents, George Lewis and Marie Alice (Boutlier) Snow were industrious but poor. George Snow worked in the mills around Nova Scotia and led hunting expeditions during moose season. Both occupations kept him away from his family for extended periods of time. Snow's mother was a homemaker, seamstress, and part-time entertainer who sacrificed a full-blown performance career in order to devote herself to raising her four children: Lillian Mae, Nina Elizabeth, "Jack," and Marion Victoria. Hank Snow inherited his musical inclinations from both of his parents—his mother habitually sang and played the organ, and his father also loved to sing.

Snow's parents divorced when he was eight years old. As the family split apart, the Snow siblings dispersed. His sisters went into foster care while Snow went to live with his grandmother. Snow's grandmother was a stern and humorless women, and Snow persistently defied her discipline. After four years his mother remarried and Snow was returned to her custody, only to discover that his new stepfather was a cruel and brutal man. Snow's new father despised his young stepson and displayed his displeasure overtly. As a result, Snow left home at age 12 and took a job as a cabin boy, working on the various fishing ships that left from the coast of Canada.

As a cabin boy, he lived in poverty and frequented the less affluent areas of the town. During those years he turned to singing as a means of expression as well as for recreation. On the ships he readily entertained during non-working hours, and his co-workers proved to be a receptive audience. When he was 16 years old, his mother gave him a guitar that she purchased through a mail-order distributor, and Snow was enamored with the instrument. As the circumstances of his life brought him through a series of odd jobs, both on and off the docks, he sang continually, played his guitar, and decided ultimately to become a singer, in the fashion of his boyhood idol, Jimmie Rodgers. Snow moved to Halifax in 1933 where he auditioned for a job with radio station CHNS. He was hired and immediately started singing on the radio that same day. He was heard on a weekly program called *Down on the Farm*, and the radio station promoted the new singer under the nickname of the Blue Yodeler: Clarence Snow and His Guitar. One of the announcers on the radio station helped Clarence Snow come up with his

stage name of Hank Snow, which reflected Snow's country music image more appropriately.

Snow performed for CHNS for three years, and initially he sang uncompensated, but he began singing professionally soon afterward. When the network took over Snow's radio show, the promoters billed Snow as "Hank, the Yodeling Ranger" and placed him on the payroll. Snow's name recognition increased further when he began to perform regularly on the *Canadian Farm Hour*. For that show he brought together a group of musicians called the Rainbow Ranch Boys. Snow then billed himself as the Singing Ranger, which led to a recording contract with RCA Victor in Montreal, Quebec, in 1936. Among his earliest recordings were his own compositions, including "The Prisoned Cowboy," and "Lonesome Blue Yodel."

Snow pursued stardom in the United States throughout the remainder of the 1930s and into the 1940s. In 1949 he signed to perform on "The Big D Jamboree" out of Dallas, Texas. As a result of that contact he made the acquaintance of a well-established country singer, the late Ernest Tubb. Tubb in turn introduced Snow to the Grand Ole Opry circuit. As Snow's popularity escalated in the United States, RCA moved to release his records outside of Canada in 1949. His first American single, released that same year, was called "Marriage Vow," and RCA marked the release by sending Snow on his first tour of the United States to promote the record. The recording received a mediocre reception and failed to bring Snow to stardom. Likewise his Grand Ole Opry debut in January of 1950 was less than spectacular. Snow, who by then was married and the father of a child, considered leaving the United States and returning to Canada.

Suddenly in July of 1950, one of Snow's recordings, "I'm Moving On" caught the ear of the record-buying public; the song held the number one position on the record charts for 21 weeks. Snow's follow-up release, "The Golden Rocket," went to number one also, as did "The Rhumba Boogie," which was released the following year. All together Snow logged 24 top ten hits between 1951-55, including "I Don't Hurt Anymore," which in 1954 held fast at the top of the record charts, spending 20 weeks in the number one position. As the appeal of Snow's country ballads and traveling songs gained him an increasing number of fans, he recorded some rockabilly tunes including, "Hula Rock" and "Rockin', Rollin' Ocean." The records failed and Snow focused on writing and performing pure country music thereafter.

During his years of budding fame, the story of an early and serendipitous professional relationship with the rock and roll phenomenon Elvis Presley became a favorite sidenote of Snow's. As a new recording star in the early 1950s, Snow shared his manager, Colonel Tom Parker, with Presley; and in 1954 Snow tested his own entrepreneurial skills and joined with Parker as a booking agent. In later years, Snow recalled proudly that it was in part through his personal intercession for Presley that the young rock and roll star eventually performed on the stage of the Grand Ole Opry, and although Presley failed to impress Opry members, he moved on to other music realms and took the world by storm.

Snow's personal career continued on a rising star throughout the 1960s. He recorded new music, performed, and produced chart-topping songs until 1974. In that year, at the age of 60, Snow released the final number one hit song of his career, a tune called, "Hello Love." With that tune he achieved the distinction of being the oldest singer to release a number one hit song. He continued to perform at the Grand Ole Opry in Nashville into the 1990s.

Snow's career spanned over six decades, and during those years he recorded more than 2,000 songs, including ten top-selling records. He released more than 80 albums and was recorded in 30 languages. Robert Hilburn of the *Los Angeles Times* said that Snow's singing "has a winning and distinctive edge, thanks chiefly to his immaculate enunciation. His up-beat hits are generally characterized by catchy, galloping rhythms." Snow's most memorable performances, according to his own recollection, were overseas program venues where he performed for United States troops worldwide.

Hank Snow married Minne Aaiders on September 2, 1935, during his years as a struggling radio singer. Their son, Jimmie Rodgers Snow, was born in 1936. In 1958 the Canadian singer adopted United States citizenship. Throughout his lifetime, certain lingering memories of childhood remained unresolved in his mind, and in 1976 he founded the Hank Snow International Foundation for Prevention of Child Abuse and Neglect of Children Inc. Thereafter Snow devoted much of his time to furthering that cause.

Hank Snow died of suspected heart failure at his Rainbow Ranch in Madison, Tennessee, on December 20, 1999. Selected pieces of the flamboyant cowboy attire that he routinely wore are enshrined along with his yellow 1947 Cadillac at the Hank Snow Country Music Centre near his home.

Selected discography

Singles

"The Prisoned Cowboy," 1939.
"Lonesome Blue Yodel," 1939.
"Marriage Vow," 1949.
"Brand on My Heart," 1949.
"I'm Moving On," 1950.
"The Golden Rocket," 1951.
"Rhumba Boogie," 1951.
"A Fool Such as I," 1952.
"I Don't Hurt Anymore," 1954.
"Big Wheels," 1958.

"Miller's Cave," 1960.
"Beggar to a King," 1961.
"I've Been Everywhere," 1962.
"Ninety Miles an Hour," 1963.
"Hello, Love," RCA, 1974.

Albums

Hank Snow Sings, RCA Victor, 1952
Just Keep A-Movin', RCA Victor, 1955
Hank Snow's Country Guitar, RCA Victor, 1957.
When Tragedy Struck, RCA Victor, 1958
Singing Ranger, RCA Camden, 1959.
Hank Snow Sings Jimmie Rodgers Songs, RCA, 1960.
The Southern Cannonball, Camden, 1961.
I've Been Everywhere, RCA Victor, 1963.
The Last Ride, Camden, 1963.
Old and Great Songs by Hank Snow, Camden, 1964.
Heartbreak Trail, RCA Victor, 1965.
This is My Story, RCA Victor, 1966.
Travelin' Blues, Camden, 1966.
The Best of Hank Snow, RCA Victor, 1966.
Tales of the Yukon, RCA Victor, 1968.
Cure for the Blues, RCA Victor, 1970.
In Memory of Jimmie Rodgers, RCA Victor, 1970.
Tracks and Trains, RCA Victor, 1971.
The Jimmie Rodgers Story, RCA Victor, 1972.
The Best of Hank Snow, Vol. 2, RCA Victor, 1972.
I'm Moving On, Pair, 1974.
Living Legend, RCA Victor, 1978.
Lovingly Yours, RCA, 1980.
The Singing Ranger: 1949-1953, Bear Family, 1989.
The Singing Ranger, Vol. 2, Bear Family, 1990.
Snow Country, RCA Victor, 1992.
The Singing Ranger, Vol. 3, Bear Family, 1994.
Yodelling Ranger (1936-1947), Bear Family, 1994.
The Essential Hank Snow, RCA Victor, 1997.
Yodelling Ranger: Young Hank Snow 1936-1943, Bear Family, 1999.

Sources

Books

Snow, Hank, *The Hank Snow Story,* University of Illinois Press, Urbana, 1994.

Periodicals

Billboard, January 8, 2000, p. 8.
Los Angeles Times, July 11, 1997, p. F-21, December 21, 1999, p. 46.
Washington Post, December 21, 1999, p. B-6.

Online

"Artist – Hank Snow," http://www.country.com/gen/music/artist/hank-snow.html (April 28, 2000).
"Hank Snow," *AMG All Music Guide,* http://allmusic.com (April 28, 2000).
"Hank Snow," Nashville Songwriters Hall of Fame website, http://vhost.telalink.net/~nsf/frame-hof.htl (June 23, 2000).

—Gloria Cooksey

Spacehog

Glam-rock band

Hiding behind faux-fur coats, brightly-colored nail polish, and dark retro shades, Spacehog adopted a truly cavalier outlook that allowed them to survive in spite of personal and professional frustrations. A band accustomed to shrugging off misfortune, the band's members endured working-class upbringings, sexual abuse, and snide remarks by critics to rein in mainstream audiences with their flamboyant, glam-rock style and spacey, distant, and subtly humorous music. Spacehog's 1995 debut album, *Resident Alien,* which contained the hit single "In the Meantime," earned gold status, while their follow-up, *The Chinese Album,* won rave reviews. All this success from a group whose members fled their hometown of Leeds in Yorkshire, England, to settle in New York City's East Village, a haven for the pretentious and unaffected.

Spacehog, who realize that they don't fit in with other 1990s rock acts, go out of their way to look and act different, taking on the outrageous mannerisms of their heroes from the 1970s. "The most important thing is not to take yourself too seriously," guitarist/vocalist Antony Langdon said to Jon Wiederhorn in *Rolling Stone,* explaining the group's eccentricities. "To me, *Spinal Tap* was the greatest truth. It was like a hand-

Photograph by Joe Giron. Corbis. Reproduced by permission.©

For The Record . . .

Members include Leeds, Yorkshire, England natives **Jonny Cragg,** drums; brothers **Antony Langdon,** guitar, vocals, and **Royston Langdon,** lead vocals, bass guitar; **Richard Steel,** lead guitar.

Formed band in New York City in 1994; signed with Sire Records, released debut album *Resident Alien,* 1995; toured with the Red Hot Chili Peppers, 1996; released *The Chinese Album,* 1998.

Addresses: *Record company*—Sire Records, 936 Broadway, 5th Floor, New York City, NY 10010, phone: (212) 253-3900, fax: (212) 253-2950.

book for being in a rock band. I think that we all admired those big, dramatic bands in the '70s, and I think one of the vital things that all the great ones had in common was a highly developed, sardonic sense of humor." However, "We're very serious about our music. But at the same time it's insane not to have a good time with it. We are certainly not like a lot of what's happening out there today," lead vocalist and bassist Royston Langdon, Antony's brother, noted for the Spacehog Site. "We sort of exploded with our own kind of hostile style."

Royston, a confident singer/songwriter with a crisp, theatrical vocal style, and Antony Langdon were born and raised in Leeds, where they went through tough times beginning at a very young age. Their negative experience began in the early-1970s, after they joined the choir of their local church. "The slogan of the church was 'We will live a godly and sober life,'" recalled Antony to Wiederhorn. "And meanwhile, some of the masters of music and their assistants and priests were either banging each other or banging the choirboys…. At the time, none of it seemed at all traumatic, but I think I struggled through my late teenage years and early 20s coming to terms with what it all meant. Suddenly I didn't want to be a part of Leeds and what Leeds was all about—going to football matches and all that—but I wasn't gay either. I was just a bit confused for a while. I still am, really."

After moving from Leeds to New York City, Antony by chance met a fellow Leeds native, drummer Jonny Cragg, who was working at an East Village café. Cragg recalled fondly the day the two met for the first time in March of 1994. "I was working at an espresso bar killing rats in the basement," he said for the Spacehog Site. "Ant came in, I never met him before, but I recognized the Leeds accent and thought it was worth a cup of tea." Soon after their initial meeting, the two British expatriates started jamming together, and before long, Antony had recruited his brother Royston and lead guitarist Richard Steel, both of whom were still living in Leeds, to move to New York to play in the band. They originally called themselves Grass, but later changed their name to Spacehog when the band Supergrass made their breakthrough in Great Britain.

With the Spacehog lineup complete, the foursome began to develop their sound, noted for its swank and melodic vocals, as well as an overall feel that lies somewhere between grunge-rock and bubblegum pop. Spacehog also picked up a flashy wardrobe and developed a pretentious stage presence, then cultivated their reputation in the fertile East Village music scene, where they became instant local favorites. Despite their later acceptance back in Britain and Europe, Spacehog always felt most comfortable in their adopted city. "We went back to England this summer [to support the debut album] and got a very healthy feeling, but New York is a lot better scene than most people realize," said Antony Langdon, as quoted by the Spacehog Site. "In New York, people can tell a good song and they let you know it."

One year after joining forces in New York, Spacehog, in early-1995, signed a deal with Sire Records and entered the studio to record an album. Proving their musical and commercial capabilities, Spacehog's 1995 debut entitled *Resident Alien* went certified gold soon after it hit store shelves. "An engrossing album," wrote Liv Cecilia in *Rock: The Rough Guide,* "veering between energetic romp and slow emotional ballads, *Resident Alien* created a trippy ambience of infectiously happy, psychedelic guitar riffs, compelling vocals and perceptive lyrics." Obviously influenced by David Bowie and Queen, two of the group's most prominent inspirations, critics also drew comparisons to the Beatles, the Kinks, the Rolling Stones, and the Velvet Underground, though some complained that Spacehog relied too heavily upon their predecessors.

"We've grown up in a world that's saturated with music," said Antony Langdon to Wiederhorn, explaining the record's similarities to the above-mentioned 1970s acts. "It's all around you, and it's all influential. Bowie would never have recorded *Resident Alien* any day of the week. It's just not an accurate comparison." Steel further added, "This is only our first album. You can't look at one picture and think that says it all."

Regardless of the negative criticism, Spacehog, infamous for their interview demeanor, wild clothes, and on-stage antics, became media darlings. The band's hit single from their debut, "In the Meantime" became a rock and roll hit in both the United States and Britain, and Spacehog subsequently gave their first concert back home at London's Paramount City club. Upon their return to America, Spacehog saw their debut top the *Billboard* Heatseekers chart, leading the group to sell out venues such as New York's Irving Plaza. Then, Spacehog set out as the supporting act for the Red Hot Chili Peppers in the spring of 1996.

In 1998, Spacehog returned with their sophomore effort, *The Chinese Album.* Although it failed to sell as well as their first album, *The Chinese Album,* which displayed the group's musical growth and maturity, earned critical support. Cecilia, for example, described the work as "A beautifully crafted masterpiece, intelligent, edgy and eclectic." With their second offering, Spacehog maintained a 1970s feel, but also built in elements of jazz, blues, rockabilly, reggae, vaudeville, and even a touch of opera, resulting in a more original sound all their own. *The Chinese Album* also featured guest vocalists such as David Byrne, Brian Eno, and R.E.M.'s Michael Stipe, who sang the lead on "Almond Kisses."

Also that year, Antony Langdon appeared in the Todd Haynes film *The Velvet Goldmine.* The Langdon brothers were also known for their relationships with high-profile women; Royston dates actress Liv Tyler, while Antony is linked with super model Kate Moss.

Selected discography

Resident Alien, includes "In the Meantime," Sire, 1995.
The Chinese Album, Sire, 1998.

Sources

Books

Buckley, Jonathan and others, editors, *Rock: The Rough Guide,* Rough Guides Ltd., 1999.

Periodicals

Billboard, February 24, 1996.
Guitar Player, June 1996.
Los Angeles Times, April 18, 1996; March 16, 1998.
Melody Maker, December 20-27, 1997; February 7, 1998; May 2, 1998.
Rolling Stone, May 16, 1996.
Spin, February 2000, p. 36.

Online

Sonicnet.com, http://www.sonicnet.com (June 4, 2000).
The Spacehog Site, http://www.spacehog.simplenet.com (June 4, 2000).

—Laura Hightower

Steely Dan

Rock duo

As the split personality of rock and roll, duo Steely Dan defied classification. With the help of studio musicians and assorted others, the two released a modest one dozen albums over a 30-year period from 1970-2000. The nebulous recording group is anchored solidly by the independent song-writing pair of Walter Becker on melodies and Donald Fagen on lyrics. Yet the mystique of Steely Dan persists in that vocalist Fagen rarely took the microphone; likewise Becker, an accomplished guitarist, was heard rarely on tape.

Individually, Becker and Fagen grew up not too far apart, Fagen hailed from Passaic, New Jersey, and Becker from New York City. The two came together over their mutual love of music, and the relationship congealed over time and became firmly cemented by their equally mutual dislike for performance. They collaborated intensely for approximately one decade before moving their separate ways, only to reunite in the mid-1990s and resume their musical relationship, seemingly without missing a beat.

Fagen, the son of an accountant and a former cabaret singer was born on January 10, 1948. He took guitar lessons briefly at age seven, on a rented guitar that

Photograph by Lynn Goldsmith, Corbis. Reproduced by permission©

was in grave disrepair. At age 11 he became enamored by jazz while he was simultaneously engrossed in learning to play an old piano, that his parents had purchased. He became virtually obsessed with the piano as he had been with music all along, and often played into the night, taking respites only to listen to jazz radio. Despite his fixation with music, he refused to take formal piano lessons. He was annoyed by the structured environment of formal training, and learned instead to play by ear. Outside of music and a casual interest in stamp collecting Fagen's interests were limited. He was quiet overall and very introverted as a child.

A brief foray into Little League ended abruptly when he became aware of the political machinery that controlled the sport; his membership in the Boy Scouts was equally short-lived because he developed a severe allergy to poison plants. Instead he spent his summers swimming in the family pool and reading books. As he entered adolescence, his obsession with music lured him into weekend outings in New York City where he gravitated to the shows at the Village Vanguard. As his visits to the Vanguard increased in regularity, he developed friendships among the club staff members and even, on occasion, with the musicians. In his enthusi-

asm at the Vanguard he sometimes lost track of the time on those boyhood excursions. On more than one occasion, having missed the last bus, he found himself stranded at the bus station where he slept contentedly on a bench until the early bus arrived the following morning.

In 1965 Fagan moved to Annandale-on-Hudson in upstate New York where he attended Bard College, initially with plans to major in the theatre arts. He soon abandoned that goal, realizing that he disliked the intrinsically exhibitionist nature of the discipline. Instead he turned to the local music scene for amusement. In 1966 he met Walter Becker, and it seemed to Becker that Fagen was a member of virtually every local band on the campus of Bard.

Becker, whose German father was in the business of importing heavy machinery from Europe, was born on February 20, 1950, and was the product of a broken home. He was raised mostly by his father and grandmother, living alternately in Queens and in Scarsdale, and back in Queens. Becker was only 16 when his father died suddenly from a heart problem while away from home on a business trip. Becker, who was very close with his father, took the loss very hard.

Shortly before his father's death, when Becker was 14, he began to learn blues guitar from a neighborhood friend. Becker went on to Bard College in 1966 where he met Fagen and a friendship gelled. Becker and Fagen bonded readily, given their mutual fascination with music and extreme affinity for jazz and blues styles. The friendship solidified as they played together in amateur bands. They also spent time writing their own music. Becker, who completed his studies under an accelerated program, finished his curriculum before Fagen, who had started one year earlier, and by 1969 both musicians had completed college. Afterward the pair moved into a Brooklyn apartment, where they began writing songs in earnest.

Eventually they secured a position writing material for a 1960s rock band called Jay and the Americans (JATA). The creative efforts of Becker and Fagen resulted in few compositions of note during those early years, although they penned one song in particular, "I Mean to Shine," that attracted some attention from Barbra Streisand. She included the song on one of her albums, and thus brought a modicum of legitimacy to the two songwriters. As for their background work with JATA, they were eventually hired as performing musicians with the band. The future Steely Dan cohorts learned quickly however that they were essentially expendable to the group, and they found themselves discarded as quickly as they were hired. It was their unique and independent approach to music that created a wedge between JATA—which subscribed to the formula-based musical contingency that governed 1960s rock and roll—and the rebellious inclinations of Becker and

Fagen. Some of Becker and Fagen's nascent songwriting efforts, written mostly during their JATA years, were later released on compact disc as retrospectives called *Android Warehouse* and *Becker and Fagen, the Early Years.*

The duo next joined a band led by Denny Dias. Dias had advertised for band members in the *Village Voice,* and he, like Fagen and Becker, was a musical nonconformist in the pending tradition of Steely Dan. The Dias band rarely performed, yet they collaborated incessantly, wrote songs, developed styles, and practiced new sounds.

Becker and Fagen moved to Los Angeles, California, in 1972 at the urging of producer Gary Katz of ABC Records. Katz hired the pair to perform studio rewrites and to create song arrangements. As always, Becker and Fagen spent their free time developing their own original creations. Soon Dias joined them in California, and once again the three musicians fused. They added new band members and performed in quartet, although performances were not the focus of their efforts. After the release of their first album—with guitarists Jeff Baxter and Denny Dias, Jim Hodder on drums, and David Palmer on vocals—the group went on tour, only under pressure from their record producer, ABC, which insisted that they tour to promote the new record.

They performed with big-name stars including Frank Zappa, the Beach Boys, and Chuck Berry, but always as the opening act and never as a headline attraction. Becker and Fagen in particular disliked the tour circuit because it was demanding, exhausting, and usurped precious time from their writing interests. Their fellow band members, in contrast, embraced performance and eventually became anxious and unsettled in the shadow of Becker and Fagen's reticence. Ultimately the Steely Dan members disbanded, leaving only Becker and Fagen, and on occasion Dias, to guide the group through its evolutionary journey.

All together between 1972-80, Steely Dan released seven albums; each displayed a high degree of professionalism and polished performances on every track. The group earned respect among aficionados of every musical taste, both for the intellectual lyrics of their tunes and for the intriguing post-boogie rhythm styles. By the release of their third album, a recording called *Pretzel Logic,* Becker and Fagen had settled into a pattern of working primarily as a production duo and hiring studio musicians to perform on the recordings, a situation that suited the taste of the Steely Dan duo conveniently. The lack of a formal assemblage of musicians precluded the possibility of persistent touring, and Becker and Fagen were gratified. Each on occasion contributed guitar or vocals to the Steely Dan records, but only on an as-needed basis whenever the studio band sound failed to meet with expectations. Indeed on the 1975 release, *Katy Lied,* neither Becker

nor Fagen contributed a single note to the final tape. Steely Dan's 1978 album, *Aja,* was the first of the group's albums to break into a top five position on the music charts. The memorable recording featured performances by some of the jazz world's well-honed artists, including Wayne Shorter, Victor Feldman, Bernard Purdie, and Lee Ritenour; it sold over one million copies.

In 1980 Steely Dan released what would be its final album for over a decade. Unaffected by the success, Becker and Fagen went each their separate ways, and the unique jazz/rock band ceased to exist for over a decade. As Steely Dan dissolved into temporary retirement, the duo left a legacy as a precursor to rock and roll classicists such as Sade and Sting. Their final recording, *Gaucho,* marked the end of their ongoing contract with ABC Records (MCA by that time) and earned a slot among the top 20.

As *Gaucho* went into the editing stages, a series of tragedies beset Walter Becker, beginning with the suicide of his girlfriend and followed by a debilitating car accident that left him with a substance dependency. Fagen, as a result, single-handedly prepared *Gaucho* for release, then undertook a series of musical projects on his own. He recorded a well-received solo album, called *Nightfly,* and then wrote an off-Broadway score called *Gospel at Colonus.* He also wrote movie soundtracks and contributed articles to *Premiere.* Becker, who abandoned virtually all vestiges of his musical career, moved to Hawaii to recuperate. He was married for a time while in Hawaii and has two children, a son named Kawai and a daughter named Sa. In 1994 he released a solo vocal recording, *11 Tracks of Whack,* including a track dedicated to his son, called "Little Kawai."

Fagen eventually married singer and songwriter Libby Titus, also a Bard College alumnus, and together the couple collaborated and produced their own musical review. In the early 1990s Fagen and Titus successfully lured Becker from his self-imposed seclusion and back to New York City and into the studio where he assisted in the production of Fagen's 1992 album, *Kamakiriad.* The reunited Steely Dan members recommenced their collaboration, and Becker and Fagen became cognizant that Steely Dan might have taken an hiatus, but the spirit never died. In 1993 and 1994, the pair toured with a backup band as the Citizen Steely Dan Orchestra, and in 2000 they released a comeback album, *Two Against Nature,* filled with classic Steely Dan nonconformity. *Rolling Stone*'s David Wild said of the Giant Records release, "As always in Steely Dan's ... world, we often don't know what ... people in the songs are actually doing, but we're pretty damn certain that they shouldn't be doing it at all."

Wild went on to christen Becker a "reluctant guitar god" and likewise praised Fagen, along with the studio musicians including session drummer Vinnie Caliuto, Rickey Lawson, and Sonny Emory. Longtime Steely Dan cohort Dias said of the pair that, "Walter and Donald are one person with two brains;" Dias was quoted by Alec Wilkinson, who went on to characterize Fagen as, "[A] cross between Abraham Lincoln and Al Capone." Descriptively, critics concur that the two are highly intelligent perfectionists—an impressive tribute to a duo that named itself after a literary illusion to a dildo.

Selected discography

Singles

"Do It Again," ABC, 1972.
"Reelin' in the Years," ABC, 1972.
"Rikki Don't Lose That Number," ABC, 1974.
"Peg."
"Hey Nineteen."

Albums

Can't Buy a Thrill, ABC, October 1972.
Countdown to Ecstasy, ABC, July 1973.
Pretzel Logic, (includes "Rikki Don't Lose That Number) ABC, 1974.
Katy Lied, ABC, 1975.
The Royal Scam, ABC, 1976.

Aja, ABC, 1977.
Greatest Hits, ABC, 1978.
Gaucho, MCA, 1980.
Two Against Nature, Giant Records, 2000.

Solo releases

Nightfly (Fagen), 1982.
Kamakiriad (Fagen), 1993.
11 Tracks of Whack (Becker), 1994.

Sources

Books

Contemporary Musicians, volume 5, Gale Research, 1991.

Periodicals

Rolling Stone, March 16, 2000, p. 72; March 30, 2000, pp. 33-38.

Online

"The History of Steely Dan," *FAQ,* http://www.steelydan .com/faq.html (May 29, 2000).

—*Gloria Cooksey*

Stereophonics

Rock band

With their melodic tunes and laid-back lyrics that relate to everyday life, the Stereophonics—a trio consisting of vocalist/guitarist Kelly Jones, bass guitarist Richard Jones (of no relation to Kelly), and drummer Stuart Cable—are considered one of the best rock bands to emerge from Wales. "Here is a great rock band that plays moody, passionate songs with literate lyrics and melodies that linger in your head," declared *Washington Post* contributor Alona Wartofsky. Much of the band's appeal can be attributed to front man Kelly Jones, who sings in a soulful, raspy style reminiscent of Rod Stewart and pens lyrics that consist of vivid observations about life in a working-class small town, exploring subjects matters like life's inevitable disappointments, infidelity, gossip, intrigue, and murder. Although the Stereophonics place their songs within a rural setting, the trio's musings are equally applicable to the big city. Because of this universality, as well as anthemic choruses that hold each song together, the Stereophonics, beginning in the late-1990s, were able to become one of Great Britains most highly touted rock acts in just a few years time.

Despite the release of two critically acclaimed, platinum-selling albums, the Stereophonics remained

For The Record . . .

Members include **Stuart Cable**, drums; **Kelly Jones**, vocals, guitar; **Richard Jones** (of no relation to Kelly), bass guitar; All were born in Cwmaman, near Aberdare, South Wales.

Formed band in 1992 in Cwmaman as the Tragic Love Company, 1992; changed name to the Stereophonics, 1996; released debut album *Word Gets Around*, 1997; released *Performance and Cocktails*, 1998 in the U.K. and 1999 in the U.S.

Awards: Brit Award for "Best Newcomer," 1998.

Addresses: *Record company*—V2 Records, 14 E. 4th St., New York City, NY 10012, phone: (212) 320-8500, fax: (212) 320-8600, website: http://www. V2music.com. *Management*—Stereophonics Ltd., P.O. Box 5594, Thatcham, Berkshire, England RG18 9YH, phone: (+44 outside U.K.) (01635) 862200, fax: (+44 outside U.K.) (01635) 866449. *Website*—Stereophonics Official Website: http://www. stereophonics .co.uk.

less popular in the United States. And while their shows regularly sold out during American tours, radio stations virtually ignored the band's music, preventing the Stereophonics, like a lot of other British acts, from building a sizable audience. Even super groups such as Oasis and Blur received limited airplay across the Atlantic. "When I first came here three or four years ago," Kelly recalled to Wartofsky, "it was all Pearl Jam, Black Crowes—bands which we were all into—on the radio, so I thought we had a fair chance of getting a decent break. But now all that's kinda changed. At the moment, radio stations are playing a lot of crap. It's either stuff like Limp Bizkit or the Backstreet Boys... No decent songs, in my opinion. It's all for 15-year-olds."

Moreover, without the backing of radio or MTV, most bands find it nearly impossible, not to mention frustrating, to achieve a breakthrough. "It bothers you that you don't get played when you think you're a better band than people who are getting played," the songwriter admitted. "But that's the way of the world. It's always the tacky [expletive] that gets known. It takes longer for something which is a bit more creative to get through. Because it's less obvious, and you got to think about it a bit more."

The members of the Stereophonic all hail from the little village of Cwmaman, near Aberdare, South Wales. Although the trio officially started writing and performing music together in 1992, the history of the band stretches way back. Kelly Jones, Richard Jones, and Stuart Cable, a few years older than his bandmates, have known each other since their infancy and started honing their musical skills in their teens, rehearsing in Cable's bedroom before landing their first local gigs. Cable and Kelly Jones grew up just eight doors down from one another, while Richard Jones lived on the other side of town. "About 1,000 people live there," noted Kelly Jones to Wartofsky about the band's hometown. "Probably about 10 people out of those thousand had guitar, so you're probably gonna bump into those other people. We'd all be at each other's houses and playing tennis rackets, thinking we were Angus Young."

The trio's earliest musical inspirations arose out of their older brothers' record collections, from which they took in the sounds of Creedence Clearwater Revival, the Kinks, Led Zeppelin, AC/DC, the Sex Pistols, the Beatles, Madness, the Specials, Stevie Wonder, Neil Young, Otis Redding, Tony Bennett, and Bob Dylan, among others. Kelly Jones, a former market trader, boxer, and budding scriptwriter, came from a musical family and naturally gravitated toward singing and playing guitar. His pal Cable, who worked on a building site and delivered school dinners before the band took flight, had participated in other local bands, while Richard Jones, a self-described pragmatist and former scaffolder, coalman, and electrician, decided to take up the bass because everyone else had guitars.

After a few years lugging their equipment to London and back under the moniker Tragic Love Company, the trio in the summer of 1996 changed their name to the Stereophonics—taken from the brand name of Cable's grandmother's gramophone—and began playing more and more dates. Soon thereafter, they received numerous offers from record labels, eventually opting to become the first band signed to Richard Branson's V2 label in August of that year. Reportedly, the Stereophonics had been courted by every major label in the United Kingdom, including all five owned by EMI Records, who normally do not compete against one another.

The Stereophonics released their first record, the double A-sided, limited edition single "Looks Like Chaplin/More Life in a Tramps Vest," in November of 1996, coinciding with supporting slots with the Manic Street Preachers, Skunk Anansie, Ocean Colour Scene, and the Who. Two months later in January of 1997, the trio played to a crowd of 250,000 at the Hogmany Festival in Edinburgh, Scotland. March of that year saw the release of a second single, "Local Boy in the Photograph," which reached number 51 on the British charts, and the start of their first headlining national tour. A third single, the previously recorded "More Life in a Tramps Vest," appeared again in May and rose to the number 33 position in the British top 40. Later that month, the Stereophonics, regarded as one of the hardest-working British bands for their busy touring schedule, played to sell-out audiences at the Hillsborough Benefit Concert, Anfield, Liverpool, and the Big Noise Festival in Cardiff Bay, followed in June with shows in Scandanavia, and in July with a performance at the Belfort Festival in France.

August of 1997 saw the release of a fourth single entitled "A Thousand Trees," which peaked at number 22, as well as the release of the Stereophonics' debut album, *Word Gets Around,* which entered the British charts at number six. "Stridently self-confident fare from a band unlikely to be one-album wonders," wrote Justin Lewis, describing the album for *Rock: The Rough Guide,* "this boasts hard-edged rock music, shot through with Kelly Jones's sense of lyrical black comedy." In support of their debut, the Stereophonics played some more festivals and made their first appearance on *Top of the Pops.* Then in September, the trio toured Europe before coming to the United States for a promotional visit. When they returned home in October, the Stereophonics toured the United Kingdom again to sell-out crowds, then toured Europe again and returned to the United States the following month. In 1997 alone, the Stereophonic played more than 100 gigs.

The band continued to tour extensively the following year, and in February of 1998, the Stereophonics were rewarded for all their hard work with a "Best Newcomer" award at the Brit Awards. But the honor didn't slow down the Stereophonics, who took on more dates in France, Holland, Belgium, the United States, Australia, New Zealand, and Great Britain. In the midst of all this activity, in April of 1998 the trio entered RealWorld Studios in Bath to begin recording a follow-up album. And after a string of summer music festival appearances, the Stereophonics in August made their first trip to Japan, followed by another national tour of Britain and a visit to Thailand to shoot a video for the song "Bartender and the Thief" in October of that year.

In November of 1998, the Stereophonics arrived with their second album, *Performance and Cocktails,* which saw its American release in 1999. Rising to number three on the British charts, the album won stellar reviews and earned a nomination for the prestigious 1999 Technics Mercury Music Prize. During the remainder of 1998 and 1999, the band toured non-stop, including a support slot for Aerosmith, Lenny Kravitz, and the Black Crowes at the Toxic Twin Towers Ball at London's Wembley Stadium and a sell-out headlining show at Morfa Stadium in Swansea, South Wales. These appearances represent just some of the rewards of the band's unshakable live ethic. "We're the type of band that tours 11 months out of the year; it's cheaper than therapy," said Kelly Jones, as quoted in *Billboard* magazine.

Not only did the Stereophonics attract millions of fans and music press accolades for their music and work ethic, but they also gained the respect of several celebrated musicians. The legendary Paul Weller, for example, expressed an interest in collaborating with the band, while Liam Gallagher of Oasis gave the Stereophonics high praises. Although the Stereophonics believe strongly in the quality of their music, they were nevertheless taken aback by all the celebrity attention. "It's unbelievable how many people are interested in the band," Kelly Jones remarked to *Melody Maker*'s Carol Clerk. "The Prodigy were watching us in Switzerland and Eric Clapton phoned us and asked us if he could go on the guest list in Germany. People like that [who] you look up to."

However, the members of the Stereophonics remained unspoiled by all the success. They continue to make their homes in Cwmaman with no plans of ever leaving for the big city. The Stereophonics started recording a third album in June of 2000, which was expected to be released in April of 2001.

Selected discography

Word Gets Around, V2, 1997.
Performance and Cocktails, V2, 1999.

Sources

Books

Buckley, Jonathan and others, eds., *Rock: The Rough Guide,* Rough Guides Ltd., 1999.

Periodicals

Billboard, August 7, 1999; February 12, 2000.
Melody Maker, October 4, 1997; December 20-27, 1997; January 9, 1999; February 6, 1999; April 17, 1999; June 26, 1999; September 4, 1999; October 23, 1999; November 3-9, 1999.
Washington Post, April 7, 2000; April 10, 2000; April 12, 2000.

Online

Sonicnet.com, http://www.sonicnet.com (June 18, 2000).
Stereophonics Official Website, http://www.stereophonics.co.uk (June 18, 2000).

—*Laura Hightower*

Leni Stern

Guitarist, composer

Regarded as the "First Lady" of jazz guitar, German-born composer Leni Stern has become a respected force on the global music scene, earning the Orville H. Gibson Award for Best Female Jazz Guitarist for five consecutive years from 1996 through 2000. With songs ranging from the delicately melodic to bebop and funk, Stern has won accolades for both her compositions and her guitar skills from the world's most respected music critics and publications. *Guitar Player* once described her work as "a case study in the interactive properties of composition and improvisation," while *Jazz Times* likewise applauded Stern's music, calling it "crisp, confident and bursting with energy."

In addition to her achievements as a musician, she also ventured into the business side of the recording industry. In the 1990s, Stern established her own record label, Leni Stern Recordings, and handled most of her own business affairs. "I have this rule," she told Andy Ellis of *Guitar Player* in 1998. "Whenever I get bad news—like I didn't get a gig—I don't get up from my chair until I've attempted to avoid the bitterness. I translate the energy into a phone call to try and get another gig." Moreover, Stern expressed that dealing with business is a necessary evil for every musician. "But it's a separate art," she further explained, "and you have to keep it in proportion. You need to admit that you'll probably never be a great businessperson. I'm sure my lawyer and accountant friends double over laughing at my business sense. But its about being part of the game, if you don't want to be treated like a child and used like a slave, you have to become a grown-up, sit at the table, and establish a level playing field. My awareness of this is probably heightened by the fact that I'm a woman. I had to get my shit together, because it was too frustrating to be ignored."

Born Magdalena Thora in Munich, Germany, in 1952, Leni (pronounced "Lay-nee") Stern was drawn to music early in life. A child prodigy, she discovered the piano at age six, started taking classical piano lessons at the age of seven, and after finding an old guitar in the attic of her home, picked up that instrument and began teaching herself jazz at age eleven. Even as a child, Stern realized she possessed a natural gift for composition. "I didn't think of it as composing at the time, but I was always sticking chords together and putting a melody on top," she recalled to Bill Milkowski and Jesse Gress in a 1993 interview with *Guitar Player*. "What I learned from studying composition was how to make that process go faster. I used to randomly search for something I liked. When you study composition, you learn to look in better places for what you like. You eliminate choices and get right to the heart of the matter. And then you also learn to analyze what other people do—and steal." Back then, Stern's primary influences included Keith Jarrett, Bill Evans, Ralph Towner, and Pat Metheny, whose "Bright Size Life," she said, later "changed my whole life."

In addition to music, Stern held aspirations in other areas of the arts, namely acting. A drama major at Falckenberg Schauspelschule, the young performer went on—upon graduating from school at the age of 17—to found her own theater company, for which she also served as musical director. Before long, Stern and her radical productions sold out houses across Europe, gaining the young artist considerable press and television coverage, especially in France and Germany. As Stern's reputation blossomed, she started attracting more job offers, for both composing and acting, and by the mid-1970s, she had written two film scores and was appearing regularly on the television hit *Goldener Sontag,* a popular German show that spoofed soap operas.

Jazz Guitar Beckoned

In 1977, Stern left behind her successful career as an actor and relocated to the United States, where she enrolled as a composition major at the renowned Berklee College of Music in Boston, Massachusetts. Here, she met and befriended guitarist Bill Frisell, who accepted Stern as a private student and also introduced her to her future husband, fellow guitarist Mike Stern. "I had asked Frisell to show me some rock and blues licks, so he took me to see Michael play at a club in Boston … and he had the chops of doom," she recalled to Milkowski and Gress. "He made all the other guitar players in the audience turn green. So I asked

For The Record . . .

Born Magdalena Thora in Munich, Germany, in 1952; married Mike Stern, a jazz guitarist. *Education*: Graduated as a drama major from Falckenberg Schauspelschule in Germany; attended Berklee College of Music in Boston, MA, as a composition major; also studied guitar with Bill Frisell, Jon Damian, and and Dave Tronzo.

Started playing piano at age six and guitar at age eleven; founded own theater company at age 17; acted in hit German television show *Goldener Sontag*; moved to U.S. to study composition at Berklee, 1977; moved to New York City, 1980; formed own band, 1983; released debut album, *Clairvoyant*, 1985; established Leni Stern Recordings and released first album featuring vocals, *Black Guitar*, 1997.

Addresses: *Record company*—Leni Stern Recordings, 143 Charlie Parker Pl., New York, NY 10009, phone: (212) 979-8221, fax: (212) 673-6817, website: http://www.lenistern.com. *Tour information and merchandise*—Leni Stern Recordings, 143 Avenue B, #10D, New York, NY 10009, above phone and fax numbers.

him if he would teach me, and that was that. Two weeks later, he brought his amp over to my place, and soon after that we were married."

While at Berklee, Stern also studied with Jon Damian, who taught the aspiring guitarist to listen and play with an open mind. "He really understands how music works, and he knows the connection between playing notes and pure sound," Stern explained to Ellis. "And he can bring you to that place. To Jon, everything is music. I think he's a genius—or the closest I've come to it. My main teacher was Bill Frisell, who also studied with Jon. Along with my husband, Mike Stern, these are my major influences."

In 1980, the couple moved to New York City when Stern's husband landed an eventful gig playing with legendary trumpeter Miles Davis. Meanwhile, Stern herself played with various rock and jazz groups before forming her own band in 1983 with Frisell and drummer Paul Motian. Two years later, in 1985, Stern arrived with her debut, *Clairvoyant*, for the now defunct Passport label. Produced by Hiram Bullock and featuring

Frisell as second guitarist alongside Stern, as well as Motian, bassist Harvie Swartz, pianist Larry Willis, and tenor saxophonist Bob Berg, the album won considerable praise.

Since then, Stern continued to form associations with some of the jazz world's leading musicians. "I've always hired the guys who were better than me," she informed Milkowski and Gress. "Michael Brecker once told me that it was the best way to learn." Her follow-up recording, 1987's *The Next Day*, featured the same lineup as her debut with producer Bullock substituting for Frisell on rhythm guitar. *Secrets*, her energized 1989 debut for the Enja label, employed a three-guitar front line, with Stern's tone contrasted against slide work by guitarist David Tronzo and superb saxophone playing by Berg, while third guitarist, Wayne Krantz, supplied the rhythm. Other featured musicians included percussionist Don Alias, drummer Dennis Chambers, and bassist Lincoln Goines—all top-notch players. Her next record, 1990s *Closer to the Light*, returned many of the same sessionists, including powerhouse drumming by Chambers and Zach Danzinger, and a special guest appearance by saxophonist David Sanborn.

Collaborated with the Best

Ten Songs, released in 1992 on the Lipstick label, also saw Stern employing a cast of renowned players, such as Bob Malach on tenor saxophone, Gil Goldstein on keys, Badal Roy on Indian percussion, Zawinul Syndicate drummer Rodney Holmes, and bassist Alain Caron from the Canadian fusion group Uzeb, as well as Chambers, Goines, and Krantz. Collaborating with the best over the years evidently paid off for the album, and critics noted Stern's expanded technique—with Stern additionally playing Spanish and slide guitar—along with her always noted compositional skills. "That's the Dave Tronzo influence," she said to Milkowski and Gress, referring to her slide guitar spotlight for the fusion track "Trouble." "I love the sound of it—it's so swampy and emotional." Following the release of *Ten Songs*, Stern returned as a sole guitarist on 1993's *Like One*, which featured Didier Lockwood on violin; teamed with keyboardist John Askew for a more stripped-down sound on 1995's *Words*; and reunited with Krantz for an album of guitar duets for 1996's *Separate Cages*.

In 1997, Stern arrived with her first recording for her own label entitled *Black Guitar*, which brought the musician's musical vision into sharp focus. The highly acclaimed work also reached out to a new audience, moving away from strictly jazz elements and adding surprisingly effective vocals alongside some of her most confident guitar playing. Although Stern had previously experimented with singing during her live performances, she had never tried recording her soft, somewhat breathy voice before until *Black Guitar.* "Be advised that *Black Guitar* is not a jazz album with some songs thrown in for balance," Jon Andrews concluded in a review for *Down Beat* in 1998. "Here, we venture into the introspective domain of the singer/songwriter, where hushed, somewhat confessional vocals and storytelling are central to a low key, intimate experience."

Stern's next release, 1998's *Recollection,* looked back on the guitarist's previous work, featuring vintage material as well as new songs that again showcased Stern's singing ability. Stern and her husband have continued to reside in Manhattan in New York throughout their careers, and each guitarist prefers to keep their professional lives separate. As for possible collaborations with her husband in the future, Stern remarked, as quoted by Milkowski and Gress, "We play together around the house, but it's so private. But I do have this vision of when we're old and grey, sitting on the stage of Carnegie Hall playing 'Body and Soul' in rocking chairs."

Triumphed over Cancer

Although Stern has enjoyed an accomplished recording career and has earned the reputation as the world's leading female jazz guitarist and composer, one of her most significant triumphs was of a more personal sort. In 1989, at the same time Stern was making great strides with her music, doctors diagnosed the guitarist with breast cancer. "I'm not the kind of person who worries and suffers in silence, who turns inward and consumes herself," she explained to Milkowski and Gress. "So I found a need to turn my amp up to 10 after I was diagnosed, to let the feedback sing for a while."

Determined to defeat the disease, Stern fought back, and following surgery, chemotherapy, and various alternative treatments—including vitamins, improved nutrition, and even magnets—she won her greatest battle and was soon in remission. "I was really afraid that this thing was going to take over my life," she admitted to Milkowski and Gress. "So I really tried to return to normal as soon as I could. I was out of the hospital for three weeks when I went right back to playing just to prove to myself that I could still do it, even though I couldn't really lift up my arm after surgery. I was deathly afraid that I wouldn't be able to move my hands. That's the first thing I told the surgeon: 'If you have to cut any tendons or nerves that affect my hands, I'd rather die. Don't do it. Don't mess up my hands.' "

Selected discography

Clairvoyant, Passport Jazz, 1985.
The Next Day, Passport Jazz, 1987.
Secrets, Enja, 1989.
Closer to the Light, Enja, 1990.
Ten Songs, Lipstick, 1992.
Like One, Lipstick, 1993.
Words, Lipstick, 1995.
(With Wayne Krantz) *Separate Cages,* Alchemy, 1996.
Black Guitar, Leni Stern, 1997.
Recollection, Leni Stern, 1998.

Sources

Books

Stern, Leni*, Composing and Composition,* CPP Belwin, 1995.
Swenson, John, editor, *Rolling Stone Jazz & Blues Album Guide,* Random House, 1999.

Periodicals

Down Beat, August 1994, p. 46; April 1998, pp. 49-50.
Guitar Player, March 1993, pp. 95-104; April 1995, p. 129; August 1998, pp. 78-85.
Village Voice, July 13, 1999, p. 71.

Online

All Music Guide, http://www.allmusic.com (April 22, 2000).
Leni Stern Recordings, http://www.lenistern.com (April 22, 2000).
"Leni Stern," *Jazz Corner,* http://www.jazzcorner.com/stern /bio.html (April 22, 2000).
"Leni Stern," *IUMA,* http://www.iuma.com/IUMA/Bands/Leni_ Stern/index.html (April 22, 2000).

—*Laura Hightower*

Mike Stern

Jazz-rock guitarist

Archive Photos. Reproduced by permission.

A hard-edged experimental guitarist who rose to fame playing with Miles Davis in the 1980s, Mike Stern has earned a reputation as a bandleader and sideman for his work in bebop and hard bop, as well as his skillful technique playing fusion, straight-ahead jazz, and jazz-rock. His extraordinary career, spanning from his 1986 Atlantic Records debut *Upside Down* through his 1999 album *Play,* illustrates his unique ability to master an array of styles, from rock, funk, and the blues, to improvised jazz and alternative music—all of which he counts as personal influences. "A heroic soloist who has the ability to push the envelope to Hendrixian heights," asserted Bill Milkowski in the guitarist's official online biography, "he also has the capacity to play with Jim Hall-like sensitivity. It is the relative ease with which he shifts from aggressive bop 'n' roll to an elegant 'walking on eggshells' gentility that makes Stern such a remarkably flexible and distinctive player."

Born on January 10, 1953, in Boston, Massachusetts, and raised in Washington, D.C., Stern began to learn guitar at the age of 12, emulating the styles of legendary blues and rock players. "I started out listening and playing along with the records of Jimi Hendrix and Led Zeppelin, and a lot of blues—B.B. King, Albert King, that kind of stuff," he told Howard Mandel of *Down Beat.* "Then I got into 'jazz' a few years later, when I was around 17, and found it was a little more involved. As an ear player, I'd get lost in about two seconds."

Realizing that he wanted to further explore the intricacies of jazz music, in 1971 Stern enrolled at the esteemed Berklee College of Music, where he studied the genre seriously. He immersed himself in the records of great bandleaders, like trumpet players Miles Davis and John Coltrane alongside pianists such as McCoy Tyner and Bill Evans. He studied guitar with Mick Goodrick, among others, and met and played with fellow guitarists Pat Metheny, Bill Frisell, and John Scofield. "Mick Goodrick had a large influence actually on Frisell, Sco and myself," Stern recalled to Mandel. "There was a whole thing around the way Mick played guitar in Boston at that time. His approach was a bit removed from traditional jazz guitar: less percussive, more legato, more string-bending and definitely more phrasing from rock and funk. My generation of players were all more into that, because we'd been in Top 40 bands playing that way coming up. For jazz guitarists today, it's impossible to ignore what everybody's playing." During his stay at Berklee, Stern also developed an appreciation for jazz guitarists such as Wes Montgomery and Jim Hall; both musicians significantly influenced his own playing, yet the guitarist would remain just as inspired by the styles of artists such as Hendrix, alternative-rock icon Beck, and blues legend Stevie Ray Vaughan over the years.

Stern's first professional gig occurred in 1976, when, upon the recommendation of Metheny, he landed a spot with the group Blood, Sweat and Tears. Remaining with this group for the next two years, Stern appeared on two Blood, Sweat and Tears albums—*More Than Ever* and *Brand New Day*—before returning to Boston to study with local jazz guru Charlie Banacos. "He's a piano player who works with all instruments. I've been studying off and on with him for years... He's the best teacher I've ever found. He gives you all kinds of stuff—classical, chromatic, horn studies. At the same time, he pulls for non-symmetrical, wide-open ideas," Stern, an avid student throughout his career, explained in an interview with *Guitar Player*'s Jesse Gress.

Called to Play with Davis

In 1979, Stern joined drummer Billy Cobham's powerhouse jazz-rock fusion band, a stint that lasted two years, before he received a call to play with Miles Davis. By now, Stern was known for his fast and fluid,

highly expressive personal style that integrated rock, blues, and jazz. Davis, too, came to appreciate the guitarist's array of influences. "Miles liked what I was doing in that regard," he recalled to Mandel, "because the first time he said, 'We're going to go on the road.' I asked, 'Who's going to play keyboards?' and he said, 'No keyboards, just you.' I said, 'Are you kidding?' And Miles said, 'Don't worry about it, just play. I'll hear it.' Miles wanted that vibe—scaled down, really raw, just guitar, without a whole lot of chords."

Accepting Davis's offer, Stern made his first public appearance with the group on June 27, 1981, at the Kix nightclub in Boston, a performance documented on the 1982 live album *We Want Miles.* Stern continued to play with Davis through 1983, appearing for two more albums with his group: 1981's *The Man With the Horn* and 1983's *Star People.* From 1983 to 1984, Stern toured with Word of Mouth, a band led by Jaco Pastorius, before returning to Davis's band for another year-long tour in 1985. After this, Stern continued to accompany other musicians. In the summer of 1986, he toured with saxophonist David Sanborn; later that year, he joined Steps Ahead, a group also featuring vibraphonist Mike Mainieri, saxophonist Michael Brecker, bassist Victor Bailey, and drummer Steve Smith. Stern's debut under his own name for Atlantic Records entitled *Upside Downside,* featuring Sanborn, Patorius, saxophonist Bob Berg, bassists Mark Egan and Jeff Andrews, keyboardist Mitch Forman, and drummers Dave Weckl and Steve Jordan, was also released in 1986.

Stern served in Michael Brecker's acclaimed quintet from 1986 though 1988, then released his second Atlantic album, 1988's *Time in Place.* Again, Stern assimilated a cast of well-known names as his backing band: Peter Erskine on drums, Jim Beard on keyboards, Jeff Andrews on bass, Don Alias on percussion, and Don Grolnick on organ. Next came 1989's *Jigsaw,* featuring Stern's tribute piece to Davis entitled "Chief," another successful album produced by fellow guitarist Steve Khan. In 1989, Stern formed a touring group with Bob Berg, drummer Dennis Chambers, and bassist Lincoln Goines; the quartet continued to work together through 1992 and appeared for the guitarist's third Atlantic release, that year's *Odds or Evens.*

An Open-minded Player

Also in 1992, Stern joined a reunited Brecker Brothers Band, and his guitar work proved one of the key reasons for the group's popular success over the following two years. In the meantime, Stern in 1993 released the acclaimed *Standards (and Other Songs),* a decidedly more introspective album for the guitarist that led *Guitar Player* magazine's readers and critics alike to name him Best Jazz Guitarist of the Year. "I love the tunes. I like memorable melodies, and obviously standards have that," he told Bill Milkowski and Jesse Gress in *Guitar Player* about making the album. "But it's hard to say what a jazz standard really is. I guess a loose definition is a song that was originally written for a Broadway musical or for a movie and has been covered by singers, which is where the whole vocal approach to playing them comes in. But from a playing standpoint, these tunes are a part of a common language. You can play them with a whole bunch of different people. You just call the tune, and they know it because they've played it a thousand times. So in that respect, I love playing standards because it's relatively easy. You don't have to scuffle through reading heads and learning the material. You can just play."

For 1994's *Is What It Is,* an album offering another great contribution by Brecker on tenor saxophone, Stern "returned to the fusion fray with a vengeance," Milkowski commented in *Down Beat.* Another hard-hitting effort, *Between the Lines,* followed in 1996 and won rave reviews for its broad musical interests. "You can't argue with your heart," Stern said, explaining his method of searching for musical direction to *Down Beat*'s Michael Point. "I try to give everything I hear a chance," the guitarist continued. "I don't think there's one musical direction that's right with all the others being wrong. I just listen for honesty, for something that touches my heart as well as my intellect, and if it's there the music catches my interest." Both the richly textured *Between the Lines* and *Is What It Is,* a collection of original compositions, earned Stern two Grammy Award nominations.

In 1996, Stern returned to an overall jazz-inspired aesthetic with *Give and Take,* a more spontaneous recording featuring John Patitucci on acoustic bass and Jack DeJohnette on drums, as well as guest appearances by Alias, Brecker, Sanborn, and Gil Goldstein on piano. "Stern's playing has never been better—he's inquisitive, excitable as always, and focused," wrote Robin Tolleson for *Down Beat* in a review of the session. Upon the strength of *Give and Take,* which included covers of Sonny Rollins' "Oleo," Coltrane's "Giant Steps," and Cole Porter's "I Love You" alongside a rendition of Hendrix's "Who Knows" and originals like the bebop "Hook Up," Stern won the Orville W. Gibson Award that year for Best Jazz Guitarist.

Trio of Guitars for *Play*

Taking a new approach for his ninth Atlantic album, 1999's *Play,* Stern decided to indulge in an idea he had held for some time—to record with other guitarists. Thus, he summoned both Scofield and Frisell to take part. "I've never recorded with another guitarist, so when I decided to do it, those two guys were the obvious choices," Stern told Darrin Fox of *Guitar Player.* "They're both good friends of mine. Bill and I

used to sit around and play standards together in the early '70s, and Sco and I played with Miles Davis. And although we're all jazz guitarists, each of us grew up in the '60s, so influences like Hendrix, B.B. King, James Brown, the Ventures, and the Beatles make up big parts of our style. Plus, the three of us listen to other instruments for ideas. My style reflects a lot of the horn influence—so does Sco's—and Frisell takes a more pianistic approach."

Recorded at the rock band Pearl Jam's studio, Litho, with appearances by Dennis Chambers and Ben Perowsky on drums, Goines on bass, and Bob Malach on saxophone, *Play* won Stern further acclaim, yet was also an enjoyable recording to make. "That's why this album's called *Play,* after all," he noted to Mandel. "Obviously, there's a lot of playing on the album, but it's supposed to be fun, too. Because if you can't have fun playing music, you're in trouble." The pleasure derived from music, Stern believed, was the single factor that kept him motivated throughout his 20-year career. As he explained to Gress: "Music is such a gift. There are times of scuffling, when you feel like you're pushing a rock up a hill and you're not where you want to be. But as soon as you start playing, it's like, 'I'm just going to develop my potential on the instrument.' When music does something for you, that's a gift. The fact that you can get lost in something so beautiful is amazing."

A fixture on the New York jazz club scene and on the jazz album charts throughout the 1990s, Stern made his home in Manhattan, where he lives with wife Leni Stern—a successful composer and guitarist in her own right—in a modest apartment. Although his wife would seem a perfect musical collaborator, Mike and Leni Stern prefer to keep their professional lives separate. They have never played on one another's albums or given interviews together. "I'm constantly asking her about my stuff. I very much respect her opinion with regard to playing and writing. She's a terrific musician," Stern explained to Milkowski and Gress. "But we draw the line at playing together. And who knows if that's forever? Sometimes your profession becomes all-encompassing, so sometimes we avoid talking about it. We'll just say, 'Talk about anything else but music.' Maybe that's why it's worked out so great."

In addition to his solo work, Stern has appeared on recordings as a sideman for numerous musicians and groups including Les Arbuckle, Thomas Barth, Marc Beacco, Jim Beard, Bob Beldon, Bob Berg, Jerry Bergonzi, Charles Blenzig, Bunny Brunel, David Clayton-Thomas, Billy Cobham, Michael Cunningham and Four Corners, Michael Gerber, Lincoln Goines, David Alan Gross, Jim Hall, Tom Harrell, Joe Henderson, Motohiko Hino, Dieter Ilg, Jazzsick, Jens Johansson, Shinichi Kato, Scott Kreitzer, Dave Larue, Eric Le Lann, Pete Levin, the Peter Linhart Group, Didier Lockwood, Michael Manther, Andrea Marcelli, Andrea Marchesini, Pat Martino, Pippo Martino, Thierry

Mineau, Dan Moretti, Shunzo O'No, Tiger Okoshi, Ed Palermo, Eddie Palmieri, Jaco Pastorius, Georg Pommer, Michael Pope, Jeff Richman, Alex Riel, Doug Robinson, Randy Roos, Arturo Sandoval, Steve Slagle, Steve Smith, Lew Soloff, Spajazzy, Mr. Spats, Harvie Swartz, Michal Urbaniak, Jukkis Uotila, Roland Vazquez, and Kimo Williams.

Selected discography

As bandleader; on Atlantic Records

Upside Downside, 1986.
Time in Place, 1988.
Jigsaw, 1989.
Odds or Evens, 1991.
Standards (and Other Songs), 1993.
Is What It Is, 1994.
Between the Lines, 1996.
Give and Take, 1997.
Play, 1999.

With Blood, Sweat and Tears

Brand New Day, 1976.
In Concert, 1976.
More Than Ever
Live and Improvised, Legacy, 1991.
What Goes Up! The Best of Blood, Sweat and Tears, Legacy, 1995.

With Michael Brecker, the Brecker Brothers, and Steps Ahead

(Steps Ahead), *Live in Tokyo,* 1986.
(Michael Brecker), *Don't Try This at Home,* Impulse!, 1988.

(Brecker Brothers), *Return to the Becker Brothers,* GRP, 1992. With Miles Davis; on Columbia Records
The Man with the Horn, 1981.
We Want Miles, 1982.
Star People, 1983.

Sources

Books

Swenson, John, *Rolling Stone Jazz & Blues Album Guide,* Random House, 1999.

Periodicals

Billboard, November 27, 1999, p. 24.
Down Beat, April 1994, p. 43; September 1994, p. 47; April 1996, p. 40; December 1997, pp. 72-73; November 1999, p. 61; April 2000, pp. 50-51.
Guitar Player, March 1993, pp. 95-104; February 1998, pp. 69-75; March 2000, p. 35.

Online

All Music Guide, http://www.allmusic.com (April 16, 2000).
"Mike Stern," Atlantic Records, http://www.atlantic-records.com/frames/Artists_Music/main.html?artistID=102 (April 16, 2000).
The Official Mike Stern Pages, http://www.mikestern.org (April 16, 2000).

—Laura Hightower

Superchunk

Indie-rock band

Although not a revolutionary band, North Carolina's Superchunk has nevertheless done more to promote the indie-pop movement than nearly any other band in existence. Along with their steady stream of well-crafted records and songs that bridged the distance between old-school power-pop and hardcore punk, the quartet displayed an unyielding appetite for touring, establishing for themselves a loyal fandom without the support of MTV (Music Television), commercial radio, or major-label distribution. Instead, Superchunk held true to a do-it-yourself ethos, never conceding to fleeting styles or marketplace trends and establishing their own label, Merge Records, a company born out of a love for music—rather than to make profits—that went on to underwrite numerous like-minded acts with great success. "As of a year and a half ago, our offices were still in Laura's house," lead singer Mac McCaughan, who co-owns the independent label along with Superchunk bass player Laura Ballance, revealed to *Rolling Stone*'s Ray Rogers in December of 1994. "We've just recently begun to operate on a similar level as most labels. We have a postage meter."

The history of Superchunk began in Chapel Hill, North Carolina, in 1989, when guitarist/vocalist Mac Mc-

AP/Wide World Photos. Reproduced by permission.

For The Record . . .

Members include **Laura Ballance** (born Laura Jane Balance on February 22, 1968), bass; **Chuck Garrison** (left band in 1991), drums; **Mac McCaughan** (born on July 12, 1967), guitar, vocals; **Jack McCook** (left band in 1990), guitar; **James "Jim" Wilbur** (born on December 22, 1966, in New London, CT; joined band in 1990; former school teacher), guitar; **Jon Wurster** (born Jonathan Patrick Wurster on October 31, 1966; joined band in 1991), drums.

Formed Superchunk and established Merge Records in Chapel Hill, NC, 1989; signed with Matador Records, released self-titled debut, 1990; released final album on Matador, *On the Mouth,* 1993; *Foolish* marked a stylistic shift for Superchunk, 1994; toured with Lollapalooza, released *Here's Where the Strings Come In,* toured worldwide, 1995; released the acclaimed *Indoor Living,* 1997; released the engaging *Come Pick Me Up,* 1999.

Addresses: *Record company*—Merge Records, P.O. Box 1235, Chapel Hill, NC 27514, phone: (919) 929-0711, fax: (919) 929-4291, e-mail: merge @Interpath.com. *Website*—Superchunk.com, http://www.superchunk.com.

Caughan, bassist Laura Ballance, drummer Chuck Garrison, and guitarist Jack McCook joined forces to form a band, as well as their own record label. Headed since its inception by McCaughan and Ballance, Merge issued most of the group's subsequent American singles and EPs, as well as later albums. Initially calling themselves simply Chunk—a moniker already taken by a free-improv band led by Samm Bennett—the group released their first record on their own Merge imprint and established a cult following for their brash, yet melodic punk tunes and energetic performances. Meanwhile, a rave review of *The Chunk* EP by the influential independent music magazine *Maximum Rock 'N' Roll* also helped channel attention. With songs like "What Do I" and a cover of Shangri La's "Train From Kansas City," the foursome illustrated their obvious love for pure pop, as well as their indebtedness to the American hardcore and British punk scenes.

The group also received support from Chapel Hill's college-town climate. Home to the University of North Carolina, the city itself ran a course often compared to other famous indie-rock areas such as Athens (Georgia), Seattle, and Chicago, producing several bands that defied a single stylistic label. Polvo, Archers Of Loaf, Corrosion of Conformity, Juliana Hatfield, Dillon Fence, and Snatches of Pink all count among Chapel Hill's other successes, as did the town's other well-known label, Mammoth Records.

After releasing their first official single as Superchunk in 1990—the galvanizing "Slack Motherf***er" that appeared as well on the band's self-titled debut, became a college radio anthem, and later placed on *Spin* magazine's list of top 20 singles of the 1990s—the group signed a record deal with another independent label, Matador Records. "I was a fan of Mac's (prior) work with Bricks and Wax, so it wasn't a huge gamble that Superchunk were gonna turn out to be a great band," Matador's Gerard Cosloy, one of the parties responsible for signing Superchunk for their first three studio albums, told *Magnet* contributor Corey duBrowa.

Arriving in 1990 with *Superchunk,* the band from the onset began to collect favorable press, attracting similar attention to other then-emerging underground acts like Nirvana and Pavement. Soon after the debut's release, however, Superchunk lost band member Mc-Cook, who cited road fatigue and his career as a softball umpire as his reason for his departure. Thus, Connecticut-born James Wilbur, a self-described "old crank" stepped in to take over guitar duties. At the time he accepted the position with Superchunk, Wilbur was teaching health at the prestigious McWilloby Friends School when a student informed him of the vacancy. Bidding farewell to the academic world in favor of playing in a rock band, Wilbur joined Superchunk, touring with the band in support of their debut and joining them in the studio for a follow-up effort.

Europe Beckoned

The group's sophomore effort, 1991's *No Pocky for Kitty,* brought Superchunk even wider attention. Recorded in Chicago earlier that year with veteran producer Steve Albini (who has also worked with the Membranes and Head of David among others), the album was noted for its more fully realized collection of tunes, appealing specifically for their catchy hooks and the emergence of McCaughan's curiously coercive lyrical expression. Despite the band's accomplishment, which featured the tracks "Tossing Seeds" and "Skip Steps 1 and 3," Garrison resigned from Superchunk a few weeks before the release of *No Pocky for Kitty*. His replacement, a former window cleaner named Jon Wurster, joined the group on drums, traveling with Superchunk abroad for their first European tour. According to the band's biography at Merge Records, Superchunk broke several of the band's former touring records during their overseas excursion, including the quickest van break-in after pulling into a venue (seven minutes in Brussels, Belgium) and the smallest audience played to (eight people in Braunschweig).

By now, numerous major labels expressed interest in signing Superchunk, but the group stood by their principles, turning down several lucrative record deals. "Major-label A&R people interested in our band will call and say, 'You guys are anti-major,' " McCaughan told Rogers. "Superchunk would love to sell a million records, but the difference is wanting to sell records in a way that you're comfortable with." Thus, forgoing millions to maintain their independence, Superchunk remained with Matador for their next studio effort, *On the Mouth,* hailed as "Roaring hook-laden, and near perfect... inarguably one of the decade's best" by Matt Hickey in *Magnet.* Released in 1993 and featuring the Buzzcocks-inspired "Precision Auto," the Jam-like "I Guess I Remembered It Wrong," and a bass-driven near-ballad that slowly builds in intensity called "Swallow That," the well-received album nonetheless would be their last project for Matador Records.

Opting to release all of their subsequent records through Merge, Superchunk returned with the acclaimed *Foolish* in 1994, an album marking an important stylistic shift for the group. While maintaining an overall punk-rock feel, Superchunk also veered away from their trademark sound with *Foolish.* As Matt Diehl explained in a 1994 review in *Rolling Stone,* "The album's opener, 'Like a Fool,' suggests a totally new direction: a melodic, lush drone in which singer Mac McCaughan's falsetto struggles against a mournful wall of guitars. And 'Driveway to Driveway' offers up chugging, New Wavish pop rock, lamenting lost love with a twangy guitar hook that wouldn't be out of place in a John Hughes teen-angst movie set in the grunge age."

A busy schedule followed the prosperity of *Foolish,* with Superchunk issuing two albums in 1995: a second singles compilation, *Incidental Music 1991-95,* and a new studio effort, *Here's Where the Strings Come In,* recorded at Boston's Fort Apache Studios and released that fall. During the summer of 1995, Superchunk performed on the Lollapalooza tour, then embarked on a worldwide tour in support of *Here's Where the Strings Come In.* The next year, Superchunk took a brief hiatus, toured Australia, issued a limited-edition EP entitled *The Laughter Guns,* and started the writing process for their forthcoming album, 1997's *Indoor Living.*

Songwriting Took Center Stage

Recorded in Bloomington, Indiana, at the Echo Park Studios with fellow Chapel Hillian John Plymale co-producing with the band, *Indoor Living* earned rave reviews and saw the group maturing to focus more on melody and songcraft, evidenced with tracks such as "Marquee," "Every Single Instinct," and "Song for Marion Brown." "Compare *Indoor Living* to the self-titled debut and you might think it's a completely different band," Hickey insisted. "Longer tracks and more complex structures, often augmented by keyboards, neatly mixed with awesome rockers; the effect is solid and strongly cohesive." Furthermore, Superchunk stretched their skills to add new instrumentation into the mix; along with keyboards, *Indoor Living* revealed piano, organ vibes, and more for a more adventurous, accessible sound.

After performing the world over beginning in October of 1997, Superchunk continued to expand their sound with 1999's *Come Pick Me Up,* adding horns, strings, and effects. Superchunk, previously recognized for their raw, gritty music, seemed to be progressively warming up to sweeter studio production. "The sound of each album gets more and more separate from our live sound," McCaughan told *Guitar Player*'s Kyle Swenson. "We want to experiment with other ways of hearing our songs." Produced with the help of Jim O'Rourke, *Come Pick Me Up* "is the most engaging album of the band's decade-long career," concluded *Washington Post* contributor Mark Jenkins.

In spite of recording and touring almost non-stop, the members of Superchunk somehow found time to participate in various side projects as well. McCaughan, for one, indulged in his quieter, more experimental side with his solo project, Portastatic, and started a new label called Wobbly Rail, devoted to releasing free-jazz records. Wilbur played in the group Humidifier with John King of Spent, while Wurster also formed his own label, Stereolaffs, that issued comedy albums. Finally, in addition to running Merge, Ballance and McCaughan also earned recognition as accomplished artists; some of their work has been displayed on Superchunk's album covers.

Superchunk's Longevity

And as Superchunk continued to grow throughout their ten-plus years as a band, so did Merge Records, building a diverse roster throughout the 1990s. Not only did Merge boast some of the best American songwriters of the decade—such as Neutral Milk Honey, the Magnetic Fields, and East River Pipe—but the company also attracted British innovators like Third Eye Foundation, Ganger, and Spaceheads. "I like the way Merge is more concerned with putting out what they like and helping bands that they care about than meeting anyone's expectations of a label sound," noted Cosloy. "I've always been impressed by the obvious respect the label has for the people who purchase their records."

Whereas many indie-rock groups seem destined to fall apart, Superchunk managed to survive—and mature musically—over time. "One reason we've been around so long is that we never really sat down and said, 'This is where we want to be in five years,'" McCaughan suggested to duBrowa. "With both the band and the label, we tend to take things one day—or one month—at a time. That's helped us get through 10 years without even so much as stopping to take a breath. Because if you did, you'd probably stop and go, 'What the hell am I doing, anyway?' I also think there's a point in any band's career where they're either going to break up from going on tour, wanting to kill each other. Or they get past that and learn how to survive. A long time ago, we figured it out, which is why we can still function as a group—write songs, make records and go on tour—without imploding."

Selected discography

Albums

Superchunk, Matador, 1990, reissued, Merge, 1999.
No Pocky for Kitty, Matador, 1991, reissued, Merge, 1999.
Tossing Seeds: Singles 89-91, Merge, 1992.
On the Mouth, Matador, 1993, reissued Merge, 1999.
Foolish, Merge, 1994.
Incidental Music 1991-95, Merge, 1995.
Here's Where the Strings Come In, Merge, 1995.
Indoor Living, Merge, 1997.
Come Pick Me Up, Merge, 1999.

EPs

The Freed Seed, Merge, 1991.
Tower, Messiah Complex, 1991.
Hit Self-Destruct, Hippy Knight, 1992.

Mower, Merge, 1992.
The Question Is How Fast?, Merge, 1992.
On Paper It Made Perfect Sense, Fellaheen, 1994.
Driveway to Driveway, Merge, 1994.
Hyper Enough, Merge, 1995.
The Laughter Guns, Merge 1996.
Hello Hawk, Merge, 1999.
1,000 Lbs, Merge, 2000.

Sources

Periodicals

Billboard, February 25, 1995; September 20, 1997.
Boston Globe, January 26, 1999; August 20, 1999; February 18, 2000.
Chicago Tribune, September 24, 1999.
Guitar Player, November 1999.
Magnet, August/September 1999, p. 91; October/November 1999, pp. 51-58.
Rolling Stone, April 16, 1992; April 15, 1993; June 16, 1994; December 1, 1994; September 2, 1999.
Washington Post, February 27, 1998; January 22, 1999; August 20, 1999.

Online

"Humidifier: History," *Geocities,* http://www.geocities.com /essbiv/humidhistory.html (April 5, 2000).
Rolling Stone.com, http://www.rollingstone.tunes.coml (April 5, 2000).
"Superchunk Biography," *Merge,* http://www.merge.cata log ue.com/bio.sc.html (April 5, 2000).
Superchunk Official Website, http://www.superchunk.com (April 5, 2000).

—Laura Hightower

Travis

Rock band

In 1999, Glasgow's Travis became one of Scotland's most popular exports, making headlines throughout the United Kingdom, gaining fans across Europe, and breaking ground in the United States. According to *Rolling Stone*'s Rob Sheffield, it's easy to hear why: "Travis play sentimental pub rock at its warmest, with gorgeous guitar hooks and boy-next-door sincerity." Heavily influenced by the classic rock sounds of Neil Young as well as British pop bands, Travis drew musical comparisons to Radiohead—minus the science fiction effects—for lead singer Fran Healy's ability to pull a song together with his choir-like, tenor-range vocals. But unlike some of Britain's most popular acts, Travis, along with other recent British groups such as Stereophonics, Gomez, and Catatonia, chose to ignore the chic London scene. Tossing life in the limelight aside, the members of Travis claim they are not in the business of making records simply for the glory, but rather for the sheer joy of performing their songs.

While the band's success, which arrived in the wake of their sophomore effort *The Man Who,* appeared to take place overnight, Travis's ascent to pop stardom actually resulted after eight years of determination. Prior to forming in Glasgow in 1991, three members of Travis—

For The Record . . .

Members include **Andy Dunlop** (attended Glasgow School of Art), guitar; **Fran Healy** (attended Glasgow School of Art), vocals, songwriting; **Dougie Payne** (attended Glasgow School of Art; joined band in 1996), bass; **Neil Primrose**, drums.

Formed band in Glasgow, Scotland, 1991; relocated to London, released debut single "All I Want to Do Is Rock," 1996; released debut album *Good Feeling,* toured with Oasis, 1997; released *The Man Who,* 1999; toured the U.S. for the first time, headlined at the Glastonbury Festival, 2000.

Awards: 1999 Brit Awards for Best Album for *The Man Who* and Best British Band, 2000.

Addresses: *Record company*—Epic/Sony, 550 Madison Ave., 22nd Floor, New York City, NY 10022, (212) 833-7188. *Website*—Travis Online, http://www.travis online.com.

singer/songwriter Fran Healy, guitarist Andy Dunlop, and bassist Dougie Payne—all held ambitions other than making records. Back then, they were attending Glasgow School of Art, where Healy, a painter, met Payne, a sculptor, at an evening life drawing class; the two artists became instant best friends. Payne later met Dunlop, a jeweler and silversmith, at the Fresher's Week at the School of Art. All three continued with their studies while playing with the group, and both Payne and Dunlop completed their courses. Healy, however, found it too difficult to concentrate on his songwriting as well as his education, and eventually dropped out of art college when he discovered that he was finishing more songs than paintings.

The fourth member of Travis, drummer Neil Primrose, previously worked at Glasgow's Horseshoe Bar and knew Dunlop through his then-current band called Running Red. One night, Healy encountered Primrose at his place of work and asked the drummer to join his new band, Glass Onion, for which Dunlop was already the lead guitarist. Uniting with Healy, Dunlop, and two other members (neither being Payne), Primrose accepted the offer, and the group spent some time playing gigs in Glasgow, hoping to land a record deal. But as the months slipped by without label interest, Healy, Dunlop, and Primrose decided to make changes. They left their manager and the local club circuit, dropping out of sight for a year to write new tunes and rehearse.

A Second Chance

Feeling more confident and ready to give music another try, the band returned to the Glasgow club scene and caught the attention of label executive Andy McDonald. McDonald encouraged Healy to sign a publishing contract with Sony/ATV Music, and he also found the group a new manager, Ian McAndrew, known for his work with the Brand New Heavies and Tim Simeon. McDonald himself was keen on signing the band to a fledgling Go! Discs, but ran into difficulties with parent company PolyGram Records. However, when Go! Discs folded and McDonald formed his own label, Independiente Records, he kept Travis in mind. Later, Travis would become the first act signed to McDonald's new company.

Meanwhile, Sony/ATV urged the group's frontman to make another change: to find a new bass player and move to London. Responding to the suggestion, Healy visited his best friend's home with a bass guitar in hand. "I put it on him and stood him in front of the mirror and said 'Woof! You were born to play the bass,'" the songwriter recalled in an online interview with Lucy Robinson. At first, Payne defiantly refused, but before long changed his mind and officially stepped in to complete the lineup in May of 1996. Subsequently, Healy, Payne, Dunlop, and Primrose, said farewell to Glasgow, packing their bags and arriving in London with a new name, Travis, taken after the character in the acclaimed Wim Wenders film *Paris, Texas.*

By now, Travis had recorded their debut single, "All I Want to Do Is Rock," released in October of 1996 in a limited edition on their own Red Telephone Box Records. And with the success of the song, the same tune that had previously inspired McDonald, Travis became the first major signing to the newly minted Independiente. A pivotal performance arrived a month later: appearing on the television program *Later With Jools Holland* alongside singer Lionel Richie, rock icon Sting, and hip-hop artist Tricky. Other opportunities arose as well, including dates with other prominent bands and more than 200 headlining club gigs, leading Travis to attract a strong, devoted following.

Debut Makes the Charts

Consequently, when Travis released their debut album *Good Feeling* in the fall of 1997, they saw the effort rise straight to the top ten of the British charts. Recorded in just four days, the mostly live album—containing memorable singles such as "U16 Girls" and "More Than Us"—illustrated the group's energetic performance style and earned favorable responses. "*Good Feeling* is clearly the most accomplished, heart-stoppingly exciting British debut album since *Definitely Maybe* by Oasis," stated *Select* magazine in October of 1997. Likewise, in its October 17, 1997, issue, *Entertainment Weekly* commented, "Healy stretches every lunkheaded syllable to its elastic limit, until those words bluster almost anthemic. And this Scot's no one-hit wonder—11 more stunners spell stardom." Nonetheless, Travis failed to make a major impression on the larger population until the band Oasis stepped in. After that group's Noel Gallagher made a personal request for Travis to accompany Oasis for a highly publicized arena tour, the up-and-coming band's popularity took off.

The single "Writing to Reach You," released in March of 1999, soared to number 14 on the British charts, after which Travis made another television appearance on *Top of the Pops.* Another single issued in May, "Driftwood" charted as well at number 13, making way for the release later that month for Travis's sophomore album, *The Man Who.* Recorded and mixed between the summer of 1998 and early 1999, the album saw Travis making music in various settings. For preliminary sessions, the band recorded for three weeks at the picturesque surroundings of producer Mike Hedge's Chateau De La Rouge Motte studio in Normandy. Then, returning to London, the quartet booked time at various studios throughout the city with Nigel Godrich, who also produced for Radiohead, Beck, R.E.M., and Pavement. "This album's a wee bit more grown-up," acknowledged Payne for the group's website. "But if you were to listen to the last song on *Good Feeling* and then put the first track of *The Man Who* on, it's just a continuation really. The best way to listen to *Good Feeling* was watching us playing it, seeing and feeling the whole thing." Healy further added: "This album's not a rock album in that way, it's more of a song album. It's an album for staying in rather than going out."

Rose to Number One

The Man Who won Travis numerous accolades, and on August 22, 1999, the album reached the number one spot on the British charts, knocking Boyzone's *By Request* from the top position. The album would go on to sell over three million copies in the United Kingdom alone, and was the fourth-biggest seller that year in Travis's homeland. Early the following year, Travis took home two main Brit Awards (the United Kingdom's equivalent to the Grammys), including the award for Best British Group as well as for Best Album. Although grateful for the recognition, Travis refused to dwell on the success, focusing instead on their music, where

they have been, and where they want to go. "If you're popular, it's a symptom of how many people have heard the songs," Healy told *Melody Maker.* "The territory where nobody has heard your music, that's how far you've got to go. It's got nothing to do with awards. It's about proper bloody songs, you know? I'm just sick of all this bollocks, celebrity bullsh**. Just give us a good song, please, somebody. We just want a nice wee song to sing."

Taking their songs overseas in February of 2000, Travis arrived in the United States for a short American tour that included dates in New York City and Los Angeles; they returned in the late spring as the supporting act on the Oasis tour. The summer of 2000 saw Travis performing at another important event, the Glastonbury Festival, the United Kingdom's massive, three-day summer concert. At Glastonbury 2000, Travis was set to share headlining duties with David Bowie and the Chemical Brothers. After this, Travis planned to head into the studio to record their third album. "I don't really ponder on what we've done, I'd always just rather ponder on what we've yet to do," Healy said, as quoted by *Melody Maker.* "We go 'Isn't it great? Isn't it magic?', but most of our energy is spent on moving forwards, rather than looking behind…"

Selected discography

Good Feeling, Independiente/Sony/Columbia, 1997.
The Man Who, (U.K) Independiente, 1999; Independiente/ Sony/Epic, 2000.

Sources

Periodicals

Melody Maker, February 16-22, 2000; February 23-29, 2000, pp. 4-5; March 8-14, 2000, p. 4; March 15-21, 2000, p. 4.
Rolling Stone, March 3, 2000; April 27, 2000, p. 66.
Spin, February 16, 2000; May 2000, p. 62.
Wall of Sound, February 2, 2000; March 3, 2000.

Online

Amazon.com, http://www.amazon.com (April 19, 2000).
Good Feeling, http://www.users.epulse.net/~ruston (April 16, 2000).
Travis Online, http://www.travisonline.com (April 16, 2000).

—Laura Hightower

Gloria Trevi

Pop singer

AP/Wide World Photos. Reproduced by permission.

During the 1990s, Gloria Trevi was, in the words of Latin America's famous talk show host Christina Saralegui, "a superstar," the "Mexican Madonna." Simultaneously childlike and sexy, the brash young singer with an aggressive sexual persona and liberal politics rightfully earned the nickname La Atrevida, meaning "the bold, insolent one." She performed in ripped tights and torn shoes, teased male members of the audience, and promised to one day run for the Mexican presidency. "This society wants to suffocate me, but I won't let it," she sang to her army of adoring fans, making pronouncements on such subjects as abortion, sexual freedom for women, and ending government corruption. Embracing her strong vocals and brazen style, an audience weary of interchangeable pop stars and romantic ballads bought her albums by the millions; her 1991 movie, the supposedly autobiographical *Pelo Suelto* ("Hair Hanging Loose"), became Mexico's biggest moneymaker of all time.

However, by the close of the decade, Trevi's star power had dwindled. She had quit touring in 1996, reportedly to help the man who discovered her, Sergio Andrade, recover from cancer. And after a 1997 attempt to host her own variety show failed, the singer's demand for appearances on television talk and panel shows was almost nonexistent. But things started to heat up again for Trevi in 1998. Although relatively unknown outside Latin America, the singer for the first time made headlines around the world for her involvement in a sex scandal with Andrade, who allegedly, with Trevi's help, routinely seduced underage fans by promising to make them pop stars.

Born Gloria de los Angeles Treviño Ruiz in the Mexican city of Monterrey on February 15, 1970, the first daughter of a well-off architect, Trevi enjoyed a privileged upbringing by comparison to other Mexican children. Whereas many drop out of school by the sixth grade in order to work, Trevi never even needed an after-school job. Thus, she spent her free time taking piano lessons and acting classes. Growing up in Monterrey, a sprawling clone of Houston, Texas, located just 100 miles from the United States border and boasting a number of American companies in operation, Trevi soaked in the influences of American culture, dreaming of becoming a pop icon herself.

Although divorce is rare in Mexico, an overwhelmingly Catholic nation, Trevi—like so many American children—watched her parents split up when she was ten years old. The embittered Trevi, along with her four brothers, remained with their mother, who struggled to raise her children alone and was known for her sometimes tough-love approach to parenting. According to Trevi, every time she brought home a poor grade, her mother would punish the child with 25 swats. When the youngster flunked eight subjects one year, Trevi recalled hiding a rope outside the family home as she contemplated killing herself. "I thought suicide would save my mother the trouble," she later joked in a 1993 interview for *People* magazine.

A star-struck and angst-ridden adolescent who wanted to put her formal training to use, Trevi at the age of 13 earned a scholarship to study voice and dance after winning a national performance contest, giving the teenager her first taste of the Mexico City show business scene. Taking advantage of the cosmopolitan lifestyle rather than the educational opportunities, before long she blew off her formal training and refused to return to Monterrey when her mother ordered her home. Instead, the young singer devoted herself to auditioning for pop bands, and at the age of 15, her determination paid off when in 1985 she became an original member—a backup singer playing a pink plastic harmonium shaped like an electric guitar—of an all-female teen-pop group called the Boquitas Pintadas, meaning in English "Little Painted Mouths."

Discovered by Sergio Andrade

While Boquitas Pintadas never provided Trevi with the opportunity to fully show off her musicianship, the band, more importantly, was the creation of Sergio Andrade Sánchez, whose power within the world of Mexican pop in the 1980s was often compared to that of Phil Spector in the United States in the 1960s. A successful producer who penned many of the hit songs his young protégés recorded, Andrade was born in 1956 to a powerful Veracruz family—his brother became a senator from Mexico's ruling party—and grew up during the days of student protest, struggles that he remained attuned to as an adult. Nevertheless, as a

songwriter, studio musician, and engineer, he concentrated his talents on the commercial, romantic pop music adored by Mexican audiences. At the time, rock and roll was more or less unheard of in Mexico and was virtually banned by the government, though a huge, yet invisible rock music scene did exist. "*Rockeros* were associated with drugs, delinquency, violence and rebellion," said Juaro Calixto Albarran, a music writer for the Mexico City daily *Excelsior*, as quoted by *Rolling Stone*'s Dan Baum. "You'd get ten kids together to hear a band and the police would show up."

Therefore, in keeping with the country's ultra-conservative stance regarding music, Andrade at first worked within the boundaries of pop. His breakthrough arrived in the early-1980s when he wrote a popular ballad for a blind singer named Crystal, a success that gave him leverage to start producing singing acts, and he immediately displayed a knack for picking and cultivating stars. In addition to his top-selling acts, Andrade created numerous lesser-known bands in order to keep the cash flowing and to serve as a breeding ground for future talent. Usually, bands like Boquitas Pintadas would perform together just long enough to record a hit, then disappeared to make room for Andrade's next venture. Unknown to Andrade at the time he hired Trevi, the teenage singer would become his greatest discovery of all time.

After Boquitas Pintadas had their brief period of fame and disbanded within months of forming, Andrade went on to his next project. Meanwhile, Trevi, then 16, had fallen in love with a 32-year-old gynecologist, who she says grew jealous of her artistic ambitions and refused to let her work. "I told him I couldn't marry him," she told *People.* "He told me to go." In any case, when the relationship ended, Trevi, whose family had cut her off for her disobedience, was left to fend for herself. Without money, food, or a home, the teenager survived on the streets, selling chewing gum, singing on buses and in the subways, and begging for money and food. During these hard times, Trevi also began to compose her own songs.

Challenged Mexican Pop

Three years later, in 1989, her luck began to change when, after returning to Monterrey in desperation, she learned that her recently deceased grandfather had left her an inheritance. Soon thereafter, she headed back to Mexico City with her money and showed up at her former producer's doorstep. Since her days with Boquitas Pintadas—spurred by the frustrations of her family, a failed relationship, and living on the street unable to find work—Trevi was ready to break with the music establishment, especially when it came to sex and women's rights. Straying from traditional Mexican ideals, Trevi firmly believed that abortion should be legalized, as well as that women, like men, should feel free to explore their sexual desires and only marry out of love.

Inspired by the 19-year-old's sharp tongue, combativeness, and fearlessness in attacking the norms and values of society, Andrade, recognizing the opportunity to sneak some rock into the Mexican music scene, agreed to help the singer. First, he changed her name from Treviño to the catchier Trevi, then produced her debut album, *Qué Hago Aquí?* ("What Am I Doing Here?"). Just two days after shopping the record, Trevi received offers from two prominent labels, and she decided to accept a deal with BMG Ariola Mexico. She also signed a contract with Televisa, the dominant mass media company in Mexico that owns a myriad of television and radio stations, newspapers, and magazines, giving the network exclusive rights to her performances.

Like Trevi, the younger generation of Mexico, bored with the interchangeable pop stars performing seemingly identical songs, felt ready for a change. The government, too, under the leadership of President Carlos Salinas de Gortari, was encouraging Mexico to open up to the rest of the world. But it wasn't simply Trevi's lyrics about sexual liberation and teenage rebellion and anger that made her stand out among the other popular singers. In her voice, "there was an undeniably exciting passion in the way Trevi tore rough edges on the lyrics, like Janis Joplin or Pat Benatar," commented Baum. "She sounded angry, and that alone made her stand out on Mexican pop radio."

Qué Hago Aquí, within a week of its release, hit number one on the album charts in Mexico, and Andrade set about marketing the young star to the fullest, dressing her in bright, patterned clothes and giving her an overdone, made-up look that appealed to adolescent girls; a Trevi doll, Trevi look-alike contests, and campy comic books came next. However, at the same time Andrade promoted Trevi's more childlike qualities, he also turned her into a sex goddess. During performances, she was known to strip a man from the audience to his shorts and whip him with his own belt. Andrade also started producing annual calendars, which sold in the millions each year, that featured Trevi in a variety of erotic poses.

From 1990 until 1995, Trevi released a series of albums that gained instant popularity. The younger generation in Mexico started dressing like the superstar, sold out her concerts, and flocked to see her movies. Beyond her native country, the singer attracted Latin audiences from Madrid to Los Angeles to Buenos Aires as well, and at the peak of her career, more than 100,000 listeners had joined Trevi fan clubs. Moreover, apart from her concerts, albums, films, anti-establishment views, and calendars, Trevi became a figure of fascination offstage as well. Brilliant in her numerous television interviews, the pop star was warm, open, daring, and intelligent, reaching millions of Mexican citizens who didn't listen to her music. By now, Trevi had also reconciled with her family.

A Scandal Unfolds

Eventually, like Andrade's other creations, Trevi's appeal started to fade, that was until April of 1998. An internationally covered scandal broke out when Andrade's ex-wife, pop singer Aline Hernandez, who he married when she was just 15, published a tell-all book entitled *La Gloria por el Infierno* ("To Heaven Through Hell") that accused the producer, with Trevi's help, of luring underage girls into virtual sexual slavery with promises of building them into stars. Trevi vehemently denied such allegations. Then, in March of 1999, the parents of a missing young girl named Karina Alejandra Yapor Gomez, who was supposed to be studying music with Andrade in Spain, received a call from Spanish authorities telling them that the teen had given birth to an abandoned son. In July of that year the Yapors filed charges against Andrade; Karina Yapor reappeared in December of 1999, disputing her parents' allegations, though her story failed to check out. Wanted by Mexican authorities, Trevi and Andrade fled the country soon thereafter, but were later found in Brazil with fellow musician Mary Boquitas and arrested in January of 2000. Andrade and Trevi were expected to be returned to Mexico for trial later that spring.

"No one has anything to forgive me for," Trevi, denying the charges, said in a Mexican press interview, as quoted by *Reuters* in February of 2000. "If I were guilty I would be asking for God's forgiveness." And few of the alleged victims hold any animosity toward the singer. "Like all the girls, Gloria is the very reverse of her stage image, extremely timid and shy," Hernandez, who wrote in her book that Trevi, out of her devotion to Andrade, sometimes slept on the floor next to his bed, told *Time International.* "She's as much a victim as an accomplice." In an unfortunate turn of events, the star who became a symbol of liberation for so many Mexican women could have, in truth, suffered under Andrade herself.

Selected discography

Qué Hago Aquí?, BMG Ariola Mexico, 1989.
Tu Angel De La Guarda, Ariola International, 1991.
Me Siento Tan Sola, Ariola International, 1992.
Mas Turbada Que Nunca, BMG U.S. Latin, 1994.
Si Me Llevas Contigo, Ariola International, 1995.
De Pelos: Lo Mejor De Gloria Trevi, BMG U.S. Latin, 1996.
Rock Milenium, BMG U.S. Latin, 1999.
No Soy Monedita De Oro, Ariola International, 1999.

Sources

AP Online, January 14, 2000.
Billboard, November 14, 1992, pp. 14-15.
Newsweek, August 16, 1999, p. 36.
Newsweek International, August 2, 1999, p. 34.
People, September 27, 1993, p. 82.
Reuters, January 13, 2000; February 11, 2000.
Rolling Stone, March 2, 2000.
Time International, January 24, 2000.

—*Laura Hightower*

Tina Turner

Singer

AP/Wide World Photos. Reproduced by permission.

Tina Turner exploded into the rhythm & blues charts as a lead singer in 1960. Forty years later, as a solo artist, she had proved herself a die-hard singer of rock and roll. By 2000, her credits included 27 top ten songs and more than 180 million records sold worldwide. She once played to a crowd of 180,000 people in Brazil and was the subject of the intense biographical film, *What's Love Got to Do with It* in 1993. Twenty years after the release of her 1960s recording of "River Deep, Mountain High," with the Ike & Tina Turner Review, the song appeared among the top 20 recordings in *Rolling Stone's* top 100 hits of all-time. Youthful, ageless, and a wellspring of energy, even as the diva turned 60 years old, she continued to entertain eager audiences, leaving her legions of fans to marvel at the music that never seemed to stop.

Turner was born Anna Mae Bullock on November 26, 1938. She grew up in Nutbush, Tennessee, not far from Brownsville, where she lived with her sharecropping family in a two-room shack. Her musical talent emerged when she was still a youngster, but it was during her teen years in St. Louis in the mid-1950s that she made her historic liaison with a band leader, named Ike Turner, whom she married in 1960. The collaboration between the couple began at the Manhattan Club in East St. Louis, Kansas. Initially Tina Turner performed under the stage name of "Little Anna," until the band's first hit single, "A Fool in Love," scurried up the Rhythm & Blues charts in 1960, with Tina Turner as lead singer. The success of that record led Ike Turner to reinvent his band to spotlight Tina Turner. Thereafter the group performed as the Ike & Tina Turner Review. They embarked on a national tour, and a succession of recordings followed, including several hit singles. During the 1960s, the Turners worked as an opening act for the Rolling Stones and released a crossover hit, called "River Deep, Mountain High," that moved them into the forefront of popular music.

Tina Turner's *Let Me Touch Your Mind,* released in 1972, during the Ike & Tina Turner Review days, was her first solo album. In 1973 she released a second album, called *The Country of Tina Turner.* The Turners' performances, enhanced with high-energy backup singers, called the Ikettes, brought them to the forefront of rock and roll between 1958 and 1978. "Proud Mary," the Turners' frenzied arrangement of a popular classic, became a trademark theme, with music erupting from a slow and soothing introduction into an unbridled melee of rhythm. "Proud Mary" peaked at number four on the record charts, and in 1971, the duo won a Grammy Award from the National Academy of Recording Arts and Sciences for "Best R&B Vocal" for their interpretation of the rhythmic, pile-driving ballad.

For The Record . . .

Born Anna Mae Bullock on November 26, 1938, in Nutbush, TN; married Ike Turner (divorced 1976); children: one son with Turner, one son from a previous relationship (Craig and Ron), and two stepsons (Ike Jr. and Michael).

Sang with Ike Turner's Kings of Rhythm, late 1950s (later changed to the Ike & Tina Turner Revue); solo career, 1976—.

Awards: Winner of seven Grammy Awards, National Academy of Recording Arts and Sciences: 1971, 1984 (3 awards), 1985, 1986, 1988; Essence Award, 1993.

Addresses: Record company—Virgin/Parlophone Records, e-mail: virgin@media.virginrecords.com.

Abuse Took a Toll

One fact that remained hidden to the public throughout the Turners' years of stardom, was the presence of severe domestic violence that plagued the Turner marriage. Tina Turner, who suffered intense physical and emotional abuse at the hands of her husband, reached her limit in June of 1976. She took a severe beating, shortly after the couple's arrival in Dallas for their first stop on a national performance tour, and in desperation at the situation she abandoned Ike Turner without warning and even though the two were committed to a major tour. She left with less than 50 cents in her pocket and spared no time to collect her baggage.

One month later, on July 27, 1976, Tina Turner filed for divorce, and emerged with a small fortune in settlement property. The money paid off lawsuits from canceled Ike & Tina Turner Review engagements, leaving Turner virtually penniless. She slumped into poverty, but only very briefly. Without a backward glance she turned her life around, and embarked on a full-blown solo career.

On Her Own

In 1977, she moved to London, England and spent the remainder of that decade living and working in Europe. Undaunted by the poor showing of her 1978 solo album, Rough, from United Artists, Turner hired manager Roger Davies in 1979. She returned to the United States in 1981, toured with the Rolling Stones, and

renewed her efforts to revitalize her career as a solo artist. She met with success in 1984 when her album, Private Dancer, sported three top ten singles, including, "What's Love Got to Do with It." The song became her first number one hit record, and she won three Grammys that year, including best female pop vocalist, best female rock vocalist, and record of the year. She veered onto a stable course as a comeback sensation, and in 1985 she scored with a number two hit, "We Don't Need Another Hero," from the movie Mad Max: Beyond Thunderdome. Additionally, her recording of "One of the Living" won the Grammy award for best rock vocal performance by a female.

Yet as she conquered the issues of her tempestuous marriage to Ike Turner, she quickly tired of explaining to the press and to the public about the years that she spent under his domineering spell. In an attempt to bring closure to the affair, she immersed herself in documenting the painful details of her ex-marriage in an autobiography, I, Tina. The book, a Morrow publication, appeared in 1986. That same year her Break Every Rule album went multi-platinum (more than one million sold), and she added a Grammy to her collection, for "Back Where You Started." In 1987, Turner took to the road for 18 months for a world tour of 25 countries that lasted into 1988. She performed 220 concerts during that promotion, including a phenomenal program in Brazil where she appeared before an audience of 182,000, among the largest concert audiences ever assembled anywhere. Turner's concert tours sold out repeatedly, her recordings registered brisk sales, and her Capitol Records release, Tina Live in Europe, won a Grammy for best rock vocal performance by a female.

Turner's image by then had solidified to legendary proportions, as she "oozed sexuality from every pore in…her gritty and growling performances …," according to John Bush in All Music Guide. She took some time to rest after the well-received tour and in 1989 returned to Europe where she bought a home in London at Notting Hill Gate and settled there. Her 1989 release, called Foreign Affair, largely self-produced, was her first album after a year's hiatus.

At the Movies

From time to time, Turner performed in selected motion pictures, although acting was never the focus of her career. In 1975, she appeared as the Acid Queen in the film version of the rock opera, Tommy, by The Who, and in 1985 she portrayed the character of Auntie Entity in Mad Max: Beyond Thunderdome. Overall, Turner rejected the majority of roles that became available to her because they failed to appeal to her sense of reality; while too many roles were characterized as sexy, Turner's preference was to appear in roles of women who emote strength.

In 1993, a British video appeared, called *Tina Turner: The Girl from Nutbush,* a documentary including rare footage from the early years of the Ike and Tina Turner years. The low-visibility project was upstaged, however, when film director Brian Gibson transformed Turner's 1976 autobiography into a feature film. Kate Lanier wrote the screenplay for the movie, which starred Angela Bassett and Laurence Fishburne, and Turner generously lent creative consultation to the project. In related interviews when the movie opened in theaters, Turner expressed her desire to let go of the memories portrayed in the film; Ike Turner meanwhile avoided endorsement of the final product.

In 1996, the indefatigable Turner released an album, called *Wildest Dreams,* featuring Bono, Sheryl Crow, Sting, and Antonio Banderas among others. Turner, nearing 60 years old by then, seemed a human dynamo. On her tenth solo album, *Twenty Four Seven,* released by Virgin Records in January of 2000, she collaborated with several younger artists. It was her first album since 1997, and critics applauded the effort. *Los Angeles Times* said of Turner that she, "successfully meshes retro-soul with techno flava ... [and] is still up to any challenge." In conjunction with the release of her album in 2000, she performed in the pre-game show of Super Bowl XXXIV, and she embarked on an international tour, beginning in South Africa and encompassing 49 cities with a grand finale at Radio City Music Hall in New York City. Turner, a bona fide rock and roll icon, displayed no sense of slowing down. When she announced her plans to retire from touring following her millenium tour in 2000, *New York Times'* Jon Pareles noted that, "Ms. Turner is not about to become a grande dame anytime soon, reflecting from a distance on past triumphs and heartbreak. The way she sings, she's still a fierce contender in the battle of the sexes." *Washington Post* said of the 61-year-old Turner, "She's got better legs than Mick Jagger and better teeth than Eric Clapton."

Private Life of "Private Dancer"

It is at times a surprise to Turner's fans that her on-stage gyrations and shouting-match singing style are exclusively a performance illusion. Personally, she is slight and calm, not raunchy at all like her stage and musical image. Writers Hedda Maye and Robyn Foyster in fact called her, "The epitome of classic chic with a classic sense of style ..." in *Ebony.* After moving to London in 1977 following her breakup with Ike Turner, she moved on to Cologne, Germany, and then Zurich, Switzerland, where she owned a luxury home with five floors, a penthouse, and a pool. By 2000, Turner had settled cozily into a custom mansion in the south of France. The dream home, which she purchased in the late 1990s, is called Anna Fleur and is located in Ville, France, overlooking Nice and the Riviera. Turner decorated all of her own homes, in part with her collection of rare statuary and with a medley of musical instruments that she collected, including several antiques.

She is the mother of two sons, Craig and Ron. Additionally, she is a grandmother and a great-grandmother. Although she never remarried, in 1986 she developed an intimate and lasting relationship with a European recording executive. Shortly before she left her husband, she became a devout student of Buddhism and retained that religion throughout the years.

Selected discography

Major single releases; solo

"Let's Stay Together," Capitol, 1984.
"Private Dancer," Capitol, 1984.
"What's Love Got to Do with It," Capitol, 1984.
"Better Be Good," Capitol, 1984.
"One of the Living," Capitol, 1985.
"We Don't Need Another Hero," Capitol, 1985.

Albums; solo

The Country of Tina Turner, United Artists, 1973.
Acid Queen, Razor & Tie, 1975.
Love Explosion, United Artists, 1977.
Rough, United Artists, 1978.
Private Dancer, Capitol, 1984.
Mad Max: Beyond Thunderdome, Capitol, 1985.
Break Every Rule, Capitol, 1986.
Tina Live in Europe, Capitol, 1988.
Foreign Affair, Capitol, 1989.
Simply The Best, Capitol, 1991.
Wildest Dreams, Virgin, 1996.
Twenty Four Seven, Virgin/Parlophone, 2000.

Major single releases; with Ike Turner

"A Fool in Love," Sue Records, 1960.
"It's Gonna Work Out Fine," Sue Records, 1961.
"You Should'a Treated Me Right," Sue Records, 1962.
"River Deep, Mountain High," Phillies, 1966.
"I've Been Loving You Too Long," Blue Thumb, 1969.
"The Hunter," Blue Thumb, 1969.
"Proud Mary," Liberty, 1971.

Albums; with Ike Turner

The Sound of Ike and Tina Turner, Sue Records, 1960.
Festival of Live Performances, United Artists, 1962.
Dance with Ike and Tina Turner, Sue Records, 1962.
Don't Play Me Cheap, Sue Records, 1963.
Dynamite, Sue Records, 1963.
Ooh Poo Pah Doo, Harmony, 1965.
Ike & Tina Show 2, Tomato, 1965.
The Ike and Tina Turner Revue Live, Kent, 1965.
The Ike and Tina Turner Revue Live, Warner Brothers, 1965.
Live/The Ike and Tina Show, Loma, 1966.
River Deep and Mountain High, Phillies, 1966.
Ike and Tina Turner's Greatest Hits, Warner Brothers, 1967.
Get It Together, Pompeii, 1969.

Outta Season, Blue Thumb, 1969.
Fantastic, Sunset, 1969.
Her Man, His Woman, Capitol, 1969.
The Hunter, Blue Thumb, 1969.
Cussin', Cryin' and Carryin' On, Pompeii, 1969.
Workin' Together, Liberty, 1970.
On Stage, Valiant, 1970.
Ike and Tina Turner's Greatest Hits, Sunset, 1970.
'Nuff Said, United Artists, 1971.
Soul to Soul, Atlantic, 1971.
Something's Got a Hold on Me, Harmony, 1971.
What You Hear Is What You Get, EMI, 1971.
Feel Good, United Artists, 1972.
Let Me Touch Your Mind, United Artists, 1972.
Nutbush City Limits, United Artists, 1973.
The World of Ike and Tina Live, United Artists, 1973.
The Best of Ike & Tina Turner, Blue Thumb, 1973.
Strange Fruit, United Artists, 1974.
Sweet Rhode Island Red, United Artists, 1974.
Greatest Hits, Vol. 3, Atlantic, 1974.
Proud Mary: The Best of Ike & Tina Turner, EMI America, 1991.
Sixteen Great Performances, ABC, 1975.
Too Hot To Hold, Charly, 1975.
Delilah's Power, United Artists, 1977.
Airwaves, United Artists, 1979.
Great Rhythm & Blues Sessions, Rhino, 1991.
20 Rare Recordings, Sound Solution, 1992.
Get It On, Sound Solution, 1993.
Shake, Sound Solution, 1993.
Funky Ball, Sound Solution, 1993.
Live at Cirkus Krone, ITM/Traditional, 1994.
Mississippi Rolling Stone, Prime Cuts, 1995.
Shake Rattle & Roll, Delta, 1995.
Keep on Pushing, Laserlight, 1995.
Rockin' and Rollin', Laserlight, 1995.

Livin' for the City, Laserlight, 1995.
Nutbush Limits, Laserlight, 1995.

Sources

Books

Contemporary Musicians, volume 1, Gale Research, 1989.

Periodicals

Ebony, November 1989, p. 166 (4); January 1992, p. 102(3); September 1996, p. 38(5); May 2000, pp. 52-63.
Entertainment Weekly, March 18, 1994, p. 105; August 2, 1996, p. 72.
Essence, May 1993, p. 93(10); July 1993, p. 50(6).
Los Angeles Times, January 31, 2000, p. CAL. 73+; January 31, 2000, p. F-2.
New York Times, April 11, 2000.
Time, June 21, 1993, p. 64(2).
Washington Post, February 9, 2000, p. C1.

Online

"Tina Turner," *All Music Guide,* http://allmusic.com/cg/x.dll (April 25, 2000).
"Tina Turner," The National Academy of Recording Arts & Sciences, http://www.grammy.com/awards/ (June 26, 2000).

—Gloria Cooksey

The Turtles

Pop group

Although they never reached the rock-star status of the Beatles, the Byrds, or Paul Revere and the Raiders, the Turtles were nevertheless one of the most enjoyable American pop groups of the 1960s. Evolving through the decade, they moved from surf-rock to a folk-rock formula inspired by the Byrds, then on to a sparkling fusion of chamber-pop and straightforward, good-time pop reminiscent of the Lovin' Spoonful. Each song was infused with the vocal harmonies of co-founders and longtime friends Howard Kaylan and Mark Volman, two singers and saxophonists whose unwavering faith in the band enabled them to navigate the Turtles through numerous personnel changes without a scratch. The Turtles are known by most for their number-one hit of 1967, "Happy Together." The group went on to score three more top ten hits before disbanding in 1970. After the split, Kaylan and Volman in the early-1970s joined Frank Zappa's Mothers of Invention and also recorded new material as the Phlorescent Leech and Eddie—later shortened to Flo & Eddie. Then in 1982, Kaylan and Volman restarted the band as a nostalgia act. Since that time, the revamped band billed as the Turtles featuring Flo & Eddie enjoyed great success on the oldies circuit.

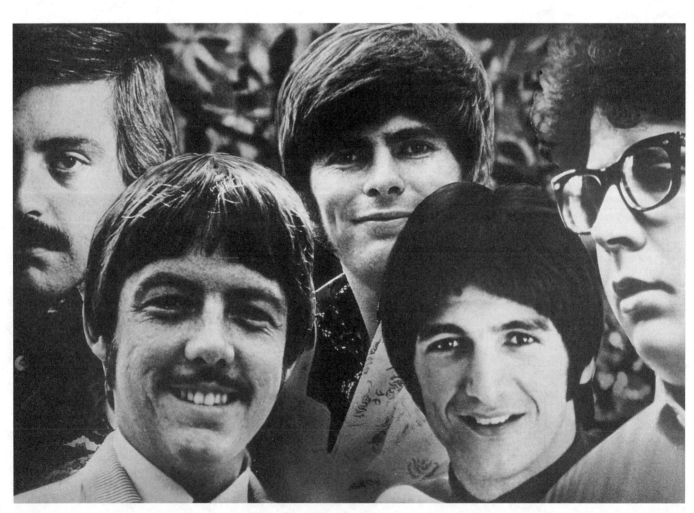

Archive Photos. Reproduced by permission.

Howard Kaylan, who in 1965 changed his last name from Kaplan, was born June 22, 1947, in the Bronx, New York, living his first eight years in Manhattan before his father accepted a job with General Electric in Utica, New York. After spending about a year in Utica, the family moved to the Los Angeles area and settled in Westchester. Mark Volman was born on April 19, 1947, in Los Angeles; his family lived in Redondo Beach for a brief time before they, too, moved to nearby Westchester. Volman and Kaylan attended Orville Wright Junior High School and Airport Junior High School respectively, and although they didn't know each other at the time, both youngsters took clarinet lessons from the same instructor in a drafty room above Westchester Music Store.

The two young men finally met at Westchester High School, where they sang in the a cappella choir; Volman sang first tenor, while Kaylan sang second tenor. It was during this time that Volman learned that Kaylan, since 1961, had been playing in an instrumental surf music group called the Nightriders with fellow choir members Al Nichol on lead guitar, Don Murray on drums, and Chuck Portz on bass guitar. In 1963, concurrent with a name change to the Crossfires, Volman joined the band, though initially as a roadie. After high-school graduation, the Crossfires continued on while its members attended area colleges, picking up rhythm guitarist Jim Tucker along the way. Inspired by Dick Dale's concept of surfer stomp—searing guitar solos over a pounding rhythm section—the Crossfires were known as one of the best local surf bands.

"If you grew up in the South Bay, you either played surf music or else were in a surf club," Volman, explaining how the singers gravitated to the instrumental style, told Bill Locey of the *Los Angeles Times.* "At that time, surf music was at its peak. It was an innocent time, and the music was reflective of that. It just allowed us to do something on the weekends instead of working at a gas station or something like that. That band got us discovered and led to a lifelong career. I blame everything on the Crossfires."

Combined Folk and Surf

After recording two singles, "Fiberglass Jungle" and "Santa and the Sidewalk Surfer," the group received a big break in 1965 when local disc jockey and club owner Reb Foster heard them play. Foster, impressed so much by the Crossfires, offered to serve as their manager, finding the group a contract with the newly formed White Whale Records. The sextet changed their name to the Tyrtles in an unveiled homage to the Byrds, but soon amended the spelling to read the Turtles. In addition, they took on a new musical direction—folk-rock—and recorded a Bob Dylan cover, "It Ain't Me Babe," as their first single. The group's version of the song, a fusion of folk music and surf-rock harmonies, reached the Top Five in August of 1965. Soon thereafter, the Turtles made their first concert appearance before 50,000 fans at the Rose Bowl, opening for Herman's Hermits, followed by a national tour and a spot with Dick Clark's Caravan of Stars.

Driven by the rebelliousness that marked the 1960s, the Turtles began to channel their energies into the whole folk-rock, protest scene. An association with songwriter/producer P.F. Sloan, known for his work with the "protest song" fad of the period, resulted in two more hits for the Turtles in 1966 with "Let Me Be" and the upbeat "You Baby." Reportedly, the Turtles passed on recording Sloan's biggest hit of the era, "Eve of Destruction," a melodramatic song recorded by Barry McGuire that touched upon every issue worth protesting.

After these successes, the Turtles commenced a seemingly endless series of lineup changes, with Murray and Portz being the first to leave. They were replaced by John Barbata and, for a short time, bassist/producer/arranger Chip Douglas. Although deeply affected by the departure of two men that had become like family, the Turtles pushed forward, finding a renewed spirit after running across two surefire hits written by Gary Bonner and Alan Gordon. In 1967, "Happy Together," one of the biggest hits of the year, held for three weeks at number one on the American charts. The Turtles' next three singles, also penned by the songwriting team of Bonner and Gordon, each hit the top 20 as well. These included the number three hit "She'd Rather Be with Me," a single that eclipsed "Happy Together" in terms of worldwide popularity, "You Know What I Mean," and "She's My Girl."

By now, the Turtles had fans across the Atlantic as well as in America, and that same year traveled to England for the first time. Here, the Beatles, Jimi Hendrix, and the Rolling Stones—all fans of the Turtles and captivated by their West Coast sound—came to see the newest stars of the pop world. Meanwhile, the Turtles underwent further changes in the lineup. Chip Douglas left the group to work with the Monkees, and was replaced by Jim Pons, a former member of the Leaves, on bass. Original member Jim Tucker, disillusioned after the tour of England amounted to nothing more than playing dingy clubs, left the group as well.

A Move Toward the Psychedelic

Surviving in spite of personnel rotations, the Turtles, now a five-piece, followed their success on the pop charts with an effort to broaden their musical scope. Beginning with "You Know What I Mean," the Turtles' revolving-door of producers, arrangers, and musicians resulted in a progressively more psychedelic sound, though they still remained much closer to mainstream rock than the era's premier psychedelic groups. In late-1967, the Turtles, in an attempt to assert their creative growth, released the self-produced "Sound Asleep." A huge disappointment, the song was the band's first single since "Happy Together" to miss the top 40. Bringing back Douglas to help with arrangement duties, the Turtles, under the gun to produce hits by White Whale, tried again with "The Story of Rock and Roll." However, that single failed to make it to the top 40 as well. Finally, a career-saving song entitled "Elenore" arrived in September of 1968, which reached the number six position on the pop chart.

Still in search of critical acclaim, the Turtles released an ambitious, self-produced concept album, *The Turtles Present the Battle of the Bands,* in November of 1968. Here, the Turtles attempted to sound like 11 different bands—one song for each group. Although it never earned the kind of breakthrough recognition the Turtles had wanted, the concept LP did contain, along with the song "Elenore," another hit entitled "You Showed Me," a song originally written and recorded by the Byrds, that peaked at number six. After recording *The Turtles Present the Battle of the Bands,* Barbata moved on to work with Crosby, Stills, & Nash, and was succeeded by drummer John Seiter.

Although the Turtles had reclaimed some of their notoriety with their concept project, White Whale continued to express dissatisfaction, attempting to follow the trend set by the Monkees and record the vocals of Kaylan and Volman with a generic studio band for a new single. But the duo, rebelling against the small label, intended to stay true to the band aesthetic. They recruited Ray Davies of the Kinks to produce their next album, 1969's *Turtle Soup.* Two singles from the album, "You Don't Have to Walk in the Rain" and "Love In the City," both failed to reach the top 40.

Disbanded the Turtles

Frustrated, Kaylan and Volman subsequently formed their own label, Blimp Records, and signed a few acts, including folk singer Judy Sill, who wrote the Turtles' last single "Lady O." Further wrangling with White Whale persisted, and their former label continued to release Turtles material without the group's consent. Moreover, the Turtles were the subjects of continuous lawsuits; managers hoping to save their images took the band to court so many times that astronomical legal bills drained most of the Turtles' earnings. By 1970, the Turtles concluded that the only alternative was to break up the group.

Soon thereafter, Kaylan, Volman and Pons joined Frank Zappa's early-1970s edition of the Mothers of Invention. According to an earlier contract, the use of the Turtles' name, and even the use of their own personal names, in a musical context remained illegal. Thus, Volman and Kaylan appeared as the Phlorescent Leech & Eddie, also known as Flo & Eddie. In addition to performing with Zappa, the trio appeared on four of his albums from 1970 to 1972—*Chunga's Revenge, 200 Motels, Live at the Fillmore* and *Just Another Band from LA*—before the bandleader was injured in an onstage altercation.

Between 1975 and 1981, the duo of Kaylan and Volman recorded some work for themselves, all the while acquiring a reputation as backing vocalists for hire, most notably for the Bruce Springsteen song "Hungry Heart." The duo also did some session work, composed music for children's movies such as *The Care Bears* and *Strawberry Shortcake,* and broadcast their own radio show in Los Angeles and later in New York City. In 1982, the reinvented the Turtles as a nostalgia act. The new group, called the Turtles Featuring Flo & Eddie, continued to perform into the year 2000 and beyond. The new lineup includes, in addition to Kaylan (Eddie) and Volman (Flo), Tristan Avakian on guitar and vocals, Joe Stefko on drums, Don Kisselbach on bass guitar and vocals, and Benjy Kingon keyboards and vocals.

Selected discography

The Turtles Present the Battle of the Bands, Sundazed, 1968.

Turtle Soup, Sundazed, 1969.
Turtle Wax: The Best of the Turtles, Vol. 2, Rhino, 1970.
20 Greatest Hits, Rhino, 1984.
Happy Together: The Very Best of the Turtles, Music Club, 1991.
Captured Live, Rhino, 1992.
30 Years of Rock 'N' Roll: Happy Together, (box set), Laserlight, 1995.

Sources

Books

Buckley, Jonathan and others, editors, *Rock: The Rough Guide,* Rough Guides Ltd., 1999.

Periodicals

Los Angeles Times, April 24, 1997.

Online

The Turtles Featuring Flo and Eddie, http://www.theturtles .com (June 20, 2000).
Yahoo! Music: The Turtles Biography, http://musicfind er.yahoo.com/shop?d=p&id=turtlesthe&cf=11 (June 20, 2000).

—Laura Hightower

Steven Van Zandt

Guitarist, songwriter, producer

An acclaimed guitarist and music producer turned character actor, the multi-talented Steven Van Zandt has been working almost non-stop since the mid-1960s, reaching one of his greatest career peaks in the late-1990s. During this period, Van Zandt recorded his first solo album in eleven years, went back on the road with Bruce Springsteen & the E Street Band after a 15-year absence, and landed a featured role playing New Jersey mobster Silvio Dante in *The Sopranos,* the acclaimed HBO cable television series about a dysfunctional mob family. "No one is more surprised at how all this has worked out than I am," Van Zandt, at the time filming episodes of his show during a break in the E Street Band tour, told *Los Angeles Times* writer Robert Hilburn. "After so many years of not doing anything really, it's funny to have it all happen at once. But it's coincidental. None of this was planned to happen simultaneously. That's the way life is."

In the midst of a budding acting career and a return to the stage with Springsteen's band, Van Zandt, who claims rock and roll music as his first love, somehow found time to resume his career as a solo recording artist. His 1999 album *Born Again Savage* signaled the end of a cycle he initiated back in 1982 when he conceived the idea to compose five albums, each dedicated to a different subject. Representative of the themes Van Zandt sought to explore included the individual, the family, the state, economics, and religion. The first four concept albums—*Men Without Women* released in 1982, *Voice of America* released in 1984, *Freedom—No Compromise* released in 1987, *Revolution* released in 1989—ranged, in terms of music, from soulful rock to world and dance music.

"I knew they would all be political records that were truthful, artistic adventures, rather than smart career moves," Van Zandt, whose albums earned critical recognition yet failed to attract the mainstream, explained to Anthony Bozza in *Rolling Stone.* "I knew their musical inconsistency would kill the possibility of a career—you can't ask that much of an audience. Looking back, you could say it was stupid, and I might agree with you. I was a bit naïve, because I forgot to think about how I was going to make a living. But I was compelled to do what I had to do." The passing of time, however, had little effect on his convictions. Years later, Van Zandt, still driven to follow his own creative energy rather than succumb to industry standards, recorded the fifth album to complete his thematic plan. Fittingly, *Born Again Savage* studies the "religion" that Van Zandt has followed his entire life: rock and roll. On the album, Van Zandt consciously saluted the spirits of an array of bands—from the Who to the Sex Pistols—who made significant contributions to rock music.

Born on November 22, 1950, in Boston, Massachusetts, to an Italian-American family, Steven Van Zandt was raised in Middletown, New Jersey, where he started playing guitar on the club circuit and formed his first band, the Source, in 1966. In the early-1970s, Van Zandt played with a number of bands, including Steel Mill and Southside Johnny Lyon's Asbury Jukes. In the middle of the decade, in addition to writing songs and producing for Lyon's first three albums, he joined Bruce Springsteen's E Street Band. As a guitarist with Springsteen's band, Van Zandt also co-produced the acclaimed *Born to Run,* helping to shape one of the world's most beloved rock and roll outfits.

Found a Kindred Spirit in "The Boss"

"We just had a thing right from the start," the guitarist said to Hilburn, recalling the bond he and Springsteen discovered soon after they first met. "I was one of the two guys in my high school of 3,000 with long hair. He was the only one in his high school with long hair. That meant you didn't really fit in. You were called a freak—especially if you were in a band. This was before everyone wanted to be in a band. But we found something in the music that we believed in—even though no one else was supportive and there was no way of realistically thinking you were going to make a living at it."

While working with the E Street Band, Van Zandt formed Little Steven and the Disciples of Soul in 1982, a 12-piece band that included horn players from the Asbury Jukes, bass guitarist Jean Beauvoir, formerly of the Plasmatics, and ex-Rascals drummer Dino Danelli. The group debuted that year with *Men Without Women,* a solid roots-rock effort produced by Van Zandt himself under his E Street name "Miami Steve." *Voice of America,* which included the song "Solidarity,"

followed two years later, illustrating the guitarist's new-found commitment to international politics. By the time he released this album, Van Zandt had retired from Springsteen's group, thus dropping the "Miami" part of his name on record.

Although Bruce Springsteen & the E Street Band had achieved success beyond their expectations, Van Zandt at the time felt he needed to follow his own musical path. "You dream about being the biggest band in the world, and I wasn't about to leave until we were, but then you are one day and I started to look around and I realized this was all I've done my whole life," the musician explained to Hilburn regarding his decision to leave the group. "I didn't regret that, but I also didn't know much about myself outside the band. I just felt like learning, learning about myself and learning about what was going on in the world. I was interested in what was going on in the world, and I wanted to express my ideas."

Became an Activist

As Van Zandt moved away from the E Street Band to pursue his own career, he became a freedom fighter through his music. In 1984, the musician made two visits to South Africa, and upon his return, gathered more than 50 of the world's most esteemed performers— including Springsteen, Bob Dylan, Miles Davis, George Clinton, Bonnie Raitt, Lou Reed, and U2's Bono—to form an organization called Artists United Against Apartheid. The group recorded a song written by Van Zandt entitled "Sun City," and out of that song grew an album by the same name co-produced by Van Zandt and Arthur Baker, a popular music video, and a concert, all of which raised funds for anti-apartheid efforts. The series of projects also helped refocus attention on the industry's longtime cultural boycott of South Africa, a trust many entertainers had neglected by performing at a lucrative, Las Vegas-style show at the South African Sun City resort.

Released in 1985, the *Sun City* album and other related projects transformed Van Zandt into an activist, and the musician spent the following years risking his life at times in order to meet with revolutionaries in South Africa, Nicaragua, and El Salvador, as well as raising public awareness of United States military involvement in Central America. "I was like a soldier," he told Bozza. "I was obsessed. I knew I was right and feared nothing. I didn't care if I lived or died. I wasn't going to look back 20 years later at a holocaust and feel that I didn't do as much as possible. It was egomaniacal and maybe delusional, but you need that to go out there and try the impossible."

Meanwhile, Van Zandt produced records for a variety of bands, from the goth-rock outfit Lords of the New Church to the alternative country band Lone Justice. In addition, he continued to produce and record his uncompromised, politically charged series of albums, which eventually alienated him from the music industry. Besides *Sun City,* none of his albums sold well, even though on *Freedom—No Compromise* Springsteen sang on "Native American" and Van Zandt duetted with Ruben Blades on "Bitter Fruit," a song about labor conditions in Central America. In 1991, he reunited with old friends Southside Johnny Lyon and Springsteen, producing Lyon's *Better Days* album.

Television Stardom

From there, Van Zandt spent the remainder of the decade continuing his activism and struggling to finish other projects—a forthcoming album, a rock musical, and a music company—without much success. "For a while, I was just kinda like walking my dog, man," he admitted to Hilburn. However, Van Zandt's luck changed when he received two job offers: to reunite with Bruce Springsteen and the E Street Band and to act as an old-school hitman living in the modern-day mob world on David Chase's Golden Globe award-winning HBO series *The Sopranos.* During the show's first 13-episode season in 1999, *The Sopranos* skyrocketed in popularity to become a national favorite.

"I'm living proof of 'It ain't over til it's over,'" he said with a laugh to Bozza. "It was a strange convergence. If it didn't happen to me, I wouldn't believe it." Oddly enough, Van Zandt was discovered while presenting at an awards show held in 1997. "I was inducting the Rascals into the Rock & Roll Hall of Fame, which I initially refused to do—I told them to get a real celebrity." Eventually, Van Zandt broke down and agreed to participate in the televised event. By chance, Chase watched the awards special, then asked Van Zandt to fly to Los Angeles for a screen test—just to make sure

he had some acting ability. Since then, the musician and now actor has maintained a busier schedule than ever.

Along with touring and a new acting career, Van Zandt was also able to complete *Born Again Savage,* released on his own RenegadeNation label to favorable reviews. Though continuing his solo work, Van Zandt hopes to record again with the E Street band. He resides in New York with Maureen, his wife of 17 years.

Selected discography

Men Without Women, Razor & Tie Music, 1982.
Voice of America, Razor & Tie Music, 1984.
Sun City (with others and as co-producer), Manhattan, 1985.
Freedom—No Compromise, Manhattan/EMI, 1987.
Revolution, 1989.
Born Again Savage, RenegadeNation/Pachyderm, 1999.

Sources

Periodicals

Chicago Tribune, January 11, 2000.
Los Angeles Times, December 19, 1999.
Rolling Stone, January 20, 2000; March 2, 2000.
USA Today, February 2, 1998.

Online

Rolling Stone.com, http://www.rollingstone.com (June 21, 2000).
Sonicnet.com, http://www.sonicnet.com (June 21, 2000).

—Laura Hightower

Elisabeth von Trapp

Singer, composer

She is sophisticated and very modern, yet unusually fond of the music of the Trapp Family Singers. A contemporary woman and a product of her times, she enjoys rock and roll, folk songs, and Jimi Hendrix; she has in fact an extremely wide musical range. Elisabeth von Trapp is a rare performer, classically trained and devoid of gimmicks who defies classification. A singer, songwriter, and pianist, her melodic compositions often focus on childhood memories set in the idyllic images of her birthplace of Vermont, enhanced by the crystal delicacy of her own voice.

Elisabeth von Trapp was born Maria Elisabeth von Trapp in Burlington, Vermont on May 12, 1957. She is one of the 29 grandchildren—there were 17 great-grandchildren—of the celebrated singers Georg and Maria von Trapp who fled Austria with their family in the 1930s and emigrated to the United States. Elisabeth von Trapp's father was among the seven oldest of the wartime von Trapp siblings who were born in Austria and traveled to America with their parents. Her mother, Erika, also a native of Austria, arrived in the United States in 1948. In the mid-1950s, around the time of Elisabeth von Trapp's birth, the Trapp Family Singers retired from performance and moved into other professions to better support the growing family. Her father purchased a dairy farm in Waitsfield, Connecticut, not far from the von Trapp family home in Stowe.

Her vivid childhood memories include the beauty of the Vermont countryside and the harshness of the winters, always with the melodies of Viennese classics adrift in the background. Also imbedded in her memory is the day when she went with her father to view the 20th Century Fox feature film, *Sound of Music,* which her grandparents, her father, her aunts, and uncles were immortalized through the music of Rogers and Hammerstein. She was 11. After the Trapp Family Singers retired from performing professionally, the family not surprisingly continued to sing and play music for personal gratification. Again, Elisabeth von Trapp's early memories include the joy of participating in the songfests and gatherings of her inspirational family.

Von Trapp's father, Werner von Trapp, who was also an accomplished guitarist and a cello player, sang nightly to his six children and kept the spirit of the Trapp Family music alive for them as they grew older. Elisabeth von Trapp studied both piano and violin and spent her tenth year in Austria, where she lived with her maternal grandmother and studied classical singing. After her high school graduation von Trapp returned to Austria intent upon expanding her classical music studies. Pragmatically she opted instead to learn the demanding albeit engaging art of Austrian dressmaking at the Anahof vocational academy. Even as she explored outside interests, by the age of 18 she was singing professionally as well as teaching music and designing clothes. When she returned to the United States, she enrolled at Vermont's Johnson State College. At her mother's bidding, she majored in education and received a master's degree in curriculum development. She funded her education largely through her skill as a dressmaker.

With her post-graduate work completed, and satisfied that she had done the sensible thing, von Trapp continued to support herself as a dressmaker, all the while indulging her passion for music. The undeniable urge was very clearly interlaced with her heritage. She performed whenever possible and in 1985 toured the former Soviet Union in concert; additionally she performed in Israel, Canada, and Austria. Her voice was heard on BBC-Radio, Vermont Public Radio, CNN Spanish Radio, and on Japanese National Radio. On multiple occasions she accepted invitations to sing the National Anthem at Boston's old Fenway Park, and she performed habitually at cafes, concerts, festivals, even weddings and special affairs. She portrayed her own grandmother, Maria von Trapp, appearing as the lead character in two separate stage productions of *Sound of Music.* Her television appearances extended from CBS appearances on *Eye on People,* and *Fast Forward,* to ABC's *Good Morning America*, Fox-TV's *Fox after Breakfast,* and BBC-TV. Her live North American performances spanned the continent, from St. Patrick's Cathedral in New York City and the Washington National Cathedral in Washington, D.C. to Los Positas Park in Santa Barbara, California. She also performed in Canada at the Bronson Center in Ottawa, Ontario.

Singing, according to von Trapp, fulfilled an innate need, and in 1994 she established her own record

For The Record . . .

Born on May 12, 1957 in Burlington, VT; daughter of Werner and Erika von Trapp; married Edward Hall, 1985; *Education*: Johnson State College, B.A., M.A.

Established Von Trapp Music, 1994; *Wishful Thinking* (recorded live), 1994; *One Heart, One Mind,* 1996; *Christmas Song,* 1996.

Addresses: *Home*— P.O. Box 827, Waitsfield, VT 05673; *E-mail*— vtm@madriver.com.

label, Von Trapp Music. That year she also released her first CD, *Wishful Thinking,* a live recording of one of her outdoor concerts. The concert album features von Trapp on vocals, guitar, and piano and the performance included renditions of Van Morrison and Jimi Hendrix songs. Throughout her career, critics marveled unceasingly at the clarity of von Trapp's voice, which habitually solicited such commentary as, "[S]he will have the crowd gasping with the sheer beauty of her voice," according to Rachel Kelley, praising von Trapp's "flawless voice" in *Narragansett Times* (Rhode Island). "Also prominent in her trademark sound is a haunting ambience that intrigues yet soothes—golden, warm, clear, ethereal …," critics applauded unanimously.

In 1996, two years after the release of her concert album, von Trapp released a second album, comprised almost exclusively of her own compositions, both lyrics and music. The title song of the album, an Elisabeth von Trapp original, was written in tribute to the von Trapp family, *One heart, One Mind.* According to von Trapp the song defines the Trapp Family's secret to their beautiful performance. Through the lyrics she extols, "One Heart, one mind, dreams met in time." Yet despite the heartwarming musical legacy she inherited from her family, von Trapp marveled publicly that she is the only living von Trapp to continue the family tradition of singing publicly. With that in mind, she successfully recruited her father to contribute some organ playing on the recording, and assorted cousins of the von Trapp clan to sing background vocals. The album, a tribute to her ancestry, inspires with subtlety a medieval mood. Others heard on the album include Erich Kory on cello, and Charles Eller on piano and keyboards. The trio of Von Trapp, Eller, and Kory in fact has performed together many times, and, as von Trapp described to Kelley, a "wonderful sonality" is achieved in the musical experience of singing with cello accompaniment.

In 1996, von Trapp also released a collection of Christmas music, called *Christmas Song,* an eloquent tribute to her childhood memories of a "farmhouse … filled with friends and family … the walls resounded with *Christmas Song."* On *Christmas Song,* von Trapp avoided the typical fare of seasonal recordings, and reviewers recommended the album for year-round listening. Among the 13 selections on the album, von Trapp sings the French folk song, *'Twas in the Moon of Wintertime;* the Appalachian carol, *I Wonder As I Wander*; Rogers and Hammerstein's *Edelweiss*; and the classic chant, *Dona Nobis Pacem.* Pamela Polston noted in *Seven Days* von Trapp's uncanny ability to "… make German sound silky … [She caresses] the syllables so lightly you can barely tell she's singing in that guttural language." Again observers and critics hailed her voice, and her remarkable music.

Von Trapp with her delicate crystal-toned voice left an indelible mark at New York City's Grand Central Terminal in 1997 where she sang in the midst of extensive renovation and construction that transpired in the background. The terminal, replete with jackhammers and assorted other irritating noises, posed a hostile venue for von Trapp. Regardless, her powerful performance, which was an audition for the Metropolitan Transportation Authority's "Music Under New York" program, left a distinct impression on the audience. Her voice resounded so clearly that, "you could hear her pitch like a bird's song traveling in the recesses of Grand Central," said one of the judges who was quoted by David Gonzalez in *New York Times.*

Von Trapp met her husband, Edward Hall, in 1974 while a student at Johnson State College, The couple married in 1985 in a chapel behind the Trapp Family Lodge in Stowe, Vermont. Hall, who is an attorney, doubles as a manager for his wife and her exhausting professional agenda. In addition to concerts and recording sessions, von Trapp lends her endorsement as celebrity spokesperson for Geiger's of Austria, Inc. Geiger's, a clothing company in Schaz, Austria, features a clothing line that, like von Trapp, imparts a distinctive and modern outlook. Her public appearances for Geiger's conform very well with her trademark "music for the people" paradigm. As with her concert in Grand Central Station, von Trapp entertains for Geiger's in unobstructed and open areas, in department stores and other venues that encourage direct interaction with the audience.

In reaching out to people, von Trapp brought her musical message to the children of Austria in May of 2000, when she visited that country at the invitation of an association of English-speaking teachers. The trip was an attempt by the educators to impart to the students the painful realities of the Second World War, events that originally led von Trapp's ancestors to abandon their life in Austria. Elisabeth von Trapp performed in concert and lectured to students, speaking of her family's experiences under Nazi repression. On her journey, prompted in opposition to a sudden surge of popularity of an extremist right-wing faction in the Austrian government, von Trapp urged her audiences to reject the neo-Nazi resurgents that threatened Austria in 2000.

Selected discography

Wishful Thinking, Von Trapp Music, 1994.
One Heart, One Mind, Von Trapp Music, 1996.
Christmas Song, Von Trapp Music, 1996.

Sources

Periodicals

Boston Sunday Globe, July 27, 1997.
Narragansett Times (Rhode Island), May 21, 1999.

New York Times, June 18, 1997.
People, October 20, 1997, p. 147(2).
Seven Days, December 15-22.
Sunday News (Lancaster, PA), January 14, 1999.

Online

"Elisabeth Von Trapp," *Weddings Vermont,* 1997, http://www.weddingsvermont.com/vontrapp/index.html (April 27, 2000).

Additional information obtained from the CD sleeve *Christmas Song,* 1996.

—*Gloria Cooksey*

Rufus Wainwright

Singer, songwriter

Rufus Wainwright makes pop music that sounds like it is of, by, and for another era—as if his competition were not Jewel, Britney Spears, and the Red Hot Chili Peppers, but rather Cole Porter, Irving Berlin, and George and Ira Gershwin. With just a single album to his name, Wainwright has already wowed critics and earned a degree of popular success. Part of the public's response may be purely physical. The singer/songwriter is tall and built on a thin frame, and his looks are of the matinee-idol variety. Though openly gay, Wainwright seems to enjoy a following that is at least as much female as it is male, perhaps more so. But if Wainwright's comely visage, seen most widely in a December 1998 Gap commercial on which he crooned the standard "New Year's Eve," has helped attract fans, his songs—subtle, complex, and nearly all of them gender-neutral ditties about love—are what hold their attention.

Wainwright's father is Loudon Wainwright III, the wry, WASPish singer/songwriter whose one top 40 hit came in 1973 with the song "Dead Skunk." The elder Wainwright made his son the subject of 1975's "Rufus is a Tit Man," which described his irrational jealousy of his then-infant boy being breast-fed by his mother. Clearly, no topic was taboo in the Wainwright household, and in years since, Loudon has written a number of stingingly self-critical songs about his failings as a father and husband. He split with Rufus' mother, Canadian songstress Kate McGarrigle (who writes and sings with her sister Anna), when Rufus was four.

"Growing up, I hardly saw my father at all," Wainwright told Mim Udovitch in *Rolling Stone* magazine. "I saw him, like, twice a year for, like, a week each time. I hated him for years, and part of it was fueled by my mother, who had no qualms about telling me she hated him for years. But he really, really helped me, in his own way, and it was very important to have him around, even though it was much less. Now that I'm actually making it and doing quite well, I think it's a little harder for him, because he's still making records, and he's still touring and doing his thing. I just think it's hard, and there's still a side of me that wants to conquer him in a certain way."

Wainwright grew up living with his mother in Montreal, Canada. He began playing piano at age six. The atmosphere of the McGarrigle home was artsy and bohemian, with various musicians dropping by all the time. The parlor was often alive with singalongs of songs from the classic American songbook, as well as talent shows, performed by Rufus and his sister Martha, for their grandmother. Opera was often heard on the family stereo. Kate, meanwhile, closely watched over her children's music lessons, making sure that if they were going to play the piano, they were going to play properly.

B orn in 1974 and raised in Canada; son of singer/songwriters Loudon Wainwright III and Kate McGarrigle (of the McGarrigle Sisters).

Signed with DreamWorks Records, 1996; contributed to *The Myth of Fingerprints* soundtrack, 1997; released debut album, *Rufus Wainwright*, 1998; joined with his family to record *The McGarrigle Hour* CD, 1998; contributed to the *Big Daddy* film soundtrack, 1999.

Addresses: *Record company*—DreamWorks Records, 100 Universal Plaza, Bungalow 477, Universal City, CA 91608. *Website*—Rufus Wainwright at DreamWorks Records: www.dreamworksrecords.com/rufus.

By his early teens, Rufus had joined the family act, which was billed as the McGarrigle Sisters and Family. They toured the United States, Europe, and Canada. When he was 14, Kate and Anna were writing music for a kids film, *Tommy Tricker and the Stamp Traveller*, and invited Rufus to contribute. He wrote his first song, "I'm a Runnin'," and wound up performing it in the film. It earned him nominations for a Juno Award, the Canadian equivalent of a Grammy, and a Genie, the equivalent of an Oscar.

Beset with fears and frustrations about his sexuality, Wainwright immersed himself in the world of opera, identifying not so much with the heroic male leads, but rather the "damned ladies" who often met an inglorious and tragic fate. Believing that it might help his son escape a seemingly unhealthy interest in opera, Wainwright's father sent him to boarding school. Wainwright attended the prestigious Millbrook School in upstate New York, and in the school's pastoral setting, he regained his emotional equilibrium. Wainwright also continued his artistic pursuits and participated in musicals, including *Cabaret*. "First I was the emcee in that, then I was Jesus in *Godspell*, then I was God in another play," he told radio station KCRW's Liza Richardson. "It was always like typecasting, either the devil or God." Afterwards, he returned to Canada to study classical composition at McGill University in Montreal, but soon dropped out, discouraged by the emphasis of technical aspects of the music over artistic inspiration.

Wainwright then began pursuing pop songwriting seriously for the first time. His mother agreed to support him, so long as he was actually working on songs. During this period, he also began playing guitar, no longer threatened by the fact that that was also his father's instrument of choice. In writing pop songs, he found his own voice, though he was certainly influenced in one way or another by his parents. "I think with my mom, I'm affected a lot by her chords and stuff, her sort of really dark sensibility and romanticism which she likes to portray," he told Richardson. "Whereas my father, I think I picked up a little of his sort of wit, his stage persona."

Learning his craft as a performer at the Montreal nightspot Sarajevo, Wainwright eventually attempted to record some of his songs, working with producer Pierre Marchand, a family friend who had also worked with his mother and aunt. The resulting tape impressed Loudon, who passed it on to his friend Van Dyke Parks. Parks, a record producer, songwriter, and recording artist in his own right, is best known for his work with Brian Wilson. Parks in turn passed the tape along to Lenny Waronker, the former Warner Brothers Records chief who had nurtured the careers of individualistic singer/songwriters like Joni Mitchell, Ry Cooder, and Parks himself. Kate and Anna McGarrile were once part of his artist roster as well. "When I was about to listen to his tape, I remember clearly I was thinking, 'Gee, if he has the mom's musicality and smarts, and the dad's smarts and voice, that'd be nice,' " Waronker told Udovitch. "Then I put it on and I said, 'Oh, my God, this is stunning.' "

Waronker had just set up shop at DreamWorks, the music arm of the company headed by Steven Spielberg, David Geffen, and Jeffrey Katzenberg. Waronker paired Rufus with producer Jon Brion, who has worked with artists such as Aimee Mann and Fiona Apple. They spent an inordinately long time making the record, most of 1996 and 1997, and recorded a large number of songs—56, spread out over 62 rolls of tape. Costs for the sessions ran an incredible $700,000.

Some would call that money well spent. With its lush melodies, songs of romantic yearning, and intricate string arrangements, provided by Parks, the songs on Wainwright's self-titled debut range from the gorgeous, neo-operatic "Foolish Love," to "Beauty Mark," a song Rufus had written about the mole above his mother's lip, to "Damned Ladies," about his beloved yet doomed ladies of opera. "Desdemona, do not go to sleep/ Brown-eyed Tosca, don't believe the creep," the erudite lyric reads. There is also "Millbrook," a wink and a nod to his boarding school compatriots, and the eerie "Matinee Idol," inspired, supposedly by the death of actor River Phoenix. "April Fools" pretty well sums up his worldview as it pertains to romance: "You will believe in love/And all that it's supposed to be," begins the chorus with an unusually upbeat attitude. "But only until the fish start to smell/And you're struck down by a hammer." The album garnered its share of rave reviews. "If the songs on *Rufus Wainwright* remind you of old pop standards, it's because they're so damn classy," wrote Neva Choni in *Rolling Stone*. Soon after,

Wainwright took the magazine's honor for Best New Artist.

Even as his own star began to rise, Wainwright joined the family act once again. *The McGarrigle Hour*, released in 1998 on Hannibal Records, is as close as the world will get to hearing one of those old parlor jam sessions where Rufus used to perform. In addition to Kate and Anna McGarrigle, the album features performances by their sister Jane, Anna's husband Dane Lanken and their offspring Lily and Sylvan, Loudon Wainwright, and both Rufus and Martha. One of the songs on the album is "What'll I Do," an Irving Berlin song that Rufus sang at his maternal grandmother's funeral which still has emotional resonance for the family.

For all that, he is still concentrating on making his own mark in the world, achieving a greater amount of respect and fame than his parents. "This *has* to happen," Rufus told Tucker. Given his talent and determination, it just might.

Selected discography

"Le Roi D'Ys," "Banks of the Wabash," *The Myth of Finger-prints* Original Soundtrack, Velvel, 1997.
Rufus Wainwright, DreamWorks, 1998.

The McGarrigle Hour, Hannibal, 1998.
(With Shoofly) "You Don't Know," *Dirty White Town*, Cool, 1999.
"Instant Pleasure," *Big Daddy* Original Soundtrack, American Recordings, 1999.

Sources

Periodicals

Daily News, December 17, 1998.
Entertainment Weekly, December 25, 1998.
New York Times, April 19, 1998.
Rolling Stone, June 11, 1998; June 10, 1999.

Online

"Rufus Wainwright," Internet Movie Database, http://us.imdb.com/Bio?Wainwright,+Rufus (June 29, 2000).

Other

"Morning Becomes Eclectic," KCRW radio interview, February 20, 1998.

Additional information provided by DreamWorks publicity materials.

—Daniel Durchholz

The
Wannadies

Post-modern rock band

Since their inception, the Wannadies—whose members include lead singer and guitarist Pär Wiksten, his keyboardist and backing vocalist girlfriend Christina Bergmark, drummer Erik Dahlgren (who replaced original drummer Gunnar Karlsson around 1997), and brothers Stefan Schönfeldt, a guitarist, and Fredrik Schönfeldt, bass guitarist—have made an unflinching attempt to counteract the world's preconceived notion about Swedish music, a stereotype brought on in the 1970s and 1980s by the success of pop acts like Abba and Roxette. And although today they seem to exist in a parallel universe with fellow countrymen like the Cardigans, a Swedish band that rose to international fame in the 1990s, the Wannadies would rather not see themselves lumped with the mini-phenomenon of Swedish acts making it big. Instead, the Wannadies wish to be judged by their music, not by their nationality. "Music breaks away borders," insisted Bergmark, as quoted by Doug Reece in *Billboard.* "We're proud to be from Sweden, but that's not really the issue. Our music is the issue."

Indeed, RCA Records executive Dave Novik, who brought the Wannadies to the label after the British affiliate Indolent released *Be a Girl* in1995 and *Bagsy Me* in 1997 in the United Kingdom, agrees that quality, not geography, sparked his interest in the band, as well as other Swedish acts like Thin Lizard Dawn, Robyn, and Le Click. "It's true that people are talking about Swedish bands, but it's all about the fact that a lot of those artists are making credible music," he told Reece. "There are different R&B-based and pop-based

bands, they are singing in English, and there's no sense at all that this is a fluke. These [bands] have a legitimate, unmanufactured, and completely honest lifestyle, which is making the music work." Wiksten, however, offered another explanation as to why so many musicians in Sweden are able to produce such worthwhile music. "One good factor is to be surrounded by boredom," the singer/guitarist jokingly told *Rolling Stone,* adding that the weather in the northern country doesn't hurt either. "During the winter you go to the place where you're rehearsing, and you stay there."

The Wannadies story begins in the small town of Skellefteå, Sweden, about a 12-hour drive north of Stockholm. Formed in 1987, the group derived their moniker, as in "wanna die," from a catalog of horror movie titles and developed their dark-laced themes into hard-edged, melody-laden pop with an overall jazzy/lounge feel. While waiting for their career as musicians to take off, the members of the Wannadies worked in their hometown as gravediggers during the summer months. However, as Wiksten explained for the band's website at RCA, the job was not as gruesome as one may expect. "It was just like shoveling ditches except in a cemetery. It wasn't very scary since, in the summer, the sun is practically shining around the clock in Sweden."

In 1989, the Wannadies released their first single in Sweden, the minor radio hit "The Beast Cures the Love," and after a rave performance at the Hultsfreds Festival that same year, the group signed their first record contract with the independent, Stockholm-based Soap/MNW label. The following year, the group released their self-titled debut album, which contained the track "My Home Town." Based on life in Skellefteå, the song became their first significant hit in Sweden. A second album, *Aquanautic,* followed in 1992 and featured another hit song entitled "Cherryman."

By now, the Wannadies were not only attracting attention in Sweden, but across Europe as well for their inventive music and lyrics, which revealed a sort of balancing act between playful pop sensibilities and a sometimes grim sense of sarcasm. "Most of our songs aren't only punky or only poppy—it's almost always mixed," Bergmark said to Reece. "If it's a really sweet song, there's bound to be a part of it that's harder in the lyrics or somewhere else so that it's a little twisted around." Wiksten, too, agreed that the group has a tendency to obscure the usual: "We like things that are vague, because anything that's too obvious becomes quite boring."

British and American Breakthrough

As the Wannadies' fanbase continued to extend beyond the borders of Sweden, the group signed with the BMG subsidiary Indolent, based in the United King-

For The Record . . .

Members include **Christina Bergmark**, keyboards, backing vocals; **Erik Dahlgren** (joined band c. 1997), drums; **Gunnar Karlsson** (left band c. 1997), drums; brothers **Fredrik Schönfeldt,** bass guitar, and **Stefan Schönfeldt**, guitar; **Pär Wiksten**, lead vocals, guitar.

Formed in Skellefteå, Sweden, in 1987; released self-titled debut album in Sweden, 1995; signed with Indolent, released *Be a Girl,* 1995; debuted in America on RCA with *The Wannadies,* an album combining *Be a Girl* and 1997's *Bagsy Me,* 1997; released *Yeah,* 2000.

Addresses: *Record company*—RCA Records, 1540 Broadway, Times Square, New York City, NY 10036, phone: (212) 930-4000, fax: (212) 930-4546.

dom, thereafter spending much of their time shuffling between Skellefteå, Stockholm, and London. In 1995, the band released their first album for Indolent, *Be a Girl.* Two songs from the record, the ubiquitous-feeling "Might Be Stars," described by Wiksten to *New Musical Express* writer Keith Cameron as "a party song," and "You and Me Song," became instant hits, with the latter winning a spot on the multi-platinum-selling *Romeo + Juliet* film soundtrack.

In 1997, the Wannadies returned with a second album for Indolent entitled *Bagsy Me,* which raked in favorable reviews and new fans as well. That same year, RCA, Indolent's affiliate, compiled material from both *Be a Girl* and *Bagsy Me* for the group's American debut, *The Wannadies.* "Might Be Stars," the self-depreciating, revved-up, guitar-laden punk anthem that had become such a hit in Great Britain, was released as the group's first United States single. "It's making fun of other bands, and at the same time it's a kick in our face, because we have one foot in that, too," Wiksten said of the song, as quoted by Reece. "The song could be a tribute to all these bands that want to make it, but it's a bit of a windup as well. The one side of the business I don't care too much for is the trying bit. When a band's main goal is to become stars, and you really get a sense of that, they're not on my shelf anymore; I like the doers."

"Our aim is not to become stars," the singer/guitarist added. "Our primary goal is totally centric. I just want to get kicks out of writing good songs and making records that sound good. Then, plan two is just to spread it

around the world." After touring to support *Bagsy Me* and their United States debut, including a handful of dates in American cities, Wiksten, Bergmark, and Fredrik Schönfeldt decided to leave the constrictions of small-town life in Skellefteå, quitting Sweden altogether in favor of settling in London.

More than "Swedish"

Meanwhile, the Wannadies were starting to feel frustrated with trying to extricate themselves completely from their former Swedish label, as well as with the way RCA wanted to market the band. Although the label had promised not to promote the Wannadies based on the fact that they came from Sweden, RCA nonetheless began resorting to such a technique, one that had worked well for another Swedish act called Take That. "They were walking into radio stations saying, 'They're great! And they're Swedish!'" Wiksten recalled to Cameron. "Suddenly we were doing interviews with *Just Seventeen* and strange stuff like that. They just didn't understand us."

As a result, the Wannadies went laid low for a year, during which time RCA underwent corporate restructuring and have since become more sympathetic to the group's desires. "We're not in this because we want to sit in board meetings, or because we want to have a solicitor here and a manager there and then some MD there," the band's frontman explained to Cameron. "We're in this because we like meeting people, talking, playing music, drinking beer and traveling. Music being the wheel, and we just run around it."

Intending to focus on music rather than on promotion, the Wannadies traveled to New York City to record a new album with Ric Ocasek, the former Cars leader who had recently produced Guided By Voices' acclaimed 1999 album *Do the Collapse.* And the producer surprised the Wannadies with his unreconstructed punk instincts, challenging them to follow in the footsteps of punk legend Iggy Pop. The resulting *Yeah,* considered the band's "hardest, most compacted, least cuddly Wannadies record yet, tapping an even purer seam of power in keeping with their mission to reclaim the word 'pop' from its debasement," wrote Cameron, won immediate acclaim upon its British release in early 2000. Standout, chart-bound songs included "No Holiday," "Can't See Me Now," and "Don't Like You (What the Hell Are We Supposed to Do)."

Selected discography

The Wannadies (Sweden), Soap/MNW, 1990.
Aquanautic (Sweden), Soap/MNW, 1992.
Be a Girl (U.K), Indolent, 1995.
Bagsy Me (U.K), Indolent, 1997.
The Wannadies (debut U.S. release; includes *Be a Girl* and *Bagsy Me*), RCA, 1997.

Yeah (Japan; includes bonus tracks), BMG International, 2000.
Yeah (U.K), RCA, 2000.

Sources

Periodicals

Billboard, December 14, 1996; September 13, 1997.
Daily Telegraph, March 4, 2000.
Independent, May 10, 1996, p. 11.
New Musical Express, March 4, 2000, p. 20.
Rolling Stone, August 21, 1997.

Online

Bugjuice.com: Wannadies, http://www.bugjuice.com/wannadies/intro.html (June 8, 2000).
Sonicnet.com, http://www.sonicnet.com (June 8, 2000).
The Wannadies, http://www.algonet.se/~fregus/wan/awan 8.htm (June 8, 2000).

—Laura Hightower

Wire

Rock band

Abrasive and idiosyncratic, Wire's contribution to rock music has been a unique one. Though it has never achieved widespread fame, the British group has been hailed as an influence on such better-known bands as REM and Sonic Youth. During its nearly 25 years of on-again, off-again existence, Wire has often subverted the rules of conventional songwriting and ensemble playing, managing to harness disjointed rhythms and fragmented lyrics that teeter on the edge of chaos. Critics have termed their revisionist approach to rock "postmodern," and the band has claimed the playfully unsettling spirit of Dada artist Marcel Duchamp as a key inspiration. Considered part of the British punk rock uprising of the mid-1970s, Wire passed through a techno-pop dance phase in the late 1980s before returning to its more abstract roots in the following decade. The band entered the twenty-first century as an active touring and recording entity, sustained by a loyal following.

Wire was an unlikely musical venture from the beginning. At the time of the band's formation in South London in October 1976, only lead guitarist George Gill had experience playing in rock groups. Among his bandmates, singer/guitarist Colin Newman, guitarist Bruce Gilbert, bassist Graham Lewis and drummer Mark Field (who adopted the pseudonym Robert Gotobed) were all art school students with only a basic familiarity with their instruments. At the time of Wire's launching, the deliberate primitism of the punk rock movement made such limitations a virtue as much as a handicap. The band's sparse, severe sound made

them seem in step with the trend, though they never felt truly a part of London's punk circles. "There was a lot about the punk scene that was social," Newman said in a February 2000 interview with *New Music Express* writer John Robinson. "And there was a definite hierarchy, a definite pecking order. We were rank outsiders, and we weren't playing by the rules. We weren't playing shoddily on purpose. We played as well as we could. We quickly evolved the kind of thing we wanted to hear."

Though Wire was more avant-garde than many of the British punk bands of the era, they shared in the rebellious spirit and sense of possibility that typified the movement. "I never thought we were a punk group, apart from the access," Gilbert told writer Jon Savage in the liner notes to Wire's 1989 compilation CD *On Returning*. "But the thing one should carry was the optimism that things can actually change. It's quite interesting to be at close quarters with a revolution, however minor."

Wire parted company with guitarist Gill before signing a record deal with the EMI-distributed Harvest label. *Pink Flag*, the band's 1977 debut album, was noteworthy for both its edgy, alienated ambiance and its biting instrumental attack. The mood of its 21 songs swung from the darkly insinuating "Reuters" to the surprisingly tuneful "Mannequin" and "Ex Lion Tamer." Such short, assaultive numbers as "1-2-X-U" provided inspiration for such 1980s American punk groups as Black Flag and the Minutemen.

More than anything else, it was the deconstruction of rock music's stylistic conventions that made *Pink Flag* such an influential release. "The structures were rock 'n' roll, but taken apart and put together in different ways," Lewis told Savage. "This is how they go, but not quite. They *swerve.*" In the same interview, Gilbert reflected on the irregular, clipped form of the band's compositions, noting that "We hadn't thought of the songs as being any length. That's how long they were, and when they stopped, another one started. It meant that you could get 22 of them into 43 minutes." Assessing *Pink Flag*, Mark Coleman wrote in the *Rolling Stone Album Guide* that "On a formal level, it's an astonishing achievement, pulling punk away from the rock revivalism of the Sex Pistols and the Clash without sacrificing its energy or gut level impact. Indeed, these songs are enormously expressive and offer much to the listener."

In 1978, the band released *Chairs Missing*, an album that refined their first album's sonic thrust and reflected greater input from producer/keyboardist Mike Thorne. Still present was the band's lyric obscurity and desire to disturb as much as to entertain. "I Am The Fly" crackled with tension and anger, while "Outdoor Miner" painted a fractured lyric landscape over a strangely sweet melody. Another track, "French Film Blurred," had overtones of a horror film soundtrack. The subtleties of texture found on *Chairs Missing* were developed further on Wire's third album, *154*, released by Harvest in Britain and by Automatic/Warner Bros. in the United States in 1979. Even greater sonic extremes were explored on this album, stretching from the quietly chiming "Blessed State" to the slow, ominous "A Touching Display" and the harsh-yet-danceable "On Returning."

Despite signs that Wire was poised to reach a larger audience, the band broke up during the summer of 1980 and went on to pursue a variety of individual projects. Newman released a series of solo albums during the early 1980s, including *A-Z, Not To* and *Commercial Suicide*. Gilbert and Lewis were even more prolific, recording together as members of Dome, Duet Emmo and He Said. Gotobed became a session drummer, working with Newman among others, and ventured into organic farming as well. Still, the possibility of Wire's return remained an open one, and by the end of 1984 the band was reactivated. The foursome began working together again in a stripped-down, keyboard-less format. "The idea was very simple—it was put together because of equipment and the fact that we didn't have any money," Newman told *Cash Box* writer Karen Woods. "We just had guitars, bass and drums... We didn't know what we were going to do, but we didn't want to get involved in a whole big comeback scene, which could have been very embarrassing and very tasteless. So we decided to start a new Wire, and see whether we liked it..."

The fruits of these efforts were realized on *The Ideal Copy*, released by Mute Records in Britain and on the

Enigma label in the United States in 1987. The album found Wire more in harmony with the tastes of the marketplace, incorporating sampled sounds and synthesizer-driven rhythms into its approach. The ironic, austere edge of the band's early days seemed in accord with dance music sensibilities of the 1980s. In his review of the album, *Rolling Stone*'s Barry Walters noted that producer Gareth Jones "takes the cool, detached approach developed by Mike Thorne for Seventies Wire and makes it attractively cold. *The Ideal Copy* is music begging for a CD player."

Appearing a year later, *A Bell Is A Cup (Until It Is Struck)* followed up the previous album with a similar mix of intriguingly oblique lyrics and pulsating beats. Such tracks as "Kidney Bingos" and "Boiling Boy" were both mysterious and instantly catchy. Critics again praised the band's ingenuity at extracting something exotic from basic elements. "Wire's music is animated architecture," wrote Michael Axerrad in his *Rolling Stone* review of the album. "Wire won't blow you out of the room; it'll just keep you from leaving it."

Wire's fondness for unusual recording strategies was evident on their next release, 1989's *It's Beginning To and Back Again.* Though it began as a collection of in-concert recordings, *IBTABA* (as the album was also known) was revised so extensively in the studio that the live tracks all but disappeared. "We removed the crowd noise from the pieces and started replacing things," Newman told *Billboard* writer Chris Morris."It's sort of addition by subtraction." The album yielded a United States single, "Eardrum Buzz," which reached the top five on *Billboard*'s Modern Rock Tracks chart.

The band entered the 1990s by releasing *Manscape,* an album that relied on computer-generated rhythms more heavily than in the past. Following its release, drummer Gotobed left the group and the band continued on as Wir, releasing *The First Letter* in 1991. While the band's output was reduced in subsequent years, its influence was evident in the music of such rising British groups as Elastica and Blur. Several compilation albums, beginning with *On Returning (1977-1979)* in 1989, helped to keep Wire's recorded legacy alive. By 2000, Gotobed had rejoined the group and Wire toured Britain and the United States once again. *Third Day*, a limited-release CD of new recordings available via the Internet, appeared early in the year.

Despite detours into individual projects, the four members of Wire have kept their band an ongoing collective effort, revising their stripped-down yet malleable sound over a quarter century. "It's an object," Newman said of Wire in his *New Music Express* interview with Robertson. "We're in it, but it isn't us. Maybe it's about having a bit of humility: if you do something and if it works it's not because I do something or he does something, it's because the energy created is greater than the sum of the individuals. There are egos involved, but when you do something really good it becomes egoless."

Selected discography

Pink Flag, Harvest, 1977; (reissue), Restless Retro, 1989.
Chairs Missing, Harvest, 1978; (reissue), Restless Retro, 1989.
154, Automatic/Warner Bros., 1979; (reissue), Restless Retro, 1989.
The Ideal Copy, Mute/Enigma, 1987.
A Bell Is A Cup (Until It Is Struck), Mute/Enigma, 1987.
It's Beginning To and Back Again, Mute/Enigma, 1989.
On Returning (1977-1979), Restless Retro, 1989.
Manscape, Mute/Enigma, 1990.

Sources

Books

DeCurtis, Anthony and Henke, James, editors, *The Rolling Stone Album Guide,* Random House, 1992.

Larkin, Colin, editor, *The Encyclopedia of Popular Music,* Muze, 1998.
Robbins, Ira A., editor, *The Trouser Press Guide To '90s Rock,* Fireside Books, 1997.

Periodicals

Billboard, July 29, 1989.
Cash Box, July 22, 1989.
Musician, July, 1987.
New Musical Express, February 5, 2000; February 19, 2000; March 11, 2000.
Rolling Stone, September 24, 1987; August 25, 1988.

Online

Pinkflag, http://www.pinkflag.com (May 18, 2000).
Wireviews, http://www.snub.dircon.co.uk (May 18, 2000).

—*Barry Alfonso*

Cumulative Subject Index

Volume numbers appear in **bold**

Britten, Benjamin **15**
Bronfman, Yefim **6**
Canadian Brass, The **4**
Carter, Ron **14**
Casals, Pablo **9**
Chang, Sarah **7**
Church, Charlotte **28**
Clayderman, Richard **1**
Cliburn, Van **13**
Copland, Aaron **2**
Davis, Anthony **17**
Davis, Chip **4**
Davis, Colin **27**
DuPré, Jacqueline **26**
Dvorak, Antonin **25**
Fiedler, Arthur **6**
Fleming, Renee **24**
Galway, James **3**
Gardiner, John Eliot **26**
Gingold, Josef **6**
Gould, Glenn **9**
Gould, Morton **16**
Hampson, Thomas **12**
Harrell, Lynn **3**
Hayes, Roland **13**
Hendricks, Barbara **10**
Herrmann, Bernard **14**
Hinderas, Natalie **12**
Horne, Marilyn **9**
Horowitz, Vladimir **1**
Ives, Charles **29**
Jarrett, Keith **1**
Kennedy, Nigel **8**
Kissin, Evgeny **6**
Kronos Quartet **5**
Kunzel, Erich **17**
Lemper, Ute **14**
Levine, James **8**
Liberace **9**
Ma, Yo Yo **24**
   Earlier sketch in CM **2**
Marsalis, Wynton **6**
Mascagni, Pietro **25**
Masur, Kurt **11**
McNair, Sylvia **15**
McPartland, Marian **15**
Mehta, Zubin **11**
Menuhin, Yehudi **11**
Midori **7**
Mutter, Anne-Sophie **23**
Nyman, Michael **15**
Ott, David **2**
Parkening, Christopher **7**
Pavarotti, Luciano **20**
   Earlier sketch in CM **1**
Perahia, Murray **10**
Perlman, Itzhak **2**
Phillips, Harvey **3**
Pires, Maria João **26**
Quasthoff, Thomas **26**
Rampal, Jean-Pierre **6**
Rangell, Andrew **24**
Rieu, André **26**
Rostropovich, Mstislav **17**
Rota, Nino **13**
Rubinstein, Arthur **11**
Salerno-Sonnenberg, Nadja **3**
Salonen, Esa-Pekka **16**
Schickele, Peter **5**
Schuman, William **10**
Segovia, Andres **6**
Shankar, Ravi **9**
Solti, Georg **13**
Stern, Isaac **7**
Stoltzman, Richard **24**
Sutherland, Joan **13**
Takemitsu, Toru **6**

Temirkanov, Yuri **26**
Thibaudet, Jean-Yves **24**
Tilson Thomas, Michael **24**
Toscanini, Arturo **14**
Upshaw, Dawn **9**
Vanessa-Mae **26**
Vienna Choir Boys **23**
Volodos, Arcadi **28**
von Karajan, Herbert **1**
Weill, Kurt **12**
Wilson, Ransom **5**
Yamashita, Kazuhito **4**
York, Andrew **15**
Zukerman, Pinchas **4**

Composers
Adams, John **8**
Adamson, Barry **28**
Adderley, Nat **29**
Allen, Geri **10**
Alpert, Herb **11**
Anderson, Wessell **23**
Anka, Paul **2**
Arlen, Harold **27**
Atkins, Chet **5**
Bacharach, Burt **20**
   Earlier sketch in CM **1**
Badalamenti, Angelo **17**
Barry, John **29**
Beiderbecke, Bix **16**
Benson, George **9**
Berlin, Irving **8**
Bernstein, Leonard **2**
Blackman, Cindy **15**
Blegvad, Peter **28**
Bley, Carla **8**
Bley, Paul **14**
Boulez, Pierre **26**
Branca, Glenn **29**
Braxton, Anthony **12**
Brickman, Jim **22**
Britten, Benjamin **15**
Brubeck, Dave **8**
Burrell, Kenny **11**
Byrne, David **8**
   Also see Talking Heads
Byron, Don **22**
Cage, John **8**
Cale, John **9**
Casals, Pablo **9**
Clarke, Stanley **3**
Coleman, Ornette **5**
Cooder, Ry **2**
Cooney, Rory **6**
Copeland, Stewart **14**
   Also see Police, The **20**
Copland, Aaron **2**
Crouch, Andraé **9**
Curtis, King **10**
Davis, Anthony **17**
Davis, Chip **4**
Davis, Miles **1**
de Grassi, Alex **6**
Dorsey, Thomas A. **11**
Dvorak, Antonin **25**
Elfman, Danny **9**
Ellington, Duke **2**
Eno, Brian **8**
Enya **6**
Esquivel, Juan **17**
Evans, Bill **17**
Evans, Gil **17**
Fahey, John **17**
Foster, David **13**
Frisell, Bill **15**
Frith, Fred **19**
Galás, Diamanda **16**

Garner, Erroll **25**
Gillespie, Dizzy **6**
Glass, Philip **1**
Golson, Benny **21**
Gould, Glenn **9**
Gould, Morton **16**
Green, Benny **17**
Grusin, Dave **7**
Guaraldi, Vince **3**
Hamlisch, Marvin **1**
Hammer, Jan **21**
Hancock, Herbie **25**
Handy, W. C. **7**
Hargrove, Roy **15**
Harris, Eddie **15**
Hartke, Stephen **5**
Henderson, Fletcher **16**
Herrmann, Bernard **14**
Hunter, Alberta **7**
Ibrahim, Abdullah **24**
Isham, Mark **14**
Ives, Charles **29**
Jacquet, Illinois **17**
Jarre, Jean-Michel **2**
Jarrett, Keith **1**
Johnson, James P. **16**
Jones, Hank **15**
Jones, Howard **26**
Jones, Quincy **20**
   Earlier sketch in CM **2**
Joplin, Scott **10**
Jordan, Stanley **1**
Kang, Eyvind **28**
Kenny G **14**
Kenton, Stan **21**
Kern, Jerome **13**
Kitaro **1**
Kottke, Leo **13**
Lacy, Steve **23**
Lateef, Yusef **16**
Lee, Peggy **8**
Legg, Adrian **17**
Lewis, John **29**
Lewis, Ramsey **14**
Lincoln, Abbey **9**
Lloyd, Charles **22**
Lloyd Webber, Andrew **6**
Loesser, Frank **19**
Mancini, Henry **20**
   Earlier sketch in CM **1**
Mandel, Johnny **28**
Marsalis, Branford **10**
Marsalis, Ellis **13**
Martino, Pat **17**
Mascagni, Pietro **25**
Masekela, Hugh **7**
McBride, Christian **17**
McPartland, Marian **15**
Menken, Alan **10**
Metheny, Pat **26**
   Earlier sketch in CM **2**
Miles, Ron **22**
Mingus, Charles **9**
Moby **27**
   Earlier sketch in CM **17**
Monk, Meredith **1**
Monk, Thelonious **6**
Montenegro, Hugo **18**
Morricone, Ennio **15**
Morton, Jelly Roll **7**
Mulligan, Gerry **16**
Nascimento, Milton **6**
Newman, Randy **4**
Nyman, Michael **15**
Oldfield, Mike **18**
Orff, Carl **21**
Osby, Greg **21**

Tangerine Dream **12**
Tesh, John **20**
Winston, George **9**
Winter, Paul **10**
Yanni **11**

Cornet

Adderley, Nat **29**
Armstrong, Louis **4**
Beiderbecke, Bix **16**
Cherry, Don **10**
Handy, W. C. **7**
Oliver, King **15**
Vaché, Jr., Warren **22**

Country

Acuff, Roy **2**
Akins, Rhett **22**
Alabama **21**
    Earlier sketch in CM **1**
Anderson, John **5**
Arnold, Eddy **10**
Asleep at the Wheel **29**
    Earlier sketch in CM **5**
Atkins, Chet **26**
    Earlier sketch in CM **5**
Auldridge, Mike **4**
Autry, Gene **25**
    Earlier sketch in CM **12**
Barnett, Mandy **26**
Bellamy Brothers, The **13**
Berg, Matraca **16**
Berry, John **17**
Black, Clint **5**
BlackHawk **21**
Blue Rodeo **18**
Boggs, Dock **25**
Bogguss, Suzy **11**
Bonamy, James **21**
Bond, Johnny **28**
Boone, Pat **13**
Boy Howdy **21**
Brandt, Paul **22**
Brannon, Kippi **20**
Brooks & Dunn **25**
    Earlier sketch in CM **12**
Brooks, Garth **25**
    Earlier sketch in CM **8**
Brown, Junior **15**
Brown, Marty **14**
Brown, Tony **14**
Buffett, Jimmy **4**
Byrds, The **8**
Cale, J. J. **16**
Campbell, Glen **2**
Carter, Carlene **8**
Carter, Deana **25**
Carter Family, The **3**
Cash, Johnny **17**
    Earlier sketch in CM **1**
Cash, June Carter **6**
Cash, Rosanne **2**
Chapin Carpenter, Mary **25**
    Earlier sketch in CM **6**
Chesney, Kenny **20**
Chesnutt, Mark **13**
Clark, Guy **17**
Clark, Roy **1**
Clark, Terri **19**
Clements, Vassar **18**
Cline, Patsy **5**
Coe, David Allan **4**
Collie, Mark **15**
Confederate Railroad **23**
Cooder, Ry **2**
Cowboy Junkies, The **4**
Crawford, Randy **25**

Crowe, J. D. **5**
Crowell, Rodney **8**
Cyrus, Billy Ray **11**
Daniels, Charlie **6**
Davis, Linda **21**
Davis, Skeeter **15**
Dean, Billy **19**
DeMent, Iris **13**
Denver, John **22**
    Earlier sketch in CM **1**
Desert Rose Band, The **4**
Diamond Rio **11**
Dickens, Little Jimmy **7**
Diffie, Joe **27**
    Earlier sketch CM **10**
Dixie Chicks **26**
Dylan, Bob **21**
    Earlier sketch in CM **3**
Earle, Steve **16**
    Also see Afghan Whigs
Estes, John **25**
Evans, Sara **27**
Flatt, Lester **3**
Flores, Rosie **16**
Ford, Tennessee Ernie **3**
Foster, Radney **16**
Frizzell, Lefty **10**
Gayle, Crystal **1**
Germano, Lisa **18**
Gill, Vince **7**
Gilley, Mickey **7**
Gilmore, Jimmie Dale **11**
Gordy, Emory Jr., **17**
Greenwood, Lee **12**
Griffith, Nanci **3**
Haggard, Merle **2**
Hall, Tom T. **26**
Harris, Emmylou **4**
Hartford, John **1**
Hay, George D. **3**
Herndon, Ty **20**
Hiatt, John **8**
Highway 101 **4**
Hill, Faith **18**
Hinojosa, Tish **13**
Howard, Harlan **15**
Jackson, Alan **25**
    Earlier sketch in CM **7**
Jennings, Waylon **4**
Jones, George **4**
Judds, The **2**
Keith, Toby **17**
Kentucky Headhunters, The **5**
Kershaw, Sammy **15**
Ketchum, Hal **14**
Kristofferson, Kris **4**
Lamb, Barbara **19**
Lambchop **29**
Lane, Fred **28**
Lang, kd **25**
    Earlier sketch in CM **4**
Lauderdale, Jim **29**
Lawrence, Tracy **11**
LeDoux, Chris **12**
Lee, Brenda **5**
Little Feat **4**
Little Texas **14**
Lonestar **27**
Louvin Brothers, The **12**
Loveless, Patty **21**
    Earlier sketch in CM **5**
Lovett, Lyle **28**
Lynn, Loretta **2**
Lynne, Shelby **29**
    Earlier sketch in CM **5**
Mandrell, Barbara **4**
Mattea, Kathy **5**

Mavericks, The **15**
McBride, Martina **14**
McCann, Lila **26**
McClinton, Delbert **14**
McCoy, Neal **15**
McCready, Mindy **22**
McEntire, Reba **11**
McGraw, Tim **17**
Messina, Jo Dee **26**
Miller, Roger **4**
Milsap, Ronnie **2**
Moffatt, Katy **18**
Monroe, Bill **1**
Montgomery, John Michael **14**
Morgan, Lorrie **10**
Murphey, Michael Martin **9**
Murray, Anne **4**
Nelson, Willie **11**
    Earlier sketch in CM **1**
Newton-John, Olivia **8**
Nitty Gritty Dirt Band, The **6**
O'Connor, Mark **1**
Oak Ridge Boys, The **7**
Oslin, K. T. **3**
Owens, Buck **2**
Parnell, Lee Roy **15**
Parsons, Gram **7**
    Also see Byrds, The
Parton, Dolly **24**
    Earlier sketch in CM **2**
Pearl, Minnie **3**
Pierce, Webb **15**
Price, Ray **11**
Pride, Charley **4**
Rabbitt, Eddie **24**
    Earlier sketch in CM **5**
Raitt, Bonnie **3**
    Earlier sketch in CM **23**
Ray Condo and His Ricochets **26**
Raye, Collin **16**
Reeves, Jim **10**
Restless Heart **12**
Rich, Charlie **3**
Richey, Kim **20**
Ricochet **23**
Rimes, LeAnn **19**
Robbins, Marty **9**
Rodgers, Jimmie **3**
Rogers, Kenny **1**
Rogers, Roy **24**
    Earlier sketch in CM **9**
Sawyer Brown **27**
    Earlier sketch in CM **13**
Scruggs, Earl **3**
Scud Mountain Boys **21**
Seals, Dan **9**
Shenandoah **17**
Skaggs, Ricky **5**
Snow, Hank **29**
Sonnier, Jo-El **10**
Statler Brothers, The **8**
Stevens, Ray **7**
Stone, Doug **10**
Strait, George **5**
Stuart, Marty **9**
Sweethearts of the Rodeo **12**
Texas Tornados, The **8**
Tillis, Mel **7**
Tillis, Pam **25**
    Earlier sketch in CM **8**
Tippin, Aaron **12**
Travis, Merle **14**
Travis, Randy **9**
Tritt, Travis **7**
Tubb, Ernest **4**
Tucker, Tanya **3**
Twain, Shania **17**

Stern, Leni **29**
Stern, Mike **29**
Stills, Stephen **5**
Stuart, Marty **9**
Summers, Andy **3**
  Also see Police, The
Tampa Red **25**
Thielemans, Toots **13**
Thompson, Richard **7**
Tippin, Aaron **12**
Toure, Ali Farka **18**
Towner, Ralph **22**
Townshend, Pete **1**
  Also see Who, The
Travis, Merle **14**
Trynin, Jen **21**
Tubb, Ernest **4**
Ulmer, James Blood **13**
Vai, Steve **5**
Van Ronk, Dave **12**
Van Zandt, Steven **29**
Vaughan, Jimmie **24**
  Also see Fabulous Thunderbirds, The
Vaughan, Stevie Ray **1**
Wachtel, Waddy **26**
Wagoner, Porter **13**
Waits, Tom **27**
  Earlier sketch in CM **12**
  Earlier sketch in CM **1**
Walker, Jerry Jeff **13**
Walker, Joe Louis **28**
Walker, T-Bone **5**
Walsh, Joe **5**
  Also see Eagles, The
Wariner, Steve **18**
Waters, Muddy **24**
  Earlier sketch in CM **4**
Watson, Doc **2**
Weller, Paul **14**
White, Lari **15**
Whitfield, Mark **18**
Whitley, Chris **16**
Whittaker, Hudson **20**
Wilson, Brian **24**
  Also see Beach Boys, The
Winston, George **9**
Winter, Johnny **5**
Wiseman, Mac **19**
Wray, Link **17**
Yamashita, Kazuhito **4**
Yoakam, Dwight **21**
  Earlier sketch in CM **1**
York, Andrew **15**
Young, Neil **15**
  Earlier sketch in CM **2**
Zappa, Frank **17**
  Earlier sketch in CM **1**

Harmonica
Barnes, Roosevelt, "Booba" **23**
Dylan, Bob **3**
Guthrie, Woody **2**
Horton, Walter **19**
Lewis, Huey **9**
Little Walter **14**
McClinton, Delbert **14**
Musselwhite, Charlie **13**
Reed, Jimmy **15**
Thielemans, Toots **13**
Waters, Muddy **24**
  Earlier sketch in CM **4**
Wells, Junior **17**
Williamson, Sonny Boy **9**
Wonder, Stevie **17**
  Earlier sketch in CM **2**
Young, Neil **15**
  Earlier sketch in CM **2**

Heavy Metal
AC/DC **4**
Aerosmith **22**
  Earlier sketch in CM **1**
Alice in Chains **10**
Anthrax **11**
Black Sabbath **9**
Blue Oyster Cult **16**
Cinderella **16**
Circle Jerks **17**
Danzig **7**
Deep Purple **11**
Def Leppard **3**
Dokken **16**
Faith No More **7**
Fear Factory **27**
Fishbone **7**
Flying Luttenbachers, The **28**
Ford, Lita **9**
Guns n' Roses **2**
Iron Maiden **10**
Judas Priest **10**
Kilgore **24**
King's X **7**
Kiss **25**
  Earlier sketch in CM **5**
L7 **12**
Led Zeppelin **1**
Megadeth **9**
Melvins **21**
Metallica **7**
Mötley Crüe **1**
Motörhead **10**
Neurosis **28**
Nugent, Ted **2**
Osbourne, Ozzy **3**
Pantera **13**
Petra **3**
Queensryche **8**
Reid, Vernon **2**
  Also see Living Colour
Reznor, Trent **13**
Roth, David Lee **1**
  Also see Van Halen
Sepultura **12**
Skinny Puppy **17**
Slayer **10**
Soundgarden **6**
Spinal Tap **8**
Stryper **2**
Suicidal Tendencies **15**
Tool **21**
Type O Negative **27**
Warrant **17**
Wendy O. Williams and The Plasmatics **26**
White Zombie **17**
Whitesnake **5**

Humor
Borge, Victor **19**
Coasters, The **5**
Dr. Demento **23**
Jones, Spike **5**
Lehrer, Tom **7**
Pearl, Minnie **3**
Russell, Mark **6**
Sandler, Adam **19**
Schickele, Peter **5**
Shaffer, Paul **13**
Spinal Tap **8**
Stevens, Ray **7**
Yankovic, "Weird Al" **7**

Inventors
Fender, Leo **10**
Harris, Eddie **15**

Partch, Harry **29**
Paul, Les **2**
Reichel, Hans **29**
Teagarden, Jack **10**
Theremin, Leon **19**

Jazz
Abercrombie, John **25**
Adderley, Cannonball **15**
Adderley, Nat **29**
Allen, Geri **10**
Allison, Mose **17**
Anderson, Ray **7**
Armstrong, Louis **4**
Art Ensemble of Chicago **23**
Avery, Teodross **23**
Bailey, Mildred **13**
Bailey, Pearl **5**
Baker, Anita **9**
Baker, Chet **13**
Baker, Ginger **16**
  Also see Cream
Barbieri, Gato **22**
Basie, Count **2**
Bechet, Sidney **17**
Beiderbecke, Bix **16**
Belle, Regina **6**
Bennett, Tony **16**
  Earlier sketch in CM **2**
Benson, George **9**
Berigan, Bunny **2**
Blackman, Cindy **15**
Blakey, Art **11**
Blanchard, Terence **13**
Bley, Carla **8**
Bley, Paul **14**
Blood, Sweat and Tears **7**
Bowie, Lester **29**
Brand New Heavies, The **14**
Braxton, Anthony **12**
Brecker, Michael **29**
Bridgewater, Dee Dee **18**
Brötzmann, Peter **26**
Brown, Clifford **24**
Brown, Lawrence **23**
Brown, Norman **29**
Brown, Ray **21**
Brown, Ruth **13**
Brubeck, Dave **8**
Burrell, Kenny **11**
Burton, Gary **10**
Calloway, Cab **6**
Canadian Brass, The **4**
Carter, Benny **3**
  Also see McKinney's Cotton Pickers
Carter, Betty **6**
Carter, James **18**
Carter, Regina **22**
Carter, Ron **14**
Chambers, Paul **18**
Charles, Ray **24**
  Earlier sketch in CM **1**
Cherry, Don **10**
Christian, Charlie **11**
Clarke, Stanley **3**
Clements, Vassar **18**
Clooney, Rosemary **9**
Cole, Holly **18**
Cole, Nat King **3**
Coleman, Ornette **5**
Coltrane, John **4**
Connick, Harry, Jr. **4**
Corea, Chick **6**
Crawford, Randy **25**
Davis, Anthony **17**
Davis, Miles **1**
DeJohnette, Jack **7**

Wilson, Cassandra **12**
Wilson, Cassandra **26**
Wilson, Nancy **28**
  Earlier sketch in CM **14**
Winter, Paul **10**
Witherspoon, Jimmy **19**
Young, La Monte **16**
Young, Lester **14**
Zorn, John **15**

Juju
Adé, King Sunny **18**

Keyboards, Electric
Aphex Twin **14**
Bley, Paul **14**
Brown, Tony **14**
Chemical Brothers **20**
Corea, Chick **6**
Davis, Chip **4**
Dolby, Thomas **10**
Eno, Brian **8**
Foster, David **13**
Froom, Mitchell **15**
Hammer, Jan **21**
Hancock, Herbie **25**
  Earlier sketch in CM **8**
Hardcastle, Paul **20**
Jackson, Joe **22**
  Earlier sketch in CM **4**
Jarre, Jean-Michel **2**
Jones, Booker T. **8**
  Also see Booker T. & the M.G.'s
Kitaro **1**
Man or Astroman? **21**
Orbital **20**
Palmer, Jeff **20**
Sakamoto, Ryuichi **19**
Shaffer, Paul **13**
Smog **28**
Sun Ra **27**
  Earlier sketch in CM **5**
Wakeman, Rick **27**
  Also see Yes
Waller, Fats **7**
Winwood, Steve **2**
  Also see Spencer Davis Group
  Also see Traffic
Wonder, Stevie **17**
  Earlier sketch in CM **2**
Worrell, Bernie **11**
Yanni **11**

Liturgical Music
Cooney, Rory **6**
Talbot, John Michael **6**

Mandolin
Bromberg, David **18**
Grisman, David **17**
Hartford, John **1**
Lindley, David **2**
Monroe, Bill **1**
Skaggs, Ricky **5**
Stuart, Marty **9**

Musicals
Allen, Debbie **8**
Allen, Peter **11**
Andrews, Julie **4**
Andrews Sisters, The **9**
Bacharach, Burt **20**
  Earlier sketch in CM **1**
Bailey, Pearl **5**
Baker, Josephine **10**

Berlin, Irving **8**
Brightman, Sarah **20**
Brown, Ruth **13**
Buckley, Betty **16**
  Earlier sketch in CM **1**
Burnett, Carol **6**
Carter, Nell **7**
Channing, Carol **6**
Chevalier, Maurice **6**
Crawford, Michael **4**
Crosby, Bing **6**
Curry, Tim **3**
Davis, Sammy, Jr. **4**
Day, Doris **24**
  Earlier sketch in CM **7**
Garland, Judy **6**
Gershwin, George and Ira **11**
Hamlisch, Marvin **1**
Horne, Lena **11**
Johnson, James P. **16**
Jolson, Al **10**
Kern, Jerome **13**
Laine, Cleo **10**
Lerner and Loewe **13**
Lloyd Webber, Andrew **6**
LuPone, Patti **8**
Martin, Mary **27**
Masekela, Hugh **7**
Menken, Alan **10**
Mercer, Johnny **13**
Merman, Ethel **27**
Moore, Melba **7**
Patinkin, Mandy **20**
  Earlier sketch in CM **3**
Peters, Bernadette **27**
Porter, Cole **10**
Robeson, Paul **8**
Rodgers, Richard **9**
Sager, Carole Bayer **5**
Shaffer, Paul **13**
Sondheim, Stephen **8**
Styne, Jule **21**
Waters, Ethel **11**
Weill, Kurt **12**
Whiting, Margaret **28**
Yeston, Maury **22**

Oboe
Lateef, Yusef **16**

Opera
Adams, John **8**
Ameling, Elly **24**
Anderson, June **27**
Anderson, Marian **8**
Austral, Florence **26**
Baker, Janet **14**
Bartoli, Cecilia **12**
Battle, Kathleen **6**
Beltrán, Tito **28**
Blegen, Judith **23**
Bocelli, Andrea **22**
Bumbry, Grace **13**
Caballe, Monserrat **23**
Callas, Maria **11**
Carreras, José **8**
Caruso, Enrico **10**
Church, Charlotte **28**
Copeland, Stewart **14**
  Also see Police, The
Cotrubas, Ileana **1**
Davis, Anthony **17**
Domingo, Placido **20**
  Earlier sketch in CM **1**
Fleming, Renee **24**
Freni, Mirella **14**
Gershwin, George and Ira **11**

Graves, Denyce **16**
Hampson, Thomas **12**
Hendricks, Barbara **10**
Heppner, Ben **23**
Herrmann, Bernard **14**
Horne, Marilyn **9**
McNair, Sylvia **15**
Norman, Jessye **7**
Pavarotti, Luciano **20**
  Earlier sketch in CM **1**
Price, Leontyne **6**
Quasthoff, Thomas **26**
Sills, Beverly **5**
Solti, Georg **13**
Sutherland, Joan **13**
Te Kanawa, Kiri **2**
Toscanini, Arturo **14**
Upshaw, Dawn **9**
von Karajan, Herbert **1**
Weill, Kurt **12**
Zimmerman, Udo **5**

Percussion
Aronoff, Kenny **21**
Baker, Ginger **16**
  Also see Cream
Blackman, Cindy **15**
Blakey, Art **11**
Burton, Gary **10**
Collins, Phil **20**
  Earlier sketch in CM **2**
  Also see Genesis
Copeland, Stewart **14**
  Also see Police, The
DeJohnette, Jack **7**
Gurtu, Trilok **29**
Hampton, Lionel **6**
Henley, Don **3**
Jones, Elvin **9**
Jones, Philly Joe **16**
Jones, Spike **5**
Krupa, Gene **13**
Mo', Keb' **21**
N'Dour, Youssou **6**
Otis, Johnny **16**
Palmieri, Eddie **15**
Parker, Leon **27**
Puente, Tito **14**
Qureshi, Ustad Alla Rakha **29**
Rich, Buddy **13**
Roach, Max **12**
Santamaria, Mongo **28**
Sheila E. **3**
Starr, Ringo **10**
  Also see Beatles, The
Walden, Narada Michael **14**
Webb, Chick **14**

Piano
Adamson, Barry **28**
Allen, Geri **10**
Allison, Mose **17**
Amos, Tori **12**
Apple, Fiona **28**
Argerich, Martha **27**
Arrau, Claudio **1**
Axton, Hoyt **28**
Bacharach, Burt **20**
  Earlier sketch in CM **1**
Ball, Marcia **15**
Basie, Count **2**
Berlin, Irving **8**
Blake, Eubie **19**
Bley, Carla **8**
Bley, Paul **14**
Borge, Victor **19**
Brendel, Alfred **23**

Shamen, The **23**
Shearing, George **28**
Sheep on Drugs **27**
Sheila E. **3**
Shirelles, The **11**
Shonen Knife **13**
Siberry, Jane **6**
Simon, Carly **22**
  Earlier sketch in CM **4**
Simon, Paul **16**
  Earlier sketch in CM **1**
  Also see Simon and Garfunkel
Sinatra, Frank **23**
  Earlier sketch in CM **1**
Sixpence None the Richer **26**
Smith, Elliott **28**
Smith, Keely **29**
Smiths, The **3**
Snow, Pheobe **4**
Sobule, Jill **20**
Sonny and Cher **24**
Soul Coughing **21**
Sparks **18**
Spears, Britney **28**
Spector, Phil **4**
Spector, Ronnie **28**
Spice Girls **22**
Springfield, Dusty **20**
Springfield, Rick **9**
Springsteen, Bruce **25**
  Earlier sketch in CM **6**
Squeeze **5**
Stafford, Jo **24**
Stansfield, Lisa **9**
Starr, Kay **27**
Starr, Ringo **24**
  Earlier sketch in CM **10**
Steely Dan **29**
  Earlier sketch in CM **5**
Stereolab **18**
Stevens, Cat **3**
Stewart, Rod **20**
  Earlier sketch in CM **2**
  Also see Faces, The
Stills, Stephen **5**
Sting **19**
  Earlier sketch in CM **2**
  Also see Police, The
Stockwood, Kim **26**
Story, The **13**
Straw, Syd **18**
Streisand, Barbra **2**
Suede **20**
Summer, Donna **12**
Sundays, The **20**
Super Furry Animals **28**
Superchunk **29**
Supremes, The **6**
Surfaris, The **23**
Sweat, Keith **13**
Sweet, Matthew **9**
SWV **14**
Sylvian, David **27**
Talk Talk **19**
Talking Heads **1**
Taylor, James **25**
  Earlier sketch in CM **2**
Taylor, Steve **26**
Tears for Fears **6**
Teenage Fanclub **13**
Temptations, The **3**
Texas **27**
The The **15**
They Might Be Giants **7**
Thomas, Irma **16**
Three Dog Night **5**
Tiffany **4**

Tikaram, Tanita **9**
Timbuk 3 **3**
TLC **15**
Toad the Wet Sprocket **13**
Tony! Toni! Toné! **12**
Torme, Mel **4**
Townshend, Pete **1**
  Also see Who, The
Trevi, Gloria **29**
Turner, Tina **29**
  Earlier sketch in CM **1**
  Also see Ike & Tina Turner
Turtles, The **29**
Valli, Frankie **10**
Vandross, Luther **2**
Vanessa-Mae **26**
Vega, Suzanne **3**
Velocity Girl **23**
Veloso, Caetano **28**
Velvet Crush **28**
Vinton, Bobby **12**
Wainwright, Rufus **29**
Walsh, Joe **5**
Warnes, Jennifer **3**
Warwick, Dionne **2**
Was (Not Was) **6**
Washington, Dinah **5**
Waters, Crystal **15**
Watley, Jody **26**
  Earlier sketch in CM **9**
Webb, Jimmy **12**
Weller, Paul **14**
Whiting, Margaret **28**
Who, The **3**
Williams, Andy **2**
Williams, Dar **21**
Williams, Deniece **1**
Williams, Joe **11**
Williams, Lucinda **24**
  Earlier sketch in CM **10**
Williams, Paul **26**
  Earlier sketch in CM **5**
Williams, Robbie **25**
Williams, Vanessa **10**
Williams, Victoria **17**
Wilson, Brian **24**
  Also see Beach Boys, The
Wilson, Jackie **3**
Wilson, Nancy **28**
Wilson Phillips **5**
Winwood, Steve **2**
  Also see Spencer Davis Group
  Also see Traffic
Womack, Bobby **5**
Wonder, Stevie **17**
  Earlier sketch in CM **2**
Yankovic, "Weird Al" **7**
Young M.C. **4**
Young, Neil **15**
  Earlier sketch in CM **2**

Producers

Ackerman, Will **3**
Afanasieff, Walter **26**
Albini, Steve **15**
Alpert, Herb **11**
Austin, Dallas **16**
Baker, Anita **9**
Bass, Ralph **24**
Benitez, Jellybean **15**
Brown, Junior **15**
Brown, Tony **14**
Browne, Jackson **3**
Burnett, T Bone **13**
Cale, John **9**
Clark, Dick **25**
  Earlier sketch in CM **2**

Clarke, Stanley **3**
Clinton, George **7**
Cohen, Lyor **29**
Collins, Phil **2**
  Also see Genesis
Combs, Sean "Puffy" **25**
  Earlier sketch in CM **16**
Costello, Elvis **2**
Cropper, Steve **12**
Crowell, Rodney **8**
Dave, Edmunds **28**
Dixon, Willie **10**
Dolby, Thomas **10**
Dr. Dre **15**
  Also see N.W.A.
Dupri, Jermaine **25**
  Earlier sketch in CM **2**
Edmonds, Kenneth "Babyface" **12**
Enigma **14**
Eno, Brian **8**
Ertegun, Ahmet **10**
Ertegun, Nesuhi **24**
Foster, David **13**
Fripp, Robert **9**
Froom, Mitchell **15**
Gabler, Milton **25**
Garnier, Laurent **29**
Gordy, Jr., Emory **17**
Gray, F. Gary **19**
Grusin, Dave **7**
Hardcastle, Paul **20**
Jackson, Millie **14**
Jam, Jimmy, and Terry Lewis **11**
Jones, Booker T. **8**
  Also see Booker T. & the M.G'.s
Jones, Quincy **20**
  Earlier sketch in CM **2**
Jordan, Montell **26**
Krasnow, Bob **15**
Lanois, Daniel **8**
Laswell, Bill **14**
Leiber and Stoller **14**
Lillywhite, Steve **13**
Lynne, Jeff **5**
Mandel, Johnny **28**
Marley, Rita **10**
Martin, George **6**
Master P **22**
Mayfield, Curtis **8**
McKnight, Brian **22**
McLaren, Malcolm **23**
Miller, Mitch **11**
Most, Mickie **29**
Osby, Greg **21**
Parks, Van Dyke **17**
Parsons, Alan **12**
Paul, Prince **29**
Post, Mike **21**
Prince **14**
  Earlier sketch in CM **1**
Queen Latifah **24**
  Earlier sketch in CM **6**
Riley, Teddy **14**
Robertson, Robbie **2**
Rodgers, Nile **8**
Rubin, Rick **9**
Rundgren, Todd **11**
Scruggs, Randy **28**
Shocklee, Hank **15**
Simmons, Russell **7**
Skaggs, Ricky **5**
Spector, Phil **4**
Sure!, Al B. **13**
Sweat, Keith **13**
Too $hort **16**
Toussaint, Allen **11**
Tricky **18**

Blessid Union of Souls **20**
Blige, Mary J. **15**
Blues Brothers, The **3**
Bolton, Michael **4**
Booker T. & the M.G.'s **24**
Boyz II Men **15**
Brandy **19**
Braxton, Toni **17**
Brown, James **16**
  Earlier sketch in CM **2**
Brown, Ruth **13**
Brownstone **21**
Bryson, Peabo **11**
Burdon, Eric **14**
  Also see War
  Also see Animals
Busby, Jheryl **9**
C + C Music Factory **16**
Campbell, Tevin **13**
Carey, Mariah **20**
  Earlier sketch in CM **6**
Carr, James **23**
Charles, Ray **24**
  Earlier sketch in CM **1**
Cole, Natalie **21**
  Earlier sketch in CM **1**
Color Me Badd **23**
Commodores, The **23**
Cooke, Sam **1**
  Also see Soul Stirrers, The
Crawford, Randy **25**
Cropper, Steve **12**
Curtis, King **17**
D'Angelo **20**
D'Arby, Terence Trent **3**
DeBarge, El **14**
Des'ree **24**
  Earlier sketch in CM **15**
Dibango, Manu **14**
Diddley, Bo **3**
Domino, Fats **2**
Dr. John **7**
Dru Hill **25**
Earth, Wind and Fire **12**
Edmonds, Kenneth "Babyface" **12**
En Vogue **10**
Evora, Cesaria **19**
Fabulous Thunderbirds, The **1**
Four Tops, The **11**
Fox, Samantha **3**
Franklin, Aretha **17**
  Earlier sketch in CM **2**
Gaye, Marvin **4**
Gill, Johnny **20**
Gordy, Berry, Jr. **6**
Green, Al **9**
Guthrie, Gwen **26**
Hall & Oates **6**
Hawkins, Screamin' Jay **29**
  Earlier sketch in CM **8**
Hayes, Isaac **10**
Hill, Lauryn **25**
Holland-Dozier-Holland **5**
Houston, Whitney **25**
  Earlier sketch in CM **8**
Howland, Don **24**
Hurt, Mississippi John **24**
Ike and Tina Turner **24**
Incognito **16**
Ingram, James **11**
Isley Brothers, The **8**
Jackson, Freddie **3**
Jackson, Janet **3**
Jackson, Michael **17**
  Earlier sketch in CM **1**
  Also see Jacksons, The
Jackson, Millie **14**

Jacksons, The **7**
Jam, Jimmy, and Terry Lewis **11**
James, Etta **6**
Jodeci **13**
John, Willie **25**
Jones, Booker T. **8**
  Also see Booker T. & the M.G.'s
Jones, Grace **9**
Jones, Quincy **20**
  Earlier sketch CM **2**
Jordan, Louis **11**
Jordan, Montell **26**
Kelly, R. **19**
Khan, Chaka **19**
  Earlier sketch CM **9**
King, B. B. **24**
  Earlier sketch in CM **1**
King, Ben E. **7**
Knight, Gladys **1**
Kool & the Gang **13**
LaBelle, Patti **8**
Los Lobos **2**
Love, G. **24**
Martha and the Vandellas **25**
Maxwell **22**
Mayfield, Curtis **8**
McKnight, Brian **22**
McPhatter, Clyde **25**
Medley, Bill **3**
Meters, The **14**
Milli Vanilli **4**
Mills, Stephanie **21**
Mint Condition **29**
Mo', Keb' **21**
Monica **26**
Monifah **24**
Moore, Chante **21**
Moore, Melba **7**
Morrison, Van **24**
  Earlier sketch in CM **3**
Ndegéocello, Me'Shell **18**
Neville, Aaron **5**
  Also see Neville Brothers, The
Neville Brothers, The **4**
O'Jays, The **13**
Ocean, Billy **4**
Ohio Players **16**
Otis, Johnny **16**
Pendergrass, Teddy **3**
Peniston, CeCe **15**
Perry, Phil **24**
Pickett, Wilson **10**
Platters, The **25**
Pointer Sisters, The **9**
Price, Lloyd **25**
Priest, Maxi **20**
Prince **14**
  Earlier sketch in CM **1**
Rainey, Ma **22**
Rawls, Lou **19**
Redding, Otis **5**
Reese, Della **13**
Reeves, Martha **4**
Richie, Lionel **2**
Riley, Teddy **14**
Robinson, Smokey **1**
Ross, Diana **1**
  Also see Supremes, The
Ruffin, David **6**
  Also see Temptations, The
Sam and Dave **8**
Scaggs, Boz **12**
Secada, Jon **13**
Shai **23**
Shanice **14**
Shirelles, The **11**
Shocklee, Hank **15**

Silk **26**
Sledge, Percy **15**
Sly & the Family Stone **24**
Soul II Soul **17**
Spinners , The **21**
Stansfield, Lisa **9**
Staples, Mavis **13**
Staples, Pops **11**
Stewart, Rod **20**
  Earlier sketch in CM **2**
  Also see Faces, The
Stone, Sly **8**
Subdudes, The **18**
Supremes, The **6**
  Also see Ross, Diana
Sure!, Al B. **13**
Sweat, Keith **13**
SWV **14**
Temptations, The **3**
Third World **13**
Thomas, Irma **16**
Thornton, Big Mama **18**
TLC **15**
Tony! Toni! Toné! **12**
Toussaint, Allen **11**
Turner, Tina **29**
  Earlier sketch in CM **1**
  Also see Ike & Tina Turner
Vandross, Luther **24**
  Earlier sketch in CM **2**
Was (Not Was) **6**
Waters, Crystal **15**
Watley, Jody **26**
  Earlier sketch in CM **9**
Wexler, Jerry **15**
White, Karyn **21**
Williams, Deniece **1**
Williams, Vanessa **10**
Wilson, Jackie **3**
Wilson, Nancy **28**
Winans, The **12**
Winbush, Angela **15**
Womack, Bobby **5**
Wonder, Stevie **17**
  Earlier sketch in CM **2**
Zhane **22**

Rock

10,000 Maniacs **3**
311 **20**
AC/DC **4**
Adam Ant **13**
Adams, Bryan **20**
  Earlier sketch in CM **2**
Aerosmith **22**
  Earlier sketch in CM **3**
Afghan Whigs **17**
Alarm **2**
Albini, Steve **15**
Alexander, Arthur **14**
Alice in Chains **10**
Alien Sex Fiend **23**
Allen, Daevid **28**
Allman Brothers, The **6**
Alvin, Dave **17**
America **16**
American Music Club **15**
Animals **22**
Anthrax **11**
Apple, Fiona **28**
Aquabats **22**
Archers of Loaf **21**
Art of Noise **22**
Audio Adrenaline **22**
Aztec Camera **22**
Babes in Toyland **16**
Bad Brains **16**

Vai, Steve **5**
Valens, Ritchie **23**
Valli, Frankie **10**
Van Halen **25**
 Earlier sketch in CM **8**
Van Zandt, Steven **29**
Vandermark, Ken **28**
Vaughan, Jimmie **24**
Vaughan, Stevie Ray **1**
Velvet Underground, The **7**
Ventures **19**
Veruca Salt **20**
Verve Pipe, The **20**
Verve, The **18**
Vincent, Gene **19**
Violent Femmes **12**
Waits, Tom **27**
 Earlier sketch in CM **12**
 Earlier sketch in CM **1**
Wakeman, Rick **27**
 Also see Yes
Wallflowers, The **20**
Walsh, Joe **5**
 Also see Eagles, The
Wannadies, The **29**
War **14**
Warrant **17**
Waterboys, The **27**
Wedding Present, The **28**
Weezer **20**
Weller, Paul **14**
Wendy O. Williams and The Plasmatics **26**
Westerberg, Paul **26**
White Zombie **17**
Whitesnake **5**
Whitley, Chris **16**
Who, The **3**
Wilson, Brian **24**
 Also see Beach Boys, The
Winter, Johnny **5**
Winwood, Steve **2**
 Also see Spencer Davis Group
 Also see Traffic
Wire **29**
Wolf, Peter **25**
Wray, Link **17**
Wyatt, Robert **24**
X **11**
XTC **26**
 Earlier sketch in CM **10**
Yardbirds, The **10**
Yes **8**
Yo La Tengo **24**
Young, Neil **15**
 Earlier sketch in CM **2**
Zappa, Frank **17**
 Earlier sketch in CM **1**
Zevon, Warren **9**
Zombies, The **23**
ZZ Top **2**

Rock and Roll Pioneers
Ballard, Hank **17**
Berry, Chuck **1**
Clark, Dick **25**
 Earlier sketch in CM **2**
Darin, Bobby **4**
Diddley, Bo **3**
Dion **4**
Domino, Fats **2**
Eddy, Duane **9**
Everly Brothers, The **2**
Francis, Connie **10**
Glitter, Gary **19**
Haley, Bill **6**
Hawkins, Screamin' Jay **29**
 Earlier sketch in CM **8**

Holly, Buddy **1**
James, Etta **6**
Jordan, Louis **11**
Lewis, Jerry Lee **2**
Little Richard **1**
Nelson, Rick **2**
Orbison, Roy **2**
Otis, Johnny **16**
Paul, Les **2**
Perkins, Carl **9**
Phillips, Sam **5**
Presley, Elvis **1**
Professor Longhair **6**
Sedaka, Neil **4**
Shannon, Del **10**
Shirelles, The **11**
Spector, Phil **4**
Twitty, Conway **6**
Valli, Frankie **10**
Wilson, Jackie **3**
Wray, Link **17**

Saxophone
Adderley, Cannonball **15**
Anderson, Wessell **23**
Ayler, Albert **19**
Barbieri, Gato **22**
Bechet, Sidney **17**
Braxton, Anthony **12**
Brecker, Michael **29**
Brötzmann, Peter **26**
Carter, Benny **3**
 Also see McKinney's Cotton Pickers
Carter, James **18**
Chenier, C. J. **15**
Clemons, Clarence **7**
Coleman, Ornette **5**
Coltrane, John **4**
Curtis, King **17**
Desmond, Paul **23**
Dibango, Manu **14**
Garrett, Kenny **28**
Getz, Stan **12**
Golson, Benny **21**
Gordon, Dexter **10**
Harris, Eddie **15**
Hawkins, Coleman **11**
Henderson, Joe **14**
Herman, Woody **12**
Hodges, Johnny **24**
Jacquet, Illinois **17**
James, Boney **21**
Kenny G **14**
Kirk, Rahsaan Roland **6**
Koz, Dave **19**
Kuti, Femi **29**
Lacy, Steve **23**
Lateef, Yusef **16**
Lloyd, Charles **22**
Lopez, Israel "Cachao" **14**
Lovano, Joe **13**
Marsalis, Branford **10**
Morgan, Frank **9**
Mulligan, Gerry **16**
Murray, Dave **28**
Najee **21**
Osby, Greg **21**
Parker, Charlie **5**
Parker, Evan **28**
Parker, Maceo **7**
Pepper, Art **18**
Redman, Joshua **25**
 Earlier sketch in CM **12**
Rollins, Sonny **7**
Russell, Pee Wee **25**
Sanborn, David **28**
 Earlier sketch in CM **1**

Sanders, Pharoah **28**
 Earlier sketch in CM **16**
Shorter, Wayne **5**
Smith, Tommy **28**
Threadgill, Henry **9**
Vandermark, Ken **28**
Washington, Grover, Jr. **5**
Winter, Paul **10**
Young, La Monte **16**
Young, Lester **14**
Zorn, John **15**

Sintir
Hakmoun, Hassan **15**

Songwriters
2Pac **17**
Acuff, Roy **2**
Adams, Bryan **20**
 Earlier sketch in CM **2**
Adams, Yolanda **23**
Afanasieff, Walter **26**
Aikens, Rhett **22**
Albini, Steve **15**
Alexander, Arthur **14**
Allen, Peter **11**
Allison, Mose **17**
Almond, Marc **29**
Alpert, Herb **11**
Alvin, Dave **17**
Amos, Tori **12**
Anderson, John **5**
Anka, Paul **2**
Apple, Fiona **28**
Armatrading, Joan **4**
Atkins, Chet **26**
 Earlier sketch in CM **5**
Autry, Gene **25**
 Earlier sketch in CM **12**
Bacharach, Burt **20**
 Earlier sketch in CM **1**
Badu, Erykah **26**
Baez, Joan **1**
Baker, Anita **9**
Barlow, Lou **20**
Basie, Count **2**
Belew, Adrian **5**
Benét, Eric **27**
Benton, Brook **7**
Berg, Matraca **16**
Berlin, Irving **8**
Berry, Chuck **1**
Björk **16**
 Also see Sugarcubes, The
Black, Clint **5**
Black, Frank **14**
Blades, Ruben **2**
Blegvad, Peter **28**
Blige, Mary J. **15**
Bloom, Luka **14**
Bond, Johnny **28**
Brady, Paul **8**
Bragg, Billy **7**
Brandt, Paul **22**
Brickell, Edie **3**
Brokop, Lisa **22**
Brooks, Garth **25**
 Earlier sketch in CM **8**
Brown, Bobby **4**
Brown, James **16**
 Earlier sketch in CM **2**
Brown, Junior **15**
Brown, Marty **14**
Browne, Jackson **3**
Buckingham, Lindsey **8**
 Also see Fleetwood Mac
Buckley, Jeff **22**

Joel, Billy **12**
  Earlier sketch in CM **2**
Johansen, David **7**
John, Elton **20**
  Earlier sketch in CM **3**
Johnson, Lonnie **17**
Jones, George **4**
Jones, Quincy **20**
  Earlier sketch in CM **2**
Jones, Rickie Lee **4**
Joplin, Janis **3**
Jordan, Montell **26**
Kane, Big Daddy **7**
Kee, John P. **15**
Keith, Toby **17**
Kelly, R. **19**
Ketchum, Hal **14**
Khan, Chaka **19**
  Earlier sketch in CM **9**
King, Albert **2**
King, B. B. **24**
  Earlier sketch in CM **1**
King, Ben E. **7**
King, Carole **6**
King, Freddy **17**
Knopfler, Mark **25**
  Earlier sketch in CM **3**
  Also see Dire Straits
Kottke, Leo **13**
Kravitz, Lenny **26**
  Earlier sketch in CM **5**
Kristofferson, Kris **4**
L.L. Cool J **5**
Landreth, Sonny **16**
Lang, K. D. **25**
  Earlier sketch in CM **4**
Larkin, Patty **9**
Lauderdale, Jim **29**
Lavin, Christine **6**
LeDoux, Chris **12**
Lee, Ben **26**
Lee, Peggy **8**
Lehrer, Tom **7**
Leiber and Stoller **14**
Lennon, John **9**
  Also see Beatles, The
Lennon, Julian **26**
  Earlier sketch in CM **2**
Lewis, Huey **9**
Lightfoot, Gordon **3**
Linkous, Mark **26**
Little Richard **1**
Loeb, Lisa **23**
Logan, Jack **27**
Loggins, Kenny **20**
  Earlier sketch in CM **3**
Love, Laura **20**
Loveless, Patty **5**
Lovett, Lyle **28**
  Earlier sketch in CM **5**
Lowe, Nick **25**
  Earlier sketch in CM **6**
Lydon, John **9**
  Also see Sex Pistols, The
Lynn, Loretta **2**
Lynne, Jeff **5**
Lynne, Shelby **29**
  Earlier sketch in CM **5**
MacColl, Kirsty **12**
MacNeil, Rita **29**
Madonna **16**
  Earlier sketch in CM **4**
Manilow, Barry **2**
Mann, Aimee **22**
Mann, Billy **23**
Marley, Bob **3**
Marley, Ziggy **3**

Marshall, Amanda **27**
Marx, Richard **3**
Mattea, Kathy **5**
Mayfield, Curtis **8**
MC 900 Ft. Jesus **16**
MC Breed **17**
McCartney, Paul **4**
  Also see Beatles, The
McClinton, Delbert **14**
McCorkle, Susannah **27**
McCoury, Del **15**
McCulloch, Ian **23**
McLachlan, Sarah **12**
McLaren, Malcolm **23**
McLean, Don **7**
McLennan, Grant **21**
McMurtry, James **10**
McTell, Blind Willie **17**
Medley, Bill **3**
Melanie **12**
Mellencamp, John **20**
  Earlier sketch in CM **2**
  Also see John Cougar Mellencamp
Mercer, Johnny **13**
Merchant, Natalie **25**
  Also see 10,000 Maniacs
Messina, Jo Dee **26**
Michael, George **9**
Miller, Roger **4**
Miller, Steve **2**
Milsap, Ronnie **2**
Mitchell, Joni **17**
  Earlier sketch in CM **2**
Moffatt, Katy **18**
Morrison, Jim **3**
Morrison, Van **24**
  Earlier sketch in CM **3**
Morrissey **10**
Morrissey, Bill **12**
Morton, Jelly Roll **7**
Mould, Bob **10**
Moyet, Alison **12**
Nascimento, Milton **6**
Ndegéocello, Me'Shell **18**
Near, Holly **1**
Nelson, Rick **2**
Nelson, Willie **11**
  Earlier sketch in CM **1**
Newman, Randy **27**
  Earlier sketch in CM **4**
Nicks, Stevie **25**
  Earlier sketch in CM **2**
  Also see Fleetwood Mac
Nilsson **10**
Nugent, Ted **2**
Nyro, Laura **12**
O'Connor, Sinead **3**
Ocasek, Ric **5**
Ocean, Billy **4**
Ochs, Phil **7**
Odetta **7**
Orbison, Roy **2**
Orton, Beth **26**
Osbourne, Ozzy **3**
Oslin, K. T. **3**
Owens, Buck **2**
Page, Jimmy **4**
  Also see Led Zeppelin
  Also see Yardbirds, The
Palmer, Robert **2**
Paris, Twila **16**
Parker, Graham **10**
Parks, Van Dyke **17**
Parnell, Lee Roy **15**
Parsons, Gram **7**
  Also see Byrds, The

Parton, Dolly **24**
  Earlier sketch in CM **2**
Paul, Les **2**
Paxton, Tom **5**
Peniston, CeCe **15**
Penn, Michael **4**
Perkins, Carl **9**
Petty, Tom **9**
  Also see Tom Petty and the Heartbreakers
Phair, Liz **14**
Phillips, Sam **12**
Pickett, Wilson **10**
Plant, Robert **2**
  Also see Led Zeppelin
Pop, Iggy **23**
Porter, Cole **10**
Price, Lloyd **25**
Prince **14**
  Earlier sketch in CM **1**
Prine, John **7**
Professor Longhair **6**
Rabbitt, Eddie **24**
  Earlier sketch in CM **5**
Raitt, Bonnie **23**
  Earlier sketch in CM **3**
Rea, Chris **12**
Redding, Otis **5**
Reddy, Helen **9**
Reed, Lou **16**
  Earlier sketch in CM **1**
  Also see Velvet Underground, The
Reid, Vernon **2**
  Also see Living Colour
Rice, Chris **25**
Rich, Charlie **3**
Richards, Keith **11**
  Also see Rolling Stones, The
Richey, Kim **20**
Richie, Lionel **2**
Richman, Jonathan **12**
Riley, Teddy **14**
Ritchie, Jean **4**
Robbins, Marty **9**
Robertson, Robbie **2**
Robillard, Duke **2**
Robinson, Smokey **1**
Rodgers, Jimmie **3**
Rodgers, Richard **9**
Roth, David Lee **1**
  Also see Van Halen
Rusby, Kate **29**
Russell, Mark **6**
Ryder, Mitch **23**
Sade **2**
Sager, Carole Bayer **5**
Sanborn, David **28**
  Earlier sketch in CM **1**
Sangare, Oumou **22**
Satriani, Joe **4**
Scaggs, Boz **12**
Scott-Heron, Gil **13**
Scruggs, Earl **3**
Scruggs, Randy **28**
Seal **14**
Seals, Dan **9**
Secada, Jon **13**
Sedaka, Neil **4**
Seeger, Pete **4**
  Also see Weavers, The
Seger, Bob **15**
Sexsmith, Ron **27**
Shannon, Del **10**
Sheila E. **3**
Shepherd, Kenny Wayne **22**
Shocked, Michelle **4**
Siberry, Jane **6**

Cumulative Musicians Index

Volume numbers appear in **bold**

10,000 Maniacs **3**
2 Unlimited **18**
23, Richard
  See Front 242
2Pac **17**
  Also see Digital Underground
3-D
  See Massive Attack
311 **20**
4Him **23**
A-ha **22**
Aaliyah **21**
Aaron,
  See Mr. T Experience, The
Abba **12**
Abbott, Jacqueline
  See Beautiful South
Abbott, Jude
  See Chumbawamba
Abbruzzese, Dave
  See Pearl Jam
Abdul, Paula **3**
Abercrombie, Jeff
  See Fuel
Abercrombie, John **25**
Abong, Fred
  See Belly
Abrahams, Mick
  See Jethro Tull
Abrams, Bryan
  See Color Me Badd
Abrantes, Fernando
  See Kraftwerk
AC/DC **4**
Ace of Base **22**
Ackerman, Will **3**
Acland, Christopher
  See Lush
Acuff, Roy **2**
Acuna, Alejandro
  See Weather Report
Adam Ant **13**
Adamendes, Elaine
  See Throwing Muses
Adams, Bryan **20**
  Earlier sketch in CM **2**
Adams, Clifford
  See Kool & the Gang
Adams, Craig
  See Cult, The
Adams, Donn
  See NRBQ
Adams, John **8**
Adams, Mark
  See Specials, The
Adams, Oleta **17**
Adams, Terry
  See NRBQ
Adams, Victoria
  See Spice Girls
Adams, Yolanda **23**
Adamson, Barry **28**
Adcock, Eddie
  See Country Gentleman, The
Adderley, Cannonball **15**

Adderley, Nat **29**
Adderly, Julian
  See Adderley, Cannonball
Adé, King Sunny **18**
Adler, Steven
  See Guns n' Roses
Aerosmith **22**
  Earlier sketch in CM **3**
Afanasieff, Walter **26**
Afghan Whigs **17**
Afonso, Marie
  See Zap Mama
AFX
  See Aphex Twin
Agnew, Rikk
  See Christian Death
Agust, Daniel
  See Gus Gus
Air Supply **22**
Aitchison, Dominic
  See Mogwai
Ajile
  See Arrested Development
Akingbola, Sola
  See Jamiroquai
Akins, Rhett **22**
Alabama **21**
  Earlier sketch in CM **1**
Alan, Skip
  See Pretty Things, The
Alarm **22**
Albarn, Damon
  See Blur
Albert, Nate
  See Mighty Mighty Bosstones
Alberti, Dorona
  See KMFDM
Albini, Steve **15**
Albuquerque, Michael de
  See Electric Light Orchestra
Alder, John
  See Gong
  See Pretty Things, The
Alex
  See Mr. T Experience, The
Alexakis, Art
  See Everclear
Alexander, Arthur **14**
Alexander, Tim
  See Asleep at the Wheel
Alexander, Tim "Herb"
  See Primus
Ali
  See Tribe Called Quest, A
Alice in Chains **10**
Alien Sex Fiend **23**
Alkema, Jan Willem
  See Compulsion
All Saints **25**
All-4-One **17**
Allcock, Martin
  See Fairport Convention
  See Jethro Tull
Allen, April
  See C + C Music Factory

Allen, Chad
  See Guess Who
Allen, Daevid **28**
  Also see Gong
Allen, Dave
  See Gang of Four
Allen, Debbie **8**
Allen, Duane
  See Oak Ridge Boys, The
Allen, Geri **10**
Allen, Jeff
  See Mint Condition
Allen, Johnny Ray
  See Subdudes, The
Allen, Papa Dee
  See War
Allen, Peter **11**
Allen, Red
  See Osborne Brothers, The
Allen, Rick
  See Def Leppard
Allen, Ross
  See Mekons, The
Allen, Wally
  See Pretty Things, The
Allison, Luther **21**
Allison, Mose **17**
Allman Brothers, The **6**
Allman, Chris
  See Greater Vision
Allman, Duane
  See Allman Brothers, The
Allman, Gregg
  See Allman Brothers, The
Allsup, Michael Rand
  See Three Dog Night
Almond, Marc **29**
Alpert, Herb **11**
Alphonso, Roland
  See Skatalites, The
Alsing, Pelle
  See Roxette
Alston, Andy
  See Del Amitri
Alston, Shirley
  See Shirelles, The
Altan **18**
Altenfelder, Andy
  See Willem Breuker Kollektief
Alvin, Dave **17**
  Also see X
Am, Svet
  See KMFDM
Amato, Dave
  See REO Speedwagon
Amedee, Steve
  See Subdudes, The
Ameling, Elly **24**
Ament, Jeff
  See Pearl Jam
America **16**
American Music Club **15**
Amon, Robin
  See Pearls Before Swine
Amos, Tori **12**

Babjak, James
  See Smithereens, The
Babyface
  See Edmonds, Kenneth "Babyface"
Bacchus, Richard
  See D Generation
Bacharach, Burt **20**
  Earlier sketch in CM **1**
Bachman, Eric
  See Archers of Loaf
Bachman, Randy
  See Guess Who
Backstreet Boys **21**
Bad Brains **16**
Bad Company **22**
Bad Livers, The **19**
Bad Religion **28**
Badalamenti, Angelo **17**
Badfinger **23**
Badger, Pat
  See Extreme
Badrena, Manola
  See Weather Report
Badu, Erykah **26**
Baez, Joan **1**
Bailey, Keith
  See Gong
Bailey, Mildred **13**
Bailey, Pearl **5**
Bailey, Phil
  See Earth, Wind and Fire
Bailey, Victor
  See Weather Report
Baker, Anita **9**
Baker, Arthur **23**
Baker, Bobby
  See Tragically Hip, The
Baker, Brian
  See Bad Religion
Baker, Chet **13**
Baker, Dale
  See Sixpence None the Richer
Baker, David
  See Mercury Rev
Baker, Ginger **16**
  Also see Cream
Baker, Janet **14**
Baker, Jon
  See Charlatans, The
Baker, Josephine **10**
Baker, LaVern **25**
Balakrishnan, David
  See Turtle Island String Quartet
Balch, Bob
  See Fu Manchu
Balch, Michael
  See Front Line Assembly
Baldes, Kevin
  See Lit
Baldursson, Sigtryggur
  See Sugarcubes, The
Baldwin, Donny
  See Starship
Baliardo, Diego
  See Gipsy Kings, The
Baliardo, Paco
  See Gipsy Kings, The
Baliardo, Tonino
  See Gipsy Kings, The
Balin, Marty
  See Jefferson Airplane
Ball, Marcia **15**
Ballance, Laura
  See Superchunk
Ballard, Florence
  See Supremes, The
Ballard, Hank **17**

Balsley, Phil
  See Statler Brothers, The
Baltes, Peter
  See Dokken
Balzano, Vinnie
  See Less Than Jake
Bambaataa, Afrika **13**
Bamonte, Perry
  See Cure, The
Bananarama **22**
Bancroft, Cyke
  See Bevis Frond
Band, The **9**
Bangles, The **22**
Banks, Nick
  See Pulp
Banks, Peter
  See Yes
Banks, Tony
  See Genesis
Baptiste, David Russell
  See Meters, The
Barbarossa, Dave
  See Republica
Barbata, John
  See Jefferson Starship
Barber, Keith
  See Soul Stirrers, The
Barbero, Lori
  See Babes in Toyland
Barbieri, Gato **22**
Bardens, Peter
  See Camel
Bardo Pond **28**
Barenaked Ladies **18**
Bargeld, Blixa
  See Einstürzende Neubauten
Bargeron, Dave
  See Blood, Sweat and Tears
Barham, Meriel
  See Lush
Barile, Jo
  See Ventures, The
Barker, Paul
  See Ministry
Barker, Travis
  See Blink 182
Barker, Travis Landon
  See Aquabats, The
Barlow, Barriemore
  See Jethro Tull
Barlow, Lou **20**
  See Dinosaur Jr.
  Also see Folk Implosion, The
  Also see Sebadoh
Barlow, Tommy
  See Aztec Camera
Barnes, Danny
  See Bad Livers, The
Barnes, Micah
  See Nylons, The
Barnes, Neil
  See Leftfield
Barnes, Roosevelt "Booba" **23**
Barnett, Mandy **26**
Barnwell, Duncan
  See Simple Minds
Barnwell, Ysaye Maria
  See Sweet Honey in the Rock
Barr, Al
  See Dropkick Murphys
Barr, Ralph
  See Nitty Gritty Dirt Band, The
Barre, Martin
  See Jethro Tull
Barrere, Paul
  See Little Feat

Barrett, (Roger) Syd
  See Pink Floyd
Barrett, Dicky
  See Mighty Mighty Bosstones
Barrett, Robert "T-Mo"
  See Goodie Mob
Barron, Christopher
  See Spin Doctors
Barrow, Geoff
  See Portishead
Barry, John **29**
Barson, Mike
  See Madness
Bartels, Joanie **13**
Bartholomew, Simon
  See Brand New Heavies, The
Bartoli, Cecilia **12**
Barton, Lou Ann
  See Fabulous Thunderbirds, The
Barton, Rick
  See Dropkick Murphys
Bartos, Karl
  See Kraftwerk
Basehead **11**
Basement Jaxx **29**
Basher, Mick
  See X
Basia **5**
Basie, Count **2**
Bass, Colin
  See Camel
Bass, Lance
  See 'N Sync
Bass, Ralph **24**
Batchelor, Kevin
  See Big Mountain
  Also see Steel Pulse
Batel, Beate
  See Einstürzende Neubauten
Batiste, Lionel
  See Dirty Dozen Brass Band
Batoh, Masaki
  See Ghost
  Also see Pearls Before Swine
Battin, Skip
  See Byrds, The
Battle, Kathleen **6**
Bauer, Judah
  See Jon Spencer Blues Explosion
Bauhaus **27**
Baumann, Peter
  See Tangerine Dream
Bautista, Roland
  See Earth, Wind and Fire
Baxter, Adrian
  See Cherry Poppin' Daddies
Baxter, Jeff
  See Doobie Brothers, The
Bayer Sager, Carole
  See Sager, Carole Bayer
Baylor, Helen **20**
Baynton-Power, David
  See James
Bazilian, Eric
  See Hooters
Beach Boys, The **1**
Beale, Michael
  See Earth, Wind and Fire
Beard, Annette
  See Martha and the Vandellas
Beard, Frank
  See ZZ Top
Beasley, Paul
  See Mighty Clouds of Joy, The
Beastie Boys **25**
  Earlier sketch in CM **8**
Beat Farmers **23**

Campbell, Glen **2**
Campbell, Isobel
 See Belle and Sebastian
Campbell, Kerry
 See War
Campbell, Luther **10**
Campbell, Martyn
 See Lightning Seeds
Campbell, Mike
 See Tom Petty and the Heartbreakers
Campbell, Phil
 See Motörhead
Campbell, Robin
 See UB40
Campbell, Sarah Elizabeth **23**
Campbell, Tevin **13**
Can **28**
Canadian Brass, The **4**
Cantrell, Jerry
 See Alice in Chains
Canty, Brendan
 See Fugazi
Capaldi, Jim
 See Traffic
Cappelli, Frank **14**
Cappos, Andy
 See Built to Spill
Captain Beefheart and the Magic Band **26**
 Earlier sketch in CM **10**
Caravan **24**
Carbonara, Paul
 See Blondie
Cardigans **19**
Cardwell, Joi **22**
Carey, Danny
 See Tool
Carey, Mariah **20**
 Earlier sketch in CM **6**
Carlisle, Belinda **8**
 Also see Go-Go's, The
Carlisle, Bob **22**
Carlos, Bun E.
 See Cheap Trick
Carlos, Don
 See Black Uhuru
Carlson, Paulette
 See Highway 101
Carmichael, Hoagy **27**
Carnes, Kim **4**
Carpenter, Bob
 See Nitty Gritty Dirt Band, The
Carpenter, Karen
 See Carpenters, The
Carpenter, Richard **24**
 Also see Carpenters, The
Carpenter, Stephen
 See Deftones
Carpenters, The **13**
Carr, Ben
 See Mighty Mighty Bosstones
Carr, Eric
 See Kiss
Carr, James **23**
Carr, Martin
 See Boo Radleys, The
Carr, Teddy
 See Ricochet
Carr, Vikki **28**
Carrack, Paul
 See Mike & the Mechanics
 Also see Squeeze
Carreras, José **8**
Carrigan, Andy
 See Mekons, The
Carroll, Earl "Speedo"
 See Coasters, The

Carruthers, John
 See Siouxsie and the Banshees
Cars, The **20**
Carter, A. P.
 See Carter Family, The
Carter, Anita
 See Carter Family, The
Carter, Benny **3**
 Also see McKinney's Cotton Pickers
Carter, Betty **6**
Carter, Carlene **8**
Carter, Deana **25**
Carter Family, The **3**
Carter, Helen
 See Carter Family, The
Carter, James **18**
Carter, Janette
 See Carter Family, The
Carter, Jimmy
 See Five Blind Boys of Alabama
Carter, Joe
 See Carter Family, The
Carter, June Cash **6**
 Also see Carter Family, The
Carter, Maybell
 See Carter Family, The
Carter, Nell **7**
Carter, Nick
 See Backstreet Boys
Carter, Regina **22**
Carter, Ron **14**
Carter, Sara
 See Carter Family, The
Carthy, Martin
 See Steeleye Span
Caruso, Enrico **10**
Cary, Justin
 See Sixpence None the Richer
Casady, Jack
 See Jefferson Airplane
Casale, Bob
 See Devo
Casale, Gerald V.
 See Devo
Casals, Pablo **9**
Case, Peter **13**
Casey, Ken
 See Dropkick Murphys
Cash, Johnny **17**
 Earlier sketch in CM **1**
Cash, Rosanne **2**
Cashdollar, Cindy
 See Asleep at the Wheel
Cashion, Doc "Bob"
 See Lane, Fred
Cassidy, Ed
 See Spirit
Catallo, Chris
 See Surfin' Pluto
Catallo, Gene
 See Surfin' Pluto
Catatonia **29**
Cates, Ronny
 See Petra
Catherall, Joanne
 See Human League, The
Catherine Wheel **18**
Caustic Window
 See Aphex Twin
Cauty, Jimmy
 See Orb, The
Cavalera, Igor
 See Sepultura
Cavalera, Max
 See Sepultura
Cavanaugh, Frank
 See Filter

Cave, Nick **10**
Cavoukian, Raffi
 See Raffi
Cazares, Dino
 See Fear Factory
Cease, Jeff
 See Black Crowes, The
Cervenka, Exene
 See X
Cetera, Peter
 See Chicago
Chamberlin, Jimmy
 See Smashing Pumpkins
Chambers, Guy
 See Waterboys, The
Chambers, Jimmy
 See Mercury Rev
Chambers, Martin
 See Pretenders, The
Chambers, Paul **18**
Chambers, Terry
 See XTC
Champion, Eric **21**
Chan, Spencer
 See Aqua Velvets
Chance, Slim
 See Cramps, The
Chancellor, Justin
 See Tool
Chandler, Chas
 See Animals, The
Chandra, Sheila **16**
Chaney, Jimmy
 See Jimmie's Chicken Shack
Chang, Sarah **7**
Channing, Carol **6**
Chapin Carpenter, Mary **25**
 Earlier sketch in CM **6**
Chapin, Harry **6**
Chapin, Tom **11**
Chapman, Steven Curtis **15**
Chapman, Tony
 See Rolling Stones, The
Chapman, Tracy **20**
 Earlier sketch in CM **4**
Chaquico, Craig **23**
 Also see Jefferson Starship
Charlatans, The **13**
Charles, Ray **24**
 Earlier sketch in CM **1**
Charles, Yolanda
 See Aztec Camera
Charm Farm **20**
Charman, Shaun
 See Wedding Present, The
Chasez, Joshua Scott "JC"
 See 'N Sync
Chastain, Paul
 See Velvet Crush
Che Colovita, Lemon
 See Jimmie's Chicken Shack
Chea, Alvin "Vinnie"
 See Take 6
Cheap Trick **12**
Cheatam, Aldolphus "Doc"
 See McKinney's Cotton Pickers
Checker, Chubby **7**
Cheeks, Julius
 See Soul Stirrers, The
Chemical Brothers **20**
Cheng, Chi
 See Deftones
Chenier, C. J. **15**
Chenier, Clifton **6**
Chenille Sisters, The **16**
Cher **1**
 Also see Sonny and Cher

Collins, Judy **4**
Collins, Mark
  See Charlatans, The
Collins, Mel
  See Camel
  Also see King Crimson
Collins, Phil **20**
  Earlier sketch in CM **2**
  Also see Genesis
Collins, Rob
  See Charlatans, The
Collins, William
  See Collins, Bootsy
Colomby, Bobby
  See Blood, Sweat and Tears
Color Me Badd **23**
Colt, Johnny
  See Black Crowes, The
Colthart, Chris
  See Papas Fritas
Coltrane, John **4**
Colvin, Shawn **11**
Colwell, David
  See Bad Company
Combs, Sean "Puffy" **25**
  Earlier sketch in CM **16**
Comess, Aaron
  See Spin Doctors
Commodores, The **23**
Common **23**
Como, Perry **14**
Compulsion **23**
Condo, Ray
  See Ray Condo and His Ricochets
Confederate Railroad **23**
Congo Norvell **22**
Conneff, Kevin
  See Chieftains, The
Connelly, Chris
  See KMFDM
  Also see Pigface
Conner, Gary Lee
  See Screaming Trees
Conner, Van
  See Screaming Trees
Connick, Harry, Jr. **4**
Connolly, Pat
  See Surfaris, The
Connors, Marc
  See Nylons, The
Conti, Neil
  See Prefab Sprout
Conway, Billy
  See Morphine
Conway, Dave
  See My Bloody Valentine
Conway, Gerry
  See Pentangle
Cooder, Ry **2**
  Also see Captain Beefheart and His Magic
  Band
Cook, David Kyle
  See Matchbox 20
Cook, Greg
  See Ricochet
Cook, Jeffrey Alan
  See Alabama
Cook, Paul
  See Sex Pistols, The
Cook, Stuart
  See Creedence Clearwater Revival
Cook, Wayne
  See Steppenwolf
Cooke, Mick
  See Belle and Sebastian
Cooke, Sam **1**
  Also see Soul Stirrers, The

Cool, Tre
  See Green Day
Cooley, Dave
  See Citizen King
Coolio **19**
Coomes, Sam
  See Quasi
Cooney, Rory **6**
Cooper, Alice **8**
Cooper, Jason
  See Cure, The
Cooper, Martin
  See Orchestral Manoeuvres in the Dark
Cooper, Michael
  See Third World
Cooper, Paul
  See Nylons, The
Cooper, Ralph
  See Air Supply
Coore, Stephen
  See Third World
Cope, Julian **16**
Copeland, Stewart **14**
  Also see Police, The
Copland, Aaron **2**
Copley, Al
  See Roomful of Blues
Coppola, Donna
  See Papas Fritas
Corea, Chick **6**
Corella, Doug
  See Verve Pipe, The
Corgan, Billy
  See Smashing Pumpkins
Corina, Sarah
  See Mekons, The
Cornelius, Robert
  See Poi Dog Pondering
Cornell, Chris
  See Soundgarden
Cornershop **24**
Cornick, Glenn
  See Jethro Tull
Corrigan, Brianna
  See Beautiful South
Cosper, Kina
  See Brownstone
Costello, Elvis **12**
  Earlier sketch in CM **2**
Coté, Billy
  See Madder Rose
Cotoia, Robert
  See Beaver Brown Band, The
Cotrubas, Ileana **1**
Cotten, Elizabeth **16**
Cotton, Caré
  See Sounds of Blackness
Cotton, Jeff "Antennae Jimmy Siemens"
  See Captain Beefheart and His Magic Band
Cougar, John(ny)
  See Mellencamp, John
Coughlan, Richard
  See Caravan
Counting Crows **18**
Country Gentlemen, The **7**
Coury, Fred
  See Cinderella
Coutts, Duncan
  See Our Lady Peace
Coverdale, David
  See Whitesnake **5**
Cowan, John
  See New Grass Revival, The
Cowboy Junkies, The **4**
Cox, Andy
  See English Beat, The
  Also see Fine Young Cannibals

Cox, Terry
  See Pentangle
Coxon, Graham
  See Blur
Coyne, Mark
  See Flaming Lips
Coyne, Wayne
  See Flaming Lips
Crack, Carl
  See Atari Teenage Riot
Cracker **12**
Cracknell, Sarah
  See Saint Etienne
Cragg, Jonny
  See Spacehog
Craig, Albert
  See Israel Vibration
Craig, Carl **19**
Crain, S. R.
  See Soul Stirrers, The
Cramps, The **16**
Cranberries, The **14**
Craney, Mark
  See Jethro Tull
Crash Test Dummies **14**
Crawford, Dave Max
  See Poi Dog Pondering
Crawford, Ed
  See fIREHOSE
Crawford, Michael **4**
Crawford, Randy **25**
Crawford, Steve
  See Anointed
Crawford-Greathouse, Da'dra
  See Anointed
Cray, Robert **8**
Creach, Papa John
  See Jefferson Starship
Creager, Melora
  See Rasputina
Cream **9**
Creed **28**
Creedence Clearwater Revival **16**
Creegan, Andrew
  See Barenaked Ladies
Creegan, Jim
  See Barenaked Ladies
Crenshaw, Marshall **5**
Cretu, Michael
  See Enigma
Criss, Peter
  See Kiss
Crissinger, Roger
  See Pearls Before Swine
Croce, Jim **3**
Crofts, Dash
  See Seals & Crofts
Cronin, Kevin
  See REO Speedwagon
Cropper, Steve **12**
  Also see Booker T. & the M.G.'s
Crosby, Bing **6**
Crosby, David **3**
  Also see Byrds, The
  Also see Crosby, Stills, and Nash
Crosby, Stills, and Nash **24**
Cross, Bridget
  See Velocity Girl
Cross, David
  See King Crimson
Cross, Mike
  See Sponge
Cross, Tim
  See Sponge
Crouch, Andraé **9**
Crover, Dale
  See Melvins

de Young, Joyce
See Andrews Sisters, The
De Borg, Jerry
See Jesus Jones
De Gaia, Banco **27**
De La Luna, Shai
See Lords of Acid
De La Soul **7**
De Lisle, Paul
See Smash Mouth
De Meyer, Jean-Luc
See Front 242
De Oliveria, Laudir
See Chicago
Deacon, John
See Queen
Dead Can Dance **16**
Dead Kennedys **29**
Dead Milkmen **22**
Deakin, Paul
See Mavericks, The
Deal, Kelley
See Breeders
Deal, Kim
See Breeders
Also see Pixies, The
Dean, Billy **19**
Death in Vegas **28**
DeBarge, El **14**
Dee, Mikkey
See Dokken
Also see Motörhead
Deee-lite **9**
Deep Forest **18**
Deep Purple **11**
Def Leppard **3**
DeFrancesco, Joey **29**
Deftones **22**
DeGarmo, Chris
See Queensryche
Deibert, Adam Warren
See Aquabats, The
Deily, Ben
See Lemonheads, The
DeJohnette, Jack **7**
Del Amitri **18**
Del Mar, Candy
See Cramps, The
Del Rubio Triplets **21**
Delaet, Nathalie
See Lords of Acid
DeLeo, Dean
See Stone Temple Pilots
DeLeo, Robert
See Stone Temple Pilots
Delonge, Tom
See Blink 182
DeLorenzo, Victor
See Violent Femmes
Delp, Brad
See Boston
DeMent, Iris **13**
Demeski, Stanley
See Luna
DeMone, Gitane
See Christian Death
Demos, Greg
See Guided By Voices
Dempsey, Michael
See Cure, The
Denison, Duane
See Jesus Lizard
Dennis, Garth
See Black Uhuru
Denny, Sandy
See Fairport Convention

Densmore, John
See Doors, The
Dent, Cedric
See Take 6
Denton, Sandy
See Salt-N-Pepa
Denver, John **22**
Earlier sketch in CM **1**
Depeche Mode **5**
Depew, Don
See Cobra Verde
Derakh, Amir
See Orgy
Derosier, Michael
See Heart
Des'ree **24**
Earlier sketch in CM **15**
Desaulniers, Stephen
See Scud Mountain Boys
Deschamps, Kim
See Blue Rodeo
Desert Rose Band, The **4**
Desjardins, Claude
See Nylons, The
Desmond, Paul **23**
Destri, Jimmy
See Blondie
Deupree, Jerome
See Morphine
Deurloo, Hermine
See Willem Breuker Kollektief
Deutrom, Mark
See Melvins
Deutsch, Stu
See Wendy O. Williams and The Plasmatics
DeVille, C. C.
See Poison
Devito, Nick
See Four Seasons, The
Devito, Tommy
See Four Seasons, The
Devlin, Adam P.
See Bluetones, The
Devo **13**
Devoto, Howard
See Buzzcocks, The
DeWitt, Lew C.
See Statler Brothers, The
Dexter X
See Man or Astroman?
di Fiore, Vince
See Cake
Di Meola, Al **12**
Di'anno, Paul
See Iron Maiden
Diagram, Andy
See James
Diamond "Dimebag" Darrell
See Pantera
Diamond, Mike "Mike D"
See Beastie Boys, The
Diamond, Neil **1**
Diamond Rio **11**
Dibango, Manu **14**
Dick, Magic
See J. Geils Band
Dickens, Little Jimmy **7**
Dickerson, B.B.
See War
Dickinson, Paul Bruce
See Iron Maiden
Dickinson, Rob
See Catherine Wheel
Diddley, Bo **3**
Didier, Daniel
See Promise Ring, The
Dietrich, Marlene **25**

Diffie, Joe **27**
Earlier sketch in CM **10**
Difford, Chris
See Squeeze
DiFranco, Ani **17**
Digable Planets **15**
Diggle, Steve
See Buzzcocks, The
Diggs, Robert "RZA" (Prince Rakeem)
See Gravediggaz
Also see Wu-Tang Clan
Digital Underground **9**
Dillon, James
See Built to Spill
Dillon, Jerome
See Nine Inch Nails
Dilworth, Joe
See Stereolab
DiMant, Leor
See House of Pain
DiMucci, Dion
See Dion
DiNizo, Pat
See Smithereens, The
Dinning, Dean
See Toad the Wet Sprocket
Dinosaur Jr. **10**
Dio, Ronnie James
See Black Sabbath
Dion **4**
Dion, Celine **25**
Earlier sketch in CM **12**
Dire Straits **22**
Dirks, Michael
See Gwar
Dirnt, Mike
See Green Day
Dirty Dozen Brass Band **23**
DiSpirito, Jim
See Rusted Root
Dittrich, John
See Restless Heart
Dixie Chicks **26**
Dixon, George W.
See Spinners, The
Dixon, Jerry
See Warrant
Dixon, Willie **10**
DJ Domination
See Geto Boys, The
DJ Fuse
See Digital Underground
DJ Jazzy Jeff and the Fresh Prince **5**
DJ Muggs
See Cypress Hill
DJ Premier
See Gang Starr
DJ Ready Red
See Geto Boys, The
DJ Terminator X
See Public Enemy
DMC
See Run DMC
DMX **25**
Doc Pomus **14**
Doe, John
See X
Dog's Eye View **21**
Dogbowl
See King Missile
Doherty, Denny
See Mamas and the Papas
Dokken **16**
Dokken, Don
See Dokken
Dolby, Monica Mimi
See Brownstone

Edison, Harry "Sweets" **29**
Edmonds, Kenneth "Babyface" **12**
Edmonton, Jerry
  See Steppenwolf
Edson, Richard
  See Sonic Youth
Edward, Scott
  See Bluetones, The
Edwards, Dennis
  See Temptations, The
Edwards, Edgar
  See Spinners, The
Edwards, Gordon
  See Kinks, The
  Also see Pretty Things, The
Edwards, John
  See Spinners , The
Edwards, Johnny
  See Foreigner
Edwards, Leroy "Lion"
  See Mystic Revealers
Edwards, Mark
  See Aztec Camera
Edwards, Michael James
  See Jesus Jones
Edwards, Mike
  See Electric Light Orchestra
Edwards, Nokie
  See Ventures, The
Edwards, Skye
  See Morcheeba
Edwardson, Dave
  See Neurosis
eels **29**
Efrem, Towns
  See Dirty Dozen Brass Band
Ehran
  See Lords of Acid
Eid, Tamer
  See Emmet Swimming
Einheit, F.M.
  See KMFDM
Einheit
  See Einstürzende Neubauten
Einstürzende Neubauten **13**
Einziger, Michael
  See Incubus
Eisenstein, Michael
  See Letters to Cleo
Eitzel, Mark
  See American Music Club
Ekberg, Ulf
  See Ace of Base
Eklund, Greg
  See Everclear
El Hefe
  See NOFX
El-Hadi, Sulieman
  See Last Poets
Elastica **29**
Eldon, Thór
  See Sugarcubes, The
Eldridge, Ben
  See Seldom Scene, The
Eldridge, Roy **9**
  Also see McKinney's Cotton Pickers
Electric Light Orchestra **7**
Elfman, Danny **9**
Elias, Hanin
  See Atari Teenage Riot
Elias, Manny
  See Tears for Fears
Ellefson, Dave
  See Megadeth
Ellington, Duke **2**
Elliot, Cass **5**
  Also see Mamas and the Papas

Elliott, Dennis
  See Foreigner
Elliott, Doug
  See Odds
Elliott, Joe
  See Def Leppard
Ellis, Arti
  See Pearls Before Swine
Ellis, Bobby
  See Skatalites, The
Ellis, Herb **18**
Ellis, Ingrid
  See Sweet Honey in the Rock
Ellis, Terry
  See En Vogue
Ellison, Rahsaan
  See Oakland Interfaith Gospel Choir
Elmore, Greg
  See Quicksilver Messenger Service
ELO
  See Electric Light Orchestra
Ely, John
  See Asleep at the Wheel
Ely, Vince
  See Cure, The
  Also see Psychedelic Furs
Emerson, Bill
  See Country Gentlemen, The
Emerson, Darren
  See Underworld
Emerson, Keith
  See Emerson, Lake & Palmer/Powell
Emerson, Lake & Palmer\Powell **5**
Emery, Jill
  See Hole
Eminem **28**
Emmanuel, Tommy **21**
Emmet Swimming **24**
Empire, Alec
  See Atari Teenage Riot
En Vogue **10**
Endo, Nic
  See Atari Teenage Riot
English Beat, The **9**
English, Michael **23**
English, Richard
  See Flaming Lips
Enigk, Jeremy
  See Sunny Day Real Estate
Enigma **14**
Eno, Brian **8**
Enos, Bob
  See Roomful of Blues
Enright, Pat
  See Nashville Bluegrass Band
Entwistle, John
  See Who, The
Enya **6**
  Also see Clannad
EPMD **10**
Epstein, Howie
  See Tom Petty and the Heartbreakers
Erasure **11**
Erchick, Peter
  See Olivia Tremor Control
Eric B.
  See Eric B. and Rakim
Eric B. and Rakim **9**
Erickson, Roky **16**
Erikson, Duke
  See Garbage
Erlandson, Eric
  See Hole
Erner, Jeff "The Shark"
  See Dropkick Murphys

Errico, Greg
  See Sly & the Family Stone
  Also see Quicksilver Messenger Service
Erskine, Peter
  See Weather Report
Ertegun, Ahmet **10**
Ertegun, Nesuhi **24**
Erwin, Emily
  See Dixie Chicks
Esch, En
  See KMFDM
  Also see Pigface
Escovedo, Alejandro **18**
Eshe, Montsho
  See Arrested Development
Eskelin, Ian **19**
Esler-Smith, Frank
  See Air Supply
Esquivel, Juan **17**
Estefan, Gloria **15**
  Earlier sketch in CM **2**
Estes, Sleepy John **25**
Estms, Shep
  See Lane, Fred
Estrada, Roy
  See Little Feat
  Also see Captain Beefheart and His Magic
  Band
Etheridge, Melissa**16**
  Earlier sketch in CM **4**
Eurythmics **6**
Evan, John
  See Jethro Tull
Evans, Bill **17**
Evans, Dick
  See U2
Evans, Faith **25**
Evans, Gil **17**
Evans, Mark
  See AC/DC
Evans, Sara **27**
Evans, Shane
  See Collective Soul
Evans, Tom
  See Badfinger
Everclear **18**
Everlast **27**
  Also see House of Pain
Everly Brothers, The **2**
Everly, Don
  See Everly Brothers, The
Everly, Phil
  See Everly Brothers, The
Everman, Jason
  See Soundgarden
Everything But The Girl **15**
Evora, Cesaria **19**
Ewen, Alvin
  See Steel Pulse
Ex, The **28**
Exkano, Paul
  See Five Blind Boys of Alabama
Exposé **4**
Extreme **10**
Ezell, Ralph
  See Shenandoah
Fabian **5**
Fabulous Thunderbirds, The **1**
Faces, The **22**
Fadden, Jimmie
  See Nitty Gritty Dirt Band, The
Fagen, Donald
  See Steely Dan
Fahey, John **17**
Fahey, Siobhan
  See Bananarama
Fairport Convention **22**

Fordham, Julia **15**
Foreigner **21**
Foreman, Chris
  See Madness
Forrester, Alan
  See Mojave 3
Forsi, Ken
  See Surfaris, The
Forster, Robert
  See Go-Betweens, The
Forte, Juan
  See Oakland Interfaith Gospel Choir
Fortune, Jimmy
  See Statler Brothers, The
Fortus, Richard
  See Love Spit Love
Fossen, Steve
  See Heart
Foster, David **13**
Foster, Malcolm
  See Pretenders, The
Foster, Paul
  See Soul Stirrers, The
Foster, Radney **16**
Fountain, Clarence
  See Five Blind Boys of Alabama
Fountain, Pete **7**
Fountains of Wayne **26**
Four Seasons, The **24**
Four Tops, The **11**
FourHim **23**
Fowler, Bruce "Fossil Fowler"
  See Captain Beefheart and His Magic Band
Fox, Lucas
  See Motörhead
Fox, Oz
  See Stryper
Fox, Samantha **3**
Foxton, Bruce
  See Jam, The
Foxwell Baker, Iain Richard
  See Jesus Jones
Foxx, Leigh
  See Blondie
Frame, Roddy
  See Aztec Camera
Frampton, Peter **3**
Francis, Black
  See Pixies, The
Francis, Connie **10**
Francis, Michael
  See Asleep at the Wheel
Francolini, Dave
  See Dark Star
Franke, Chris
  See Tangerine Dream
Frankenstein, Jeff
  See Newsboys, The
Frankie Lymon and The Teenagers **24**
Franklin, Aretha **17**
  Earlier sketch in CM **2**
Franklin, Elmo
  See Mighty Clouds of Joy, The
Franklin, Kirk **22**
Franklin, Larry
  See Asleep at the Wheel
Franklin, Melvin
  See Temptations, The
Franti, Michael **16**
  Also see Spearhead
Frantz, Chris
  See Talking Heads
Fraser, Elizabeth
  See Cocteau Twins, The
Frater, Shaun
  See Fairport Convention

Frazier, Stan
  See Sugar Ray
Frederiksen, Lars
  See Rancid
Fredriksson, Marie
  See Roxette
Freeman, Matt
  See Rancid
Freese, Josh
  See Suicidal Tendencies
Frehley, Ace
  See Kiss
Freiberg, David
  See Quicksilver Messenger Service
  Also see Jefferson Starship
French, Frank
  See Cake
French, John "Drumbo"
  See Captain Beefheart and His Magic Band
French, Mark
  See Blue Rodeo
Freni, Mirella **14**
Freshwater, John
  See Alien Sex Fiend
Frey, Glenn **3**
  Also see Eagles, The
Fricker, Sylvia
  See Ian and Sylvia
Fridmann, Dave
  See Mercury Rev
Friedman, Marty
  See Megadeth
Friel, Tony
  See Fall, The
Fripp, Robert **9**
  Also see King Crimson
Frischmann, Justine Elinor
  See Elastica
Frisell, Bill **15**
Frishmann, Justine
  See Suede
Frith, Fred **19**
Frizzell, Lefty **10**
Froese, Edgar
  See Tangerine Dream
Front 242 **19**
Front Line Assembly **20**
Froom, Mitchell **15**
Frusciante, John
  See Red Hot Chili Peppers, The
Fu Manchu **22**
Fuel **27**
Fugazi **13**
Fugees, The **17**
Fulber, Rhys
  See Front Line Assembly
Fuller, Blind Boy **20**
Fuller, Craig
  See Little Feat
Fuller, Jim
  See Surfaris, The
Fulson, Lowell **20**
Fun Lovin' Criminals **20**
Funahara, O. Chosei
  See Wendy O. Williams and The Plasmatics
Fuqua, Charlie
  See Ink Spots
Furay, Richie
  See Buffalo Springfield
Furler, Peter
  See Newsboys, The
Furr, John
  See Treadmill Trackstar
Furuholmen, Magne
  See A-ha
Futter, Brian
  See Catherine Wheel

G. Love **24**
Gabay, Yuval
  See Soul Coughing
Gabler, Milton **25**
Gabriel, Peter **16**
  Earlier sketch in CM **2**
  Also see Genesis
Gadler, Frank
  See NRBQ
Gaffney, Eric
  See Sebadoh
Gagliardi, Ed
  See Foreigner
Gahan, Dave
  See Depeche Mode
Gaines, Steve
  See Lynyrd Skynyrd
Gaines, Timothy
  See Stryper
Galás, Diamanda **16**
Gale, Melvyn
  See Electric Light Orchestra
Galea, Darren
  See Jamiroquai
Gallagher, Liam
  See Oasis
Gallagher, Noel
  See Oasis
Gallup, Simon
  See Cure, The
Galore, Lady
  See Lords of Acid
Galway, James **3**
Gambill, Roger
  See Kingston Trio, The
Gamble, Cheryl "Coko"
  See SWV
Gane, Tim
  See Stereolab
Gang of Four **8**
Gang Starr **13**
Gannon, Craig
  See Aztec Camera
Gano, Gordon
  See Violent Femmes
Garbage **25**
Garcia, Dean
  See Curve
Garcia, Jerry **4**
  Also see Grateful Dead, The
Garcia, Leddie
  See Poi Dog Pondering
Gardiner, John Eliot **26**
Gardner, Adam
  See Guster
Gardner, Carl
  See Coasters, The
Gardner, Suzi
  See L7
Garfunkel, Art **4**
  Also see Simon and Garfunkel
Gargiulo, Lulu
  See Fastbacks, The
Garland, Judy **6**
Garner, Erroll **25**
Garnes, Sherman
  See Frankie Lymon and The Teenagers
Garnier, Laurent **29**
Garrett, Amos
  See Pearls Before Swine
Garrett, Kenny **28**
Garrett, Peter
  See Midnight Oil
Garrett, Scott
  See Cult, The
Garrison, Chuck
  See Superchunk

Goldstein, Jerry
  See War
Golson, Benny **21**
Gong **24**
Gonson, Claudia
  See Magnetic Fields, The
Goo Goo Dolls, The **16**
Gooden, Ramone Pee Wee
  See Digital Underground
Goodie Mob **24**
Goodman, Benny **4**
Goodman, Jerry
  See Mahavishnu Orchestra
Goodridge, Robin
  See Bush
Googe, Debbie
  See My Bloody Valentine
Gordon, Dexter **10**
Gordon, Dwight
  See Mighty Clouds of Joy, The
Gordon, Jay
  See Orgy
Gordon, Jim
  See Traffic
Gordon, Kim
  See Sonic Youth
Gordon, Mike
  See Phish
Gordon, Nina
  See Veruca Salt
Gordy, Berry, Jr. **6**
Gordy, Emory, Jr. **17**
Gore, Martin
  See Depeche Mode
Gorham, Scott
  See Thin Lizzy
Gorka, John **18**
Gorman, Christopher
  See Belly
Gorman, Steve
  See Black Crowes, The
Gorman, Thomas
  See Belly
Gorter, Arjen
  See Willem Breuker Kollektief
Gosling, John
  See Kinks, The
Gossard, Stone
  See Brad
  Also see Pearl Jam
Goswell, Rachel
  See Mojave 3
Gotobed, Robert
  See Wire
Gott, Larry
  See James
Goudreau, Barry
  See Boston
Gould, Billy
  See Faith No More
Gould, Glenn **9**
Gould, Morton **16**
Goulding, Steve
  See Gene Loves Jezebel
Grable, Steve
  See Pearls Before Swine
Gracey, Chad
  See Live
Gradney, Ken
  See Little Feat
Graffety-Smith, Toby
  See Jamiroquai
Graffin, Greg
  See Bad Religion
Graham, Bill **10**
Graham, Glen
  See Blind Melon

Graham, Johnny
  See Earth, Wind and Fire
Graham, Larry
  See Sly & the Family Stone
Gramm, Lou
  See Foreigner
Gramolini, Gary
  See Beaver Brown Band, The
Grandmaster Flash **14**
Grant, Amy **7**
Grant, Bob
  See The Bad Livers
Grant, Gogi **28**
Grant Lee Buffalo **16**
Grant, Lloyd
  See Metallica
Grappelli, Stephane **10**
Grateful Dead, The **5**
Gratzer, Alan
  See REO Speedwagon
Gravatt, Eric
  See Weather Report
Gravediggaz **23**
Graves, Denyce **16**
Gray, David
  See Spearhead
Gray, Del
  See Little Texas
Gray, Ella
  See Kronos Quartet
Gray, F. Gary **19**
Gray, James
  See Spearhead
Gray, James
  See Blue Rodeo
Gray, Luther
  See Tsunami
Gray, Tom
  See Country Gentlemen, The
  Also see Seldom Scene, The
Gray, Walter
  See Kronos Quartet
Gray, Wardell
  See McKinney's Cotton Pickers
Greater Vision **26**
Grebenshikov, Boris **3**
Grech, Rick
  See Traffic
Greco, Paul
  See Chumbawamba
Green, Al **9**
Green, Benny **17**
Green, Carlito "Cee-lo"
  See Goodie Mob
Green, Charles
  See War
Green, David
  See Air Supply
Green Day **16**
Green, Grant **14**
Green, James
  See Dru Hill
Green, Peter
  See Fleetwood Mac
Green, Susaye
  See Supremes, The
Green, Willie
  See Neville Brothers, The
Greene, Karl Anthony
  See Herman's Hermits
Greenhalgh, Tom
  See Mekons, The
Greensmith, Domenic
  See Reef
Greenspoon, Jimmy
  See Three Dog Night

Greentree, Richard
  See Beta Band, The
Greenwood, Al
  See Foreigner
Greenwood, Colin
  See Radiohead
Greenwood, Gail
  See Belly
Greenwood, Jonny
  See Radiohead
Greenwood, Lee **12**
Greenwood,Colin
  See Radiohead
Greer, Jim
  See Guided By Voices
Gregg, Dave
  See D.O.A.
Gregg, Paul
  See Restless Heart
Gregory, Bryan
  See Cramps, The
Gregory, Dave
  See XTC
Gregory, Keith
  See Wedding Present, The
Gregory, Troy
  See Prong
Greller, Al
  See Yo La Tengo
Grey, Charles Wallace
  See Aquabats, The
Grice, Gary "The Genius"
  See Wu-Tang Clan
Griffin, A.C. "Eddie"
  See Golden Gate Quartet
Griffin, Bob
  See BoDeans, The
Griffin, Kevin
  See Better Than Ezra
  Also see NRBQ
Griffin, Mark
  See MC 900 Ft. Jesus
Griffin, Patty **24**
Griffin, Rodney
  See Greater Vision
Griffith, Nanci **3**
Grigg, Chris
  See Treadmill Trackstar
Grisman, David **17**
Grohl, Dave
  See Nirvana
  Also see Foo Fighters
Grotberg, Karen
  See Jayhawks, The
Groucutt, Kelly
  See Electric Light Orchestra
Grove, George
  See Kingston Trio, The
Grover, Charlie
  See Sponge
Grundy, Hugh
  See Zombies, The
Grusin, Dave **7**
Guaraldi, Vince **3**
Guard, Dave
  See Kingston Trio, The
Gudmundsdottir, Björk
  See Björk
  Also see Sugarcubes, The
Guerin, John
  See Byrds, The
Guess Who **23**
Guest, Christopher
  See Spinal Tap
Guided By Voices **18**
Gunn, Trey
  See King Crimson

Hart, Douglas
  See Jesus and Mary Chain, The
Hart, Hattie
  See Memphis Jug Band
Hart, Lorenz
  See Rodgers, Richard
Hart, Mark
  See Supertramp
Hart, Mark
  See Crowded House
Hart, Mickey
  See Grateful Dead, The
Hart, Robert
  See Bad Company
Hart, Tim
  See Steeleye Span
Hart, William Cullen
  See Olivia Tremor Control
Hartford, John 1
Hartke, Stephen 5
Hartley, Matthieu
  See Cure, The
Hartman, Bob
  See Petra
Hartman, John
  See Doobie Brothers, The
Hartnoll, Paul
  See Orbital
Hartnoll, Phil
  See Orbital
Harvey, Bernard "Touter"
  See Inner Circle
Harvey, Philip "Daddae"
  See Soul II Soul
Harvey, Polly Jean 11
Harvie, Iain
  See Del Amitri
Harwell, Steve
  See Smash Mouth
Harwood, Justin
  See Luna
Haseltine, Dan
  See Jars of Clay
Hashian
  See Boston
Haskell, Gordon
  See King Crimson
Haskins, Kevin
  See Bauhaus
  Also see Love and Rockets
Haslinger, Paul
  See Tangerine Dream
Hassan, Norman
  See UB40
Hassman, Nikki
  See Avalon
Hastings, Jimmy
  See Caravan
Hastings, Pye
  See Caravan
Hatfield, Juliana 12
  Also see Lemonheads, The
Hathaway, Jane
  See Lane, Fred
Hatori, Miho
  See Cibo Matto
Hauser, Tim
  See Manhattan Transfer, The
Havens, Richie 11
Hawes, Dave
  See Catherine Wheel
Hawkes, Greg
  See Cars, The
Hawkins, Coleman 11
Hawkins, Erskine 19
Hawkins, Lamont "U-God"
  See Wu-Tang Clan

Hawkins, Nick
  See Big Audio Dynamite
Hawkins, Richard (Dick)
  See Gene Loves Jezebel
Hawkins, Roger
  See Traffic
Hawkins, Screamin' Jay 29
  Earlier sketch in CM 8
Hawkins, Sophie B. 21
Hawkins, Taylor
  See Foo Fighters
Hawkins, Tramaine 17
Hawkins, Xian
  See Silver Apples
Hay, George D. 3
Hayden, Victor "The Mascara Snake"
  See Captain Beefheart and His Magic Band
Hayes, Christian "Bic"
  See Dark Star
Hayes, Gordon
  See Pearls Before Swine
Hayes, Isaac 10
Hayes, Roland 13
Haynes, Gibby
  See Butthole Surfers
Haynes, Warren
  See Allman Brothers, The
Hays, Lee
  See Weavers, The
Hayward, David Justin
  See Moody Blues, The
Hayward, Richard
  See Little Feat
Haza, Ofra 29
Headliner
  See Arrested Development
Headon, Topper
  See Clash, The
Healey, Jeff 4
Healy, Fran
  See Travis
Heard, Paul
  See M People
Hearn, Kevin
  See Barenaked Ladies
Heart 1
Heath, James
  See Reverend Horton Heat
Heaton, Paul
  See Beautiful South
Heavy D 10
Hecker, Robert
  See Redd Kross
Hedford, Eric
  See Dandy Warhols
Hedges, Eddie
  See Blessid Union of Souls
Hedges, Michael 3
Heggie, Will
  See Cocteau Twins, The
Heidorn, Mike
  See Son Volt
Heitman, Dana
  See Cherry Poppin' Daddies
Helfgott, David 19
Hell, Richard
  See Television
Hellauer, Susan
  See Anonymous 4
Hellerman, Fred
  See Weavers, The
Hellier, Steve
  See Death in Vegas
Helliwell, John
  See Supertramp

Helm, Levon
  See Band, The
  Also see Nitty Gritty Dirt Band, The
Helmet 15
Hemingway, Dave
  See Beautiful South
Hemmings, Paul
  See Lightning Seeds
Henderson, Andy
  See Echobelly
Henderson, Billy
  See Spinners, The
Henderson, Fletcher 16
Henderson, Joe 14
Hendricks, Barbara 10
Hendricks, Jon
  See Lambert, Hendricks and Ross
Hendrix, Jimi 2
Henley, Don 3
  Also see Eagles, The
Henrit, Bob
  See Kinks, The
Henry, Bill
  See Northern Lights
Henry, Joe 18
Henry, Kent
  See Steppenwolf
Henry, Nicholas "Drummie"
  See Mystic Revealers
Hensley, Ken
  See Uriah Heep
Hepcat, Harry 23
Hepner, Rich
  See Captain Beefheart and His Magic Band
Heppner, Ben 23
Herdman, Bob
  See Audio Adrenaline
Herman, Maureen
  See Babes in Toyland
Herman, Tom
  See Pere Ubu
Herman, Woody 12
Herman's Hermits 5
Herndon, Mark Joel
  See Alabama
Herndon, Ty 20
Heron, Mike
  See Incredible String Band
Herrema, Jennifer
  See Royal Trux
Herrera, R. J.
  See Suicidal Tendencies
Herrera, Raymond
  See Fear Factory
Herrlin, Anders
  See Roxette
Herrmann, Bernard 14
Herron, Cindy
  See En Vogue
Hersh, Kristin
  See Throwing Muses
Hester, Paul
  See Crowded House
Hetfield, James
  See Metallica
Hetson, Greg
  See Bad Religion
  Also see Circle Jerks, The
Heveroh, Ben
  See Oakland Interfaith Gospel Choir
Hewitt, Bobby
  See Orgy
Hewitt, Steve
  See Placebo
Hewson, Paul
  See U2

Huld, Hafdis
  See Gus Gus
Human League, The **17**
Humes, Helen **19**
Humperdinck, Engelbert **19**
Humphreys, Paul
  See Orchestral Manoeuvres in the Dark
Hunnekink, Bernard
  See Willem Breuker Kollektief
Hunt, Darryl
  See Pogues, The
Hunter, Alberta **7**
Hunter, Charlie **24**
Hunter, Jason "The Rebel INS" (Inspectah Deckk)
  See Wu-Tang Clan
Hunter, Mark
  See James
Hunter, Shepherd "Ben"
  See Soundgarden
Hurley, George
  See fIREHOSE
Hurst, Ron
  See Steppenwolf
Hurt, Mississippi John **24**
Hutchence, Michael
  See INXS
Hutchings, Ashley
  See Fairport Convention
  Also see Steeleye Span
Hutchinson, Trevor
  See Waterboys, The
Huth, Todd
  See Primus
Hütter, Ralf
  See Kraftwerk
Hutton, Danny
  See Three Dog Night
Huxley, Rick
  See Dave Clark Five, The
Hyatt, Aitch
  See Specials, The
Hyde, Karl
  See Underworld
Hyde, Michael
  See Big Mountain
Hyman, Jerry
  See Blood, Sweat and Tears
Hyman, Rob
  See Hooters
Hynd, Richard
  See Texas
Hynde, Chrissie
  See Pretenders, The
Hyslop, Kenny
  See Simple Minds
Ian and Sylvia **18**
Ian, Janis **24**
  Earlier sketch in CM **5**
Ian, Scott
  See Anthrax
Ibbotson, Jimmy
  See Nitty Gritty Dirt Band, The
Ibold, Mark
  See Pavement
Ibrahim, Abdullah **24**
Ice Cube **25**
  Earlier sketch in CM **10**
  Also see N.W.A
Ice-T **7**
Idol, Billy **3**
Iglesias, Enrique **27**
Iglesias, Julio **20**
  Earlier sketch in CM **2**
Iha, James
  See Smashing Pumpkins
Ike and Tina Turner **24**

Illsley, John
  See Dire Straits
Imbruglia, Natalie **27**
Immergluck, David
  See Monks of Doom
Imperial Teen **26**
Incognito **16**
Incredible String Band **23**
Incubus **23**
Indigo Girls **20**
  Earlier sketch in CM **3**
Inez, Mike
  See Alice in Chains
Infante, Frank
  See Blondie
Ingber, Elliot "Winged Eel Fingerling"
  See Captain Beefheart and His Magic Band
Inge, Edward
  See McKinney's Cotton Pickers
Ingram, Jack
  See Incredible String Band
Ingram, James **11**
Ink Spots **23**
Inner Circle **15**
Innes, Andrew
  See Primal Scream
Innis, Dave
  See Restless Heart
Insane Clown Posse **22**
Interior, Lux
  See Cramps, The
INXS **21**
  Earlier sketch in CM **2**
Iommi, Tony
  See Black Sabbath
Iron Maiden **10**
Irons, Jack
  See Red Hot Chili Peppers, The
Isaak, Chris **6**
Isabelle, Jeff
  See Guns n' Roses
Isacsson, Jonas
  See Roxette
Isham, Mark **14**
Isles, Bill
  See O'Jays, The
Isley Brothers, The **8**
Isley, Ernie
  See Isley Brothers, The
Isley, Marvin
  See Isley Brothers, The
Isley, O'Kelly, Jr.
  See Isley Brothers, The
Isley, Ronald
  See Isley Brothers, The
Isley, Rudolph
  See Isley Brothers, The
Israel Vibration **21**
Iuean, Dafydd
  See Catatonia
Ives, Burl **12**
Ives, Charles **29**
Ivey, Michael
  See Basehead
Ivins, Michael
  See Flaming Lips
J, David
  See Bauhaus
  Also see Love and Rockets
J.
  See White Zombie
J. Geils Band **25**
Jabs, Matthias
  See Scorpions, The
Jackson 5, The
  See Jacksons, The

Jackson, Al
  See Booker T. & the M.G.'s
Jackson, Alan **25**
  Earlier sketch in CM **7**
Jackson, Clive
  See Ray Condo and His Ricochets
Jackson, Eddie
  See Queensryche
Jackson, Freddie **3**
Jackson, Jackie
  See Jacksons, The
Jackson, Janet **16**
  Earlier sketch in CM **3**
Jackson, Jermaine
  See Jacksons, The
Jackson, Joe **22**
  Earlier sketch in CM **4**
Jackson, Karen
  See Supremes, The
Jackson, Mahalia **8**
Jackson, Marlon
  See Jacksons, The
Jackson, Michael **17**
  Earlier sketch in CM **1**
  Also see Jacksons, The
Jackson, Millie **14**
Jackson, Milt **15**
Jackson, Pervis
  See Spinners, The
Jackson, Quentin
  See McKinney's Cotton Pickers
Jackson, Randy
  See Jacksons, The
Jackson, Stevie
  See Belle and Sebastian
Jackson, Tito
  See Jacksons, The
Jacksons, The **7**
Jackyl **24**
Jacobs, Christian Richard
  See Aquabats, The
Jacobs, Jeff
  See Foreigner
Jacobs, Parker
  See Aquabats, The
Jacobs, Walter
  See Little Walter
Jacox, Martin
  See Soul Stirrers, The
Jacquet, Illinois **17**
Jade 4U
  See Lords of Acid
Jaffee, Rami
  See Wallflowers, The
Jagger, Mick **7**
  Also see Rolling Stones, The
Jairo T.
  See Sepultura
Jalal
  See Last Poets
Jam, Jimmy, and Terry Lewis **11**
Jam, Jimmy
  See Jam, Jimmy, and Terry Lewis
Jam Master Jay
  See Run DMC
Jam, The **27**
James **12**
James, Alex
  See Blur
James, Andrew "Bear"
  See Midnight Oil
James, Boney **21**
James, Cheryl
  See Salt-N-Pepa
James, David
  See Alien Sex Fiend

Jones, Mic
  See Big Audio Dynamite
  Also see Clash, The
Jones, Michael
  See Kronos Quartet
Jones, Mick
  See Foreigner
Jones, Mick
  See Clash, The
Jones, Orville
  See Ink Spots
Jones, Paul
  See Catatonia
Jones, Paul
  See Elastica
Jones, Philly Joe 16
Jones, Quincy 20
  Earlier sketch in CM 2
Jones, Randy
  See Village People, The
Jones, Richard
  See Stereophonics
Jones, Rickie Lee 4
Jones, Robert "Kuumba"
  See Ohio Players
Jones, Robin
  See Beta Band, The
Jones, Ronald
  See Flaming Lips
Jones, Russell "Ol Dirty Bastard"
  See Wu-Tang Clan
Jones, Sandra "Puma"
  See Black Uhuru
Jones, Simon
  See Verve, The
Jones, Spike 5
Jones, Stacy
  See Letters to Cleo
  Also see Veruca Salt
Jones, Steve
  See Sex Pistols, The
Jones, Terry
  See Point of Grace
Jones, Thad 19
Jones, Tom 11
Jones, Will "Dub"
  See Coasters, The
Jonsson, Magnus
  See Gus Gus
Joplin, Janis 3
Joplin, Scott 10
Jordan, Lonnie
  See War
Jordan, Louis 11
Jordan, Montell 26
Jordan, Stanley 1
Jorgenson, John
  See Desert Rose Band, The
Jos
  See Ex, The
Joseph, Charles
  See Dirty Dozen Brass Band
Joseph, Kirk
  See Dirty Dozen Brass Band
Joseph-I, Israel
  See Bad Brains
Josephmary
  See Compulsion
Jourgensen, Al
  See Ministry
Journey 21
Joy Division 19
Joy Electric 26
Joyce, Mike
  See Buzzcocks, The
  Also see Smiths, The
Judas Priest 10

Judd, Naomi
  See Judds, The
Judd, Wynonna
  See Judds, The
  Also see Wynonna
Judds, The 2
Juhlin, Dag
  See Poi Dog Pondering
Jukebox
  See Geto Boys, The
Jungle DJ "Towa" Towa
  See Deee-lite
Jurado, Jeanette
  See Exposé
Jurgensen, Jens
  See Boss Hog
Justman, Seth
  See J. Geils Band
Jym
  See Mr. T Experience, The
K-Ci
  See Jodeci
Kabongo, Sabine
  See Zap Mama
Kahlil, Aisha
  See Sweet Honey in the Rock
Kain, Gylan
  See Last Poets
Kakoulli, Harry
  See Squeeze
Kale, Jim
  See Guess Who
Kalligan, Dick
  See Blood, Sweat and Tears
Kamanski, Paul
  See Beat Farmers
Kaminski, Mik
  See Electric Light Orchestra
Kamomiya, Ryo
  See Pizzicato Five
Kanal, Tony
  See No Doubt
Kanawa, Kiri Te
  See Te Kanawa, Kiri
Kand, Valor
  See Christian Death
Kane, Arthur
  See New York Dolls
Kane, Big Daddy 7
Kane, Nick
  See Mavericks, The
Kang, Eyvind 28
Kannberg, Scott
  See Pavement
Kantner, Paul
  See Jefferson Airplane
Kaplan, Ira
  See Yo La Tengo
Karajan, Herbert von
  See von Karajan, Herbert
Karges, Murphy
  See Sugar Ray
Karlsson, Gunnar
  See Wannadies, The
Karoli, Michael
  See Can
Kath, Terry
  See Chicago
Kato, Nash
  See Urge Overkill
Katrin
  See Ex, The
Katunich, Alex
  See Incubus
Katz, Simon
  See Jamiroquai

Katz, Steve
  See Blood, Sweat and Tears
Kaukonen, Jorma
  See Jefferson Airplane
Kavanagh, Chris
  See Big Audio Dynamite
Kay Gee
  See Naughty by Nature
Kay, Jason
  See Jamiroquai
Kay, John
  See Steppenwolf
Kaye, Carol 22
Kaye, Tony
  See Yes
Kaylan, Howard
  See Turtles, The
Keaggy, Phil 26
Kean, Martin
  See Stereolab
Keane, Sean
  See Chieftains, The
Kee, John P. 15
Keelor, Greg
  See Blue Rodeo
Keenan, Maynard James
  See Tool
Keene, Barry
  See Spirit
Keifer, Tom
  See Cinderella
Keitaro
  See Pizzicato Five
Keith, Jeff
  See Tesla
Keith, Toby 17
Keithley, Joey "Shithead"
  See D.O.A.
Kelly, Betty
  See Martha and the Vandellas
Kelly, Charlotte
  See Soul II Soul
Kelly, Ed
  See Oakland Interfaith Gospel Choir
Kelly, Hugh
  See Wedding Present, The
Kelly, Johnny
  See Type O Negative
Kelly, Kevin
  See Byrds, The
Kelly, Matt
  See Dropkick Murphys
Kelly, R. 19
Kelly, Rashaan
  See US3
Kelly, Scott
  See Neurosis
Kelly, Sean
  See Sixpence None the Richer
Kelly, Terrance
  See Oakland Interfaith Gospel Choir
Kemp, Rick
  See Steeleye Span
Kendrick, David
  See Devo
Kendricks, Eddie
  See Temptations, The
Kennedy, Delious
  See All-4-One
Kennedy, Frankie
  See Altan
Kennedy, Nigel 8
Kenner, Doris
  See Shirelles, The
Kenny, Bill
  See Ink Spots

Krusen, Dave
  See Pearl Jam
Kruspe, Richard
  See Rammstein
Kuba
  See D.O.A.
Kulak, Eddie
  See Aztec Camera
Kulick, Bruce
  See Kiss
Kunkel, Bruce
  See Nitty Gritty Dirt Band, The
Kunzel, Erich 17
Kurdziel, Eddie
  See Redd Kross
Kurihara, Michio
  See Ghost
Kuti, Fela 7
Kuti, Femi 29
L.L. Cool J. 5
L7 12
LaBar, Jeff
  See Cinderella
LaBelle, Patti 8
LaBrie, James
  See Dream Theater
Lack, Steve
  See Veruca Salt
LaCroix, Dimples
  See Lane, Fred
Lacy, Steve 23
Lady Miss Kier
  See Deee-lite
Ladybug
  See Digable Planets
Ladysmith Black Mambazo 1
Lafalce, Mark
  See Mekons, The
Lagerburg, Bengt
  See Cardigans, The
Laine, Cleo 10
Laine, Denny
  See Moody Blues, The
Laird, Rick
  See Mahavishnu Orchestra
Lake, Greg
  See Emerson, Lake & Palmer/Powell
  Also see King Crimson
LaKind, Bobby
  See Doobie Brothers, The
Lally, Joe
  See Fugazi
LaLonde, Larry "Ler"
  See Primus
Lamb, Barbara 19
Lamb, Michael
  See Confederate Railroad
Lambchop 29
Lambert, Dave
  See Lambert, Hendricks and Ross
Lambert, Hendricks and Ross 28
Lamble, Martin
  See Fairport Convention
Lamm, Robert
  See Chicago
Lampkin, Troy
  See Oakland Interfaith Gospel Choir
Lancaster, Brian
  See Surfin' Pluto
Landers, Paul
  See Rammstein
Landreth, Sonny 16
Lane, Fred 28
Lane, Jani
  See Warrant
Lane, Jay
  See Primus

Lane, Ronnie
  See Faces, The
Lanegan, Mark
  See Screaming Trees
lang, k. d. 25
  Earlier sketch in CM 4
Lang, Jonny 27
Langan, Gary
  See Art of Noise
Langdon, Antony
  See Spacehog
Langdon, Royston
  See Spacehog
Langford, Jon
  See Mekons, The
Langford, Willie
  See Golden Gate Quartet
Langley, John
  See Mekons, The
Langlois, Paul
  See Tragically Hip, The
Langosch, Paul
  See Ralph Sharon Quartet
Langston, Leslie
  See Throwing Muses
Lanier, Allen
  See Blue Oyster Cult
Lanker, Dustin
  See Cherry Poppin' Daddies
Lanois, Daniel 8
LaPread, Ronald
  See Commodores, The
Larkin, Patty 9
Larson, Chad Albert
  See Aquabats, The
Larson, Nathan
  See Shudder to Think
Last Poets 21
Laswell, Bill 14
Lataille, Rich
  See Roomful of Blues
Lateef, Yusef 16
Latimer, Andrew
  See Camel
Lauderdale, Jim 29
Laughner, Peter
  See Pere Ubu
Lauper, Cyndi 11
Laurence, Lynda
  See Supremes, The
Lavin, Christine 6
Lavis, Gilson
  See Squeeze
Lawler, Feargal
  See Cranberries, The
Lawnge
  See Black Sheep
Lawrence, Tracy 11
Lawry, John
  See Petra
Laws, Roland
  See Earth, Wind and Fire
Lawson, Doyle
  See Country Gentlemen, The
Layzie Bone
  See Bone Thugs-N-Harmony
Le Bon, Simon
  See Duran Duran
Le Mystère des Voix Bulgares
  See Bulgarian State Female Vocal Choir, The
Leadbelly 6
Leadon, Bernie
  See Eagles, The
  Also see Nitty Gritty Dirt Band, The
Lear, Graham
  See REO Speedwagon

Leary, Paul
  See Butthole Surfers
Leavell, Chuck
  See Allman Brothers, The
LeBon, Simon
  See Duran Duran
Leckenby, Derek "Lek"
  See Herman's Hermits
Led Zeppelin 1
Ledbetter, Huddie
  See Leadbelly
LeDoux, Chris 12
Lee, Ben 26
Lee, Beverly
  See Shirelles, The
Lee, Brenda 5
Lee, Buddy
  See McKinney's Cotton Pickers
Lee, Buddy
  See Less Than Jake
Lee, Garret
  See Compulsion
Lee, Geddy
  See Rush
Lee, Peggy 8
Lee, Pete
  See Gwar
Lee, Sara
  See Gang of Four
Lee, Stan
  See Incredible String Band
Lee, Tommy
  See Mötley Crüe
Lee, Tony
  See Treadmill Trackstar
Leeb, Bill
  See Front Line Assembly
Leen, Bill
  See Gin Blossoms
Leese, Howard
  See Heart
Leftfield 29
Legg, Adrian 17
Legowitz, Herr
  See Gus Gus
Leherer, Keith "Lucky"
  See Circle Jerks
Lehrer, Tom 7
Leiber and Stoller 14
Leiber, Jerry
  See Leiber and Stoller
LeMaistre, Malcolm
  See Incredible String Band
Lemmy
  See Motörhead
Lemonheads, The 12
Lemper, Ute 14
Lenear, Kevin
  See Mighty Mighty Bosstones
Lenners, Rudy
  See Scorpions, The
Lennon, John 9
  Also see Beatles, The
Lennon, Julian 26
  Earlier sketch in CM 2
Lennox, Annie 18
  Also see Eurythmics
Leonard, Geno
  See Filter
Leonard, Glenn
  See Temptations, The
Lerner, Alan Jay
  See Lerner and Loewe
Lerner and Loewe 13
Lesh, Phil
  See Grateful Dead, The

Lucas, Trevor
  See Fairport Convention
Luccketta, Troy
  See Tesla
Lucia, Paco de
  See de Lucia, Paco
Luciano, Felipe
  See Last Poets
Luke
  See Campbell, Luther
Lukin, Matt
  See Mudhoney
Luna 18
Lunsford, Bret
  See Beat Happening
Lupo, Pat
  See Beaver Brown Band, The
LuPone, Patti 8
Luscious Jackson 27
  Earlier sketch in CM 19
Lush 13
Luttell, Terry
  See REO Speedwagon
Lydon, John 9
  Also see Sex Pistols, The
Lyfe, DJ
  See Incubus
Lymon, Frankie
  See Frankie Lymon and The Teenagers
Lynch, David
  See Platters, The
Lynch, Dermot
  See Dog's Eye View
Lynch, George
  See Dokken
Lynch, Laura
  See Dixie Chicks
Lynch, Stan
  See Tom Petty and the Heartbreakers
Lyngstad, Anni-Frid
  See Abba
Lynn, Lonnie Rashid
  See Common
Lynn, Loretta 2
Lynne, Jeff 5
  Also see Electric Light Orchestra
Lynne, Shelby 29
  Earlier sketch in CM 5
Lynott, Phil
  See Thin Lizzy
Lynyrd Skynyrd 9
Lyons, Leanne "Lelee"
  See SWV
M People 27
  Earlier sketch in CM 15
M.C. Hammer
  See Hammer, M.C.
M.C. Ren
  See N.W.A.
Ma, Yo-Yo 24
  Earlier sketch in CM 2
Mabry, Bill
  See Asleep at the Wheel
MacColl, Kirsty 12
MacDonald, Barbara Kooyman
  See Timbuk 3
MacDonald, Eddie
  See Alarm
MacDonald, Pat
  See Timbuk 3
Macfarlane, Lora
  See Sleater-Kinney
MacGowan, Shane
  See Pogues, The
MacIsaac, Ashley 21
Mack Daddy
  See Kris Kross

MacKaye, Ian
  See Fugazi
Mackey, Steve
  See Pulp
MacNeil, Michael
  See Simple Minds
MacNeil, Rita 29
MacPherson, Jim
  See Breeders
Macy, Robin
  See Dixie Chicks
Madan, Sonya Aurora
  See Echobelly
Madder Rose 17
Madness 27
Madonna 16
  Earlier sketch in CM 4
Mael, Ron
  See Sparks
Mael, Russell
  See Sparks
Magehee, Marty
  See 4Him
Maghostut, Malachi Favors
  See Art Ensemble of Chicago, The
Maginnis, Tom
  See Buffalo Tom
Magnetic Fields, The 28
Magnie, John
  See Subdudes, The
Magoogan, Wesley
  See English Beat, The
Mahavishnu Orchestra 19
Maher, John
  See Buzzcocks, The
Mahogany, Kevin 26
Mahoney, Tim
  See 311
Maida, Raine
  See Our Lady Peace
Maillard, Carol
  See Sweet Honey in the Rock
Maimone, Tony
  See Pere Ubu
Maines, Natalie
  See Dixie Chicks
Maïtra, Shyamal
  See Gong
Majewski, Hank
  See Four Seasons, The
Makeba, Miriam 8
Makino, Kazu
  See Blonde Redhead
Malcolm, Hugh
  See Skatalites, The
Malcolm, Joy
  See Incognito
Male, Johnny
  See Republica
Malherbe, Didier
  See Gong
Malin, Jesse
  See D Generation
Malins, Mike
  See Goo Goo Dolls, The
Malkmus, Stephen
  See Pavement
Malley, Matt
  See Counting Crows
Mallinder, Stephen
  See Cabaret Voltaire
Malmsteen, Yngwie 24
Malo, Raul
  See Mavericks, The
Malone, Russell 27
Malone, Tom
  See Blood, Sweat and Tears

Malone, Tommy
  See Subdudes, The
Mamas and the Papas 21
Man or Astroman? 21
Mancini, Henry 20
  Earlier sketch in CM 1
Mandel, Johnny 28
Mandrell, Barbara 4
Maness, J. D.
  See Desert Rose Band, The
Mangione, Chuck 23
Manhattan Transfer, The 8
Manic Street Preachers 27
Manilow, Barry 2
Mann, Aimee 22
Mann, Billy 23
Mann, Herbie 16
Manninger, Hank
  See Aqua Velvets
Manson, Shirley
  See Garbage
Manuel, Richard
  See Band, The
Manzarek, Ray
  See Doors, The
March, Kevin
  See Shudder to Think
Marie, Buffy Sainte
  See Sainte-Marie, Buffy
Marilyn Manson 18
Marini, Lou, Jr.
  See Blood, Sweat and Tears
Marker, Steve
  See Garbage
Marks, Toby
  See De Gaia, Banco
Marley, Bob 3
Marley, Rita 10
Marley, Ziggy 3
Marr, Johnny
  See Smiths, The
  Also see The The
Marriner, Neville 7
Mars, Chris
  See Replacements, The
Mars, Derron
  See Less Than Jake
Mars, Mick
  See Mötley Crüe
Marsalis, Branford 10
Marsalis, Ellis 13
Marsalis, Jason
  See Los Hombres Calientes
Marsalis, Wynton 20
  Earlier sketch in CM 6
Marsh, Ian Craig
  See Human League, The
Marshal, Cornel
  See Third World
Marshall, Amanda 27
Marshall, Arik
  See Red Hot Chili Peppers
Marshall, Brian
  See Creed
Marshall, Jenell
  See Dirty Dozen Brass Band
Marshall, Steve
  See Gene Loves Jezebel
Martensen, Vic
  See Captain Beefheart and His Magic Band
Martha and the Vandellas 25
Martin, Barbara
  See Supremes, The
Martin, Barrett
  See Screaming Trees
Martin, Carl
  See Shai

McDonald, Richie
  See Lonestar
McDonald, Steven
  See Redd Kross
McDorman, Joe
  See Statler Brothers, The
McDougall, Don
  See Guess Who
McDowell, Hugh
  See Electric Light Orchestra
McDowell, Mississippi Fred **16**
McElhone, John
  See Texas
McEntire, Reba **11**
McErlaine, Ally
  See Texas
McEuen, John
  See Nitty Gritty Dirt Band, The
McFarlane, Elaine
  See Mamas and the Papas
McFee, John
  See Doobie Brothers, The
McFerrin, Bobby **3**
McFessel, Sean
  See Cake
McGearly, James
  See Christian Death
McGee, Brian
  See Simple Minds
McGee, Jerry
  See Ventures, The
McGeoch, John
  See Siouxsie and the Banshees
McGinley, Raymond
  See Teenage Fanclub
McGinniss, Will
  See Audio Adrenaline
McGrath, Mark
  See Sugar Ray
McGraw, Tim **17**
McGuigan, Paul
  See Oasis
McGuinn, Jim
  See McGuinn, Roger
McGuinn, Roger
  See Byrds, The
McGuinness
  See Lords of Acid
McGuire, Christine
  See McGuire Sisters, The
McGuire, Dorothy
  See McGuire Sisters, The
McGuire, Mike
  See Shenandoah
McGuire, Phyllis
  See McGuire Sisters, The
McGuire Sisters, The **27**
McIntosh, Robbie
  See Pretenders, The
McIntyre, Joe
  See New Kids on the Block
McJohn, Goldy
  See Steppenwolf
McKagan, Duff
  See Guns n' Roses
McKay, Al
  See Earth, Wind and Fire
McKay, John
  See Siouxsie and the Banshees
McKean, Michael
  See Spinal Tap
McKee , Julius
  See Dirty Dozen Brass Band
McKee, Maria **11**
McKeehan, Toby
  See dc Talk

McKenna, Greg
  See Letters to Cleo
McKennitt, Loreena **24**
McKenzie, Christina "Licorice"
  See Incredible String Band
McKenzie, Derrick
  See Jamiroquai
McKenzie, Scott
  See Mamas and the Papas
McKernan, Ron "Pigpen"
  See Grateful Dead, The
McKinney, William
  See McKinney's Cotton Pickers
McKinney's Cotton Pickers **16**
McKnight, Brian **22**
McKnight, Claude V. III
  See Take 6
McLachlan, Sarah **12**
McLagan, Ian
  See Faces, The
McLaren, Malcolm **23**
McLaughlin, John **12**
  Also see Mahavishnu Orchestra
McLean, A. J.
  See Backstreet Boys
McLean, Dave **24**
McLean, Don **7**
McLean, John
  See Beta Band, The
McLennan, Grant **21**
  Also see Go-Betweens, The
McLeod, Rory
  See Roomful of Blues
McLoughlin, Jon
  See Del Amitri
McMackin, Bryon
  See Pennywise
McMeel, Mickey
  See Three Dog Night
McMurtry, James **10**
McNabb, Travis
  See Better Than Ezra
McNair, Sylvia **15**
McNeilly, Mac
  See Jesus Lizard
McNew, James
  See Yo La Tengo
McPartland, Marian **15**
McPhatter, Clyde **25**
McPherson, Graham "Suggs"
  See Madness
McQuillar, Shawn
  See Kool & the Gang
McRae, Carmen **9**
McReynolds, Jesse
  See McReynolds, Jim and Jesse
McReynolds, Jim
  See McReynolds, Jim and Jesse
McReynolds, Jim and Jesse **12**
McShane, Ronnie
  See Chieftains, The
McShee, Jacqui
  See Pentangle
McTell, Blind Willie **17**
McVie, Christine
  See Fleetwood Mac
McVie, John
  See Fleetwood Mac
McWhinney, James
  See Big Mountain
McWhinney, Joaquin
  See Big Mountain
Mdletshe, Geophrey
  See Ladysmith Black Mambazo
Meat Loaf **12**
Meat Puppets, The **13**
Medley, Bill **3**

Medlock, James
  See Soul Stirrers, The
Meehan, Tony
  See Shadows, The
Megadeth **9**
Mehldau, Brad **27**
Mehta, Zubin **11**
Meine, Klaus
  See Scorpions, The
Meisner, Randy
  See Eagles, The
Mekons, The **15**
Melanie **12**
Melax, Einar
  See Sugarcubes, The
Mellencamp, John **20**
  Earlier sketch in CM **2**
Melvin, Eric
  See NOFX
Melvins **21**
Memphis Jug Band **25**
Memphis Minnie **25**
Menck, Ric
  See Velvet Crush
Mendel, Nate
  See Foo Fighters
Mendel, Nate
  See Sunny Day Real Estate
Mengede, Peter
  See Helmet
Menken, Alan **10**
Menuhin, Yehudi **11**
Menza, Nick
  See Megadeth
Mercer, Johnny **13**
Merchant, Jimmy
  See Frankie Lymon and The Teenagers
Merchant, Natalie **25**
  Also see 10,000 Maniacs
Mercier, Peadar
  See Chieftains, The
Mercury, Freddie
  See Queen
Mercury Rev **28**
Merman, Ethel **27**
Merritt, Stephin
  See Magnetic Fields, The
Mertens, Paul
  See Poi Dog Pondering
Mesaros, Michael
  See Smithereens, The
Messecar, Dek
  See Caravan
Messina, Jim
  See Buffalo Springfield
Messina, Jo Dee **26**
Metallica **7**
Meters, The **14**
Methembu, Russel
  See Ladysmith Black Mambazo
Metheny, Pat **26**
  Earlier sketch in CM **2**
Mew, Sharon
  See Elastica
Meyer, Eric
  See Charm Farm
Meyers, Augie
  See Texas Tornados, The
Mhaonaigh, Mairead Ni
  See Altan
Michael, George **9**
Michaels, Bret
  See Poison
Michel, Luke
  See Emmet Swimming
Michel, Prakazrel "Pras"
  See Fugees, The

Morriss, Reginald Ilanthriy
  See Bluetones, The
Morrissett, Paul
  See Klezmatics, The
Morrissey **10**
  Also see Smiths, The
Morrissey, Bill **12**
Morrissey, Steven Patrick
  See Morrissey
Morton, Everett
  See English Beat, The
Morton, Jelly Roll **7**
Morvan, Fab
  See Milli Vanilli
Mosbaugh, Garth
  See Nylons, The
Mosely, Chuck
  See Faith No More
Moser, Scott "Cactus"
  See Highway 101
Mosher, Ken
  See Squirrel Nut Zippers
Mosley, Bob
  See Moby Grape
Moss, Jason
  See Cherry Poppin' Daddies
Most, Mickie **29**
Mothersbaugh, Bob
  See Devo
Mothersbaugh, Mark
  See Devo
Mötley Crüe **1**
Motörhead **10**
Motta, Danny
  See Roomful of Blues
Mould, Bob **10**
Moulding, Colin
  See XTC
Mounfield, Gary
  See Stone Roses, The
Mouquet, Eric
  See Deep Forest
Mouskouri, Nana **12**
Mouzon, Alphonse
  See Weather Report
Moye, Famoudou Don
  See Art Ensemble of Chicago, The
Moyet, Alison **12**
Moyse, David
  See Air Supply
Mr. Dalvin
  See Jodeci
Mr. T Experience, The **29**
Mudhoney **16**
Mueller, Karl
  See Soul Asylum
Muir, Jamie
  See King Crimson
Muir, Mike
  See Suicidal Tendencies
Muldaur, Maria **18**
Mulholland, Dave
  See Aztec Camera
Mullen, Larry, Jr.
  See U2
Mullen, Mary
  See Congo Norvell
Mulligan, Gerry **16**
Murcia, Billy
  See New York Dolls
Murdoch, Stuart
  See Belle and Sebastian
Murdock, Roger
  See King Missile
Murph
  See Dinosaur Jr.
Murphey, Michael Martin **9**

Murphy, Brigid
  See Poi Dog Pondering
Murphy, Chris
  See Sloan
Murphy, Dan
  See Soul Asylum
Murphy, John
  See Gene Loves Jezebel
Murphy, Michael
  See REO Speedwagon
Murphy, Peter **22**
  Also see Bauhaus
Murray, Anne **4**
Murray, Dave **28**
Murray, Dave
  See Iron Maiden
Murray, Dee
  See Spencer Davis Group
Murray, Don
  See Turtles, The
Murray, Jim
  See Quicksilver Messenger Service
Musburger, Mike
  See Fastbacks, The
Mushroom
  See Massive Attack
Musselwhite, Charlie **13**
Mustaine, Dave
  See Megadeth
  Also see Metallica
Mutter, Anne-Sophie **23**
Mwelase, Jabulane
  See Ladysmith Black Mambazo
My Bloody Valentine **29**
Mydland, Brent
  See Grateful Dead, The
Myers, Alan
  See Devo
Myles, Alannah **4**
Mystic Revealers **16**
Mystikal **29**
Myung, John
  See Dream Theater
'N Sync **25**
N.W.A. **6**
N'Dour, Youssou **6**
Na'dirah
  See Arrested Development
Naftalin, Mark
  See Quicksilver Messenger Service
Nagler, Eric **8**
Najee **21**
Nakai, R. Carlos **24**
Nakamura, Tetsuya "Tex"
  See War
Nakatami, Michie
  See Shonen Knife
Naked, Bif **29**
Nana
  See Rasputina
Narcizo, David
  See Throwing Muses
Nas **19**
Nascimento, Milton **6**
Nash, Graham
  See Crosby, Stills, and Nash
Nash, Leigh
  See Sixpence None the Richer
Nashville Bluegrass Band **14**
Nasta, Ken
  See Royal Trux
Nastanovich, Bob
  See Pavement
Naughty by Nature **11**
Navarro, Dave
  See Red Hot Chili Peppers

Navarro, David
  See Jane's Addiction
Navarro Fats **25**
Nawasadio, Sylvie
  See Zap Mama
Ndegéocello, Me'Shell **18**
Ndugu
  See Weather Report
Near, Holly **1**
Neel, Johnny
  See Allman Brothers, The
Negron, Chuck
  See Three Dog Night
Negroni, Joe
  See Frankie Lymon and The Teenagers
Neil, Chris
  See Less Than Jake
Neil, Vince
  See Mötley Crüe
Nelson, Brett
  See Built to Spill
Nelson, Brian
  See Velocity Girl
Nelson, David
  See Last Poets
Nelson, Errol
  See Black Uhuru
Nelson, Gabe
  See Cake
Nelson, Nate
  See Platters, The
Nelson, Rick **2**
Nelson, Shara
  See Massive Attack
Nelson, Willie **11**
  Earlier sketch in CM **1**
Nero, Peter **19**
Nesbitt, John
  See McKinney's Cotton Pickers
Nesmith, Mike
  See Monkees, The
Ness, Mike
  See Social Distortion
Netson, Brett
  See Built to Spill
Neufville, Renee
  See Zhane
Neumann, Kurt
  See BoDeans
Neurosis **28**
Nevarez, Alfred
  See All-4-One
Neville, Aaron **5**
  Also see Neville Brothers, The
Neville, Art
  See Meters, The
  Also see Neville Brothers, The
Neville Brothers, The **4**
Neville, Charles
  See Neville Brothers, The
Neville, Cyril
  See Meters, The
  Also see Neville Brothers, The
Nevin, Brian
  See Big Head Todd and the Monsters
New Grass Revival, The **4**
New Kids on the Block **3**
New Order **11**
New Rhythm and Blues Quartet
  See NRBQ
New York Dolls **20**
Newman, Colin
  See Wire
Newman, Randy **27**
  Earlier sketch in CM **4**
Newmann, Kurt
  See BoDeans, The

Orr, Benjamin
　See Cars, The
Orr, Casey
　See Gwar
Orrall, Frank
　See Poi Dog Pondering
Ortega, Leonor "Jeff"
　See Five Iron Frenzy
Ortega, Micah
　See Five Iron Frenzy
Orton, Beth **26**
Orzabal, Roland
　See Tears for Fears
Osborne, Bob
　See Osborne Brothers, The
Osborne Brothers, The **8**
Osborne, Buzz
　See Melvins
Osborne, Joan **19**
Osborne, Sonny
　See Osborne Brothers, The
Osbourne, Ozzy **3**
　Also see Black Sabbath
Osby, Greg **21**
Oskar, Lee
　See War
Oslin, K. T. **3**
Osman, Mat
　See Suede
Osmond, Donny **3**
Ostin, Mo **17**
Otis, Johnny **16**
Ott, David **2**
Otto, John
　See Limp Bizkit
Our Lady Peace **22**
Outler, Jimmy
　See Soul Stirrers, The
Owen, Randy Yueull
　See Alabama
Owens, Buck **2**
Owens, Campbell
　See Aztec Camera
Owens, Henry
　See Golden Gate Quartet
Owens, Ricky
　See Temptations, The
Oyewole, Abiodun
　See Last Poets
P.M. Dawn **11**
Pace, Amedeo
　See Blonde Redhead
Pace, Simone
　See Blonde Redhead
Page, Jimmy **4**
　Also see Led Zeppelin
　Also see Yardbirds, The
Page, Patti **11**
Page, Steven
　See Barenaked Ladies
Paice, Ian
　See Deep Purple
Paliotta, Cherie
　See Avalon
Palmer, Bruce
　See Buffalo Springfield
Palmer, Carl
　See Emerson, Lake & Palmer/Powell
Palmer, Clive
　See Incredible String Band
Palmer, David
　See Jethro Tull
Palmer, Jeff
　See Sunny Day Real Estate
Palmer, Jeff **20**
Palmer, Keeti
　See Prodigy

Palmer, Phil
　See Dire Straits
Palmer, Richard
　See Supertramp
Palmer, Robert **2**
Palmer-Jones, Robert
　See King Crimson
Palmieri, Eddie **15**
Paluzzi, Jimmy
　See Sponge
Pamer, John
　See Tsunami
Pankow, James
　See Chicago
Panter, Horace
　See Specials, The
Pantera **13**
Papach, Leyna
　See Geraldine Fibbers
Papas Fritas **29**
Pappas, Tom
　See Superdrag
Parazaider, Walter
　See Chicago
Paris, Twila **16**
Park, Cary
　See Boy Howdy
Park, Larry
　See Boy Howdy
Parkening, Christopher **7**
Parker, Charlie **5**
Parker, Evan **28**
Parker, Graham **10**
Parker, Kris
　See KRS-One
Parker, Leon **27**
Parker, Maceo **7**
Parker, Tom
　See Animals, The
Parkin, Chad
　See Aquabats, The
Parks, Van Dyke **17**
Parnell, Lee Roy **15**
Parsons, Alan **12**
Parsons, Dave
　See Bush
Parsons, Gene
　See Byrds, The
Parsons, Gram **7**
　Also see Byrds, The
Parsons, Ted
　See Prong
Parsons, Tony
　See Iron Maiden
Partch, Harry **29**
Parton, Dolly **24**
　Earlier sketch in CM **2**
Partridge, Andy
　See XTC
Parvo, Carpella
　See Rasputina
Pasemaster, Mase
　See De La Soul
Pash, Jim
　See Surfaris, The
Pasillas, Jose
　See Incubus
Pass, Joe **15**
Passons, Michael
　See Avalon
Pastorius, Jaco
　See Weather Report
Paterson, Alex
　See Orb, The
Patinkin, Mandy **20**
　Earlier sketch CM **3**

Patrick, Richard
　See Filter
Patti, Sandi **7**
Patton, Charley **11**
Patton, Mike
　See Faith No More
Paul, Alan
　See Manhattan Transfer, The
Paul III, Henry
　See BlackHawk
Paul, Les **2**
Paul, Prince **29**
　Also see Gravediggaz
Paul, Vinnie
　See Pantera
Paulo, Jr.
　See Sepultura
Pavarotti, Luciano **20**
　Earlier sketch in CM **1**
Pavement **14**
Pavia, John
　See Four Seasons, The
Paxton, Tom **5**
Payne, Bill
　See Little Feat
Payne, Dougie
　See Travis
Payne, Richard
　See Bluetones, The
Payne, Scherrie
　See Supremes, The
Payton, Denis
　See Dave Clark Five, The
Payton, Lawrence
　See Four Tops, The
Payton, Nicholas **27**
Pearce, David
　See Flying Saucer Attack
Pearl Jam **12**
Pearl, Minnie **3**
Pearls Before Swine **24**
Pearson, Dan
　See American Music Club
Peart, Neil
　See Rush
Pedersen, Chris
　See Monks of Doom
Pedersen, Herb
　See Desert Rose Band, The
Peduzzi, Larry
　See Roomful of Blues
Peek, Dan
　See America
Peeler, Ben
　See Mavericks, The
Pegg, Dave
　See Fairport Convention
　Also see Jethro Tull
Pegrum, Nigel
　See Steeleye Span
Peligro, Darren H.
　See Dead Kennedys
Pelletier, Mike
　See Kilgore
Pence, Jeff
　See Blessid Union of Souls
Pendergrass, Teddy **3**
Pendleton, Brian
　See Pretty Things, The
Pengilly, Kirk
　See INXS
Peniston, CeCe **15**
Penn, Michael **4**
Penner, Fred **10**
Pennywise **27**
Pentangle **18**

Portman, Dr. Frank
  See Mr. T Experience, The
Portman-Smith, Nigel
  See Pentangle
Portnoy, Mike
  See Dream Theater
Portz, Chuck
  See Turtles, The
Posa, Dylan
  See Flying Luttenbachers, The
Posdnuos
  See De La Soul
Post, Louise
  See Veruca Salt
Post, Mike 21
Potter, Janna
  See Avalon
Potts, Sean
  See Chieftains, The
Povey, John
  See Pretty Things, The
Powell, Baden 23
Powell, Billy
  See Lynyrd Skynyrd
Powell, Bud 15
Powell, Cozy
  See Emerson, Lake & Palmer/Powell
Powell, Kobie
  See US3
Powell, Owen
  See Catatonia
Powell, Paul
  See Aztec Camera
Powell, William
  See O'Jays, The
Powers, Kid Congo
  See Congo Norvell
  Also see Cramps, The
Prater, Dave
  See Sam and Dave
Pratt, Awadagin 19
Prefab Sprout 15
Presley, Elvis 1
Preston, Leroy
  See Asleep at the Wheel
Pretenders, The 8
Pretty Things, The 26
Previn, André 15
Price, Alan
  See Animals, The
Price, Leontyne 6
Price, Lloyd 25
Price, Louis
  See Temptations, The
Price, Mark
  See Archers of Loaf
Price, Ray 11
Price, Rick
  See Electric Light Orchestra
Pride, Charley 4
Priest, Maxi 20
Prima, Louis 18
Primal Scream 14
Primettes, The
  See Supremes, The
Primrose, Neil
  See Travis
Primus 11
Prince 14
  Earlier sketch in CM 1
Prince Be
  See P.M. Dawn
Prince, Prairie
  See Journey
Prince, Vivian
  See Pretty Things, The
Prine, John 7

Prior, Maddy
  See Steeleye Span
Proclaimers, The 13
Prodigy 22
Professor Longhair 6
Promise Ring, The 28
Prong 23
Propatier, Joe
  See Silver Apples
Propellerheads 26
Propes, Duane
  See Little Texas
Prout, Brian
  See Diamond Rio
Pryce, Guto
  See Super Furry Animals
Psychedelic Furs 23
Public Enemy 4
Puccini, Giacomo 25
Puente, Tito 14
Puff Daddy
  See Combs, Sean "Puffy"
Pullen, Don 16
Pulp 18
Pulsford, Nigel
  See Bush
Pusey, Clifford "Moonie"
  See Steel Pulse
Pyle, Andy
  See Kinks, The
Pyle, Artemis
  See Lynyrd Skynyrd
Pyle, Chris
  See Royal Trux
Pyle, Pip
  See Gong
Pyro, Howie
  See D Generation
Q-Tip
  See Tribe Called Quest, A
Quaife, Peter
  See Kinks, The
Quasi 24
Quasthoff, Thomas 26
Queen 6
Queen Ida 9
Queen Latifah 24
  Earlier sketch in CM 6
Queens, Hollis
  See Boss Hog
Queensryche 8
Querfurth, Carl
  See Roomful of Blues
Quicksilver Messenger Service 23
Qureshi, Ustad Alla Rakha 29
R.E.M. 25
  Earlier sketch in CM 5
Raaymakers, Boy
  See Willem Breuker Kollektief
Rabbitt, Eddie 24
  Earlier sketch in CM 5
Rabin, Trevor
  See Yes
Radiohead 24
Raekwon
  See Wu-Tang Clan
Raffi 8
Rage Against the Machine 18
Raheem
  See Geto Boys, The
Rainey, Ma 22
Rainey, Sid
  See Compulsion
Rainford, Simone
  See All Saints
Rainwater, Keech
  See Lonestar

Raitt, Bonnie 23
  Earlier sketch in CM 3
Rakim
  See Eric B. and Rakim
Raleigh, Don
  See Squirrel Nut Zippers
Ralph Sharon Quartet 26
Ralphs, Mick
  See Bad Company
Rammstein 25
Ramone, C. J.
  See Ramones, The
Ramone, Dee Dee
  See Ramones, The
Ramone, Joey
  See Ramones, The
Ramone, Johnny
  See Ramones, The
Ramone, Marky
  See Ramones, The
Ramone, Ritchie
  See Ramones, The
Ramone, Tommy
  See Ramones, The
Ramones, The 9
Rampage, Randy
  See D.O.A.
Rampal, Jean-Pierre 6
Ramsay, Andy
  See Stereolab
Ranaldo, Lee
  See Sonic Youth
Rancid 29
Randall, Bobby
  See Sawyer Brown
Raney, Jerry
  See Beat Farmers
Rangell, Andrew 24
Ranglin, Ernest
  See Skatalites, The
Ranken, Andrew
  See Pogues, The
Rankin, Cookie
  See Rankins, The
Rankin, Heather
  See Rankins, The
Rankin, Jimmy
  See Rankins, The
Rankin, John Morris
  See Rankins, The
Rankin, Raylene
  See Rankins, The
Ranking, Roger
  See English Beat, The
Rankins, The 24
Rapp, Tom
  See Pearls Before Swine
Rarebell, Herman
  See Scorpions, The
Rasboro, Johnathen
  See Silk
Rasputina 26
Rat Fink, Jr.
  See Alien Sex Fiend
Ratcliffe, Simon
  See Basement Jaxx
Ravel, Maurice 25
Raven, Paul
  See Prong
Rawls, Lou 19
Ray, Amy
  See Indigo Girls
Ray Condo and His Ricochets 26
Ray, East Bay
  See Dead Kennedys
Raybon, Marty
  See Shenandoah

Robinson, Louise
  See Sweet Honey in the Rock
Robinson, Prince
  See McKinney's Cotton Pickers
Robinson, R.B.
  See Soul Stirrers, The
Robinson, Rich
  See Black Crowes, The
Robinson, Romye "Booty Brown"
  See Pharcyde, The
Robinson, Smokey **1**
Roche, Maggie
  See Roches, The
Roche, Suzzy
  See Roches, The
Roche, Terre
  See Roches, The
Roches, The **18**
Rockenfield, Scott
  See Queensryche
Rocker, Lee
  See Stray Cats, The
Rockett, Rikki
  See Poison
Rockin' Dopsie **10**
Rodford, Jim
  See Kinks, The
Rodgers, Jimmie **3**
Rodgers, Nile **8**
Rodgers, Paul
  See Bad Company
Rodgers, Richard **9**
Rodney, Red **14**
Rodriguez, Rico
  See Skatalites, The
  Also see Specials, The
Rodriguez, Sal
  See War
Roe, Marty
  See Diamond Rio
Roeder, Jason
  See Neurosis
Roeder, Klaus
  See Kraftwerk
Roeser, Donald
  See Blue Oyster Cult
Roeser, Eddie "King"
  See Urge Overkill
Roessler, Kira
  See Black Flag
Roger, Ranking
  See English Beat, The
Rogers, Dan
  See Bluegrass Patriots
Rogers, Kenny **1**
Rogers, Norm
  See Jayhawks, The
Rogers, Roy **24**
  Earlier sketch in CM **9**
Rogers, Willie
  See Soul Stirrers, The
Rogerson, Roger
  See Circle Jerks
Roland, Dean
  See Collective Soul
Roland, Ed
  See Collective Soul
Rolie, Gregg
  See Journey
Rolling Stones, The **23**
  Earlier sketch in CM **3**
Rollins, Henry **11**
  Also see Black Flag
Rollins, Sonny **7**
Rollins, Winston
  See Jamiroquai

Romanelli, Chris "Junior"
  See Wendy O. Williams and The Plasmatics
Romano, Ruben
  See Fu Manchu
Romm, Ronald
  See Canadian Brass, The
Ronstadt, Linda **2**
Roomful of Blues **7**
Roots, The **27**
Roper, Dee Dee
  See Salt-N-Pepa
Roper, Reese
  See Five Iron Frenzy
Roper, Todd
  See Cake
Rorschach, Poison Ivy
  See Cramps, The
Rosas, Cesar
  See Los Lobos
Rose, Axl
  See Guns n' Roses
Rose, Felipe
  See Village People, The
Rose, Johanna Maria
  See Anonymous 4
Rose, Michael
  See Black Uhuru
Rosen, Gary
  See Rosenshontz
Rosen, Peter
  See War
Rosenshontz **9**
Rosenthal, Jurgen
  See Scorpions, The
Rosenthal, Phil
  See Seldom Scene, The
Rosenworcel, Brian
  See Guster
Ross, Annie
  See Lambert, Hendricks and Ross
Ross, Diana **1**
  Also see Supremes, The
Ross, Malcolm
  See Aztec Camera
Rossdale, Gavin
  See Bush
Rossi, John
  See Roomful of Blues
Rossington, Gary
  See Lynyrd Skynyrd
Rossy, Jose
  See Weather Report
Rostill, John
  See Shadows, The
Rostropovich, Mstislav **17**
Rota, Nino **13**
Roth, C. P.
  See Blessid Union of Souls
Roth, David Lee **1**
  Also see Van Halen
Roth, Gabrielle **26**
Roth, Ulrich
  See Scorpions, The
Rotheray, Dave
  See Beautiful South
Rotsey, Martin
  See Midnight Oil
Rotten, Johnny
  See Lydon, John
  Also see Sex Pistols, The
Rourke, Andy
  See Smiths, The
Rowberry, Dave
  See Animals, The
Rowe, Dwain
  See Restless Heart

Rowe, Simon
  See Mojave 3
Rowlands, Bruce
  See Fairport Convention
Rowlands, Tom
  See Chemical Brothers
Rowntree, Dave
  See Blur
Roxette **23**
Roy, Jimmy
  See Ray Condo and His Ricochets
Royal Trux **29**
Rube Waddell **29**
Rubin, Mark
  See Bad Livers, The
Rubin, Rick **9**
Rubinstein, Arthur **11**
Rucker, Darius
  See Hootie and the Blowfish
Rudd, Phillip
  See AC/DC
Rudd, Roswell **28**
Rue, Caroline
  See Hole
Ruffin, David **6**
  Also see Temptations, The
Ruffin, Tamir
  See Dru Hill
Ruffy, Dave
  See Waterboys, The
Ruffy, Dave
  See Aztec Camera
Run DMC **25**
  Earlier sketch in CM **4**
Run
  See Run DMC
Rundgren, Todd **11**
RuPaul **20**
Rusby, Kate **29**
Rush **8**
Rush, Otis **12**
Rushlow, Tim
  See Little Texas
Russell, Alecia
  See Sounds of Blackness
Russell, Graham
  See Air Supply
Russell, Hal
  See Flying Luttenbachers, The
Russell, John
  See Steppenwolf
Russell, Mark **6**
Russell, Mike
  See Shudder to Think
Russell, Pee Wee **25**
Russell, Tom **26**
Rusted Root **26**
Rutherford, Mike
  See Genesis
  Also see Mike & the Mechanics
Rutsey, John
  See Rush
Ryan, David
  See Lemonheads, The
Ryan, Mark
  See Quicksilver Messenger Service
Ryan, Mick
  See Dave Clark Five, The
Ryan, Pat "Taco"
  See Asleep at the Wheel
Rybska, Agnieszka
  See Rasputina
Ryder, Mitch **23**
  Earlier sketch in CM **11**
Ryland, Jack
  See Three Dog Night

Sedaka, Neil **4**
Seeger, Peggy **25**
Seeger, Pete **4**
  Also see Weavers, The
Seger, Bob **15**
Segovia, Andres **6**
Seidel, Martie
  See Dixie Chicks
Seldom Scene, The **4**
Selena **16**
Selway, Phil
  See Radiohead
Sen Dog
  See Cypress Hill
Senior, Milton
  See McKinney's Cotton Pickers
Senior, Russell
  See Pulp
Sensi
  See Soul II Soul
Sepultura **12**
Seraphine, Daniel
  See Chicago
Sermon, Erick
  See EPMD
Sete, Bola **26**
Setzer, Brian
  See Stray Cats, The
Severin, Steven
  See Siouxsie and the Banshees
Severinsen, Doc **1**
Sex Pistols, The **5**
Sexsmith, Ron **27**
Sexton, Chad
  See 311
Seymour, Neil
  See Crowded House
Shabalala, Ben
  See Ladysmith Black Mambazo
Shabalala, Headman
  See Ladysmith Black Mambazo
Shabalala, Jockey
  See Ladysmith Black Mambazo
Shabalala, Joseph
  See Ladysmith Black Mambazo
Shabo, Eric
  See Atomic Fireballs, The
Shade, Will
  See Memphis Jug Band
Shadow, DJ **19**
Shadows, The **22**
Shaffer, James
  See Korn
Shaffer, Paul **13**
Shaggy **19**
Shaggy 2 Dope
  See Insane Clown Possee
Shai **23**
Shakespeare, Robbie
  See Sly and Robbie
Shakur, Tupac
  See 2Pac
Shallenberger, James
  See Kronos Quartet
Shamen, The **23**
Shane, Bob
  See Kingston Trio, The
Shanice **14**
Shankar, Ravi **9**
Shannon, Del **10**
Shannon, Sarah
  See Velocity Girl
Shannon, Sharon
  See Waterboys, The
Shanté **10**
Shapiro, Jim
  See Veruca Salt

Shapiro, Lee
  See Four Seasons, The
Shapps, Andre
  See Big Audio Dynamite
Sharon, Lois & Bram **6**
Sharon, Ralph
  See Ralph Sharon Quartet
Sharp, Dave
  See Alarm
Sharp, Laura
  See Sweet Honey in the Rock
Sharpe, Matt
  See Weezer
Sharrock, Chris
  See Lightning Seeds
Sharrock, Sonny **15**
Shaw, Adrian
  See Bevis Frond
Shaw, Artie **8**
Shaw, Martin
  See Jamiroquai
Shaw, Woody **27**
Shea, Tom
  See Scud Mountain Boys
Shearer, Harry
  See Spinal Tap
Shearing, George **28**
Sheehan, Bobby
  See Blues Traveler
Sheehan, Fran
  See Boston
Sheep on Drugs **27**
Sheila E. **3**
Shellenberger, Allen
  See Lit
Shelley, Peter
  See Buzzcocks, The
Shelley, Steve
  See Sonic Youth
Shenandoah **17**
Shepherd, Hunter "Ben"
  See Soundgarden
Shepherd, Kenny Wayne **22**
Sheppard, Rodney
  See Sugar Ray
Sherba, John
  See Kronos Quartet
Sherinian, Derek
  See Dream Theater
Sherman, Jack
  See Red Hot Chili Peppers, The
Shields, Kevin
  See My Bloody Valentine
Shines, Johnny **14**
Shirelles, The **11**
Shirley, Danny
  See Confederate Railroad
Shively, William
  See Big Mountain
Shives, Andrew
  See Fear Factory
Shock G
  See Digital Underground
Shocked, Michelle **4**
Shocklee, Hank **15**
Shogren, Dave
  See Doobie Brothers, The
Shonen Knife **13**
Shontz, Bill
  See Rosenshontz
Shore, Pete
  See Boss Hog
Shorter, Wayne **5**
  Also see Weather Report
Shovell
  See M People

Shuck, Ryan
  See Orgy
Shudder to Think **20**
Siberry, Jane **6**
Sice
  See Boo Radleys, The
Sidelnyk, Steve
  See Aztec Camera
Siebenberg, Bob
  See Supertramp
Siegal, Janis
  See Manhattan Transfer, The
Sikes, C. David
  See Boston
Silk **26**
Sills, Beverly **5**
Silva, Kenny Jo
  See Beaver Brown Band, The
Silver Apples **23**
Silver, Horace **19**
Silver, Josh
  See Type O Negative
Silverchair **20**
Silveria, David
  See Korn
Simeon
  See Silver Apples
Simien, Terrance **12**
Simins, Russell
  See Jon Spencer Blues Explosion
Simmons, Gene
  See Kiss
Simmons, Joe "Run"
  See Run DMC
Simmons, Patrick
  See Doobie Brothers, The
Simmons, Russell **7**
Simmons, Trinna
  See Spearhead
Simms, Nick
  See Cornershop
Simon and Garfunkel **24**
Simon, Carly **22**
  Earlier sketch in CM **4**
Simon, Paul **16**
  Earlier sketch in CM **1**
  Also see Simon and Garfunkel
Simone, Nina **11**
Simonon, Paul
  See Clash, The
Simons, Ed
  See Chemical Brothers
Simple Minds **21**
Simpson, Denis
  See Nylons, The
Simpson, Derrick "Duckie"
  See Black Uhuru
Simpson, Mel
  See US3
Simpson, Ray
  See Village People, The
Simpson, Rose
  See Incredible String Band
Sims, David William
  See Jesus Lizard
Sims, Matt
  See Citizen King
Sims, Neil
  See Catherine Wheel
Sin, Will
  See Shamen, The
Sinatra, Frank **23**
  Earlier sketch in CM **1**
Sinclair, David
  See Camel
  Also see Caravan

Spence, Alexander "Skip"
　See Jefferson Airplane
　Also see Moby Grape
Spence, Cecil
　See Israel Vibration
Spence, Skip
　See Spence, Alexander "Skip"
Spencer Davis Group 19
Spencer, Jeremy
　See Fleetwood Mac
Spencer, Jim
　See Dave Clark Five, The
Spencer, Jon
　See Boss Hog
　Also see Jon Spencer Blues Explosion
Spencer, Thad
　See Jayhawks, The
Spice Girls 22
Spin Doctors 14
Spinal Tap 8
Spindt, Don
　See Aqua Velvets
Spinners, The 21
Spirit 22
Spiteri, Sharleen
　See Texas
Spitz, Dan
　See Anthrax
Spitz, Dave
　See Black Sabbath
Sponge 18
Spring, Keith
　See NRBQ
Springfield, Dusty 20
Springfield, Rick 9
Springsteen, Bruce 25
　Earlier sketch in CM 6
Sproule, Daithi
　See Altan
Sprout, Tobin
　See Guided By Voices
Squeeze 5
Squire, Chris
　See Yes
Squire, John
　See Stone Roses, The
Squires, Rob
　See Big Head Todd and the Monsters
Squirrel Nut Zippers 20
St. Hubbins, David
　See Spinal Tap
St. James, Rebecca 26
St. John, Mark
　See Kiss
St. Marie, Buffy
　See Sainte-Marie, Buffy
St. Nicholas, Nick
　See Steppenwolf
Stacey, Peter "Spider"
　See Pogues, The
Stacy, Jeremy
　See Aztec Camera
Staehely, Al
　See Spirit
Staehely, J. Christian
　See Spirit
Stafford, Jo 24
Stahl, Franz
　See Foo Fighters
Staley, Layne
　See Alice in Chains
Staley, Tom
　See NRBQ
Stanier, John
　See Helmet
Stanisic, Ched
　See Cobra Verde

Stanley, Bob
　See Saint Etienne
Stanley, Ian
　See Tears for Fears
Stanley, Paul
　See Kiss
Stanley, Ralph 5
Stansfield, Lisa 9
Staples, Mavis 13
Staples, Neville
　See Specials, The
Staples, Pops 11
Stapp, Scott
　See Creed
Starcrunch
　See Man or Astroman?
Starkey, Kathryn La Verne
　See Starr, Kay
Starkey, Richard
　See Starr, Ringo
Starks, Tia Juana
　See Sweet Honey in the Rock
Starling, John
　See Seldom Scene, The
Starr, Kay 27
Starr, Mike
　See Alice in Chains
Starr, Ringo 24
　Earlier sketch in CM 10
　Also see Beatles, The
Starship
　See Jefferson Airplane
Statler Brothers, The 8
Stax, John
　See Pretty Things, The
Stead, David
　See Beautiful South
Steaks, Chuck
　See Quicksilver Messenger Service
Stebbins, Jone
　See Imperial Teen
Steel, John
　See Animals, The
Steel Pulse 14
Steel, Richard
　See Spacehog
Steele, Billy
　See Sounds of Blackness
Steele, David
　See English Beat, The
　Also see Fine Young Cannibals
Steele, Jeffrey
　See Boy Howdy
Steele, Michael
　See Bangles, The
Steele, Peter
　See Type O Negative
Steeleye Span 19
Steely Dan 29
　Earlier sketch in CM 5
Stefani, Gwen
　See No Doubt
Stefansson, Baldur
　See Gus Gus
Steier, Rick
　See Warrant
Stein, Chris
　See Blondie
Steinberg, Lewis
　See Booker T. & the M.G.'s
Steinberg, Sebastian
　See Soul Coughing
Stephenson, Van Wesley
　See BlackHawk
Steppenwolf 20
Sterban, Richard
　See Oak Ridge Boys, The

Stereolab 18
Stereophonics 29
Sterling, Lester
　See Skatalites, The
Stern, Isaac 7
Stern, Leni 29
Stern, Mike 29
Steve
　See Fun Lovin' Criminals
Stevens, Cat 3
Stevens, Ray 7
Stevens, Roger
　See Blind Melon
Stevens, Vol
　See Memphis Jug Band
Stevenson, Bill
　See Black Flag
Stevenson, Don
　See Moby Grape
Stevenson, James
　See Gene Loves Jezebel
Steward, Pat
　See Odds
Stewart, Dave
　See Eurythmics
Stewart, Derrick "Fatlip"
　See Pharcyde, The
Stewart, Freddie
　See Sly & the Family Stone
Stewart, Ian
　See Rolling Stones, The
Stewart, Jamie
　See Cult, The
Stewart, John
　See Kingston Trio, The
Stewart, Larry
　See Restless Heart
Stewart, Rex
　See McKinney's Cotton Pickers
Stewart, Rod 20
　Earlier sketch in CM 2
　Also see Faces, The
Stewart, Sylvester
　See Sly & the Family Stone
Stewart, Tyler
　See Barenaked Ladies
Stewart, Vaetta
　See Sly & the Family Stone
Stewart, William
　See Third World
Stewart, Winston "Metal"
　See Mystic Revealers
Stiff, Jimmy
　See Jackyl
Stills, Stephen 5
　See Buffalo Springfield
　Also see Crosby, Stills, and Nash
Sting 19
　Earlier sketch in CM 2
　Also see Police, The
Stinson, Bob
　See Replacements, The
Stinson, Tommy
　See Replacements, The
Stipe, Michael
　See R.E.M.
Stockman, Shawn
　See Boyz II Men
Stockwood, Kim 26
Stoll
　See Clannad
　Also see Big Mountain
Stoller, Mike
　See Leiber and Stoller
Stoltz, Brian
　See Neville Brothers, The
Stoltzman, Richard 24

Tepper, Jeff "Morris"
 See Captain Beefheart and His Magic Band
Terminator X
 See Public Enemy
Terrell, Jean
 See Supremes, The
Terrie
 See Ex, The
Terry, Boyd
 See Aquabats, The
Terry, Clark **24**
Tesh, John **20**
Tesla **15**
Texas **27**
Texas Tornados, The **8**
Thacker, Rocky
 See Shenandoah
Thain, Gary
 See Uriah Heep
Thayil, Kim
 See Soundgarden
The The **15**
Theremin, Leon **19**
They Might Be Giants **7**
Thibaudet, Jean-Yves **24**
Thielemans, Toots **13**
Thin Lizzy **13**
Third Eye Blind **25**
Third World **13**
Thirsk, Jason
 See Pennywise
Thistlethwaite, Anthony
 See Waterboys, The
Thomas, Alex
 See Earth, Wind and Fire
Thomas, David Clayton
 See Clayton-Thomas, David
Thomas, David
 See Pere Ubu
Thomas, David
 See Take 6
Thomas, Dennis "D.T."
 See Kool & the Gang
Thomas, George "Fathead"
 See McKinney's Cotton Pickers
Thomas, Irma **16**
Thomas, John
 See Captain Beefheart and His Magic Band
Thomas, Mickey
 See Jefferson Starship
Thomas, Olice
 See Five Blind Boys of Alabama
Thomas, Ray
 See Moody Blues, The
Thomas, Richard
 See Jesus and Mary Chain, The
Thomas, Rob
 See Matchbox 20
Thomas, Rozonda "Chilli"
 See TLC
Thompson, Chester
 See Weather Report
Thompson, Danny
 See Pentangle
Thompson, Dennis
 See MC5, The
Thompson, Dougie
 See Supertramp
Thompson, Lee
 See Madness
Thompson, Les
 See Nitty Gritty Dirt Band, The
Thompson, Mayo
 See Pere Ubu
Thompson, Porl
 See Cure, The

Thompson, Richard **7**
 Also see Fairport Convention
Thomson, Kristin
 See Tsunami
Thoranisson, Biggi
 See Gus Gus
Thorn, Christopher
 See Blind Melon
Thorn, Stan
 See Shenandoah
Thorn, Tracey
 See Everything But The Girl
 Also see Massive Attack
Thornalley, Phil
 See Cure, The
Thornburg, Lee
 See Supertramp
Thornhill, Leeroy
 See Prodigy
Thornton, Big Mama **18**
Thornton, Kevin "KT"
 See Color Me Badd
Thornton, Teri **28**
Thornton, Willie Mae
 See Thornton, Big Mama
Threadgill, Henry **9**
Three Dog Night **5**
Throwing Muses **15**
Thunders, Johnny
 See New York Dolls
Tickner, George
 See Journey
Tiffany **4**
Tikaram, Tanita **9**
Tilbrook, Glenn
 See Squeeze
Tiller, Mary
 See Anointed
Tilley, Sandra
 See Martha and the Vandellas
Tillis, Mel **7**
Tillis, Pam **25**
 Earlier sketch in CM **8**
Tilson Thomas, Michael **24**
Timberlake, Justin
 See 'N Sync
Timbuk 3 **3**
Timmins, Margo
 See Cowboy Junkies, The
Timmins, Michael
 See Cowboy Junkies, The
Timmins, Peter
 See Cowboy Junkies, The
Timms, Sally
 See Mekons, The
Tinsley, Boyd
 See Dave Matthews Band
Tippin, Aaron **12**
Tipton, Glenn
 See Judas Priest
TLC **15**
Toad the Wet Sprocket **13**
Toback, Jeremy
 See Brad
Tobias, Jesse
 See Red Hot Chili Peppers
Todd, Andy
 See Republica
Tolhurst, Laurence
 See Cure, The
Tolland, Bryan
 See Del Amitri
Toller, Dan
 See Allman Brothers, The
Tolliver, T.C.
 See Wendy O. Williams and The Plasmatics

Tolson, Peter
 See Pretty Things, The
Tom Petty and the Heartbreakers **26**
Tone-Loc **3**
Tong, Winston
 See Tuxedomoon
Tontoh, Frank
 See Aztec Camera
Tony K
 See Roomful of Blues
Tony Williams **6**
Tony! Toni! Toné! **12**
Too $hort **16**
Toohey, Dan
 See Guided By Voices
Took, Steve Peregrine
 See T. Rex
Tool **21**
Toomey, Jenny
 See Tsunami
Topham, Anthony "Top"
 See Yardbirds, The
Topper, Sharon
 See God Is My Co-Pilot
Tork, Peter
 See Monkees, The
Torme, Mel **4**
Torres, Hector "Tico"
 See Bon Jovi
Toscanini, Arturo **14**
Tosh, Peter **3**
Toure, Ali Farka **18**
Tourish, Ciaran
 See Altan
Toussaint, Allen **11**
Towner, Ralph **22**
Townes, Jeffery
 See DJ Jazzy Jeff and the Fresh Prince
Towns, Efrem
 See Dirty Dozen Brass Band
Townshend, Pete **1**
 Also see Who, The
Traffic **19**
Tragically Hip, The **18**
Trammell, Mark
 See Greater Vision
Travers, Brian
 See UB40
Travers, Mary
 See Peter, Paul & Mary
Travis **29**
Travis, Abby
 See Elastica
Travis, Merle **14**
Travis, Randy **9**
Treach
 See Naughty by Nature
Treadmill Trackstar **21**
Tremonti, Mark
 See Creed
Trevi, Gloria **29**
Tribe Called Quest, A **8**
Trick Daddy **28**
Tricky **18**
 Also see Massive Attack
Trimble, Vivian
 See Luscious Jackson
Trimm, Rex
 See Cherry Poppin' Daddies
Tripp, Art "Art Marimba"
 See Captain Beefheart and His Magic Band
Tritsch, Christian
 See Gong
Tritt, Travis **7**
Trotter, Kera
 See C + C Music Factory

Volodos, Arcadi **28**
Volz, Greg
  See Petra
von Karajan, Herbert **1**
von Trapp, Elisabeth **29**
Von Bohlen, Davey
  See Promise Ring, The
Von, Eerie
  See Danzig
Von, Jon
  See Mr. T Experience, The
Vox, Bono
  See U2
Vrenna, Chris
  See Nine Inch Nails
Vudi
  See American Music Club
Waaktaar, Pal
  See A-ha
Wachtel, Waddy **26**
Waddell, Larry
  See Mint Condition
Wade, Adam
  See Shudder to Think
Wade, Chrissie
  See Alien Sex Fiend
Wade, Nik
  See Alien Sex Fiend
Wadenius, George
  See Blood, Sweat and Tears
Wadephal, Ralf
  See Tangerine Dream
Wagner, Kurt
  See Lambchop
Wagoner, Faidest
  See Soul Stirrers, The
Wagoner, Porter **13**
Wahlberg, Donnie
  See New Kids on the Block
Wailer, Bunny **11**
Wainwright III, Loudon **11**
Wainwright, Rufus **29**
Waits, Tom **27**
  Earlier sketch in CM **12**
  Earlier sketch in CM **1**
Wakeling, David
  See English Beat, The
Wakeman, Rick **27**
  Also see Yes
Walden, Narada Michael **14**
Waldroup, Jason
  See Greater Vision
Walford, Britt
  See Breeders
Walker, Clay**20**
Walker, Colin
  See Electric Light Orchestra
Walker, Ebo
  See New Grass Revival, The
Walker, Jerry Jeff **13**
Walker, Joe Louis **28**
Walker, Matt
  See Filter
Walker, T-Bone **5**
Wallace, Bill
  See Guess Who
Wallace, Ian
  See King Crimson
Wallace, Richard
  See Mighty Clouds of Joy, The
Wallace, Sippie **6**
Waller, Charlie
  See Country Gentlemen, The
Waller, Dave
  See Jam, The
Waller, Fats **7**
Wallflowers, The**20**

Wallinger, Karl **11**
  Also see Waterboys, The
Wallis, Larry
  See Motörhead
Walls, Chris
  See Dave Clark Five, The
Walls, Denise "Nee-C"
  See Anointed
Walls, Greg
  See Anthrax
Walsh, Joe **5**
  Also see Eagles, The
Walsh, Marty
  See Supertramp
Walter, Tommy
  See eels
Walter, Weasel
  See Flying Luttenbachers, The
Walters, Richard
  See Slick Rick
Walters, Robert "Patch"
  See Mystic Revealers
Wannadies, The **29**
War **14**
Ward, Andy
  See Bevis Frond
  Also see Camel
Ward, Bill
  See Black Sabbath
Ward, Michael
  See Wallflowers, The
Ware, Martyn
  See Human League, The
Wareham, Dean
  See Luna
Wariner, Steve **18**
Warner, Les
  See Cult, The
Warnes, Jennifer **3**
Warnick, Kim
  See Fastbacks, The
Warrant **17**
Warren, Diane **21**
Warren, George W.
  See Five Blind Boys of Alabama
Warren, Mervyn
  See Take 6
Warwick, Clint
  See Moody Blues, The
Warwick, Dionne **2**
Was (Not Was) **6**
Was, David
  See Was (Not Was)
Was, Don **21**
  Also see Was (Not Was)
Wash, Martha
  See C + C Music Factory
Washington, Chester
  See Earth, Wind and Fire
Washington, Dinah **5**
Washington, Grover, Jr. **5**
Wasserman, Greg "Noodles"
  See Offspring
Waterboys, The **27**
Waters, Crystal **15**
Waters, Ethel **11**
Waters, Muddy **24**
  Earlier sketch in CM **4**
Waters, Roger
  See Pink Floyd
Watkins, Christopher
  See Cabaret Voltaire
Watkins, Tionne "T-boz"
  See TLC
Watley, Jody **26**
  Earlier sketch in CM **9**
Watson, Doc **2**

Watson, Guy
  See Surfaris, The
Watson, Ivory
  See Ink Spots
Watt, Ben
  See Everything But The Girl
Watt, Mike **22**
  Also see fIREHOSE
Watters, Sam
  See Color Me Badd
Watts, Bari
  See Bevis Frond
Watts, Charlie
  See Rolling Stones, The
Watts, Eugene
  See Canadian Brass, The
Watts, Lou
  See Chumbawamba
Watts, Raymond
  See KMFDM
Watts, Todd
  See Emmet Swimming
Weather Report **19**
Weaver, Louie
  See Petra
Weavers, The **8**
Webb, Chick **14**
Webb, Jimmy **12**
Webb, Paul
  See Talk Talk
Webber, Andrew Lloyd
  See Lloyd Webber, Andrew
Webber, Mark
  See Pulp
Webster, Andrew
  See Tsunami
Wedding Present, The **28**
Wedgwood, Mike
  See Caravan
Wedren, Craig
  See Shudder to Think
Weezer **20**
Weider, John
  See Animals, The
Weiland, Scott
  See Stone Temple Pilots
Weill, Kurt **12**
Weir, Bob
  See Grateful Dead, The
Weiss, Janet
  See Sleater-Kinney
  Also see Quasi
Weissman, Marco
  See Waterboys, The
Welch, Bob
  See Fleetwood Mac
Welch, Brian
  See Korn
Welch, Bruce
  See Shadows, The
Welch, Justin
  See Elastica
Welch, Mcguinness
  See Lords of Acid
Welch, Sean
  See Beautiful South
Welk, Lawrence **13**
Weller, Paul
  See Jam, The
Weller, Paul **14**
Wells, Cory
  See Three Dog Night
Wells, Junior **17**
Wells, Kitty **6**
Welnick, Vince
  See Grateful Dead, The

Willsteed, John
　See Go-Betweens, The
Wilmot, Billy "Mystic"
　See Mystic Revealers
Wilson, Anne
　See Heart
Wilson, Brian **24**
　Also see Beach Boys, The
Wilson, Carl
　See Beach Boys, The
Wilson, Carnie
　See Wilson Phillips
Wilson, Cassandra **26**
　Earlier sketch in CM **12**
Wilson, Chris
　See Love Spit Love
Wilson, Cindy
　See B-52's, The
Wilson, Dennis
　See Beach Boys, The
Wilson, Don
　See Ventures, The
Wilson, Eric
　See Sublime
Wilson, Gerald **19**
Wilson, Jackie **3**
Wilson, Kim
　See Fabulous Thunderbirds, The
Wilson, Mary
　See Supremes, The
Wilson, Nancy **28**
Wilson, Nancy **14**
　Also see Heart
Wilson, Orlandus
　See Golden Gate Quartet
Wilson, Patrick
　See Weezer
Wilson Phillips **5**
Wilson, Ransom **5**
Wilson, Ricky
　See B-52's, The
Wilson, Robin
　See Gin Blossoms
Wilson, Ron
　See Surfaris, The
Wilson, Shanice
　See Shanice
Wilson, Wendy
　See Wilson Phillips
Wilson-James, Victoria
　See Soul II Soul
　Also see Shamen, The
Wilton, Michael
　See Queensryche
Wimpfheimer, Jimmy
　See Roomful of Blues
Winans, Carvin
　See Winans, The
Winans, Marvin
　See Winans, The
Winans, Michael
　See Winans, The
Winans, Ronald
　See Winans, The
Winans, The **12**
Winbush, Angela **15**
Winfield, Chuck
　See Blood, Sweat and Tears
Winston, George **9**
Winter, Johnny **5**
Winter, Kurt
　See Guess Who
Winter, Paul **10**
Winthrop, Dave
　See Supertramp
Winwood, Muff
　See Spencer Davis Group

Winwood, Steve **2**
　Also see Spencer Davis Group
　Also see Traffic
Wire **29**
Wire, Nicky
　See Manic Street Preachers
Wiseman, Bobby
　See Blue Rodeo
Wiseman, Mac **19**
WishBone
　See Bone Thugs-N-Harmony
Withers, Pick
　See Dire Straits
Witherspoon, Jimmy **19**
Wolf, Kurt
　See Boss Hog
Wolf, Peter
　See J. Geils Band
Wolfe, Gerald
　See Greater Vision
Wolstencraft, Simon
　See Fall, The
Womack, Bobby **5**
Wonder, Stevie **17**
　Earlier sketch in CM **2**
Woo, John
　See Magnetic Fields, The
Wood, Chris
　See Traffic
Wood, Danny
　See New Kids on the Block
Wood, Ron
　See Faces, The
　Also see Rolling Stones, The
Wood, Roy
　See Electric Light Orchestra
Woodgate, Dan
　See Madness
Woods, Gay
　See Steeleye Span
Woods, Terry
　See Pogues, The
　Also see Steeleye Span
Woods-Wright, Tomica **22**
Woodson, Ollie
　See Temptations, The
Woodward, Keren
　See Bananarama
Woody, Allen
　See Allman Brothers, The
Woolfolk, Andrew
　See Earth, Wind and Fire
Worley, Chris
　See Jackyl
Worley, Jeff
　See Jackyl
Worrell, Bernie **11**
Wray, Link **17**
Wreede, Katrina
　See Turtle Island String Quartet
Wren, Alan
　See Stone Roses, The
Wretzky, D'Arcy
　See Smashing Pumpkins
Wright, Adrian
　See Human League, The
Wright, David "Blockhead"
　See English Beat, The
Wright, Heath
　See Ricochet
Wright, Hugh
　See Boy Howdy
Wright, Jimmy
　See Sounds of Blackness
Wright, Norman
　See Country Gentlemen, The

Wright, Rick
　See Pink Floyd
Wright, Simon
　See AC/DC
Wright, Tim
　See Pere Ubu
Wu-Tang Clan **19**
Wupass, Reverend
　See Rube Waddell
Wurster, Jon
　See Superchunk
Wurzel
　See Motörhead
Wyatt, Robert **24**
Wyman, Bill
　See Rolling Stones, The
　Also see Bill Wyman & the Rhythm Kings
Wynette, Tammy **24**
　Earlier sketch in CM **2**
Wynne, Philippe
　See Spinners, The
Wynonna **11**
　Also see Judds, The
X **11**
Xefos, Chris
　See King Missile
XTC **26**
　Earlier sketch in CM **10**
Ya Kid K
　See Technotronic
Yale, Brian
　See Matchbox 20
Yamamoto, Hiro
　See Soundgarden
Yamamoto, Seichi
　See Boredoms, The
Yamano, Atsuko
　See Shonen Knife
Yamano, Naoko
　See Shonen Knife
Yamashita, Kazuhito **4**
Yamataka, Eye
　See Boredoms, The
Yamauchi, Tetsu
　See Faces, The
Yamazaki, Iwao
　See Ghost
Yang, Naomi
　See Damon and Naomi
Yankovic, "Weird Al" **7**
Yanni **11**
Yardbirds, The **10**
Yarrow, Peter
　See Peter, Paul & Mary
Yates, Bill
　See Country Gentlemen, The
Yauch, Adam
　See Beastie Boys, The
Yearwood, Trisha **25**
　Earlier sketch in CM **10**
Yella
　See N.W.A.
Yes **8**
Yeston, Maury **22**
Yo La Tengo **24**
Yo Yo **9**
Yoakam, Dwight **21**
　Earlier sketch in CM **1**
Yoot, Tukka
　See US3
York, Andrew **15**
York, John
　See Byrds, The
York, Pete
　See Spencer Davis Group
Yorke, Thom E.
　See Radiohead